Speaking

ACL–MIT Press Series in Natural-Language Processing

Aravind Joshi, editor

Speaking: From Intention to Articulation (1989)
Willem J. M. Levelt

Speaking

Willem J. M. Levelt

From Intention to Articulation

A Bradford Book
The MIT Press
Cambridge, Massachusetts
London, England

Fifth printing, 1998
First MIT Press paperback edition, 1993

This book was set in Times Roman by Asco Trade Typesetting Ltd. in Hong Kong and printed and bound by Halliday Lithograph in the United States of America.

Library of Congress Cataloging-in-Publication Data

Levelt, W. J. M. (Willem J. M.), 1938–
  Speaking: from intention to articulation / Willem J. M. Levelt.

     p.   cm.
  "A Bradford book."
  Bibliography: p.
  Includes index.
  ISBN 0-262-12137-9 (HB), 0-262-62089-8 (PB)
  1. Psycholinguistics. 2. Speech. I. Title.
P37.L44 1989   88-19144
401'.9—dc19

to nobody Els but you

Contents

Contents

Preface

Talking is one of our dearest occupations. We spend hours a day conversing, telling stories, teaching, quarreling, ... and, of course, speaking to ourselves. Speaking is, moreover, one of our most complex cognitive, linguistic, and motor skills. Articulation flows automatically, at a rate of about fifteen speech sounds per second, while we are attending only to the ideas we want to get across to our interlocutors.

This fascinating human skill has not received the attention it deserves within psycholinguistics. Psycholinguistics is the science of human language production, comprehension, and acquisition, but the main body of research and teaching relates primarily to the latter two topics. Language production is the stepchild of psycholinguistics. Butterworth's (1980c, 1983b) excellent two-volume anthology is the only source on the subject; there is no text and no coherently written handbook.

When the European Science Foundation invited me to lecture on "speaking" at a summer course in psycholinguistics to be held in Brussels in 1985, I gladly accepted and began writing what I thought would be an introductory text. A year and a half would suffice, I thought, in view of the rather limited psycholinguistic literature on the subject.

My main discovery was that the literature on speaking is gigantic. But the majority of it is not to be found in standard psycholinguistic sources. Other disciplines have asked the questions that psycholinguists have ignored. Students of conversational analysis, pragmatics, discourse semantics, artificial intelligence, syntax, phonology, speech communication, and phonetics have contributed myriad theoretical insights and empirical findings. The major problem with this huge literature, however, is that it is compartmentalized—phoneticians ignore phonology, conversational analysts ignore discourse semantics and phonetics, students of AI ignore psycholinguistics, and so on.

The present book gives a bird's-eye view of this highly heterogeneous research field. It is an effort to provide a theoretical integration of hitherto disparate approaches to the speaker in us, but without relaxing the psycholinguist's main objective: to understand the mental information processing that underlies our capacity for speech.

The book's organization is straightforward. After an introductory chapter on the speaker as information processor and a subsequent chapter on the speaker as interlocutor, the text follows the generation of speech step by step. The steps consist of message generation, grammatical encoding, phonological encoding, and articulation. The final chapter deals with the speaker's self-monitoring and self-repair. Each processing step computes its own kind of output or representation, and I always discuss these representations before discussing the issues of processing themselves. Not surprisingly, the representational chapters or sections have a more strongly linguistic flavor than the parts of the book that discuss processing.

My strategy in this book has been to exemplify theoretical issues rather than to formalize them. The text contains few formulas and acronyms, little computer jargon, and few statistics, but many worked-out cases, many examples, and much graphic support. It should be readable not only by psycholinguists and their advanced students, but also by anyone interested in the other disciplines mentioned above.

While plowing through the mound of literature, I decided that neither you nor I should bite off more than we can chew. The book concentrates on the normal spontaneous speech production of adults. It does not cover the neurological basis of speech and language. In particular, it contains nothing on aphasia and other relevant neurological disorders, nor does it discuss reading (although there are occasional references to experimental work in which reading materials have been used). Reading aloud differs from spontaneous speech in many important ways, and results on reading therefore cannot, as a rule, be generalized to conditions of spontaneous speech. Speaking is usually accompanied by gestures, gaze patterns, body movements, and so forth. In spite of its communicative importance, this so-called paralinguistic behavior is not reviewed. The book, finally, does not deal with the history of research in speech and speaking, despite occasional references to Wilhelm Wundt, Karl Bühler, and other pioneers.

What people can do with words is incredible, and its psychology is still largely a mystery. By necessity, this book is incomplete and theoretically wanting, even in the areas on which it focuses. I look forward to the day when it can be replaced by something better.

Acknowledgments

This book emerged in the stimulating circle of the Max-Planck-Institut für Psycholinguistik and Nijmegen University. Numerous colleagues can't give up educating me in matters linguistic and psycholinguistic, and I would be at a loss without them. Also, many distinguished visitors from all over the world have given me help and advice. I am sincerely grateful to all of them.

Some, from within and without this circle, have taken the effort to read drafts of chapters and to formulate comments, either orally or in writing. Before mentioning them, I must say that each of these efforts has deeply touched me. Time and again I experienced it as a great privilege to be taken so seriously and with so much friendship. In alphabetical order, these angels were Manfred Bierwisch, Melissa Bowerman, Herbert Clark, Anne Cutler, Jane Edwards, Lyn Frazier, Merrill Garrett, Gerard Kempen, Wolfgang Klein, Aditi Lahiri, and John Marshall. I would also like to thank Gerard van Galen, who gave me a special tutorial on psychomotor theory.

Though I typed the manuscript myself with two index fingers on a terminal, finishing touches have been made by Uschi de Pagter and Edith Sjoerdsma, especially in completing the bibliography. Our librarian, Karin Kastens, also helped me on countless occasions. Many thanks to all three of them.

The graphic work was done by Wil Maas during three months of ideal cooperation.

Nijmegen, February 29, 1988

Author's Notes

On Pronominalization

I will contribute to the present chaos of person pronominalization in English by adhering to the following conventions: Speakers, whether male, female, or generic, will receive masculine pronominalization. Hearers or addressees will be treated as female. When there are two or more interlocutors (i.e., speakers/hearers), the first one will be male, the second one female, and so on in alternation. General use of these conventions in psycholinguistics will, given the bias for language-comprehension research, make most person reference female.

On Transcription

I will follow the transcription conventions of the International Phonetic Alphabet. The phonetic symbols used are listed in the appendix.

Chapter 1

The Speaker as Information Processor

Speaking is one of man's most complex skills. It is a skill which is unique to our species. Each normal child starts acquiring it in infancy, clearly driven by a genetically given propensity for language. The mature skill takes all of childhood to develop. It requires extensive interaction between the child and its parents, peers, teachers and other members of the language community. There is, in fact, never a steady state. The mature language user keeps expanding his lexicon as new words are needed or arise in the language. There is also often a continuing growth of rhetorical and narrative abilities in the adult speaker.

The present book is about the organization of this skill. It will consider the speaker as a highly complex information processor who can, in some still rather mysterious way, transform intentions, thoughts, feelings into fluently articulated speech. The dissection of this skill is a scientific endeavor in its own right. It is, in particular, not enough to study the functions of speaking—the kinds of intentional acts a language user can perform through speech, such as referring, requesting, and explaining. Nor is it enough to study the patterns of spoken interaction between interlocutors—the ways they engage in conversation, take turns, signal misunderstanding, and so forth. These are, it is true, of crucial importance for the understanding of speakers as interlocutors. Indeed, these perspectives cannot be ignored with impunity when the skill of speaking is dissected. But they do not suffice. Developing a theory of any complex cognitive skill requires a reasoned dissection of the system into subsystems, or processing components. It also requires a characterization of the representations that are computed by these processors and of the manner in which they are computed, as well as specification of how these components cooperate in generating their joint end product. A theory of speaking will involve various such processing components, and the present chapter will make a first go at partitioning the processing system that underlies the generation of speech.

By way of introduction, I will present a case study of a speaker's generation of a single utterance. This case study is phenomenological in nature, but it is not theory-free. Its purpose is to set the scene for conjecturing an architecture for the processing system that underlies speech production. Such an architecture will be proposed in section 1.2. It consists of various processing components which, together, translate the speaker's intentions into overt speech.

The nature of these processors is discussed further in sections 1.3 and 1.4. It will, in particular, be stressed that processing components are specialized and that they do their work in rather autonomous fashion. Most of the components underlying the production of speech, I will argue, function in a highly automatic, reflex-like way. This automaticity makes it possible for them to work in parallel, which is a main condition for the generation of uninterrupted fluent speech. The special way in which this cooperation between components is organized so as to result in "incremental production" is the subject of section 1.5.

The rest of the book is straightforward in structure. It will basically follow the components of the proposed architecture one by one, from the speaker's initial conception of something to express to his eventual articulation of an appropriate utterance. However, before venturing upon that voyage, I devote a second introductory chapter to the speaker as interlocutor. Many aspects of a speaker's information processing cannot be correctly evaluated if we lose sight of the canonical ecological context of talking: the speaker's participation in conversation.

1.1 A Case Study

The case to be analyzed is taken from page 868 of Svartvik and Quirk 1980. It appears in a tape-recorded exchange between two male academics, aged about 40, and a male about 18 years old who is applying for admission to college. The academics are apparently testing the student's knowledge of Shakespeare, and the following pair of turns emerges:

Academic 1:   [e:m] ... would you say Othello was [e:] ... a tragedy of circumstance ... or a tragedy of character.

(lapse)

Student: I I don't know the way ... play WELL enough sir.

The target of analysis here will be the student's utterance. The academic's utterance invited the student to provide certain information about the play *Othello*, presumably not because the academic lacked that knowledge but rather because he wanted to find out more about the student's informedness. And this, one might assume, was mutually known between the academics and the student. All three parties knew and accepted that the conversation was an interview, and that defined their roles.

The student started his utterance after a lapse, a long silence. Since academic 1 had addressed the question to the student (*would you say* ...), the situation obliged the cooperative student to take the floor. Hence, the lapse could not have been due to the student's expecting somebody else to take the floor. The student was, rather, involved in serious information processing. Of what sort? Was he retrieving whatever he knew about the play in order to infer a probable answer? This would mean that the student had conceived of the intention to assert the requested information, and that he was now engaged in inferring it. There is evidence in the interview that this was not what was going on.

The student was probably aware, but academic 1 apparently was not, that academic 2 had asked almost the same question five or ten minutes earlier (*Would you call Othello a tragedy of circumstance or of character?*) and that the student had then expressed his ignorance (*I don't know much about Othello, so I couldn't say*). It may or may not have been the case, moreover, that academic 2's subsequent turn in that sequence (*Well which others would you characterize as tragedies of circumstance?*) had given away the answer to the student. Although the student may have tried to remember that earlier discussion in order to come up with the correct answer, it is more likely that he was embarrassed by this repeated question and that he considered another move (namely, reminding academic 1 that academic 2 had preempted him on this issue, or some similar speech act). Under this interpretation, the lapse resulted from a conflict of intentions: What move should be made? The student's final decision was apparently to let politeness prevail, and to avoid embarrassing academic 1 by suggesting that he hadn't been very attentive. The student would, instead, express his ignorance again.

So far, the analysis suggests that, in planning an utterance, there is an initial phase in which the speaker decides on a purpose for his next move. This decision will depend on a variety of factors, and not in the last place on the speaker's needs, beliefs, and obligations. The speaker's choice of purpose relates in particular to what has been said before in the conversation, of which he must have kept some record. In the present example, the student took into account the previous turn (i.e., the academic's question, the topic of the discourse—Shakespeare's plays) and, presumably, the earlier part of the discourse concerning *Othello*. This first step in planning an utterance is the conception of a communicative intention. In view of this end, appropriate means will have to be marshaled.

Let us return to the student's utterance. Having decided to politely reveal his ignorance, the student had to decide on the information he would have to express in order to convey that intention. The academic left the student with two alternatives: saying that *Othello* is a tragedy of circumstance and saying that it is a tragedy of character. Strictly speaking, the question left no other option open for the student. In particular, the interviewer did not explicitly allow for the possibility that the student did not know the answer. In that case, the question should have been phrased like this: *Do you know whether Othello was a tragedy of circumstance or a tragedy of character?* Neither of the two options given could be chosen to express the intention. What would have conveyed the intention would have been for the student to tell the academic straightaway that he couldn't give the answer. Because of the interview character of the conversation, that condition was on everybody's mind in any case. Still, the information the student selected for expression was slightly different. The student expressed less informa- tion than was required, because he did not say *I cannot answer your ques- tion*; at the same time, he expressed more than was required by saying that he didn't know the play well enough. Why did the student select the latter information as a means of conveying his intention?

There may have been two reasons. First, given the decision to answer politely, the student may have rejected the option of directly expressing information that would presuppose a third option, one not overtly given by the academic. It is, after all, slightly impolite for a questioner to ignore the listener's potential ignorance, and it would be equally impolite for the answerer to implicate that there had been a flaw in politeness. The student, rather, left it to academic 1 to *infer* his inability to answer the question (*well enough* for what?). That was the main implication of the information expressed, and the issue of impoliteness thus faded into the background. Second, the student may have wanted to reveal something else at the same time: that he did know *Othello*, contrary to what academic 1 might have inferred from a straight "I don't know" answer.

The content selected for expression was not an atom but a structured concept. It consisted of an experiencer ("me"), of whom it is predicated that his state of knowledge about subject matter X doesn't meet criterion Y, where X is Shakespeare's play *Othello* and Y is "sufficient for inferring the type of tragedy". This selection also reflected the speaker's decision not to spell out criterion Y, so that the inference could be left to the interviewer. In addition, there was the decision to use a polite addressing form (which surfaced as *sir*).

The speaker's elaboration of a communicative intention by selecting the information whose expression may realize the communicative goals will be called *macroplanning* in this book.

In the example above, there were also other decisions taken with respect to the information to be expressed. Among them were (i) to refer to *Othello* in reduced but definite form because that referent had been introduced explicitly in the previous turn (surfacing as *play*), (ii) to acknowledge that *Othello* and the student's knowledge thereof was the topic the answer had to be about (resulting in sentence-initial placement), and (iii) to focus on the degree of knowledge of the play as the new information (surfacing as sentence-final and receiving tonic stress, *WELL enough*). All these decisions related in some way or another to the state of the student's record of the discourse so far. They determined the informational perspective of the utterance, its topic, its focus, and the way in which it would attract the addressee's attention. Conceptual planning activities of this kind—i.e., planning an informational perspective for an utterance—will be called *microplanning*.

So far, we have seen reasons to distinguish two phases in the planning of an utterance after a communicative intention has been conceived. During macroplanning the speaker selects and molds information in such a way that its expression will be an appropriate means for conveying the intention. In this phase the speaker spells out his communicative intention and marshals the appropriate information whose expression will reveal the intention to the addressee. This fixes the "speech act," i.e., the commitments the speaker is prepared to make by expressing a particular informational content as well as the chosen levels of directness and politeness. These bits of information are not independent. In the example, the degree of directness appeared to affect the content to be expressed. During the second phrase—microplanning—the speaker brings all this information into perspective, marking the information status of referents as "given" or "new" for the addressee, assigning topic and focus, and so on.

The student had to cast this highly structured package of information (which will be called the *message*) in an utterance of some sort—a phrase, or a rather elliptical sentence. He began with *I*, and there was still some hesitation. There may not have been a final decision on the information to be expressed—we will never know precisely—but the long silence made it important to do something. At any rate, *I* appeared again. It is the deictic term referring to the experiencer "me" in the conceptual structure to be expressed. It is, moreover, in the nominative case (not *my*, *mine*, or *me*), which indicates that the speaker had selected it as the grammatical subject of the sentence. This choice does justice to treating the experiencer as the given topic of discourse, a reflection of the academic's *you*. It is the one about whom the comment is to be made. The choice also clearly restricts what the speaker can do next: He must select a verb that allows *I* to be its grammatical subject. If indeed the speaker had started to say *I* out of urgency, and before the necessary information had been made available, this restriction may explain the hesitation on *I*. The speaker selected as the main verb *know*, which does express the concept of "state of knowledge". Ignoring the *don't* for the moment, observe that the student realized the substance of that state of knowledge—Shakespeare's play *Othello*—as the grammatical object of *know*. In fact, he mapped that concept, to be expressed in reduced form, onto the noun *play*. The final part of the conceptualization, "not meeting criterion *Y*", and eliding *Y*, was mapped on an adverbial phrase: (not) *WELL enough*. To complete his utterance, the student accessed a polite address form for a male addressee: the conventional *sir*.

The way in which a speaker maps the package of information to be expressed onto spoken words involves, of course, the retrieval of lexical items from what I will call the *mental lexicon*—the store of information about the words in one's language. The speaker will use parts of the conceptual structure to retrieve the appropriate words (i.e., the lexical items that correctly express the intended meanings) from the lexicon. A lexical item is a complex entity. It is retrieved on the basis of its meaning, but in addition it contains syntactic, morphological, and phonological information.

There is evidence, to be discussed in chapters 6 and 7, that speakers construct the "framework" of an utterance without much regard for the phonology of words. Apart from the semantic information, they use the syntactic information (and sometimes aspects of the morphological information) contained in the retrieved items to build this framework. This nonphonological part of an item's lexical information will be called the item's *lemma information* (or, for short, the *lemma*). So, when we say that a speaker has retrieved a lemma, we mean that the speaker has acquired access to those aspects of a word's stored information that are relevant for the construction of the word's syntactic environment. Take, for instance, the word *know*, which our speaker used in his utterance. The lemma *know* requires a subject that expresses the role of experiencer, and an object (or a complement) that expresses what is known, and there is a certain order in which these grammatical elements should appear. By some process, (which we will call *grammatical encoding*), the speaker retrieves the appropriate lemmas for the concepts to be expressed and puts the lemmas in the right order. It is presumably as part of this process that the negative element (in "not meeting criterion Y") is mapped onto an auxiliary verb, which eventually yields *don't*. In addition, certain features are assigned to lemmas during grammatical encoding, such as that they are definite (for *play*), that they should receive pitch accent (as for *WELL*), or that they should have a certain case (e.g., nominative for *I*). This initial move in mapping the information to be expressed onto words creates what will be called a *surface structure*.

But how then could the speech error *way* appear? In order for the lemma *way* to become active, the speaker should have been thinking of its meaning. Maybe the speaker thought of something like "I don't know the way". If the above phenomenology is correct, however, the meaning of *way* was not part of the message, and its lemma therefore did not appear in the surface structure. The error presumably arose when the phonological forms of the words were accessed. It is not far-fetched to suppose that *way* is the result of blending the sound realizations of *WELL* and *play*. At the critical moment in time, the student had both lemmas available in his surface structure, and a slight mistiming in the activation of their phonological patterns created the blend. Note that *way* was not accented; rather, it carried the level prosody intended for *play*, not the raised pitch that *WELL* should receive. Such speech errors are an important argument for distinguishing an independent level of *phonological encoding*. After retrieving the phonological forms for the lemmas in the surface structure, the speaker can build a *phonetic* or *articulatory plan* for the utterance.

The transcription of the above conversation doesn't tell us how the utterance really sounded. It will have been delivered with some specific pitch and loudness contour, it will have displayed the student's characteristic timbre, and there will have been some degree of blending or "co-articulation" between successive speech sounds. All these and many other features of the utterance are aspects of the speaker's articulation—the execution of the phonetic plan by the delicately tuned musculature of the vocal apparatus.

It is, finally, not trivial that the student *noticed* that he had said *way* instead of *play*. In fact, he noticed it right after he said it. He stopped the flow of speech, there was a short moment of silence, and he replaced the error by an edited version. How did the student know that something had gone wrong? Had he listened to himself speaking and noticed that *way* was not what he had intended to say? Or would he have discovered the error even without listening to himself? And why did he replace *way* with *play*, and not with *the play* or *know the play*? There is, apparently, some way for the speaker to monitor his own speech and to adapt things correspondingly. In conversation, moreover, interlocutors send various signals to the speaker which tell him that something wasn't clear (*eh?*), or that he should go on (*mhm*), or that one waits for him to take the turn, and so on. Much of this can be done by gaze or gesture. A speaker, while delivering his utterance, is continuously monitoring himself and his interlocutors, and this feeds back to what he is doing.

The student's utterance may not have helped him much in the interview, but it has been most helpful for us in distinguishing various steps in a speaker's production of an utterance. There is the initial choice of purpose ("conceiving the intention") and there is selection of the means to make this intention apparent to the interlocutor. These conceptual processes depend on the speaker's state of motivation, the knowledge shared with the interlocutors, and especially the speaker's discourse record. They create a "message" to be expressed. Furthermore, there are more specifically linguistic steps to be taken. Words have to be accessed. Syntactic forms that map the concepts and their relations onto a grammatical surface structure have to be constructed. These surface structures, in turn, have to be developed into phonetic plans that serve to instruct the articulatory apparatus of the speaker. On top of all this, the speaker apparently manages to monitor and, where necessary, improve what he is doing.

In the next section a framework will be proposed in which these processing notions are brought together.

1.2 A Blueprint for the Speaker

Figure 1.1 proposes a partitioning of the various processes involved in the generation of fluent speech. It consists of a number of processing components, each of which receives a certain kind of input and produces a certain kind of output. The output of one component may become the input for another. In the subsequent sections some preliminary motivation will be given for proposing the flow of information depicted in the figure, but first the different processing components will have to be introduced.

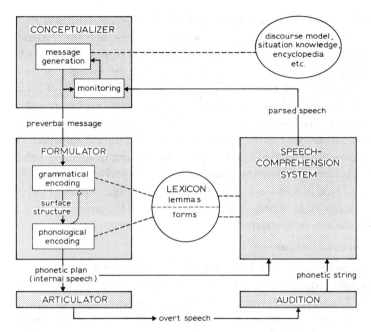

Figure 1.1
A blueprint for the speaker. Boxes represent processing components; circle and ellipse represent knowledge stores.

1.2.1. Conceptualizing

Talking as an intentional activity involves conceiving of an intention, selecting the relevant information to be expressed for the realization of this purpose, ordering this information for expression, keeping track of what was said before, and so on. These activities require the speaker's constant attention. The speaker will, moreover, attend to his own productions, monitoring what he is saying and how (see subsection 1.2.4). The sum total of these mental activities will be called *conceptualizing*, and the subserving processing system will on occasion be called the *Conceptualizer* (in full awareness that this is a reification in need of further explanation—we are, of course, dealing with a highly open-ended system involving quite heterogeneous aspects of the speaker as an acting person). The product of conceptualizing will be called the *preverbal message*.

In order to encode a message, the speaker must have access to two kinds of knowledge.

The first kind is *procedural* knowledge; it has the format IF X THEN Y. For instance:

IF the intention is to commit oneself to the truth of p, THEN assert p.
Here p is some proposition the speaker wants to express as being the case, and the indicated procedure is to build an assertion of that proposition. The Conceptualizer and its message generator can be thought of as a structured system of such condition/action pairs (to which we will return in section 1.3). These procedures can deposit their results in what is called *Working Memory* (Baddeley 1986). Working Memory contains all the information currently accessible to the speaker, i.e., all the information that can be processed by message-generating procedures or by monitoring procedures. It is the information *attended to* by the speaker.

The second kind of knowledge is *declarative* knowledge. A major kind of declarative knowledge is *propositional* knowledge. The variable p above could, for instance, be given the value

"Manhattan is dangerous".

This is a unit of propositional knowledge. The speaker has access to a huge amount of declarative knowledge. That knowledge is, in the first place, available in *Long-Term Memory*—the speaker's structured knowledge of the world and himself, built up in the course of a lifetime (and also called *encyclopedic knowledge*). But there is also declarative knowledge of the present discourse situation. The speaker can be aware of the interlocutors—where they are and who they are. The speaker, moreover, may be in the perceptual presence of a visual array of objects, of acoustic information about the environment, and so forth. This *situational knowledge* may also be accessible as declarative knowledge, to be used in the encoding of messages. Finally, the speaker will keep track of what he and the others have said in the course of the interaction. This is his *discourse record*, of which only a small, focused part is in the speaker's Working Memory. Figure 1.1 represents declarative knowledge within circles. Procedural knowledge is not represented independently in the figure; it is part of the processors themselves, which are given rectangular shape.

When the speaker applies the above IF X THEN Y procedure to the proposition "Manhattan is dangerous", the message will be the assertion of this proposition. The message generated is not only the output of the Conceptualizer; it is also the input to the next processing component, which will be called the *Formulator*. As we will see in subsection 4.4.5, the Formulator can handle only those messages that fulfill certain language-specific conditions. Hence, the adequate output of the Conceptualizer will be called a *preverbal* message. It is a conceptual structure that can be accepted as input by the Formulator.

We have already distinguished two stages in the planning of a preverbal message: macroplanning and microplanning. Macroplanning involves the elaboration of some communicative goal into a series of subgoals, and the retrieval of the information to be expressed in order to realize each of these subgoals. Microplanning assigns the right propositional shape to each of these "chunks" of information, as well as the informational perspective (the particular topic and focus) that will guide the addressee's allocation of attention.

1.2.2   Formulating: Grammatical and Phonological Encoding

The formulating component, or *Formulator*, accepts fragments of messages as characteristic input and produces as output a *phonetic* or *articulatory plan*. In other words, the Formulator translates a conceptual structure into a linguistic structure. This translation proceeds in two steps.

First, there is *grammatical encoding* of the message. The Grammatical Encoder consists of procedures for accessing lemmas, and of syntactic building procedures. The speaker's lemma information is declarative knowledge, which is stored in his mental lexicon. A lexical item's lemma information contains the lexical item's *meaning* or *sense*, i.e., the concept that goes with the word. Two examples of such information are that *sparrow* is a special kind of bird and that *give* involves some actor X causing some possession Y to go from actor X to recipient Z. Also, the *syntax* of each word is part of its lemma information. The lemma *sparrow* is categorized as a count noun; the verb *give* is categorized as a verb (V) which can take a subject expressing the actor X, a direct object expressing the possession Y, and an indirect object expressing the recipient Z (as in *John gave Mary the book*); and so forth. A lemma will be activated when its meaning matches part of the preverbal message. This will make its syntax available, which in turn will call or activate certain syntactic building procedures. When, for instance, the lemma *give* is activated by the conceptual structure of the message, the syntactic category V will call the verb-phrase-building procedure. This procedural knowledge (stored in the Grammatical Encoder) is used to build verb phrases, such as *gave Mary the book*. There are also procedures in the Grammatical Encoder for building noun phrases (e.g. *the sparrow*), prepositional phrases, clauses, and so on.

When all the relevant lemmas have been accessed and all the syntactic building procedures have done their work, the Grammatical Encoder has produced a *surface structure*—an ordered string of lemmas grouped in phrases and subphrases of various kinds. The surface string *John gave Mary the book* is of the type "sentence," with the constituents *John* (a noun phrase which is the sentence's subject) and *gave Mary the book* (a verb phrase which is its predicate). The verb phrase, in turn, consists of a main verb and two noun phrases: the indirect object and the direct object. The grammatical encoding procedures can deposit their interim results in a buffer, which we will call the *Syntactic Buffer*.

Second, there is *phonological encoding*. Its function is to retrieve or build a phonetic or articulatory plan for each lemma and for the utterance as a whole. The major source of information to be accessed by the Phonological Encoder is *lexical form*, the lexicon's information about an item's internal composition. Apart from the lemma information, an item in the lexicon contains information about its morphology and its phonology—for instance, that *dangerous* consists of a root (*danger*) and a suffix (*ous*), that it contains three syllables of which the first one has the accent, and that its first segment is /d/. Several phonological procedures will modify, or further specify, the form information that is retrieved. For instance, in the encoding of *John gave Mary the book*, the syllable /buk/ will be given additional stress.

The result of phonological encoding is a *phonetic* or *articulatory plan*. It is not yet overt speech; it is an internal representation of how the planned utterance should be articulated—a program for articulation. Not without hesitation, I will alternatively call this representation *internal speech*. The term may, of course, lose some of its everyday connotation when used as an equivalent for the technical term "phonetic plan." In particular, the speaker will, in the course of fluent speech, often not be aware of his phonetic plan. The term "internal speech," however, entails a certain degree of consciousness (McNeill 1987). A more precise way to put things would be to say that internal speech is the phonetic plan as far as it is attended to and interpreted by the speaker—i.e., the phonetic plan as far as it is *parsed* by the speaker (see below). I will ignore this fine distinction where it is without consequence. This end product of the Formulator becomes the input to the next processing component: the Articulator.

1.2.3 Articulating

Articulating is the execution of the phonetic plan by the musculature of the respiratory, the laryngeal, and the supralaryngeal systems. It is not obvious that the Formulator delivers its phonetic plan at just the normal rate of articulation. In fact, the generation of internal speech may be somewhat ahead of articulatory execution. In order to cope with such asynchronies, it is necessary that the phonetic plan can be temporarily stored. This storage device is called the *Articulatory Buffer*. The Articulator retrieves successive chunks of internal speech from this buffer and unfolds them for execution. Motor execution involves the coordinated use of sets of muscles. If certain muscles in a set are hampered in their movement, for instance when the speaker chats with a pipe in his mouth, others will compensate so that roughly the same articulatory goal is reached. In other words, though the articulatory plan is relatively independent of context, its execution will, within limits, adapt to the varying circumstances of articulation. The product of articulation is *overt speech*.

1.2.4 Self-Monitoring

Self-monitoring involves various components that need no detailed treatment in a book on language production since they are the processing components of normal language comprehension. A speaker is his own listener. More precisely, a speaker has access to both his internal speech and his overt speech. He can listen to his own *overt* speech, just as he can listen to the speech of his interlocutors. This involves an *Audition* processing component. He can understand what he is saying, i.e., interpret his own speech sounds as meaningful words and sentences. This processing takes place by means of what is called the *Speech-Comprehension System* in figure 1.1. It consists, of course, of various subcomponents, which are not at issue here and hence not indicated in the figure. The system has access to both the form information and the lemma information in the lexicon, in order to recognize words and to retrieve their meanings. Its output is *parsed speech*, a representation of the input speech in terms of its phonological, morphological, syntactic, and semantic composition.

The speaker can also attend to his own *internal* speech (Dell 1980). This means that parsed internal speech is representable in Working Memory. How does it get there? Figure 1.1 expresses the assumption that internal speech is analyzed by the same Speech-Comprehension System as overt speech. In this way the speaker can detect trouble in his own internal speech before he has fully articulated the troublesome element. This happened, presumably, in the following self-correction (from Levelt 1983).

(1) To the left side of the purple disk is a v-, a horizontal line

There is reason to assume (see chapter 12) that the speaker of these words intercepted articulation of the word *vertical* at its very start. Presumably, the plan for *vertical* was internally available, understood, and discovered to have a nonintended meaning. In other words, the monitor can compare the meaning of what was said or internally prepared to what was intended. But it can also detect form errors. The Speech-Comprehension System allows us to discover form errors in the speech of others. In the same way, it is able to notice self-generated form failures. This is apparent from a self-correction such as the following (from Fay 1980b).

(2) How long does that has to – have to simmer?

Dell (1980) found that speakers also discover form failures in their own internal speech. In short, speakers monitor not only for meaning but also for linguistic well-formedness (Laver 1973).

When the speaker detects serious trouble with respect to the meaning or well-formedness of his own internal or overt speech, he may decide to halt further formulation of the present utterance. He may then rerun the same preverbal message or a fragment thereof, create a different or additional message, or just continue formulation without alteration, all depending on the nature of the trouble. These processes are not of a different nature than what is going on in message construction anyhow.

The speaker no doubt also monitors messages *before* they are sent into the Formulator (see chapter 12), considering whether they will have the intended effect in view of the present state of the discourse and the knowledge shared with the interlocutor(s). Hence, there is no good reason for distinguishing a relatively autonomous monitoring component in language production. The main work is done by the Conceptualizer, which can attend to internally generated messages and to the output of the Speech-Comprehension System (i.e., parsed internal and overt speech).

1.3   Processing Components as Relatively Autonomous Specialists

The architecture in figure 1.1 may, on first view, appear to be rather arbitrary, and at this stage it is. There is no single foolproof way of achieving the partitioning of a complex processing system. There are always various empirical and theoretical considerations that have to be taken into account before one decides on one partitioning rather than another. It doesn't help much at this stage to say that the blueprint reflects earlier proposals by Garrett (1975), Kempen and Hoenkamp (1987), Bock (1982, 1987a), Cooper and Paccia-Cooper (1980), Levelt (1983), Dell (1986), and others. In fact, it is one of the aims of this book to argue that these proposals make sense. The present chapter can only give some background considerations for deciding whether a particular partitioning of the system is more attractive than another.

A first argument for distinguishing a particular processing component is that it is *relatively autonomous* in the system. The central idea is that a processing component is a *specialist*. The Grammatical Encoder, for instance, should be a specialist in translating conceptual relations into grammatical relations; no other component is able to build syntactic phrases. Moreover, in order to execute these specialized procedures, the Grammatical Encoder needs only one kind of input: preverbal messages. That is its characteristic input. And in order to do its work, it need not consult with other processing components. The characteristic input is necessary and sufficient for the procedures to apply. More generally, it makes no sense to distinguish a processing component A whose mode of operation is continuously affected by feedback from another component, B. In that case, A is not a specialist anymore, it won't come up with the right result without the "help" of B. There is only one component then: AB.

There is another way in which the idea of components as autonomous specialists can be ducked, namely by assuming that all components receive as characteristic input the output of all other components (plus feedback of their own output). In that way each component has access to all information in the system. But this is tantamount to saying that components have no *characteristic* input—that they are general problem solvers that weigh all the available information in order to create their characteristic output. The Grammatical Encoder, for example, would access one lemma rather than another not only on the basis of the concept to be expressed, but also taking into consideration the morphology assigned to the previous word, the intonation pattern of the current sentence, the next intention the speaker has just prepared, and so forth. Some theorists like such models, which make each component an intelligent homunculus. The problems are, of course, to define the algorithm the component applies in considering this wide variety of information, and to realize this algorithm by a processing mechanism that can work in real time.

Generally speaking, one should try to partition the system in such a way that (a) a component's characteristic input is of a maximally restricted sort and (b) a component's mode of operation is minimally affected by the output of other components.

The combination of these two requirements is sometimes called *informational encapsulation* (Fodor 1983). In the blueprint of figure 1.1, these two requirements are met. Each component is exclusively provided with its characteristic input: the Grammatical Encoder with preverbal messages, which are conceptual structures; the Phonological Encoder with surface structures, which are syntactic entities; the Articulator with internal speech, which consists of phonetic representations; and so forth. The functioning of these processors is affected minimally, or not at all, by other input. There is no feedback from processors down the line (except for some Formulator-*internal* feedback). The Articulator, for instance, cannot affect the Formulator's subcomponents. The only feedback in the system is via the language-comprehension components. This makes self-monitoring possible. But there is not even any *direct* feedback from the Formulator or the Articulator to the Conceptualizer. The Conceptualizer can recognize trouble in any of these components only on the basis of feedback from internal or overt speech.

These are strong and vulnerable hypotheses about the partitioning of the system. If one could show, for instance, that message generation is directly affected by the accessibility of lemmas or word forms, one would have evidence for direct feedback from the Formulator to the Conceptualizer. This is an empirical question, and it is possible to put it to the test. Studies of this kind will be reviewed in section 7.5. So far, the evidence for such feedback is negative.

A processing component may itself consist of subcomponents of varying degrees of autonomy. The Formulator in figure 1.1, for instance, consists of two subcomponents, which may be less autonomous than the Formulator as a whole. There is, in fact, convincing experimental evidence in the literature for the possibility of feedback from phonological to grammatical encoding (Levelt and Maassen 1981; Dell 1986; Bock 1987b; see also chapters 7 and 9 below).

And partitioning can even go further. It will, for instance, be argued in the course of this book that both of these subcomponents consist of even smaller building blocks, such as a noun-phrase processor and a verb-phrase processor within the Grammatical Encoder.

On the notion that a processing component is a relatively antonomous specialist, the following questions should be asked for each component that is proposed:

1. What are the characteristic kinds of information, or types of representation, the component accepts as input and delivers as output?
2. What sort of algorithm is needed to transform the input information into the characteristic output representation?
3. What type of process can execute that algorithm in real time?
4. Where does the input information come from, and where does the output information go to? A component can have one or more sources of input, and can transmit information to one or more other components.

In the course of this book these questions will return like the main theme of a rondo. For each component to be discussed, the nature of the target output will be considered first. One cannot specify the operations of a component without an explicit characterization of the representation it computes. The Grammatical Encoder, for instance, produces what we called "surface structures" as output. Making a theory of grammatical encoding requires one to be explicit about what kinds of objects surface structures are. They are the target representations of the syntactic building operations (the grammatical encoding algorithm). Question 1 above has a certain priority over questions 2 and 3. In the following chapters I will honor that priority by considering a component's output representation before turning to its operations. Still, the questions are, in fact, interdependent. One may have good independent reasons for assuming a particular kind of operation. Speech errors, as we shall see, reveal much about the processes of grammatical encoding. We will naturally prefer to conjecture an encoding algorithm that does justice to such empirical observations. But the choice of algorithm, in turn, limits the kind of target representations that can be generated. Processes and representations cannot be studied independent of one another.

A component's output representation is, at the same time, the characteristic input for the next processor down the line. For each processor, we must ask whether there are circumstances under which it can be affected by information other than its characteristic input (issue 4 above). I have already mentioned the issue of feedback; in the next section I will discuss components' sensitivity to "executive control."

In subsequent chapters, a discussion of a component's output representation will always be followed by a treatment of its algorithm and its processes (i.e., issues 2 and 3 above). This will involve reviewing both theoretical proposals and empirical research. In all cases the depth of treatment is crucially dependent on the amount of detail provided by the existing literature.

The procedures an algorithm consists of are taken to be *productions* in the sense defined by Newell and Simon (1972) and used extensively by Anderson (1983). It was mentioned earlier that these productions are condition/action pairs of the kind IF X THEN Y, where X is the condition and Y the action. The example given was the conceptual procedure *IF the intention is to commit oneself to the truth of p, THEN assert p*. Here the IF clause is the condition. It states the speaker's prevailing intention. The THEN clause states the action. A speech act of the type "assertion" is to be made (such as *Manhattan is dangerous*, and not *Is Manhattan dangerous?*; the latter would be a question). Productions can contain variables, such as *p* in the example. That gives them generality, and it keeps them apart from declarative knowledge (i.e., from the set of insertable propositions). Not only can conceptual algorithms be stated in the formal language of productions; the same holds for the algorithms of grammatical and phonological encoding.

Algorithms must run in real time. This means that the brain must be able to execute an algorithm—in fact, the sum total of all algorithms involved in speaking—in such a way that fluent speech results (see issue 3 above). This will make certain proposals for algorithms less attractive than others. Take, for instance, an algorithm for the planning of speech melody or intonation. It is known that speech melody bears some relation to the syntactic structure of the sentence. One might therefore be tempted to propose an algorithm that inspects the full surface structure before generating the appropriate melody for a sentence. But such an algorithm would violate the real-time requirement. Since no word can be pronounced without melody, the full surface structure of a sentence would have to be stored in the Syntactic Buffer before the sound form of its first word could be generated. This would create huge dysfluences between sentences, except when one would make the unlikely assumption that the speaker articulates sentence i while formulating sentence $i + 1$. I will return to this issue in the next paragraph, but first let me state that a main real-time restriction on speech planning should be that it run "from left to right" with very little lookahead.

One might want to go one step further and propose neural-network structures that could run the algorithm. This is still a very long shot for the algorithms involved in the process of speaking. Still, proposals of a quasi-neurological sort are being made for various aspects of language processing. These are the "*connectionist*" or "*spreading activation*" accounts (I will use the more accurate term "activation spreading"). In these accounts an algorithm is implemented in a network of connected nodes. The nodes can be in various states of activation, and they can spread their activation to the nodes with which they are connected. Figure 1.2 gives an example. It represents, in a highly simplified way, how the above procedure of accessing a lemma's corresponding sound form could be implemented in detail. Each lemma node in the lexicon is connected to a set of syllable nodes. The figure represents this state of affairs for just two lemmas, *construct* and *constrain*. The network connections are relatively permanent. What varies is the states of activation of the nodes. When the lemma *construct* is part of the surface structure, its node is in a state of high activation. The node "fires" and spreads its activation to its two constituent syllable nodes in the form lexicon: *con* and *struct*. Initially, *con* should be more highly activated

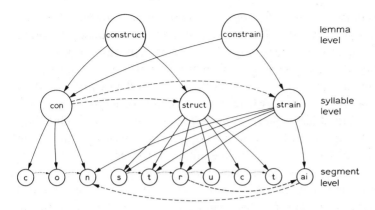

Figure 1.2
Example of an activation-spreading network.

than *struct*; otherwise the speaker may happen to say *structcon* instead of *construct*—a type of slip that is absent from collections of speech errors. In order to realize this, a directed inhibitory connection (dotted line) can be supposed to exist between the syllable nodes *con* and *struct*. When the syllable node *con* is sufficiently activated, it will, in turn, fire and spread its activation to the so-called segment nodes, *c*, *o*, and *n*. And again, their ordering of activation has to be controlled by a system of inhibitory connections. If everything runs well, the segment nodes will fire in the right order. It can further be assumed that a node, after spreading its activation, returns to a low state of activation. When this happens to the syllable node *con*, the inhibition on *struct* will fade away so that it can reach threshold activation and fire. Its constituent segments will be activated, and the inhibitory mechanism will make them fire in the right order. The lemma *constrain* is connected to a large part of the same network, and so are other lemmas that share syllables or segments with *construct*.

This is not meant to be more than an example. Activation-spreading or connectionist accounts vary enormously in detail (Anderson 1983; Dell 1986; Rumelhart et al. 1986; MacKay 1987). They differ in the kinds of nodes, the use of excitatory and inhibitory connections between nodes, the directions of spreading, the time characteristics of activation spreading, the summation function of input activations to a node, the possible range of activation states of a node, and the nodes' output function. They also differ in the control of timing and order. It may or may not be the case that *any* explicit process can be implemented in a "spreading activation" network.

Connectionism is, in the first place, a *formal language* for the expression of cognitive processes. It is not a *theory about* cognitive processes. Theories, whether expressed in the language of spreading activation or in the language of production systems, are coherent sets of principles which *restrict* the domain of possible processes. In other words, a theory *forbids* certain states of affairs to occur, whereas a sufficiently rich formal language doesn't. A formal language is a vehicle for the expression of interesting theoretical principles, which can be more or less convenient. And it can provide a complexity measure for the output generated by an algorithm. The connectionist formal language is especially convenient for the representation of principles of parallel processing, and there is much parallel processing in the generation of speech. In the course of this book we will meet certain restricted theoretical proposals that use the connectionist language of parallel distributed processing—in particular, Dell's (1986, 1988) theory of phonological encoding.

1.4   Executive Control and Automaticity

Speaking is usually an intentional activity; it serves a purpose the speaker wants to realize. An intentional activity is, by definition, under central control (Carr 1979; Bock 1982; Fodor 1983). A speaker can decide on one course of verbal action rather than another on the basis of practically any sort of information: his state of motivation, his obligations, his believing this rather than that, his previous speech acts or other actions, and so forth. The speaker will invest his attention on matters of this sort in planning what to say next.

Given the existence of central or *executive* control, an important question is to what degree the various processing components are subject to such control. When a component is not subject to central control, its functioning is *automatic*. The distinction between controlled and automatic processing is fundamental to cognitive psychology, and is based in a firm research tradition (LaBerge and Samuels 1974; Posner and Snyder 1975; Schneider and Shiffrin 1977; Flores d'Arcais 1987a).

Automatic processes are executed without intention or conscious awareness. They also run on their own resources; i.e., they do not share processing capacity with other processes. Also, automatic processing is usually quick, even reflex-like; the structure of the process is "wired in," either genetically or by learning (or both). This makes it both efficient and, to a large extent, inflexible; it is hard to alter automatic processes. Since automatic processes do not share resources, they can run in parallel without mutual interference.

Controlled processing demands attentional resources, and one can attend to only a few things (the items in Working Memory) at a time. Attending to the process means a certain level of awareness of what one is doing. Human controlled processing tends to be serial in nature, and is therefore slow. But it is not entirely fixated in memory. In fact, it is highly flexible and adaptable to the requirements of the task.

Let us now look again at the components of the blueprint in figure 1.1. Clearly, the Conceptualizer involves highly controlled processing. Speakers do not have a small, fixed set of intentions that they have learned to realize in speech. Communicative intentions can vary in infinite ways, and for each of these ways the speaker will have to find new means of expression. This requires much attention. And introspection supports this. When we speak, we are aware of considering alternatives, of being reminded of relevant information, of developing a train of thought, and so forth. Message construction is controlled processing, and so is monitoring; self-corrections are hardly ever made without a touch of awareness. The speaker can *attend* to his own internal or overt speech. The limited-capacity resource in conceptualizing and monitoring is Working Memory. The system allows only a few concepts or bits of internal speech to be highly active, i.e., available for processing (Miller 1956; Broadbent 1975; Anderson 1983). On the other hand, not all processing in message encoding is under executive control. An adult's experience with speaking is so extensive that whole messages will be available in long-term memory and thus will be retrievable. Many conversational skills (such as knowing when and how to take or give a turn in conversation and deciding how direct or how polite one's speech act should be) have been acquired over the course of a lifetime and are quite directly available to the speaker. They are not invented time and again through conscious processing. Still, even these automatic aspects of conceptualizing are easily attended to and modified when that is required by the conversational situation. They are not "informationally encapsulated."

All the other components, however, are claimed to be largely automatic. There is very little executive control over formulating or articulatory procedures. A speaker doesn't have to ponder the issue of whether to make the recipient of GIVE an indirect object (as in *John gave Mary the book*) or an oblique object (as in *John gave the book to Mary*). Neither will much attention be spent on retrieving the word *horse* when one wants to refer to the big live object that is conventionally named that way. These things come automatically without any awareness. They also come with very high speed. Speech is normally produced at a rate of about two to three words per second. These words are selected at that rate from the many tens of thousands of words in the mental lexicon. There is just no time to consciously weigh the alternatives before deciding on a word. Articulation runs at a speed of about fifteen phonemes per second. One should be grateful that no attention need be spent on the selection of each and every individual speech sound. Formulating and articulating are "underground processes" (Seuren 1978) that are probably largely impenetrable to executive control even when one wishes otherwise. (See Pylyshyn 1984 for more on cognitive impenetrability.)

There may be marginal forms of executive control, however. They are evidenced, for instance, in the fact that a speaker can abruptly stop speaking when he detects an error (Levelt 1983). The sentence or the phrase is then typically not completed. One can stop a word in the middle of its articulation, even ignoring syllable boundaries. It is apparently possible to send an executive "halt" signal to the individual processing components. Maybe similar signals can be sent to control other global aspects of processing, such as speaking rate, loudness, and articulatory precision.

The notions of automaticity, informational encapsulation, and cognitive impenetrability also figure centrally in the ongoing "modularity" discussions (Fodor 1983, 1985, 1987; Garfield 1987; Marshall 1984). The issue is whether, in an interesting number of cases, automatic components of processing also show several other features, such as being genetically given to the species, being located in specialized neurological tissues, and showing highly specific breakdown patterns. It is by no means excluded that some or all of these additional features have a certain applicability to the automatic processing components that underlie speech production. Only man can speak; there are dedicated neurological substrates for the production of speech in the left hemisphere; their disruption creates specific disorders such as agrammatism; and in the course of this book we will observe a multitude of characteristic breakdown patterns for different processing components, in particular speech errors. A processing component that shares most of these features is called a *module*. Whether the automatic components proposed in the blueprint above share the additional features that would make them modules will, however, not be a major issue in this book; hence, we will not call them modules.

1.5   Units of Processing and Incremental Production

1.5.1   Units of Processing

Much ink has been spilled on the question of what units of processing are involved in speech production, and in part for the wrong reasons. Many authors have tried to delineate *the* unit of speech, and this search for the Holy Grail has enriched the literature with an astonishing gamma of units. Others, surely, have recognized that there is no single unit of speech production, but have spent much attention on one particular unit. Here are some of the units one regularly encounters in the literature, with references to selected sources:

cycle (Goldman-Eisler 1967; Beattie 1983)
deep clause (Ford and Holmes 1978)
idea (Butterworth 1975; Chafe 1980)
information block (Grimes 1975)
information unit (Halliday 1967a; Brown and Yule 1983)
I-marker (Schlesinger 1977)
message (Fodor, Bever, and Garrett 1974)
phonemic clause (Boomer 1965)
phrase (Bock 1982)
proposition or propositional structure (Clark and Clark 1977; Herrmann 1983)
sentence (Osgood 1971, 1980; Garrett 1980a)
spurt (Chafe 1980)
surface clause (Hawkins 1971)
syntagma (Kozhevnikov and Chistovich 1965; McNeill 1979)
tone group (Halliday 1967a)
tone unit (Lehiste 1970).
total conception [*Gesamtvorstellung*] (Wundt 1900)
turn-constructional unit (Sacks, Schegloff, and Jefferson 1974).

And one can easily double or triple the length of this list. Foss and Hakes (1978) correctly remark that "speech has many planning units: words, syllables, phonological segments, and even phonological features."

The empirical evidence marshaled for one unit rather than another has been very diverse, including pause patterns, intonational structure, speech errors, and speech-accompanying gestures. Much of this evidence will be reviewed in the following chapters. The point to be stressed here is that there is no single unit of talk. Different processing components have their own characteristic processing units, and these units may or may not be preserved in the articulatory pattern of speech. If, for instance, grammatical encoding involves units such as "noun phrase," "verb phrase," "sentence," and "clause," then these units need not be preserved in the prosody of the utterance. Later stages of processing—particularly the stage of phonological encoding—may undo these units of surface structure and impose a somewhat different organization (one more appropriate for fluent articulation). Still, the presumed absence of syntactic-clause boundaries in an utterance's prosody has been used as argument against multistage models of speech generation (McNeill 1979).

1.5.2 Incremental Production

A major reason for some theorists to object to multistage models and to prefer "multi-faceted single-stage speech production" (McNeill 1979) may be what Danks (1977) calls the "lock-step succession" of processing stages. It would indeed be disturbing if processing were strictly serial in the following way: First, the speaker generates the complete message to be communicated. Then, he generates the complete surface structure for the message. Next, the speaker starts building a phonetic plan for the utterance. Only after finishing this can the speaker begin to work on the articulation of the first word of the utterance. After completion of the utterance, the speaker can start preparing the next message. This would, of course, create serious dysfluences in discourse.

There is, however, nothing in stage models that requires this kind of seriality. Even though there can be no formulating without some conceptual planning, and there can be no articulating without a phonetic plan, message encoding, formulating, and articulating can run in parallel. Fry (1969) and Garrett (1976) made the obvious assumption that the next processor can start working on the still-incomplete output of the current processor (i.e., can start working before the current processing component has delivered its complete characteristic unit of information). Kempen and Hoenkamp (1982, 1987) called this *incremental processing*. All components can work in parallel, but they all work on different bits and pieces of the utterance under construction. A processing component will be triggered by any *fragment* of characteristic input. As was already noted in section 1.3, this requires that such a fragment can be processed without much lookahead—i.e., that what is done with the fragment should not depend on what will be coming in later fragments. Intoning the first few words of a sentence, for instance, should not depend on the way in which the sentence will finish. Some lookahead is, of course, necessary in certain cases. A speaker who is going to say *sixteen dollars* should not pronounce

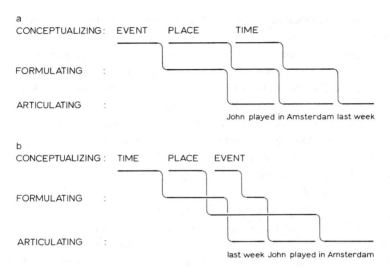

Figure 1.3
Incremental production without (a) and with (b) inversion of order. (After
Kempen and Hoenkamp 1987.)

sixTEEN (a correct accentuation of the word) and then *DOllars*; rather, he
should say *SIXteen DOllars*, with word stress shifted to SIX. In other
words, in order for the right stress pattern to be generated for the first word,
the stress pattern of the second word must be available. This is lookahead.
But in order to make incremental processing possible, this lookahead
should, for each processor, be quite limited. This puts interesting restrictions on the kind of algorithm that is allowable for each component.

It should immediately be added that a processing component will, on
occasion, have to reverse the order of fragments when going from input to
processed output. Figure 1.3 depicts incremental processing without (a)
and with (b) inversion of fragment order. The first case is meant to
represent an instance in which the speaker conceptualizes for expression
an EVENT (John's playing before "now"), then the PLACE of the event
(it took place in Amsterdam), then the TIME of the past event (during
last week). When the first fragment of the message (the EVENT) becomes
available, the Formulator starts working on it. While the Formulator is
encoding the EVENT, the Conceptualizer generates the next piece of the
message (the PLACE information). It is sent to the Formulator, which has
just completed *John played*. This piece of the phonetic plan is now up for
articulation. While this articulation proceeds, the Formulator encodes the
PLACE information. At the same time, the Conceptualizer generates the

message fragment concerning the TIME information. And so on. This is pure incremental processing.

But the order of words doesn't always follow the order of thoughts. Figure 1.3(b) gives the case where the message fragments come in the order TIME, PLACE, EVENT. The formulation and articulation of the TIME information can follow the normal course, leading to the articulation of *last week*. But the Formulator cannot deliver its encoding of the PLACE information before having encoded the EVENT information; this would produce *last week in Amsterdam John played*. The Formulator, which is built to produce English syntax, will reverse the order and come up with *last week John played in Amsterdam*.

Other languages will have other ordering problems. A speaker of German, for instance, will have to swap fragments in the formulation depicted in figure 1.3(a), where they come in the order EVENT, PLACE, TIME, and should cast the sentence as *Hans spielte letzte Woche in Amsterdam*. It is obvious that, where such reversals are necessary, certain fragments must be kept in abeyance. In other words, components must have storage or buffering facilities for intermediate results. Three such facilities have already been mentioned: Working Memory (which can store a small number of message fragments as well as fragments of parsed speech), the Syntactic Buffer (which can store results of grammatical encoding), and the Articulatory Buffer (which can store bits of the phonetic plan). These buffers will, at the same time, absorb the asynchronies that may arise from the different speeds of processing in the different components.

Although there is a need for a theory of processing that will handle ordering problems of this kind, the main job will be to do as much as can be done with strictly incremental production. This is a time-honored principle in psycholinguistics. Wundt (1900) said that word order follows the successive apperception of the parts of a total conception [*Gesamtvorstellung*]. Of course Wundt added that this can hold only to the degree that word order is free in a language, but the principle is there. Let us call it *Wundt's principle*, but broaden it somewhat for the present purposes: *Each processing component will be triggered into activity by a minimal amount of its characteristic input*. In the following chapters we will, time and again, have to consider how small that minimal amount can be. How large a fragment of surface structure is needed for phonological encoding to do its work? How much of a phonetic plan must be available for articulation to be possible? And so forth. When these amounts are all small, articulation can follow on the heels of conceptualization.

But the theoretical assumption of incremental processing (i.e., of parallel processing activity in the different components of speech generation) hinges on automaticity. Only automatic processors can work without sharing resources and, thus, work in parallel. If each processor were to require access to attentional resources (i.e., to Working Memory), we would be in the situation that Danks (1977) called "lock-step succession." Then speaking would be more like playing chess: an overt move now and then, but mostly silent processing.

Summary

The intentional use of speech is subserved by information-processing skills that are highly complex and little understood. A case analysis of a single utterance appearing in a natural conversation gave a first impression of the intricacy of the processing that underlies speech. It also suggested a variety of kinds of information and of processing steps involved in the generation of an utterance.

How to partition such a system in a psychologically meaningful way? There is no single foolproof approach to this issue. This chapter's sketch of a framework for such a partitioning will be filled in and elaborated in subsequent chapters. The blueprint for the speaker consists of the following components: (i) *A Conceptualizer, which generates preverbal messages.* These messages consist of conceptual information whose expression is the means for realizing the speaker's intention. (ii) *A Formulator consisting of two subcomponents.* The Grammatical Encoder retrieves lemmas from the lexicon and generates grammatical relations reflecting the conceptual relations in the message. Its output is called "surface structure." The Phonological Encoder creates a phonetic plan (or "internal speech") on the basis of the surface structure. It has access to the form information in the lexicon, and it also incorporates procedures for generating the prosody of an utterance. (iii) *An Articulator, which unfolds and executes the phonetic plan as a series of neuromuscular instructions.* The resulting movements of the articulators yield overt speech. (iv) *The Speech-Comprehension System,* which makes self-produced internal and overt speech available to the conceptual system; this allows the speaker to monitor his own productions.

Each of these components, we assume, is an autonomous specialist in transforming its characteristic input into its characteristic output. The procedures apply largely without further interference or feedback from other components. The theoretical task ahead of us is to describe, for each component, what kind of output representations it generates, and by what kind of algorithm. Also, we will have to consider how that algorithm is implemented as a mechanism operating in real time.

Next, the distinction between controlled and automatic processing was applied to these components. Message generation and monitoring were described as controlled activities requiring the speaker's continuing attention. Grammatical encoding, form encoding, and articulating, however, are assumed to be automatic to a large degree. They are speedy and reflex-like, require very little attention, and can proceed in parallel.

The proposed architecture allows for a mode of processing which Kempen and Hoenkamp (1987) called *incremental*. It combines serial and parallel processing in the following way: Each fragment of information will have to be processed in stages, going from the conceiving of messages to articulation. Still, all processing components can work in parallel, albeit on different fragments. If the fragments are small (i.e., if the components require little lookahead), incremental processing is efficient, producing fluent speech without unintended interruptions. That it is sufficient for a processing component to be triggered into activity by only a minimal fragment of characteristic input was called "Wundt's principle."

Intermediate representations, such as preverbal messages, surface structure, and the phonetic plan, have their own kinds of units; there is no *single* unit of processing in the production of speech. There must be storage facilities for buffering such intermediate representations as they become available. Working Memory can store messages and parsed internal speech. A Syntactic Buffer can store bits of surface structure. And an Articulatory Buffer can store stretches of articulatory plan for further execution as motor programs.

The chapters to follow will trace the blueprint of figure 1.1 from message generation to self-monitoring, considering the kinds of representations generated by the processors, the algorithms involved, and the real-time properties of these algorithms. In the course of this journey, certain parts of the blueprint can be worked out as theoretical statements with predictive potential. In many more cases, however, we will be able to do no more than "zoom in" a little closer on the details of the architecture, and in particular on empirical studies of these details. But first, we will give attention to the speaker as interlocutor—in particular, to his role in conversation.

Chapter 2
The Speaker as Interlocutor

The most primordial and universal setting for speech is conversational, free interaction between two or more interlocutors. Conversation is primordial because the cradle of all language use is the conversational turn-taking between child and parent (Bruner 1983). Unlike other uses of language, conversation is also universal; it is the canonical setting for speech in all human societies. The speaker's skills of language use cannot but be tuned to the requirements of conversation. Of course, this does not mean that they can be derived from or explained by conversational usage. One cannot deduce a car's construction from the way it does its canonical job of driving along the road, but it would be silly to ignore that behavior when studying the car's internal construction and operations. Similarly, one cannot dissect the speaker's skill into components without carefully considering the tasks these components, alone and together, have to perform. We know that they should at least allow the speaker to converse. The present chapter will review some essential aspects of a speaker's participation in conversation.

Conversation is, first, a highly contextualized form of language use. There is, on the one hand, the participant context. A speaker will have to tune his talk to the turns and contributions of the other persons involved; his contributions should, in some way or another, be relevant to the ongoing interaction. There is, on the other hand, a spatio-temporal setting, shared by the interlocutors, which serves as a source of mutual knowledge. By anchoring their contributions in this shared here and now, interlocutors can convey much more than what is literally said. Nonconversational forms of speech are usually less contextualized. The addressees may be scattered (as in radio reporting), the spatial setting may not be shared (as in telephone talk), the temporal setting may also not be shared (as in tape-recording), there may be turn taking without the other party's talking (as in speaking to one's baby), there may also be very limited turn-taking (as in lecturing), and so on.

Conversation is, second, an intentional, goal-directed activity. People talk together with the more or less explicit purpose of informing one another of certain states of affairs, of sharing feelings of joy, sorrow, or indignation, of committing one another to certain actions, and so forth. Eibl-Eibesfeldt (1984) suggested that, phylogenetically, the main purpose of conversation is the regulation and ritualization of social relations. Conversation originates from communicative intentions.

One may thus define the *canonical setting for speech* as one in which speakers interact, in a shared spatio-temporal environment, for some purpose. These three properties will be discussed in the present chapter. Section 2.1 deals with the *interactional* character of speech—with issues of turn-taking and cooperation. Section 2.2 discusses speaking's dependence on the spatio-temporal context (also called its *deictic* character). Section 2.3 is concerned with speaking as purposeful action—the *intentional* character of speech.

2.1 Interaction

2.1.1 Cooperation

A speaker who participates in a conversation is subject to a system of rules governing the proper conduct of conversation. These rules are to be distinguished from purely *linguistic* standards of speech to which speakers adhere. They are rules of *appropriate social conduct*, regulating the acceptability, fluency, politeness, and effectiveness of social interaction. If a speaker adheres to these rules, he is said to be *cooperative* (Grice 1975). So, for example, speaker Betty is not fully cooperative in the following conversation:

Arnold: Could you tell me the way to Stephen's Church?

Betty: Yes, I could.

(Betty turns away).

Clearly, Arnold was requesting street directions, but Betty uncooperatively replied to a literal interpretation of the question—namely, whether she has the competence to give the directions. By turning away, moreover, Betty did not allow Arnold to make a new move in the conversation, which might have remedied the trouble.

The rules governing cooperation in conversation are of two sorts:

(1) Rules for the allocation of turns. They ensure everybody's right to talk, while generally preventing the simultaneous talk of different parties, and they regulate engaging in and disengaging from conversation.

(2) Rules governing the character of the contributions. They ensure that contributions are relevant to the conversation and that participants can infer a speaker's communicative intention from the utterance and the context.

These two types of rule are in the baggage of every normal speaker. Let us consider them one by one.

2.1.2 Turn Taking, Engagement, and Disengagement

The basic and perhaps universal rules for turn taking in conversation were discovered by Sacks, Schegloff, and Jefferson (1974). Many refinements and qualifications have been added since, but the central insights have gone unchallenged. The major features of the system are as follows:

Turn-constructional units

A turn consists of one or more *units* which are *projectable*. Being project-able means that the completion of the unit can be roughly predicted from its type, so an interlocutor can know where to take over. In *Could you tell me the way to* ... there is a sentential unit that is likely to be completed by a noun phrase, for instance *Stephen's Church*. Other projectable units are clausal, phrasal, and lexical ones, and we will shortly return to the issue of units in turn taking. Given these units, the following rules apply.

Turn-assignment rules

(1) A speaker who has the turn is initially entitled to utter one such unit. The end of a unit is a so-called *transition-relevance place*. When that place is reached, rule 2 applies.

(2) The current speaker can assign the right and obligation to speak to a particular party in the conversation. This is called the *current speaker selects next* technique of turn allocation.

The technique of rule 2 was applied in the conversation above, where the speaker directed a question to a particular person (*Could you tell me the way to Stephen's Church?*) and thus assigned her the right and the obligation to the next turn. Notice that other parties are not entitled to take the next turn, and that the addressed party should not start before the transition-relevance place.

If the current speaker in fact selects the next speaker, according to this rule, the next rule to apply is rule 5. If the option is not used, then rule 3 applies.

(3) Any other party may claim the next turn at the transition-relevance place. This is called *self-selection*. The one who starts first has the right to the turn. There is, however, no obligation for anyone to take the next turn.

If someone takes the next turn, rule 5 is the next one to be applied. If no one does, rule 4 is next.

(4) The current speaker may, but need not, continue with a further unit. If he does, the cycle starts all over again at rule 1. This may be done recursively until transfer to a next speaker is effectuated. If the option is not used, the conversation halts.

(5) The next speaker becomes the current speaker, and rule 1 applies again.

The rule system is exemplified by the following conversation. The numbers in parentheses indicate places where the above rules apply.

Arnold: (1) I didn't sleep well last night.   (2, 3, 4, 1)   (To Betty:)
Did you hear me clumping down the stairs?   (2, 5)

Betty: (1) No, I didn't.   (2, 3, 5)

Christian: (1) I thought there was a burglar in the house.   (2, 3, 4)

Rule 4 allows for discontinuing the conversation at this point.

The rules of turn taking guarantee that at most one speaker talks at a time (except when under rule 3 two or more interlocutors "tie" in being first, which we will return to below). A turn of a speaker can be any length, not only because there is no formal limit on the size of a unit but also because recursive application of the rules allows an unlimited number of units to be strung together in a single turn. The latter possibility, however, can only be realized cooperatively; it can occur only if no participant claims the next turn when the current speaker reaches a transition-relevance place, so that the current speaker is allowed to produce an additional utterance.

Rule 3 almost guarantees that any participant in the conversation can claim the floor. The right is fully guaranteed in a two-party conversation. Even if the current speaker doesn't select the next speaker (by rule 2), the other party can "break in" at the end of the current unit. In conversations involving three or more parties, however, two or more participants can form a coalition by making turns one unit long and always selecting one another, thus bypassing rule 3. Though this is a far-fetched and rude possibility, even such corrupted conversations follow the rules of turn taking.

Conversations can contain moments of silence, three sorts of which can be distinguished. A speaker can be silent at some moment *within* a unit, as in the following.

Arnold: Can we really (pause) afford to do this?

Such a silence is called a *pause*. It can happen, for instance, when the speaker has difficulty finding the appropriate word; or it may also be rhetorical, as a kind of upbeat for something important to follow. For a silence to be a pause, the speaker and the listener should experience it as interrupting an ongoing unit. In the above example, the unit is sentential and intonational; there is no transition-relevance place after "really".

The second type of silence occurs *between* units, and it is called a *gap*. Gaps result from rules 3 and 4. The following conversation contains two gaps:

Arnold: He kept playing all night. (gap)
It is hard to stop an amateur. (gap)
Betty: Do you play an instrument yourself?

The first gap occurred after Arnold completed a unit (*He kept playing all night*). Nobody claimed the floor at that moment, and Arnold decided to go on (by rule 4). After completing the next unit, Arnold left the floor open again, but did not resort to rule 4 this time when silence occurred. After some time, Betty claimed the floor (by rule 3) and introduced another topic. Beattie (1978) reported that only 34 percent of turn transitions in dyadic conversations are "seamless" (i.e., have gaps shorter than 200 milliseconds). The other turn transitions involve gaps of about 500 msec, on average.

A *lapse* occurs when the silence between units is particularly extended. This can occur when a conversation draws to conclusion, signaling disengagement of the participants (Goodwin 1981).

A major feature of conversations, modeled by the turn-allocation rules above, is that, overwhelmingly, speakers talk in turns and not simultaneously. But the rules are idealized in this respect, since overlap does occur in real-life conversations. Beattie (1983) found that in dyadic university tutorials 11 percent of turn starts interrupt the previous turn, and this rises to 31 percent in multi-student tutorials. There are two major causes of overlap: multiple self-selection and projection trouble. Multiple self-selection, as was observed above, can occur when interlocutors tie in claiming the next turn at a transition-relevance place. By rule 3, the right to the floor goes to the one who speaks first, and overlap will occur if two speakers are nearly simultaneous in starting. The following real-life example is taken from Sacks et al. 1974.

A: I know who d'guy is.

B: ⎡He's ba::d

C: ⎣You know the gu:y?

After A's turn, B and C start simultaneously (indicated by the bracket), and both complete a short unit. (The colon stands for a vowel lengthening or "drawl," which often occurs in unit-final segments.)

Projection trouble may occur when interlocutors misjudge the moment at which a unit is to be completed. A speaker preparing to claim the next turn must estimate the current speaker's place of completion; and in order to be first (see rule 3), or to maintain a fluent course of conversation, he cannot just wait till the unit is factually completed. The right timing of speech onset requires preparation, and hence requires anticipation of the transition-relevance place. Miscalculation easily arises when the current speaker adds a term of address (*sir, dear, John*) or of etiquette (*please*), a tag question (*isn't it?, right?*), or an apposition (*I think*). Here is an example taken from Jefferson 1985.

A: ez soon ez he said the do:gs'r okay somehow I c'd handle the

whole thing. ⎡Y'know?

B: ⎣The whole thing yeah

An important feature of the conversational turn-taking system is what Sacks et al. (1974) called its *local management*. The allocation of the next turn is not pre-established (there is no "chairman"). Either it is free (when self-selection, by rule 3, is used) or it is determined during the current turn (in cases of current-speaker-selects-next; rule 2). Turn assignment is local in that it involves adjacent pairs only. This does not rule out the existence of turn-assignment biases that go beyond the niche of adjacent turns. A participant can become dominant in a conversation by self-selecting a great deal. Or, if there is somebody important among the interlocutors, others will self-select less, so that the important person can keep the floor for longer stretches of speech (following rule 4). Another bias, quite generally observed, is to allocate the next turn to the previous speaker and thus create an A-B-A sequence. This is not completely surprising; in coherent conversation, B is likely to react to something A said, and if this involves a request for clarification, expansion, explanation, or something similar, A is automatically selected as the next speaker.

There is a substantial literature on so-called *turn-yielding cues*—i.e., means by which a speaker can signal that his turn is over or that he wants to keep the floor in spite of his having completed some unit (see Duncan and Fiske 1977 and, for a review, Beattie 1983). There are prosodic cues, such as rising or falling pitch at the end of a clause; however, Schaffer (1983) found these cues to be only moderately effective, and it is not certain that they are consistently used by speakers (Cutler and Pearson 1986). More important, according to Schaffer, are syntactic and lexical cues. And rhythmic cues, such as pausing and vowel lengthening or "drawl" in clause-final syllables (as in *He's ba:d* above), seem to play a role in signaling ends of turns. There are, in addition, nonverbal means for regulating floor apportionment, especially through gaze and gesture. For instance, speakers tend to establish eye contact by the end of a turn. Speakers have a whole arsenal of means to secure and to keep an interlocutor's attention, and to induce participants to reply.

The empirical issue of what can count as a transition-relevance place is complicated. Sacks et al. (1974) defined it in terms of the turn-constructional units, and these are of a syntactic nature: sentential, clausal, phrasal, or lexical. At the same time, as has already been discussed, Sacks et al. stressed the importance of "projectivity" of units, the degree to which recognition of the unit's type allows one to anticipate the completion of the unit token. There is, however, no reason to expect that syntax and projectivity will converge on this matter. There is, surely, abundant evidence that smooth transitions do occur at places corresponding to each of the above-mentioned syntactic-unit types. Questions, for instance, can be sentences (*How do you feel today?*), clauses (*Because he couldn't come?*), phrases (*The windmill?*), or lexical items (*What?*), and each of these can lead up to a seamless transition of turn. But this is not true for just any unit of these types; in that case, the completion of every word, phrase, or clause would be a transition-relevance point, and that is clearly false. Should one, in addition, require projectivity, granting that syntactic units are not always projectable? This doesn't work either. Nothing is so projectable as a word's completion. Experimental work by Marslen-Wilson and Tyler (1980) has demonstrated that the recognition of spoken words occurs as soon as the word can be distinguished from all other words in the language that have the same initial sound structure. On average this occurs roughly halfway through the word, and words in context are recognized even earlier than isolated words (Tyler and Wessels 1983). Upon recognition, the word's completion is projectable. But this would again mean that almost every word's ending is a transition-relevance point.

Clearly, other factors are involved here. Interlocutors are probably not projecting just any units, but only units that are conversationally *relevant*— i.e., *semantic* units. Halliday (1967a) called them "information units," whereas Butterworth (1975) and Chafe (1980) talked about "idea units" in this connection. It is a matter of controversy to what degree these units become prosodically encoded in speech (see Brown and Yule 1983); however, it is an empirical issue beyond the concerns of this book whether and how a listener projects such semantic units to predict transition-relevance points in a conversation. The projectivity of an utterance is probably multiply determined by its prosody, its syntax, and its meaning. How a listener combines these sources of information to compute transition-relevance places in actual discourse is largely untouched in the extensive literature on discourse analysis (for an experimental study see Grosjean 1983).

How do interlocutors engage in a conversation, sustain it, and disengage from it? The turn-taking rules above do not specify how interlocutors engage in a conversation, and although these rules allow for terminating a conversation (by rule 4), nothing in the theory predicts when that option will be chosen. Given the system of rules, the most obvious way to engage another person in a conversation is for a speaker to use the current-speaker-selects-next technique (rule 2). Moves can be made that invite a reply. Schegloff and Sacks (1973) called such pairs of turn "adjacency pairs." Though the most typical example is the question-answer sequence, there are many other adjacency pairs that can open a conversation. Instances are greeting-greeting (*Morning sir – Good morning*), complaint-denial (*Don't push me – He did*), challenge-rejection (*You won't complete this in time – I sure will*), and so forth (see Schegloff 1972 on conversational openings). Also, adjacency pairs can be used to *sustain* conversation (Wells, MacLure, and Montgomery 1981)—i.e., to signal that one does not yet want to disengage (*Tell me more about your friend*).

There is much more to opening and sustaining conversation than the exploitation of adjacency pairs. If the purpose is to attain and maintain mutual orientation between participants, there are many ways to realize that. Particularly important is what Yngve (1970) called "backchannel behavior": a variety of indications to the current speaker implying that he should continue (nods, *hmms*, etc.). According to an analysis by Goodwin (1981), to gaze at an interlocutor is to propose further talk, and an interlocutor's gaze may be attracted by pausing, repairing, or vowel lengthening. Goodwin's evidence is that speakers who gaze at the listener display more interrupt-restarts when the interlocutor is not gazing than when she is. Changing the topic is another means of saving an ebbing conversation, but eventually all conversation gets disengaged.

The intention to disengage can be signaled in several ways. There may be longer pauses, i.e., instances where participants do not immediately use their options for self-selection. There may be increased involvement in side activities (such as walking around or blowing one's nose), which may decrease the participants' other-directed orientation. But the interactant's culture may also provide ritualized means of bringing a conversation to a close without violating standards of politeness. Levinson (1983) gives the following example from a telephone conversation:

A: Why don't we all have lunch

B: Okay so that would be in St. Jude's would it?

A: Yes

  (gap)

B: Okay so:::

A: One o'clock in the bar

B: Okay

A: Okay?

B: Okay then thanks very much indeed George

A: All right. ⌐See you there

B: └See you there

A: Okay

B: Okay ⌐bye

A: └Bye

This interaction displays some ritual closing moves. Levinson mentions the introduction of a "closing implicative" topic (proposing having lunch), the use of topicless "passing turns" (*okay, all right*), a "typing" of the conversation (in this case, the phone call as a grant favored—*thanks very much indeed*), and an exchange of "terminal elements" (*bye*). These and other rituals may be accompanied by nonverbal rituals. For instance, Goodwin (1981) observed exchanges of eyebrow flashes in the closing of conversations, and this may well be universal across cultures (Eibl-Eibesfeldt 1974).

The rules for turn taking discussed in this section are not a grammar. The system of rules is not a device for distinguishing well-formed from ill-formed sequences of turns, but rather a specification of principles of conduct normally adhered to by cooperative participants in a conversation. Or, more precisely, each interlocutor can assume that the others will normally adhere to these rules. But more important is the assumption of cooperativeness. Interlocutors will take for granted that whatever another party does in a conversation serves some purpose in the ongoing exchange of talk, even when that party flouts certain turn-taking rules. An example may illustrate this.

According to rule 2, the addressee is supposed to take the next turn when the current-speaker-selects-next technique is used. This rule is violated in the following conversation:

Teacher: Betty, what happened to your father last week?

Betty: (silence)

Teacher: I am so sorry for you.

The teacher's question selects Betty as the next turn speaker, but she flouts the convention and keeps silent. In spite of this, the teacher assumes Betty's cooperativeness and interprets the silence as her inability to express her sorrow in a well-formed reply (or, more precisely, interprets this as what Betty intended to convey). The teacher's next move expresses that this is accepted. This conversation is certainly well formed, but the break of rules gives it a special character.

Similarly, violation of rule 3 can produce a strong rhetorical effect in conversation. When a next speaker self-selects before the transition-relevance place, the interlocutors will overlap. But this may be a highly effective means of communication, as in the following conversation from Schiffrin 1985:

Henry: Standards are different. But I'm tellin'y' –
           if the father is respected ⌜an:d eh
Irene: ⌞Henry, le me ask you a
           question. Le- you made a statement that the mothers
           run the house, right?

Here Henry starts making a statement, but is interrupted by Irene. Henry initially continues his utterance, so that there is some overlap. By violating rule 3, Irene's question acquires the character of a challenge, and this is intended. This conversation is cooperative in the sense that, in spite of their disagreement, both parties address the same issue and interpret each other's contributions as relevant to that issue. Deviation from the rules is used to make intentions and emotions apparent that would otherwise be hard to get across. There are, probably, even *rules* of conversational rhetoric, which relate particular deviations to particular effects. Henry and Irene's conversation is well formed, though in a nonstandard way. This kind of behavior will be called *marked*, as opposed to the *unmarked* behavior that follows the normal turn-taking rules.

To put this differently: No finite set of rules can ever delineate the full set of well-formed conversations. As long as participants assume cooperativeness, each violation of a rule will be interpreted as conveying a certain intention which contributes to the conversation. And if the effectiveness of rule breaking is itself rule governed, then flouting that rule can itself be put to effective communicative use, and so on. The turn-taking rules only specify what is the normal or unmarked standard of appropriate behavior in turn taking.

2.1.3 Saying and Conveying

The state of affairs is similar when one considers the *character* of contributions to a conversation. The assumption of cooperativeness applies not only to the ways in which parties in the conversation take turns, but also to what they have to say when at turn. Also, there are normal standards of conduct here, which are mutually assumed by the parties. But when a speaker deviates from such a standard, the assumption of cooperativeness will prevail, and parties in the conversation will interpret the speaker's contribution as conveying some intention in a marked way.

These standards of conduct have been discussed throughout the history of rhetoric. It has, in particular, been argued that contributions to dialogue should be appropriate, correct, clear, intelligible, pleasant, and so forth (Franck 1980). It was Grice (1975, 1978) who reintroduced these notions into the modern discussion of pragmatics, and the subsequent development has been very similar to what happened to the theory of turn taking set forth by Sacks et al. (1974): There have been many changes and additions, but the essential insights have stood the test of time.

There is, first and foremost, the *cooperative principle* (Grice 1975): "Make your conversational contribution such as is required, at the stage at which it occurs, by the accepted purpose or direction of the talk exchange in which you are engaged." According to Grice, parties in a conversation mutually assume that their contributions are governed by this principle. Grice then proceeds to distinguish four sets of rules of conduct which are particular realizations of this principle. These *maxims* were labeled in a slightly arbitrary way (following Kant's terminology), and much of the subsequent discussion in the literature has centered around the necessity, sufficiency, and completeness of the set. Here they are:

Maxims of quantity

1. Make your contribution as informative as required (for the current purpose of exchange).
2. Do not make your contribution more informative than is required.

An example suffices to show what can happen if a speaker violates the first quantity maxim:

Arnold: I sold my house today.

Betty: Are you going to move?

Arnold: No, I still own the house I live in.

What Arnold said was truthful, because he did sell a house he owned. But the way he said it was misleading, since without further specification *my house* means the place where one lives. By not saying something like *I sold my second house*, Arnold *underspecified* the object of the transaction, in violation of the first maxim.

The following would be a violation of the second quantity maxim:

Arnold: How long does it take to walk to the shops?

Betty: Three minutes and twelve seconds.

This is—if true at all—an overspecification. But the same answer might be an underspecification in response to the question: "What's the world's record for running the mile"? Then, tenths of seconds may count, and should be included in the answer.

Maxims of quality
1. Do not say what you believe to be false.
2. Do not say that for which you lack adequate evidence.

These are almost like the commandment "Do not lie"; still, there are no ethical implications. The important point is that parties in a conversation normally assume that a speaker *commits* himself to what he is saying. It is therefore very odd to say *The sun is shining, but I don't believe it*. The art of lying is indeed to commit oneself to the lie; one should speak *as if* one believes what one says and be consistent (see Wunderlich 1976).

Maxim of relation
Be relevant, or make your contributions relate to the ongoing exchange of talk.

This maxim has been the source of a great deal of confusion, not least because Grice (1975) seriously underspecified it (in violation of his own first quantity maxim). It may be taken as just an alternative formulation of the principle of cooperation itself instead of a particular instantiation of it. But then the maxim is redundant. Some authors have taken a different route, interpreting the maxim of relation in such a way that the other three sets of maxims are special cases (see Wilson and Sperber 1981 and especially Sperber and Wilson 1986). In the following conversation, Betty's contribution doesn't seem to relate to Arnold's (though the reader might be able to create a context in which it does).

Arnold: Can you pass the pepper?

Betty: Bananas are yellow.

Here, given Arnold's question, Betty makes an irrelevant remark.

Maxims of manner

1. Avoid obscurity of expression.
2. Avoid ambiguity.
3. Be brief (avoid unnecessary prolixity).
4. Be orderly.

Grice himself suggested that this list is probably not complete, and others have argued that it contains too much already. For instance, every single utterance in a conversation contains some ambiguity, but still this clearly does not violate any tacit standards of manner. Orderliness is at stake in the following example.

Arnold: He drove away and started his car.

This utterance does not follow the natural ordering of actions, in which one first starts a car and then drives away. The orderly (unmarked) way to put this is *He started his car and drove away*. Maxim 4 explains, by the same token, the difference in implicatures between *She married and became pregnant* and *She became pregnant and married* (Levelt 1981).

It is not the aim of the present discussion to achieve more orderliness in Grice's maxims, and we will ignore most of the literature on these issues (but see Gazdar 1979, Levinson 1983, and Sperber and Wilson 1986). The major points of relevance for a theory of the speaker are, however, (i) that a cooperative speaker will adhere to certain standards of conduct with respect to the character of his contributions, (ii) that by adhering to these standards the speaker can convey information without formulating it explicitly, and (iii) that a cooperative speaker can flout these rules to produce particular communicative effects. By listing Grice's maxims, I have indicated the sorts of rules that may be at issue. Notice that these rules are not just conventions. For a rule to be a convention, not only must it be shared within a community; it must also be arbitrary to a certain degree (see Lewis 1969). Accepting that conversational maxims are shared in a community, one should still doubt that they are arbitrary. They are, rather, general ways of being rational. One would, therefore, expect them to be universal to an interesting degree. This is an empirical issue, and indeed it has been argued that Grice's maxims are not necessarily universal (Ochs-

Keenan 1976; see also various papers in Gumperz and Hymes 1972). Ochs-Keenan, for instance, discusses cases such as the following: In Malagasy, one can answer the question "Where is your mother" with "She is either in the house or at the market" *without* implicating that one doesn't know which of the two is the case. Ochs-Keenan adduces this to a general reluctance in the culture to reveal one's small bits of news in a society where everything is under public gaze.

One wonders how much cross-cultural misunderstanding is due to slight variations in conversational conventions (see Perdue 1984). Still, one should not exclude the possibility that, at a more abstract level, universally valid maxims of conversation can be formulated.

Let us now turn to the other two points: how a speaker can convey information over and above what he says, and the effective use of violating the rules.

When it is mutually assumed among the parties to a conversation that one adheres to maxims of the sort described, a speaker can communicate more than what is strictly implied or entailed by what he is saying. This "more" is called *implicature*. The following example presupposes Betty's respecting the maxims of quantity.

Arnold: Did you see Peter and Joan yesterday?

Betty: I saw Peter.

The implicature here is that Betty didn't see Joan. The quantity maxims require Betty to give just the right amount of information in answer to Arnold's question. Since Betty neither said *Yes* nor *Indeed, I saw Peter and Joan yesterday* but singled out her seeing Peter, Arnold can infer that Betty could not sincerely assert that she had seen Joan as well. Hence, he can conclude that she didn't see Joan.

The following example shows the implicative power of the maxim of relation.

Arnold: My cough is getting very bad today.

Betty: There is a doctor across the street.

The implicature of Betty's remark is that that doctor could be consulted in connection with Arnold's problem. If Betty believed that the doctor across the street was not consultable, her contribution would not have entertained a relation of relevance to Arnold's lamentation. Arnold knows this and, hence, can infer that the doctor is consultable.

Such examples can be constructed *ad libitum*. But, more important, when one reads transcripts of everyday conversations (an important source book is Svartvik and Quirk 1980), implicatures appear everywhere. They lubricate the conversation. It is often enough for a speaker to just hint at a certain piece of information; the addressee will interpret that information as relevant to the ongoing interaction and will infer the speaker's intention. Sperber and Wilson (1986) argued that this facilitates processing for the listener. It probably also does so for the speaker. There is normally no need to formulate one's intentions in all detail in order for communication to be effective. The challenge for a psycholinguistic theory of the speaker is precisely to understand how speakers manage to select for expression just the relevant information.

A blatant failure to respect a conversational maxim can have pointed communicative effects. When a speaker flouts a maxim for cooperative purposes (i.e., to convey some intention in a marked way), Grice (1975) talks of the *exploitation* of a maxim. Here is an example of exploitation: Arnold and Betty jointly attend a harpsichord performance. When it is over, the following conversation ensues.

Arnold: How did you like it?

Betty: It was a nice piano recital.

Betty's answer violates the first maxim of quality, since she knows perfectly well that the instrument was a harpsichord. This is in fact mutually known (i.e., Arnold knows that Betty knows this, and that this is in turn known to Betty, and so forth). Arnold therefore infers that Betty is flouting a maxim, and, on the assumption that Betty is cooperative, Arnold will try to find out what Betty intended to convey. The most likely interpretation here is that the performer played the harpsichord *as if* it were a piano—i.e., without real feel for the instrument. A less likely but possible interpretation is that the harpsichord was such an awful make that it sounded like a piano. Which interpretation Arnold will adduce to Betty's answer depends entirely upon the mutually known context. There is no standard or conversational way to infer the intention in this case of flouting a maxim. A speaker who exploits a maxim (for instance, to produce irony, as in the above example) must estimate whether enough contextual conditions are fulfilled in order for the addressed interlocutor to make the inference. It should further be noticed that Betty's remark does not convey the same information that would have been conveyed if she had said *The performer played without real feel for the instrument*. That would not have been ironical; the breaking of the maxim conveys the latter proposition, but it also creates the special effect of irony. (See the discussion between Jorgenson, Miller, and Sperber [1984] and Clark and Gerrig [1984].)

Grice suggested that other figures of speech, such as hyperbole and metaphor, also result from exploiting the maxims. More extended treatments of metaphor in this framework can be found in Lyons 1981, Levinson 1983, and Sperber and Wilson 1986.

To sum up the discussion so far: There are more or less culture-specific conversational maxims. By adhering to these, speakers can convey intentions they don't utter literally. Speakers can also use the violation of normal rules of conduct to create special dramatic effects in communication. All this requires interlocutors to be cooperative and to share relevant knowledge and relevant contextual information.

It is, however, by no means the case that Grice's conversational maxims are the only sources of implicatures. Grice himself mentioned implicatures that are conventionally attached to certain words in certain contexts (he called them *conventional*, as opposed to *conversational*, implicatures). A speaker can convey very different attitudes toward what he is saying by merely choosing *and* or *but* to conjoin clauses. *Tom is honest but brave* implicates that the speaker experiences some contrast between being honest and being brave. This implicature is absent in *Tom is honest and brave*. The point will not be further elaborated here; the latter examples are taken from Osgood's interesting essay on the psychological effects of connectives (1980). At this point we will ignore other ways of conveying without saying—in particular, those that are transmitted by nonverbal means in a conversation.

Conversing is the archetypical form of speaking. The present section reviewed, first, the turn-taking rules that speakers tend to follow in normal conversations. It should be kept in mind, though, that the rules are different in other types of discourse. Second, attention was given to other aspects of cooperativeness in conversation—particularly those that have to do with the character of contributions. In order for an addressee to be able to derive the speaker's intention from what is said, the speaker will adhere to certain rules of conduct, or maxims. However, all rules of these kinds, whether turn-taking rules or Gricean maxims, can be bypassed as long as the addressee can assume that what the speaker does is relevant to the interaction.

2.2   Deixis

2.2.1   Types of Deixis

A particularly important way in which interlocutors make their contributions relevant to the situation of discourse is by anchoring what they talk about to the spatio-temporal context of utterance. Starting again from conversation as the canonical setting for speech, the spatio-temporal context of an utterance involves (apart from the speaker) at least one addressee, an audio-visual scene which is more or less shared between the interlocutors, the places and orientations of the interlocutors in this scene at the moment of utterance, and the place of the utterance in the temporal flow of events (including past and future utterances). The German psychologist Karl Bühler (1934) called utterance anchoring of this sort *deixis*, a technical term for pointing with words. An example may be helpful.

Arnold: Have you seen this?
        (He points to a Min dynasty vase, which displays a horrifying pattern of fresh cracks)
Betty: You asked me that before, but I haven't been here since yesterday.

This interaction involves, first of all, *person deixis*. Arnold's *you* refers to Betty, but Betty's *you* refers to Arnold. *You* is a deictic pronoun; it refers to the addressee. But the person *you* points at is variable, depending on the spatio-temporal setting of the utterances. Many languages have two (or even more) versions of *you*—for instance, *Sie* and *du* in German, which depend on the status relation between speaker and addressee. This is sometimes called *social deixis*. Another case of person deixis in the conversation above is the use of *I*. The referent of *I*, like that of *you*, shifts depending on who is at turn.

There is, furthermore, *place deixis*. A's *this* points to something that is mutually available in the situation. The word *this* can refer to practically anything in the speaker's vicinity, but the cooperative speaker should make sure that the addressee can identify the intended referent. There are various ways to do this effectively, but making a pointing gesture by hand or head, or visibly gazing at the object, is an obvious procedure. Another case of place deixis can be found in Betty's utterance in the last example. By using *here*, Betty probably refers to the place of conversation; but how much this includes is not obvious. If she is cooperative, it includes at least all places from which the cracks can be seen, and not just the place where she is presently sitting.

There is also *time deixis*, which is most apparent in Betty's *before* and *yesterday*. *Before* means something like "at a moment earlier than the present exchange of turns", but only mutual knowledge can help to delineate how much earlier. It may or may not have been during the present conversation, for instance. *Yesterday* is the day preceding the day on which the conversation takes place. By using this term, Betty anchors her period of absence with respect to the moment at which she delivers her utterance.

There is another type of time deixis in these utterances, namely the verb tenses used. *Have seen* refers to a moment before the present utterance, and the same holds for *asked* and *have been*. There is, moreover, a subtle difference, in references to the past, between perfect tense (*have seen*) and past tense (*asked*); we will return to this below.

A final type of deixis in the above conversation can be called *discourse deixis*. It is exemplified by Betty's use of *that* in referring to Arnold's question *Have you seen this?* Betty thus points to an earlier piece of discourse, which is identifiable by Arnold.

The above example contains all major types of deixis distinguished in the literature (see especially Lyons 1977 and Levinson 1983): person and social deixis, place, time, and discourse deixis.

The meaning of a deictic expression depends critically on its relation to the context of utterance. Bühler (1934) calls the relevant context of utterance the *indexical field* [*Zeigfeld*], and the anchoring point of this field the *origin* [*Origo*]. The person origin is the speaker ("I"), the social origin is the role or status of the speaker, the locative origin is the speaker's place ("here") at the moment of utterance, the temporal origin is the time of utterance ("now"), and the origin of discourse is the stretch of talk being produced by the present speaker. In other words, the anchoring point of deictic expressions is egocentric (or, better, speaker-centric).

Adult speakers skillfully relate what they are talking about to this me-here-now. However, this skill is by no means an obvious one—as is apparent from the long and twisting road children have to travel before finally mastering the deictic systems of a language (E. Clark 1977; Deutsch and Pechmann 1978; Tanz 1980; Boehme 1983). Though there have been important developments in the linguistic analysis of deictic systems (Lyons 1977; Jarvella and Klein 1982; Weissenborn and Klein 1982), psycholinguists have not shown an overwhelming interest in the adult speaker's use of these linguistic devices. (Miller and Johnson-Laird 1976 is a major exception.)

Examples of some of the complexities a speaker faces in producing deictic utterances by considering reference to space and to time, respectively, will be given below.

2.2.2 Place Deixis

There are at least three things a speaker can do through locative deictic expressions: identifying, informing, and acknowledging (Fillmore 1982). Though these functions are not exclusively deictic but rather general functions of language, they offer an easy way to bring some order to the phenomena of place deixis.

Identifying

The speaker can single out an object in space by indicating its place. In the example above, this happens when Arnold says *have you seen this?* The *this* plus the corresponding gesture identifies the object of concern: the mutilated vase. Identifying is typically (but not necessarily) done by means of demonstrative determiners, such as *this*, *that*, *these*, and *those*. They vary on the deictic dimension of *proximity to the speaker*, which is a universal space-deictic feature in the languages of the world, and on the nondeictic dimension *number* (singular-plural), which is by no means universal. The identifying function can be realized only between interlocutors who share a great deal of knowledge. Basically, the function is a two-step one. First, the speaker informs the listener of what is called the *demonstratum*. The speaker directly refers to some place, which may or may not suffice to identify the demonstratum. In the example, Arnold intends to refer to the ruinous state of the vase, and he does this by singling out the vase as the demonstratum. But by pointing at the vase, Arnold also points at some central region of the vase, and at a certain area in the room. Only mutual knowledge can guide Betty's attention to the vase—for instance, that there are no other objects in front of it, that it is a highly valuable object, or that Arnold is always calling her attention to the vase. The vase is a better candidate than the empty region of space just behind it, or in front of it. Let us assume that the context is indeed sufficiently clear for Betty to single out the vase as the demonstratum.

But the vase is not the intended referent; the speaker intends to refer to the disastrous state of the vase. How does the speaker guide the listener from the demonstratum (the vase) to the referent (its cracked state)? This requires a second step. According to Nunberg (1979), the speaker makes use of a *referring function*, which maps the demonstratum onto a likely referent. Cooperative interlocutors can compute this function on the basis of mutual knowledge. Let us see how that might work here. The vase is the demonstratum; could it also be the referent? Hardly so if the situation is such that Arnold and Betty mutually know that the vase has been standing there within living memory. This excludes, by Gricean principles, that Arnold wanted to convey the question *have you seen this vase?* Arnold can therefore expect Betty to identify a referent other than the vase, something that had not been mutually available before. *Salience* is one possible guide in directing Betty's attention, and the pattern of cracks will be salient to even a moderate connoisseur of valuables. This may be enough for Betty to identify the referent. In many cases, the demonstratum will be the referent. When Arnold and Betty are quite close to the big vase, and there is one clear crack, Arnold could be pointing at that crack, and Betty might identify it as the demonstratum and at the same time as the referent. However, the demonstratum and the referent may also be quite distinct (examples will soon be given), and it is necessary to distinguish them.

Nunberg's theory of referring is a general one, including deictic reference. Miller (1982) further analyzed its applicability to demonstrative reference, and Clark, Schreuder, and Buttrick (1983) published the first empirical study on how listeners compute the referent given the demonstratum, salience being one important cue. The distinction between demonstratum and referent is also of paramount importance for other types of space deixis.

Informing

The second function Fillmore (1982) distinguished is *informing*. A deictic term can be used to inform the interlocutor about the place of an object. This is typically (but not exclusively) done by deictic adverbials and prepositions, such as *here, there, above, below, in front of, behind, left*, and *right*. A father can tell his child *Your ball is behind the tree*; this is not identifying an object, but informing the interlocutor where some object is (in this case, by predicating the location of the object).

How can a place be indicated? In order to get this done, a speaker always needs what we will call a *relatum*—an entity with respect to which the referent object can be localized. To indicate the place of some dog, the speaker could say *the dog is near me, near you*, or *near the table*. The relatum is *me, you*, or *table*. The speaker will, in addition, often need a *coordinate system*, which makes it possible to orient the referent object with respect to the relatum. This is clear from expressions such as *the dog is under the table, in front of the table*, or *to the left of the table*. Using the preposition *under* acknowledges the existence of a vertical dimension, whereas *in front of* and *to the left of* presuppose the existence of two horizontal dimensions of orientation.

It is now possible to categorize the most important systems of localization that are used in verbal communication, by cross-classifying kinds of relatum and kinds of coordinate system. A first, incomplete categorization is presented in table 2.1. Three of the four cells in this table are actually used by speakers. Let us consider them in turn. The most basic system of local reference is the one depicted in cell I: *primary deictic reference*. Here the speaker is both the relatum and the origin of the coordinate system. What kind of coordinate system is this? It is three-dimensional, consisting of a

COORDINATE	RELATUM	
SYSTEM	speaker	other entity
speaker	(I) primary deictic reference	(II) secondary deictic reference
other entity	(III) ---	(IV) intrinsic reference

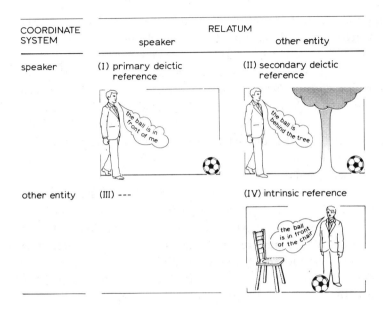

Table 2.1
Three basic systems of local reference.

vertical dimension and two horizontal dimensions, and it has the speaker as the origin. The orientation of the vertical dimension is determined by what can be called "perceived verticality"; the speaker senses the vertical direction largely through the pull of gravity on his vestibular and muscular systems. But there is also a role played by the orientation of the surrounding visual frame (rooms have a clear ceiling/floor orientation, and outdoors one has cues such as upright trees, houses, the sky, and the horizon), as well as by other cues (see Levelt 1984a; on astronauts' problems in this respect, see Friederici and Levelt 1986). The vertical dimension is quite special for two reasons: First, it is rather independent of the speaker's physical orientation. When the speaker lies down, the sensed vertical changes only to a small extent (Mittelstaedt 1983)—particularly when the visual frame is maintained. Second, the orientation of the vertical dimension is normally shared between interlocutors. In what I have called "the canonical setting for speech" (following H. Clark 1973), the interlocutors are relatively close together and mutually visible. They share the pull of gravity as well as important aspects of the visual frame. As a consequence, they all have about the same sense of verticality.

The two horizontal dimensions, however, are not normally shared between interlocutors. The first one is the speaker's front/back dimension.

The picture in cell I of the table shows the use of this dimension. The speaker is uttering *the ball is in front of me*. The ball is *in front of* the speaker because it is located along what is usually called the "positive" half of the dimension, towards which the speaker is oriented. When two interlocutors are facing one another (which is quite normal in conversation), their front/back orientations are opposite and thus not shared. The same holds for the second horizontal dimension, which runs perpendicular to the front/back dimension. It is the speaker's behaviorally more symmetrical left/right dimension. What is "left" for the speaker is "right" for the interlocutor facing him.

Given the constant threat of nonalignment of coordinate systems between interlocutors, the latter have what Klein (1978) calls a *coordination problem*: The addressee must know where the speaker is located and what his orientation is in order to interpret his deictic expressions, and the speaker must be aware of the addressee's ability or inability to have access to such information. You will plan your deictic expressions quite differently when on the phone than when in full view of your interlocutor.

Let us now consider cell II, secondary deictic reference. This involves the same coordinate system as primary deixis, with the speaker as origin and with his vertical and horizontal (front/back and left/right) dimensions as coordinates. The relatum, however, is not the speaker but some other object. The scene in cell II of the table depicts a tree as relatum. In order to locate the ball, the speaker says *the ball is behind the tree*. It is important to notice that trees have no front and back sides of their own. The ball's being behind the tree is dependent on the speaker's coordinate system. The ball and the tree are located on the speaker's front/back dimension, with the ball further removed from the speaker than the tree. If the speaker would move 90° clockwise around the tree, always facing it, he could say *the ball is to the left of the tree*. The tree has no left side of its own. Deictic spatial reference always depends on where the speaker is and on his orientation in the scene. In order to interpret a deictic expression, the listener must be aware of these spatial properties of the speaker.

How the relation between speaker, relatum, and referent is mapped onto deictic terms varies from language to language. Hill (1982), for instance, described an African language (Hausa) in which a speaker in the scene of cell II uses the equivalent of *in front of the tree* to localize the ball. In fact, Hill found that the same is done in certain English-speaking communities.

In the lower cells of the table, the situation changes drastically. The system of coordinates is no longer dependent on the speaker; now it depends on some other entity. In the standard case, the relatum is also the source of the coordinate system. This is so for the scene depicted in cell IV. The chair has a vertical dimension and two horizontal ones, a front/back and a left/right dimension. The ball lies on the positive half of the chair's front/back axis, and that makes it possible for the speaker to say that the ball is *in front of* the chair. This kind of reference is called *intrinsic*, because localization is relative to intrinsic dimensions of some entity. Note that the position and the orientation of the speaker with respect to the scene are irrelevant. If the speaker were to turn around or move behind the chair, it would not affect intrinsic reference. The ball would continue to be *in front of* the chair. This is quite different from secondary deictic use, as in the scene of cell II, where the ball is *behind, in front of, left of,* or *right of* the tree, depending on where the speaker is.

There are situations where deictic and intrinsic reference can lead to conflicting expressions. Take again the scene in cell IV. The speaker in that scene could as well use secondary deictic reference. He would then have to say *the ball is to the left of the chair,* because from his point of view the ball is further to the left on his left/right dimension. It should be obvious that such conflicts can lead to trouble in communicating. The interlocutor must be able to guess which coordinate system the speaker is using. Usually, speakers are not very explicit about this. It is the exception rather than the rule that a speaker says *from my point of view ...* or something similar (Levelt 1982b; Ehrich 1985; Bürkle, Nirmaier, and Herrmann 1986; Herrmann, Bürkle, and Nirmaier 1987). The potential clashes of deictic and intrinsic reference, and some ways in which they are resolved, are discussed in Levelt 1984a.

The fact that cell III of the table is empty means that it is unusual, if not entirely impossible, for a speaker to use himself as relatum in an intrinsic coordinate system. The speaker in the scene of cell IV would then have to say something like *the ball is to the right of me,* because the speaker and the ball are roughly aligned along the chair's left/right dimension.

It was mentioned above that the representation of local reference systems in table 2.1 is not complete. For one thing, there are other coordinate systems besides the two mentioned so far. An important one is the system of *geographic reference.* An object can be *north, west,* etc. of some relatum. There are linguistic communities in which this or similar systems of geographic reference are used intensively. For our present concern, the speaker as interlocutor, a second extension of the system is of great relevance. It concerns intrinsic reference. Within this cell of the table (cell IV), the speaker could also take the addressee as a basis for the coordinate system. This is exemplified in figure 2.1. When the speaker says *the ball is in front*

Figure 2.1
Intrinsic reference with the addressee as basis for the coordinate system.

of you, as in the left picture, the addressee is taken both as the relatum and as the origin of the coordinate system, just as the chair is in cell IV of table 2.1. But the speaker could also say *the ball is to the right of the lamp*, as in the right picture. Here the lamp is the relatum, but the addressee is still the basis for the coordinate system. It is only from the addressee's perspective that the ball is to the right of the standing lamp. Bürkle et al. (1986) and Herrmann et al. (1987) showed that such addressee-based intrinsic reference is spontaneously used by speakers, especially when the speaker has reason to suppose that the addressee might have trouble determining what kind of coordinate system the speaker is using. Still, it is a general finding that the dominant or default system for most speakers is deictic reference, either primary or secondary (Bürkle et al. 1986; Ehrich 1985; Herrmann et al. 1987; Hill 1982; Levelt 1982b, 1984a; Wunderlich 1981; Zubin and Choi 1984).

A third point, which may have been blurred by the analysis of table 2.1, is that there is local reference without an implicit or an explicit coordinate system. The most basic case is in the use of *here*. This deictic term means roughly "near the speaker", but it does not specify any orientation of the located entity with respect to the speaker. Klein (1978) asked himself the question "where is here?", and especially how close an entity should be to the speaker to be "here". If the locus of *here* is some region including the speaker, that region is highly variable in size. It may or may not include the addressee, for instance. If speaker Arnold says *It's more comfortable here than in your chair*, the region of *here* does not include the addressee (Betty). But when he says *it's warm here*, it is more likely that the region is meant to include both himself and Betty; it is probably an atmospheric condition of the room. In a certain state of mind Arnold could complain *There is no justice here*, expanding the region to all of the sublunary world. Klein (1978) calls this the *delimitation problem* the interlocutors have to solve.

Deictic *there* indicates some place outside the region of *here*, but it requires in addition some specification of direction, just as in demonstrative reference. This direction presupposes an origin (the speaker), but no particular coordinate system; *there* need not be in front of the speaker, or above the speaker. It is, rather, the direction pointed to (or otherwise indicated by nonverbal means). The delimitation problem is the problem interlocutors have of distinguishing the regions for *here* and for *there*, given the prevailing context of discourse. In languages other than English the delimitation problem can be even more complicated. The proximal/distal distinction underlying the uses of *here* and *there* happens to be dichotomous in English, but some other languages (among them Latin, Spanish, Javanese) organize that dimension in a three-step fashion: proximal-medial-distal (Fillmore 1982; Weissenborn and Klein 1982). The speaker must make sure that the addressee can derive the intended region from what he is saying and from the context of conversation.

Another case of local reference without a coordinate system, involving only a relatum, is the use of terms like *near*, *close to*, and *by*. In *the balloon is near the house*, neither the speaker's nor the house's system of coordinates is used as a base; all that is said is that the balloon is in the *region* of the house.

A final but important point to be made concerns *deixis-by-analogy* (Bühler 1934). Nunberg's distinction between demonstratum and reference also applies to informing an addressee about a place. The place *demonstrated* by deictic or intrinsic reference is not necessarily the place *referred to*. One example suffices to show this.

Arnold: Does John have scars after the accident?

Betty (touching her right cheek with her index finger):   Yes, he got a big one here.

The demonstratum is evidently the indicated region on Betty's right cheek, but it is equally obvious that it cannot be the referent: How could John's scar be located on Betty's cheek? The intended referent is the analogical region on John's cheek, and Arnold is supposed to understand that Betty is using her own body as a model for John's. Note that the information Betty conveys in this way is quite different from what is literally said— another demonstration of Grice's cooperative principle.

One's own body can also function deictically as a model for animals and even cars (example: Philip, who loves old-timers, tells his father in great excitement *I saw one with a wheel here* while making a turning hand gesture near his right side, thus indicating the locus of the car's spare wheel). Still, analogical deixis is not limited to using one's own body as a model. If Arnold and Betty occupy similar rooms in a dormitory, and Arnold is visiting Betty in her quarters, he could say *I put my floor lamp there* (indicating some place in Betty's room) or even *I hung my lamp just to the right of where your table is.* Bühler (1934) referred to this as a shift of origin from where the speaker is now to the analogical place elsewhere—i.e., from the demonstratum to the referent.

There are also models that have been designed to function as models. One can point on a map and say *I live there.* The demonstratum is the spot on the map. The referred-to place, however, is the place in the real world corresponding to the locus in the model. Deixis-by-analogy is a powerful tool speakers use for referring to place.

Acknowledging

There are, finally, spatial deictic uses that do not have the function of identifying an object or of informing the interlocutor about an object's location. The location is, rather, presupposed. The clearest cases in English are some uses of deictic verbs of motion, such as *come* and *go*. When a speaker says *Christian is going to the library*, this "acknowledges" the fact that at the moment of utterance the speaker is *not* in the library. If the speaker happens to be in the library, he should say *Christian is coming to the library.* These uses of *come* and *go* thus depend on where the speaker is; they are deictic uses.

Come, but not *go*, easily allows for a shift of origin from speaker to addressee. When the addressee is in the library, and the speaker calls from some other place, it is all right to say *Christian is coming to the library*, thus shifting the deictic origin to the addressee. Fillmore (1973) showed that this happens especially when the addressee is "at home base." One will say *May I come in?*—not *May I go in?*— when an addressee answers the doorbell. In other words, deictic *come* is used when the goal of motion is a region around the deictic origin. When the origin is not shifted, this region includes the speaker and may or may not include the addressee. When it is shifted, it includes the addressee. Deictic *go* is used when the goal of movement is outside the speaker's region.

There are three other deictic verbs of motion in English: *bring*, *send*, and *take*. E. Clark (1974) analyzed them as causative verbs (*bring* as *cause to come*, and the other two as variants of *cause to go*). They have deictical properties similar to those of *come* and *go*, respectively. The acknowledging uses of deixis are not limited to verbs of motion; there are languages that require a speaker to mark nouns for proximity or visibility of the object to the speaker (see Dixon 1972 on the Australian language Dyirbal), and English has other forms of deictic acknowledgement than verbs of motion alone (Fillmore 1982).

2.2.3   Time Deixis

Deictic time—i.e., time with respect to the speaker's "now"—is expressible in all languages, but the means are very different. Probably all languages have temporal adverbs of some sort or another, such as *tomorrow*, *today*, and *yesterday*. English and many (but not all) other languages also have tense systems to express, among other things, deictic time. In English, but not in all other tensed languages, tense markers are inflections on the verb. With *Francis was cashing the check* the speaker refers to an event preceding "now," whereas *Francis is cashing the check* refers to the present.

In the canonical setting for speech, the deictic temporal origin is shared by the interlocutors. They all have the same "now." (Remember, they don't necessarily have the same "here.") Let us start by considering some short-lived event, such as Francis' cashing a check. (One may, of course, spend hours on cashing a check, but in what follows let us assume that it is a rather instantaneous event.) The moment of the event can be symbolized by e. The speaker can say something about the event, and let the moment of utterance be u. The tense of the utterance may or may not reveal some temporal relation of precedence or coincidence between e and u. Here is the simplest case (where $<$ means "precedes," $=$ means "coincides," and $=<$ means "coincides and/or precedes"):

Past tense: $e < u$
Example: Francis was cashing the check.

Present tense: $u =< e$
Example: Francis is cashing the check.

Both examples have progressive aspect (*cashing*), but the tense difference is the one between *was* and *is*.

Both of the above cases are examples of what Lyons (1977) called *primary tense*—i.e., deictic uses of tense where the speaker's time of utterance is the reference (just as in primary local deixis, where the speaker's place is the relatum). But just as a different spatial relatum can be chosen in local deixis, a different reference time can be chosen in time deixis. By using the perfect tense, a speaker of English can create a "past in the past" by introducing a *reference time*, r, that is different from u and between e and u:

Pluperfect: $e < r < u$
Example: Francis had been cashing a check (when Peter arrived).

A speaker who says this refers to a time r in the past (for instance, the moment that Peter arrived) and relates to it the moment of cashing the check, e. This new moment, r, can be thought of as the moment at which the event was or became *relevant*, so r can stand for both "relevance time" and "reference time." Notice that the newly created relation between e and r is itself nondeictic; it is independent of the speaker's "now." It can be paraphrased as *Francis' cashing of the check precedes Peter's arriving*, which merely orders two events in time. But the pluperfect expresses that the reference time is in the past, i.e., preceding the speaker's "now," and that relation is deictic. Hence we have in the pluperfect two temporal relations: a deictic one between utterance time u and relevance time r, namely $r < u$, and a nondeictic (or *intrinsic*) one between event time and relevance time, namely $e < r$.

In the example, the newly introduced relevance time—the moment of Peter's arrival—was explicitly mentioned. But this is not always necessary. There are situations in which a speaker can just say *Francis had been cashing a check*. Such an utterance *acknowledges* some relevance time mutually known to the interlocutors.

Many authors (following Reichenbach 1947) prefer to use the notion of relevance time also for the simple present tense and past tense. In that case, one should say for the present tense that the utterance time and the relevance time coincide—i.e., the deictic temporal relation is $r = u$, and the intrinsic component for the present tense is $e = r$. For the past tense, the relevance time precedes the utterance time (i.e., the deictic relation is $r < u$) but the relevance time coincides with the event time (i.e., $e = r$). Applying this two-component analysis generally, we get the following.

(a) *Present*
Deictic component: $r = u$.   Intrinsic component: $e = r$.

(b) *Past*
Deictic component: $r < u$.   Intrinsic component: $e = r$.

(c) *Pluperfect*
Deictic component: $r < u$.   Intrinsic component: $e < r$.

This analysis can now be extended to other tenses. Take the present perfect, as in *Francis has been cashing the check* (i.e., he has the money now). Here the relevance time coincides with the speaker's "now." The speaker expresses that what happened is still actual; the present availability of money could even be the topic of the ongoing conversation. Compare this with the past tense: *Francis was cashing the check* does not express that the event is presently relevant. Thus, for present perfect we have the following.

(d) *Present perfect*
Deictic component: $r = u$. Intrinsic component: $e < r$.

The English tense system does not allow for future marking on the verb. Reference to the future is often accomplished by using the auxiliary *will* in the present tense, as in *Francis will be cashing the check*. In this case the relevance time is the speaker's "now," but the event is in the future:

(e) *Future*
Deictic component: $r = u$. Intrinsic component: $r < e$.

This future construction, however, has a strong modal overtone. It expresses the speaker's attitude with respect to the definiteness of the expected event (Lakoff 1970).

A final and especially instructive case is future perfect, as in *Francis will have been cashing the check* (by the time Peter arrives). In this example, the speaker takes the future moment of Peter's arrival as the relevance time and predicates that the event (cashing the check) precedes it. The latter relation is the nondeictic one ($e < r$), but the moment of Peter's arrival is deictically located after the speaker's "now" (i.e., $u < r$). In this case, nothing follows with respect to the relative timing of e and u; the only thing we know is that both precede the relevance time. Thus, the speaker leaves unspecified whether, at the moment of speaking, the check has already been cashed. For future perfect we have the following.

(f) *Future perfect*
Deictic component: $u < r$. Intrinsic component: $e < r$.

It will not always be necessary for the speaker to mention the time of relevance explicitly. If it is mutually known to the interlocutors, it can be left unmentioned. The speaker can just say *Francis will have been cashing the check* (or perhaps better, without progressive aspect, *Francis will have cashed the check*). In that case the future perfect just acknowledges the existence of such a relevance time, and the interlocutors will be able to retrieve it. Finally, there is a modal aspect to the future perfect that expresses a strong expectation on the part of the speaker that this will be the course of events. Lyons (1981) calls this an *epistemic commitment*.

So far we have only considered deictic reference to events. However, temporal reference can also be made to a state, such as being in love or knowing a telephone number. The state may be more or less enduring, and it may or may not overlap with the utterance time, with the relevance time, or with both. These cases will not be discussed here, but see Steedman 1982.

I began this section by saying that tense is but one device for expressing time deictically. The use of time adverbials is a more universal means in the languages of the world. *Today* is the day including the interlocutor's "now," *yesterday* is the day preceding the day of the utterance, and so on. Many societies have developed a quasi-objective system of time reference: *calendar time.* "June 18, 1832" denotes a day without reference to a deictic, speaker-dependent origin. Still, most uses of calendar time are still deictic to a certain extent. When a speaker asks *Will you be here in June?*, the addressee will interpret this as the first June from "now"; and similarly for references to days of the week and times of the day.

The present discussion of time deixis owes much to Steedman 1982 and to Ehrich 1987. Other major sources the reader might want to consult are Miller and Johnson-Laird 1976 and Lyons 1977.

In conclusion: Everyday conversations are inherently deictical. Interlocutors anchor their contributions steadily in the spatio-temporal context of their conversation. When this is done by reference to a speaker-centric origin—and this is the normal or the default case—the reference is deictic. Speakers can identify objects and events by deictic reference, they can inform one another about locations of objects and about times of events and states by reference to their spatio-temporal origin, and they can deictically acknowledge place and time. Deixis allows speakers to refer indirectly by shifting the origin, by setting up spatial analogies or additional "relevant" moments in time. All this is done fluently, and mostly unawares. These basic and astonishing abilities of speakers have received relatively little psycholinguistic attention.

2.3. Intention

2.3.1 Speech Acts

It is generally assumed, and it seems to be supported by introspection, that speakers produce utterances in order to realize certain communicative intentions. Although this need not be true for everything uttered, people generally talk for some purpose. They intend to inform an interlocutor, or they want to be informed; they wish the other party to take some action; they want to share feelings of sympathy, sorrow, or happiness; they want to commit themselves to some action; and so on. This communicative intention of an utterance is called its *illocutionary force* (Austin 1962). An utterance with an illocutionary force is called a *speech act*; it is an intentional action performed by means of an utterance.

Each speech act begins with the conception of some intention. Where intentions come from is not a concern of this book. They may arise from previous discourse, for instance from a question by the interlocutor. In many cases they have other origins: a need for information or help during the execution of some activity, a wish to please or to impress someone, and so forth. Not all intentions are communicated (thank heaven), and speech acts are only one way of expressing intentions.

In fact, the intentions that underlie speech acts (as well as some other acts of communication) are of a special kind. We will call them *communicative intentions*, and this needs some elaboration. For a speech act to be effective, the addressee must be able not only to understand the utterance but also to recognize the speaker's intention to communicate this information. In other words, a speaker's communicative intention involves more than the intention to convey a thought, a wish, or whatever. In addition it involves the intention that the utterance makes it possible for the addressee to recognize the speaker's purpose to convey just this thought, wish, or whatever. A communicative intention always involves this purpose of *intention recognition* by the addressee.

This point was made by Grice (1957, 1968) and has been elaborated by various other authors (see especially H. Clark 1985; Recanati 1986; Sperber and Wilson 1986). It is not a trivial point. Take for instance the case where a speaker says something in order to impress an interlocutor. If the speaker does not want to be perceived as a boaster, it is essential that the interlocutor not recognize that intention. The utterance should merely cause the addressee to be impressed. It is an intention, but not a *communicative* intention in the strict sense used here. For an intention to be a communicative intention, it must involve the purpose of being recognizable as such by the other party. The content of the utterance, moreover, should be instrumental in making the addressee recognize that intention.

Not all speech acts are effective in conveying the speaker's communicative intention. A speech act's effectiveness will depend on a variety of factors, among them (i) what the speaker says, (ii) the context in which it is said, (iii) the way in which it is said in terms of prosody, accompanying gestures, gaze, etc., and (iv) various listener factors, such as attention, willingness, and available background information. Illocutionary force, defined as the intended effect of an utterance, is a speaker-centered notion. Because of the mentioned listener factors, it would be wrong to define an utterance's illocutionary force operationally in terms of what a listener infers from it. But it is certainly important, empirically and theoretically, to ask under which conditions speech acts are effective (i.e., are successful in conveying the speaker's communicative intention to the addressee(s)). The following utterances are speech acts if the conversants deliver them with the illocutionary force indicated in parentheses and with the purpose of conveying their intention

Arnold: Wolfgang has torn his Achilles tendon.   (a *statement* made to inform interlocutor B of a presumably unknown fact)

Betty: Oh no! Is he in the hospital?   (an *exclamation* intended to express one's feelings, followed by a *question* made to invite Arnold to provide certain information unknown to Betty)

Arnold: Yes.   (an *answer* intended to comply with B's invitation)

Betty: Send him a bunch of flowers.   (a *command* intended to get A to a certain course of action)

Arnold: I'll do that.   (a *promise* intended to commit oneself to the mentioned course of action)

These speech acts have the illocutionary forces of statement, exclamation, question, answer, command, and promise, respectively. Although the variety of speech acts is unlimited, at least some major classes of illocutionary force can be distinguished. Searle (1979) proposed the following taxonomy:

(i) *Assertives*   The intention of an assertive is to commit a speaker to something's being the case. The first turn above commits Arnold to the truth of Wolfgang's having torn his Achilles tendon, and in the third turn Arnold commits himself to the truth of Wolfgang's being in the hospital. Grice's maxims of quality require the speaker to behave (in subsequent turns) as if he believes in the truth of whatever he has asserted. Searle calls this the *sincerity condition* of the speech acts that share this illocutionary force. It would not be sincere for Arnold to answer *Yes, but I do not believe him to be in the hospital*. The sincerity condition is a necessary condition for the utterance to be an assertive speech act.

Speakers can commit themselves in various ways to something's being the case; they can state, boast, conclude, complain. These types of speech act differ in intention, and thus they differ in illocutionary force. Still, they share the basic feature of the speaker's committing himself to the truth of some proposition.

(ii) *Directives*   The purpose of a directive is to get the addressee(s) to do something. The question in the second turn of the above conversation is an attempt on Betty's part to get Arnold to provide certain information, namely whether Wolfgang is in the hospital. A question is a directive, and so is a command. The command in the fourth turn is an attempt by Betty to get Arnold to send a bunch of flowers to Wolfgang. There are marked differences between these two directives; in the one case the intended action is a reply, and in the other it is some activity external to the conversation. And there are other directives, such as orders, requests, pleas, and challenges, which are still different in illocutionary detail. All of them are attempts by the speaker to have the addressee do something. The sincerity condition for a directive is that the speaker behave as if he wants the addressee to do the action and as if he has a certain right to request it. It would be odd for a cooperative speaker to say *Send him a bunch of flowers, but I don't want you to.*

(iii) *Commissives* The intention of a commissive is for the speaker to commit himself to some future course of action. Arnold's *I'll do that* in the fifth turn commits him to sending the flowers. Such commitments can be made by promises, by pledges, by vows, or by threats, and the commitments can differ in other aspects (such as strength and content). The sincerity condition of a commissive is the speaker's intention to perform the action. It would be rather extraordinary for Betty to say *I'll do it, but I don't intend to.* The speaker has taken on a certain obligation.

(iv) *Expressives* The intention of an expressive is for the speaker to make known his feelings with respect to some state of affairs that concerns him and/or the addressee. The exclamation *Oh no!* in the second turn above expresses Betty's feelings with respect to the state of affairs mentioned in Arnold's previous turn. Some other types of expressives are thanks, congratulations, apologies, welcomes, and condolences. The sincerity condition for an expressive is that the speaker commit himself to the feeling expressed. Betty couldn't have sincerely exclaimed *Oh no, but I don't care!*

(v) *Declarations* The purpose of a declaration is to bring about a change that makes reality correspond to what is declared. When Roosevelt declared war on Japan, that declaration changed reality from a state of nonwar to a state of war. It is obvious that Roosevelt could do this only by virtue of his institutional rights, and most declarations work by virtue of the speaker's special role in some institution (as with baptizing, marrying, and the granting of degrees). Searle gives as a counterexample "I define ...''; one doesn't need to have a degree in mathematics to define a new term. According to Searle, declarations have no sincerity conditions—and sure enough, Roosevelt's declaration of war changes the state of the world whether or not he believes it, finds it inevitable, wants it, or whatever. None of these speaker attitudes is necessary for the utterance to be a declaration. Still, it is pretty absurd for a doctor to say "I hereby pronounce the patient dead, but I don't believe it". Insofar as declarations *are* intentional (and thus speech acts), their sincerity condition is the speaker's belief in the change of state occasioned by the declaration.

These five types of illocutionary force involve, in their sincerity conditions, two modalities of psychological attitude on the part of the speaker (Lyons 1981): *epistemic* and *deontic* commitment. Epistemic commitment is committing oneself to factuality—to something's being the case. This commitment is at issue in assertives and expressives. In performing these speech acts, the speaker commits himself to, respectively, the truth of some proposition and the real presence of the feeling expressed. Deontic commitment is a commitment to desirability—to the necessity of some course of action. The speaker expresses his will that something be so. This commitment is involved in directives (with which the speaker commits himself to wanting some action on the part of the addressee), in commissives (with which the speaker commits himself to the necessity of his own course of action), and in declarations (with which the speaker is committed to bringing about the change of state that is expressed in the declaration). It is the speaker's communicative intention that the commitment he makes be recognized as such by the addressee.

Such commitments can come in degrees. Degrees of epistemic commitment can, for instance, be expressed by way of modal verbs (*Wolfgang will be in the hospital*; *Wolfgang can be in the hospital*), by adverbial phrases (*It is possible that Wolfgang is in the hospital*), by subtle variations of intonation, and so on. Similarly, variations in deontic commitment can be expressed (*You may buy a bunch of flowers*; *It is necessary that you buy a bunch of flowers*, and so on).

Is this set of speech-act types universal and complete? Probably neither. Cultures can differ substantially in the actions people perform by talking. What about praying? Is it asserting, directing, committing, expressing, declaring, all of these at the same time, or something really different? What about the varieties of magic? No doubt there are types of speech act that are unknown to Western culture, and they may even involve other *classes* of illocutionary force than the ones mentioned here.

2.3.2 Speech-Act Type and Sentential Form
A theory of the speaker should explain how language users map intentions onto linguistic form. It is therefore of central importance to analyze whether there are systematic relations between types of speech act and types of sentence uttered by speakers. Linguists and philosophers have generally maintained that such systematic relations exist, and I agree. Some have also

argued that the relation is a very strict one—specifically, that there is a one-to-one correspondence between illocutionary force and sentence form, and here I must disagree. I will not review the arguments in favor of or against the latter position; others have done so in great detail (Gazdar 1979; Levinson 1983; Sperber and Wilson 1986; Wilson and Sperber 1988). Rather, in the following pages I will review some of the regular and the less regular relations that have been observed between speech-act type and sentence form. It should be stressed that regularities of this sort are, in part, *conventional* regularities resulting from standards of use shared by inter-locutors in a community of language and culture. Still, certain conventions may hold universally in the world's societies—that does seem to be the case. But language users can deviate from standards; in fact, cultures grow elaborate systems to regulate such deviations, thereby imposing new standards. These can, in turn, be flouted by language users, and so forth. Before turning to these issues in the next section, I will introduce some of the regularities.

Sentence types
Sentences come in different *types* (sometimes called *moods*). The three main types found in the world's languages are declarative, interrogative, and imperative (Sadock and Zwicky 1985). These types are often reflected in the mood of the verb. Again depending on the language, a verb can be morphologically marked for indicative, imperative, optative, subjunctive, and still other moods. Such moods clearly relate to characteristic functions of these sentence types in everyday conversation—in particular, to the kinds of commitment made by uttering such sentences. Also, the type of a sentence can determine its word order and its melody or intonation, as is reflected in the difference between the declarative and the interrogative sentence form in English.

Declarative sentences (with the verb in indicative mood) are characteristically used to assert and to declare (*Wolfgang is in the hospital*; *Hereby I open the meeting*). These types of speech act, as we saw above, have in common the speaker's attitude of epistemic commitment (a belief in something's being or becoming the case). It may, depending on the context, be a good first choice for a speaker who intends to assert or declare something to opt for a declarative sentence.

Imperative sentences (with the verb in imperative mood, and/or with particular imperative word order) are characteristically used to order and to forbid (*Send him a bunch of flowers*; *Don't walk on the lawn*). They typically function to impose on the addressee some obligation to perform or desist from a course of action.

Interrogative sentences—for which languages don't seem to have a particular mood of the verb, but which may be marked by word order, rising intonation, and the use of particles (such as *please*)—also have a directive function. They characteristically put the addressee under an obligation to provide information of some sort (*Is he in the hospital?*; *What is the time?*).

Both imperatives and interrogatives, whether or not they are grammaticized in a language, are typically used to create deontic commitment of some sort for the addressee. Languages seem to be less rich in the means they provide to commit the speaker to some action (i.e., promising or pledging). Rather, speakers indicate their commitment indirectly by putting the action in the future (*I'll do that*). As we have seen, however, future is also used to express the speaker's degree of certainty when he makes an assertion; it is a way of indicating the modality of a speech act.

Though certain sentence types do seem to relate to particular types of speech act, the relationship to Searle's five kinds of speech acts is by no means one-to-one. If anything, declarative sentences relate to both assertions and declarations, imperative and interrogative sentences both relate to directives, and there are no major characteristic sentence types for either commissives or expressives. As will be discussed below, the relations are, moreover, highly context-dependent. Practically any sentence type can be used to perform practically any kind of speech act. Wunderlich (1979), Gazdar (1979), Levinson (1983), and Wilson and Sperber (1988) have proposed ways of dealing with these context dependencies, which will not be discussed here. But some of the regularities noticed here do seem to exist, at least as *tendencies* of use. It would indeed be remarkable, for example, to find a language in which assertives are typically made by means of interrogative or imperative sentences. If a linguist were to find such a language, one would rather doubt the usefulness of his criteria for calling certain sentence types in that language interrogative or imperative.

Performative verbs
The most direct means a speaker has to express the illocutionary force of his intention is by explicitly using verbs of a particular class: the so-called performatives. A speaker can make an assertive by saying *I state that ...*, *I believe that ...*, *I conclude that ...*, and so on. Directives can, similarly, be made by using performatives, such as *order*, *forbid*, *request*, and *ask*. Examples of performative verbs for making commissives are *promise*, *vow*, and *pledge*. For making expressives, a speaker has verbs like *congratulate* and *thank*. Declarations can be made by using *declare*, *define*, *baptize*, and so on. At one point linguists even suggested that all sentences with illocu-

tionary force have some performative verb in their underlying structure (Ross 1970), but that idea has been abandoned. Note that for some illocutionary forces there are no performative verbs; for example, one cannot say *I boast that* ... (Searle 1979).

Performative verbs are very direct means of expressing illocutionary force, and Deese (1984), who called them "psychological verbs," found that they are frequently used for that purpose in natural discourse.

2.3.3 Politeness and Indirect Speech Acts

Conversation, and most other talk, is a collaborative activity that can be successful only if the speaker respects, or takes into account, the rights, capabilities, propensities, and feelings of the other parties. The use of straightforward linguistic means of the sorts discussed in the previous paragraph may be orthogonal to this requirement, and cultures have developed rather intricate systems to cope with potential conflicts in conversation. These systems, which regulate politeness and formality, are no less conventional than the uses of sentence form discussed above. Over and above this, speakers will remain creative and use nonconventional means to act with words.

It should not be surprising that politeness-regulating devices are especially apparent where directives are concerned. Directives are speech acts that put certain obligations on other parties, and their successful execution depends crucially on the interlocutor's willingness and ability to take on the obligation. Cultures have developed remarkably efficient conventions for expressing the speaker's awareness of addressee factors. If Betty wants to commit Arnold to sending Wolfgang a bunch of flowers, Betty can refrain from using the imperative (1).

(1) Send him a bunch of flowers.

Instead, she can inquire about Arnold's ability or willingness to act, or even to attend to a question:

(2) Can you send him a bunch of flowers?

(3) Would you mind sending him a bunch of flowers?

(4) May I ask you to send him a bunch of flowers?

There are still other ways to phrase such questions. (The conventions also differ considerably between languages.) Questions of this sort perform two functions simultaneously: They overtly express the speaker's concern for the addressee's condition, and they function as a request to perform the action. Clark and Schunk (1980) have shown that the above question forms are judged to be very polite requests. Let us consider this requesting use of questions in some detail.

A question, we have seen, is a directive that invites the addressee to provide certain information. Sentences 2, 3, and 4 are questions; the addressee is invited to provide information about his ability or willingness to perform a certain action, or to attend to a request. And the addressee may indeed provide that information, especially when it is negative (for instance, to question 2, *I cannot, I have to leave now*). The addressee's certainty as to whether the speaker is already in the possession of the requested information may vary; however, if the addressee has good contextual reasons to believe that the speaker already knows about her ability or readiness to perform the action, she knows that the speaker cannot have sincerely asked for it. By Grice's maxim of relation, the speaker must have meant something else—most probably a request to perform the mentioned action. Utterances that ask a question but implicate a request are called *indirect requests*. Herrmann and his collaborators (see Herrmann 1983) have studied experimentally what factors induce speakers to make requests by implicature and, if they do, what condition they will question. These results will be discussed further in chapter 4, but it can already be said that they clearly indicate that a speaker's doubt with respect to the listener's readiness to comply with the directive is an especially important factor in the speaker's decision to request by implicature. Under such conditions of doubt, speakers choose question forms that Clark and Schunk's subjects judged to be very polite.

A cooperative addressee will react to the request (*I'll do that*), but it is not unusual to answer to both the question and the implicated request. To question 2 above, Arnold could react with *Yes* (to the question), *I'll do that* (to the request). H. Clark (1979) analyzed the factors inducing a speaker to respond to the question, to the request, or to both. His technique was to make telephone calls to shops, banks, and restaurants and ask questions such as these:

(5) Can you please tell me what the interest is on your regular savings account?

(6) Can you tell me what the interest is on your regular savings account?

(7) Are you able to tell me what the interest is on your savings account?

The respondents' answers depended on, among other things, the degree of conventionality or idiomaticity of the question. Question 5 is highly idiomatic, with *Can you please*; as was mentioned above, *please* is a regular request marker. Question 6 doesn't contain *please* but still has the conventional *Can you* idiom. Question 7 is a far less idiomatic way of questioning about a person's capability. Clark's results show unequivocally that the less conventional the question form, the more likely it is that respondents will answer to the question. The answer type *Yes, four percent* (as opposed to *Four percent*) occurred in 8 percent of the responses to question 5, in 16 percent of the responses to question 6, and in 30 percent of the responses to question 7.

These results demonstrate not only the effectiveness of requesting by implicature, but also the power of convention in doing so. Considerations of politeness and cooperativeness can induce speakers to bypass direct conventional mappings of speech-act type to sentence form. However, speakers can adopt conventional means of deviating from these standards. The more conventional the means, the less ambiguous the intention conveyed.

Still, Clark's results show that, even in the less idiomatic cases of indirect requests, the request intention is usually conveyed. The least idiomatic question (7), for instance, still almost always induced respondents to mention the interest rate. This is no doubt due to the Gricean rationality of these conversations: Why would a person call a bank if he assumes that the bank cannot provide him with a datum as basic as the interest rate? The respondent will normally assume that belief in this ability is mutual.

And this possibility to implicate speech acts is by no means restricted to requests. Just about any speech act can be made indirectly, as long as context and Gricean cooperativeness guarantee that the addressee can infer the speaker's intention. Here is an example:

Child, after the washing up: Everything clean!

Mother, after quick inspection: You call that clean?

The mother's interrogative question implicates the assertive that things are not clean, and probably the order to do it all over again. The information asked for in the question (namely, whether the word "clean" was applied to the situation) was already mutually available to the interlocutors, and hence the sincerity condition for that question was not fulfilled. By violating the sincerity condition for asking a question, the mother induced her child to infer her real intention and, at the same time, created a special rhetorical effect. Another example:

Teacher: Assume w to be the number of different English words.

The teacher's imperative sentence is first of all a declaration ("I define w to be ..."), not a directive. The special conventions of teaching will immediately induce the alert student's inference that from now on w stands for the number of different English words, whether he assumes it or not.

Performative verbs can also be used obliquely, as in the following.

Husband to his wife's lover: I thank you for taking such good care of Amelia.

The same holds for the use of *please*—

Lover's answer: Please!

The endless varieties of performing speech acts indirectly are especially enhanced by prosodic and paralinguistic means. The sentence

So, you are going to the station

can be used as a statement, a question, an order, an expressive, and even a declarative (imagine a stage director defining roles for the actors), depending on prosody and context. Gestures, gaze, and facial expression can be crucial cues for the listener's inference of intended speech act.

The main points of this section are these: Speakers usually talk with some communicative intention, and there is no limit to the number of expressible intentions. The expression of a communicative intention through language is called a speech act, and speech acts commit their speakers epistemically or deontically. These commitments can vary in degree. There are certain regularities in the use of linguistic means to express different types of speech act. They have to do with syntactic type and with choice of performative verb. But speakers can override these standard ways, especially when restrictions on polite interaction are at stake. There are more or less conventional ways of doing this, but in all cases the resulting speech act is implicit or indirect. The speaker draws on the cooperative rationality of the interlocutors. In short, there are certain conventions for the linguistic utterance of intentions, but there are no fixed mapping rules. The situation is highly open-ended.

Summary

This chapter has introduced the speaker as an interlocutor, a participant in conversation, the "foundation stone of the social world" (Beattie 1983). In this canonical setting for speech, parties alternate their contributions, thus creating a running context for the cooperative interpretation and generation of utterances. There are rules of conduct regulating the way in which parties to a conversation allocate their turns. These rules minimize the chance of simultaneous talk (which would interfere with the distribution of attention) and maximize the occasion for all interlocutors to contribute to the interaction. There are also rules that regulate the cooperative character of contributions, i.e., the ways in which a contribution relates to what is mutually known and intended. These are known as Grice's maxims.

Participants in a conversation also share a nonlinguistic spatio-temporal context, in which they deictically anchor their utterances. In particular, there is deictical reference to persons, to social status, to place, to time, and to loci in the ongoing discourse. As far as space and time are concerned, interlocutors tacitly assume the speaker's "here" and "now" to be the origin of his deictic expressions. In primary place deixis, the speaker uses himself as relatum for place and also as origin of a spatial coordinate system. In secondary deixis, the relatum is another object but the speaker-centric spatial coordinate system is maintained. Spatial reference can also be made with respect to a coordinate system which is intrinsic to some oriented object in the context of conversation or to the addressee. The locus indicated by deictic or intrinsic means is in all cases the "demonstratum"; it is not necessarily the intended referent. Interlocutors draw heavily on mutual knowledge to "jump" from demonstratum to referent. This is particularly apparent in deixis-by-analogy, which involves a shift in deictic origin. The deictic origin is also often just "acknowledged," particularly in the use of verbs like *come* and *go*.

Deictic reference to time is accomplished by the use of deictic adverbials (*yesterday*, *tomorrow*) and by the use of tense. Most of the attention in the chapter was given to tense. It appeared that speakers express two temporal relations by means of tense: a deictic relation between the moment of utterance and some implicit or explicit moment of reference (the "relevance time"), and an intrinsic relation between that moment of relevance and the time of the event or the state talked about. Not all languages have tense systems, but the same two components can also be referred to by adverbial means.

Speakers' contributions to a conversation are intentional. They are means to achieve certain social ends, and they are intended to be recognized as such. Speakers can express their communicative intentions in more or less direct ways, depending on the requirements of politeness, and drawing on shared knowledge. It may be possible to distinguish different types of speech act (intentional contributions), and Searle's categorization into assertives, directives, commissives, expressives and declarations was reviewed. But there is less hope for theories proposing a direct reflection of speech-act type in linguistic form. The relations between speech acts and linguistic forms are highly context-dependent. Moreover, speakers can always flout existing regularities and reap the harvest by creating pointed effects in conversation.

Chapter 3
The Structure of Messages

This chapter marks the beginning of our odyssey through the speaker's processing components, and our guide will be the blueprint in figure 1.1. The voyage will have the Conceptualizer as both its point of departure and its point of arrival. We will first consider it as a generator of messages; in the final chapter, coming full circle, we will return to its monitoring function. Messages and their generation are the subject of this chapter and the next. The present chapter will deal with the issue of representation: What kind of structures are preverbal messages? The next chapter will then turn to procedures of message generation.

According to the blueprint, preverbal messages form the only kind of input representations to the Formulator. This means that a message should contain the features that are necessary and sufficient for that next stage of processing—in particular, for grammatical encoding. One could call a preverbal message that contains all such features a "well-formed" message. It can be accepted by the Formulator as characteristic input. The ultimate goal for a theory of message structure is to specify in a precise way what makes a message well formed. One could, for instance, think of a "message grammar" that generates precisely the well-formed messages. But, alas, such a grammar doesn't exist, nor is it in the offing. The present chapter can only present a global review of the message features that are required at later stages of processing, and indicate why they are needed. Among these features are that messages are propositional, that they have thematic structure, and that they have perspective. There are, in addition, obligatory language-specific features of various sorts.

Messages are the vehicles of reference and predication. Speakers intend their messages to refer to persons, objects, states of affairs, emotions, or what have you. At the same time, messages are often used to predicate things about these referents. They can assert or deny things about them, assign properties to them, question things about them, and so on. And when something is predicated about a referent, that predication can be true, or false, or undecidable. Such representations are often called *propositional*. Let us adopt this practice, but be aware that messages do not always have truth values. When you say *Congratulations!* or *What?*, the underlying message is probably not a proposition. So, "propositional" will stand for a mode of representation of which propositions are a special case. The present chapter is largely concerned with detailing this representational mode of messages.

In the section 3.1 it will be argued that the propositional mode of messages is only one of a number of formats in which the mind can internally communicate with itself. There is more than a single "language of thought"; however, if a thought is to be expressed in natural language, the mediating code must be propositional.

An initial step in specifying the structure of messages is to characterize their vocabulary, i.e., the concepts that figure in reference and predication, as well as the relations that can hold between them. In section 3.2, preverbal conceptual structures (which will be called "semantic") will be described as function/argument structures, which can be built up hierarchically. Some of the semantic functions involved, such as CAUSE and FROM, are of a very central and frequent sort. They make it possible to characterize certain arguments in a semantic structure as carrying a particular role, such as agent, source, or goal. These roles define the *thematic structure* of the message, which will be discussed in section 3.3.

The speaker will also put the message in some *perspective*. He will, in particular, mark the topic—the entity about which the message is intended to make a predication. He will also mark referents for their news value, i.e., whether they are given or to be focused. This structure of foregrounding and backgrounding, the "information structure" of the message, will be treated in section 3.4.

Further, the speaker's message should indicate the intended mood of the utterance, i.e., whether it will be declarative, imperative, or interrogative. These features, as well as those of aspect and deixis, will be considered in section 3.5.

A final issue to be raised is whether messages must, to some degree, be *tuned* to the target language. Will a message for an English Formulator have to differ from one that is fed into a Dutch Formulator, merely because of language-specific requirements? The answer given in section 3.6 is positive: Using a particular language requires the speaker to think of particular conceptual features.

3.1 Modes of Knowledge Representation and Preverbal Messages

In chapter 2 we made a distinction between declarative and procedural knowledge. The inner workings of a processing component, we assumed, are guided by procedural knowledge—i.e., by a system of condition/action pairs. The procedures apply to declarative knowledge items. Message generation makes reference to declarative knowledge about the world, which is permanently available in long-term memory, and to situational knowledge (about the present context of interaction, the ongoing discourse, and so forth).

It is likely that declarative knowledge comes in different modes. The two most studied modes are spatial and propositional representations. One can know (or remember, or construe) a state of affairs as a spatial image. This is probably the main mode of representing scenes such as one's office, house, street, and town. These representations can be made subject to transformational procedures of various kinds: They can be rotated, enlarged, or reduced, one can move objects or oneself around in them, and so on (Shepard and Metzler 1971; Kosslyn 1980; Levelt 1982b). One can also represent states of affairs in propositional form, as sets of relations holding between concepts. A proposition is true or false of the state of affairs it refers to, and we are endowed with a rich system of procedures for evaluating the truth or falsity of propositions on the basis of the truth or falsity of other propositions. If a person believes the proposition "All city centers are dangerous" and also the proposition "Manhattan is a city center", he will be able to evaluate the truth of the proposition "Manhattan is dangerous".

It is, to some extent, possible to go from one mode of representation to the other. When somebody asks me "What is the form of the table in your living room?", I can retrieve a spatial image and extract the propositional information that the table is round. I can then decide to assert this proposition in response to the question. Inversely, propositional information can often be evaluated by constructing some sort of image of the state of affairs referred to by the propositions. If I am given the propositional information that Arnold is taller than Betty, and also that Betty is taller than Christian, then I can evaluate the truth of Arnold's being taller than Christian by imagining three people—Arnold, Betty, and Christian—such that Arnold stands head and shoulders above Betty, and similarly for Betty and Christian. In fact, the construction of such working models or "mental models" is rather more the rule than the exception when we reason or listen to discourse (Johnson-Laird 1983).

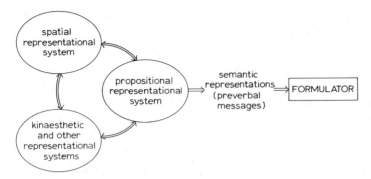

Figure 3.1
Some representational systems involved in thought and language.

There may be still other kinds of declarative knowledge that we use in conceptualizing the world. Anderson (1983) argues that we have a special mode for representing the sequential structure of events, Posner and Snyder (1975) talk about kinesthetic codes, and there may be other sense-related modes of representation for sounds (especially music), tastes, and smells. This is obviously not the topic of the present book. The point to be made, however, is that there is no *single* language of thought; we can move from one type of code to another, depending on the requirements of the task. If, however, the intention is to speak, then the code must eventually be propositional in nature. The preverbal message is a semantic representation that refers to some state of affairs. That state of affairs can be in any mode of thought, but the message must be in propositional form.

This is represented in figure 3.1. The cognitive system communicates internally by means of a number of conceptual codes: propositional ones, spatial ones, kinesthetic ones, and probably others. There are procedures for going from one code to another, and there is no reason to assume that the propositional language of thought is the one that should mediate between all others. Also, there is no reason to assume that the propositional language of thought is unique to man (Premack 1976). What *is* unique to man is that this internal language became externalized as a vehicle of interpersonal communication (Sperber and Wilson 1986).

A message is a semantic representation that is cast in the propositional language of thought but that, at the same time, meets conditions that make it expressible in natural language. It may be the case that *any* conceptual representation in the propositional language of thought is directly expressible (i.e., can be a preverbal message). This is tantamount to saying that a propositional representation is a conceptual representation that can be directly expressed verbally. In this way, the propositional language of thought is very much like a natural language. Fodor (1975) and Dik (1987) have argued for this position, and they have my sympathy. Still, we shouldn't exclude the possibility that expressibility imposes its own requirements on semantic representations. For example, when a language has a tense system, preverbal messages *must* include codes for deictic and intrinsic time; otherwise the message cannot be formulated. But do we then also impose this condition on all conceptual respresentations that are created for mere internal communication, even when temporal codes are totally irrelevant? Figure 3.1 leaves open the possibility that preverbal messages, though in the propositional language of thought, are of a special kind.

3.2 Semantic Entities and Relations

3.2.1 Semantic Representations
The human mind organizes the world of experience in categories such as persons, objects, events, actions, states, times, places, directions, and manners. Propositional structures are composed of elements representing entities of these sorts, and so are messages.

In the literature, these structures have been analysed in extremely divergent ways (see, e.g., Anderson 1976, 1983; Barth and Wiche 1986; Barwise and Perry 1983; Bresnan 1982; Dik 1978; Frijda 1972; Jackendoff 1983; Kintsch 1974; McNeill 1979; Miller 1978; Miller and Johnson-Laird 1976; Montague 1974; Norman and Rumelhart 1975; Schank 1975; Seuren 1985; Sowa 1984). This is, for the most part, due to differences in purpose. Take, for instance, two extreme cases: Anderson's and Montague's semantic representations.

Anderson's original purpose was to account for experimental results in sentence memory. When a subject is given a list of sentences or a text to read, the sentences are not memorized verbatim; rather, the memory trace is propositional, i.e., in terms of entities referred to and relations holding between these entities. As a consequence, subjects make characteristic errors in recognition tasks. When the text contained *John gave the book to Mary* and subjects were afterwards asked whether *John gave Mary the book* had been in the list, they tended to affirm this because the two sentences encode the same semantic relations. Also, their reaction times in retrieving sentences or parts of sentences when given particular cue words (such as *Mary* or *book*) showed patterns revealing an underlying propositional structure. Anderson proposed a so-called *propositional network representation* to account for such results—a formalism not without its problems, as we will shortly see. In a propositional network, nodes stand for concepts and arcs stand for relations between them. So, leaving details aside, the two sentences above could be represented as follows:

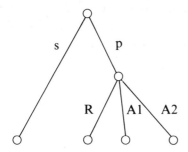

JOHN   GIVE   MARY   BOOK

Here, the proposition as a whole is represented as the top node. The proposition relates some subject, JOHN, to a predicate. The predicate is a semantic relation, GIVE, with two arguments: MARY and BOOK. In this case the network is a tree structure. But propositional networks are not always trees. The sentence *John gave the book to himself* would be represented as follows:

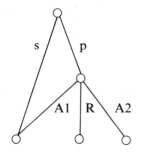

JOHN   GIVE   BOOK

In other words, the same concept or referent will always be represented by the same node. If there are several predications about JOHN in memory, they are all linked to the one JOHN node. Such representations may become especially useful when combined with notions of activation spreading. When I hear a sentence about John, activation will spread to the node JOHN, and from there to all nodes that encode further attributes of John, such as that John is a friend of Mary, that he has a child called Peter, and so forth. There are experimental procedures for measuring whether such attributes are indeed activated when I hear a sentence about John.

But is this kind of representation fit for the representation of preverbal messages? One may grant that an individual (person, object, etc.) is *represented* only once in the mind of the language user, but a characteristic property of language is that there can be repeated *mention* of that individual. One would like preverbal messages to represent such repeated mention. This is not easily done in a network representation, but can be done by using tree structures with indexed nodes. For instance:

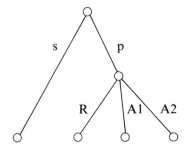

JOHN$_i$ GIVE JOHN$_i$ BOOK

Here the same individual, JOHN$_i$, is referred to twice. The Formulator will have to recognize this identity of reference in the message in order to come up with *himself* for the second mention (notice that *John gave the book to John* can only mean that there are two different persons *John* involved).

Network representations are less handy for other reasons as well. They can handle the scope of quantifiers only with difficulty. Compare the two sentences *Everyone gave a book to everyone* and *Everyone gave a book to himself*. These sentences clearly differ in meaning; however, the practice mentioned above would project both of them onto the same network:

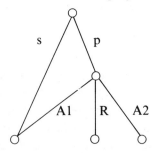

EVERYONE   GIVE BOOK

This network representation is, therefore, ambiguous. In other words, the Formulator receiving it as input cannot know which of the two sentences to generate. Such problems can probably be remedied (Anderson 1976, chapter 7), but networks are certainly not the most transparent vehicles for expressing quantification. This is more easily done by means of indexed trees. The representational ambiguity disappears, for instance, when the two sentences are represented as follows (leaving irrelevant details aside):

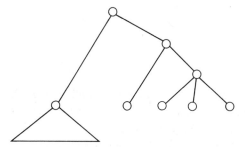

ALL PERSON X   X   GIVE   X   BOOK

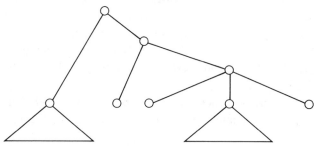

ALL PERSON X   X   GIVE   ALL PERSON X   BOOK

Montague (1974), on the other hand, had no taste for the psychological relevance of his semantic representations. His interest was in logic and formal semantics. His aim was to do for natural language what others had done for formal languages, namely to write a rigorous system of rules by which the truth value of a sentence could be derived from the denotations of its constituents plus the syntactic relations holding between these constituents. Montague's research program is now in full swing, but revealing applications to issues of psycholinguistic processing are still to come. We will return to some of these notions below in subsection 3.2.5, where the subject will be semantic types.

It is too early to make a principled choice between existing systems of semantic representation. For one thing, there are many problems of completeness to be solved, such as whether the system is *in principle* capable of making the semantic distinctions that native speakers make between expressions in the language. Second, there are many processing issues to be considered. None of these systems has ever been thoroughly combined with a psychologically realistic algorithm for language generation. It is only in such working models that one can evaluate the pros and cons of different types of semantic representation. Nevertheless, some more general things can be said about what preverbal messages should consist of.

3.2.2   Kinds of Messages

One way of looking at declarative messages is that they contain answers to tacit questions. These answers express certain categories of experience: persons, objects, events, and so on. This is exemplified in table 3.1. Similarly, interrogative messages, such as the ones underlying the questions in table 3.1, express *gaps* of the same kinds of category. Given the question and the state of affairs to which it refers, each answer can be true or false. Still, only the answers of categories EVENT and STATE express full propositions; the others are elliptical. In a later paragraph it will be proposed that the underlying messages are elliptical in the same way—e.g., that the message underlying *Peter* denotes an individual and no more. This brings the preverbal message very close to the utterance.

The categories of experience combine in systematic ways, and their relations can be expressed in language: A THING and a PLACE can

Table 3.1
Declarative messages as answers to questions.

Question	Answer	Category
Who dropped the milk?	Peter	PERSON
What did you get?	A pencil	THING
What happened?	I lost my purse	EVENT
What did Peter do?	Drop the milk	ACTION
What was the case?	The tire was flat	STATE
When was the fire?	Yesterday	TIME
Where was the flood?	In Holland	PLACE
Where did he point?	Toward the soldier	DIRECTION
What color was the house?	White	ATTRIBUTE
How did he travel?	By plane	MANNER

combine into a state (*the newspaper is here*), a PERSON and an ACTION can combine into an EVENT (*Peter dropped the milk*), an EVENT and a MANNER can combine into an EVENT (*Peter dropped the milk abruptly*), and so on. From this point of view, messages are more or less complex conceptual structures that relate entities of different categories to one another. But, as was already mentioned, theories differ in how semantic categories and their relations in a message should be represented. If one has reservations about network theories, there are still a wide variety of indexed tree-type representations to choose from. One of them is type theory, which was developed in the framework of Montague semantics. Another is Jackendoff's (1983) theory of conceptual structure. (For recent developments of the theory, see Jackendoff 1987a and, especially, Jackendoff 1987b.) In the following, I will first present some main notions from Jackendoff's theory, which explicitly claims "psychological reality." I will then use some of these notions to illustrate a type-theoretical account of semantic categories. In Jackendoff's theory, conceptual or semantic categories of the kinds mentioned above combine in essentially two ways: as function/argument structures, and as head/modifier structures. Let us consider these in turn.

3.2.3 Function/Argument Structures

When somebody asks *Where is Peter?*, the answer may be as simple as *here* or *home*. These words denote places in the world of experience. But place concepts are often more complex. When the answer is *in the tree*, the place is relative to a thing: the tree. One can say that there is a *place function*, IN, that takes a THING as argument and yields a PLACE as value in just the same way as the function $x(x + 1)$ takes a value of x (say 3) as argument and yields a numeral (12, in that case) as the function's value. We will be using capitals to denote conceptual functions, arguments, and modifications. When the THING concept is TREE, the PLACE is a function/argument structure, which can be represented as a graph in which the function and the argument(s) are put in left-to-right order:

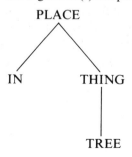

(This ordering is, of course, only a notational convention; it does not designate any temporal concatenation of conceptual entities.) A fully equivalent representation is a bracket notation in which the categories PLACE and THING expressed in the graph are added as subscripts to the parentheses:

($_{PLACE}$IN($_{THING}$THE TREE)).

In the following, the graph and bracket notations will be used interchangeably. However, when we use a bracket notation we will, as a rule, ignore the subscripts of the brackets. Hence, the simplified notation for the example will be (IN(TREE)). Also, the outer brackets can be deleted without creating ambiguity: IN(TREE).

The concept BE is a *state function*. In its so-called locative use, it can take a THING or PERSON and a PLACE as arguments, and the value is a STATE: the location of the THING or PERSON. The conceptual structure for *Peter is in the tree* looks like this:

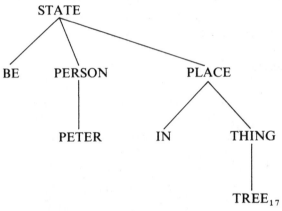

Here TREE$_{17}$ stands for a particular token tree.

An *event function* takes a maximum of three arguments, which can be THINGs, PERSONs, PLACEs, TIMEs, EVENTs, STATEs, or other categories, though not just any of these; for each event function, particular categories are required for the different arguments. The event function PUT, for instance, can take a PERSON, a THING, and a PLACE as arguments. The sentence *Joe put the key under the doormat* corresponds to this propositional structure:

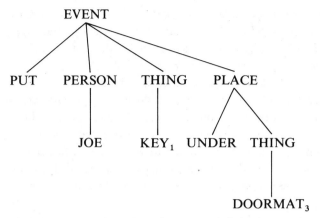

The numerals indicate, again, some definite key and some definite door-mat.

Some functions can take arguments of their own category. There are, for instance, event functions that take EVENTs as arguments. Consider CAUSE, which can take a PERSON or THING and an EVENT as arguments. A message of that sort underlies the sentence *Cynthia saw that Joe put the key under the doormat.* As a graph, it looks like

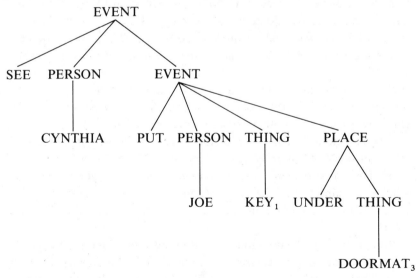

As a formula, it reads

SEE(CYNTHIA, PUT(JOE, KEY$_1$, (UNDER(DOORMAT$_3$)))).

This means that conceptual structures can be *recursively embedded*: EVENTs can contain EVENTs; STATES can contain EVENTs, and these, in turn, can contain STATES; and so on. For example, the sentence *Fred is happy about becoming a doctor* is about FRED's STATE. The STATE expressed contains an EVENT referred to as *becoming a doctor*, which involves the eventual STATE of Fred's being a doctor. This recursiveness allows conceptual structures to be arbitrarily large. There is no upper limit on the size of conceptual structures. This does not mean that messages of just any size will be generated by speakers; there are surely limitations of attention, which will keep the size of messages fairly small. It means only that nothing in the nature of concepts prohibits arbitrarily complex structures.

There are other important function/argument structures; however, they will not be treated in detail here. They involve what are sometimes called *logical* operations: negation, NEG(X); conjunction, AND(X,Y); disjunction, OR(X,Y); and condition, IF/THEN(X,Y), where X and Y are the arguments of the logical functions.

3.2.4 Head/Modifier Structures

Certain categories, such as MANNER and PROPERTY, do not behave like arguments of functions. Rather, complete function/argument structures are further specified, or qualified, or quantified by such modifiers. The sentence *Joe put the key under the doormat* expresses a complete conceptual structure, with all arguments specified (see above), but the EVENT can be further qualified, as in *Joe quickly put the key under the doormat*. Similarly, THINGs can be modified (*the red house*) or quantified (*two houses*), and most other categories accept modification too.

One characteristic of modification is that it leaves the category unchanged. A modified EVENT is an EVENT, a modified THING is a THING, and so on. This property of modification is easily expressed in type theory, as we will see in subsection 3.2.6. A more extensive discussion of modifier/head versus function/argument relations is to be found in Hawkins 1984.

Broken lines will be used to represent modification in semantic graphs. The following examples represent a modified THING, a modified PLACE, a modified EVENT, and a modified PROPERTY. Verbal expressions of these conceptual structures are given in parentheses.

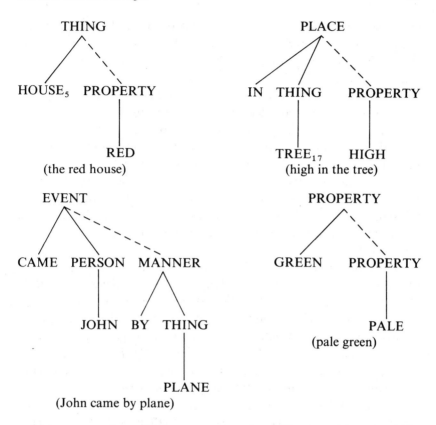

(John came by plane)

This apparently uniform treatment of modification, however, hides important semantic differences. A red house is not red in the same way that a big house is big. A red house is both a house and red, but a big house can be small in comparison with other buildings. And these PROPERTY modifications differ again from MANNER modifications. In other words, the broken lines do not always express the same kind of semantic modification.

In some of the above examples I added numerals to refer to token entities (TREE$_{17}$, KEY$_1$, DOORMAT$_3$). Before turning to type theory, I should say something about Jackendoff's type/token distinction.

3.2.5   Types and Tokens
In the above examples, the concepts JOHN, JOE, CYNTHIA, and HARRY represent individuals in the world of experience (notice that they need not exist in reality; they can be believed to exist or imagined). TREE$_{17}$, KEY$_1$, and DOORMAT$_3$ also represent individuals or *tokens* in the world of

experience. In the same way, one can speak of token PLACES (this particular place, e.g. in the tree), token STATES (this particular state, e.g. Peter's being in the tree), token EVENTS (this particular event, e.g. John's coming by plane) and of other individual instances of abstract categories.

Speakers do not exclusively speak about tokens or individuals (these technical terms are used interchangeably here); they can also mention types. In *John came by plane*, the word *plane* does not refer to a particular PLANE in the world of experience. According to Jackendoff, it does not refer at all; it expresses a *type* of transport. When a speaker says *Cynthia is a girl*, *Cynthia* refers to a particular individual; however, *girl* doesn't—it denotes a type, and the sentence expresses that CYNTHIA is an instance of this type. The speaker's next sentence could be *But the girl behaves like a boy*. Here *the girl* is referring to an already-introduced individual, namely CYNTHIA.

The entities the speaker refers to in his utterance are tokens (individual PERSONs, EVENTs, THINGs, and so on), but these tokens are implicitly or explicitly instances of types. When a speaker introduces CYNTHIA with the word *Cynthia*, the addressee will have the implicit belief that the individual is of type FEMALE HUMAN BEING. The speaker can, of course, prevent this by explicitly introducing CYNTHIA as *my dog Cynthia*. Shared type knowledge is essential for cooperative discourse. Interlocutors mostly assume mutual knowledge of the types of the individuals talked about. When necessary, a speaker can count on the addressee's tacit type inference, such as that a particular CHAIR is of the type FURNITURE, a particular DOG of the type ANIMAL, a particular EVENT (say Peter's silently picking Robert's pocket) is of the type THEFT, and so on. The type/token distinction is essential in reasoning and in the expression of thought.

We have great flexibility in moving back and forth between types and tokens. Not only do the tokens a speaker refers to tacitly carry the kinds of type information just mentioned, but types tend to be represented to consciousness by token exemplars, thus individuating them. It is hard, if not impossible, to think of the type concept BIRD or GAME without imagining some particular bird or game. These may or may not be prototypical exemplars, such as a robin or the game of baseball. Johnson-Laird (1983) argues that much reasoning with types consists in manipulating tokens set up in consciousness to represent these types. There is, moreover, no limit to the number of types, since a type can be generated from each token. If CYNTHIA is a token individual, then GIRL LIKE CYNTHIA is a type. When PICASSO is an individual, *a Picasso* can denote a type of painting (see Clark and Clark 1979 for an analysis of such cases).

Each category in a message is either a type or a token. This was not explicitly represented in the above examples (except by way of numerals), and it will mostly be obvious in any case. The following semantic structures, however, are, by way of example, explicitly marked in this respect:

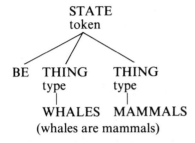

(whales are mammals)

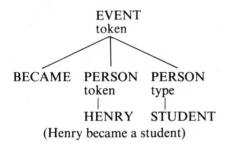

(Henry became a student)

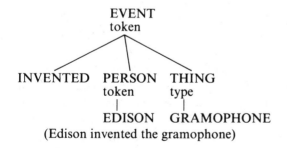

(Edison invented the gramophone)

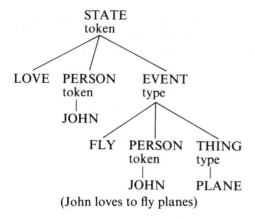

(John loves to fly planes)

3.2.6 Semantic Types

The notion of messages as answers to questions, introduced above, gave us a handle for distinguishing kinds of messages, i.e., semantic categories expressed in messages. Type theory can be viewed as a principled, formal way of approaching the same issue. In this subsection, some more technical notions from type theory will be introduced. They are helpful, but not really essential for understanding the subsequent sections. In other words, the reader can skip what follows without losing continuity.

Take the following two question/answer pairs:

(1) What happened?   John fell

(2) Who fell?   John

In (1) the answer expresses some EVENT; in (2) it expresses a PERSON. Of the two answers, only *John fell* is a full proposition which can be true or false with respect to some state of affairs the speaker has in mind. Because it can have a truth value, such an expression is said to be of type *t* in type theory. Only full propositions are of type *t*. The second answer, *John*, can only be true or false with respect to the (tacit) question. It has no truth value in itself; it is merely a referring expression. Expressions denoting individual entities, such as PERSONs or THINGs, are of type *e* in type theory. To know whether the answer *John* is true or false, we need a predicate. The tacit predicate in the question is *fell*. Combined with *John* it yields an expression of type *t*, i.e., one that can have a truth value. From this it can be deduced that the underlying one-place predicate FALL is of type $\langle e,t \rangle$. This notation means the following: FALL is of type $\langle e,t \rangle$ because when applied to an expression of type *e* (for instance JOHN) it yields an expression that has a truth value (for instance FALL (JOHN)) of type *t*.

More generally, in type theory an expression is of type $\langle a,b \rangle$ if, applied to a, it yields an expression of type b. To take an example from Jackendoff's analysis above: The place function IN is of type $\langle e,p \rangle$ because if it is applied to a THING (for instance TREE, which is of type e) it yields a PLACE, which can be said to be of type p.

The types e and t are the only two basic types in type theory. All other types are recursively built up by the following simple combination rule:

If a and b are types, then $\langle a,b \rangle$ is a type.

Let us see how this works. We know that e and t are types; therefore $\langle e,t \rangle$ is a type. This type we have already met. The example above was FALL. Other examples are SKATE and SLEEP. All one-place first-order predicates are of type $\langle e,t \rangle$. Since e is a type, $\langle e,e \rangle$ should also be a type. Expressions of this type should yield individuals when applied to individuals. An example is the semantic function MOTHER OF. When applied to the individual JOHN it yields MOTHER OF (JOHN), which is an individual. Other examples are PRESIDENT OF and FRIEND OF. Similarly, $\langle t,t \rangle$ is a type. An expression of this type is a function that, when applied to an expression of type t, produces an expression of type t. They are expressions that modify a whole proposition—for instance, NOT, as in NOT(FALL(JOHN)). An important function of this sort is the tense function, which locates the state of affairs expressed in the proposition along the time scale. When the speaker prepares a message about a past event, he will introduce the function PAST, which is of type $\langle t,t \rangle$, as in PAST(FALL(JOHN)). In diagram form this is simply expressed as follows:

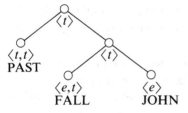

This information will then induce the Formulator to generate the right tense for the verb (*fell*). The situation is, in actuality, slightly more complex. In the previous chapter we saw that the determination of tense requires *two* functions: a deictic one and an intrinsic one. Both are of type $\langle t,t \rangle$.

One can go further building up types. The speaker may want to modify the predicate SKATE so as to express the idea that John skated fast. SKATE is of type $\langle e,t \rangle$; however, so is FAST(SKATE), because, if applied to an individual (for instance JOHN), it yields an expression with a truth value. FAST is therefore of type $\langle\langle e,t\rangle,\langle e,t\rangle\rangle$; it modifies a predicate into a predicate. More generally speaking, what was called modification in subsection 3.2.3 is always of type $\langle a,a\rangle$. In type theory, modifiers are functions that map some semantic type (say, a) onto the *same* semantic type (a). What is the type of a predicate like LOVE? If the speaker wants to predicate of John that he loves Mary, LOVE(MARY) should be a one-place predicate (i.e., of type $\langle e,t\rangle$). The function LOVE takes an entity of type e (MARY) to yield this type. Therefore, LOVE is of type $\langle e,\langle e,t\rangle\rangle$. Similarly, a three-place predicate such as GIVE is of type $\langle e,\langle e,\langle e,t\rangle\rangle\rangle$. It needs, successively, three arguments of the type $\langle e\rangle$ to yield an expression that can have a truth value, such as the message underlying *John gave Mary the book* (where the three entities are MARY, BOOK, and JOHN, respectively).

Categories such as EVENT and STATE are not always expressed in the same semantic type. Compare the sentence *John skated* with the noun phrase *John's skating*. The sentence can have a truth value; the underlying message SKATE(JOHN) is therefore of type $\langle t\rangle$. In other words, it is an *event-proposition*. The second one, however, is of type $\langle e\rangle$, because it must combine with a one-place predicate (of type $\langle e,t\rangle$) to form an expression with a truth value (e.g., BEAUTIFUL(SKATING(JOHN)), which underlies *John's skating is beautiful*). How can SKATING(JOHN) be of type $\langle e\rangle$? Since JOHN is of type $\langle e\rangle$, SKATING must be of type $\langle e,e\rangle$, just like MOTHER OF. When the speaker conceives of an event as an entity (i.e., of type $\langle e\rangle$), the Formulator will express it as a noun phrase (e.g., *John's skating*). In other words, messages can also denote event-*entities*. Similarly, they can represent state entities, such as the message underlying *John's becoming a doctor*.

One major reason for the further development of type theory is Montague's ideal of closely matching the semantics and the syntax of natural languages. One should develop the semantics in such a way that the various types will match hand in glove with syntactic categories. Or, to put it in terms of a speaker model (something completely ignored by Montague and most of his followers): Given the hierarchy of semantic types in a message, the Formulator would ideally "know" what kinds of syntactic constituent to develop for all parts of the message. If the message is of type $\langle t\rangle$, the Formulator should build a sentence; if it contains a part of type $\langle e\rangle$, the Formulator will create a noun phrase for that part; and so forth. But there is still a long way to go, if indeed the approach is at all correct (see Williams 1983 and Partee and Rooth 1983).

3.2.7 What Are Possible Messages? The Problem of Ellipsis

Is every conceptual structure that is built according to the rules of semantic composition a possible message? Could, for instance, all of the examples of function/argument and head/modifier structures given in the previous subsections be messages? This question is easier to ask than to answer, but the tentative answer here is Yes. The issue is not one of size or complexity. Very large messages may be impossible to construct for an attention-limited speaker, as we saw in subsection 3.2.3. But the question here is whether there is anything in the *nature* of messages that excludes certain types of conceptual structure.

One might, for instance, ask whether a speaker can refer without predicating something about the referent. Can a message be LIZ, or can it only be some predication such as WALK (LIZ)? I take it that, in certain contexts, the mere PERSON concept LIZ can be a message. When the speaker's interlocutor asks *Who did Peter visit?*, the speaker's answer can be *Liz*. What is his message? Is it something like PAST(VISIT(PETER, LIZ), or is it LIZ? If it is the former, the Formulator must cancel most of the message and encode only LIZ. This looks like a wasteful procedure: First generate a lot of conceptual structure, then do away with most of it. Still, this may be the case.

The alternative is that what the speaker generates for expression is just the message LIZ. Of course, the speaker will surely have been *thinking* about Peter's visiting some person in response to the interlocutor's question. But all that is not selected for expression. This solution of the so-called *ellipsis problem* (first proposed in Bühler 1934) is, however, not without problems either (see Klein 1984). Under certain circumstances the speaker can answer the question *Who did Peter visit?* with *her*, a pronominal expression for LIZ. But notice that the answer *she* is impossible. Apparently, the answer must have accusative case. But if the message is a mere LIZ, how can the Formulator know that it has to assign accusative case? It is not enough for it to know that LIZ is the patient of some action, since patients of actions do not always receive accusative case. It should, rather, know that the active verb *visit* is involved, which requires that its patient is the grammatical object and carries accusative case. So, how can the Formulator know about *visit* if VISIT is not in the message?

The conjecture is that the Formulator knows about *visit* because the speaker had just parsed the interlocutor's question, which contained the verb and requested information about the patient. But this is no more than a conjecture, and it requires the Formulator to have access to recent parsing output. (Some independent evidence that the Formulator has such access will be considered in subsection 4.2.5 and in section 7.5)

If this solution can be held up, there is nothing against messages that just refer without making predications. Or, put more generally: No semantic type is excluded as a message. The message can be a proposition, an entity, a predicate, a modifier, or any other semantic type. It will, however, be apparent in later subsections that, in order for a propositional representation to be a message, it should embody certain specific features that make it verbally expressible.

Some kinds of messages are very special indeed. What about the messages underlying such utterances as *yes*, *congratulations*, *ow!*, and *please!*? No effort will be made here to analyze these in detail. They express psychological attitudes; the speaker expresses the relation he has to a proposition or to some state of affairs. When I answer *yes* to the question *Is John asleep?*, I commit myself to the truth of the proposition ASLEEP(JOHN). In other words, I am expressing TRUE(ASLEEP(JOHN)). But the message is elliptical; it involves only the concept TRUE. In terms of type theory, the message underlying this use of *yes* is of type $\langle t, t \rangle$.

3.3   The Thematic Structure of Messages

The arguments of a function/argument structure usually fulfill certain abstract *roles* in the conceptual structure, and several authors have argued that these roles are drawn from a rather limited universal set (Gruber 1965; Fillmore 1968; Schank 1972; Jackendoff 1972, 1983). The distribution of roles within a message is called its *thematic structure*. The notion of conceptual role is, for reasons to be discussed shortly, most easily clarified in the framework of concepts of motion and location.

3.3.1   Thematic Roles

Take the sentence *the ball is in the garden*. It expresses the state-proposition BE (BALL$_3$, (IN (GARDEN$_7$))), relating a THING and a PLACE. (In the following, I will delete the individuating numbers.) Here BALL is said to fulfill the role of *theme*, and IN (GARDEN) the role of *location*. The next example incorporates two additional roles, which are fulfilled by arguments of so-called *path functions*. These roles are *source* and *goal*. Take, for example, the sentence *The ball rolled from the chair to the table*. It represents a theme (BALL) traversing a PATH—namely, from CHAIR to TABLE— which extends from one PLACE, the source (CHAIR), to another PLACE, the goal (TABLE). In other words, the path function FROM/TO has two arguments: CHAIR and TABLE. They fulfill the roles of source and goal. But the PATH can also be bounded at just one side: the source or the goal. The path functions are FROM and TO in these cases, and they take just one argument: either the source or the goal. Such a function/argument structure would underlie the sentence *The ball rolled to the table*, where only the goal is specified.

DIRECTIONs are paths that do not *contain* the reference object; they only go toward or away from some location. They figure in sentences such as *Frederick pointed toward the sun* and *Little Red Riding-Hood ran away from the wolf*, where neither SUN nor WOLF is part of the PATH. Here the path functions (or, more specific, the direction functions) are TOWARD and AWAY FROM, each with one argument.

So far we have distinguished the thematic roles of theme, location, source, and goal. We are now going to add *agent*, which is less obviously spatial in nature. The role of agent appears most clearly in causative events of the form CAUSE (PERSON, EVENT). In the sentence *The witch fed Hansel*, the witch is the person who caused Hansel to eat; she is the agent. There is disagreement about whether the causation should be intentional. If one limits agentivity to intentional causation (i.e., causing something on purpose), THINGs cannot be agents. A less restrictive interpretation of agentivity is that it merely involves causation. In that case, THINGs can be agents. So, for instance, in the sentence *The root made Tom Thumb tumble*, the EVENT is TUMBLE (TOM THUMB), where TOM THUMB is the theme. The EVENT is caused by a THING: ROOT; it is the agent. The root, clearly, has no intention to cause TOM THUMB's tumbling (though one never knows in fairy tales). Whatever interpretation one adopts, a necessary condition for agentivity is causation.

The next thematic role to be considered is *actor*, which should not be confused with agent. The definition of actor requires the notion of ACTION. Certain EVENTs involve ACTIONs. Their linguistic diagnostic is to make the following paraphrase: *What x did was* . . . . The sentence *John put the key under the doormat* can be paraphrased as *What John did was put the key under the doormat*. The ACTION is the conceptual structure expressd by *put the key under the doormat*. The actor, then, is the x mentioned in *what x did*—in this case, JOHN. In other words, the EVENT consists of the PERSON (the actor) and whatever he did (the ACTION).

Actors may or may not be agents; he who CAUSEs an EVENT is. In *Peter dropped the milk*, *Peter* denotes the PERSON who is actor by the just-mentioned diagnostic, and *dropped the milk* denotes the ACTION. But this

ACTION conceptually involves the causation of an EVENT. The EVENT is FALL (MILK), where MILK is theme, and the causation is a permissive LET. Hence, the message structure underlying this sentence is

LET (PETER (FALL (MILK))),

and PETER fulfills the thematic roles of both agent and actor. If the actor does not cause an EVENT, it is not an agent. This is exemplified in sentences such as *the child wept* and *Henry took the train*, where CHILD and HARRY are actors but not agents. Notice that an actor can be a theme. By the litmus test for actor/action, TOM THUMB is actor of FALL (TOM THUMB), i.e., *what Tom Thumb did was fall*, but TOM THUMB is also the theme (the object being displaced). We will return to this issue of multiple thematic roles.

Four final thematic roles often mentioned but not very uniformly analyzed in the literature are those of *patient, recipient, experiencer,* and *instrument*. A patient can only figure in an ACTION; it is the animate entity (if any) subjected to the ACTION. In *Gretel grabbed Hansel, Hansel* denotes the patient of *Gretel*'s ACTION. A recipient is also an animate entity; it is the one who receives the theme in some ACTION. It is usually, at the same time, the goal. In *The witch gave Hansel a hamburger, Hansel* is in the role of recipient. The experiencer is somewhat like a patient and a recipient; it is the person subject of a state or experience, like *Hansel* in *Hansel was hungry* or *I* in *I don't know the play well enough*. Instruments are apparent in sentences such as *John came by plane* and *I opened the door with the key*; PLANE and KEY are instrumental concepts here. Instruments tend to appear in the conceptual category of MANNER, as in these two examples.

To sum up: The theme is the argument being localized or displaced in a physical or mental "space." Source and goal are reference locations in such a space. Agentivity is a feature of the first argument in causative structures. The actor is the argument "doing" something. The patient is the animate entity subjected to some ACTION. The recipient is the one who receives the theme. The experiencer is the animate subject of a state or experience, and an instrument is the means by which some ACTION is effected.

One should be very careful not to confuse thematic roles with concepts or categories. The role of theme, for instance, can be fulfilled not only by the categories PERSON and THING, as already discussed, but also by EVENTs, STATEs, and other categories, as will be discussed shortly. Similarly, the roles of location, source, and goal can be played not only by PLACEs and THINGs but also by PERSONs, STATEs, and other arguments. The thematic role of an argument is probably determined solely by the kind of function it is an argument of. But then, how can different functions involve the same thematic roles? What is it in, say, HIT and SPILL that makes their first argument an agent?

It is surely unsatisfactory when thematic roles are not *explicitly* represented in the message structure. The difficulties in representing thematic structure in semantic networks or trees have moved some theorists (including Anderson [1976]) to give up the notion altogether. But thematic roles are important for grammatical encoding, as will be discussed in chapter 7. Hence, they should, in some way or another, be represented in the message. Other theorists have, therefore, proposed to decompose semantic functions in such a way that thematic roles are tied to certain constants in semantic functions (Bierwisch 1986). Take, for instance, the role of agent. The condition for something to be an agent, we saw, is that it cause something. Hence, any message involving an agent must have an underlying predicate CAUSE; and when there is a predicate CAUSE in the message there is an agent, namely the first argument of CAUSE. Similarly for the role of actor: Since the actor is the argument "doing" something, a necessary and sufficient condition for there to be an actor is that there be an underlying predicate DO in the message. In the same vein, source and goal are arguments of underlying predicates FROM and TO. An advantage of this approach is that it might give a principled account of multiple thematic roles. Something is, for instance, both an agent and an actor when it *does* something that *causes* something. In *John teaches Peter the alphabet*, John does something by which he causes Peter to know the alphabet; hence John is both actor and agent.

This approach requires messages to be semantically *decomposed* to a certain extent. For instance, the sentence *Gretel killed the witch* would not have the predicate KILL(X,Y) in its underlying message; it would have something like CAUSE(X, DIE (Y)), where X is the agent. It is, however, one thing to say that speakers *know* that killing normally involves the causation of death, but quite another thing to require that this knowledge become an explicit part of the preverbal message. The problem is that there is no end to semantic decomposition. DIE is to become not alive, BECOME has temporal aspects to be spelled out, and so forth. However, it is also arbitrary to impose some cutoff point. Semantic decomposition is probably not an all-or-none matter when we consider the process of speaking. Rather, depending on the intention to be conveyed, certain semantic components or predicates will have a higher level of saliency or activation in the speaker's mind than others. In chapter 6, these levels of saliency will turn out to play an important role in the accessing of lemmas. When, in the following, a certain level of semantic decomposition will be maintained in the representations of messages, this matter of saliency should be kept in mind. Some of the spelled-out message structures are "ideal cases" involving various components that *could* be salient in the speaker's mind; no claim is made that all of them *must* be highly salient. Arguments against semantic decomposition are reviewed in Fodor et al. 1980.

3.3.2 Semiotic Extension of Thematic Roles

Thematic roles are not only implicit in semantic representations of physical motion and action, they can also be apparent in other conceptual domains (see especially Jackendoff 1983, whose analysis we follow here, and Fauconnier 1985). The domain of time is an obvious case. Consider as an example the sentence *Helen worked from nine to five.* There is an EVENT, expressed by *Helen worked*, and there are two reference points in time: 9 and 5 o'clock. Here, the EVENT is the theme, and it starts at the source TIME, 9 o'clock (the FROM-argument) and extends over, or traverses, a PATH in time till the goal TIME, 5 o'clock (the TO-argument). Notice, moreover, that the use of past tense expresses the fact that the EVENT, and thus the whole temporal PATH it traversed, preceded the speaker's "now." The tense, one could say, expresses the DIRECTION of the speaker's time perspective; it "points" toward the past.

The temporal domain is a one-dimensional space in which EVENTs are located just as THINGs in three-dimensional space. EVENTs can be momentary (*he arrived at five*), i.e., located at a reference TIME just as THINGs or PERSONs are located at a reference PLACE (*he arrived at the airport*). EVENTs can also extend over time in much the same way as THINGs extend over, or traverse, a PATH in space (*She worked from nine to five*; *The road twisted from Zermatt to Saas Fee*).

It is less common, but not impossible, for TIMEs to appear in the role of actor. Jackendoff (1983), following H. Clark (1973), gives as an example *Tuesday crept by*, which is like the spatio-temporal *the train crept by*. In a decomposed semantic representation there is a DO underlying both sentences: DO(X, CREEP BY(X)), where X can be TUESDAY or TRAIN. On the decomposition hypothesis introduced above, this explains the actorship in both cases.

It is probably no accident that the thematic roles of space and physical action extend to time and, as will shortly be discussed, to other domains of experience. McNeill (1979) names this "semiotic extension." Our categories of experience, he argues, develop ontogenetically from a matrix of "sensory-motor ideas"—notions pertaining to physical motion and action.

Many other semantic domains show a similar pattern of thematic roles. Take the notions of possession expressed by such verbs as *have*, *keep*, *give*, and *take*. Having in possession fulfills the role of location. In *Tanya has the book* there is a theme, BOOK, which is possession-located at TANYA. In *Tanya gave the book to Martin*, the theme (BOOK) traverses a PATH from a source-possessor to a goal-possessor or recipient. In other words, it follows from the underlying predicate FROM/TO that there is a source and a goal. TANYA, moreover, is an agent in a causative EVENT. TANYA, namely, CAUSED the EVENT of the theme's going from source to goal. When we denote the concept of traversing a "possessional" path by GOposs, the message structure underlying the sentence (ignoring tense indicators) can be represented by the following event-proposition:

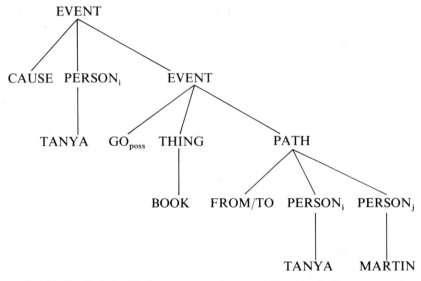

On this level of detail, the structure that underlies *give* is the same as the one for *receive*. The above structure also applies to the sentence *Martin received the book from Tanya*. Whether the speaker will formulate the one or the other sentence in the presence of this semantic structure depends on, among other things, whether TANYA or MARTIN is the topic (see subsection 3.4.1).

3.3.3 Some Concluding Remarks

The Conceptualizer produces messages as output; they can be representations of different types, such as propositions, predicates, entities, and modifiers. Messages and their constituent parts can denote such categories of experience as EVENTs, STATEs, THINGs, PERSONs, ACTIONs,

PLACEs, PATHs, and MANNERs. The present section has outlined the type of representation in which these categories participate. They can be conceived of as hierarchically organized function/argument structures and head/modifier relations, allowing for quantification, for binding of variables, and for repeated reference to the same entity.

It was further discussed that arguments in these structures play a rather limited set of abstract roles, such as theme, source, goal, agent, actor, patient, recipient, experiencer, and instrument. These roles presumably depend on the underlying predicates. If there is CAUSE(X,Y) in the message, then X is an agent; if there is FROM(X), X is a source; and so on. Not only is this the case for the domains of space and action; it also applies to other semantic fields. We considered as examples the domain of time and that of possession, but various authors have extended the analysis to such disparate fields as circumstantials (as in *Lisa began/kept/stopped working*), properties and measures (as in *the metal melted* or *I don't know the play well enough*), and perception (as in *he showed us a picture on the screen*). Some of the Formulator's procedures make reference to the thematic structure of the message.

The issue of semantic decomposition was also touched on. To what degree are underlying predicates indeed spelled out in the speaker's message? This is probably not an all-or-none matter. Rather, semantic components in a message show various degrees of saliency or activation. The Formulator will acknowledge these degrees of saliency in the kinds of lemma it accesses, in the detail of modification it generates, and in the word order it will generate. This brings us to a final point.

There is no reason to assume a specific temporal left-to-right ordering in message structures. The left-to-right structure in the examples above is due only to the notational conventions we adopted. It is a so-called *set-system* (see Levelt 1974, volume 2). For a given message, however, the order of activation of the different parts may vary. And since (according to Wundt's principle) the Formulator will start working on the part that first becomes available, the order of activation may affect the sentence structure generated by the Formulator.

3.4 Perspective and Information Structure

3.4.1 Nuclear Thematic Structure
Let us return to the notion that thematic relations in a message may differ in importance, saliency, or centrality for the speaker. He may want to pull

certain relations more into the foreground, and to leave others in the background. Another way of saying this is that the speaker brings the conceptual structure into some *perspective* (Fillmore 1977; MacWhinney 1977). Different perspectives may lead to different formulations of the same thematic structure.

An example was given in subsection 3.3.2. The sentence *Martin received the book from Tanya* expresses the same thematic structure as the sentence *Tanya gave the book to Martin*, but the perspectives are different. The former sentence describes the scene from the recipient's perspective, whereas the latter takes the agent as the point of departure. A speaker must decide not only which roles in a scene he wants to express (he may want to ignore the agent completely and say *Martin received the book*) but also which of those roles are to be foregrounded. Let us call the latter the *nuclear elements*, following Fillmore 1977. And, as will be discussed in chapters 6 and 7, these nuclear elements tend to be encoded in the major grammatical functions of subject, direct object, and (maybe) indirect object. Backgrounded elements, on the other hand, tend to end up in less important and often optional grammatical functions. (These are usually called *oblique* functions.)

Here is another example, from Fillmore 1977:

(1) I hit the stick against the fence

(2) I hit the fence with the stick

The speaker who uttered sentence 1 had I (SPEAKER) and STICK as foregrounded or nuclear elements in his message, whereas the speaker of sentence 2 drew I (SPEAKER) and FENCE into the foreground. In both cases the nuclear elements were encoded as subject and direct object, whereas the non-nuclear element was in each case given a minor grammatical function.

The problem is, of course, to determine what is nuclear for the speaker without taking recourse to the sentence he utters. That will be needed to prove Fillmore's claim that nuclear elements get assigned to major grammatical functions. Some empirical approaches to this problem will be discussed in chapter 7. Here it suffices to suggest that certain elements in a message are highlighted by the speaker. For a good understanding of what follows it is not necessary to give a formal characterization of this foregrounding. It is, however, necessary to consider one particular foregrounded element in more detail: the *topic* of the message.

3.4.2   The Topic

If a speaker wants to make some predication about some referent, he had better make sure that the addressee understands which referent is being commented upon. This is not obvious from the message structures considered so far. Even if we know what the nuclear elements are, it is still not clear which of them is the one the speaker intends to make a predication about. Take, for instance, the following event-proposition:

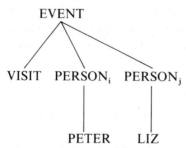

Here VISIT is a function with $PERSON_i$ (the agent) as first argument and $PERSON_j$ (the patient) as second argument. This representation does not tell us whether it is PETER or LIZ about whom the predication is made. It doesn't matter for the truth value of the message, but it makes a substantial difference from a psychological point of view. If it is PETER, the addressee is given information she is supposed to integrate with whatever she knows about PETER. If it is LIZ, the addressee must look up what she knows about LIZ and add that Peter visited her. Hence, for the benefit of the addressee, the topic has to be somehow marked in the utterance; it will be encoded as *sentence topic*. But the Formulator can perform the appropriate grammatical encoding only if the preverbal message indicates which entity is the topical one, the one the message is about.

Our convention will be to add TOPIC = X to the message, where X is the topic argument. So if the above message is about LIZ, we add TOPIC = LIZ. Speakers tend to encode the topic element in sentence-initial position (e.g., *Liz was visited by Peter*), but this is an issue for chapter 7.

Not just any entity in the message can be the topic. First of all, the topic should be among the nuclear elements of the message. If one asks *What about the stick?*, it is peculiar to get the answer *I hit the fence with the stick*, but *I hit the stick against the fence* is all right. Only the message underlying the latter sentence has the topical STICK among its nuclear elements, if Fillmore's analysis is correct. Second, the topic should be referential in the sense that the listener can know *which* object or set of objects is meant. Reinhart (1982), whose analysis of topic we follow here, gives the example

There is a fly in my tea. This would be a very odd answer to the question *What about a fly?*. In other words, the indefinite concept FLY is not the topic here. The reason is that the sentence would hold for just any fly; there is no specific fly referred to about which the comment is made.

How many topics does a message have? Just as many as should appear as sentence topics. A sentence becomes topicless when the underlying message is. Of course there is no topic when there is no comment. A message without predication, for instance one that only refers (like *LIZ*), has no topic. Also, when there is a predication, the speaker may want to leave it undecided what the topic of the predication is, i.e., where he wants the listener to store the information. In that case the Formulator will also produce a sentence without sentence topic. The above sentence *There is a fly in my tea* is of this kind; it may be about the tea, about the speaker, or about the state of the tea. Can there be more than one topic? Reinhart (1982) assumes not. One can, of course, conjoin sentences that have different topics (*It was Tom who cooked the meal and it was Mary who served it*), but otherwise this is an assumption we will adopt. A nonconjoined sentence has at most one sentence topic (the constituent the sentence is about), and that happens in just those cases where the underlying message has a topic-marked element.

Must a topic be *given* information in the discourse? Definitely not. A speaker can introduce a brand-new entity and at the same time make a comment about it. If I say *Constantine wrote more than six hundred compositions*, my addressee will take Constantine as topic even if she has never heard of him. She will probably hope that I will clarify at some point who Constantine is (it is Constantine Huygens), but she does store the comment under a newly created address for the unknown.

In subsection 4.2.2 we will distinguish the present limited use of topic, namely the message-level feature responsible for the grammatical encoding of sentence topic, from a broader notion of topic: the *discourse topic*.

3.4.3   Givenness and Inferability

It is clear from the above example that referents about which predications are made can be more or less accessible to the addressee. A cooperative speaker usually marks the givenness of the referents in a message. To take an obvious example: If the referent was mentioned in the previous sentence, it is given in the discourse and is highly accessible. The speaker will then tend to pronominalize it, as in *I saw John.* He *was at the meeting.* A referent not given in the previous discourse may still be inferable, as when one opens a conversation with *The pope was here today.* We will assume that the inferability or noninferability of each referent in the message is given in the message. These issues of givenness and inferability will be discussed extensively in subsection 4.5.1.

3.4.4 Focus

The speaker will further mark what is the new focus in the message. (This too will be treated in chapter 4.) The new focus is the information that the addressee was not attending to but should be attending to now. In formulating, there are two important ways for the speaker to mark the focused information: to give it pitch accent and to put it at the end of the sentence. Both means are used to mark the focus shift from the first to the second sentence in the following: *Peter saw much of Mary recently. But yesterday he visited LIZ.*

The items listed in the present section all contribute to what is sometimes called the *information structure* of an utterance. The speaker creates a message in order to convey certain intentions. For the message and the utterance proceeding from it to be effective, the addressee must be able to make the intended inferences. It is therefore important for the speaker to mark clearly what the message is about; whether the referents are given, inferable, or brand new; what information is to be focused; and so on. This will all facilitate the addressee's processing. I will not introduce formal ways of representing givenness, inferability, and new focus in message structures, but we must assume that they are—in some way—marked at the message level. It will be argued in subsequent chapters that various aspects of grammatical encoding are controlled by these message-level features.

3.5 Mood, Aspect, and Deixis

The procedures of the Formulator—particularly those that have to do with the assignment of word order and verb morphology—will depend on indicators for mood, aspect, and deixis in the message.

3.5.1 Mood and Modality

It should, first of all, be specified in the message whether a declarative, an imperative, or an interrogative utterance is intended. For the interrogative mood, a further distinction must be made between a polar interrogative and a content interrogative. Let us consider these cases from the viewpoint of the underlying message.

The unmarked mood is declarative. As was already discussed in chapter 2, using declarative mood is the neutral or privileged way of making an epistemic commitment (to assert or declare something). When the speaker indeed intends to express his epistemic commitment in this neutral way, the message may contain a marker to that effect. Let us indicate it by DECL. It can be taken as a proposition-modifying function, just like tense. A speaker preparing the utterance *John fell* would create the preverbal message

DECL(PAST(FALL(JOHN))).

Similarly, imperative mood in sentences such as *Let us go* and *Go away* expresses a deontic commitment of the type "I want you/us to do something". According to Wilson and Sperber (1988), imperatives are typically used to express the desirability of some state of affairs (for instance, that we go or that you go). It does not necessarily commit anybody; for instance, *Get well soon* expresses a desirable state but doesn't commit the addressee. When the speaker wants to express such an attitude in a neutral way, he will—we assume—code his preverbal message with an imperative marker, IMP. The message underlying *Let us go* would thus be IMP(GO(WE)).

When the speaker wants to know something (i.e., wants to express the desirability of some information or thought), he may construct a message marked for interrogative mood. The interrogative mood comes in two subtypes: polar and content. The *polar* interrogative invites an answer that is a confirmation or an invalidation of some proposition; it is therefore also called a "yes/no question." The *content* interrogative requests a missing piece of information, and what is missing is indicated by a so-called WH-element, such as *What* or *where* (see subsection 3.2.2); such questions are called "WH-questions." The marker we will use for interrogative messages is "?". (It is mostly self-evident whether the mood is polar or content.) The message underlying *Did John fall?* will thus be expressed as

?(PAST(FALL(JOHN))).

Expressing the desirability of some information will often commit the addressee to present that information.

Since declarative mood can be seen as the standard or unmarked mood, we will, when there can be no ambiguity, leave out the DECL marker. Hence, the message PAST(FALL(JOHN))) is to be interpreted as marked for declarative.

Commitments and desirablenesses, whether epistemic or deontic, come in degrees, as was discussed in subsection 1.3.1. These *modalities* of commitment may also be expressed in the message, but we will not introduce formal ways of representing them. They can induce the Formulator to select modal verbs (*can*, *may*) or "future" modals (*will*, *shall*). See Seuren

1985 for a treatment of modality and Doherty 1987 for an analysis of mood and modalities of commitment.

But the expression of attitudes is far more complex than what has been suggested so far. A speaker can, for instance, ask a question by way of a declarative sentence with rising sentence intonation, as in *John came?*. This differs subtly from the interrogative *Did John come?*. The declarative form expresses surprise, or the presupposition that John wasn't going to come. The interrogative form is more neutral in these respects. Also, emotional attitudes, such as indignation, irony, submissiveness, and excitement, are readily expressed by prosodic means—in particular, sentence melody (van Bezooijen 1984; Scherer 1986). At this point, we will probably have to qualify the assumption that everything relevant to formulating is encoded at the message level. If the message-level code is propositional in nature, emotional attitudes that are "directly" expressed in a high-pitched or shrieky voice are probably affecting phonological encoding and articulation via a different route. We should not exclude the possibility that the Phonological Encoder and the Articulator are independently sensitive to speakers' attitudes of this sort. For that reason, I will defer discussion of what is commonly called "intonational meaning" to chapter 8, which deals with the output representations of phonological encoding.

3.5.2 Aspect
Depending on the language, the Formulator will not only mark deictical time in verb morphology; it will also mark such temporal features as whether an action is durative or punctual (for instance, reading versus hitting), whether it is just beginning, and whether it is an iterative activity. These temporal properties are called *aspectual*. The clearest case of aspect in English is the grammatical distinction between simple and progressive duration (e.g., between *John read the book* and *John was reading the book*). When such semantic features are to be expressed, the message should contain modifiers to this effect. I will refrain from introducing semantic functions or symbols for this purpose.

3.5.3 Deixis
The deictic anchoring of an utterance should, of course, be prepared in the message. In a language that has a tense system, such as English, Spanish, or German, the expression of time is obligatory. In chapter 2 we saw that this anchoring involves two temporal relations: a deictic one and an intrinsic one. Both must be expressed in the message. The deictic time expresses the relation between the "now" of the utterance and the moment of relevance;

the intrinsic temporal relation is between the moment of relevance and the event. Where there can be no confusion, we will express these together as PAST, PRESENT, or FUTURE. In terms of the analysis in subsection 3.2.6, these can be seen as predicates operating on the proposition as a whole, as in PAST(FALL(JOHN)). Notice that intrinsic time is a semantic feature of the same kind as the aspectual features mentioned above; it is a non-deictic temporal aspect of the event, state, or activity.

Also, person and space deictical features should be expressed in the message. A speaker who makes reference to himself, or to the addressee, will encode these as such, and not as just any other person. When Fritz is talking to Heida, these roles immediately appear in such sentences as *I want to ask you something*; it would be very odd indeed if Fritz said *Fritz wants to ask Heida something*, which might be interpreted as referring to another Fritz and another Heida. In other words, it is encoded in the message which referent is the speaker and which is the addressee of the current expression.

Similarly, the speaker will, where necessary, encode the spatial relations between entities in the speech situation and himself. This is required for the correct grammatical expression of spatial deixis, as in *the book is here* (see subsection 2.2.2).

3.6 Language-Specific Requirements

There are different Formulators for different languages, and the question should be asked whether there are any language-specific requirements on what should be encoded for expression in a message. Consider, for instance, the feature of deictic proximity. In chapter 2 some properties of the English system for spatial deixis were discussed, and we noticed that the distinction between *here* and *there* and between *this* and *that* has to do with the proximity to ego. The English system (like the Dutch) acknowledges a two-step contrast here: PROXIMAL versus DISTAL. These are the categories in which distances to ego are cast. But other languages differ on this point. Spanish makes a three-step contrast: *aquí–ahí–allí* for the here/there dimension, and *este–ese–aquel* for the this/that dimension. This opposes the categories PROXIMAL, MEDIAL, and DISTAL. The Japanese deictical system is also tripartite, with different morphological markers for the three categories (Fillmore 1982).

It is highly unlikely (*pace* Whorf [1956]) that English and Dutch speakers *perceive* distance to ego differently than Spanish and Japanese speakers. But when they prepare distance information for expression, English and Dutch speakers must represent that information in their messages in a bipartite way, whereas Spanish and Japanese speakers must use a tripartite code. Hence, we have a language-specific difference in encoding at the message level.

This point was explicitly argued by Schlesinger (1977) on a more general level. And indeed, the PROXIMAL/DISTAL distinction is not the only example that can be given. Earlier in this chapter another important case of a language-specific system was discussed: tense marking. There are languages without a tense system, i.e., without obligatory marking of temporal features such as PAST or PRESENT in the inflection of the finite verb. Malay is such a language. Speakers of Malay can, of course, still express these temporal relations in other ways, but it is not obligatory to express them, as it is in English. And there is no reason to suppose that the message of a Malayan speaker will contain the temporal information when he has no intention to express it. An English speaker, however, must encode it even if it is of no communicative value.

Another famous case is the system of classificatory particles in Kilivila (an Austronesian language), first described by Malinowski (1920). Demonstratives, numerals, and adjectives carry affixes that relate to the *class* of object they modify. They acknowledge such properties of objects as whether they are wooden and long or round and stony, whether they consist of leaves or fibers, whether they are forked branches, clay pots, or cut-off parts, and so on. Malinowski found 42 categories of this (for Western cultures) haphazard sort which are grammaticalized in the language's morphology. (For an analysis of present-day Kilivilan particles, see Senft 1985.) Speakers of this language *must* encode such features in their messages; otherwise the morphology cannot come out right.

These and similar examples raise an interesting question about the separability of conceptual and grammatical encoding: Is a representation at the message level really built without recourse to the linguistic information encapsulated in the Formulator, or are the two systems less autonomous than was conjectured in the previous chapter?

Slobin (1982) argued that the list of features that obtain an obligatory grammatical marking in one language but not in another is fairly small. In other words, if there is a "leakage" between the two systems, it will be of a limited sort. But there is really no reason to suppose interaction between the two systems to start with. In learning the language, the speaker (the child) must surely have realized that the language requires him to attend to certain perceptual or conceptual features when he encodes a message. And, as Slobin and others have shown, the child makes characteristic errors that reveal his successive hypotheses about the conceptual properties required for the assignment of his language's morphology.

But although conceptualizing and grammatical encoding *are* interacting for the language-acquiring child, the mature speaker has learned what to encode when preparing a message for expression. He knows by experience whether his language requires a category of medial proximity, number, tense, object shape, or whatever is needed, and he will select the appropriate information in building his preverbal messages. It is no longer necessary for the Conceptualizer to ask the Formulator at each occasion what it likes as input. In short, the systems have become autonomous. The language-specific requirements on semantic structure have become represented in the Conceptualizer's procedural knowledge base.

Summary

This chapter has outlined the target representations of the conceptual system when it prepares messages for expression. These representations have been called *propositional*, because they involve expressions that can have truth values, or constituent parts of such expressions. The propositional mode of representation is by no means the only language of thought. It is not even a central code in the sense that it must mediate between other mental codes, such as spatial, musical, or kinesthetic ones. But as soon as concepts are to be expressed verbally, they must be coded in the propositional mode of representation.

Preverbal messages are propositional structures of a special kind, which we have called *semantic*. They entail several features that are material for their role as input to the Formulator. They need not be complete propositions; various other types of semantic structure, such as expressions denoting individuals, predicates, and modifiers, can be preverbal messages. The nonpropositions are, in a way, elliptical messages. Messages involve function/argument relations of various degrees of complexity. They can be built up hierarchically to express complex conceptualizations. Some of the arguments play abstract roles, such as agent, actor, source, or goal. The character of these roles is probably determined by the function. Some semantic functions, such as $DO(X,Y)$, $CAUSE(X,Y)$, $FROM(X)$, and $TO(X)$, are so basic that they tend to appear in the most diverse conceptualizations. Their presence in a semantic representation imposes a certain "thematic structure" on the message.

In order for a message and the resulting utterance to be effective, the message should incorporate a particular perspective. A potential addressee must be able to find out what the utterance is about, what information is already available in the ongoing discourse, what is to be newly focused, and so on. These and other "control" aspects should be marked in the message.

In order for the Formulator to accept it as input, the message should indicate mood—i.e., whether the utterance is to be declarative, imperative, or interrogative. In addition, the message should contain the aspectual and deictical features required for the generation of verb morphology.

Languages differ in the kinds of semantic features that are grammatically acknowledged. As a consequence, the encoding of messages is not the same for speakers of different languages. The message-encoding procedures must take into account that certain semantic components are obligatory in a message. When, for instance, the speaker's language has a tense system, each and every message of the type proposition must be provided with temporal markers. It is irrelevant whether this temporal information is of any communicative value.

Chapter 4
The Generation of Messages

The construction of a preverbal message is a first step in the generation of speech. This step is usually initiated by the conception of some communicative intention; the speaker wants to achieve some purpose by means of saying something, and he wants the addressee to recognize that intention from what is said. Given the communicative intention, the speaker will select information for expression that is expected to be instrumental in realizing the goal. This information should make it possible for the co-operative addressee to infer the intention. These issues are discussed in section 4.1.

But information can be instrumental only if it is relevant to the situation of interaction, and that situation is a continuously changing one. As discourse proceeds, intermediary goals are achieved or blocked, new relevant facts appear, and so forth. A major task of the speaker while constructing messages for expression is to keep track of what is happening in the discourse situation. This "bookkeeping" is the topic of section 4.2.

We will then proceed to message construction proper. It will be suggested that the preparation of a message involves two steps. The first one will be called *macroplanning*. It consists in the elaborating of the communicative intention as a sequence of subgoals and the selection of information to be expressed (asserted, questioned, etc.) in order to realize these communicative goals. This determines the content of the subsequent speech acts. The second step, *microplanning*, is concerned with the further shaping of each speech act to bring it into the format required by a preverbal message.

Sections 4.3 and 4.4 are devoted to macroplanning. The former discusses in greater detail how a speaker selects information instrumental to the communicative goal; the latter is concerned with the speaker's linearization problem, i.e., how a speaker orders for expression complex information involving several messages.

Section 4.5 explores some of the processes underlying microplanning. A speaker will mark referents in a message for their accessibility in such a way as to guide the listener's attention to what is already given in the discourse or to signal that a new entity is being introduced. He may also want to mark a particular referent as the topic. The speaker must further take care that all information is given the necessary propositional format, and that each preverbal message acknowledges the language-specific requirements of the Formulator.

4.1   From Intention to Message

The mother of each speech act is a communicative intention. This notion was introduced in chapter 2. The speaker's "proximal" purpose in planning a speech act, we saw, is *intention recognition* by the addressee. The present chapter discusses how a speaker goes from a communicative intention to a preverbal message that, when formulated, will make the cooperative addressee recognize that intention. We will be only marginally concerned with other, more "distal" intentions of speakers, which are not to be recognized as such by the other party. It should, however, be added that such more distal intentions are by no means uninteresting for a theory of the speaker; they may affect the selection of information to be expressed (see subsection 4.3.5) as well as the prosodic features of speech, such as loudness, rate, or intonation.

Let us begin with an example, a case of informing. Speaker Simon wants to tell hearer Hanna that Wubbo is an astronaut. More formal, Simon's message encoding begins with the intention to bring about a situation in which

KNOW (HANNA, INTEND (SIMON, BELIEVE (HANNA, ASTRONAUT (WUBBO)))).

The goal state is Hanna's knowing that Simon intended her to believe that Wubbo is an astronaut. There may be several ways for Simon to achieve this goal state. They need not even be verbal means. Simon could, for instance, show Hanna a picture with Wubbo in an astronaut's outfit. If Hanna knows Wubbo but didn't know that he is an astronaut, Simon's showing the picture can fulfill the communicative intention. But if Simon's communicative intention is *illocutionary* (i.e., if the intention is to use *verbal* means to bring about the goal state), Simon must encode a message. In order to achieve his goal, Simon could encode the message DECL (ASTRONAUT (WUBBO)). When formulated, this message would be uttered as *Wubbo is an astronaut*. If Hanna is cooperative, she will derive not only the proposition that Wubbo is an astronaut but also that Simon intended her to believe this proposition.

The journey from intention to message will, normally, involve more than a single step. Often, the goal will have to be expanded into subgoals. If the intention is, for example, to give a person a route direction, the speaker must create a whole plan consisting of subgoals ("first direct her to the city center, then inform her about the precise location of the museum") and sub-subgoals ("to go to the city center first take the freeway, then turn right at the second traffic light"), and so forth. The speaker will have to plan and order the various subgoals to be achieved. For each of the subgoals he will have to decide on a speech act to be expressed—that is, on an assertion, a command, a question, or whatever. This involves, for each speech act, the planning of information to be expressed to the interlocutor in order to satisfy the goal. As was extensively discussed in chapter 2, much can be conveyed without being explicitly formulated. The speaker will, normally, count on the capacity of a cooperative interlocutor to *infer* the goal or subgoal from an utterance that expresses only a fraction of the information to be conveyed; speech acts can be indirect. The sum total of these activities will be called *macroplanning* (roughly following Butterworth 1980b). Its output is an ordered sequence of what we will call *speech-act intentions* (sometimes shortened to "speech acts"). These are messages as far as specified for intended mood (declarative, interrogative, imperative) and content.

But the speaker must not only plan and order the contents of successive speech acts. The contents of each speech act should also be brought into perspective, and a particular information structure has to be assigned. The distribution of what should be expressed as topical, focused, or new information must be assigned, and the speaker will have to acknowledge certain language-specific requirements the message has to satisfy. These activities on the part of the speaker will be called *microplanning*. The output of microplanning is, for each intended speech act, a preverbal message.

It is tempting to view macroplanning and microplanning as two stages in the process of message encoding. In macroplanning a speaker elaborates a communicative intention down to the level of the content of individual speech acts; in microplanning the content of each intended speech act is given informational perspective and is assigned all the features that are obligatory for a preverbal message. Such a two-stage theory should, of course, be of the incremental sort. It is not necessary for a speaker to complete all macroplanning before microplanning can start. One can begin

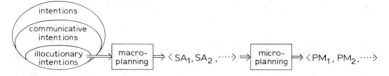

Figure 4.1
From intention to preverbal message.

giving a route direction without having planned all its details. This two-stage view may eventually turn out to be too restrictive; there may be situations in which macroplanning is affected by microplanning. Until then, however, the two-stage view is to be preferred because it is more restrictive.

The issues discussed so far are summarized in figure 4.1, which shows that communicative intentions are a subclass of intentions and that only a subset of communicative intentions are to be realized by means of speech acts. There are, then, two kinds of process involved in message encoding: First, the speaker must elaborate the intention. For each of its subgoals, the speaker should plan a speech act (SA)—i.e., should select information whose expression would be instrumental in realizing the goal. This is macro-planning. Second, each informational unit to be expressed must be shaped into a preverbal message (PM) by giving it an information structure, a propositional format, and a perspective that will guide the addressee's attention in the intended way and meet the input requirements of the Formulator. This is microplanning.

Both sides of the message-encoding process are heavily context-dependent. In order to elaborate his goals and to select *effective* information for expression, the speaker must take into account the precise discourse situation, and the same holds for the assignment of informational perspective. A discourse context is a continuously changing situation, and the processes of message encoding must therefore refer to the records the speaker keeps of the ongoing discourse. We will take up this important issue of the speaker's discourse records before we turn to the processes depicted in the figure.

4.2   Bookkeeping and Some of Its Consequences for Message Construction

The defining characteristic of coherent discourse is that every new move of a speaker is in some way related to whatever was said before. A cooperative speaker's contributions are supposed to be relevant to the ongoing discourse. But this requires bookkeeping or storage on the part of the speaker. He will have to keep track of what was said and what was conveyed by himself and by the interlocutors. The sum total of the information about the discourse that is currently available or accessible to the speaker is called the speaker's *discourse record*; it is the speaker's internal representation of the discourse as it evolved.

A discourse record is by nature a dynamic entity. It changes with each new contribution made to the conversation, whether by the speaker or by another participant. The speaker's record is not just a superficial trace of all utterances made; it is a structured interpretation of what happened in the conversation. An interesting but little-studied issue is which aspects of discourse lead to deep encoding (i.e., to long-term storage) and which aspects are transient (i.e., kept in working memory for only short periods of time). Let us review some of the major titles in the speaker's account books.

4.2.1 The Type of Discourse
There are different types of discourse, and they require different kinds of contributions on the part of the speaker. There is, first and foremost, *informal everyday conversation*. This may be a less unified type than is generally supposed. For instance, it is doubtful that everyday chatting with peers is of the same nature as everyday chatting with parents or children. Among the defining characteristics are, at any rate, the interlocutors' awareness of informality, of roughly equal rights to the floor, and of the freedom to change topic. When a speaker experiences the discourse as everyday conversation, he tacitly knows which turn-taking rules to follow—namely, the ones discussed in chapter 2.

Analysts of conversation have distinguished and studied various other types of discourse. *Narrations* (Beaugrande 1980; Labov 1972; Scollon and Scollon 1981)—including the telling of stories (Jefferson 1978; Ryave 1978) or dirty jokes (Sacks 1978)—can happen inside everyday conversations, but they require an awareness on the part of the interlocutors that a single speaker has the preferential right to the floor until the narrative is completed. The speaker can count on the suspension of disruptive self-selection by other participants, but has to pay by having to generate a structured sequence of messages. *Lectures* (Goffman 1981) are similar in the latter respect, but they are usually not embedded in conversation; they are more serious and impersonal. The speaker is supposed to impart his views to a spatially marked audience. *Examinations* and *interviews* (Atkinson and Drew 1979) are characterized by a fixed question-answer turn order, in which roles are clearly divided as to who does the questioning and who gives the answers. *Debates* (Walton 1982) share much of the question-answer nature of examinations, but the role of questioner is now equally distributed between the participants, and each participant has some thesis to defend. This list is by no means complete. The many other types of discourse include *planning discourse* (Linde and Goguen 1978; Goguen and Linde 1983), *route direction* (Klein 1982; Wunderlich and Reinelt 1982), *spatial description* (Ehrich 1982; Ehrich and Koster 1983; Levelt 1981, 1982a,b; Linde and Labov 1975), *radio talk* (Goffman 1981), and *therapeutic discourse* (Labov and Fanshel 1977). A good source on kinds of discourse is volume 3 of van Dijk 1985.

The speaker has to keep track of the type of discourse in which he is engaged, and of the special role assigned to him. The speaker makes a category mistake if he constructs his messages in the framework of the wrong discourse type—for example, if he takes an examination to be a debate, or air-traffic-control discourse to be everyday conversation. It is especially important that the type of discourse in which interlocutors are engaged be mutually known, so that the participants will be on common ground. Establishing agreement on the discourse type may require explicit negotiation at the outset, but usually the type of discourse is *invoked* by the way the talk is conducted (Schegloff 1987). For instance, it is in the way one person talks like a doctor (i.e., speaking of a "hematoma" instead of a "bruise") that the interlocutor recognizes that the discourse is of the doctor-client type.

4.2.2 The Topic of Discourse

The *discourse topic* is what is being talked about, and thus mutually experienced, by the participants. A conversation can be about the cost of living, an interview about one's medical condition, a planning discourse about tonight's burglary, and so on. The maxim of relation requires the speaker to make his contribution relevant to the ongoing discourse. Normally, a contribution will relate to the discourse topic. That is what makes discourse coherent. Brown and Yule (1983) call this "speaking topically."

But a speaker may want to change the topic in order to realize some goal not related to the present topic. This involves establishing agreement with the interlocutors about the topic shift. There are myriad devices with which a speaker can initiate a shift of topic. It can be done by explicit declaration (*The next issue I want to address is . . .*); this is what Grosz and Sidner (1985) call a *true interruption*. It may also be done unobtrusively by suggesting a relation to the current topic (*That reminds me of . . .*); this introduces a *digression*. A *flashback* (*Whoops, I forgot to tell you that . . .*), finally, is a kind of interruption a speaker will make in order to satisfy some subgoal that should have been handled at an earlier stage; it is usually followed by a return to the main topic. And there are prosodic means of marking the introduction of a new topic, such as raising the pitch (Brown, Currie, and Kenworthy 1980). The choice of means for effecting a shift will also depend on the type of discourse, and especially on the distribution of power among participants in that type of discourse.

Brown and Yule (1983) point out that a speaker's topic may or may not develop into a discourse topic, depending on whether it meets with mutual agreement. The speaker has to keep track of what is the current discourse topic, and he should not confuse it with his private "speaker topics." It is exactly confusion of this kind that makes schizophrenic speech incoherent (Brown 1973; Rochester and Martin 1979).

Though the notion of discourse topic is intuitively obvious and its relevance for discourse understanding has been demonstrated over and again (Bransford and Johnson 1973; Sanford 1985), it is notoriously hard to formalize. When a conversation is about the cost of living, it can at the same time be about the cost of food, and about the cost of bread. Most interesting topics of conversation are hierarchical in structure, and participants in a discourse can move up and down through the hierarchy in making their contributions. Grosz and Sidner (1985) relate this to the intentional structure of the discourse, i.e., the hierarchy of goals and subgoals being developed. When a subgoal is introduced, interlocutors descend a step in the hierarchy; when the subgoal is satisfied, one can return to considering a higher-level goal. Large moves are like topic shifts, and may require some negotiation; small moves occur from utterance to utterance.

The lowest-level subgoals eventually evoke individual messages and their topics (see subsection 3.4.2); they are the smallest ingredients in the hierarchy of discourse topics.

A speaker who keeps track of what is being talked about doesn't do so by keeping a running but unstructured list of topics. What is kept is (i) a structured mental representation of the discourse content as it developed and (ii) a pointer to the part of the content structure and the goal structure that is now being elaborated. Let us consider these two elements in turn.

4.2.3 The Content of Discourse: Discourse Models and Presuppositions
Interlocutors introduce and reintroduce referents (persons, things, events, etc.) and make predications about them. In doing so, they build "mental models" (Johnson-Laird 1983) of these entities, their relations, and their

properties. A *discourse model* is a speaker's record of what he believes to be shared knowledge about the content of the discourse as it evolved (Johnson-Laird and Garnham 1980; Kamp 1984; Prince 1981; Seuren 1985; Webber 1981).

Discourse models are populated by representations of token events, persons, and so forth—i.e., entities to which reference can be made. Also, it is possible to make reference to finite or infinite *sets*, as in *the world wars* or *the natural numbers*. Each of these referents is said to have an *address* in the discourse model. And when something is communicated about that referent, the predication is added to its address.

Every new speech act of a participant changes the state of the discourse model. It may add an address, which is typically done by using an indefinite expression. If a speaker says *there is a baby in the bath*, he invites his interlocutor to add BABY as an address but he is not yet *referring* to any particular baby. The predication is true if any baby is in the bath. With respect to the discourse up to that point, this is *new information*.

A speech act may also add information to an existing address. The former speaker's next sentence may be *the baby is crying*. The speaker is now making reference to a particular baby. The sentence is true only if the baby in the bath cries, not just any baby. Typically, a definite expression ("*the* baby") is used for referring to an already existing address. The baby is now *given information*. (See subsection 4.5.1 for an elaboration of these notions.)

Depending on their intentions, speakers may convey information concerning existing or newly introduced entities or may invite other participants to provide such information. Put more formally: Speech acts can be conceived of as mappings of the current discourse model onto the next. They change the shared set of referents, or the shared information about them. The shared information includes, in particular, information about the interlocutors. When a speaker gives a command, for example, he adds to his information about the addressee that the addressee now knows his intention to commit her to a certain action.

The speaker's utterance invites the addressee to infer the communicative intention, i.e., to construct a representation of the information to be conveyed. This may involve the creation of new addresses and the storage of new information under old or new addresses. Normally, the speaker's purpose will be that the listener's representation agree in essential points with his own.

In the simplest case—two-person interaction—there are four knowledge structures involved in this part of a speaker's bookkeeping. To distinguish among these, let us consider a fictitious example in which Marcia and Seth are conversing about their travel experiences. The topic of discourse is, more specifically, travels in Italy. Marcia's and Seth's mental representations are depicted in figure 4.2. The nodes represent addresses for referents, such as places, persons, and events. The figure represents only some of the major tokens referred to in the conversation. Many are left out (for instance, the egos of the two participants). What is said about the referents is not really represented either. It should consist of lists of predications stored under each address. In the figure, arcs have been drawn between nodes that figure in the same proposition. If Seth says *the food is nice in Rome*, an arc is drawn between the nodes for FOOD and ROME, suggesting that the predication relates them in some way in the discourse model.

The first kind of knowledge that is relevant to a speaker's discourse planning is the knowledge the speaker believes he shares with the listener, independent of the present discourse interaction. Let us call this *common ground*. For example, Seth may believe that Marcia knows about the existence of the pope and about the fact that the pope lives in Rome. Figure 4.2 represents for both Seth and Marcia the entities POPE and ROME, as well as the arc connecting them (which stands for their locative relation). POPE and ROME are inside the balloon labeled "common ground." The common ground may also include knowledge of a less general type. Seth and Marcia may have shared knowledge about a common friend, Harry. Seth may, moreover, believe that they mutually know that Marcia wants to talk about Italy, and so on. It is irrelevant for the present discussion whether the common ground is *really* shared by the interlocutors; what matters is that the speaker believes it is. A last item in the common ground is the shared context of discourse—the local scene the speaker believes to be sharing with the interlocutor. Seth knows, from perceptual evidence, where Marcia is located in the scene and how she is oriented. He believes that Marcia shares this knowledge, and that she knows that Seth knows it, and so forth.

The second knowledge structure is what the speaker believes to have successfully conveyed to the listener during the discourse up to now; it is the shared knowledge arising from the speaker's *own contributions*. Seth, for instance, talked about his experiences in Rome but not about the pope. Rather, he discussed the food, the tipping habits, and other matters that he believed Marcia didn't know about. This information, which Seth believes he has conveyed to Marcia, is represented in figure 4.2 as own contributions in Seth's representation. Marcia's own contribution concerns information she conveyed about Florence (where their common friend Harry lives) and

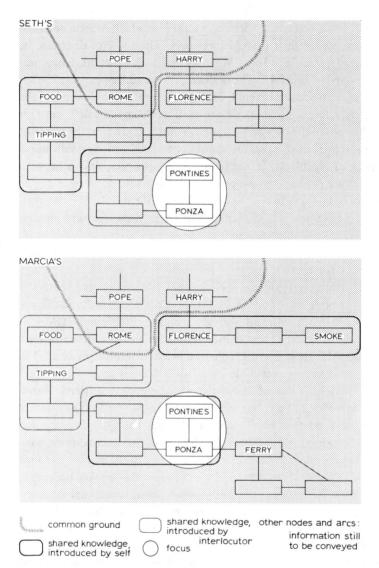

Figure 4.2
Types of knowledge involved in example conversation.

about Ponza (an island previously unknown to Seth). These items are demarcated as own contribution in Marcia's representation.

The third knowledge structure is the information the speaker believes the interlocutor to have intended to convey to him in the discourse as it developed. From the speaker's point of view, this is shared knowledge emanating from the interlocutor; it is the *interlocutor's contribution*. Seth, for instance, takes it that Marcia talked about Ponza (an island he had never heard about) and Florence (where their common friend Harry lives). Ideally, the own-contribution part of a speaker's mental representation should be identical to the interlocutor's part of the addressee's mental representation. However, a speaker's belief that this knowledge is shared may be mistaken, and thus may lead to later misunderstanding. Marcia, for instance, believes that she mentioned the smoke poisoning the air in Florence; however, Seth failed to register this, owing to his inattentiveness.

The fourth knowledge structure is information which the speaker still intends to convey but which has not been up for expression yet. This *information to be conveyed* by the speaker is also depicted in figure 4.2. Marcia wants to say more about Ponza's ferryboats, while Seth wants to relate what Marcia said about Florence to his own experiences in Rome. The knowledge intended to be conveyed—i.e., the communicative goal—develops by plan or association as the discourse proceeds.

The speaker's discourse model can now be defined as "own contributions plus interlocutor's contributions"—that is, the knowledge structure the speaker believes he has conveyed to the interlocutor plus the knowledge structure the speaker believes the interlocutor intended to convey in the discourse up to now. The picture will obviously be more complicated for multiparty discourse, but that will not concern us here.

Every move in the conversation changes the knowledge pattern of the interlocutors. When Seth introduces a new entity and believes that Marcia has grasped it, Seth's "own contribution" part is expanded by that element. If indeed Marcia has grasped it, her "interlocutor's contribution" part is correspondingly expanded, and so on. Discourse models change continually.

It is characteristic of coherent discourse that a new contribution relates to what was said before, i.e., is relevant to the current state of the discourse model. It will either add further linking information to existing addresses or introduce new referents by linking them to existing ones. An important notion here is *presupposition*. To maintain coherent discourse, the presuppositions of a new message must be satisfied or satisfiable in the discourse model. If Marcia were to say *The ferry is convenient* without having previously referred to a ferry, her contribution would violate a so-called *existential* presupposition, because her use of a definite expression presupposes the existence of a FERRY address in the discourse model or in the common ground. If Seth were to ask *When did you stop taking your vacations in Italy?*, there would be the *factive* presupposition that Marcia had indeed stopped taking her vacations in Italy. Such a question is a coherent contribution only when that fact is somewhere in the discourse model or in the common ground.

Still, speakers often ignore presuppositions in making their contributions. They rely on the interlocutor's intelligence to realize what Seuren (1985) calls *backward suppletion* of the presupposed information. When Marcia talks about *the ferry*, Seth will derive that there must be some ferry, and he will set up a provisional address for it in the hope and expectation that he will soon be informed about which ferry Marcia means. Similarly, Marcia, in response to Seth's question, will think "Ah, he thinks I am not going to Italy anymore". Marcia adds Seth's apparent belief to the discourse model, and may then either deny it when it is false (*Oh, I haven't stopped going*) or answer the question if it is a true belief (*Since 1985*).

But backward suppletion is impossible when information contrary to the presupposition is already in the discourse model. In that case the presupposition is really violated, and the discourse is incoherent. This happens in the following bit of discourse.

Marcia: I always go to Italy for vacation.

Seth: When did you stop taking your vacations in Italy?

This led Seuren (1985), following van der Sandt (1982), to propose the following presupposition test: If S is the formulation of a message, then P is the formulation of a presupposition of the message if and only if

(i) P, but/and S is coherent

and

(ii) perhaps not P, but/and S is incoherent.

The presupposition of Seth's question can be formulated as *You stopped taking your vacations in Italy*. The first test requires the following sequence to be coherent: *You stopped taking your vacations in Italy, and when did you stop doing so?* It clearly is coherent. The second test predicts incoherence for the sequence *Perhaps you didn't stop taking your vacations in Italy, but when did you stop doing so?*, which is incoherent indeed. Therefore, Marcia's having stopped taking her vacations in Italy is indeed a presupposition for the message in Seth's question. The same pair of tests can easily be applied to the earlier existential presupposition about the ferryboat. In generating a message, a cooperative speaker will introduce referents and will maintain reference in such a way that no violation of presupposition results.

It should be obvious that, for any sizable discourse, the speaker cannot keep the whole discourse model in his center of attention. The discourse model is, rather, stored in long-term memory. But it is easily accessible. At any one moment, only a small fragment of this information is attended or "pointed" to. This fragment is called the *focus*.

4.2.4   The Focus

The attention span of a speaker is fairly limited. He can work on only one or a few notions at a time in planning his discourse. And the same holds for the listener who is interpreting the speaker's utterances. The information to which the speaker is attending at a particular moment in time is called his *focus*. Similarly, there is a listener's focus. If the speaker believes that their foci are shared, there is a unique part of the discourse model which the speaker marks as "jointly attended to." In the conversation between Seth and Marcia, this can be the food in Rome, the island of Ponza, or any of the other discourse entities. There is, of course, more in focus than just individual referents. The speaker focuses on a particular goal or subgoal to be satisfied; there is some communicative intention to be jointly attended to.

The notion of attentional focusing is classical in psychology, and is not limited to the study of language use. Wilhelm Wundt (1896) called it apperception; William James (1892) called it apprehension or primary memory. These and many other authors have argued that one can consciously attend to only a few disconnected elements at a time. Miller (1956) spoke of a "magical number seven plus or minus two," and Broadbent (1975) of a "three-slot register." But when information is structured, the span of attention can be larger—and that is often the case when the speaker is planning a message. Our present use of "focus" in the planning of discourse agrees with the way in which Chafe (1979, 1980), Grosz (1981), Grosz and Sidner (1985), Herrmann (1983), and Sanford and Garrod (1981) use the term "focusing."

The encircled parts of the networks in figure 4.2 are supposed to be "currently in focus" for the interlocutors. Seth and Marcia are in the happy circumstance that their foci are aligned. They are both concentrating on Ponza and the Pontines and the information being conveyed about them.

One can further distinguish a *focal center*, as proposed by Grosz, Joshi, and Weinstein (1983). This is what the speaker is newly attending to in making the current utterance; it is the most salient part of his focus. It is more the rule than the exception that the speaker's focal center differs from the hearer's. By his utterance the speaker is trying to make the hearer attend to something she is not yet attending to. It is, therefore, important to distinguish between the *speaker's focal center* and the *hearer's focal center*. It is a major concern for the speaker to align the focal centers. When the speaker shifts his focal center to a new referent, his utterance should tell the interlocutor where to go; the speaker's and the interlocutor's foci are not yet aligned. In the example, Marcia may shift her focus to the Ponza ferry, intending to say something about it. If she believes that Seth's focus is still as depicted in figure 4.2, she may say *The island can be reached by an old ferryboat*. In this way Marcia connects the new information to what Seth is presently focusing on (Ponza island), and by using an indefinite expression (*an old ferryboat*) she signals that the newly focused element is not yet in the discourse model or in the common ground.

More generally, the speaker's way of instructing the listener where to focus next is dependent not only on the speaker's new focal center but also on the listener's current focal center. The cooperative speaker thus has to keep track of the interlocutor's current focus and its current center. They are represented in the discourse model. Whether the representation is veridical is not relevant. "The interlocutor's current focus" and "the inter-locutor's focal center" are what the speaker *believes* to be the interlocutor's focus and focal center—that is, what the speaker will take into account in constructing messages. Whether his belief is warranted is not at issue.

A newly focused element will usually not be the topic of the speaker's message. In *The island can be reached by an old ferryboat*, the message is about the island Ponza, whereas the speaker's new focal center is the ferry. Still, the topic and the new focal center may coincide. Seth could, out of the blue, say *The pope didn't say much in five languages*. The pope is newly focused here, and he is the topic of the message.

Usually, speakers place newly focused or newly introduced information later in the sentence than information that is currently focused or is already in the discourse model. Clark and Haviland (1977) have shown how this principle of ordering helps the addressee to connect new information to tokens currently or recently shared between speaker and hearer. The Formulator will, of course, have to "know" all this. It will, in other words, be necessary for the speaker to encode in the message where the referents can be found—i.e., in the current focus, elsewhere in the discourse model, or in the common ground—or that they are "brand new." We will turn to this issue in subsection 4.5.1.

4.2.5 What Was Literally Said

Interlocutors listen, in the first place, for content. But there is evidence that, within limits, they also register the literal wording of what was said. There has been substantial laboratory research on listeners' memory for spoken text (see Levelt and Kempen 1975 and Levelt 1978 for reviews). The major finding is that it is short-lived. Recall and recognition are generally very good for the last clause or sentence heard, but quickly decline to nearly chance level for less recent materials (Jarvella and Herman 1972).

However, three studies performed in more natural settings and with more naturalistic materials have demonstrated that the literal wording of conversational materials affects long-term memory. Kintsch and Bates (1977) tested students' memories of statements from a lecture they had attended and found especially good memory for the literal form of jokes and for statements extraneous to the topic of the lecture. These effects were still measurable five days after the lecture. Keenan, MacWhinney, and Mayhew (1977) recorded the conversation of a lunchroom discussion group and tested memory for the literal wording of what they called "high interactional content" statements. (This notion is somewhat vague; what it means is that there is a high personal involvement of speaker or interlocutors in a statement such as *Do you always put your foot in your mouth?*.) Literal memory was much better for such statements than for "low interactional" statements. These two studies show that listeners do register the literal form of utterances that are interactionally salient. Bates, Masling, and Kintsch (1978) used conversations from a television drama as test materials and specifically analyzed literal memory for the ways in which referents were introduced or maintained in the video conversations. Among many other things, they found that their subjects had better memory for statements in which a person's name was used than for statements in which a personal pronoun was used, and that elliptical sentences were remembered less well than nonelliptical ones. These results seem to show that when the pragmatic role of an utterance is to introduce new referents (which is not done by way of pronouns) or to introduce new statements about referents (which is not done by elliptical clauses), there is more than chance memory for the literal wording used.

Surprisingly, there has been almost no research on what speakers remember of what they have said themselves. Deutsch and Jarvella (1983) compared memory for own speech and interlocutor's speech and found that, under certain restricted experimental conditions, the recall for self-produced speech is better than that for other-produced speech. But this difference can be explained entirely by the speaker's giving more attention to the *content* of self-produced speech than to the *content* of other-produced speech. Or, in terms of discourse models, a speaker will keep a better record of self-conveyed information than of interlocutor-conveyed information. The fact that one's own speech is *self-articulated* may be entirely irrelevant.

Does memory for what was literally said have any significance for what a speaker is going to say? There is observational (Schenkein 1980; Harley 1984) and experimental (Levelt and Kelter 1982) evidence that the wording of the interlocutor's last turn can affect the wording of the current speaker's turn. In one of Levelt and Kelter's experiments, shopkeepers were telephoned and asked the Dutch equivalent of one of the following four questions:

(1) What time do you close?

(2) At what time do you close?

(3) What time do you close, since I will have to come downtown especially for this, you know?

(4) At what time do you close, since I will have to come downtown especially for this, you know?

These questions differ in two ways: They contain or do not contain the preposition *at*, and they are short (without additional clause) or long. The preposition *at* (or more precisely the Dutch equivalent thereof) has no meaningful function whatsoever. The answers were scored for the presence of *at* in the shopkeeper's time phrase (e.g., *five o'clock* or *at five o'clock*). It was possible for *at* to occur or not to occur in an answer to any of the four questions. For questions 1 and 2, it turned out that the answers tended to follow the question in the use of *at*. Question 2 elicited significantly more *at* answers than question 1; question-to-answer correspondence was 61 percent. In other words, the interlocutor's *at* must have been registered by the shopkeeper, in spite of the fact that it had nothing to do with the content of the question. For questions 3 and 4, however, there was no systematic question-to-answer correspondence at all; it dropped to a random 47 percent. This makes it likely that, in conversation, literal recall not supported by salient content or pragmatic significance is short-lived, probably going back only as far as the last clause uttered.

When, however, the literal wording *is* important for conversational purposes, speakers will make a record of it and use that wording with profit. Clark and Wilkes-Gibbs (1986) had subjects communicate information about a set of tangram figures—irregular geometrical shapes that are hard to name. After some give and take, interlocutors settled upon a fixed referring expression for each of the shapes (e.g., *the angel*). This was conversationally far more practical than giving again and again the full initial descriptions of the same figure (e.g., *sort of an angel flying away or something; it's got two arms*). Of course, this requires the speaker to maintain a record of the literal expression that was used previously by himself or by the interlocutor.

This completes our list of the items in the speaker's discourse record. It will become apparent from the following sections that the speaker refers to these records continually, both in macroplanning and in microplanning.

4.3 Macroplanning 1: Deciding on Information to Be Expressed

Illocutionary intentions are intentions to commit oneself or an interlocutor to the factuality or desirability of something. The speaker's utterances should make these intentions recognizable to the person concerned. Depending on the character of the illocutionary intention, this may involve the construction of one or more speech acts. When the intention is to inform an addressee that a train is arriving, a single speech act may suffice (namely the assertion that the train is arriving). When, however, the intention is to inform the hearer about the route from Florence to Rome, a sequence of several declarative speech acts may be necessary. Conversely, one speech act can realize several communicative intentions at the same time. When Marcia asks Seth whether he met Harry recently, Seth may answer *I saw the bastard in Florence*. This answer communicates to Marcia both a commitment to the factuality of Seth's having seen Harry in Florence and a commitment to an opinion about the character of Harry. This many-to-many mapping from communicative intentions onto speech acts complicates the analysis of macroplanning greatly.

The major requirement in order for the information to be expressed in the speaker's message is that it be *instrumental* in changing the addressee's discourse model in the intended way. An instrumental message need not express each and every detail of the information to be conveyed to the listener. The speaker will assume that the cooperative listener will be able to *infer* the communicative intentions from well-chosen bits of information expressed in the message. The relations between the information to be conveyed and the information to be expressed are governed by Gricean principles (discussed extensively in chapter 2). In particular, the maxims of quantity require the speaker to sail a middle course between being over-informative and being underinformative. Information that is readily inferable from shared knowledge—be it in the discourse model or in the common ground—should, as a rule, not be expressed in the message; the speaker will transmit it by implicature. When, in a route description, a speaker says *Then turn right at the church*, he conveys by implication that there is some road or pathway there. This need not be expressed; the intelligent addressee can infer it. It is, indeed, instrumental to convey information by implication. First, it is efficient; the speaker will have to express only a part of the whole package of information. Herrmann (1983) calls this the *pars-pro-toto principle*. Second, it is a way to acknowledge the addressee's intelligence and cooperativeness. Third, it can be a way to express secondary communicative intentions, such as the intention to be polite. Finally, expressing every detail of the information to be conveyed would induce the interlocutor to interpret the speaker's contribution as flouting a maxim of quantity, and this may lead to inferences not intended by the speaker.

In the following, we will first consider the format of macroplanning procedures. We will then turn to empirical psycholinguistic studies of macroplanning—in particular, the use of attentional resources in elaborating communicative intentions, the speaker's selection of information for making reference to objects, and the construction of requests.

4.3.1   The Format of Macroprocedural Knowledge

Chapter 1 described procedural knowledge as a collection of condition/action pairs of the following form: IF a certain set of conditions are met, THEN perform a certain action. What sort of IF/THEN pairs are involved in macroplanning? In other words, if macroplanning is procedural in nature, what form will these procedures have? In view of the assumed process depicted in figure 4.1, the condition for a procedure should, at least, involve one or more illocutionary intentions. And the action to be performed must be a speech act, or a string of speech acts (such as assertions or questions). Only students of artificial intelligence have begun to formulate such procedures explicitly (see especially Appelt 1985), and they do not claim psychological reality for their proposals. Still, it is worthwhile to consider one or two such theoretical proposals before we turn to empirical studies of macroplanning.

Let us first take up the simplest cases of informing. Section 4.1 gave the example of a speaker, Simon, who had the illocutionary intention to inform a hearer, Hanna, that Wubbo is an astronaut. Simon realized the intention by asserting that Wubbo is an astronaut. This can be put in more general terms (roughly following Appelt 1985): Assume that the speaker's illocutionary intention is to bring about the state

KNOW(H, INTEND(S, BELIEVE(H, P))),

where H is the hearer, S the speaker, and P the proposition to be believed. One way of realizing this intention is to assert P. This, in turn, can be done by encoding the message DECL(P). In fact, this is a general message-encoding procedure for informing:

IF the goal state is KNOW(H, INTEND(S, BELIEVE(H, P))), THEN encode message DECL(P).

In other words, it is part of the speaker's procedural knowledge that the speech act of asserting P will, under certain conditions, bring about the effect that the hearer believes that the speaker intended her to believe that P is the case (for instance, that Wubbo is an astronaut). The conditions have to be further specified. The speaker must, among other things, believe that the hearer can hear him. The speaker must, moreover, believe that the hearer doesn't yet know P. Simon will probably not assert to Hanna that Wubbo is an astronaut when this is already mutual knowledge. If he does, he is probably realizing another communicative intention, for instance to reveal to Hanna that he envies Wubbo. These conditions, and probably several more, must be added to the IF-statement above.

A similar condition/action pair can be formulated for the intention of requesting some action. Simon may want Hanna to buy a stamp. The intended goal state is that Hanna know that Simon intends her to intend to buy a stamp. A speech act realizing this intention is a request. More formally:

IF the goal state is KNOW(H, INTEND(S, INTEND(H, DO(A)))), THEN encode message ?(FUTURE (DO(H, A)))),

where A is the intended action.

If this is part of Simon's procedural knowledge, he will ask Hanna *Will you buy a stamp?* But here, too, there are additional conditions. There is the same physical condition as before: It must be mutual knowledge that Simon believes that Hanna can hear him. Also, Simon must believe that Hanna doesn't yet intend to buy a stamp. If Hanna's intention to buy a stamp is already mutual knowledge, requesting that Hanna buy a stamp involves another communicative intention (for instance, to let her know that she should hurry a bit). In other words, several IF-conditions will have to be added for this procedure to work. In fact, the conditions for different request forms (*Can you buy a stamp?*; *Please, buy a stamp*; etc.) are quite complex, as is apparent from psycholinguistic studies on requesting (see subsection 4.3.3). There is, obviously, still a long way to go in the explicit formulation of even the most elementary macroplanning procedures. Let us now turn to some empirical studies of macroplanning.

4.3.2 Macroplanning and Attentional Resources

Which information has to be conveyed to the addressee depends entirely on the speaker's intentions and on the current state of the discourse model. The information may already be in the speaker's focus. It may, alternatively, involve an elaborate memory search. An example of the former is a situation in which a speaker happens to look out a window, notices a rainstorm, and develops the intention to inform an addressee about this. The event is in the speaker's focus; no further information has to be retrieved. An instance of the latter is a situation in which another party asks for a route direction. A cooperative and knowledgeable speaker will aim at filling the gap in the interlocutor's discourse model by retrieving the locative information that constitutes the path from "here" to the goal place. This may involve several steps of retrieval. The speaker will use the source and goal positions as retrieval cues for accessing a relevant part of his cognitive map of the town, which is in his long-term memory. He will then infer a shortest or easiest route connecting the two positions. He will retrieve landmarks, such as churches and viaducts, to identify successive parts of the route for the addressee, and so on. Retrieving information to be expressed can involve substantial memory search, inference, and planning.

Elaborate search is characteristic for certain discourse types. Not only route directions, but also narrations, lectures, speeches, and other monological forms of discourse are in this category. Interviews and debates are other examples. Such planning and search is under executive control and requires the speaker's attention. At the same time, the speaker must keep some attention available for the further preparation of each message—the microplanning—so that speech can keep flowing while information is being retrieved.

There is some evidence that in longer monologues speakers slowly alternate between phases in which they spend much attention on information retrieval and inference (i.e., on macroplanning) and phases in which they concentrate on finalizing messages for expression (i.e., on microplanning). This evidence stems from work by Henderson. Goldman-Eisler, and Skarbek (1966), Goldman-Eisler (1968), Butterworth (1975, 1980b), and Beattie (1983) on the distribution of pausing and speaking in longer stretches of speech or monologues. (See Petrie 1988 for a different kind of experimental evidence.)

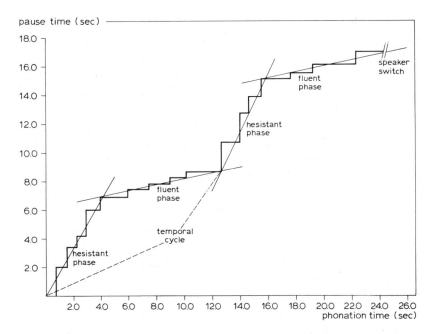

Figure 4.3
Alternation of hesitant and fluent phases in a monologue. (After Beattie 1983.)

Henderson et al. (1966) represented speech-pause alternations in what I will call "Henderson graphs." One such graph is presented here as figure 4.3. Both coordinates represent time—the horizontal axis speaking time, the vertical axis pausing time. Each successive segment of either speech or silence is traced in the corresponding horizontal or vertical direction. What counts as silence is any nonphonation period longer than 200 or 250 milliseconds (200 in the case of figure 4.3). The general slope of the resulting curve is the ratio of silence to speech for the stretch of talk represented.

The relevant observation by the above-mentioned authors is that there seems to be a rhythmic alternation of slope in Henderson graphs; steep and flat phases follow one another in a rather regular fashion. The steep parts are called phases of *hesitant speech*, since there is much pausing. These authors also suggest that this pausing is due to speaker's attentional preoccupation with goal elaboration and information retrieval—with macroplanning. The flat parts represent phases of *fluent speech*, with relatively little pausing. Jaffe, Breskin, and Gerstman (1972) and Power (1983, 1984) have warned that these fluctuations may be random, but other studies have made that interpretation less likely (see Beattie 1980, 1983, 1984). The curve in figure

4.3 is derived from a sample of videotaped teacher-student interactions. Beattie (1980) analyzed all single-speaker stretches of talk longer than 30 seconds. These monologues showed a mean cycle time (hesitant phase plus fluent phase) of 22 seconds, with a rather large standard deviation of 16 seconds. Beattie (1980) demonstrated the nonrandomness of these cycles by means of a judgment experiment in which subjects received transcripts of successive sentences from these monologue parts in random order and the task was to reestablish their original order. This turned out to be significantly easier for sentences occurring within the same cycle than for sentences that succeeded one another over a cycle break. In other words, there is more conceptual coherence within a cycle than between cycles. The cycle, it seems, involves the elaboration of some communicative goal into a series of speech acts. This results in a coherent discourse segment. When the speaker then shifts his focus to a new goal or subgoal, a new cycle of elaboration will start, resulting in the next coherent discourse segment.

Though these are suggestive results, one should be careful not to generalize the cycle notion to each and every kind of monologue. If the speaker's attention fluctuates between macroplanning and microplanning, this will lead to overt alternations in fluency only when macroplanning is effortful. Indeed, there have been independent experimental demonstrations of the relation between speech fluency and the "cognitive load" imposed by selecting information for expression. Goldman-Eisler (1968), for instance, showed that there is more fluency in the execution of a cartoon-description task than in that of a cartoon-interpretation task. Good and Butterworth (1980) asked subjects to give route descriptions. One comparison the authors made was between a familiar route (that from home to work) and a relatively unfamiliar one. The familiar route was described slightly but significantly more fluently than the unfamiliar route, as measured by the total percentage of silence time in a description (33 percent and 37 percent, respectively). When a subject was asked to repeat the description of the familiar route, the silence ratio dropped to 27 percent. Selecting information for expression is presumably much easier in the latter case because it is still highly available in memory.

The latter situation approaches one that Clark and Clark (1977) called "ideal delivery"; the subject already knows what he wants to say, and utters it fluently. Clark and Clark suggested that speakers strive for smooth delivery of clauses; they try to minimize within-clause pauses. Good and Butterworth (1980) indeed found that within-clause pauses (over 250 milliseconds long) were substantially less frequent in the repeated descriptions than in the original descriptions (28 percent and 41 percent of the total number of pauses, respectively). In other words, when the information-selection task is less demanding, the speaker can spend more attention on delivering "clause-ready" messages—i.e., on microplanning.

Attentional lapses in macroplanning sometimes lead to all-out speech errors. Harley (1984) reported several such cases. In one of them the speaker wavered between saying that he got up at 8:52 and that he felt fine at 8:52, and this led to *I felt up fine at 8:52*. Freudian speech errors are also said to be due to attentional lapses, and we will return to them in chapter 6.

4.3.3   Selecting Information for Making Reference to Objects

Olson (1970) made the almost trivial but highly seminal observation that a speaker's referring expression indicating some object in the environment is a function of what alternative objects there are in the context of reference. The same object may be referred to differently, depending on the set of contextual alternatives. If a speaker wants to make reference to a big black ball in a situation where speaker and addressee jointly observe only two black balls, a big one and a small one, the referring expression is likely to be *the big one* or *the big ball*. If, however, the alternative object is a big white ball, the speaker's referring expression will be *the black one* or *the black ball*. The choice of attribute depends on whether it can be distinctive for the addressee. A speaker who wants to convey the identity of an object to an addressee will almost never have to list all the object's properties; he will select for expression some subset which is *instrumental* for the addressee to uniquely identify the object in the context of reference.

As was mentioned above, Grice's quantity maxims require the speaker to sail between the Scylla of underdetermination or ambiguity and the Charybdis of overspecification or redundancy. In the above-mentioned situation, an example of underdetermination would be the use of the referring expression *the ball*, which does not discriminate sufficiently; an example of overdetermination would be the use of *the big black ball*, which contains more information than is necessary. What do speakers do in actuality?

The general finding is clear (see Deutsch and Pechmann 1982 for a review): Referring expressions are almost always sufficient or nonambiguous, but they tend to be redundant. The latter seems to contradict a Gricean maxim and needs further scrutiny. An example can be found in the cited paper by Deutsch and Pechmann. They asked children and adults to select from an array of eight toys the one they would most like to give as a birthday present to a child. The toys in the array were of two to four different kinds (for instance, combs, spoons, cars, and cups); some were large and some small, and they were of three or four different colors. The combinations of these attributes were varied over different arrays. Only 6 percent of the adults' referential expressions were underspecifications, but 28 percent were redundant. In a similar experiment, Pechmann (1984) found that more than 60 percent of adults' referential expressions were redundant.

Pechmann analyzed some of the reasons for this seeming deviancy from the maxim of quantity. In his 1984 study the adult subjects were presented with a sequence of slides, each containing a variable number of objects, which could differ in kind, color, or size. One of the objects in a slide was marked with a star. The subjects' task was to tell an imaginary listener, who would see the same slide but not the star, which object was marked.

Figure 4.4 gives an example of an initially presented array of four objects (Pechmann used blue and red rather than black and white) and three potential subsequent arrays of three objects. For each array, the Dutch subjects' characteristic response is given in English translation; capitalization indicates prosodic accent. The response to array A is typically *the black bIrd*. Neither *black* nor *bIrd* alone would have been sufficient for the

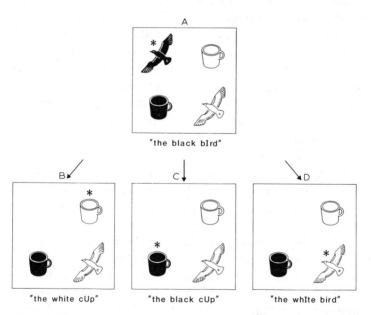

Figure 4.4
Stimuli used in an object-naming experiment. (After Pechmann 1984).

listener to identify the object. The referential expression is nonredundant. If it is array B that follows array A, subjects typically respond with *the white cUp*. In this case too both the color and the object name are necessary to distinguish the referent from the alternatives; there is another white object, and there is also another cup. But what happens if either the color or the object name suffices to discriminate the object? In array C it is the color name that would suffice; there is only one black object in the array, and it is the referent. Still, most subjects refer to it as *the black cUp*, in spite of the fact that *cUp* is redundant and moreover nondiscriminating (there is another cup in the array). Also, when the object name is the only discriminating information, subjects tend to include the color name as well. This is the case for array D, where *bird* would be enough. Subjects typically say *the whIte bird* in this case. Note also that for both array C and array D the *non*discriminating information is given prosodic prominence: *cUp* in array C and *whIte* in array D. We will return to this finding shortly.

It would be wrong to conclude from this example that speakers talk redundantly because they simply supply the listener with *all* information concerning the referent. This doesn't hold in general for Pechmann's results, and it is also contradicted by the findings reported in Herrmann and Deutsch 1976, Deutsch and Pechmann 1982, Herrmann 1983, and several other papers. Especially when there are more than two attributes involved, speakers start economizing on their referential expressions. It is also unlikely that speakers introduce some redundancy in their object names in order to help the addressee cope with "degraded communication"; if one discriminating attribute is missed by the listener, he will still be able to identify the referent by means of another discriminating attribute. We saw, however, that speakers also make their descriptions redundant by adding nondiscriminating attributes.

There are at least two other reasons for a speaker to overspecify the referent. One is that redundant nondiscriminating information can help the addressee find the referent. Deutsch (1976), Mangold (1986), and Sonnenschein (1982, 1984) showed that it is easier for listeners to identify an overspecified referent than a minimally specified object in an array of objects. Listeners apparently create a "gestalt" of the object for which they have to search. It is harder to search for "something red" than for "a big red bird", even if the color would be sufficiently discriminating. Information about the *kind* of object to be looked for (e.g., a bird) is especially helpful for constructing such a gestalt. This would explain a general tendency in the experimental findings on object naming to include the noun in the referential expression even when redundant (e.g., *the red bird* instead of *the red one*). The nature of the "distractor" objects is irrelevant here.

Another reason for the apparent redundancy has to do with the speaker's discourse model. A speaker cannot refer only by mentioning what discriminates the object in the situation perceptually shared with the addressee (i.e., in what was earlier called "common ground"); he can also refer by contrasting it to the last one focused by the listener. In other words, the new focal center can be introduced by expressing information that makes it contrast to what is in the addressee's current focal center. This is presumably what happened for arrays C and D in figure 4.4. We observed that in both cases speakers gave nondiscriminating information (*cUp* and *whIte*, respectively). The speakers apparently contrasted the new referent object with the previous one (*black bird*), in spite of the fact that the old referent was no longer *perceptually* present. That comparison required mentioning the differing feature, whether it was perceptually redundant or not. In other words, in terms of the discourse model *cUp* and *whIte* express the *non*redundant information, whereas *black* and *bird* are redundant because the previous object in the focal center was a black bird. Pechmann (1984) calls this latter kind of redundancy (i.e., with respect to the discourse model) *endophoric* redundancy, as opposed to the *exophoric* redundancy which derives from the set of perceptually given alternatives. Especially noteworthy is that the endophorically discriminating information (*cUp* and *whIte*, respectively) was given prosodic stress. This is a quite general finding in the studies by Pechmann and in those by Terken (1984): There is systematic accentuation of endophorically discriminating information (such as *whIte* in figure 4.4D), but no systematic accentuation of exophorically discriminating information (such as *bird* in figure 4.4D). I will return to this in discussing microplanning in subsection 4.5.1.

What information the speaker will express for referring to one object among alternatives will depend on both endophoric and exophoric factors. Endophoric reference—i.e., reference from the perspective of the previously mentioned object—is especially cooperative when the current referent differs only slightly from the previous one. By stressing the differing feature, the speaker instructs the addressee to just adapt the previous gestalt correspondingly: "Don't construct a totally new template for your search; the previous one, slightly modified, will do." If there are too many differences, however, it is more economical for the addressee to compute a new target gestalt. This is probably the case for the referent in figure 4.4B. It is not efficient for the addressee to construct the target concept WHITE

CUP by deriving it from BLACK BIRD. In that case, exophoric reference is indicated.

Grice's maxims are too general to be experimentally refutable, but the results discussed so far certainly show that there is more than one way to be cooperative in referring to objects. What violates the maxims of quantity from the exophoric point of view doesn't do so from the endophoric. There is still another perspective, which has received surprisingly little attention. Deutsch and Pechmann (1982) pointed out that speakers, especially younger children, underspecify because they *exploit* cooperativeness. When an array contains many similar objects, it would be too much work for a speaker to determine all the relevant exophoric contrasts. Instead he mentions a few salient features, and counts on the cooperative addressee to ask further if the referent cannot be uniquely identified. Deutsch and Pechmann showed that children (and sometimes adults) do this even when they are fully able to distinguish the exophorically relevant features of the referent object.

Clark and Wilkes-Gibbs (1986) turned this vice into a virtue. They stressed that referring to objects in conversation is always a *collaborative* process. Speakers try to establish the mutual belief with their interlocutors that the object reference is understood well enough for the current purposes. And establishing this mutual belief often requires some turn-taking. In the experiment of Clark and Wilkes-Gibbs (already mentioned in subsection 4.2.5), pairs of subjects conversed about arranging irregular shapes for which there are no easy names. Here is a typical effort to establish reference to such a tangram figure:

A: Uh, person putting a shoe on.

B: Putting a shoe on?

A: Uh huh. Facing left. Looks like he's sitting down.

B: Okay.

The first person, A, proposes a referential expression. His partner, B, indicates that it doesn't suffice. A adds some information, and B says *Okay*, creating the belief that he has identified the intended referent. Referring situations are not always as complicated as this one, but Clark and Wilkes-Gibbs argued that simpler cases of referring are not essentially different. The speaker presents a referring expression, and the addressee indicates in some way that it suffices for the current purposes. Isaacs and Clark (1987) provided additional experimental evidence for this theory.

Herrmann (1983) reviewed several more findings about a speaker's selection of information for expression in object reference, such as the finding by Herrmann and Deutsch (1976) that if there are two features, each of which is sufficiently discriminating in the exophoric sense, speakers tend to choose the feature that captures the most perceptually salient difference between the referent object and the alternatives. The choice, in other words, is perceptually driven. These authors also found strong set effects. If a feature, such as color, has been instrumental time and again, speakers will keep using it even when it becomes redundant. A speaker's cooperativeness displays a certain inertia, apparently.

What is still to be developed is a theory about indirect means of object reference. Chapter 2 mentioned Nunberg's (1979) notion of *referring function*, which relates the demonstratum to the referent. The referent, we saw, need not be the object pointed to. It also need not be the object named. One of Nunberg's examples involved a restaurant waiter going off duty and reminding his replacement that *the ham sandwich is sitting at table 20*. The object named (the demonstratum) is the ham sandwich; the entity referred to is a customer. The demonstratum and the context make it, presumably, possible for the addressee to derive the function and thus the referent. But how does a speaker, who has the referent in mind, discover a referring function that allows him to refer indirectly? And why does he want to do so? What a speaker selects for expression can be quite distinct from the information to be conveyed and can still be instrumental.

4.3.4   Selecting Information for Construction of Requests

A speaker who makes a request conveys a multitude of information to the addressee. As was discussed in chapter 1, the addressee should know that the speaker wants her to perform a certain action. But that is not sufficient; the addressee should also know how strongly she is being obliged to perform the action. It must be mutually known between speaker and addressee what the speaker's right is to request this action. Herrmann (1983) calls this the *legitimacy* of a request. A soldier who wants his trousers ironed by his colonel will probably have a hard time transmitting the legitimacy of the request to the colonel. It must also be mutually known that the addressee is able and willing to perform the action. The addressee's willingness will depend, in part, on the legitimacy of the request. Hence, the information to be conveyed by means of a request involves at least the following points: The speaker wants, with a certain degree of firmness or commitment, a particular action on the part of the addressee; the speaker has a certain legitimacy to oblige the addressee to this course of action, and is aware of the latter's ability and willingness to perform the action.

It is, however, a rarity that all information to be conveyed in a request is also explicitly expressed. Given the current discourse model and the common ground of the interlocutors, a speaker can economize substantially on what is to be said. The addressee will infer the implicated information. What the speaker will select for expression depends on the firmness of his wanting the action, his feeling of being legitimized to request the action, and his estimates of the partner's willingness and ability to perform the action.

Herrmann (1983) and his co-workers manipulated some of these factors in experimental studies of requesting. One experiment consisted of a two-person game played by an accomplice of the experimenter and the subject, whose speech was analyzed. The players were in the role of detectives who had to perform certain tasks. The subjects were 144 young German adults. The game was organized in such a way that at some moment the subject couldn't do anything else than request the partner to hand over his pistol. It was, however, mutually known that the partner also needed the pistol himself; the willingness of the partner was not self-evident. What Herrmann varied in this experiment was the degree to which the speaker could view himself as being legitimized to request the pistol. The pistol was either his own property or his partner's. This factor strongly affected the speakers' choice of request form. When a speaker owned the pistol, he perferably used the German equivalent of a request form such as *give me the pistol, you must give me the pistol,* or *I need the pistol.* These forms do not express any concern about the addressee's willingness or ability to hand over the weapon. The first two forms, moreover, express the addressee's obligation to act, whereas the third one formulates the firmness of the speaker's want. If, however, the partner owned the pistol, the speaker was more likely to say *could you give me the pistol, would you give me the pistol,* or *I would like to use the pistol.* The first two of these express concern for the listener's condition, leaving a loophole for the addressee to deny fulfillment. The third form expresses the want but not its firmness, nor does it specify the action or any obligation to perform it.

In other experiments, Herrmann (1983; see also Winterhoff-Spurk, Herrmann, and Weindrich 1986) varied the perceived willingness of the partner to comply with the request, and found that speakers tended to express their concern for the partner's conditions of willingness or ability when these were in doubt. However, this was seldom done when the speaker was in a strong position of legitimacy to make the request. Politeness increased with diminishing rights. The rule is, apparently, that the information to be expressed should be two-way instrumental. It should, on the one hand, be sufficient for the addressee to derive the intended obligation; i.e., she should be led to believe not that the utterance is *just* an assertion, a question, or an expressive but that it indeed conveys a request. The utterance should, on the other hand, minimize the risk that the addressee will decline to comply because bad feelings have been provoked. The latter risk is small when the speaker's right to oblige is very evident.

Also, Francik and Clark (1985) found that speakers construct requests in such a way as to overcome potential obstacles on the part of the addressee. When a speaker is put in a position to ask the time of somebody who is clearly not wearing a watch, the request tends to be of the form *Do you have a watch?* If, however, the addressee does wear a watch, the typical request is *Do you know what time it is?*.

So far, we have considered two cases of a speaker's selecting information for expression: in referring to objects and in making requests. The experimental results showed that, as a rule, speakers do not utter all the information that is to be conveyed. Rather, they select for expression information that is instrumental in achieving the communicative goal. In referring, this is the information that will be effective in focusing the addressee's attention on the new referent, be it endophoric or exophoric information. In requesting, it is information that will minimize the risk of a noncomplying response on the part of the addressee; this, in turn, depends on the distribution of rights, the perceived willingness of the addressee, and so forth.

4.3.5   Selecting Main-Structure and Side-Structure Information

The problems of information selection are substantially more complicated when we consider complex verbal activities, such as giving route directions, describing scenes, narrating, and planning joint actions. In these and other cases, a main goal is successively unfolded in subgoals and sub-subgoals. We will return to some of these issues in the next section; here we will note one rather general feature of a speaker's selection of information—a feature that is common to almost all these complex types of discourse: Speakers categorize the information they select for expression in what Klein and Stutterheim (1987) call *main-structure* and *side-structure* information. For instance, one speaker, when asked to relate her plans for the future, said (among other things) the following:

(5) So, I will go to the university and study something, probably French. And then, I will become a teacher, *although the chances are bad right now*. And then of course, I will marry and have children. *I am very traditional here, I love babies.*

The main structure of this text consists of the subsequent future steps. They are straightforward elaborations of the main goal the speaker set for herself in response to the interviewer's question. The side structure (italicized in the text) consists of additional comments, associations, embellishments, and so forth. Hopper (1979) and Reinhart (1984) have called the latter *background* information and the former *foreground* information. It is, in general, much easier to see how the selected main-structure or foreground information relates to the speaker's communicative intention than to explain why the background or side-structure information is selected for expression. The speaker can generate all sorts of "side intentions," such as to give reasons for actions, plans, or decisions; or he can develop noncommunicative intentions (in the sense discussed in section 4.1), such as to appear knowledgeable, pleasant as a conversant, etc. Whatever the grounds are for the selection of side-structure information, the speaker gives it special treatment in the generation of the message. For instance, it is not given the same temporal deictic perspective as the main-structure information. In example 5, the future tense of the main structure does not appear in the side structure. Also, the side messages express states rather than events, and there are various other remarkable differences (see Klein and Stutterheim 1987).

In one experimental study in which the linguistic differentiation of main-structure and side-structure information in speech production was examined, Brown and Dell (1987) asked subjects to retell stories. Each story involved an action performed by means of some instrument (e.g., a stabbing). One experimental variable was the kind of instrument used. It could be the typical instrument for the action (a knife) or an atypical instrument (an icepick). When speakers retold such a story, the typical instrument was less often explicitly mentioned than the atypical instrument. Since the default instrument for stabbing is a knife, the speaker can refrain from selecting that information for expression; it is inferable. When a speaker nevertheless decides to mention the knife explicitly, this must be due to a "side intention"—to embellish the story, to be very explicit, or what have you. The atypical instrument, however, is main information to be expressed. Brown and Dell found a characteristic difference in the grammatical encoding of atypical and typical instruments. Main information (i.e., the atypical instruments) tended to be encoded in the same clause as the action (*The robber stabbed the man with an icepick*), whereas side information (i.e., the typical instruments) tended to end up in an earlier clause (*The robber grabbed a knife and stabbed the man*). In other words, the speaker's message expressed a more intimate relation between action and instrument when the instrument belonged to the story's main structure than when it belonged to its side structure.

4.4 Macroplanning 2: Ordering Information for Expression

Whenever a speaker wants to express anything more than the simplest assertions, requests, declarations, etc., he has to solve what will be called the *linearization problem*: deciding what to say first, what to say next, and so on. The linearization problem has been the subject of rhetorical treatises since Aristotle; an educated speaker was supposed to give special attention to the ways in which he would order or arrange information for expression. That such arrangement (even of two simple propositions) can have dramatic effects on the addressee's interpretation is apparent from the following examples:

(6) She married and became pregnant.

(7) She became pregnant and married.

Each of these sentences contains the same two propositions; however, their order differs, and the implicatures differ correspondingly.

It is important to distinguish the linearization of propositions from the kind of ordering that is due to topicalizing or taking perspective in a message. (The latter is called "linearization" in Chafe 1970.) The two sentences in example 8 differ in this respect; the second one is "topicalized."

(8) I will send you the money next week.

The money I will send you next week.

Such topicalizing effects will be discussed in subsection 4.5.3. Here our main focus is the linearization of entire propositions or predications.

There are two major sets of determinants for a speaker's ordering of information for expression: *content-related* and *process-related* determinants.

4.4.1 Content-Related Determinants

The content-related determinants of linearization derive from the following principle:

Principle of natural order   Arrange information for expression according to the natural ordering of its content.

What counts as natural ordering is different for different domains of discourse, and there is no general definition. Still, for certain important cases the notion is obvious. For event structures, the natural order is the chronological order of events. Unless the speaker explicitly indicates otherwise, the interlocutor will assume that the order of mention corresponds to chronological order. This is what happens in examples 6 and 7 above; it is the default case. A cooperative speaker will mark deviations from chronology, as in the following:

(9) She became pregnant after she married.

The word *after* signals to the addressee that chronology is not preserved. It is known that children have a hard time acquiring these deviant structures (E. Clark 1970); preserving chronological order is one of the earliest rhetorical skills in children.

There are also other domains that have natural ordering. Linear spatial structures are a good example. Above, we considered a speaker's retrieval of the shortest or easiest route from a source place to a goal place in town. It is not enough for a speaker to make this spatial information conceptually available; the information should also be ordered for expression. The natural order is the connective sequence of loci from source to goal. It is not necessarily the case that this is also the order in which a speaker retrieves the shortest route from memory. He may well happen to become aware of the final part of the route before he has worked out the initial part in detail. In other words, the natural order has to be imposed for the listener's sake. That speakers indeed follow source-to-goal spatial connectivity when giving route directions is evident from several empirical studies (Klein 1979, 1982; Munro 1977; Wunderlich and Reinelt 1982).

Why is natural order so natural? The principle of natural order will be effective only in domains of discourse where there is tacit agreement between the interlocutors as to what will constitute a natural order. This tacit agreement may be due to universal principles of memory organization, or to more culture-specific "scripts" (Schank 1975). An example of the former is, probably, the chronology principle for temporal domains. If people normally organize and remember related events as temporally ordered structures, it should be relatively easy or natural for a speaker to retrieve the information, and for a listener to decode it, in that order. A *script* gives a further specification of what the order should be in a particular culture. The order of courses in a meal, for instance, is not universal; within a culture, however, there will be a script, shared by the language community, which can provide a set of default values for arranging messages about meals.

4.4.2 Process-Related Determinants

The process-related determinants of linearization are most apparent when there is no natural order, and especially when the speaker has to express a multidimensional informational structure. A classical example is the task of describing the layout of one's apartment (Linde and Labov 1975). Two-

or three-dimensional spatial information has to be mapped onto some linear order for expression, and there is no single natural way to proceed. The major limiting factor is the speaker's bookkeeping ability. The speaker must keep track of what has been said and what is still to be expressed, and this requires special memory operations. Also, the speaker may show some concern for the memory limitations of the addressee, who will have to reconstruct an image of the multi-dimensional array from the successive bits of information.

Results from experimental studies of the process-related principles of linearization are reported in Levelt 1981, 1982a,b, and 1983. Subjects in the experiments were asked to describe spatial-grid-like networks, such as those in figure 4.5, which were put on the table in front of them. These networks consisted of differently colored dots, connected by horizontal and vertical lines. (In the figure, the colors are replaced by their names.) The subjects were asked to start their descriptions at the node indicated by an arrow, and to describe the network in such a way as to enable the next subject to correctly draw it on the basis of the tape-recorded description. Here is one subject's description (translated from Dutch) of pattern a:

(10) Begin in the middle, a gray node. From there upwards a red node. Then to the left, a pink node from the red. Then from pink again to the left a blue node. Then back again to red. Then from red to the right a yellow node. And from yellow again to the right a green node.

The precise models that successfully predicted the subjects' linearizations (Levelt 1982a) are less important here than the principles on which they are based. It is likely that these principles will, *mutatis mutandis*, hold for other spatial and nonspatial domains of description, because they reflect quite general properties of perception and memory. Let us review them with reference to the various patterns in figure 4.5.

Principle of connectivity   Wherever possible, choose as the next node to be described one that has a direct connection to the current node.

This principle predicts that a speaker will go over a pattern as much as possible "without lifting the pencil," the mental pencil's point being the speaker's focus of attention. In example 10 above, the speaker goes in a connected fashion from GRAY to RED to PINK to BLUE, and again from RED to YELLOW to GREEN. Speakers rarely violated the connectivity principle for string-like parts of patterns. Nobody ever went from RED to GREEN to YELLOW in pattern a. For pattern b, every subject went in connected fashion from GREEN to PINK, mentioning all intermediary nodes as if giving route directions.

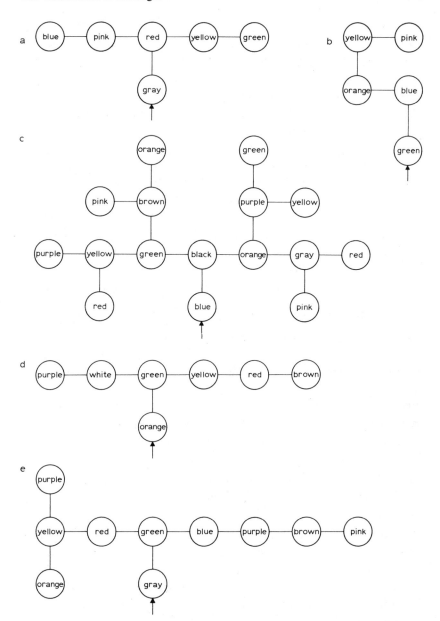

Figure 4.5
Patterns to be described in a linearization experiment (After Levelt 1982a).

Ehrich and Koster (1983) found a high degree of connectivity in the description of furniture arrangements in a doll house. This was especially marked when the arrangements were chaotic or nonfunctional; the speaker would make small jumps from one object to the nearest one. There was far less connectivity of this sort when the furniture arrangement was natural (e.g., chairs around a table). In that case, natural order took over; a speaker would introduce the central object (the table) and mention all objects with some functional relation to the table (the chairs, the lamp, the vase).

The connectivity principle is certainly not limited to spatial domains of discourse. Whenever possible, a speaker who is asked to list his relatives selects as the next person to mention one who has direct kinship to the last person mentioned (Levelt, unpublished data). One goes from ME to PARENT to UNCLE or AUNT to COUSIN, never straight from PARENT to COUSIN. Connectivity is a general ordering principle in perception and memory.

It is, of course, not always possible for a speaker to introduce new nodes (new items of information) in a connected way without repeating old ones. This problem appears when the speaker reaches the end of a string in patterns such as the ones in figure 4.5. In example 10, the speaker leaps from the end point (BLUE) back to the choice node (RED) in order to complete the description of the right part of the pattern. The return leap violates connectivity, but two-thirds of the subjects do this. The only way to preserve connectivity would be to return step by step to the choice node, retracing the old items. This is what one-third of the subjects do. Here is an example description for the same pattern (figure 4.5a):

(11) I start at node gray. Go straight on to red. Go left to pink. Go straight on to blue. Turn around, go back to pink. Go back, uh straight on to red. Straight on to yellow. Straight on to green.

The speaker preserves connectivity by adding that one should "turn around" and by rementioning PINK. The speaker is, clearly, involved in a mental tour through the pattern. Repeating old items preserves connectivity but violates a quantity maxim. Most subjects opt to respect the latter.

How do "leaping" subjects keep track of the returns to be made? This is a simple matter for pattern a, where there is only one choice node to leap back to. The speaker mentally flags "back to RED upon reaching the end of a string." But if the speaker passed two or more choice nodes before reaching the end of a string, in which order should he return to these nodes? This problem arises when pattern c is described. When the speaker starts his description by mentioning in connected fashion BLUE, BLACK,

ORANGE, PURPLE, and GREEN, there are three choice nodes in the queue for the speaker to return to: BLACK, ORANGE, and PURPLE. The next principle expresses how speakers handle this.

Stack principle Return to the last choice node in the waiting line.

The just-mentioned speaker who reached GREEN will first return to PURPLE, and will mention the YELLOW node to the right of PURPLE. He will then go back to ORANGE and mention GRAY, which is itself a choice node. After mentioning RED (or PINK), the speaker will return to GRAY, the last choice node in the line, in order to mention PINK (or RED); only then will he return to BLACK. The speaker's bookkeeping for return addressees is like putting them on a stack and always returning to the top item on the stack after reaching the end of a connected string. The experimental data show almost no exceptions to this principle.

This stack principle is well known in the psychology of problem solving (see, for instance, Newell and Simon 1972); it is a dominant way of keeping track of hierarchically organized structures. It is not unlikely that speakers will also follow the principle in linearizing other spatial or nonspatial domains that are multiply branching. Linde and Labov's (1975) findings for apartment descriptions are in full agreement with the principle.

The third and final principle regulates what speakers will do upon reaching a multiply branching node. In which order do they treat the outgoing branches? Consider pattern d in figure 4.5. Which branch will the speaker describe first upon reaching the GREEN choice node: the left branch, or the right one? There is a probabilistic rule governing such choices:

Minimal-load principle Order alternative continuations in such a way that the resulting memory load for return addresses is minimal.

For pattern d, this principle predicts that speakers will tend to describe the left branch first. The speaker will have to keep the GREEN choice node flagged in memory for return, whether he goes left or right first. But if he goes left first, the duration of the load will be shorter; there are only two further nodes before the return leap can be made. When the speaker goes right first, as many as three nodes have to be described before memory can be relieved of its flag. And indeed, speakers mostly describe shorter branches before longer branches.

Another example is pattern e. Which branch will be taken first from the GREEN choice node? Both branches contain the same number of nodes and arcs. Still the principle predicts a preference for going right first. There are two choice nodes in the pattern: GREEN and YELLOW. When the speaker goes right first, he will keep GREEN on the stack until he reaches

PINK. But after the return leap to GREEN, the stack is empty until YELLOW is reached. There is, in other words, never more than one return address to be remembered at a time. However, when the speaker goes left first, he will have to flag GREEN and (after two more moves) YELLOW as well; he will then have two return addresses on his stack. Hence, the memory load will be minimized by going right first. And that is indeed what speakers prefer to do in the experiments.

When there are more alternatives, the principle says "Do the simplest thing first." And one can expect this to apply to other domains of discourse as well. When one has to give instructions for shopping involving two different shops, a big food store where a large range of items has to be purchased and a dry cleaner where a skirt has to be picked up, one will probably start the instructions by mentioning the dry cleaner. But only further research can tell us how general this principle and the previous two are as process-related determinants of linearization.

This section and the previous one have discussed aspects of macroplanning, the processes by which a speaker selects and orders information for expression. The result of marcoplanning is a speech-act intention, or a series of speech-act intentions. The speaker selects and orders information whose expression with declarative, interrogative, or imperative mood will be instrumental in realizing the goals that proceed from the original communicative intention. In other words, macroplanning produces the substance of the messages, such as that the message should declare a particular proposition or interrogate a certain state of affairs. But more has to be done in order for a message to become expressible. Its contents must be presented in such a way that the addressee can attend to it, find the referents, register what is new, and so forth. Also, the contents must be put in a propositional format that the Formulator can understand. This is microplanning, to which we now turn.

4.5 Microplanning

Four major aspects of microplanning will be discussed in this section. The first one is the assignment of what I will call *accessibility status* to the referents in the message. Each referent in the message will be provided with an index which states where it can be found—for instance, in the current focus or elsewhere in the discourse model. This index will be taken into account in grammatical encoding, giving rise to cues in the utterance that guide the addressee's attention to where the referent is to be identified. The second aspect of microplanning to be treated is topicalization, the assignment of the topic role to one of the referents. The third is the "propositionalization" of the information to be expressed. It will be argued that translating information into propositional format necessarily involves the assignment of perspective. The final aspect of microplanning to be discussed is the acknowledgment of the Formulator's language-specific requirements.

4.5.1 Assigning Accessibility Status to Referents

A speaker will introduce and reintroduce referents (persons, objects, events, etc.) into the discourse in such a way that the addressee can create or locate them in her own discourse model. What matters here is the estimated *accessibility* of the referent for the addressee ("estimated" because it is the speaker's judgment that matters, not the real accessibility as experienced by the addressee). Recall from section 4.2 the conversation between Marcia and Seth. Marcia had, at some point, said something about the smoke of Florence. Owing to a lapse of attention, Seth had not registered that remark. When Marcia, not aware of this, wants to say more about this smoke, she will judge that it is accessible as a referent for Seth. She may then refer to it as *the smoke*. But Seth, who cannot locate the referent in his discourse model, will ask *what smoke?* or something similar.

The accessibility status of a referent can be conceived of as a complex value or index attached by the speaker to each referent in a message. This value is an important determinant of the linguistic shape the Formulator will compute for the referent. Marcia's discourse entity SMOKE may surface in her utterance as *the smoke, smoke, that*, or *it*, depending on what she thinks is the entity's accessibility to Seth.

The speaker can derive the accessibility status of a referent from his content and focus accounts (see subsections 4.2.3 and 4.2.4). This involves three dichotomies, which are of central relevance for further grammatical encoding: whether the referent is estimated to be accessible at all to the addressee, whether it is assumed to be in the addressee's discourse model, and whether it is guessed to be in the addressee's current focus. These three dichotomies are not orthogonal. They are, rather, embedded in this way:

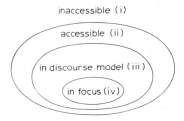

This embedding of dichotomies naturally corresponds to four cases, numbered in the diagram. For different languages, the consequence for grammatical encoding of a referent's accessibility status on these dichotomies may be quite different. But it seems that most languages acknowledge these dichotomies in some way or another. In discussing the four cases, I will give examples for English only. The examples cannot be simply generalized to other languages.

(i) The discourse record tells the speaker that the listener cannot find or infer the entity. It is neither in the common ground nor in the discourse model; it is also not inferable (see (ii) below) from entities in these shared knowledge structures. Prince (1981) calls these referents "brand new. ' The ferry Marcia wants to introduce in the discussion (see figure 4.2) is not represented for Marcia as something Seth knows about. The English speaker will normally encode a referent with the feature "inaccessible" as indefinite. For instance:

One can reach the island by an old ferryboat.

Marcia would not be very cooperative if she used a definite expression, as in

One can reach the island by the old ferryboat.

Marking a referent as inaccessible is inviting the listener to create a new address for the entity referred to.

(ii) Though the referent is neither in the discourse model nor in the common ground, the discourse record makes it seem likely to the speaker that the addressee can *infer* the referent. Marcia believes that she has successfully introduced the information that Ponza is an offshore island, one of the Pontines. She also believes that Seth is focusing on this information. Marcia may now rely on Seth's general knowledge about Italian offshore islands, and in particular that such islands tend to have old ferries. Seth, she thinks, can infer that Ponza has such a ferry. She may then say

One day I took the old ferryboat.

It is essential that Ponza, from which the existence of the ferry can be inferred, is supposed to be in the addressee's focus. When Marcia believes that Seth is focusing on Florence, she cannot refer to Ponza's ferryboat by *the old ferryboat*. By using a definite expression, a speaker tells an addressee that a referent can be uniquely identified—either in their common ground (Seth could talk about *the pope*), or in their shared discourse knowledge, or by inference from what is currently in focus. In the last case, the listener will create a new address by backward suppletion.

The following two cases concern reference to entities that are already in the discourse model. When the entity is uniquely identifiable, the speaker will make definite reference to tell the addressee "you can identify the referent". But the speaker can do more to guide the addressee's attention. He can make nonprominent or reduced reference.

(iii) The entity is in the discourse model, but it is not in the addressee's current focus. As in the previous case, such a referent is uniquely identifiable; it receives the index "accessible". The English speaker will express this by making definite reference. But in addition to this, the referent is indexed for being available in the discourse model. It has, in that sense, no news value. When an entity is newly introduced into the discourse it does have news value. This notion, called *conceptual prominence*, will be discussed in the next subsection.

An item already in the discourse model, and not prominent for other reasons, will receive prosodic deaccentuation in the (English) utterance. Pitch accent will be withheld. When Marcia talks about Florence after relating her experiences at Ponza, she may, as an afterthought, want to add something about Ponza's church:

The island [or Ponza] has a beautiful chUrch.

The word *island*, or *Ponza*, whichever is used, can be uttered in a non-prominent way. Accentuation goes to the referent that is *outside* the discourse model: Ponza's church.

The speaker's tendency to deaccent the expression for a referent that is already in the discourse model has been revealed in various empirical studies. It is, for instance, in excellent agreement with the findings of Brown and Yule (1983), who instructed speakers to describe visual diagrams containing colored geometrical figures, words, and connecting colored lines. Each speaker had as addressee a person who could not see the diagram, but who was to draw it from the speaker's description. Here is a typical description:

halfway down the page draw a red horizontal line of about two inches on eh the right hand side just above the line in black write "ON".

When the tapes were analyzed for prosodic prominence or nonprominence of referential expressions, the results shown in table 4.1 emerged. These clear findings are also in good agreement with those of MacWhinney and Bates (1978), Marslen-Wilson, Levy, and Tyler (1982), Terken (1984), and Fowler and Housum (1987). Fowler and Housum compared speakers' utterances of words produced for the first and for the second time in a monologue (both times referring to the same entity). It turned out that

Table 4.1
Prominence and nonprominence in diagram descriptions (data from Brown and Yule 1983).

	Referent is			
	not in discourse model		in discourse model	
	inaccessible	inferable	not in focus	in focus
Prominent	87%	79%	4%	0%
Nonprominent	13%	21%	96%	100%

speakers distinguished old referents by attenuating their names. These words were shorter, lower in pitch, and less loud at second use.

Let us now return to Marcia, who said *The island has a beautiful church*. Notice that, under the same circumstances, she should not say *It has a beautiful church*; the pronoun *it* would have been interpreted by Seth as referring to Florence, which is in Seth's current focus. This brings us to the fourth case.

(iv) The referent is in the addressee's current focus. Such a referent is given the status feature "in focus". Because of the embedding relation depicted above, each "in focus" referent is also in the discourse model and accessible. This means that the English speaker will, normally, deaccent the referring expression and make it definite. But the specific "in focus" feature has an additional consequence: The referring expression will be reduced. When Marcia believes Seth is focusing on the island of Ponza, she can say *It also has a beautiful church* or *I have seen a beautiful church there*. The proforms *it* and *there* tell the addressee "Don't search; you have the referent in focus." This use of reduction has been especially well documented by Chafe (1976), Prince (1981), Marslen-Wilson, Levy, and Tyler (1982), and Brown and Yule (1983). But it should be added that there are degrees of reduction (or "attenuation," as Chafe called it). Marcia would probably not say *The island of Ponza has a beautiful church*, which contains a very full referential phrase (*the island of Ponza*). Less full are *Ponza island*, *the island*, and *Ponza*; very reduced are *there* and *it*. Speakers tend to reduce the size of referential expressions when an entity is repeatedly referred to in discourse. Empirical evidence to this effect has been reported by Krauss and Weinheimer (1964), Osgood (1971), Brown and Yule (1983), Clark and Wilkes-Gibbs (1986), Redeker (1986), Isaacs and Clark (1987), and Sridhar (1988). Adjectives, relative clauses, and other modifiers tend to be dropped. Interlocutors follow Grice's maxim of quantity by economizing on the size of referential expressions. This economizing is also done for discourse entities that are not in focus. However, when a referent is believed to be in the addressee's focus, and especially in her focal center, reference is, as a rule, made by the use of "pro-forms," such as *it*, *he*, *that*, and *this*.

These four cases illustrate a referent's status on the three accessibility features "accessible", "in the discourse model", and "in focus". The speaker's assignment of this three-valued index to each referent can be seen to be governed by procedural knowledge. The underlying procedures can be put this way:

IF the referent $\left\{ \begin{array}{l} \text{can be uniquely identified} \\ \text{is in the discourse model} \\ \text{is in the addressee's current focus} \end{array} \right\}$,

THEN assign it the value $+ \left\{ \begin{array}{l} \text{accessible} \\ \text{in discourse model} \\ \text{in focus} \end{array} \right\}$;

otherwise assign it the opposite (negative) value.

The English encoding of these three features employs, in particular, definiteness, deaccentuation, and reduction (pronominalization), respectively. Other languages express these features differently, and even in English there are known exceptions to these rules of thumb. One of the exceptions has to do with the assignment of prosodic prominence: An item already in the discourse model is not necessarily subject to deaccentuation; it may have conceptual prominence for independent reasons. We will turn to this now.

4.5.2 Conceptual Prominence

When a speaker introduces a new referent into the discourse, it has what we called "news value" for the addressee; it is conceptually *prominent*. But a referent that is already in the discourse may also become prominent. Consider the following example.

Assume that Seth and Marcia shift to a new topic: a quarrel between three boys and a girl they know, Sam, Saul, Simon, and Tessie. After introducing the protagonists, Seth could say

First, Tessie pestered SAm, then she insulted SAUl, and finally she hit SImon.

All three victims (i.e., patients of some action) are given pitch accent here in spite of the fact that they are all represented in the discourse model. Nooteboom and Terken (1982) pointed out, and showed experimentally, that pitch accent gets assigned to successive but different referents appearing in the same role. In our example this is the case for Sam, Saul, and Simon, who are all figuring as patients in Tessie's actions. (Pechmann's [1984] experimental evidence to this effect was discussed above.) One could say that in these cases the referents *contrast* in the same thematic role (in Pechmann's terms: there is endophoric contrast). The news value is in the fact that the same role, the one in the listener's focus of attention, is now fulfilled by a different referent. In order to express this, the speaker will mark it in the message by assigning prominence to the item. This, in turn, may lead to accentuation of the referential expression.

When, however, the *same* referent reappears in the *same* role, it is made nonprominent. In the example that happens to Tessie, who continues to be actor. Whatever the prominence of the first mention, the second and third (both *she*) are deaccented.

Since repeated mention is usually made by anaphoric means—that is, by terms that stand for the original referential expression (e.g., *she* for *Tessie*)—one would expect anaphors, and in particular anaphoric pronouns, to become deaccented; they refer to entities already in the discourse model. But pronouns may also become accented when their referents contrast in the same conceptual role. Consider the following example:

Tessie went after SImon, and then hE chased hEr.

Here *Tessie* and *Simon* are reduced to pronouns (*her* and *he*), but these reduced forms receive pitch accent. It signals, for both referents, contrast in the same role (the actor was first Tessie, then Simon; the patient was first Simon, then Tessie). Here the reduction to pronouns tells the addressee that the referents are still in focus; the accentuation tells the addressee that the same kind of action is continued, but with the roles swapped. Note that the roles in the action must indeed be very similar if this contrastive prominence is to be used. The following could not be said:

Tessie went after SImon, and then hE kissed hEr.

Going after and chasing are similar in a way that going after and kissing are not. These cases show that speakers not only mark referents for being in the discourse model or not; they also mark them for contrastive roles between what is in the addressee's current focus and what is in the speaker's new focus.

The assignment of prominence to elements in a message is not restricted to referring items. Predications can also be marked as prominent by the speaker; this again depends on their estimated news value for the addressee, as is particularly apparent in question answering. Consider the following exchange.

Q: What happened to your uncle?
A: He dIEd last week.

The answer provides the new information, which the questioner presumably asked for. This new information is given prominence in the message. And conceptually prominent information is usually formulated with pitch accent, also when it is a predication.

In short, a conceptual entity in a message is assigned the feature " + prominent" when it has news value. Though this notion is hard to formalize, three clear cases are recognizable: A speaker will refer with prominence when the entity is newly introduced in the discourse, i.e., when it has the accessibility feature " − in discourse model". He will also refer with prominence when the referent is contrasting in a focused role. And he will assign prominence to a new predication, especially when this is an answer to a question about some referent.

4.5.3   Topicalizing

When a speaker has selected certain information for expression, he will use various devices to guide the listener's attention. One such device, treated in the previous subsection, is to signal to the addressee the location of a particular referent or the need to add a new address to the discourse model. But there is more to be done (see section 3.4). It may often be necessary for the speaker to topicalize a referent.

A speaker will mark as topic the referent that the message is about. In this way the speaker may tell the addressee where to store the information being expressed. If the speaker intends to inform the other party about his sister Jane, he could say

Jane is married to Peter.

Here, *Jane* is topic, and the addressee is invited to store the new information (being married to Peter) under Jane's address in the discourse model. If there is also an address for Peter (i.e., when Peter is accessible inside or outside the discourse model), the listener may, in addition, store the corresponding information (Peter's being married to Jane) under Peter's address. However, the speaker probably intends only the former when he makes Jane the topic. In procedural terms:

IF the goal is that the listener store the information under address X,
THEN assign topic status to X.

Why this should become a goal is a different issue; it should, in some way, proceed from the speaker's illocutionary intention. One obvious reason for setting oneself such a goal is an interlocutor's explicit question, for instance

Is your sister married?. Another important reason for topicalizing a referent is that it is particularly *salient* in the state of affairs to be communicated. A human agent is more easily topicalized than a nonhuman theme (*Peter cut the tree* versus *The tree was cut by Peter*), big or moving objects are more easily topicalized than small or immobile ones, and so on. We prefer to entertain addresses for salient items; they are the pegs for storing our information about the world. Notice that as soon as these salient items have been introduced into the discourse model, the speaker will tend not to mark them for prominence any more. Instead, the predications made about them—that is, the new information items which the addressee is invited to hang upon these pegs—will be prominent. The relation between topicalization and saliency will be taken up again in chapter 7, where the grammatical encoding of topicalized and nuclear elements will be discussed.

In running discourse there is often a sequential relation between focusing and topicalizing. This is exemplified by the following:

I have a sIster. She is mArried.

The first sentence brings a new referent into the addressee's focus of attention: the speaker's sister. Since it is as yet inaccessible to the hearer, the speaker uses an indefinite full form of reference with prosodic prominence. In this way the listener is invited to set up a new address in her discourse model. The next sentence has this referent as topic. It is now in the addressee's current focus, and it is therefore referred to in short pronominal form (*she*) and without prosodic prominence. Now the predication receives prominence. It often takes two subsequent steps to introduce a referent and to say something about it: focusing and topicalizing.

When a referent is topicalized in a speaker's message, it will be given a kind of priority treatment in grammatical encoding. It will, for instance, tend to be expressed as the grammatical subject. Entities that are not topicalized but are still quite salient (i.e., the other nuclear entities of the message) will also be given special treatment; they will tend to be encoded in a major grammatical function. We will return to these issues in chapter 7.

4.5.4 Assigning Propositional Format and Perspective
A speaker often decides to communicate information that is not yet in propositional format. Take again the case of giving route directions. A speaker, when asked to tell the way to the Concertgebouw, will do the macroplanning that will give him the successive moves to be made by the addressee. But each of these moves will, initially, not be in propositional

form. Rather, these moves will be spatio-temporal images. An important aspect of microplanning is to translate these images into propositional form. The main point of this subsection is that this translation necessarily implies the assignment of perspective.

The notion of perspective-taking is easily exemplified by descriptions 10 and 11 above, which were given by two subjects in the experiment on linearization mentioned (Levelt 1982b). The descriptions refer to the pattern in figure 4.5a. Let us consider a single move in these descriptions, namely the one concerning the connection PINK-BLUE. The first subject, who gave description 10, put it this way: *Then from pink again to the left, a blue node.* The second subject, giving description 11, said: *Go straight on to blue.* Apart from the difference in ellipsis, the descriptions show a contrast in the directional terms used: *to the left* in example 10, *straight on* in example 11. Although the perceptual structures were identical for the two subjects (a pink node and a blue node connected by a black horizontal arc), they were categorized in different ways; the spatial relation of BLUE to PINK is TO THE LEFT OF in example 10 and STRAIGHT ON in example 11. The speakers agreed on their choice of PINK as the reference location for BLUE; nobody in the entire experiment said *Pink is to the right of blue.*

Both the commonality and the difference observed reveal the workings of perspective-taking. That all subjects relate BLUE to PINK and not the other way round is a consequence of the linearization strategy they have taken, namely to describe the pattern in a connected fashion as if making a tour. After the speaker has reached and mentioned the pink node, the continuation of the tour requires him to relate the next node to the last one mentioned—i.e., BLUE to PINK, since PINK is the current focus. There can be no doubt that all the speakers in the study would have related PINK to BLUE if they had been asked to start the entire pattern description from the BLUE node. When a speaker is not bound by instruction and neither PINK nor BLUE is currently in focus, he can freely take either perspective, and his categorizations of the binary spatial relations will be dependent on his choice of reference point. Note, however, that *some* choice is to be made; either BLUE or PINK is to be the relatum for putting the spatial relation between BLUE and PINK in propositional form.

The difference between the two subjects is a subtle one that reveals another degree of freedom in perspective-taking.

The first subject describes the pattern in terms of deictic perspective, taking himself as the basis for the coordinate system (see subsection 2.2.2). The mental tour made by the subject is a gaze tour; all directional terms tell the addressee where the gaze moves in terms of a speaker-centered base.

The speaker, who examines the pattern on the table in front of him, has to move his gaze to the left in order to go from the pink node to the blue node. Strong evidence that speakers who say *left* here apply categories of gaze movement to the pattern is that almost all these speakers also say *up* or *upwards* in describing the first move from the gray to the red node, *never straight* or *ahead*. The gaze's move is indeed upward for this first step in the tour, in spite of the fact that the pattern is flat on the table. In Levelt 1982b I proposed a gaze-tour theory for the frequent use of vertical dimension terms (*up*, *down*, etc.) for spatial relations that are essentially in a horizontal plane. The principle was later also put forward by Shepard and Hurwitz (1984). In short, speakers who take a deictic perspective choose *categories of gaze movement* (UP, DOWN, LEFT, RIGHT) as functions for locative predications.

The other speaker, who said *straight on*, doesn't make a gaze tour from a fixed deictic perspective; rather, she makes a kind of body tour, as if driving through the pattern by car (remember her mention of "turning around"). For every move through the pattern, the direction of the line moved along previously is taken as the new intrinsic basis for the coordinate system. It is reoriented as moves are made. The *straight on* derives from just having driven from the red node to the pink node, and continuing the same direction of movement. And indeed, in her description this subject uses *straight on* for all cases where the same direction is continued. Notice also that, as it should be in a flat array of streets, there are no *ups* or *downs* for the body-tour subjects.

This example shows that the same visual pattern can be propositionally expressed in quite different ways, depending on the deictic or intrinsic perspective taken. It determines which entities are reference locations for which other entities, and it determines the direction of these relations. Most subjects in the experiment preferred to take deictic perspective. But one-third of the speakers used the body-tour strategy, which asks for a pattern-based intrinsic perspective (the factual orientation of the speaker being irrelevant). This is, apparently, a matter of cognitive style. Is this a trivial difference? One should stay on the alert; it turned out that subjects with left-handedness among their parents or siblings were less inclined to take deictic perspective than other participants in the experiment. One wonders whether hemispheric lateralization plays a role in perspective-taking.

The example made it especially clear that there is no single *necessary* way of assigning propositional format to the visual information (and this was confirmed in a similar experiment; see Garrod and Anderson 1987).

One would expect such necessity if the visual system's output were itself in propositional form. In that case the perspective inherent in the proposition would simply be forced upon the mind. There is, however, substantial freedom in putting the perceived structure, which is spatially represented, into one or another propositional form. They are all *equivalent* descriptions of the same perceptual pattern. But they differ in perspective. This does not mean that perceptual factors play no role in assigning perspective. They do. Speakers prefer to express figure/ground relations such that the ground is taken as reference. They tend to say *The cat is in front of the wall* rather than *The wall is behind the cat*. What is smaller is preferably located with respect to what is larger. A chair-and-table scene is preferably described as *A table and a chair next to it* rather than *A chair and a table next to it*. When there is a moving object and a stable object, the moving object (A) tends to be located with respect to the stable one (B): *A approaches B*, or *A passes by B*. A contained object tends to be located with respect to the container: *A triangle in a circle* rather than *A circle around a triangle*. Rosch (1975) has argued that there are natural reference points not only in perceptual categories but also on such an abstract dimension as that of natural numbers.

We will finish this section by considering one empirical study of perspective-taking in the description of spatial scenes. Ehrich (1985) asked subjects to describe the arrangement of furniture in a doll house and analyzed the factors that determined the choice of reference objects and relations. These choices *must* be made when a spatial scene is expressed in propositional format. The study shows the systematicity of some of these choices. Ehrich varied a number of factors: the size and relative position of the objects, their locations and orientations with respect to the speaker, and the presence or absence of a background wall. But the subjects were left completely free in their choice of words.

Ehrich presented her subjects with furniture arrangements such as the ones in figure 4.6. Each subject inspected a single room through the door opening. In one condition the room had no walls. This, however, had very little effect on the speakers' descriptions; it can be ignored for the present purpose. The subjects examined the room with its six objects for some time, playing an "I spy" game with the experimenter. After this the room was removed, and the subject was unexpectedly asked to describe the furniture arrangement in such a way that a listener could reconstruct it. There were four major results:

(i) Speakers, in large majority, took a deictic perspective. In the case of the arrangement on the left in figure 4.6, they preferred to say *In front of the*

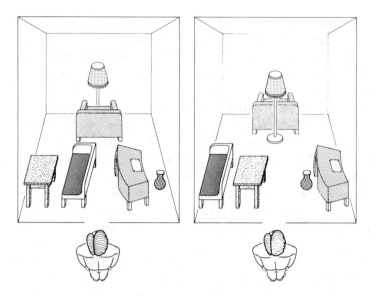

Figure 4.6
Examples of furniture arrangements to be described. (After Ehrich 1985.)

lamp is a chair, not *In front of the chair is a lamp*. In the case of the other arrangement, they even preferred to say *There is a lamp in front of the chair*, though the lamp was intrinsically behind the chair.

(ii) Speakers preferred to use the more peripheral object as reference for the location of an object that is closer to ego. In describing the arrangement shown at left, most speakers located the chair with respect to the lamp; in describing the other arrangement they located the lamp with respect to the chair.

(iii) Speakers preferred a larger object as the reference object for a smaller object. In describing the left arrangement, a substantial minority of subjects said *Behind the chair is a lamp*, whereas almost nobody said *Behind the lamp is a chair* in describing the right arrangement.

(iv) Speakers generally preferred to express relative location in terms of *in front of* rather than in terms of *behind*. Being IN FRONT OF is presumably a more salient relation than being BEHIND.

These findings show that there are preferred ways of expressing spatial relations propositionally, depending on intrinsic functional and gestalt properties of the scene. Moreover, Bürkle et al. (1986), using similar arrangements, showed that the place and the role of the interlocutor could affect the perspective chosen. But all of these are tendencies, not iron laws. A speaker is free to choose one perspective rather than another. And indeed, the ways in which the same scene is described by different subjects are surprisingly variant. When one looks over Ehrich's protocols, one is struck by the fact that no two descriptions of the same furniture arrangement are identical. Each subject added a personal touch in terms of the objects, the relations, the qualities attended to, and the choice of perspective.

4.5.5 Acknowledging Language-Specific Requirements

Section 3.6 described some cases where there is obligatory grammatical encoding of particular conceptual features, even if these are irrelevant for communication. In a language that has a tense system, for instance, it is obligatory to encode in the preverbal message the deictic and intrinsic temporal properties of a state or event. This may not be part of the speaker's macroplanning, because it need not proceed from elaborating the communicative intention. Rather, in finalizing the preverbal message for expression the speaker will retrieve these pieces of conceptual information if they are not yet represented. However, this is necessary only for speech-act intentions of the types DECL(P) and ?(P); imperatives have fixed tense in English. The speaker will then, for declaratives and interrogatives, insert the two tense functions as proposition modifiers (see subsection 3.2.6).

We must assume that the speaker has at his disposal a set of routine procedures that perform this acknowledgment function automatically for whatever the language requires. It is unlikely that these computations require special attentional effort. And this may be a more general property of microplanning. Most of a speaker's attention is spent on macroplanning, on elaborating the illocutionary intention, and on retrieving information for expression.

The end result of microplanning is a preverbal message. There is no reason to assume that preverbal messages are delivered as integral wholes. In incremental speech production, bits and pieces of the message under construction may become available one after the other. Each bit is immediately picked up by the Formulator for grammatical encoding. As we will see in chapter 7, the order in which the chunks are delivered will affect the course of grammatical encoding.

Summary

This chapter began with a characterization of communicative and illocutionary intentions. Performing a speech act involves more than just transmitting information to an addressee; it also involves making a communicative intention recognizable from what is said. The process of generating messages was then analyzed as a two-step process, with macroplanning followed by microplanning. Macroplanning consists of elaborating the communicative intention in a sequence of goals and subgoals and, for each subgoal, selecting information whose expression will be a realization of the subgoal. Microplanning finalizes each speech act for expression by providing the message with an information structure that will guide the addressee in inferring the communicative intention.

Both macroplanning and microplanning are highly context-dependent, and the context of discourse is in continuous flux. We examined several aspects of the discourse context which speakers must keep track of in order to make relevant contributions. They must register the type of discourse they are involved in (such as an interview, or a lecture). They must also take into account the topic(s) of the discourse. Speakers also build an internal representation of the contents that have been contributed by themselves and by the interlocutors; this shared knowledge is called the speaker's discourse model. They also monitor what is currently in focus. And there is, finally, some record of what was literally said, especially where this was pragmatically important or salient.

The chapter then turned to macroplanning. It was discussed that selecting information for expression may involve substantial planning, memory search, and inference-making. A speaker's attention will move back and forth between performing these activities and finalizing the messages for expression. This can lead to characteristic rhythms in monological speech, which make it likely that most attention is spent on macroplanning.

A speaker can often make complex intentions recognizable by expressing rather limited amounts of information. The information must only be instrumental in inviting the intended inference on the part of the listener. We reviewed some experimental work on what speakers select for expression when they make reference to objects and when they construct requests. There turns out to be more redundancy in object naming than one would expect from Grice's maxims. But these deviations are not really irrational or unmotivated; overspecification of an object is helpful, especially when it reveals the *kind* of object focused by the speaker. Also, speakers give seemingly redundant information when they contrast the intended referent with a previously mentioned object. This is an effective way of guiding the addressee's search. The request studies also showed that speakers select efficient information for expression—information that acknowledges the addressee's position in terms of willingness or ability to comply with the request and which, at the same time, makes it likely that the addressee will draw the intended inference. The elaboration of the original communicative intention may lead the speaker to conceive of what we called "side intentions," which may or may not be communicative in the restricted sense of this chapter. Side intentions tend to be encoded as rather independent messages, which can often be recognized as such in the speaker's discourse.

When the information to be expressed is complex, involving several successive speech acts, the speaker will have to decide on how to order the information for expression. This was called the speaker's linearization problem. Its solution depends, in the first place, on the content of what is to be expressed. A principle of natural order dictates default solutions for particular domains of discourse. The major example is that in the temporal domain events should be expressed in chronological order. In the second place, there are general restrictions on working memory that induce a speaker to prefer one linearization over another. These restrictions are well defined, and are quite general in nature.

Microplanning was the topic of the chapter's final section. The first aspect discussed was the assignment of an accessibility index to each referent in the message. This is done to inform the listener where the referent can be found: in the current focus, in the discourse model, somewhere else, or nowhere. Languages have a range of means for the grammatical encoding of this accessibility index. Also, a referent may be given the special status of topic. This is done to invite the interlocutor to store the new information under that referent's address in the discourse model. Referents may have varying degrees of saliency. A salient entity will have a better chance of getting an address in the discourse model than a nonsalient one. As a consequence, salient items are more easily topicalized than nonsalient ones. Items in the message will also vary in prominence. A speaker will make an item prominent if the listener has to store it as something new—a new referent, a new entity in a focused role, or a new predication.

Information selected for expression must eventually be encoded in a propositional format. This necessarily involves the assignment of perspective, in particular the choice of relations and reference points for these relations. These choices depend on various factors, such as the speaker's linearization strategy, the gestalt relations in a spatial scene, and the speaker's cognitive style.

Finally, the speaker will automatically retrieve the conceptual information to be acknowledged for the specific language spoken, such as temporal
information when the language has a tense system. The final result of
microplanning is a preverbal message that can be recognized by the Formulator as its characteristic input.

Chapter 5
Surface Structure

Once a message, or a fragment of a message, has been prepared for expression, the process of formulating can be initiated. Successive message fragments will trigger the Formulator to access lemmas, to inspect the message for functions, arguments, and modifiers, to specify grammatical relations, and to map these onto inflectional and phrasal structure.

This first stage of the formulating process was called "grammatical encoding" in chapter 1, and was distinguished from a second, phonological encoding stage in which word forms are accessed and prosodic patterns are generated. The present chapter will characterize the type of representation that forms the hinge between these two stages. It will be called "surface structure" (which involves an allusion but not a full commitment to particular grammatical theories). A surface structure is, by definition here, the output of grammatical encoding, and the input to phonological encoding. We will, however, stay rather close to Bresnan's (1982) notion of surface structure.

In order to understand the processes of grammatical encoding, which are discussed in subsequent chapters, we must have a sufficiently explicit specification of their target structures. It is, on the one hand, necessary to consider the way in which a surface structure expresses semantic relations through grammatical functions. This semantics-to-function mapping depends on the internal structure of lemmas, which are the terminal elements of a surface structure. It is, on the other hand, necessary to specify the way in which these grammatical functions are realized in a surface structure's hierarchical organization of phrases and in its case marking. This organization is essential input for phonological encoding.

These theoretical notions have, in general, not evolved from empirical analyses of the speaking process. They mostly stem from linguistics and computer science. Still, they do provide a much-needed framework for a theory of the speaker, which is not independently available. The theory we will assume in the present chapter is somewhat along the lines of Bresnan (1978, 1982), for three reasons. First, it is an explicit theory that allows us to formulate explicit procedures of surface-structure generation. Second, it is—as will be discussed—lexically based, and that makes it an attractive starting point for a theory of grammatical encoding. The following chapters will argue that lemmas are the driving force behind the speaker's construction of the surface structure. It is in the lemmas of the mental lexicon that conceptual information is linked to grammatical function. A lexically based grammar is a natural companion in developing this notion. Third, Bresnan's theory combines well with the psycholinguistic theory of grammatical encoding developed by Kempen and Hoenkamp (1987), which we will follow in chapter 7. Both are lexically based, and both operate with dual constituent/functional representations, as will be discussed. It should be kept in mind, however, that no grammatical theory can claim to be the correct one. We will not be committed to all details of Bresnan's theory; it will only be used as an attractive explicit framework for approaching the problems of grammatical encoding. The present chapter will be limited to the phrasal and functional aspects of surface structure. The internal grammatical structure of lemmas will be taken up in the next chapter, where the speaker's accessing of lemmas will be discussed.

The assumption that grammatical encoding is in the first instance independent of phonological encoding in no way implies that a speaker generates complete surface structures for clauses or sentences before accessing the inventory of word forms and computing phonetic patterns. The notion of incremental sentence production is also valid at this level; any terminal fragment of surface structure that becomes available will immediately trigger its phonological encoding, following Wundt's principle. Some of the word forms may already have become available with their lemmas; others are still to be retrieved. It is likely that failure to find a word's phonological form within some critical period of time may trigger grammatical revisions (see Levelt and Maassen 1981 and section 7.5). As a first approximation, however, grammatical encoding can be treated as an autonomous process that takes messages as input and produces surface structures, unspecified for phonological form, as output.

5.1 Syntactic Aspects

5.1.1 Surface Structures as Expressions of Grammatical Functions
On a theory like Bresnan's (1982), grammatical functions such as "subject", "direct object", and "indirect object" are primitives and are the basis

of syntactic structures in all languages. But these grammatical functions are realized differently in the surface structures of languages. They are, broadly speaking, realized either by case or by word order. Take, for example, the message in figure 5.1, and how it can be grammatically encoded in English and in Malayalam, a language spoken in southern India (Mohanan 1982). The message is an event proposition. There is no mood indicator, so it has the default mood DECLARATIVE. Its time indicator is represented as a proposition modifier; it is PAST. The entities CHILD, CAT, and MOTHER are all token referents, represented in the discourse model, but their accessibility index is ignored for the present purpose.

In English, grammatical functions are largely expressed by word order and phrase order; they are assigned to positions in a phrase structure. The subject of a sentence, for instance, is the noun phrase (NP) directly dominated by the sentence node (S). In the English surface structure of the figure, the NP for *the child* is the only NP that branches directly from S, and hence *the child* is the subject of the sentence. Similarly, the indirect-object function is carried by the first NP in the verb phrase (VP), i.e., *the mother*. The direct-object function is assigned to the second NP in the verb phrase, *the cat*. In other words, the grammatical functions are expressed in the configurations of surface structure. Hence, languages such as English are called *configurational* languages (see Webelhuth 1985 for an excellent discussion of this notion).

In Malayalam, however, grammatical functions are expressed through case-marking morphology (Mohanan 1982). The subject NP, for instance, is marked by assigning nominative case to the head noun (*kutti*). The subject NP is not the only NP that is directly dominated by S (as was the case in English); the two object NPs are also. Moreover, the order of the NPs is irrelevant for the assignment of grammatical function. The subject NP need not be in first position. The order of the two object NPs is also immaterial; they are grammatically distinguished by dative and accusative case markers. Compare this with the English example, where the order of the two object NPs does matter; *the child gave the mother the cat* and *the child gave the cat the mother* mean different things. Malayalam is called a *nonconfigurational* language because grammatical functions are not encoded in phrase-structural configurations. Nonconfigurational languages have great freedom of word order, and their surface phrase structures tend to be "flat" (i.e., without much hierarchy).

These examples show that the target structures of grammatical encoding are highly language-dependent; a language may be more or less configuraa message:

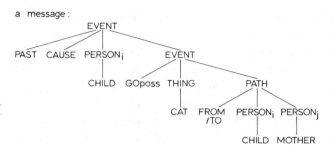

b english surface structure:

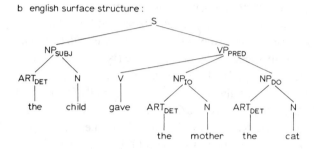

c malayalam surface structure:

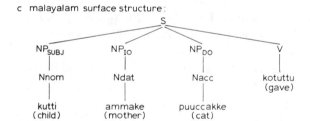

Figure 5.1

(a) A message. (b) Its expression in the surface structure of English, a configurational language. (c) Its expression in the surface structure of Malayalam, a nonconfigurational language.

tional, depending on how much grammatical function is encoded positionally and how much is encoded by morphological case marking. And many languages (such as German) encode certain functions both ways. The process of grammatical encoding, which generates these target structures, must be correspondingly language-dependent. It is a fascinating question how much, and along what dimensions, the psychological mechanisms of grammatical encoding can vary.

5.1.2 Surface Structures as Input to Phonological Encoding

A surface structure is not only the result of grammatical encoding; it is also the input for the subsequent phonological-encoding stage of the formulating process. It is not exceedingly clear how much phrase structure is needed for the accurate generation of segmental (lexical) and suprasegmental (prosodic) form information. Minimally, the following items are required:

• A string of pointers to form information in the lexicon for all content and function words in the sentence, in the correct grammatical order. Let us call these pointers *lexical pointers*. A lemma's lexical pointer indicates an address where the corresponding word-form information is stored. In figure 5.1 these lexical pointers are represented as words (*the, child*, etc). This is convenient as long as one is aware that these do not represent the word forms themselves, but only the addresses where they can be found.

• All diacritic features for each lexical pointer. The pointer to a form address may be indexed with various features that will affect the word form retrieved. We will call them *diacritic features*. The surface structure should indicate case, number, person, tense, aspect, definiteness, pitch accent, and whatever other features are to be morphologically or phonologically marked on the word form pointed to. Note that the inflections themselves are not yet specified; case, number, and so on are only abstract instructions for inflectional procedures to be run in the second phase. And the same holds for the pitch-accent feature. If a lemma is marked for pitch accent (for instance, because the corresponding concept is prominent), this will have various consequences for the subsequent phase of phonological encoding. It is generally recognized that semantically motivated pitch accent is a main determinant of sentence intonation and sentence rhythm (Bolinger 1972, 1983, 1986; Cutler and Isard 1980; Halliday 1967b; Ladd 1980; Schmerling 1976; Selkirk 1984a). We will return to the assignment of pitch accent in section 5.2.

• Phrasal information. This is, in the first place, important for the correct assignment of prosodic structure—particularly the allocation of sentence rhythm. Two utterances may involve the same string of words but different surface phrase structures. Compare, for instance, sentences 1 and 2, where major phrases are indicated by parentheses:

(1) (The widow) (discussed (the trouble)) (with her son)

(2) (The widow) (discussed (the trouble with her son))

A noncasual speaker pronounces such sentences differently (Levelt, Zwanenburg, and Ouweneel 1970; Wales and Toner 1980). There appears a slight rhythmic/melodic caesura after *trouble* in sentence 1, but not in sentence 2. Phonological encoding acknowledges such phrasal properties of surface structure. A sentence's rhythm reflects to some extent the grouping of words in surface structure. This phrasal information is certainly not the only determinant of rhythm or of intonation (pitch accent, for instance, is more important), but it does play a role, as we will see in chapters 8 and 10.

Further, phrasal information can be an important determinant of a word's pronunciation. A word's position in a phrase, for instance, can determine whether it will be phonologically reduced. A phrase-final preposition (as in *who were you thinking of?*) will not be as easily weakened as a non-phrase-final preposition (*a blade of* [əv] *grass*). These and many more examples can be found in Selkirk 1972. Like Selkirk, Kenstowicz and Kisseberth (1979) and Kaisse (1985) analyzed various other phrase-structural properties that may affect the final phonetic form of words in a sentence. These issues will be taken up in chapter 10.

So much can be said that, depending on the language, *some* phrase-structural information will be needed for the phonological encoding of a sentence. It is, however, unlikely that *all* such information is relevant for a speaker of a configurational language. The full phrase structure, with all its phrases categorized according to type (NP, VP, etc.), represents an upper limit. It is, however, still justifiable to consider linguistically fully specified surface structures as the hinging representations between the two stages of formulating, as long as one takes a procedural view. The generation of the minimally required information (listed above) will require procedural steps involving all the grammatical categories and phrasal relations represented in the "full" surface structure. They are essential *intermediary* results or outputs of grammatical encoding, as will become apparent in chapter 7.

5.1.3   Some Properties of Surface Phrase Structure

At least the following properties are essential ingredients of surface structure as far as a theory of the speaker is concerned:

(i) Surface structures are phrase structures; i.e., they can be represented as
hierarchical tree structures without crossing branches (such as in figures
5.1b and 5.1c). Phrases and subphrases (also called *constituents*) are represented in their correct left-to-right order (Levelt 1974, volume 2). The
terminal nodes of surface structures are of two sorts: lemmas with pointers
to form addresses in the lexicon (these pointers are indexed with diacritic
features), and empty elements, which have no lexical pointer but which do
carry a grammatical function. An example of the latter appears in the
sentence *the story is hard to explain (e) to Peter*, where (e) marks the
position of the empty element. Here the empty element is the direct object
of *explain*; it is, however, lexically expressed as the subject (*the story*) of the
main clause.

(ii) Surface structures represent categorial information for all nodes. This
involves, in the first place, four *major lexical categories*—noun (N), verb
(V), adjective (A), and preposition (P)—that can have the grammatical
function of head-of-phrase (see property iii below). In figure 5.1b, the
lexical item *child* in the English surface structure is of category N and
functions as head-of-phrase in the noun phrase (NP) *the child*. Similarly,
gave is of category V and functions as head of the verb phrase (VP). There
are also *minor lexical categories*, such as article (Art; e.g., *the*) and conjunction (Conj; e.g., *but*), which cannot be heads-of-phrase.

The phrases of which the major lexical categories N, V, A, and P can be
heads are, respectively, noun phrase (NP), adjective phrase (AP), verb
phrase (VP), and prepositional phrase (PP). These are called *phrasal categories* or *major constituents*. Examples in figure 5.1b are the NPs *the child*,
the mother, and *the cat* and the VP *gave the mother the cat*. In turn, these
phrasal categories can figure as heads of still more complex phrases, usually
indicated by NP′, AP′, VP′, and PP′. In the sentence *the child gave the
mother the cat on request*, the phrase *gave the mother the cat on request* is a
VP′, with the VP *gave the mother the cat* as head. Finally, there is the
phrasal category S, which may have as head a VP (or a VP′), as in English,
or a V, as in Malayalam and in many configurational languages, probably
including German and Dutch. When a language has a VP as head of S, the
head-of-phrase function is sometimes called "predicate" (PRED), and the
sentence is said to have a predicate as head-phrase.

The left-to-right order, mentioned under property i, is restricted by the syntactic category of the phrase. In chapter 7, we will consider phrasal categories as *procedures* or syntactic specialists that impose order on their parts.

It is not the case that every surface structure has S as a root. Almost any phrase can be an expressible surface structure. When the root is not S, the resulting utterance is said to be *elliptic*. So, *A church* as answer to the question *What did you see?* is elliptic. Its surface structure is of the category NP. We saw in chapter 3 that the underlying message is also elliptic; i.e., it is not a full proposition, but just an entity.

(iii) Surface structures represent functional information for all phrases except the root S. This functional information is of two kinds.

First, the surface structure indicates the *head-of-phrase function* for each phrase. The main head-of-phrase functions were specified under property ii. They assign a unique head to each constituent. What does it mean to be head-of-phrase? The notion was developed (see, especially, Jackendoff 1977) to account for the fact that one element in the phrase imposes some of its features on the phrase as a whole. For instance, if the head noun of a noun phrase is plural, then the whole noun phrase is plural; i.e., if *houses* is plural, then *the red houses* is also plural. This does not hold for the non-head elements. The noun phrase *the kings' crown* is singular in spite of the plurality of *kings*, because the head noun, *crown*, is singular. Similar relations between head and phrase exist for such features as gender, person, definiteness, and case. The head-of-phrase relation is also important in the generation of sentences. In chapter 7 we will see that the head-of-phrase can call the procedure for building the whole phrase around it.

Since for each phrase it is uniquely determined what the head-of-phrase is, it is usually not explicitly marked in our graphic representations of surface structure. In figure 5.1b, this would have amounted to adding the subscript "Head" to V, the two N's, and VP. The head carries the grammatical function of the phrase as a whole. So when a noun phrase is subject of the sentence, thus carrying a particular case (nominative or ergative), then the head noun will carry the same case. Still, a particular grammatical function, such as subject, may be distributed over different phrases. This is especially apparent in nonconfigurational languages. Their free word order allows for discontinuous expressions. If a subject of a sentence is an adjective-noun pair, the two elements may be far apart in surface structure, and even be interwoven with the adjective and noun of the object, roughly as in *Elephant mouse big small kill*. In Warlpiri, an Australian noncon-figurational language studied by Hale (1981), the two parts of the subject will both get one type of case morphology (ergative case), and the two object parts will both be in another type of case (called "absolutive"). A discontinuous expression doesn't have a unique head, but each of its continuous phrasal parts has one, and all of them are assigned the same grammatical function by means of case morphology, thus marking their functional togetherness.

Second, phrases are labeled with respect to their *grammatical functions*, if any. Examples in figure 5.1 are subject (SUBJ), predicate (PRED), two kinds of object (IO and DO for indirect and direct object, respectively), and determiner (DET). Apart from these grammatical functions, there can be obliques (OBL), such as the NP following *by* in passive sentences (*the child* in *the cat was given by the child*), and verbal complements (V-COMP), such as *steal the money* in the sentence *Grabber tried to steal the money*. These grammatical functions originate from specifications in the lemmas of verbs, nouns, adjectives, and prepositions; this will be taken up in the next chapter.

Heads-of-phrase are said to *subcategorize* other elements in the phrase. The verb *give* in figures 5.1b and 5.1c, for instance, can take three NPs, which express the conceptual arguments of giving: the one who gives, the object given, and the one who receives. These arguments are encoded as subject, direct object, and indirect object, respectively. Of these, only the last two appear in the verb phrase of which *give* is the head; they are the ones subcategorized by the verb. "Subject" is called an *external argument* of the verb.

Phrases can also have grammatical functions that do not express a conceptual argument of the head but rather express some *modification*. This is mostly the case for adjectives (A) or adjective phrases (AP), which modify an N or NP. In *the little child*, *little* has a modifying function; it is not an argument of *child*. But other phrases can also carry modifying functions. In *the child gave the mother the cat on request*, the prepositional phrase *on request* is such a modifying adjunct. Unlike the direct-object and indirect-object phrases (*the cat* and *the mother*), which *are* subcategorized by *give*, the oblique prepositional phrase *on request* is attached to the VP'-node in the surface structure, not to the VP of which *give* is the head. Modifier phrases generally attach one level up in the phrase struc-ture. Both subcategorized and modifier (or adjunct) phrases are called *complements*.

Finally, certain elements in the surface structure are *specifiers*. The NPs *the child*, *the mother*, and *the cat* all contain the article (*the*) which has the specifier function of determiner (DET). A determiner can, among other things, express definiteness or indefiniteness. There are also specifiers for number (NUM), as in *two children*, and for degree (DEG) (e.g., *very* in the AP *very large*), and there are other types of specifier. The category is rather heterogeneous and will not be elaborated here.

In summary: From the viewpoint of grammatical function, each constituent consists of at most four types of elements: the head, the complements that are subcategorized by the head and which express its conceptual arguments (if any), complements which express modifications (if any), and specifiers (if any). As a notational convention, these functions will be labeled as subscripts to the category name of the phrase, except for the function of head. Moreover, it is often convenient to leave out most or all of the function labels as long as no ambiguity arises.

(iv) The lowest-level or terminal nodes in a surface structure are (if not empty elements) lemmas with their lexical pointers indexed for diacritic features (as discussed in the first two items at the beginning of subsection 5.1.2).

This suffices as a specification of the syntactic aspects of surface structure. More extensive treatments can be found in Bresnan 1982, Gazdar et al. 1985, Jackendoff 1977, and Levelt 1974. The above notions will all return in chapter 7 when we deal with the speaker's generation of surface structure.

5.2 Prosodic Aspects

A surface structure has no prosody, but it does contain the information required in subsequent phases for the generation of prosodic patterns that will do justice to the speaker's intentions. In particular, the surface structure must contain specifications of *mood* and *focus*. Let us consider these in turn.

5.2.1 Mood and Modality

The preverbal message includes a marker for the intended mood of the utterance: declarative, interrogative, or imperative (see subsection 3.5.1). The intended mood has, of course, syntactic consequences in sentence generation. The messages DECL(PAST(LEAVE(JOHN))) and ?(PAST (LEAVE(JOHN))) lead to the generation of different surface structures, namely those for the sentences *John left* and *Did John leave?*, respectively. The mood marker in a message will, like the temporal markers, lead to a feature of the tensed verb in surface structure. This, in turn, selects for a particular syntactic structure.

But there is an additional consequence of the mood marker: It will co-determine the melody of the sentence. There may, in fact, be a neutral or default way of intonating a declarative sentence in a language, and similarly for an imperative or an interrogative sentence. These default intonations are then largely realized in the sentence-final *boundary tone*—a falling tone for declarative and imperative moods, a rising tone for interrogative mood. If this is so, and the surface structure is the hinging representation between grammatical and phonological encoding, the surface structure should, for each of the three moods, contain some cue by which the Phonological Encoder can know what tone to select. Still, there is reason to be quite careful with such generalizations. It was mentioned in subsection 3.5.1 that a speaker's presuppositions and attitudes can, in complex ways, interact with what one would optimistically take to be "standard" tones for the major sentence moods. Whether there are such default tones is, honestly, an open issue. It seems, therefore, premature to specify how they are indicated in surface structure.

The situation is even less clear for the other modalities and attitudes a speaker can express in the prosody of his utterance. This issue is nicely treated by Cutler and Isard (1980), who show that proposals to the effect that a speaker has an "intonational lexicon" in which each contour has its own specific expressive meaning are untenable. One and the same contour can express very different speaker moods (such as surprise and indignation), and different contours can express the same emotional attitude of the speaker. These intonation "meanings" are highly context-dependent. We will return to them in chapter 8. Here it suffices to say that, eventually, intonational specifications for mood and modality may have to be introduced in surface-structure representations. But it remains to be seen how this should be done.

5.2.2 Prosodic Focus

The second message ingredient that will affect the prosody of an utterance is prominence. Subsection 4.5.2 mentioned three grounds for an entity to become prominent in the message: being newly introduced into the discourse model as a referent, contrasting in a focused role with a previously mentioned entity, or involving a new predication. These three grounds have in common that the entity has "news value" for the addressee. The present subsection discusses how prominence becomes expressed in surface structure. Though one should not exclude the possibility that prominence is expressed differently in these three cases (Cutler and Isard 1980 presents evidence for a speaker's special treatment of contrastive prominence), we will ignore this for the present purposes.

Prominence, then, becomes expressed in surface structure through what is called *prosodic focus*. This is not to be confused with focus in the discourse record (the speaker's attentional "pointer"). There is some relation, of course; what is in the speaker's new focus will often be new information for the addressee and therefore be given prominence by the speaker. That prominence, in turn, results in prosodic focus. Where there can be no confusion in the discussion of prosodic focus, we will talk of just "focus."

Syntactic phrases that correspond to prominent parts of the message will be marked for focus; we will designate this by putting an f before the syntactic-category symbol in the surface structure. But when a syntactic phrase receives a focus marker, at least one of its constituent phrases will also be marked for focus, and so all the way down to the level of lemmas. Let us, by way of example, return to Seth and Marcia's ongoing conversation. At some point Marcia answers a question by Seth with the following utterance:

(3) I saw a chUrch.

What question was this an answer to? There are at least three different questions to which this could have been a natural-sounding reply:

(4) Did you see a palace?

(5) What did you see?

(6) What did you do?

In example 4 there is contrastive prominence; the concept CHURCH carries the news value by contrast to PALACE. Hence the noun *church* is given focus in surface structure. In example 5 it is the *theme* argument of SEE that is prominent in the message. This is expressed as a focus on the whole corresponding NP in surface structure: *the church*. In example 6, the whole ACTION was at issue (i.e., to go and see a church). Since the ACTION is mapped onto the surface VP, the whole VP *saw the church* is assigned focus. These three states of affairs can be represented as follows in terms of surface structure (trimmed of functional and other details which are irrelevant for the present discussion):

(i)

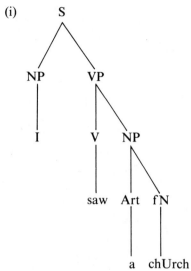

(ii)

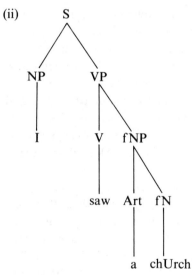

(iii)

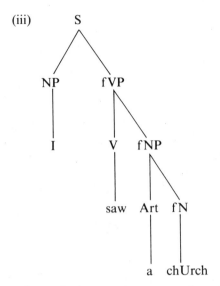

In producing a sentence, a speaker will somehow have to realize the focus information as a pattern of *pitch accents*. Pitch accent is a prosodic parameter assigned to certain lemmas in the surface tree. All three surface trees above have pitch accent assigned to the lemma for *church*. As a notational convention, a lemma that carries pitch accent in surface structure will be printed with the accented vowel capitalized. It cannot be emphasized enough, however, that pitch accent is an *abstract parameter* of a lemma; the surface structure does not contain word-form information. When the lemma carries pitch accent, this means that the lemma's lexical pointer has a diacritic feature for pitch accent.

The way in which speakers "compute" the pattern of pitch accents will be taken up in chapter 7. Here I will only present some regularities that seem to govern the patterns of focus and pitch accents in surface structures. The presentation will largely follow Selkirk 1984a. The major issue is how the prominence of some message fragment becomes represented in the surface structure a speaker generates, and how it is handed down to the level of lemmas. The main rule seems to be the following.

Phrasal-Focus Rule

The prominence of a concept in the message is expressed by assigning focus to the surface-structure phrase representing it. In a focused phrase, either the head or any of the complements that express conceptual arguments of the head should be focused.

This rule guarantees, as will be discussed, that eventually there will always be some lemma that receives focus when a higher-level phrase is focused. What happens to the lemma is given in the next rule.

Pitch-Accent Rule
A focused lemma receives pitch accent.

There is a subsidiary rule that distinguishes between heads of phrases and conceptual arguments of the head:

Focus-Interpretation Rule
Focus can be assigned to an argument only if that argument expresses a prominent concept in the message, but it can be assigned to the head irrespective of whether it represents a prominent concept.

These rules are fairly abstract, so let us consider how they work in practice by considering some examples. Examples 4–6 above are a good start.

When Seth asked *Did you see a palace?*, Marcia had to introduce *church* in a contrasting role; her having seen something indefinite was presupposed in the discourse. So Marcia gave prominence to the concept CHURCH in her message, and to nothing else. By the Phrasal-Focus Rule, the noun representing the concept was assigned focus; since the noun is a lemma, the focus was expressed as pitch accent (chUrch in diagram i) through the pitch-accent rule. Nothing else was given focus or pitch accent.

In example 5, Seth asked *What did you see?* The question carries the presupposition that something had been seen, and Marcia introduced the *theme* of her seeing (some church) in the discourse model by making it prominent in the message, and she made nothing else prominent. The theme in the message was mapped onto the object NP in the surface structure, and the NP was assigned focus in accordance with the Phrasal-Focus Rule. The NP contains no arguments, only a head and a specifier, so the same Phrasal-Focus Rule requires focus to be assigned to the head noun. The head noun is a lemma, and by the Pitch-Accent Rule it is given pitch accent (chUrch).

Example 6 is somewhat more complicated. Seth asked *What did you do?*, presupposing that some ACTION on the part of Marcia had taken place. Marcia's task was now to introduce her ACTION into the discourse. Since it was still absent from the discourse model, Marcia gave the ACTION prominence in the message. The ACTION got represented as a VP in surface structure, which received focus by the Phrasal-Focus Rule. The Phrasal-Focus Rule now requires the head or one of its subcategorized complements to receive focus—either the V (*saw*), or its object NP (*a church*), or both. It does not specify which. Marcia opted for the NP (why she did so will be discussed shortly). From here on, the story proceeds as in example 5, leading to pitch accent for the head noun (chUrch).

Why did the NP get focused? The Focus-Interpretation Rule allows focusing of NP only in cases where it expresses a concept that is prominent in the message. Apparently, Marcia had marked not only the ACTION as prominent in her message, but also the *theme* argument (CHURCH). The Phrasal-Focus Rule required the NP expressing the prominent theme to be focused anyhow; the NP was thus focused for independent reasons. But, this being the case, the condition of the Phrasal-Focus Rule with respect to the VP was already fulfilled; there was a focused argument, and nothing more was required. There is an additional reason why *church* will become more stressed than *saw*: It receives *nuclear stress*, which will be discussed at the end of this subsection.

Would it ever be possible for the head verb, but none of its complements, to become focused when the ACTION is prominent in the message? Ladd (1980) and Selkirk (1984a) argue that this can happen, and provide various examples. In our discussion between Seth and Marcia, the following exchange might arise:

(7) Seth: Did you have a chance to see the Saint Peter?
    Marcia: I sAw the church.

Neither the seeing nor its conceptual argument (*the Saint Peter*) was newly introduced in the discourse by Marcia. She could figure that both were in Seth's focus of attention. This is apparent not only from the fact that *the church* is an anaphor for *the Saint Peter* but also from the fact that Marcia could even have answered *Yes, I did*, which would have involved a reduction of both function and argument. Still, sAw was given pitch accent. Marcia made the ACTION prominent in her message for the purpose of confirmation, which was the new information asked for by Seth. The Focus-Interpretation Rule now excluded the possibility of giving prosodic focus to the complement NP *the church*, since it was not prominent in the message. More generally, an anaphor—a substitute for an expression used earlier (as *church* is for *Saint Peter*)—will, as a rule, be deaccented. This tells the listener that the referent is at hand. The only case where an anaphor can become focused in surface structure is when the referent is marked for contrastive prominence in the message. An instance of this kind was discussed in subsection 4.5.2: *Tessie went after SImon, and then hE chased hEr*. But the head V (*saw*) in the present example could receive focus, and thus pitch accent, in spite of the fact that it represents a nonprominent part of the message. This follows from the Focus-Interpretation Rule. Selkirk calls this "default accent." The resulting surface focus structure is shown in diagram iv.

(iv)

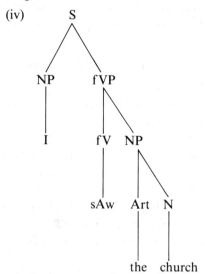

Notice that this differs essentially from the situation where *saw* receives contrastive accent. That would have happened in the following exchange:

(8) Seth: Did you PAINT the Saint Peter?
    Marcia: No, I only SAW the church.

The focus structure here is as in diagram v, with "narrow" focus on the verb only.

(v)

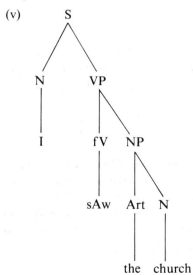

The possibility of default pitch accent on the head-of-phrase exists not only for verb phrases but also for the other three main phrasal categories. In example 9, there is default accent on the prepositional head of a PP. (The acceptability of this example depends to some degree on the dialect of English one speaks.)

(9) Shopkeeper: Did you manage to deliver the wine to Mr. PEters?
       Assistant: Yes sir, I got it tO him.

Here, the preposition is in no way contrastive, and the assistant can assume that Mr. Peters is in the shopkeeper's center of attention. Thus, neither the *direction* nor the *goal* is prominent in the assistant's message. What *is* made prominent, for reasons of confirmation, is the PATH, which is mapped onto the PP (*tO him*). Notice that the same PATH was also the prominent part of the shopkeeper's question, but there Mr. Peters was also prominent for an independent reason: He was being newly introduced into the discourse. Thus, it was possible for the shopkeeper to realize the PP focus by focusing its NP complement (*Mr. PEters*), according to the Phrasal-Focus Rule.

Before we leave the issue of focus assignment, a word should be said about the role of modifiers. The Phrasal-Focus Rule mentions the conceptual arguments of the head, but not its modifiers. Can a constituent be focused by focusing a modifier complement or a specifier? Is it indeed necessary that the complement represent a conceptual *argument?* Probably so. Focusing a modifier or a specifier tends to involve narrow focus only, as is clearly the case in a deviant case such as the following one.

(10) Seth: What did you see today?
        Marcia: I saw an Old church.

The adjective *Old* cannot carry the focus of the NP (*an old church*); it can only be contrastive to another adjective (such as *new*) in previous discourse. Here is an example in which the temporal adverbial cannot carry the focus for the verb phrase as a whole:

(11) Seth: What did you do?
        Marcia: I visited the church todAY.

This is by no means a full account of how prominence in the message is grammatically encoded in surface structure. The essential point, however, is that focus and (in its wake) pitch accent are conditioned by the prominence structure of the message, i.e., of its functions, arguments, and modifiers. There are no independent syntactic reasons for the assignment of pitch accent; syntax has only a mediating role.

The assignment of focus should not be confused with the assignment of nuclear stress. It is a general rule of English that, in any major phrase, one word receives more stress than any of the others. This word is the rightmost non-anaphoric word of the rightmost constituent in the phrase. When a speaker opens a conversation by saying

(12) Peter's father had a terrible accident

father will normally receive more stress in the NP *Peter's father* than *Peter's*, because *father* is the rightmost constituent of the noun phrase. Similarly, *accident* will be most stressed in the NP *a terrible accident*. In the VP *had a terrible accident* the word *accident* will be most stressed, because it is the most stressed word in the VP's rightmost constituent, namely the NP. In the sentence as a whole, *accident* will be the most stressed word, because it is the most stressed word in the rightmost constituent of the sentence, the VP (see also subsection 10.2.2).

When Marcia answered Seth's question *What did you do today?* with *I saw a church*, the Phrasal-Focus Rule allowed for the focusing of both *saw* and *church*. If Marcia had focused both, *church* would still have become more accented than *saw*, owing to the assignment of nuclear stress. We will return to these issues in chapters 8 and 10.

The treatment of focus in this section was based largely on facts of English. It should be kept in mind that rules can be rather different for other languages. (See Bierwisch 1965 for a classical analysis of the rule system for intonation in German.)

Summary

This chapter discussed the representation mediating between grammatical encoding and phonological encoding. It was called "surface structure." The processes of grammatical encoding project the concepts and their relations in the preverbal message onto a phrase-structural organization of lemmas and grammatical relations.

The first section reviewed various syntactic aspects of this organization and their relevance for phonological encoding. The way in which surface structures represent grammatical relations ranges between two extremes in the languages of the world. Configurational languages express grammatical functions in the hierarchical and left-to-right organization of surface constituents. Nonconfigurational languages use case marking on words to express grammatical functions; word order is less relevant. Phrase structure and inflectional features are important for phonological encoding. The lemmas in a surface structure point to addresses where the corresponding word-form information is stored. These pointers are indexed for the inflections the word stem should undergo. The way in which a word becomes articulated also depends on its position in the phrase, and on other properties of the phrase structure. The phrase structure is, in particular, relevant for the generation of sentence rhythm and melody.

The constituents of a surface structure are of different syntactic categories and fulfill different grammatical functions. The major phrasal categories are Sentence, Noun Phrase, Verb Phrase, Prepositional Phrase, and Adjective Phrase. Each of these phrases has a head. In English the head of a sentence is the VP; it fulfills the function of predicate. The other heads are Noun, Verb, Preposition, and Adjective; they may be subcategorized within the same phrase for complements, such as the objects of verbs or prepositions, and they may have modifiers and specifiers. Heads play an important role in the generation of sentences. A head can call the syntactic procedures that will build its characteristic phrase around it, assigning the correct grammatical functions to its complements within the phrase.

The second section reviewed the way in which the surface structure embodies instructions for the generation of sentence prosody. This is done by means of indicators for mood and modality, and by focus markers. How mood and modality are indicated in surface structure is not well known; we suppose that such indicators are recognized by the Phonological Encoder, which generates the appropriate pattern of intonation (in particular, the characteristic boundary tones).

Focus is, initially, assigned to each syntactic constituent that expresses a prominent concept in the preverbal message. These focus markers will "percolate down" to the lemma level. In the end, each focused constituent contains at least one focused lemma. The lexical pointer of that lemma will be indexed for pitch accent; the word will be pronounced in a prosodically prominent way. The prosody of an utterance, finally, depends on the phrasal organization of its surface structure. The assignment of nuclear stress was given as an example.

Chapter 6
Lexical Entries and Accessing Lemmas

A main thesis of this and the following chapters will be that formulation processes are lexically driven. This means that grammatical and phonological encoding are mediated by lexical entries. The preverbal message triggers lexical items into activity. The syntactic, morphological, and phonological properties of an activated lexical item trigger, in turn, the grammatical, morphological, and phonological encoding procedures underlying the generation of an utterance. The assumption that the lexicon is an essential mediator between conceptualization and grammatical and phonological encoding will be called the *lexical hypothesis*. The lexical hypothesis entails, in particular, that nothing in the speaker's message will *by itself* trigger a particular syntactic form, such as a passive or a dative construction. There must always be mediating lexical items, triggered by the message, which by their grammatical properties and their order of activation cause the Grammatical Encoder to generate a particular syntactic structure.

The crucial role of the mental lexicon in the generation of speech makes it necessary to consider in some detail the internal structure and organization of entries in the mental lexicon. This is done in the first two sections of this chapter. Section 6.1 deals with the structure of lexical entries and their mutual relations. Section 6.2 analyses in more detail the aspect of lexical entries that we called "lemmas" in chapter 1. After these more structural sections we will turn to issues of processing. Section 6.3 reviews some major theories of lemma access in speech. This theoretical section is followed by two more empirical ones. Section 6.4 addresses accessing failures, their taxonomy and their potential causes. The time course of accessing lexical items is the subject of section 6.5.

6.1 The Structure and Organization of Entries in the Mental Lexicon

6.1.1 The Internal Structure of a Lexical Entry

A speaker's mental lexicon is a repository of declarative knowledge about the words of his language. From the point of view of language production, each item in the lexicon is a listing of at least four kinds of features. There is, first, a specification of the item's *meaning*. This is the set of conceptual conditions that must be fulfilled in the message for the item to become selected. For the entry *eat*, the meaning is something like "to ingest for nourishment or pleasure". Second, there is a set of syntactic properties, including the category of the entry (V for *eat*), the syntactic arguments it can take (an external subject and an internal object for *eat*; i.e., the verb is transitive), and other properties. Certain items in the lexicon are activated during grammatical encoding by the fulfillment of their syntactic conditions. There is, third, a morphological specification of the item. For *eat* this is, among other things, that it is a root form (i.e., it is not further analyzable into constituent morphemes), that its third-person present-tense inflection is *eats*, and that its past-tense inflection is *ate*. Fourth, there is a form specification—in particular, the item's composition in terms of phonological segments, its syllable and accent structure. For *eat*, the segment structure is a monosyllabic vowel/consonant sequence, with /i/ as vowel and /t/ as consonant. (See figure 6.1.)

There are, moreover, internal relations among these four kinds of information. In particular, there are systematic relations among the morphology of an item, its meaning, and its syntax. Take, for instance, the word *painter*. Its meaning relates to its morphology *paint-er*, the *er* affix

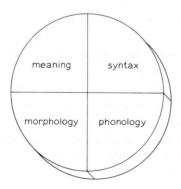

Figure 6.1
Internal structure of an item in the mental lexicon.

expressing the agentive of the action expressed by the verb stem—"one who paints." The *er* affix is, moreover, related to the syntactic category N, and so forth.

There are, probably, additional properties stored with an item. It may have particular pragmatic, stylistic, and affective features that make it fit one context of discourse better than another. The item *policeman* fits better in formal discourse than the item *cop*, which is otherwise very similar in meaning. Certain so-called *registers* (talk to babies, talk between lovers, etc.) seem to select for lexical items with particular connotational properties. Whether such features should be considered as conceptual conditions on the item's use is a matter of much dispute; we will not go into it.

6.1.2 Relations between Items in the Mental Lexicon

Entries in the lexicon are not islands; the lexicon has an internal structure. Items are connected or related in various ways. Let us explore some such relations that are relevant to language production. There are item relations *within* and *between* entries.

Not all lexical items are lexical entries. The various inflections of a verb (e.g., *eat, eats, ate, eaten, eating*) are items belonging to the same lexical entry. They are related *within* an entry. The diacritic features for person, number, tense, mood, and aspect will take care of selecting the right item within the lexical entry. We assume that this is generally the case for inflections. Hence, the items *dog* and *dogs* are to be found under the same lexical entry or address, and similarly for *man* and *men*, for *he, him,* and *his,* for *big, bigger,* and *biggest* (we take comparatives to be inflections), and so forth. But it is not the case for derivations; *act, action, active, activity,* etc. are different lexical entries (Butterworth 1983a).

The relations *between* lexical entries in the mental lexicon are of two kinds: intrinsic and associative. The intrinsic relations derive from the four kinds of features listed for an entry. Items may connect in the mental lexicon because they share certain features. Let us consider each of the four kinds of feature. First, items may have special connections on the basis of meaning. There is evidence in the literature that such connections exist between a word and its hypernym (e.g., between *dog* and *animal,* or between *green* and *color*), between a word and a co-hyponym (e.g., *dog* and *cat,* or *green* and *blue*), between a word and a near-synonym (e.g., *close* and *near*), and so on (Noordman-Vonk 1979; Smith and Medin 1981). Sets of meaning-related items are called *semantic fields*. There is a semantic field of color names, one of kinship terms, and so on (see Miller 1978 for a concise review of this notion). Sometimes speech errors reveal such connections;

for instance, *Irvine is quite clear* involves a blend of *close* and *near* (Fromkin 1973). Second, morphologically determined connections may hold between entries with the same morphological stem. Such entries are said to be *derivationally related*, such as *nation, national* and *nationalize*, or *likely* and *unlikely*. Not surprisingly, there are almost always meaning relations involved as well in these cases. There are, third, clear phonological connections between entries in the mental lexicon. Words with the same initial or final speech sounds show connections in speech production, sometimes leading to characteristic errors such as *open* for *over* or *week* for *work* (Fay and Cutler 1977). This suggests (but doesn't prove) that phonologically similar items are, in some way or another, connected in the mental lexicon (other evidence will be discussed in chapter 8). Finally, there is, as yet, no convincing experimental evidence for syntactically conditioned relations between lexical items in the mental lexicon. Are all nouns mutually connected, or all transitive verbs? Surely each such class plays characteristic roles in the generation of speech. This can be dramatically apparent in neurological cases; there are amnesic disorders in which the whole class of nouns has become virtually inaccessible in production. But this does not imply that their members have special mutual connections in the mental lexicon.

The nature of intrinsic relations is an issue in itself. There may be *direct* connections between lexical items, or the relations can be *mediated*. A direct semantic relation, for instance, would be one in which all cohyponyms of an item were listed with the item. The entry for *green* would contain a listing of co-hyponym addresses—the ones for *blue, red,* and so forth. A mediated semantic relation would be one where there is a relation between the *concepts* GREEN and BLUE, but without mutual reference at the level of the lexical entries *green* and *blue*. This distinction is important for the analysis of lexical intrusions in section 6.4. Intrinsic connections are not a *necessary* consequence of feature sharing between lexical entries. Entries connect on the basis of shared word-initial consonants, but a shared first-syllable-final consonant is probably irrelevant.

Associative relations between entries have no necessary basis in their semantic properties; rather, the basis lies in the frequent co-occurrence of the items in language use. *War* and *death* and *truth* and *beauty* are two cases in point. Though these connections are initially mediated by complex conceptual relations, they have become direct associations between lexical items. When the one item is used, the other one will be primed, even when the original conceptual connection is not at issue in the ongoing discourse. It is to be expected that some intrinsic-meaning relations will also develop into strong associative relations, because meaning-related items tend to co-occur in discourse. Antonyms such as *left* and *right* and *big* and *small* are cases in point. (See H. Clark 1970 for a semantic analysis of associative relations.)

6.1.3   Retrieving versus Constructing Words

The mental lexicon is, we assume, a passive store of declarative knowledge about words. It does not contain procedural knowledge, which makes possible the generation of new words. Do speakers generate new words when they speak? The answer is probably Yes for all languages, but the degree of spontaneous new-word formation during normal speech varies drastically between languages.

English is at one extreme of the distribution. English speakers seldom produce words they have never used before. An extreme case cited by Bauer (1983) occurred in the spontaneous utterance *I feel particularly sit-around-and-do-nothing-ish today*. Less extravagant cases are new constructions with *-ful* (such as *bucketful*) or *un-* (such as *unnarrow* or *unobscure*), and new compounds (such as *my lecture-tie*). For English one of the most productive cases is number names, as Miller (1978) observed. Their unlimited amount makes storage in the mental lexicon impossible (we probably have no lexical entry for a number such as 4,257). Still, the use of such new formations is exceptional in everyday language. By and large, English speakers use words that they have frequently used before, and these words are probably stored in the mental lexicon. The other extreme occurs in speakers of certain agglutinative languages, such as Turkish and Finnish. In these languages, words consist of strings of morphemes—a root plus affixes, each adding to the meaning of the word. These strings can become very long—perhaps *arbitrarily* long, as Hankamer (forthcoming) argues for Turkish. In Turkish, the root morpheme for *house* is *ev*. Adding *ler* makes it plural (*ev-ler*), adding *den* creates a word meaning "from the houses" (*ev-ler-den*), and so on. The word for "to the ones of those that are in our pockets" is *ceb-lar-lmlz-da-ki-kar-nln-ki-n-ya*. Hankamer computes that, even if one ignores the existing possibility for affixes to recur in a string, a single Turkish noun can appear in more than 4 million different forms. It is obvious that most of these forms are never used by a Turkish speaker; they are not stored forms in his mental lexicon. But they will be recognized as possible words, and they will be interpreted correctly. This situation is quite comparable to the case of number names for an English speaker. However, for the Turkish speaker this is the normal case rather than the exception. The stored forms in his mental lexicon will probably consist of all stems (such as *ev* for "house"), all possible affixes, and a certain number of frequently used multimorphemic words. In order to use this "passive" store productively, the Turkish speaker must have access to *lexical procedural knowledge*—ways of building new words, given the conceptualizations in the preverbal message. In other words, such a speaker must have a strongly developed processing component dedicated to *lexical encoding*, which produces new words as output.

The conclusions to be drawn from this comparison are that speakers can produce more words than just the ones stored in their mental lexicon and that they have the capacity to construct new words while they are speaking. But languages differ enormously in the degree to which they exploit these word-constructional capabilities. While a Turkish speaker's grammatical encoding consists for the most part of such lexical encoding, an English speaker is extremely "conservative" in the sense that he normally uses words he has used often in the past. For the English speaker, lexical encoding plays a very minor role in grammatical encoding; the action is in syntactic encoding. A theory of the speaker should, of course, encompass both kinds of grammatical encoding. As a matter of fact, however, almost nothing is known about the psychology of lexical encoding. Of necessity the rest of this chapter, as well as chapter 9, will deal with lexical access in the sense of retrieving items stored in the mental lexicon, and these items are all *words* (but see subsection 6.1.4). This does not preclude the possibility that these word items have strong morphemic relations to one another; see Butterworth 1983a and Cutler 1983a for reviews of the evidence.

Little attention will be given to word-constructional processes. This is not a dramatic restriction of my discussion as far as speakers of English or Chinese are concerned, but it will underexpose theoretical issues in the production of Turkish or Japanese, where lexical items are often morphemes, not words.

6.1.4   Phrases and Idioms

Speakers have, over and above a stock of words, stocks of phrases and idioms. Certain concepts map directly onto phrases, such as *Dutch uncle* or *red tape*. That these are phrases, not compound words, is apparent from their stress patterns; they do not have compound-word stress, as do *blAckbird* and *hOt dog*. But they are special in that their meaning is opaque; it does not—as in the case of syntactic phrases—derive from the meanings of their parts. The difference between *red tape* and *green tape* is not in their color, as is the difference between *red apple* and *green apple*. They have *idiomatic* meanings. Such idiomatic phrases also have restricted syntactic possibilities. It is all right to pluralize *hot dog* to *hot dogs*, but it is less good to use it in the comparative degree (*I have a hotter dog than you*). Or take an idiomatic expression like *to kick the bucket*. It has, like the earlier examples, no transparent meaning. It also has rather restricted syntactic possibilities. One can say *he has kicked the bucket*, but one cannot very well say *he is kicking the bucket* (although one can say *he is dying*). Also impossible are constructions such as *the bucket was kicked by John* and *it was the bucket that John kicked*.

There is an extensive linguistic literature on these issues (see e.g. Makkai 1972 and Cruse 1986), but not much is known about the speaker's generation of idioms. We will assume that idiomatic collocations are entries in the mental lexicon. Each entry consists of one or more items. The entry for *kick the bucket* contains items for infinitive and for past tense, but none for progressive. The entry for *red tape* contains the singular and plural item, but no comparative one. Idioms, like words, have their characteristic conceptual conditions. If such a condition is met in the message, the idiom will be accessed.

6.1.5 Lexical Entries, Lemmas, and Morpho-Phonological Forms

The processes of grammatical encoding are, to a first approximation, independent of the phonological information in lexical entries. In addition, for languages without much lexical encoding, a word's morphological composition is, on first approximation, irrelevant for grammatical encoding. Only a lexical entry's meaning and syntax are relevant. There is now a tradition of following the terminology introduced by Kempen and Huijbers (1983) and calling this part of an entry's composition a *lemma*. The entry's morphological makeup and its phonological properties, on the other hand, are essential for phonological encoding; the entry's lemma is, by and large, irrelevant at that stage of processing. Hence, from the viewpoint of language production a lexical entry can be split up into two parts: its lemma and its form information (figure 6.2). This theoretical distinction can be extended to the mental lexicon as a whole: Lemmas can be said to be "in the lemma lexicon," and morpho-phonological forms to be "in the form lexicon." Each lemma "points" to its corresponding form; i.e., it can refer to the address in the form lexicon where the information for that item is stored. This was discussed in subsection 5.1.2.

The partitioning of the mental lexicon in two kinds of store is no more than a spatial metaphor acknowledging the existence of two kinds of

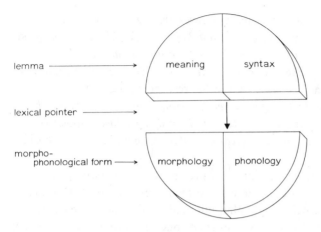

Figure 6.2
A lexical entry consisting of a lemma and a morpho-phonological form. (After
Levelt and Schriefers 1987.)

internal organization in the mental lexicon: one according to the meaning
of items and one according to their form properties. These two rather
independent kinds of organization appear in various production phenomena, such as speech errors and tip-of-the-tongue phenomena (which
we will consider in subsequent chapters). The distinction should, however,
not be overstated. In particular, we should not conclude that a lexical entry
cannot be retrieved as a whole—i.e., that retrieval of the lemma must
always precede retrieval of the item's form. This is still an open issue (see
subsection 6.5.4).

6.2   The Structure of Lemmas

6.2.1   Semantic and Syntactic Properties
The *semantic* information in a lemma specifies what conceptual conditions
have to be fulfilled in the message for the lemma to become activated; it is
the lemma's *meaning*. These conditions can be stated in the same propositional format as messages. Let us consider as an example the conceptual
specification for the verb *give* as it appears in the sentence *the child gave the
mother the cat*. The message structure underlying that sentence was represented in figure 5.1a.

   The conceptual specification for *give* is something like the following.

• Conceptual specification:

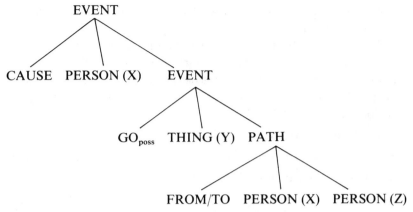

This conceptual specification involves three variables: X, a PERSON, which is both the agent of the causative EVENT and the source of the PATH; Y, a THING, which is the theme, and Z, a PERSON, which is the goal of the PATH. This can be viewed as a conceptual "template" to be matched with substructures of the message. It is irrelevant in what way the variables X, Y, and Z are bound in the message. But the fact that the conceptual specification *has* these three slots for conceptual arguments will turn out to be important. They are the three variables in the conceptual structure to which grammatical functions can be assigned. This must be explicitly stated for the lemma.

• Arguments of the conceptual function: (X, Y, Z).

These arguments fulfill certain thematic roles in the message; they depend on the functions CAUSE, GOposs, and PATH. As we will shortly see, some important grammatical generalizations about lemmas can be expressed in terms of thematic roles.

It is, moreover, important that the three arguments are of the conceptual categories PERSON, THING, and PERSON, respectively. These are called *selectional restrictions* on the use of *give*.*

The message of figure 5.1 binds the conceptual variables as CHILD, CAT, and MOTHER. (We are assuming that an animal is a special kind of THING.) When there is a match between conceptual specification and message (and in this case there is), the lemma is retrieved, which means that

---

*The selectional restrictions PERSON, THING, and PERSON may, in fact, be too restrictive for *give*. Take for instance the use of *give* in the sentence *The bright lights gave Santa's arrival a colorful appearance*. Selectional restrictions on the kinds of entities that can fill argument slots in the conceptual specification of a lemma are often very hard to define. We will ignore the issue entirely, but see Bresnan 1982.

its syntactic properties become available. This brings us to the syntactic properties of a lemma.

A lemma's *syntactic* information specifies the item's syntactic category, its assignment of grammatical functions, and a set of diacritic feature variables or parameters. Let us consider again the lemma for *give* as an example. It has the following specifications for syntactic category and functions.

- Syntactic category: V.

This means that the lemma will act as a main verb in grammatical encoding.

- Grammatical functions: (SUBJ, DO, IO).

This means that the lemma for *give* requires a subject, a direct object, and an indirect object. In the example these grammatical functions are fulfilled by the phrases *the child*, *the cat*, and *the mother*, respectively. Nothing, however, is said about the ordering of these three. In fact, the sentence *the child gave the mother the cat* has them in the order SUBJ-IO-DO. Still, the order of listing grammatical functions is not arbitrary. It will, by convention, correspond to the order in which the arguments are listed. The first argument (X) has to be realized as the first grammatical function (SUBJ), the second argument (Y) as the second grammatical function (DO), and the third argument (the goal/recipient) as the third grammatical function (IO). It should be remembered that the ordering of the arguments in the message is no more than a notational convention (subsection 3.3.3). But the lemma includes a specification of which conceptual argument is to be mapped onto which grammatical function.

This mapping is not always of the simple one-to-one sort, as for *give*. It is, in particular, not always the case that the number of grammatical functions is equal to the number of arguments; there may be more functions than arguments. This is often the case when the lemma requires a complement of the type V-COMP or S-COMP. Examples of verbs requiring a V-COMP are the so-called raising verbs, such as *believe*. The conceptual structure specification for *believe* has two variables, X and Y, where X is the one who believes, the experiencer, and Y is some state of affairs. But *believe* assigns three grammatical functions in sentences such as *Atilla believed the world to be flat*: SUBJ, DO, and V-COMP. The "additional" direct object *the world* is, in fact, the "raised" subject of the verbal complement that expresses the state of affairs, namely that the world is flat. The lemma for *believe* specifies where the additional grammatical function comes from: DO = V-COMP's SUBJ. It also requires V-COMP to be in the infinitive (*to be flat*). So, for *believe* we have the following additional syntactic specification.

- Relations to COMP: DO = V-COMP's SUBJ
                         V-COMP has diacritic parameter "inf".

The lemma for *give*, however, has no such functional relations specified.

Let us now turn to the last two items on the lemma's list. Subsection 6.1.4 discussed the sense in which a lemma "points to" a morpho-phonological form. The lemma relates to specific form information; it "points to a form address." Let the address for the form information of *give* in the speaker's lexicon be 713.

- Lexical pointer: 713.

That address or entry contains several word forms: the inflections of *give*, i.e., *give*, *gives*, *gave*, *given*, *giving*. They can be distinguished only by assigning values to several features or diacritic variables. These parameters are listed in the final item on the lemma's list.

- Diacritic variables: tense, mood, aspect, person, number.

Also to be included here is the lemma's pitch-accent value. The verb *give* may or may not receive focus and hence pitch accent during the generation of the utterance, as was discussed in the previous chapter. The values of all these variables are collected during the process of generating the surface structure. The word-form inventory can be successfully addressed only when all of a lemma's diacritic parameters have been fixed.

The lemma for *give*, before these parameters have been collected, is summarized in figure 6.3. This example was given to itemize the different

```
give :  conceptual specification :
             CAUSE ( X,(GOposs ( Y, ( FROM/TO (X, Z ))))))

        conceptual arguments : ( X, Y, Z )

        syntactic category : V

        grammatical functions : ( SUBJ,DO, IO )

        relations to COMP : none

        lexical pointer : 713

        diacritic parameters :   tense
                                 aspect
                                 mood
                                 person
                                 number
                                 pitch accent
```

Figure 6.3
Lemma for *give*.

types of knowledge a speaker has stored in a lemma. The knowledge *content* under these items will, of course, differ from lemma to lemma. In the next subsection we will consider some further aspects of verb lemmas—in particular, the ways in which verbs relate conceptual arguments to grammatical functions. In subsection 6.2.3, more will be said about other major lemma categories (nouns, adjectives, and prepositions) and about auxiliaries.

6.2.2   Grammatical Functions and Conceptual Arguments

The way in which grammatical functions are assigned to conceptual arguments is not entirely arbitrary in the world's languages. When the verb has an agent as a conceptual argument, it is usually paired with the subject function, as in the example for *give*. If it has a theme or a patient over and above an agent, this argument tends to occupy an object slot, as in *John kicked the ball* (where *ball* is theme) or *George killed the dragon* (where *dragon* is patient). If, however, the subject slot is not occupied, patient and theme are preferably expressed by the subject function. This happens, for instance, for verbs like *fall*, which require a theme but require no agent as argument: *the bottle fell*. If the verb has a source or goal over and above an agent and a theme or patient, this tends to be mapped on an oblique grammatical function. This happens for a verb like *send*; *Henry sent the letter to Japan* has an agent, a theme, and a goal. Here the goal (*Japan*) ends up in oblique function, in a prepositional phrase. But source or goal is "promoted" when object or subject functions are not occupied by other arguments. The verb *leave*, for instance, has a theme and a source, and they map onto subject and object, respectively: *Marcia left Italy*. One could say that there is a preference hierarchy for grammatical functions, from subject via direct and indirect object to oblique functions. In addition there is a "pecking order" for thematic roles, from agent via theme and recipient to source and goal (see Pinker 1985 and Bock and Warren 1985 for a further discussion of these issues).

But not all verbs show this canonical order of assigning grammatical functions to their conceptual arguments. An example is *receive*, where the goal is encoded as subject and the agent as oblique (*the mother received the cat from the child*). More important, the grammar of a language may provide quite regular means for changing the mapping order. The mapping order for *give*, as presented in figure 6.3, is the following:

X(agent), Y(theme), Z(goal)
   | | |
SUBJ,   DO,   IO

But there is another possible mapping for *give*:

X(agent), Y(theme), Z(goal)
   | | |
SUBJ,   DO,   OBL

This mapping is used in the generation of sentences such as *the child gave the cat to the mother*. It has the three arguments in canonical mapping order. This means that the specifications for the lemma *give* in figure 6.3 are not complete. Under "grammatical functions" the alternative mapping (SUBJ, DO, OBL) should also be given. This pair of mappings for *give* is not an exception; there are similar pairs for other verbs, such as *send*, *sell*, and *buy*. In each of these cases there is an alternation between an indirect object function and an oblique function. This regularity—called a *lexical rule* by Bresnan (1978, 1982)—is the "dative shift" rule.

Another lexical rule is "passive". In English most transitive verbs have an active and a passive mapping of conceptual arguments onto grammatical functions. They differ in the way grammatical functions are assigned to two of their arguments, mostly agent and patient:

Active lemma   **Passive lemma**
agent patient   agent patient
  | | | |
SUBJ OBJ   OBL SUBJ

Take the verb *kill*. In the active *George killed the dragon*, agent and patient are in their canonical grammatical functions, subject and direct object. The passive variant imposes a different function assignment—either as in *the dragon was killed*, where the patient has moved up to subject position and the agent is without grammatical encoding, or as in *the dragon was killed by George*, where the agent appears as an object in the oblique *by*-phrase. In the case where the passive variant is chosen for the grammatical encoding of conceptual arguments, the lexical pointer gets the diacritic parameter for perfect-tense morphology. This will select for *killed* in phonological encoding. It will also lead to retrieving an auxiliary verb (*was*), as will be discussed in subsection 6.2.4.

Most languages have passives, and one wonders what they can do for a speaker. What they seem to have in common is that they demote the argument that would otherwise be encoded as subject, i.e., the argument that occupies the top of the pecking order. This will often be the agent, but in the agentless case it may be the theme (*the cat was given to the mother*). Why would a speaker want to deny the top argument its canonical position when assigning grammatical functions? The pragmatic reason is probably that the grammatical subject is universally the preferred way to encode the topic (see Keenan 1976). Usually the sentence topic coincides with the top argument, but it need not. When another argument is assigned the role of topic in the message, a mapping will be needed that allows it to appear as the grammatical subject. This is what passive mappings provide for. They "demote" the top argument from the subject position, freeing that slot for the topicalized argument.

What happens to the demoted argument? The passive does not require its grammatical encoding. If the argument (say, the agent) is absent from the message, it will also be absent from the sentence (*the dragon was killed*). But if it is still an argument to be expressed (though not as a topic), the passive in English allows for at least the agent's encoding at the very bottom of the functional hierarchy: in an oblique *by*-phrase (*the dragon was killed by George*). This is not a very essential property of passive verb forms, and many languages do not have it. What is essential is the lexical possibility of demoting the top argument in order to topicalize a lower one. Normally this results in the reduction of the number of arguments by one. This state of affairs can be pictured as follows (in correspondence with Pinker 1985):

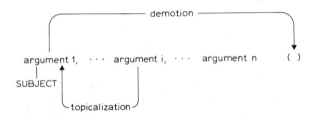

Note that the promoted argument need not be the second in line; the passive variant of *give* can be used to express a topicalized theme (*the cat was given to the mother*) or a topicalized goal (*the mother was given the cat*).

6.2.3   Prepositions, Adjectives, and Nouns
Though the lemmas for verbs play the major role in assigning grammatical functions during speech, formulating is impossible without lemmas for nouns, adjectives, prepositions, adverbials, and other categories such as auxiliaries, determiners, conjunctions. Prepositions, nouns, and adjectives can be heads of PPs, NPs, and APs, respectively, and they may subcategorize for other elements in these phrases. A few words about each of these are presented in this subsection. Subsection 6.2.4 will touch on auxiliaries and other minor categories.

Prepositions

Subcategorization by prepositions is usually obligatory; for example, *toward* requires an NP which expresses the direction argument (*Frederic pointed toward the sun*). The lemma for the preposition specifies the argument and the grammatical function. For *toward* they are the goal and a prepositional object function. The latter becomes expressed as a case feature on the subcategorized NP (*toward him*, not *toward he*). The lemmas of most prepositions have, furthermore, a conceptual specification. For *toward* it specifies that the concept is a DIRECTION, i.e., a PATH that does not contain the goal or reference object (see subsection 3.3.1). Miller and Johnson-Laird (1976) give detailed conceptual specifications for various prepositional lemmas.

But there are also prepositions with empty conceptual specifications. These are sometimes called *idiomatic* prepositions. The *for* in *George waited for the dragon* has an idiomatic relation to the verb and is otherwise meaningless. Still, it does specify case for the NP it is heading. Because it is idiomatic, it is listed in the verb's lemma.

wait:
  conceptual arguments: (X, (Y))
  grammatical functions: (SUBJ, (for OBJ))

This means that *wait* has two conceptual arguments: the one who waits and the entity waited for. The first one is obligatory, the second one optional (as in *John waited*). The optional argument will be grammatically encoded as "for OBJ". But what is the status of this "for"? We will assume that it is the address of the nonidiomatic lemma *for*, i.e., of the meaningful preposition. Activating the lemma *wait* when there is an object argument will automatically involve addressing the lemma *for*. Notice that in this case the conceptual activation conditions of *for* play no role in its activation, and they are also irrelevant in the further generation of the prepositional phrase. Only the syntactic features of *for* and its lexical pointer are relevant.

Adjectives

Adjectives can appear as specifiers in NPs (*hard work*), but also as heads in APs. In the latter case the adjective can subcategorize various elements in the phrase, and the adjective lemma specifies how this is done. One somewhat overworked example should suffice to show this. *Eager* and *easy* can head the adjectival phrases *eager to please* and *easy to please* in *John is eager/easy to please*. Both lemmas are of category A and specify the following grammatical functions:

grammatical functions: (SUBJ, S-COMP)

In both examples the subject is *John* and the S-COMP is *to please*. The difference is in the relations to COMP specified in the lemmas.

eager:

Relations to COMP: SUBJ = S-COMP's SUBJ

                                 S-COMP has diacritic parameter "inf"

easy:

Relations to COMP: SUBJ = S-COMP's OBJ

                                 S-COMP has diacritic parameter "inf"

This makes *John* the subject of *please* when *eager* is the adjective and the object of *please* when *easy* is the adjective. In both cases S-COMP's verb will be in the infinitive. The specifications of relations to COMP in the lemmas function as instructions in the sentence-generation process to create a subjectless phrase to represent the S-COMP of *eager* and an objectless phrase for the S-COMP of *easy*. These are only examples of *grammatical* specifications in the lemmas of adjectives; I will refrain altogether from discussing their conceptual and form specifications.

Nouns

Nouns as heads of phrase can have specifiers such as determiners and quantifiers, but some nouns also subcategorize for complements. The expression of these complements is, however, always optional. Such complements can be PPs (as in *the father of Sylvia*), NPs (as in *Germany's president*), or Ss (as in *the claim that the world is flat*). In all three cases the complement expresses a proper argument of the noun's conceptual specification: a father's child, a president's domain, and the state of affairs the claim is about. They should be distinguished from complements that are not subcategorized by the noun, such as in *the father with money* or *France's cheese*. These complements represent conceptual modifications, not arguments, and they are not specified in the head noun's lemma.

Noun lemmas fall into two major classes: *proper nouns* and *common nouns*. Each proper-noun lemma specifies a conceptual *token*; the conceptual specification need be no more than a pointer to the token's address in memory. Examples of proper names are *Mount Everest, Hans Brinker*, and *World War II*. It may well be, however, that a proper name is not purely referential but has additional intentional features as well. It is, for instance, unlikely for *Mount Everest* to be a war, or *World War II* to be a mountain. There is usually some type information in the kind of name given to a token (Carroll 1983a,b).

Common nouns are nouns whose lemmas contain exclusively *type* information as conceptual specification. Examples are *horse, furniture*, and

democracy. The lemma for *democracy* specifies several conceptual properties which a type or token concept in the message must display in order for
the lemma to become activated: rule by the people, free elections, or what
have you. The problems about the precise structure of these conceptual
specifications are horrendous; they will be left undiscussed here, but some
of them will be taken up in section 6.3.

The common nouns further subdivide along syntactic lines into *count
nouns* and *mass nouns*. The lemmas of English count nouns (such as *dog,
event, belief*) have a diacritic variable for number, which can have the value
'single' or 'plural'. They can also accept either definite or indefinite determiners. Lemmas of mass nouns (such as *sugar, happiness, furniture*), on the
other hand, have the fixed syntactic feature 'singular' and usually accept
definite determiners only. Though the distinction between a count noun
and a mass noun is correlated with properties of the conceptual specifications of these lemmas (count nouns tend to refer to concepts that are
countable; mass nouns refer to substances), it is principally a grammatical
distinction. There is, for instance, no conceptual difference in countability
or substantialness between *the paintings in my house* and *the furniture in my
house*, or between *the blessings of my marriage* and *the happiness of my
marriage*.

6.2.4 Auxiliaries and Minor Categories
As we saw above, the retrieval conditions for idiomatic prepositions are not
of a conceptual kind. This can also be the case for certain auxiliaries—in
particular, English *have, be,* and *do*. When a speaker generates the sentence
The child has given the cat to the mother, the message involves a particular
time index (see subsection 2.2.3) which will induce the grammatical encoder
to generate a perfect-tense verb phrase. This is done by a special VP
procedure (to be discussed in the next chapter), which activates the lemma
of the auxiliary verb *have* and provides it with the appropriate diacritic
features (in the example: third person singular, present). In other words, the
auxiliary lemma is not conceptually activated; rather, it is addressed by a
syntactic building procedure. Since there are no direct conceptual conditions for the lemma's activation, its meaning specification is empty.

But this is not so for all auxiliaries. The *modal* auxiliary verbs (such as
can, may, and *shall*) do have independent semantic activation conditions,
relating to possibilities and necessities in the message (Lyons 1977; Seuren
1985). They can be treated as main verbs that take verbal complements
(Bresnan 1982; Pinker 1985). The syntactic specifications in their lemmas
are the following.

modal verb: Syntactic category: V
              Grammatical functions: (SUBJ, V-COMP)
              Relations to COMP: SUBJ = V = COMP's SUBJ,
                                    V-COMP has diacritic value 'inf'

The surface structure for *Olithia can go* will thus be

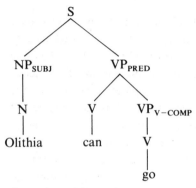

where the subject of *go* has become the subject of *can*, and where *go* is indexed for infinite form.

Most English auxiliaries have rather degenerate inflectional possibilities (see Pinker 1985). The verb *may*, for instance, cannot be used as an infinitive, a perfective, or a progressive (there is no *to may*, *mayed*, or *maying*). The English Formulator cannot do what a Dutch one can, namely produce constructions such as *to may go*. There are no conceptual reasons for this to be impossible; it is due entirely to the syntactic properties of the lemmas involved.

Certain lemmas can (I repeat) be directly addressed by syntactic procedures, whether or not they have a semantic specification. This is the case not only for certain prepositions and auxiliaries, but also for other, especially minor syntactic categories which cannot be heads of phrases. In chapter 7 we will see this happen for certain determiners—in particular, English *the* and *a*. The next section will, however, be devoted entirely to the *conceptual* activation of lemmas.

6.3   Theories of Lemma Access

If indeed the process of grammatical encoding is lexically driven, the way in which lemmas are accessed is a key issue for theories of language production. However, very little is known about how lemmas become activated by fragments of the message. This is not totally surprising, in view of the magnitude of the problem. A speaker with a normal speech rate produces some 150 words per minute (Maclay and Osgood 1959)—on the average, one every 400 milliseconds. Under time pressure the rate can easily be doubled to one every 200 milliseconds. A normal educated adult speaker of English has an active vocabulary—i.e., words he actually uses in his everyday speech—of about 30,000 words.* A speaker makes the right choice from among these 30,000 or so alternatives not just once but, in fluent speech, continuously two to five times per second—a rate that can be maintained without any clear temporal limit. There is probably no other cognitive process shared by all normal adults whose decision rate is so high. Still, the error rate is very low. Collectors of speech errors know that a day's catch is meager. Garnham, Shillcock, Brown, Mill, and Cutler (1982) found 191 slips of the tongue in a text corpus of 200,000 words—about one slip per 1,000 words. Almost half of these (86) were lexical errors. Hotopf (1980) did not find more than 125 whole-word slips of the tongue in the tape recordings of eight conference speakers.

The major issue for a theory of lemma access is how the conceptual specification of a verb, a common noun, an adjective, or another content word comes to "resonate" with some fragment of the message, and how a speedy and accurate choice is made between different lemmas at these high processing rates. The present section will review some theories of access. To begin, let us consider two theoretical issues which are crucial for evaluating any theory of lexical access.

6.3.1 Parallel Processing and Convergence

Parallel Processing

High-speed access requires parallel processing. It would, for instance, be disastrous if, for any concept to be expressed, all lemmas in the mental lexicon would have to be successively checked for their appropriateness until a fitting one was found. This would involve several thousands of tests (from two to five per second) for each new word in the sentence. A touchstone for theories of access will be the degree to which they can reduce such sequential testing. Not only is a parallel account of access necessary for theoretical reasons; there is also convincing empirical evidence for parallel lexical access in speech. Speech errors (blends, in particular) often

---

*The number will vary greatly from speaker to speaker and is, moreover, hard to measure. Oldfield's 1963 estimate for Oxford undergraduates was a vocabulary size of about 75,000 words, but these were words *understood* by students (i.e., their *passive* vocabularies). Their *active* vocabularies must have been substantially smaller.

reveal the simultaneous activation of two near-synonyms, such as in *stummy* for *tummy* and *stomach* (Fromkin 1973).

There is similar evidence for another kind of parallel processing in lexical access. Different message fragments can trigger lemmas in parallel. If two or more fragments are available at the same time, their activation of lemmas need not be serial. If, for instance, some function/argument structure is to be expressed (say, that the text fits the page), all conceptual fragments—FIT, TEXT, and PAGE—may be simultaneously available for expression in the speaker's mind, each initiating its own search for a lemma. One gains a factor of 3 in speed if there are, on average, three different but overlapping accessing processes running during fluent speech production. This type of parallelness may also lead to a characteristic type of errorproneness. A speaker may happen to say *the page fits the text*, and this type of speech error is indeed not uncommon.

Convergence
Whatever the accessing algorithm, it must eventually converge on a single item, the correct one. With E. Clark (1987, 1988), we will assume that there exists no real synonymy in a language. There is a "principle of contrast" which says that all forms in a language contrast in meaning. If word *a* correctly expresses notion A, then word *b* cannot also correctly express notion A.

Convergence would be guaranteed when concepts and words would entertain a simple one-to-one relationship. This is, to some degree, realized for proper nouns and the individuals they refer to. In these cases, as we saw in subsection 6.2.3, the conceptual specification of the lemma might be no more than a pointer to the token individual's address in memory. If all concept-to-word relations were of this kind, accessing lemmas would be like typewriting: Each concept would hit its own key, printing its own lemma character. In more psychological terms: Activating a lemma is a simple reaction involving no choice. Since Donders (1868), we have known that these mental reactions are the speediest of all. The one-to-one mapping ensures high speed as well as faultless convergence.

The alternative, "componential" view is that a word's conceptual specification (its meaning) is some conglomerate of conceptual components, or features, which have to be checked against smaller or larger fragments of the message. In a procedural theory, such as the one developed by Miller and Johnson-Laird (1976), the components are predicates, and for each predicate there is a testing procedure that can evaluate whether the predicate is true or false for the concept at hand. The conceptual specification for the lemma *give* in figure 6.3 is such a conglomerate of predicates or functions, such as CAUSE, GOposs, and FROM/TO. To test the lemma's applicability, the concept should probably be checked for the presence of each of these components, and for their correct relations, since none of them should contradict the concept. It should be obvious that the more detailed the componential structure of a lemma's cognitive specification, the more tests will have to be executed in order to converge on the correct lemma. And this will be to the detriment of accessing speed if the tests are not run in parallel. Though some degree of componentiality is unavoidable in a theory of word meaning, there is a virtue in carefully testing its empirical necessity, particularly for a theory of access in speech production. Fodor, Garrett, Walker, and Parkes (1980) argue against the componential view and provide some empirical results in support of their position. In discussing his language-production model, Garrett (1982) also proposes a close match between the conceptual inventory of which messages are composed and the words of a language.

There is one particularly nasty convergence problem that has not been solved by any theory of lexical access. I will call it the *hypernym problem*. It appears in different guises for different theories, as we will see, but a short formulation is this:

The hypernym problem   When lemma A's meaning entails lemma B's meaning, B is a hypernym of A. If A's conceptual conditions are met, then B's are necessarily also satisfied. Hence, if A is the correct lemma, B will (also) be retrieved.

To give an example, if the speaker intends to express the concept DOG, then all conceptual conditions for the activation of the lemma *animal* are satisfied because the meaning of *dog* entails the meaning of *animal*. Why then does the speaker not say *animal* instead of *dog*? To put it more casually, why do speakers not talk in hypernyms, such as *the person moves* instead of *the man walks*, *the thing travels* instead of *the plane flies*, or *the event caused an event* instead of *his leaving made her weep*?

The hypernym problem is a touchstone for theories of lexical access. After reviewing access theories, I will formulate a processing principle whose incorporation in theories of access will solve the problem. The principle will also shed another light on the issue of convergence in general.

6.3.2   Logogen Theory

Logogen theory, as developed by Morton (1969, 1979), was intended as a general theory of lexical access, i.e., access in both language comprehension and language production. Though most research in this framework has been devoted to language comprehension (particularly word recognition), the theory has been stimulating for production research as well. The present discussion will be limited to the latter. Lexical items are mentally represented as *logogens* in this theory. Logogens are devices that collect evidence for the appropriateness of a word. They are sensitive to information that may indicate the appropriateness of "their" word. All logogens are simultaneously active in collecting their specific information; that is, the logogen system is a parallel accessing device. In normal speech production, the information that activates logogens originates from the so-called Cognitive System, which is the repository of all conceptual, syntactic, and higher-order functions.

Each logogen has a threshold. As soon as the collected bits of evidence exceed the threshold, the logogen "fires" (i.e., makes the word's form available for use). This means that the logogen sends a phonological code to the so-called Response Buffer, where it has a short existence. At the same time, the logogen's activation level drops back to zero, and its threshold is temporarily lowered. The Response Buffer can use the phonological code to initiate a vocal response. It can also return the phonological code to the Logogen System. In that case, the logogen will be reactivated, and since the logogen's threshold is still low, it will normally fire again, which means that the same phonological code is returned to the Response Buffer. This may go on indefinitely. In this way a phonological code may be kept available for use, even when it cannot be immediately uttered. This will often be the case in fluent speech, where words have to be correctly ordered for output. The threshold of a logogen will vary with how frequently the logogen has been activated in the past and how recently that happened. Figure 6.4 is a schematic diagram of this part of the model.

The Cognitive System is equivalent to our Conceptualizer, except that it also generates syntactic information. Logogens are like lemmas, in that they are tuned to specific conceptual and syntactic information. The phonological codes they send to the Response Buffer are the lexical items' form information.

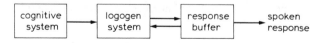

Figure 6.4
Diagram of the Logogen Model. Only parts involved in the generation of speech are represented.

Logogen theory has been used to account for a range of empirical findings in fluent speech production. Here are two examples:

(1) If a logogen's threshold is higher when it has been less frequently used in the past, one expects longer accessing times for low-frequency logogens than for high-frequency ones. This is because more evidence has to be accumulated to surpass a high threshold. Is it the case that low-frequency words are more often preceded by prelexical hesitation pauses than high-frequency words? Findings by Maclay and Osgood (1959) and Martin and Strange (1968) provide some indirect evidence. Function words (articles, pronouns, and other minor category words), which are of high-frequency, were far less often preceded by pauses than content words (such as nouns, verbs, and adjectives), which are, on the average, of far lower frequency. Beattie and Butterworth (1979) argued that it is the *predictability* of a word, not its frequency, that correlates with pausing. Since the predictability and the frequency of words are highly correlated in fluent speech, their effects must be statistically disentangled. Beattie and Butterworth found no frequency effect when predictability was taken into account. However, Levelt (1983) found a strong frequency effect but almost no predictability effect. The data were the prelexical filled-pause hesitations in subjects' descriptions of colored spatial networks (the task was discussed in subsection 4.4.2). Speakers used . . er . . more often before a low-frequency color word, such as *purple*, than before a high-frequency color word, such as *red*.

Predictability is again at issue in the second example.

(2) According to the model, a logogen also gathers relevant *contextual* information from the Cognitive System. The word *table*, for example, is easier to recognize when it follows the sentence fragment *The cup was placed on the*—than when it follows *They went to see the new*—. The first context gives a high *transitional probability* for *table*, whereas the transitional probability is low after the second sentence fragment. This latter fragment makes *film* easy to recognize (Morton 1979). Are there similar context effects in the *production* of a word? Lounsbury (1954) predicted that speakers would hesitate more at transitions of low transitional probability, and Goldman-Eisler (1958, 1968) showed this to be the case; it was subsequently confirmed by Tannenbaum, Williams, and Hillier (1965), by Butterworth (1972), and by Beattie and Butterworth (1979). (See Butterworth 1980b for a review.)

Though these two phenomena are in agreement with logogen theory, one should keep in mind that hesitation data can almost always be interpreted in multiple ways. In terms of lemma and word-form access, the word-frequency effect in example 1 above may be due either to accessing of the lemma or to accessing of the word form. This is not a relevant distinction in logogen theory, since the lexical item is accessed as a whole. Arguments for a form-based interpretation of the frequency effect can be found in Garrett 1982 and in Levelt 1983.

The context effect in example 2, moreover, may be due not to lowered thresholds for the logogen *table* or *film* in the appropriate context but rather to the greater availability of the concept TABLE or FILM in contexts where one is talking about placing objects or going out. This was Goldman-Eisler's interpretation of the data. She supported it with the finding that the sentence fragment *following* a target word was equally predictive of hesitation before that target word. Prelexical hesitation indicates, according to Goldman-Eisler, that the speaker is involved in complicated conceptual planning, and this may also cause the following words to be less obvious or expectable continuations of the "hesitant" word. In other words, the context effect on prelexical hesitation originates not at the level of accessing logogens but at the preliminary state of conceptual planning or message construction.

The major attractive property of logogen theory for fluent language production is its distributed control structure. All lemmas are simultaneously testing their characteristic features against the message or message fragments available. The first logogen that reaches threshold activation will "fire." This predicts that, normally, many more logogens are activated to some degree than just the one that is finally used in the sentence. This is all right as long as there is a unique solution for convergence. But does the system guarantee that, eventually, the correct logogen will fire? This property will not fall out naturally. Consider the hypernym problem. If the speaker intends to express the concept DOG, the Cognitive System will make available conceptual features relevant to the activation of the logogen for *dog*. But these features have as a subset those that will activate the logogen for *animal*. Why would *dog* fire but not *animal*? One answer could be that *dog* has a lower threshold than *animal* and so is quicker in reaching threshold stimulation. But then this should hold across the board for all hypernym relations: Hypernyms should have higher thresholds. This, however, cannot be true, since a word's hypernyms can be used with much more frequency than the word itself. Compare *dog* and *collie*. The former is a hypernym of the later; it is also of much higher frequency, and hence of lower threshold. A speaker intending to express the concept COLLIE will necessarily end up saying *dog*. The convergence problem has not been solved in logogen theory.

6.3.3   Discrimination Nets

Discrimination networks were originally proposed in computer models of verbal learning (Feigenbaum 1963), and have since then been widely used in artificial intelligence. Goldman (1975) was the first to construct a discrimination net for handling lexical access in an artificial language-producing system (which was called BABEL). In essence, his discrimination nets are binary tree structures. Each nonterminal node in the tree represents some predicate that is either true or false for the conceptualization at hand. Terminal nodes correspond to lexical items. The access procedure starts by running the test for the tree's root predicate. If it evaluates to "true" for the concept at hand, control moves to the node's left daughter; if it evaluates to "false", it goes to the right daughter node. The next test concerns the daughter node's predicate. The procedure is self-terminating; it iterates till a terminal node is reached. The lexical item at that terminal node is the system's lexical response to the concept.

A made-up example is presented in figure 6.5a. It discriminates among four lemmas which express pieces of furniture: *chair, stool, table,* and *bed.* If the speaker intends to express the concept STOOL, and the tree in figure 6.5a is his discrimination net, he will first run a test determining whether the concept involves the presence of a seat. This test will evaluate to "true". Control then shifts to the left daughter of the first test node. It represents the test whether the notion to be expressed involves a backrest. In the case of STOOL it will evaluate to "false". This brings the procedure to the terminal node that represents the lemma *stool.* In other words, the lemma is retrieved by executing a sequence of two semantic tests; this also holds for retrieving any of the other three lemmas in the network. A rather less symmetrical case is represented in figure 6.5b. It is a network discriminating among *table, chair, cabinet,* and *bed.* Here it involves only one test to

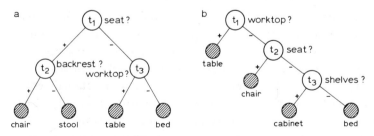

Figure 6.5
An elementary discrimination net for four pieces of furniture.

retrieve *table*, but three sequential tests to come up with either *cabinet* or *bed*.

Goldman did not claim psychological reality for his discrimination-net approach. Still, one might ask whether it is an attractive option for a psychological theory of lexical access in production. Well, it isn't. Let us consider some of the major drawbacks of this approach.

(i) Discrimination nets are sequential testing devices, and won't operate in real time. A few numbers may serve to highlight this problem. If the speaker's lexicon contains 30,000 content words, the speaker's discrimination net will contain 30,000 terminal nodes. How many sequential tests will, on the average, be involved to reach such a terminal node? This depends on the structure of the discrimination net. The optimal case is one where the structure is like that shown in figure 6.5a and where all lemmas involve an equal number of tests. Though this is possible only if the number of lemmas is a power of 2, it can be closely approached in other cases. For such a network, the average number of tests approaches $2 \log N$, where N is the number of lemmas. For a lexicon of 30,000 this number is about 15. In other words, it takes about 15 sequential tests to reach a terminal node in such a network. The worst case is a network like the one in figure 6.5b, where at least one outcome of any test produces a lemma. The average number of tests in this case is $0.5(N + 1) - 1/N$. For our example lexicon, this number is about 15,000. This extreme case may be judged unrealistic, but so is the optimal case. We know that concepts vary in complexity, and there will thus be variation in the number of tests needed to discriminate them; more complexity involves more tests. The average number of sequential tests needed to retrieve a lemma will, in short, be somewhere between 15 and 15,000. To do this between 2 and 5 times per second, a speaker must run his tests at a rate of between 30 and 75,000 per second. This is not very appealing for a real-time model of lexical access.

(ii) The access time for a lemma will be a monotonic increasing function of the number of tests. If, for example, figure 6.5b is accurate for the four lemmas involved, it will take less time to access *table* than to access *bed*. Nothing in the literature supports this prediction. Levelt, Schreuder, and Hoenkamp (1978) and Schreuder (1978) showed that the reaction times for choosing among four verbs of motion (*take along*, *pass*, *launch*, and *pick up*) in the presence of a visual event were not compatible with *any* of the possible discrimination nets. In naming tasks where a subject was free to call the perceived movement whatever he liked, the more generic verbs (such as *move*)—i.e., the verbs with fewer conceptual features—always had longer naming latencies than the more specific verbs (such as *launch*). On any reasonable theory, the former verbs involve fewer conceptual components than the latter ones and should therefore display shorter speech-onset latencies if the lexicon is organized like a discrimination net. In short, the theory makes the wrong kinds of prediction with respect to access times.

(iii) Discrimination nets of the kind proposed fail on the criterion of correct convergence. In particular, they cannot handle the hypernym problem, for quite principled reasons. If lemma *a* is a hypernym of lemma *b* (as are, for instance, *animal* and *bear*), then *a* and *b* cannot be represented on the same discrimination net. Why not? In order for *a* and *b* to be located at different terminal nodes on the same binary tree, there must be at least one test that discriminates between the underlying concepts A and B (ANIMAL and BEAR in the example). But since *a* is a hypernym of *b*, all tests on which A evaluates to "true" will also evaluate to "true" for B (everything that will be true for ANIMAL will be true for BEAR), and what is true for B is either true or irrelevant for A. In other words, there cannot be a test on which A and B receive opposing values. This is, indeed, a serious problem. The mental lexicon abounds with hypernym relations, but these cannot be represented by way of binary discrimination nets. Hence, they cannot be realistic psychological models, for purely structural reasons. For the same reason, they will fail as lexical representations in artificial natural-language generators.

(iv) It is, finally, an illusion to think that the mental lexicon is organized in the manner of a hierarchical taxonomy. Many semantic relations between lexical items are of a quite different nature, as is immediately obvious when one considers semantic relations between kinship terms, color names, names for days of the week, and so on (Miller and Johnson-Laird 1976; Lyons 1977).

6.3.4 Decision Tables

A major improvement over discrimination nets was proposed in Miller and Johnson-Laird 1976 (see also Steedman and Johnson-Laird 1980). Their *decision-table* proposal still involves a speaker who runs a set of tests in order to retrieve a lemma, but the tests can be run in parallel. The example in table 6.1 will serve to introduce the notion of a decision table.

A decision table is a matrix representing a set of IF/THEN or condition/action pairs. The rows in the upper half of the table represent the outcomes of semantic tests. They are the same kinds of tests as those discussed in the

tests	outcomes					
(semantic conditions)	1	2	3	4	5	6

IF

	1	2	3	4	5	6
t1	+	+	-		+	-
t2	-	-	+	-	+	+
t3	+	-		+	-	
t4	+	+	-	+	-	+

lemmas						
(lexical actions)						
a	x					
b ◄——THEN——►	x	x				
c				x		
d		x				
e				x		

Table 6.1
Example of a decision table.

previous section. If, for instance, the decision table concerns pieces of furniture, there will be tests for properties like "worktop", "seat", and "shelves". (A detailed example is worked out in Miller and Johnson-Laird 1976.) If the speaker considers expressing the notion STOOL, he will run all tests in parallel and come up with a value (+ or −) for each test. This pattern of results is called the outcome. Let us assume that the outcome for testing STOOL is the one encircled in column 2 of table 6.1. This outcome is a condition for an action specified in the lower half of the table. The x in column 2 is in the row of lexical action *b*; in the example that action is to retrieve *stool*. In other words, IF the outcome specified in column 2 arises, THEN lemma *b* is to be used. It should be noticed that certain cells in the upper half of the table are blank. This means that the corresponding test values are irrelevant. The action will be performed in case there is a match for all + and − values in the column, whatever the value on the "blank" test. We will return to this important property of decision tables shortly.

The lower half of table 6.1 also has some noteworthy properties. First, can there be two or more crosses in a single row, as is the case for row *b*? Yes; this is a natural way to represent homonymy, the same word expressing different concepts. For instance, columns 2 and 3 could represent outcomes for the notions BANK (of river) and BANK (financial institution), respectively. They would both occasion the lexical action of accessing the word *bank*. What about two crosses appearing in the same column, as in column 5 of the example? This should not be allowed. It violates the theoretical criterion of convergence. A single concept would lead to two different lexical actions. Decision tables can always be arranged in such a way that this does not happen. Can there be outcomes without lexical action, i.e., without a corresponding x in the lower table? This situation is exemplified by the outcome in column 6. It should be noticed that the number of possible outcome patterns increases rapidly with the number of tests in the table. There may, then, not be enough possible lexical actions to take care of each of these outcomes. Miller and Johnson-Laird (1976) talked about the "exponential specter." They tried to curb this threatening explosion by introducing "table-linkage," which will be discussed shortly.

But what does it really mean that there are outcome patterns for which there is no lexical action? Cases where there is a unitary concept without a corresponding lexical item are called "lexical gaps." Such cases are not disastrous for a theory of language production, since most conceptualizations we entertain are not expressible in single words. Under such circumstances the speaker will resort to a syntactic solution, i.e., he will create a phrase or sentence that expresses the concept. If the concept to be expressed is a dead animal, the tests will converge on the lemma *corpse*; if it is a dead tree, they will not converge on a lemma. The speaker will then resort to formulating the phrase *dead tree*. We could accommodate this by adding to the bottom of the table a row *f* standing for "syntactic action". All outcome patterns for which there is no lexical action will have xs in row *f*.

Of course, this leaves unanswered the difficult question of how a speaker partitions a message into "unitary concepts"—i.e., conceptual fragments for which there will normally be words in the language.

Though the "exponential specter" doesn't seem to be much of a problem for a theory of the speaker, there may be other reasons to consider reducing the size of a decision table. Anyone who has ever tried to construct a decision table for a set of lexical items will have noticed that almost every new item in the set requires the addition of a new test. Even if one assumes that, on the average, a new test is needed for every tenth item, one will have 3,000 tests for a 30,000-word mental lexicon. This implies that the IF-statement for the retrieval of each lexical item is a pattern of 3,000 test outcomes, and this is quite far from the ideal case where, for each item, one or a few tests would suffice for its identification.

Table linkage is a way of cutting up the large decision table into a set of smaller ones. There will be a table for each semantic domain: one for furniture terms, one for verbs of motion, one for kinship terms, and so on. Each of these tables involves a small number of tests, so the number of outcome patterns will never be excessive. The tables are linked in that each table can make reference to one or more other tables (called "successor tables"), depending on the outcome pattern of the tests. Testing begins at some privileged table. If an outcome pattern results for which there is no lexical action, control is transferred to a successor table. This will iterate until some table in the sequence comes up with a lexical action. But notice that this is seriality again. How many successive tables a speaker will, on the average, have to go through in order to come up with a lexical action will depend on the way the tables are linked.

How does the decision-table approach handle convergence? Is the correct item indeed found? The touchstone is again the handling of hypernyms. In the previous subsection we observed that discrimination nets cannot represent hypernym relations. But decision tables can. There is an example in table 6.1. Word d is a hypernym of word a (as in *diplomat* and *ambassador*). How is this visible in the table? Compare the outcomes of columns 1 and 4. They are identical except for the cells in the upper row; whereas column 1 displays a $+$, column 4 has a blank. This means that outcome 1 implicates outcome 4, but not conversely. That defines the hypernym relation. Consider the example: If someone is an ambassador, he or she is a diplomat; but a diplomat need not be an ambassador. There are diplomats who do not share the special feature of ambassadors of being a country's representative. Test 1 concerns this feature. It is irrelevant for deciding whether a person is a diplomat (the blank cell in column 4), but it is essential for deciding whether a person is an ambassador.

But though hypernym relations are representable in decision tables, they create a violation of our convergence criterion. The obvious reason is that if the column for the specific term (i.e., *ambassador*) is satisfied, the column for its hypernym is by necessity also satisfied. As a consequence, there will be *two* lexical actions if the more specific concept (e.g., AMBASSADOR) is to be expressed; the hypernym will also be accessed. Since many words have a whole hierarchy of hypernyms (*ambassador–diplomat–person–human*–etc.), there will be permanent cluttering of lexical actions. Later we will see that even when there is cluttering (as in blends of words) it hardly ever involves a term and a hypernym.

Decision tables are a major improvement over discrimination nets in that they allow for real-time parallel processing. However, in their present form they defy proper convergence, and this is a serious drawback.

6.3.5 Activation Spreading

Could there be a connectionist account of lexical access? In chapter 1, where we discussed connectionism as a potentially powerful formal language for the description of parallel processing, we went through an example of word-form access (see figure 1.2). The top-level nodes in that example were lemmas, and we traced the activation spreading down to the level of segments or phonemes. Substantive proposals have been made with respect to this process (see especially Dell 1986, 1988); we will turn to these in chapter 9. Our present problem concerns the preceding phase of activation: How are the lemma-level nodes activated? At the time of this writing, the literature contains no serious proposals.

One approach could be to distinguish a level of nodes representing conceptual components. Returning to our furniture example, we could think of such properties as having a worktop or shelves, being a seat, and so on. In a connectionist account, such properties can be represented as input nodes. Let us call them A, B, C, etc. On this account a concept is nothing more than an activated collection of such nodes. This is called a *distributed* representation. The output nodes will be lemmas: *stool*, *chair*, and so forth. The simplest account is one in which these are the only two levels of nodes, with each input node connected to all the output nodes:

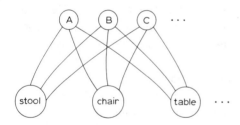

We can now further specify the system by defining the characteristic state of activation of the input nodes for different concepts (this may or may not involve a binary activation scale), the output function of each node (i.e., how the degree of the node's activation determines the level of its output), the input function of the lemma nodes (i.e., how the propagated activity impinging on an output unit summates to activate that unit), and so on. We will not go through this exercise. In fact, there are only casual suggestions in the literature as to how this should be done for the modeling of lexical access.

We will, rather, limit the present discussion to two observations. The first is that, as a parallel-activation account, activation spreading is an excellent candidate for taking care of real-time limitations. The number of steps from input nodes to output nodes is one or (if there is a level of hidden nodes) two. The second observation is that, so far, no one has even begun to account for convergence. Not only is the structure over which the activation should spread not known; there is also no principled approach to solving the hypernym problem.

6.3.6   Toward a Solution of the Hypernym Problem

As was observed above, convergence is a major stumbling block for all theories of lemma access. In particular, none of the existing theories involves a correct treatment of the hypernym problem. In the following, three principles will be proposed that, if incorporated in a processing model, guarantee correct convergence for a term and its hypernyms.

The first principle will use the notion of *core*. A lemma's core meaning or conceptual core condition is a privileged, "most salient" meaning component. There is an empirical basis for assuming the existence of core meanings. Miller (1969) suggested a "negation test" procedure for determining a lemma's core, and this procedure was used by Levelt et al. (1978) and Schreuder (1978) to analyze verbs of motion and by Noordman (1979) to study kinship terms.

The idea underlying the negation test is that negation will, when there is no restriction on the set of alternatives, affect only a word's core. Here is an example from the study of verbs of motion: Subjects were asked to complete sentences such as *They do not ski, but they....* No subject ever completed this sentence with a verb like *breathe* or *think*. The most frequent response was *skate*. Subjects apparently apply minimal negation, in that most of the meaning of *ski* is preserved under negation; like *ski*, *skate* denotes some form of human locomotion over a frozen surface, involving some instrument attached to the feet. Only the character of the instrument is different. The instrument's character is the only conceptual component changed under negation. By this test it constitutes the core component of the lemma for *ski*. Miller called the unchanged part (in the present instance the meaning shared by *ski* and *skate*) the lemma's *presupposition*.

Though the negation test is helpful in demonstrating the notion of core meaning, it is not a foolproof procedure for finding an item's core. When the set of alternatives to the negated item is restricted in the situation of discourse, the test easily fails. If you happen to know that John is either skiing or working, then the completion *John isn't skiing, he is working* is quite natural.

Let us now turn to the first principle. It is a stronger version of what was introduced earlier as E. Clark's (1987, 1988) principle of contrast: "Every two forms contrast in meaning." This principle denies the existence of full synonyms in a language. Restricting this principle to core meanings, we have the uniqueness principle.

The uniqueness principle   No two lexical items have the same core meaning.

In other words, there are as many core meanings as there are lexical items. This principle captures the intuition described above in the discussion of decision tables: Every new item added to a table seems to require a new idiosyncratic test. The following two principles formulate the role of core meaning in lexical access.

The core principle   A lexical item is retrieved only if its core condition is satisfied by the concept to be expressed.

This is not a very strong principle, but it is a first step toward solving the hypernym problem. The reason is that, by the uniqueness principle, a term and a superordinate or hypernym never have the same core. To keep to the above example: Both *skiing* and *skating* are forms of *gliding*; hence, *glide* is a superordinate of these verbs. When the negation test is applied to *glide*, it will yield verbs like *stick* where there is no smooth continuity in the motion. The core of *glide* is, apparently, this manner feature of smooth continuity. Hence, *ski* and *glide* have different core conditions. If the speaker now intends to express the notion GLIDE, the core principle guarantees that no subordinate term will be used. The speaker will not erroneously retrieve *ski*, since that word's core condition is not met by the concept GLIDE.

But the reverse may still happen. If the notion SKI entails the notion GLIDE, then if SKI is the concept the speaker intends to express, the core condition of GLIDE is necessarily satisfied by that concept. Hence we need an additional principle to prevent retrieval of the hypernym:

The principle of specificity   Of all the items whose core conditions are satisfied by the concept, the most specific one is retrieved.

This principle prevents the retrieval of *glide* when SKI is the concept. Since the meaning of *ski* entails the meaning of *glide*, *ski* is the more specific word item. It will be the one retrieved.

These principles are reminiscent of Grice's maxims of quantity. One should not say *glide* when one intends to express the notion SKI. That is like (truthfully) saying "I have two sisters" when one has in fact three.

Lexical access, then, involves essentially recognizing the most entailing predicates in the concept and finding the unique lemmas that have these as their core conditions (when they exist). We began the present section by considering the "ideal" case of a one-to-one relationship between concepts and words. In that case, retrieving a word would be a simple mental reaction. Under the present assumptions this ideal situation is closely approached. Each lexical item can be seen as a testing device for the realization of its own core condition, roughly as in logogen theory. Implementation of the principle of specificity will guarantee correct convergence.

6.4   Failures of Lemma Access

6.4.1   A Taxonomy of Causes

Anthony Cohen, one of the initiators of speech-error research in modern psycholinguistics (Cohen 1965, 1968), called speech errors "blabbers." That speech errors are thoughtless or even indiscrete exposures of the underlying formulating machinery was not only the view of the pioneers in this field, Meringer and Mayer (1895) and Freud (1904); it is the main impetus for what is now one of the most flourishing empirical methods in the study of the formulation of speech. There are three major anthologies in this field: Fromkin 1973, Fromkin 1980, and Cutler 1982a. Cutler 1982b is an exceptionally complete bibliography.

The three classes of speech errors to be discussed in this section have different etiologies in the production process. All are due to derailments in the retrieval of lemmas, but the mechanisms involved are different. We will have to distinguish two major causes of word errors: *conceptual intrusion* and *associative intrusion.** Conceptual intrusion occurs when lemma selection is disturbed by the simultaneous activity of two or more concepts. Associative intrusion occurs when lemma selection is interfered with by associations between lemmas, better known as *word associations*. We will assume that associative relations between lemmas are *direct* relations, i.e., not mediated by anything else (see subsection 6.1.2). A further distinction should be made: The intruding element may or may not be related in meaning to the intended element. Since the latter distinction is independent of the former, we end up with a four-way taxonomy (figure 6.6).

---

*It is not a matter of concern here *why* a person happens to have an alternative thought in mind, or *why* he built up a particular association in his lifetime. See Cutler 1982a for a distinction between these more remote causes of error and the proximal causes and mechanisms we are dealing with here.

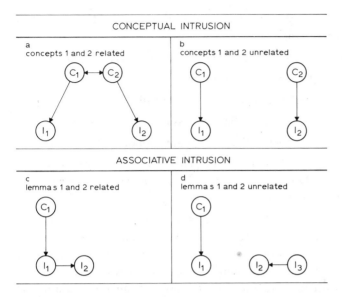

Figure 6.6
Conceptual and associative intrusion in lemma access. The intruding concept, C_2, is either (a) meaning related to the intended one, C_1, or (b) not. Also, the intruding lemma, l_2, may (c) or may not (d) be meaning related to the intended lemma, l_1.

In the figure the intended concept, the one to be expressed, is always C_1. The appropriate lemma to express this concept in the context of use is always ℓ_1. Conceptual intrusion is caused by the presence of another concept, C_2. It activates its own lemma ℓ_2, and this interferes with the activity of ℓ_1. Concepts C_1 and C_2 can be closely related in meaning, as in figure 6.6a, or they can be unrelated, as in figure 6.6b. Associative intrusion is caused by one lemma's directly activating another one. In figure 6.6c the intended lemma, ℓ_1, activates a closely associated lemma, ℓ_2, which may then interfere with ℓ_1's activity. In figure 6.6d the intruding lemma, ℓ_2, is unrelated to ℓ_1; it is activated by the independent but still active lemma ℓ_3, to which it is closely associated. Let us now make these notions more concrete by applying them to the three classes of speech error: blends, substitutions, and exchanges of words.

6.4.2 Blends

In a word blend two words are fused into one. Two lemmas are retrieved, which compete for the same syntactic slot. Semantically speaking, there are two kinds of word blends. The first kind involves words of similar meaning;

the second kind involves what we will call distractions. Here is a set of examples of the first kind:

(1) The competition is a little stougher [stiffer/tougher] (Fromkin 1973)

(2) Irvine is quite clear [close/near] (Fromkin 1973)

(3) To determine watch [what/which] (Fromkin 1973)

(4) At the end of today's lection [lecture/lesson] (Garrett 1975)

(5) and would like to enlict [enlist/elicit] your support (Garrett 1980a)

(6) "Lexikon" ist ein Terminus, der sich eingebildet [herausgebildet/ eingebürgert] hat (*"Lexicon" is a term that has emerged/has become familiar*) (Bierwisch 1982)

The major observation about this class of word blends is that the two words are roughly equivalent in meaning in the context of the message as a whole. Is this relatedness of meaning a conceptual relation, as in figure 6.6a, or a lemma association, as in figure 6.6c? The empirical evidence is in favor of the former interpretation. In the case of lemma association one would expect the two blended words to be close associates. Among the closest associates in word-association tables (see, for instance, Palermo and Jenkins 1964) are antonyms. But antonym blends are highly exceptional. Meringer and Mayer's (1896) sample contains only two: *wehr* [*weniger/ mehr*] and *Beneinung* [*Bejahung/Verneinung*]. Fromkin's (1973) list of 65 blends contains no antonym blends, and Hotopf (1980) also presents numbers testifying to this exceptionality. The few cases observed may have originated at the conceptual level. The speaker who produced *wehr* may have had two closely related concepts in mind, namely LESS (activating the lemma for *weniger*) and NOT MORE (activating the lemma for *mehr*). Antonyms are semantically related, but only as far as their presuppositions are concerned; their core meanings are mutually exclusive. Only equivalence or similarity of core meaning seems to count for this category of blends.

The latter restriction also excludes blends of a term and a hypernym. In subsection 6.3.6 it was proposed that a term's core meaning is always different from the core meanings of its hypernyms. And indeed, as Hotopf (1980) shows, such blends hardly ever occur. There are, for instance, only three potential cases of word/superordinate merges among Fromkin's (1973) 65 published blends: *dealsman* [*dealer/salesman*], *hegraines* [*headaches/migraines*], and *swifting* [*shifting/switching*]. I say "potential" because the two core meanings may have been *functionally* equivalent in the contexts where these blends occurred (Bierwisch 1982).

It is not characteristic of blended words to be close associates of one another. It may just happen to be the case, but it may equally well not be the case. The etiology of blends of related words, therefore, seems to be that the message (fragment) itself contains a certain ambivalence with respect to two equally appropriate concepts (there are "alternative plans," as Butterworth 1982 called this kind of interference). These closely related concepts trigger their lemmas almost simultaneously. Both lexical items, whether word associates or not, are retrieved, and they are both inserted in the same surface-structure slot. This induces their word forms to become blended at the level of phonological processing. In short, these blends are due to conceptual intrusion.

The same can be said about blends-by-distraction. The speaker who is in the train of expressing concept C_1 through lemma ℓ_1 may get an intruding thought by distraction or whatever Freudian cause (Butterworth called this the "competing plan" kind of interference). A concept C_2, not part of the message, will independently activate a lemma ℓ_2. If both lemmas fire simultaneously, a blend can arise. Example 7 is of this sort.

(7) Dann aber sind Tatsachen zum Vorschwein [Vorschein/Schweinereien] gekommen (*But then facts came to appearance/filthinesses*) (observed by both Mayer and Freud, and cited in Meringer and Mayer 1895 and Freud 1904)

The speaker of these famous words agreed to the two observers that he was thinking of "filthinesses" when he was speaking his rather neutral sentence. The intruding thought (C_2) activated an intruding lemma (ℓ_2), and the two word forms merged. Clearly, the two concepts involved were unrelated, and there was no association between the two words. Blends-by-distraction are of the type shown in figure 6.6b.

Two blended words are usually of the same syntactic category, as is the case in all of examples 1–7. On first view this is surprising; if lemmas of content words are triggered solely on the basis of their conceptual specifications, syntactic category information should be irrelevant, and lemmas of different categories but similar meaning might be prone to amalgamation as well. One should, however, imagine what would happen if two such lemmas were to compete. They cannot appear in the same phrasal environment because of their category difference, and at this point one of two things may happen. The first one is that the already existing phrasal restrictions are such that only a lemma of a particular category can be accepted for insertion. In that case, the other lemma will be unfit for use and without effect for further processing. One can say that it is "filtered out" by subsequent syntactic processing. If the phrasal environment is not sufficiently restrictive to filter one lemma out right away, a second thing may happen: Each lemma may trigger the construction of its own phrasal environment, and some phrasal blend may occur. These cases are exceptional; the following example, reported in Fay's (1982) corpus of sentence blends, may be due to such a process:

(8) And that is how I got interested into it [into/interested in]

The notion of filtering out is also important for the explanation of other aspects of word blends. Many word blends are words themselves; this is, for instance, the case for examples 2, 3, 4, and 6 above. Dell and Reich (1981) provided statistical evidence that there is a slight overrepresentation of real words among blends. This may be the result of filtering at a later stage, namely when word forms are generated. Selective filtering at that stage may also be the cause of blends between words that are similar in word form, as in *herrible* [*terrible/horrible*] (see Butterworth 1982 for an analysis of this phenomenon). These issues are discussed further in chapter 9.

Though the blends discussed in the present subsection are due to conceptual interference of one kind or another, there are also blends with different (for instance, phonological) etiologies. See Butterworth 1982, Harley 1984, and Stemberger 1985a for a wider discussion of blending.

6.4.3 Substitutions
Word substitutions can be of various sorts. The following are some examples of the selection errors that concern us here:

(9) He's a high–low grader [low → high] (Fromkin 1973)

(10) Don't burn your toes [fingers → toes] (Fromkin 1973)

(11) Der hat so'n Ding geheiratet–ich meine geerbt [geerbt → geheiratet] (*He married–I mean inherited–this thing* [*inherited → married*]) (Bierwisch 1982)

(12) I just put it in the oven at a very low speed [temperature → speed] (Garrett 1982)

(13) Met een blauw vlakje, een blauw rondje aan de bovenkant [rondje → vlakje] (*with a blue spot, a blue disk at the upper end* [*disk → spot*]) (Levelt 1983)

This set of examples is somewhat biased, in that no substitutions in which the target word and the substitution are unrelated are included. They do occur. However, we will first look into the most frequent type of substitution, which involves some semantic relation between the target and the error. This means that we are first dealing with cases a and c in figure 6.6. The question then is whether the intrusion is conceptual or associative.

The most frequently observed cases involve antonyms or other cases of semantic opposition, as in example 9, or co-hyponyms (i.e., words from the same semantic field), as in example 10. This is a pattern one typically encounters with word associations: similarity in presupposition, but difference in core. Fromkin's (1973) list of word substitutions is again a goldmine here; one finds substitutions such as *last → first, wine → beer, later → earlier, come → gone, little → much,* and *sun → world.* There are also more remote co-hyponyms where the common class is less immediate, as in examples 11 and 12. Hotopf (1980) claims that these cases more or less exhaust the semantic relations to be found in word substitutions.

These facts show that word substitutions, unlike blends, often reflect associative relations. This betrays an etiology like that in figure 6.6c. In *don't burn your toes,* for instance, the concept FINGERS activates the lemma *fingers,* which has *toes* as a close associate, which it activates. For some reason, the activation of *toes* reaches threshold before *finger* "fires" and the accident is created.

What could cause the associate lemma to become available before the target lemma? An obvious suggestion is that the associate has a lower threshold in the sense of logogen theory (subsection 6.3.2). According to logogen theory, high-frequency words have lower thresholds than low-frequency ones, and one wonders whether the substituting words in association-caused substitutions are of higher frequency than the target words. This would predict that a high-frequency word is more likely to substitute for a low-frequency one than inversely. I substantiated this by analyzing the word substitutions listed by Fromkin (1973), using the word-frequency tables of Kucera and Francis (1967). In the list of substitutions there were 23 cases where the substitution was clearly an associate of the target word (e.g. *question → answer, east → west*) and for which word frequences were available. Of these, 17 cases were in the predicted direction; only 6 went the other way. This difference is significant at the 0.02 level. No frequency difference between target and substitute can be discerned if *all* substitutions are taken into account. It only holds for those errors that can be interpreted as intrusions by a word that is *associated* to the target word. The demonstrated frequency effect does not contradict Hotopf's (1980) statistical finding that the substituting word tends to be of the *same* frequency class as the target word. That finding is not surprising, insofar as, quite generally, a word and its first associates are of the same frequency class. The demonstrated frequency difference holds *within* such frequency classes.

The next question is whether we can exclude *conceptual* intrusion as a cause of word substitutions. Surely examples 11–13, though of a less frequent sort, do not involve very close associates. What about words that are conceptually equivalent in the context? Synonyms and superordinates (e.g. *animal* for *dog*) do not appear in Hotopf's data. Garrett (1982) also called attention to these missing cases. As we have seen, synonyms (or, better, equivalent terms in the context) are the normal case for blends; why are they missing in substitution data? This may not be more than an artifact. If A and B are near-synonyms in the message context, it really doesn't matter which lemma is triggered first. In both cases the selected word will be appropriate, and nobody will ever notice that there was a "race" between the two activation processes. In blends, however, A and B get merged, and this will strike the attentive ear as a slip. In substitutions nothing so striking happens; we cannot exclude that a near-synonym may substitute for the target word.

Can a similar argument account for the near absence of superordinates (hypernyms) in word substitutions? At least in part. How can one know that a speaker should have said *dog* instead of the actually used word, *animal*? It will often go unnoticed, but the speaker may reveal it by making a correction. An anaysis of speaker's spontaneous repairs (Levelt 1983) shows that it is not at all unusual for speakers to replace a word by a more specific one. Example 13 is such a case. The speaker was describing visual patterns composed of colored disks connected by black arcs. In this context a disk (*rondje* in Dutch) is clearly a spot (*vlakje*), but the inverse need not be the case. *Spot* is a superordinate of *disk*. Still, even in these cases it is undecidable whether the concept triggered a hypernym. One cannot know whether the concept DISK was already active at the moment that *spot* was used; it could have been an afterthought. In that case, example 13 is not a substitution at all. In short, we can neither confirm nor deny that hypernym substitutions occur. But if, as we suppose, word association is a major cause of substitutions, one would expect substitutions by superordinates to occur. Word associations like *dog → animal* are not infrequent.

So far, we have considered substitutions involving some semantic relation, and we have tried to interpret them as either of type a or of type c in figure 6.6. We found that there is good evidence for an etiology as in c, associative intrusion; there may or may not be conceptual intrusion. What about semantically unrelated intrusions? Can one find cases like b and d among word substitutions? Two cases from Fromkin 1973 that seem to be of type d are the following:

(14) a branch falling on the tree [roof → tree]

(15) Q: when are you going to have the ale?

   A: with the beer [dinner → beer]

In example 14, *tree* is not meaning-related to the target word *roof*, but it is
a close associate of *branch*. The constellation is as in figure 6.6d, where the
intended concept (C_1) is ROOF and the intended lemma (ℓ_1) is *roof*. The
intruding lemma (ℓ_2) is *tree*, which is a close associate of still another
lemma *branch* (ℓ_3). Similarly, in example 15 *beer* (ℓ_2) is associated to the
interlocutor's *ale*, which became also activated in the speaker's mind (ℓ_3).
So, recently activated lemmas other than the target word can also cause
intrusion by a nonintended but associated lemma, and this case is not at all
infrequent in the published data (see especially Harley 1984).

   Example 15 shows that the priming may be due to a word *perceived* by
the speaker. Recall the experimental data collected by Levelt and Kelter
(1982) and presented in subsection 4.2.5. When shopkeepers were asked the
question *At what time do you close?*, the answer was more likely to contain
at (e.g., *At six*) than when the question was *What time do you close?* (typical
answer: *Six o'clock*). This is a case of *identity priming* in production; the
interlocutor's use of a word (*at*) increases the probability that the speaker
will use that word in the next turn.

   Though associative intrusion of the sort presented in figure 6.6d is clearly
a cause of many word substitutions, one cannot exclude the possibility that
other cases are due to *conceptual* intrusion, as in figure 6.6b. Example 16,
also from Fromkin's sample, is probably of this sort.

(16) he's not that happy in Hawaii [Illinois → Hawaii]

The speaker was already thinking of Hawaii, which was going to come up
in the next sentence. This example forms a natural bridge to the last kind of
access errors to be discussed here: word exchanges.

6.4.4   Exchanges of Words

It was suggested earlier that word exchanges result from different message
fragments' being active at the same time. Two characteristic examples from
the many that have been published suffice as demonstrations:

(17) Well you can cut rain in the trees [rain ↔ trees] (Garrett 1982)

(18) This spring has a seat in it [spring ↔ seat] (Garrett 1980a)

In word exchanges it is no more than accidentally the case that the two
words are close associates. They typically express different concepts that are

both about to be formulated, mostly as parts of the same sentence. (Butterworth 1982 calls this kind of interference "plan internal.") Example 16 may have been a case of a beginning exchange between two consecutive sentences. This puts word exchanges in the category represented in figure 6.6b. Word exchanges are the clearest evidence available for parallelness of the second type discussed in subsection 6.3.1, i.e., the simultaneous accessing of different lemmas by different fragments of the message. Such parallel processing probably contributes to the speed and fluency of speech; it apparently also creates some accident-proneness.

In word exchanges of this type the two words are always of the same syntactic category. This is what one would expect if the insertion of the lemma in the developing surface structure were to require a fitting syntactic category. Garrett (1980a) observed that the exchanging words belong to different phrases and play similar roles in their respective phrases. It is hard to define what a similar role is, but something functional seems to be at stake. The elements are often both heads of phrase, and they tend to be similar in the thematic arguments they express or in the grammatical functions they fulfill. We will return to these issues in the next chapter.

6.5   The Time Course of Lexical Access

6.5.1   Stages of Access

How rapidly is an object's name retrieved? When speakers are shown pictures of objects and asked to name the objects as quickly as possible, it takes some 600 to 1,200 milliseconds from picture presentation to the initiation of the vocal response. This speech-onset latency is the result of several stages of processing, which may or may not show some overlap in time. The speaker will first process the picture visually. This involves extracting visual features, borders, corners, shades, overlaps, foreground/ background relations, and so on. The next stage will be to categorize the visually emerging object as a car, a table, a clock, or whatever the kind of object presented. This category or concept is the occasion for retrieving the corresponding lexical item: car, table, etc. We are not sure whether the latter stage involves one or two steps, but at any rate both the lemma and the form information will be retrieved. Finally, the articulatory response has to be prepared; only then can the overt naming be initiated.

It is, of course, not the case that all accessing of content words in speech passes through all of these stages. The visual processing and categorization is not an essential part of lexical access. There are other ways of conceiving of a concept to be expressed. Still, studies of the time course of lexical access have almost exclusively been studies of naming—the naming of objects or of visual relations. The present section is concerned with these studies.

The speech-onset latency in naming depends on several factors which exert their effects in one or another of the conjectured stages. There are visual effects, conceptual effects, word-frequency effects, and so on. We will first discuss latency effects, which are largely caused during the visual and conceptual stages of processing; then we will turn to effects that are due to lexical accessing proper. Next we will consider the issue of lemma versus form retrieval; are they two successive steps or rather two aspects of the same retrieval operation? Finally, a few remarks will be made about potential overlap between the stages of categorization and lexical access.

6.5.2   Visual Processing and Categorization

How is a visually represented object categorized? This question deserves a book in itself and will not be extensively discussed here. But naming latencies do reveal preferences of categorization. Rosch and colleagues (see especially Rosch, Mervis, Gray, Johnson, and Boyes-Braem 1976) introduced the notion of *basic object level*. It is the preferred level of categorization of visual objects: apple, shoe, chair, car, etc. There is a superordinate level of categories (fruits, clothing, furniture, vehicles, and so on), and there are subordinate categories for each of the basic-level terms (cooking apple, pump, Ottoman, convertible, etc.). Several studies, nicely reviewed by Seymour (1979) and including some of his own, have shown that naming latencies are shortest when a speaker uses basic-level terms for the objects he is presented with. When a subject receives a mixed set of fruits, furniture items, vehicles, and so on, and is required to say *fruit, furniture, vehicle*, etc. (that is, to use superordinate categories instead of basic-level terms like *apple* and *chair*), the naming latencies are substantially longer. But latencies are also longer when subordinate terms have to be used. This finding can probably not be explained by the lower frequency of usage of non-basic-level terms. It shows, rather, that there are preferred ways of categorizing visually presented objects.

The process of visual object categorization can further be traced by the so-called priming paradigm. The picture to be named is preceded by another visual stimulus (the prime) which can entertain some relation to the target object, and this relation may effect the naming response to the target. Flores d'Arcais and Schreuder (1987) used a picture-naming task where the prime was another picture. It appeared 450 milliseconds before the presentation of the target and was visible for 200 milliseconds. The prime could be related to the target in various ways, among them the following

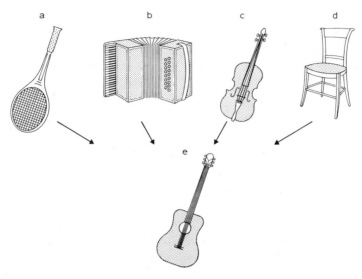

Figure 6.7
A target picture (e) and four prime pictures entertaining different relations to
the target: only perceptually related (a), only functionally related (b), both
perceptually and functionally related (c), and unrelated (d).

two: (i) the prime and the target could be *perceptually similar*, i.e., could
share certain visual features; or (ii) they could be of the same superordinate-
level category, making them *functionally similar*. By realizing both, one, or
none of these two, four kinds of prime result. An example of a target picture
and instances of these four kinds of prime are presented in figure 6.7.

Flores d'Arcais and Schreuder conjectured that there are two "priming
routes," depicted here in figure 6.8. The first route involves visual perceptual features shared by the prime and the target picture; the second one
involves functionally shared features. The bottom part of figure 6.8 is
similar to figures 6.6a and 6.6b, but the figure represents the additional
levels of perceptual and functional feature nodes. The target picture activates a set of visual features, among them P_1 and P_i. The prime picture
activates another set of features, among them P_i and P_m. Hence, P_i is a
perceptual feature activated both by the prime and by the target. If the two
pictures are very similar, they share a large number of perceptual features.
The target picture's features will activate the corresponding concept node,
C_1, and the prime's perceptual features will activate C_2. The first, visual
priming route goes from prime picture to shared perceptual feature (P_i in
the figure) to target concept (C_1). When the prime preactivates P_i, the

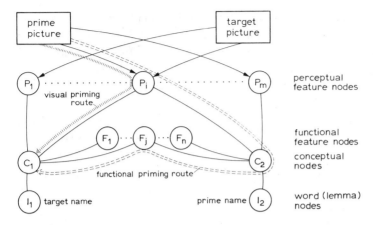

Figure 6.8
Two priming routes. There is direct visual priming, not involving the prime's concept node, and there is functional or conceptual priming which does involve the prime's concept node.

speaker will be quicker in categorizing the target object. This, in turn, will speed up the naming response. Notice that this route does not involve C_2; the prime concept need not be activated.

This is different for the second, functional priming route. The prime's visual features activate the prime's concept node, C_2. This, in turn, shares a functional (or conceptual) feature, F_j, with the target concept (both being musical instruments, for instance), through which activation spreading may take place. The prime/target pairs in figure 6.7 make it possible to test which of these routes is the more effective in speeding up the naming response.

The results are clear-cut. When a prime like that in figure 6.7a was used (i.e., one that shares visual features with the target), the naming response was sped up by some 35 milliseconds as compared to when an unrelated prime was used (figure 6.7d). The visual route, therefore, is quite effective. A prime like 6.7b, however, was not very effective. Naming latency decreased by a nonsignificant 16 milliseconds. The best prime was 6.7c, which has both perceptual and functional features in common with the target. It sped up the naming response by 125 milliseconds.

Huttenlocher and Kubicek (1983), in a very similar experiment, found substantial priming by functionally related pictures (e.g., a drum and a guitar). Some of these pairs were also perceptually related (e.g., a violin and a guitar). In those cases, however, they had been depicted from a different visual perspective (or angle) so that low-level visual processing of the target would not be aided by the prime. These cases were independently studied by Flores d'Arcais and Schreuder, who found that there was substantial priming (47 milliseconds) between functionally related objects when they were physically similar (e.g., a guitar and a violin), even when the visual perspective was different.

Many authors have not used a prime *picture*, but a prime *word*. The printed word doesn't share visual features with the target picture; this excludes the visual priming route. This work is well reviewed in Glaser and Düngelhoff 1984. Here we will consider a major set of results obtained by these authors. An important variable in their study was the delay between presentation of prime word and target picture. This is called the *stimulus-onset asynchrony* (SOA). If the prime precedes the target, the SOA is negative; if it follows the target, the SOA is positive. In all cases the subjects' task was simply to name the picture, and their speech-onset latencies were measured. It is, of course, possible that a prime word can have an effect on naming latency even if it is presented shortly after the picture (i.e., with a positive SOA).

What kinds of prime words did the authors use? First, the prime could be conceptually related to the target. If the picture showed a church, the prime word could be *house*. This is a *related* prime word. Second, the prime word could be *unrelated*. If the picture was a church, an unrelated prime could be *car*. Third, the prime word could be the picture's name. If the picture to be named displayed a church, the *identical prime* was the word *church*. And fourth, the prime could be *neutral*. In this case the "word" presented was just the row xxxxxx. The latter condition was taken as the baseline condition. If a prime word caused picture naming to be faster than in the neutral condition, there was *facilitation*. If naming was slower than in the neutral condition, there was *inhibition*. Figure 6.9 shows the inhibition and facilitation observed for related, unrelated, and identical primes given at different SOAs.

It is clear from figure 6.9 that the identical prime generally caused facilitation, even if it came as late as 200 milliseconds after the target picture. However, the other two kinds of prime—the related and unrelated primes—generally produced an inhibitory effect; their presentation slowed down the naming response. The strongest inhibition resulted from the related prime. The latter result seems to contradict the above-mentioned findings of Huttenlocher et al. and Flores d'Arcais et al. They found that a related picture prime caused shorter naming latencies than an unrelated picture prime. However, both these studies used negative SOAs with an

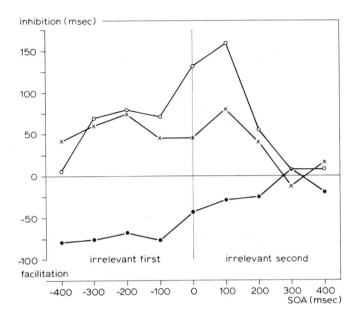

Figure 6.9
Facilitation and inhibition scores for three kinds of prime—related (o),
unrelated (x), and identical (●)—and for different stimulus-onset asynchronies.
(After Glaser and Düngelhoff 1984.)

absolute value of more than 400 milliseconds, the extreme leftmost value in
figure 6.9. There may well be a crossover of related and unrelated curves in
that region. The interpretation of the results in the figure is a matter
of much dispute (see especially Vorberg 1985). For our present purposes it
suffices to conclude that if the prime activates a concept other than the
target, whether related or unrelated, there is interference with the naming
response. The naming response is facilitated only when the identical prime
is given—which shouldn't be surprising, because it activates the target
concept.

    In what on first view seems to be a very different set of experiments,
Schriefers (1985) also found evidence for interference by a second concept,
but now in the naming of a relationship. He presented the subjects with
pairs of figures, such as in figure 6.10.

    Consider the pair of triangles in figure 6.10a. The subject is first pre-
sented with a +, either in the left or in the right side of the field. After 1.5
seconds the pair of triangles is presented. The subject's task is to say
"bigger" or "smaller", indicating whether the triangle in the position of the

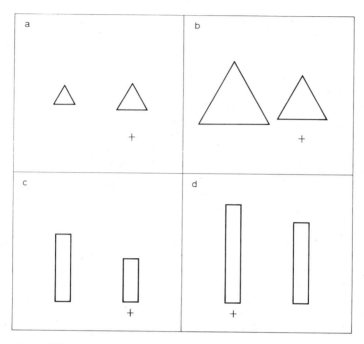

Figure 6.10
Pairs of triangles (a, b) and of sticks (c, d) used in comparative-judgment
experiments by Schriefers (1985). The subject's task was to say whether the
figure marked by + was *bigger* or *smaller*, *taller*, or *shorter* than the other one.

cross is the bigger or the smaller one of the pair. Schriefers complicated this
relation-naming task by mixing pairs of relatively small triangles (as in
6.10a) with pairs of big triangles (as in 6.10b). The obtained naming
latencies showed a strong *congruency effect*: When there was a pair of small
triangles the subjects were quicker in saying "smaller" than in saying
"larger", but with pairs of large triangles they were quicker to say "larger"
than to say "smaller". Exactly the same pattern of results was obtained for
pairs of sticks that varied in tallness, as in figures 6.10c and 6.10d. Saying
"taller" was easier when both sticks were tall, as in 6.10d; saying "shorter"
was the speedier response when both were short, as in 6.10c. In other words,
the latency of the naming response is shortest when the to-be-judged
relative size of a figure is congruent with the *absolute* size of the pair.
Schriefers explained this result by assuming a conflict in the decision-
making (or categorization) stage. When there is a pair of big figures, the
concept **BIG** is automatically created in the subject's mind. This will

interfere with the preparation of the judgment SMALLER, but it will facilitate the preparation of the judgment BIGGER.

This congruency result is very much like the previously discussed findings. When, together with the target concept, a different concept is created in the speaker's mind, there will be interference with the naming of the target. An essential question for all these findings is whether this is, as I have suggested, a matter of interference at the conceptual level, or whether the retrieval of the lexical item for one concept may suffer from activation of the other lexical item. Schriefers tested this explicitly. If it is really a matter of interference at the level of lexical access, the congruency effect should disappear when no verbal response is required. To test this, Schriefers repeated the experiment with tall and short sticks (figures 6.10c and 6.10d), but now requiring the subject to press one button when the taller of two sticks was marked and another button when the shorter stick was marked. The outcome showed an undiminished congruency effect, revealing that the interference occurs really at the judgmental, conceptual level.

6.5.3   Lexical Access

In the same series of experiments Schriefers also found a *semantic-markedness effect*. When triangle pairs of only one size category were presented, as in figure 6.10a, the response "bigger" was systematically given with shorter latency than the response "smaller". Similarly, for pairs of tall and short bars, as in figure 6.10c, the response "taller" came reliably more quickly than the response "shorter".

Adjectives such as *big* and *tall* are called *semantically unmarked*. These terms can neutrally denote the whole dimension of size or vertical extension. For example, the question "how big is your dog?" does not presuppose that the dog is big, whereas "how small is your dog?" does presuppose that the dog is small. (See Clark and Clark 1977 for a detailed discussion of the markedness notion.)

What Schriefers found, therefore, was that it takes more time to retrieve a semantically marked relation name than it takes to retrieve an unmarked one. Is this a matter of judgment, like the congruency effect? To test this, Schriefers repeated the experiment with tall and short bars, but now with push-button reactions. Would the markedness effect stay, as did the congruency effect? The result was unequivocal: There was no longer any trace of the markedness effect. To obtain the effect, it is apparently necessary to have a *verbal* response. In other words, the effect is due to finding or articulating the word. Schriefers ruled out the latter possibility by measuring pure articulation latencies independently. The semantic markedness effect is due entirely to accessing of the lexical item.

Another effect that is also generally considered to arise at the level of lexical access is the *word-frequency effect*, already mentioned in the discussion of logogen theory (subsection 6.3.2). On a picture-naming task, Oldfield and Wingfield (1965) found a high correlation between naming latency and the frequency with which the object name occurs in language use. Speech onset for *basket*, for instance, took 640 milliseconds from picture onset; *syringe* took 1,080 milliseconds on the average.

Is this difference due to visual processing and categorization, i.e., to the time needed to *recognize* the object? Wingfield (1968) showed that this was not the case by measuring recognition latencies for the same objects. To measure the recognition latency for a basket, for instance, subjects were repeatedly given the same set of pictures, but now with the task of pushing a button every time they saw a basket and giving no response otherwise. Such a recognition test was done for each object in the set. Word frequency showed no correlation with these recognition latencies. Like the semantic-markedness effect, the frequency effect arises in the phase of lexical access, not earlier. The two effects may, moreover, be connected; semantically marked adjectives are usually of lower frequency of usage than unmarked ones.

The word-frequency effect was also found in the above-mentioned study by Huttenlocher and Kubicek, who found that pictures with high-frequency names were responded to more rapidly (by some 100 milliseconds) than ones with low-frequency names. This effect was independent of the priming effect; i.e., the same frequency effect was found whether or not the priming picture was related to the target. This again testifies to the stage view of lexical access: The categorization stage is sensitive to semantic priming, the following lexical accessing stage is sensitive to word frequency, and the two effects are additive. Schriefers's congruency and markedness effects were also additive, the same two stages being involved.*

Huttenlocher and Kubicek showed, further, that the 100-millisecond word-frequency effect they found was not due to the initiation of articulation. The effect vanished almost completely when the same words that had been given as names in the original experiment were simply read. Like Schriefers, these authors excluded an articulatory explanation.

---

*A recent study by Humphreys, Riddoch, and Quinlan (1988) provides some evidence that the frequency effect is not *always* independent of semantic priming. Some interaction may arise when very long (negative) SOAs are used (-5 seconds in their experiment).

6.5.4 Accessing Lemmas and Word Forms: Two Stages?

So far we have recognized the following stages or levels of processing in picture naming: There is, first, a stage of visual processing. At this level there is a facilitating effect of visual similarity between prime and target. There is, second, a stage of conceptual categorization. At this level of processing, conceptual or functional closeness of prime and target has an effect on naming latency. Third, there is the level of lexical access proper. Here word frequency and semantic markedness have their effects. The semantic conditions for the retrieval of an item at this stage are created at the second level of processing, during conceptual categorization.

A question deserving further scrutiny is this: Are an item's lemma and form properties retrieved *simultaneously* or *successively* during the phase of lexical access? The issue is, of course, not whether lemma and word-form information are distinct kinds of information in the lexical entry, nor whether these kinds of information are relevant in subsequent phases of the formulating process (viz., during grammatical and phonological encoding, respectively). Rather, the issue is whether the lexical retrieval stage has to be further partitioned into two subsequent retrieval steps. Let us anticipate the conclusion: We do not know.

One phenomenological argument for a two-step retrieval process is the "tip-of-the-tongue phenomenon," which will be discussed in chapter 9. Everyone has had the experience that—even in fluent speech, and often to the speaker's surprise—an intended word just doesn't come. Still, one knows that something has been accessed—that the word is on the tip of one's tongue. One may even know the initial consonant or the number of syllables. It is tempting to say that in such cases the lemma has been accessed. The word's syntax has become available; the troublesome word is correctly embedded in the syntactic environment. The phonological form, however, resists retrieval.

But no critical experiments have been done to show that under tip-of-the-tongue conditions the item's syntactical properties, such as its gender, have indeed been retrieved. Does the French speaker who is in the tip-of-the-tongue state know whether the word is a *le* word or a *la* word? It might still be the case that as soon as an item's conceptual conditions are met, syntax and word form are simultaneously retrieved. In the tip-of-the-tongue state this *joint* retrieval would then be blocked.

Butterworth (forthcoming) presents an excellent review of the evidence for the two-stage theory of lexical access. There is indeed convincing experimental support (Kempen and Huijbers 1983; Levelt and Maassen 1981) for the notion that semantic activation precedes form activation in lexical access. The problem is that we do not know the status of this semantic activation. Is it "mere" stage-2 activation, i.e., activation of the concepts to be expressed? Or is it stage-3 activation, i.e., lemma activation involving a word's semantic/syntactic composition? This question is, as yet, unanswered.

6.5.5 Are Categorization and Lexical Access Nonoverlapping Stages?

A related question still under scrutiny is whether the second and third levels of processing, categorization and lexical access, are not only successive but also temporally *nonoverlapping* stages. Does lexical access begin only after the categorization has been completed, or is it rather the case that lexical activation occurs as soon as there is *any* categorization response? It could, in particular, be the case that a first, vague categorization response activates a semantically related set of lexical items—a *semantic cohort*—which is further narrowed down as the categorization becomes sharper and more definite. We considered this possibility to explain blends such as *clear* [*close/near*] in subsection 6.4.2.

Evidence that there is temporal overlap between the phases of categorization and lexical access can be found in Humphreys et al. 1988. Levelt et al. (in preparation) found that, on an object-naming task, phonological activation follows the categorization response with a very short delay. There may be a short period during which there is both semantic and phonological activation. The latter kind of activation, however, is maintained till the moment of speech onset, whereas the categorization response fades out quickly after the picture's presentation. In other words, the two phases are successive, but there may be a short period of overlap.

The fact that it is possible to demonstrate the existence of a "late" phase in object naming, in which there is activation of an item's form but no longer any activation of its meaning, is of course supportive of the idea that there can be form activation without lemma activation.

Summary

The mental lexicon plays a central role in the generation of speech. It is the repository of information about the words the speaker has available for production. This information involves, at least, the meaning of each item and its syntactic, morphological, and phonological properties. Some authors distinguish between an item's lemma information, which is essential for grammatical encoding, and its form information, which is used in the subsequent phase of phonological encoding. Entries in the mental lexicon are mutually related in various ways, according to both meaning and form.

Not all the words a speaker uses are stored in the lexicon. Words can be newly constructed on the spot. But languages differ enormously in the amount of lexical encoding they require. Speakers of English rely to a great extent on their store of frequently used words and idioms.

A lexical item's lemma information consists of the conceptual specifications for its use (including pragmatic and stylistic conditions), and of various kinds of (morpho-)syntactic properties. Among the latter are the lemma's syntactic category, the grammatical functions it imposes, and the relations between these functions and the conceptual variables or thematic roles in the conceptual structure. Also, lemmas have various diacritical variables whose parameters have to be set during grammatical encoding. Among them are such variables as person, number, tense, aspect, mood, case, and pitch accent.

There is a preference hierarchy for grammatical functions, with the subject function being the most highly valued one. Similarly, there is a "pecking order" for thematic roles, with agent as the highest-ranking one. The highest-ranking thematic role tends to be mapped onto the most preferred grammatical function. This alignment of functions and roles is acknowledged by most verbs, though not by all. Often verbs have alternative mapping orders, such as active and passive. The latter makes it possible to assign the subject function to a lower-ranking argument (e.g., for purposes of topicalization).

How are lexical items accessed during fluent speech? There are two essential criteria on which theories of access should be judged. The first one is how a theory accounts for the speed of access. Theories that are strongly sequential in character fail on this criterion. The fast access that occurs in fluent speech, as well as various speech-error phenomena, are revealing of parallel processing. The second criterion is convergence. Can a theory account for accessing of the correct item, given a speaker's intention to express a particular concept? The touchstone for correct convergence is a theory's solution of the hypernym problem: Given a concept to be expressed, how does the theory ensure that the corresponding item is accessed but none of its hypernyms? A review of various theories showed that some fail on the speed criterion (discrimination nets, maybe table linkage), and that all fail on the criterion of convergence (i.e., also logogen theory, decision-table theory, and activation spreading). A step toward the remedying of this lack of convergence was the formulation of three principles that, when implemented in a processing theory, guarantee correct convergence without creating insurmountable problems for meeting the speed criterion.

Speech errors such as word blends, substitutions, and exchanges are not random phenomena. The tongue slips in patterns, revealing aspects of the machinery involved in lexical access. Blends have their prime cause at the conceptual level: Two or more concepts compete for expression. The intruding term is often a near-synonym, but a blend can also be due to an intruding (Freudian) thought. Substitutions, on the other hand, are caused mainly (though not solely) by word association—i.e., direct associative connections between lemmas. Exchanges, finally, can arise when two different concepts in a message simultaneously trigger lexical items that are of the same syntactic category. This last kind of error causation will be taken up extensively in the next chapter. In all cases, speech errors reveal the parallel activation of more than a single lexical item.

The final section of the present chapter discussed the time course of lexical access, in particular the processing stages involved in the naming of objects or of visual relations. Three stages or levels of processing were distinguished. The first is the visual processing of the picture. This stage is sensitive to interference by visually similar material. The second stage is concerned with categorizing the visual pattern. There is a preference for using "basic-level" categories at this level of processing. This stage is differentially sensitive to interference by primes of the same and of different semantic categories. The third stage is lexical access proper, the speed of which is highly dependent on the frequency of usage of the addressed item. There is reason to suppose that this last process evolves over time in such a way that an item's lemma information decays before its form information.

Chapter 7
The Generation of Surface Structure

According to our lexical hypothesis, grammatical encoding is lexically driven. Conceptually activated lemmas instigate a variety of syntactic procedures to construct their proper syntactic environments. The procedures build the phrasal, clausal, and sentential patterns that express the required grammatical functions by means of phrasal ordering and case marking. Grammatical encoding is the process by which a message is mapped onto a surface structure.

In the present chapter we will first consider the kind of architecture needed for a Grammatical Encoder that is not only lexically driven but also incremental in its operation. The requirement of incrementality, as we saw in chapter 1, implies that a surface structure is, by and large, generated "from left to right" as successive fragments of the message become available. Wundt's principle requires that the generation of surface structure occur without much lookahead or backtracking, so that each surface unit produced can immediately be processed by the Phonological Encoder. The only explicit or computational theory of grammatical encoding that is both lexically driven and incremental in its operation is the Incremental Production Grammar (Kempen and Hoenkamp 1982, 1987; Kempen 1987; De Smedt and Kempen 1987; Hoenkamp 1983; for a review of other computational models of language generation, see Kempen 1988). The sketch of the Grammatical Encoder in section 7.1 will follow the main lines of this theory, which is a natural companion to Bresnan's Lexical Functional Grammar. The first aim of this sketch is to show that an incremental lexically driven Grammatical Encoder is a coherent and possible notion. The second aim is to demonstrate the notion's empirical potential. I will do this by mixing the presentation of the architecture with analyses of speech errors. Errors of grammatical encoding can be quite revealing of the underlying mechanisms. Are they consistent with the proposed architecture, or are they occasionally problematic?

After the rather "algorithmic" section 7.1, we will turn to the more classical research tradition in the psycholinguistics of grammatical encoding. Section 7.2 will deal with units of grammatical encoding. What do pauses and speech-onset latencies tell us about "chunks" of grammatical encoding? Section 7.3 addresses the question of how the speaker assigns grammatical functions to more or less prominent arguments in the message. The accessibility of concepts and the need to topicalize can affect the course and the outcome of grammatical encoding. Section 7.4 reviews some research on cohesion in grammatical encoding. How does the speaker make use of referential expressions and syntactic means in order to make his ongoing sentence cohesive with previous discourse? Section 7.5 approaches the issues raised in chapter 1: whether grammatical encoding can feed back to message encoding (this should not be the case in a modular theory) and whether grammatical encoding can, in turn, be affected by feedback from the next processing component—phonological encoding.

For a solid review of the psycholinguistic research in grammatical encoding, see Bock 1987a.

7.1 The Architecture of Grammatical Encoding

7.1.1 Some Basic Kinds of Operation
The claim that grammatical encoding is lexically driven implies that the encoding operations are largely controlled by the grammatical properties of the lemmas retrieved. It does not mean that lexical elements are *procedures*. The previous chapter treated lemmas rather as bundles of *declarative* knowledge about a word's meaning and grammar. This declarative knowledge becomes available when a lemma is retrieved. The grammatical encoding procedures of the Formulator will then be guided by the information the lemmas make available. The lemma *give*, for instance, requires slots for its subject and for its direct and indirect objects. This causes dedicated syntactic procedures to set up the appropriate frame. More generally, lemmas call specialized syntactic procedures in some orderly fashion, so as to produce a unified surface structure as eventual output. It is in this vein that Kempen and Hoenkamp (1987) made a procedural package of what verbs require of their syntactic environment, and similar packages for nouns, adjectives, and prepositions. These packages are the specialists that build S-, NP-, AP-, and PP-constituents around the major category lemmas. They contain the necessary procedural knowledge for dealing with the grammatical constraints that the different kinds of lemma impose on their syntactic environment.

Our initial sketch of the architecture proposed by Kempen and Hoenkamp will be made from a concrete example: the generation of the simple declarative sentence *the child gave the mother the CAT* (with pitch accent on CAT), for which the groundwork has already been laid in chapters 5 and 6. Since the example is an English sentence, some adaptations of the algorithm will be necessary—in particular, the addition of a VP-procedure (which is probably not necessary for the generation of Dutch, Kempen and Hoenkamp's target language). There are seven major kinds of procedure involved in the generation of such a sentence.

1. A lemma is retrieved if a fragment of the message satisfies its conceptual specifications. This semantically conditioned retrieval of lemmas was discussed extensively in chapter 6.

The message underlying the example sentence was given in figure 5.1a and is repeated here.

message:

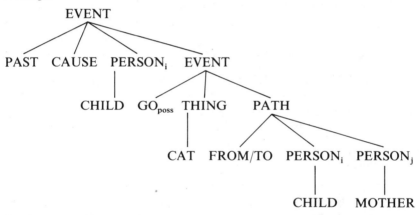

In chapter 5 the accessibility status of the referents in this message was ignored. Here we will assume that all three referents (CHILD, CAT, and MOTHER) are " + accessible." We will, moreover, assume that CAT is " + prominent" (see subsection 4.5.1). Remember, moreover, that the left-to-right ordering is merely a notational convention. The order in which the message fragments become available may be a different one. That order can be a major determinant of the eventual syntactic form, as we will see.

Suppose that the concept CHILD was the first message fragment delivered by the conceptualizer. Only the lemma *child* out of the speaker's 30,000 or so lemmas finds its conceptual conditions satisfied. It is retrieved, and its internal grammatical specifications become available.

2. The lemma's syntactic category calls a *categorial procedure*, namely a building instruction for the phrasal category in which the lemma can fulfill the function of head. This holds for lemmas of types N, V, A, and P; the categorial procedures are NP, VP, AP, and PP, respectively.

The lemma *child* is of syntactic category N, and N can only be head of a noun phrase, NP (see subsection 5.1.3). So, *child* calls procedure NP, which is specialized in building noun phrases.

Categorial procedures can be called not only by lemmas but also by higher-order functional procedures—procedures that try to realize a certain head-of-phrase function (e.g., predicate for S, main verb for VP, head noun for NP) or a certain grammatical function (e.g., subject, direct object).

3. The categorial procedure inspects the message for conceptual material that can fill its obligatory or optional complements and specifiers and can provide values for diacritic parameters. Categorial procedures can also inspect the message for relevant head-of-phrase information.

The NP categorial procedure with *child* as head looks for modifying or specifying information attached to the concept CHILD in the message. In particular, it checks the accessibility status of CHILD, and it finds the value " + accessible". In addition, since *child* is a count noun, the procedure inspects the concept for number and comes up with the parameter "singular". The NP procedure derives the parameter value "third person" from the lemma's syntactic category N.

4. The categorial procedure transfers control to subroutines—functional procedures for handling all the complements, specifiers, and parameter values it has found. These subroutines work in parallel.

In the example, NP calls upon the functional procedure DET, which can generate a definite specifier expressing the conceptual information " + accessible". DET calls the lemma *the*, which consists largely of a pointer to the word form. In other languages, such as French and Dutch, DET will have to inspect the gender and number parameters of the NP-head and insert their values in the list of diacritic parameters of the article lemma. This is, of course, required for finding the appropriate word form (*le*, *la*, or *les* in French; *de* or *het* in Dutch). In German and various other languages, the functional procedure DET also needs case information, since the word form of the article depends on the grammatical function of the NP by which it was called (subject of the sentence, object of the prepositional phrase, etc.). So far, this grammatical function is still undetermined for *the child*.

NP also hands the "singular" information to the head-of-phrase procedure, which inserts it as a diacritic parameter value in the lemma for *child*.

Generally, the functional procedures deliver their results to the categorial specialist that called them. In the example, DET delivers the lemma *the* to the NP, and the head noun procedure does the same with *child*.

5. The categorial procedure determines the order of the materials it receives back from the functional procedures it called. Each categorial procedure has a "holder" with a number of slots, and there are certain restrictions on the order in which the slots can be filled by the procedure. There is, however, an important psychological principle here: *Materials will be put in the leftmost slot they are allowed to occupy.*

The latter is an implementation of the "left-to-right" incremental principle. Fragments of a message are grammatically expressed as much as possible in the order in which they became available. As we will see in the more empirical sections of this chapter, topical or salient concepts tend to be expressed early in the sentence. In terms of the model, one could say that their categorial procedures are initiated early because their lemmas are available early. Left-to-right filling of contiguous slots in the holders of categorial procedures at the earliest possible moment contributes to the fluency of speech, because phonological encoding can proceed "on line" (i.e., incrementally from left to right).

In the example, the NP procedure puts the lemma *the* to the left of the lemma *child*. This is an obligatory order for English. However, the fact that the whole NP *the child* will end up as the leftmost constituent of the sentence is due not to an obligatory ordering but to Wundt's principle (subsection 1.5.2). CHILD being the first conceptual fragment to become available causes the noun phrase *the child* to end up in sentence-initial position.

6. The categorial procedure chooses a grammatical function for its output; that is, it decides on its *functional destination*. It will become a head or a complement of some higher-order categorial procedure. Higher-order categorial procedures are ones that do not have lemmas but phrases as heads. They are NP', VP', AP', PP', and S (the latter takes a VP or VP' as head or predicate). The main rule for functional destination is that it is precisely the head or complement function of the higher-order procedure that called the categorial procedure to start with. If there is no such higher-order calling procedure, there is a preferential destination (and in fact a preferential destination *order*) for each categorial procedure.

Let us see how this works in the above example. Remember that the NP categorial procedure that generated *the child* was called by the noun lemma *child*, not by any higher-order categorial procedure. The default destination for the output of the NP procedure is "subject of S". Or, in the format of chapter 5: The NP acquires the subscript SUBJ and hence subordinates itself to the categorial procedure S. This provides NP, at the same time, with the diacritic case feature "nominative", which is then available for the procedures DET and N when their lemmas require diacritic case values. (They don't in the present example.) Later we will consider cases where there *is* a higher-order calling procedure.

7. The preferential higher-order categorial procedure is activated by receiving the output of a lower-order procedure.

In this way, NP$_{SUBJ}$ calls the categorial procedure S, which is a specialist in building sentences. S accepts the noun phrase as its subject, and registers its person (third) and number (singular) parameters. S also inspects the message for a mood marker. It finds none, which induces S to impose the default declarative constituent order (see subsection 3.5.1). S can then assign the subject noun phrase to its leftmost slot by an operation of type 5. (When there is a mood marker, IMP or ?, this will lead to a diacritic feature on the verb. Such a mood-marked verb calls the appropriate categorial procedure for imperative or interrogative word order.)

These are the seven main kinds of procedures underlying the architecture of grammatical encoding in the Kempen-Hoenkamp model. Each individual procedure can be written as a production—a condition/action pair of the kind IF X THEN Y, where X is the condition and Y is the action.

Let us see what stage we have reached in the generation of the surface structure of *the child gave the mother the CAT*. It is easily displayed by the following bit of tree structure:

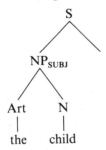

This may not seem much; however, *the child* has reached its final, leftmost position in the sentence. There is nothing to prevent its phonological encoding while the grammatical encoding for the remainder of the sentence is still in (parallel) operation. This is incremental production.

The following encoding steps are essentially of the same kind as the previous ones. The categorial procedure S, once called, will execute procedures of type 3. It will, in particular, scan the message for a conceptual function that has CHILD as an argument. The only function in the message satisfying this property is CAUSE. More precise:

CAUSE (PERSON$_i$, EVENT)

where PERSON$_i$ = CHILD.

The procedure S also inspects the modifiers of the CAUSE function to set its tense parameter (and similarly for aspect, which will be ignored here). It finds PAST (which was shorthand for deictic r < u and intrinsic e = r; see subsections 2.2.3 and 3.2.6). This induces S to assign the value "past tense" to its tense parameter.

Having localized the function of which CHILD is an argument and registered its temporal modifiers, S turns to a type 4 operation. It calls the functional procedure that can construct its head of phrase, or predicate: the PRED procedure. S provides it with the collected diacritic parameters: "past tense", "third person", and "plural". S reserves its second slot for the predicate output: the verb phrase (the first slot being occupied by the subject NP). Since this slot is consecutive to the already-filled leftmost slot, S allows the PRED procedure to make its output incrementally available to the Phonological Encoder.

PRED, in its turn, calls the categorial specialist VP, which inspects the message to localize materials for its head of phrase, the verb. The structure of the tree emanating from the CAUSE function is compatible with the conceptual specifications of *give* (see subsection 6.2.1). But it is also compatible with the semantics of *receive* (subsection 6.2.2). However, only a lemma that maps the agent onto SUBJ of S can comply with the already-generated functional destination of the NP *the child*. The lemma *receive* would assign the SUBJ function to the goal argument, which is inappropriate. The lemma *give*, however, makes the mapping

X(agent), Y(theme), Z(goal)
  | | |
SUBJ   DO   IO

(and we momentarily disregard the other lemma for *give*, which also assigns the agent a subject role; see subsection 6.2.2). VP accepts this lemma as its head of phrase.

Procedure VP transmits its diacritic parameters to V, its head of phrase, which initiates the functional main-verb procedure. It assigns the parameters to the main-verb lemma *give*. The parameters are set to create a so-called tensed verb, i.e., a verb which is marked for tense and which agrees with the sentence subject in terms of person and number. This being completed, the main-verb procedure will report its output to VP, which, by an operation of type 5, assigns the first or leftmost slot in its holder to this lemma, by which it becomes available for phonological encoding.

In the example we are constructing, the retrieval of *give* was initiated by a syntactic procedure (the VP procedure). There was a need for a main verb. But *give* could also have been retrieved without syntactic intervention, in just the same way as *child* was—that is, by mere "resonance" with the corresponding fragment of the message. In that case, the retrieved verb lemma would have called the categorial procedure VP, which would eventually have delivered its output to S, its preferential destination.

How far have we proceeded? After the lemmas *the* and *child*, *give* has now reached its final destination in the surface structure. The situation is this:

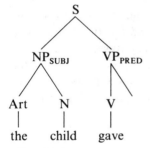

The phonological properties of *give* with parameters "3rd person", "singular", and "past" (the graph presents this as *gave*) can now be retrieved by the phonological encoding procedures concurrent with the further generation of the surface structure.

Next VP calls the functional procedures direct object (DO) and indirect object (IO) to inspect the message (operations of type 3). This is done in order to find the *theme* and the *goal*, respectively, as required by the head verb. Remember that the lemma for *give* dictates the *theme* to map onto a direct-object complement, and the *goal* onto an indirect-object complement.

The functional procedures DO and IO, which may run in parallel, identify CAT and MOTHER (respectively) in the message. They both call the categorial procedure NP to lexicalize these conceptual fragments. The NP procedure is of type 3, and it may run in parallel for DO and IO. Both running NP procedures call the head-noun procedure to inspect the message fragments made available by DO and IO. This can, again, be done in parallel fashion. It leads to the retrieval of the lemmas *cat* and *mother*, respectively. Meanwhile, the NP-procedures perform operations of type 3; i.e., they look for modifying or specifying information attached to the message fragments they are working on (CAT and MOTHER). Both register the property " + accessible", and the one working on CAT also finds the feature " + prominent". The former feature leads to the NP's calling a definite DET procedure. The registered prominence of CAT causes NP to produce a focus feature (f). The head-noun procedures deliver their lemmas (*cat* and *mother*) to their respective NP procedures, which accept these lemmas as heads of phrase. From here on, both NPs are constructed in the way we have seen for the NP *the child*. The head of phrase *cat* receives the focus feature (f), which will, in turn, be translated into a pitch-accent parameter for the lemma *cat* in accordance with the rules discussed in section 5.2. The parallel-running NP procedures have DO and IO as functional destinations for their output in the type 6 operation. This is because they had been called to fill these VP slots to start with.

When the functional procedures DO and IO receive the trees the NP procedures have built (i.e., those for *the cat* and *the mother*), they assign accusative and dative case, respectively, just as SUBJ assigned nominative case to the NP for *the child*. It is important to note that, according to this algorithm, case is assigned at a fairly late stage—namely *after* the NPs return their trees to the functional procedures that called them. One motive for organizing the control structure in this way derives from the nature of certain speech errors; we will return to this shortly.

Operations of type 5 make VP arrange the NPs in the order IO → DO. Finally, VP turns to a type 6 procedure, choosing the predicate functional procedure that called it as its functional destination. The predicate information is then delivered to S, which puts it in the second slot of its holder. Because nothing remains to be covered in the message, S halts the procedure. The produced surface structure is

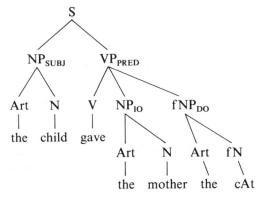

(where *gave* is shorthand for *give* with its diacritic parameters, and *cAt* stands for *cat* plus pitch accent).

This picture is misleading insofar as it is a static representation of what was built up and transmitted over time. If one were to draw only the *active* nodes at any one moment, one would never see the whole graph. At the final stage, just after NP_{DO} has put the lemma *cat* in its second slot, the only active part of the tree is

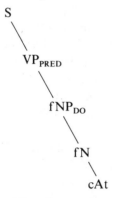

The Kempen-Hoenkamp algorithm shows a strict alternation in the calling of procedures: Categorial procedures call functional procedures, and functional procedures call categorial procedures. Also, a categorial procedure always delivers its output to the functional procedure that called it (if any), and normally a functional procedure delivers its output to the categorial procedure that called it.

Lemma structure plays a central role in the generation of surface structure. In particular, the main verb dictates what arguments have to be checked in the message, and which grammatical functions will be assigned to them. In the Kempen-Hoenkamp algorithm the activation of lemmas is, to some degree, guided by procedures of type 3. The control structure of the encoding operations dictates which parts of the message are accessed for gramatical encoding at what moments. This may activate certain lemmas that would otherwise have stayed asleep for a while.

But the control structure itself depends on the availability of the different message fragments (incremental production). In the example, CHILD was available early in the message. It activated the lemma *child* without the intervention of a type 3 procedure. As a consequence, the first categorial procedure to run was NP. The order in which grammatical encoding procedures operate depends, in part, on the order in which lemmas become available. And this, in turn, depends on the order in which message fragments are produced by the speaker. Fluent speech requires incremental production. Lemmas are grammatically and phonologically processed as soon as possible after retrieval. Subsequent grammatical encoding procedures will adapt to already available structure rather than revise it. An example is the choice of *give* after the NP *the child* had been generated. To keep the NP in its leftmost position, the lemma *receive*—which did fit the conceptual specification in the message, and might have been used, was filtered out by the categorial procedures. Its use would have created extra waiting time in order to construct the NP *the mother* for appearance in leftmost position, and for revising the subject assignment of *the child*. It is probably too strong to say that such "on the fly" revisions never occur; they are, however, kept to a minimum.

Incremental production can also explain the choice of a passive lemma for *give* when *cat* would have been the first available lemma. The noun *cat* would have called NP, and this categorial procedure would have claimed the subject function for *the cat*. S would have assigned this NP its leftmost slot. But then the passive-verb lemma, which maps the *theme* argument onto SUBJ (subsection 6.2.2), would be the only appropriate choice for further processing. The final result would have been the surface structure corresponding to *The cat was given to the mother by the child*. It is, of course, an important question what determines the availability or primacy of a lemma. It clearly has to do with the topichood of the corresponding concept in the message. This factor and other determinants will be considered in section 7.3.

Parallel processing is a main contributor to fluency. In the example, the direct-object and indirect-object constituents were constructed in parallel. There are no control problems here as long as the active procedures are all connected, as in the example. But imagine the situation in which both CHILD and CAT are available early in the message such that both lemmas *child* and *cat* are independently and more or less simultaneously retrieved. Both will call NP procedures. These, in turn, will both deliver their output to S as a preferential destination; both will claim the subject function for their output (*the child* and *the cat*, respectively). The simplest control measure is that prior entry will decide such cases. If the NP procedure that constructs *the child* is the first to call S, the other one (constructing *the cat*) will be given its second preferential destination. This is a procedure of type 6. This second preference will be the direct-object function. The only verb lemma that can satisfy both the conceptual specifications in the message and the grammatical functions now assigned to the conceptual arguments is the alternative active lemma for *give* (which has so far been ignored in the discussion). It will then govern the generation of the sentence *The child gave the cat to the mother*, where *cat* is the direct object. Empirical evidence in support of this analysis will be presented in section 7.3.

It is not obvious that the rate of left-to-right delivery of surface structure fragments corresponds perfectly to the rate of the subsequent phonological encoding of these fragments. Hence, fragments may occasionally have to wait for further processing. This requires a buffering facility for output of grammatical encoding: the Syntactic Buffer. The Phonological Encoder retrieves subsequent fragments from this buffer.

7.1.2 Speech Errors: Exchanges of Same-Category Phrases and Words

The algorithm so far can provide a better understanding of how certain word and phrase exchanges arise in fluent speech. In chapter 6 word exchanges were adduced to parallel processing of different message fragments. In the example above, there is parallelness in the grammatical encoding of MOTHER and CAT. The two NPs are constructed simultaneously, according to the algorithm. Let us consider how the following error could arise:

(1) The child gave the cat the mOther [*instead of*: The child gave the mother the cAt]

The error may arise at an early stage of generation, namely when the two NP procedures accept their head nouns. We saw that, according to the algorithm, each NP called a head-noun procedure that would retrieve the lemmas for the corresponding arguments in the message (MOTHER and CAT). These head-noun procedures may err in the destination of their output, the lemmas *mother* and *cat*. The NP procedures blindly accept whatever noun is made available at the time they need one. In a parallel-processing environment, this may on occasion be the wrong one. The only thing that counts at this level of processing is that the head slot of NP is filled by a lemma of syntactic category N.

The consequences of such a destination error are quite interesting. First, the NP working on CAT will equally blindly assign its focus feature (f) to its head noun, which is now the lemma *mother*. As a consequence, *mother* will receive pitch accent. This is called *stranding*: The pitch accent stays in place, detached from its exchanging target lemma. The replacing element (*mother*) is said to *accommodate* the stranded feature. Second, each NP will call the appropriate DET procedure, i.e., the procedure involved in expressing the intended referent's accessibility status. The effect is invisible in example 1, because both NPs required definite determiners. But if the target sentence had been *The child gave the mother a cAt*, the exchange error would have produced *The child gave the cat a mOther*.

And indeed, real word reversals tend to show both properties . Examples 2 (from Fromkin 1973) is a case in point.

(2) Seymour sliced the knife with a salAmi [*instead of*: the salami with a knIfe]

Here the nouns *knife* and *salami* are exchanged. Stranding of accent occurs, according to expectation. In fact, Fromkin noted that this is the general rule in word reversals. The accent-stranding phenomenon—probably first noticed by Boomer and Laver (1968)—has been extensively analyzed by Fromkin (1971), Garrett (1982),* and others. In addition, the example error shows stranding of (in)definiteness: The determiners *the* and *a* appear in the right places, but with the wrong nouns.

What should happen to the number feature, on the present theoretical analysis? It was suggested that, by a procedure of type 3, the NP procedure registers the conceptual information that would be relevant for computing the number parameter of its head count noun. And, by a procedure of type 4, NP hands the computed number feature to the head-of-phrase procedure, which inserts it as a diacritic parameter in its lemma. This predicts that number should strand in word reversals as well. When NP accepts the wrong head of phrase, it will blindly provide it with the originally derived number feature. And indeed, such cases occur. Here is an example from Fromkin 1973:

(3) a hole full of floors [*instead of*: a floor full of holes]

If the number feature had exchanged as well, the result would have been *holes full of a floor*.

However, there are cases where number does move with its "own" lemma, as in the following (from Fromkin 1971):

(4) examine the horse of the eyes [*instead of*: the eyes of the horse]

The error was not *examine the horses of the eye*. Stemberger (1985a) reported that stranding of the plural, as in example 3, is about four times as frequent as non-stranding cases, such as example 4. This suggests that examples 3 and 4 have different etiologies. In example 4 we probably have to deal with an exchange of whole noun phrases (*the horse* and *the eyes*) instead of a mere exchange of head nouns. Where could this arise in the

---

*Garrett (1982) gives examples that suggest that there is less or no stranding of *contrastive* accent. This agrees with Cutler and Isard's (1980) special treatment of contrastive stress, referred to in subsection 5.2.2.

sketched algorithm? It could occur at the later stage where the NP procedures deliver their output to their functional destinations, direct object (of
examine) and oblique object (of *of*). These are procedures of type 6. If the
DO and OBL (oblique object) procedures are, in parallel, waiting to receive
a noun phrase, a destination error may occur: DO accepts *the horse* and
OBL takes *the eyes*, probably because of some slight mistiming.

That destination errors for complete NPs indeed occur is apparent from
the following two examples:

(5) I have to smoke my coffee with a cigarette [*instead of*: I have to
smoke a cigarette with my coffee] (from Fromkin 1973)

(6) I got into this guy with a discussion [*instead of*: I got into a
discussion with this guy] (from Garrett 1980a)

In each of these cases there is an exchange of full noun phrases: *my
coffee* and *a cigarette* in example 5, *this guy* and *a discussion* in example 6.

If indeed the noun phrases were delivered to the wrong functional
destinations, one would expect a stranding of case marking but not a
stranding of plural. Remember that the algorithm assigns case to a constituent only *after* it has been returned to the functional procedure that
instigated its construction. The speech-error data are not conclusive in this
respect. English has rather poor case morphology, and the published
speech-error corpora do not contain much relevant material. One interesting example can be found in Fay (1980b):

(7) If I was done to that [*instead of*: If that was done to me]

Here the subject (*that*) and the prepositional object (*me*) switched places.
But the error did not become *If me was done to that*; the first person
pronoun was given nominative case (*I*), as it should in a subject function.
This is in agreement with the algorithm.

German is richer in case marking, and indeed Meringer and Mayer's
(1896) corpus contains a few word exchanges involving case. Some of
them clearly follow the predicted pattern of case stranding, such as the
following:

(8) Bis er es bei Dir abholt [*instead of*: Bis Du es bei ihm abholst] (*English
translation*: Until he collects it from you)

If case had moved with the pronouns, the speaker would have said *Bis ihm
es bei Du abholt*. However, the subject pronoun receives nominal case
marking, as it should. Similarly, the prepositional object (*Dir*) has the
correct dative case. A more recent, negative example is this, from the
Bierwisch corpus:

(9) Wenn der Wand aus der Nagel fällt [*instead of*: Wenn der Nagel aus der Wand fällt] (*English translation*: when the (dative) wall falls from the (nominative) nail)

If case had stranded, the error would have been *Wenn die Wand aus dem Nagel fällt* (*When the* (nominative) *wall falls from the* (dative) *nail*).

Berg (1987) reports other examples of failing case accommodation in German. Where such accommodation does not occur, one must conclude that case is assigned *before* the noun phrases are delivered to their functional destination.

Generally, however, case, number, and other inflections have a strong tendency to be stranded (Garrett 1982, Stemberger 1983a, 1985a). This is supportive of the notion that the corresponding diacritical features are assigned *after* the lemma is inserted into its grammatical slot.

Berg (1987), in a careful analysis of accommodation in various languages, concluded that, as a rule, an erroneous element adapts to its new environment, as Garrett (1980b) suggested. But the environment usually does not adapt to the erroneous element. This is precisely the pattern of results one would expect if diacritic features are assigned to the lemma "from the environment." In example 3 above, for instance, it is the NP procedure that assigns the plurality feature to its head noun, whatever noun lemma happens to show up. Examples 4 and 5 do not contradict this, because here whole NPs—not just nouns—are delivered to the wrong destination.

Analyses of this kind show the advantage of an explicit algorithm for grammatical encoding: It helps us predict particular *kinds* of speech error, and to exclude others as impossible. It can even tell us something about the mutual dependency of different kinds of speech error, and therefore on their relative frequencies. For instance, on the above analysis, if plural strands, then case should strand as well, but not vice versa. This is because the assignment of the plural feature occurs at a lower level of destination than the assignment of the case feature. Violation of such predictions will force us to abandon or revise the model.

The Kempen-Hoenkamp Incremental Production Grammar assumes the existence of "syntactic specialists," a collection of grammatical and functional procedures. These procedures, we saw, function in a highly modular fashion. They do their thing when called and provided with their characteristic input, and they deliver their own special kind of output to a particular address. They do their work automatically (i.e., without using the speaker's attentional resources) and in parallel fashion. And they are stupid. They blindly accept the wrong input if it is of the right kind. The speech errors discussed so far testify to this witless automaticity of grammatical encoding.

7.1.3 Some More Complex Cases

In Chapter 6, a few remarks were made on "raising" verbs, such as *believe*. It was observed that in a sentence like *Attila believed the world to be flat*, the verb in the main clause imposes certain restrictions on the structure of the complement: that the subject of V-COMP should be realized as the direct object of the main clause, and that the tense of V-COMP should be infinitive. Let us see what is needed to generate such a sentence, given the seven kinds of procedures discussed in subsection 7.1.1.

Much depends on which lemma is triggered first. Let us assume that *Attila* sets the stage. *Attila*, being a noun, calls a categorial procedure in which it can figure as head, according to a type 2 operation. This procedure is NP, which accepts it as a proper (head) noun. NP does not call DET in case of proper nouns, but immediately chooses a default destination— namely SUBJ (a type 6 operation). This activates the categorial procedure S (type 7), and S puts the acquired subject in the leftmost slot of its holder. S then scans the conceptual structure for a function of which ATILLA is an argument (type 3). It comes up with the concept BELIEVE, which has two conceptual arguments: an experiencer and a state of affairs (or *theme*). This fragment, plus the information that SUBJ = experiencer, plus the diacritic parameters for person, number, and tense, are then handed over by S to its head-of-phrase procedure (PRED), which calls VP.

VP's main verb procedure causes BELIEVE to trigger the retrieval of the lemma *believe*. This lemma specifies three grammatical functions: SUBJ, DO, and V-COMP (see subsection 6.2.1). Can VP accept this lemma, in view of the present state of generation? Yes, since the only existing restriction comes from the already-available information on the subject as experiencer. The lemma specifies that the SUBJ function should be reserved for the conceptual experiencer argument, and that is exactly the case.

Given the lemma *believe*, VP must reserve two further slots in its holder. It reserves the second one for DO and the third one for V-COMP. But here something special happens. VP does not call the procedure DO, but only V-COMP (a call-procedure operation of type 4). It reserves its DO slot for V-COMP's subject; this is what the structure of the lemma dictates. For the same reason, the call to V-COMP specifies that it should be infinitival.

V-COMP calls categorial procedure S to inspect the state-of-affairs argument. The S procedure is also provided with the diacritic feature

" + infinitive". This feature suffices for S to "know" that the functional destination of its subject noun phrase is DO of the main VP; there will be no SUBJ functional destination for that noun phrase. Also, that feature causes the functional destination of the predicate VP to be the V-COMP slot of the main VP, not the predicate slot of S. In other words, V-COMP's S procedure will behave in a deviant fashion. It will not set up a holder of its own, and it induces external destinations for its subject NP and predicate VP. We will soon see the consequences.

Inspecting the state-of-affairs argument of BELIEVE, S finds a STATE function like this:

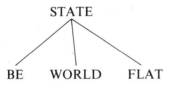

STATE

BE   WORLD   FLAT

S calls a SUBJ and a PRED functional procedure, and assigns the fragments WORLD and BE FLAT to them, respectively. The functions may or may not work in parallel. The SUBJ procedure calls the categorial procedure NP to lexicalize the WORLD fragment. This leads to the retrieval of *world*, and to the eventual construction of the noun-phrase tree *the world*, which is handed back to SUBJ. SUBJ, in turn, delivers it to the DO slot of the main VP, where it receives case. This case assignment is not quite visible in the present sentence, but an otherwise equivalent sentence shows this clearly: *Attila believed her to be flat.* Here *her* has the accusative case required for direct objects, not the nominative case of subjects (as in *Attila believed she to be flat*).

The PRED procedure, meanwhile, has called the categorial procedure VP to lexicalize its message fragment BE (FLAT). The main-verb procedure comes up with lemma *be*, which requires a subject. (If the SUBJ procedure had not started independently, it would have been called now.) The main-verb procedure not only realizes "infinitive" as a (zero) inflectional parameter on the lemma *be*; it also activates the preposition *to*. VP accepts this ordered pair and puts it in its leftmost slots.

The head verb *be*, finally, requires an adjectival complement, on which the property (FLAT) in the message is to be mapped. Hence, VP calls an AP procedure to lexicalize FLAT. This leads to the retrieval of the adjective *flat*, which becomes the head (and only element) of the adjective phrase, ending up in VP's third slot. VP now has its holders filled, and the PRED procedure that called it will deliver this output to the main-clause VP. It puts this verb phrase in the latter's third slot, which was reserved for the

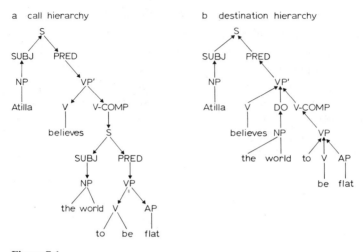

Figure 7.1
Call hierarchy and destination hierarchy for the sentence *Attila believed the world to be flat*.

output of V-COMP. The output of the main-clause VP will, finally, end up in the main S-predicate slot, and S will halt.

It is useful to distinguish the two verb phrases generated in this example. The main verb phrase will be denoted by VP′ and the other by VP, in accordance with the notation proposed in subsection 5.1.3.

The above example is important because the *call hierarchy* differed from the *destination hierarchy*. This distinction (introduced in Hoenkamp 1983) is probably relevant for the interpretation of certain experimental findings in sentence production, as will be discussed in section 7.2. Figure 7.1 presents the two hierarchies for the present example sentence. In 7.1a the arrows indicate which procedures called which; in 7.1b the arrows indicate where the procedures delivered their output (certain less relevant details are left out).

The major difference between the two hierarchies is that the call hierarchy has an embedded call to S, but in the destination hierarchy nothing is delivered to S at that level. In other words, the embedded S procedure is involved in inspecting the message for subject and predicate information, but it is not involved in ordering the output of the procedures it called; the ordering of constituents is exclusively handled by VP′. Let us call these the *inspecting* and *ordering* tasks of the S procedure, respectively.

The difference is also reminiscent of the distinction made by rather diverse linguistic theories between *deep structure* and *surface structure*. The point will not be elaborated here; see Hoenkamp 1983 and Kempen and Hoenkamp 1987.

The distinction between call and destination hierarchies can be exploited with profit to handle other cases as well. The S-COMP of certain adjectives (as in *John is eager to please*) and the V-COMP structure of auxiliaries (as in *Olithia can go*), discussed in subsections 6.2.3 and 6.2.4, are handled in rather analogous ways. In questions (*Can Olithia go?*), S will order the output of VP's constituents (*can* and *go*). So-called *Wh-movement*, as in *Who do you think John saw?*, where the *who* in front is the output of the object procedure of the embedded sentence (and where an "empty element" is left after *saw*—see subsection 5.1.3), can also be handled in an elegant way; see Kempen and Hoenkamp 1987. It is essential to the character of all these solutions that the speaker can incrementally produce from left to right, without any backtracking.

7.1.4 Ellipsis

The algorithm can also account for the incremental production of ellipsis in coordinative sentences (e.g., *John met the president, and Peter the secretary*). It involves skipping certain otherwise iterative operations in the generation of the second clause. We will not pursue this issue here, but see De Smedt and Kempen 1987. This is also the main mechanism involved in the generation of repairs, to which we will return in chapter 12.

Somewhat less straightforward are the cases of ellipsis discussed in subsection 3.2.7. There we considered the possibility that messages can be of any semantic type—proposition, entity, predicate, or whatever. Take an entity message, e.g., CHILD. If it has the feature " + accessible", the algorithm discussed will generate the noun phrase *the child*, and the NP procedure will deliver it as subject of S, by which S is called into operation. S gives the noun phrase nominative case and inspects the message for a function of which CHILD is an argument—in vain this time; there is nothing more to be found. It can, of course, be specified that the procedure will halt in such a state. But is this what we want? Let us return to the example in subsection 3.2.7 where the interlocutor asks *Who did Peter visit?*. If the answer message is the same (i.e., CHILD), then a seemingly correct surface structure is generated: *the child*. But it carries the wrong case. This would come to the surface in a pronominal answer, which could be *her* (accusative) but not *she* (nominative).

How could it be organized that the NP procedure claims the object function for *the child*? Would it be enough to mark CHILD in the message as patient? The algorithm should then be extended so as to claim object slots for patients in messages. But this is clearly not what we want either. A patient can easily appear in subject position (as in *The child was visited by Peter*), and the algorithm would no longer be able to generate such cases correctly. What is worse is that in certain languages the same thematic role will be expressed in different cases, depended on the verb used. A good German example involves the quasi-synonymous verbs *treffen* and *begegnen* (*to meet*):

Question	Answer
Wirst Du Helmut treffen?	Nein, den Präsidenten (accusative)
Wirst Du Helmut begegnen?	Nein, dem Präsidenten (dative)
(Will you meet Helmut?)	(No, the president)

The elliptical answers have the case marking that is required by the verb. This forces us to recognize that the elliptical production does, in some way or another, involve the particular verb lemma, in spite of the fact that it is not overtly used in the answer. A categorial procedure can apparently inspect the surface structure of the question to which it is generating an elliptical answer. There are no concrete proposals as to how this is done.

7.1.5 Ordering Errors
The categorial procedures S, NP, VP, AP, and PP have holders containing more than a single slot. The procedures are specialists in ordering returned constituents in these slots. The control structure of incremental production guarantees that the ordering is, as much as possible, done from left to right as materials are returned, but there are obligatory restrictions which may lead to necessary inversions. I have not discussed in any detail the ordering rules applied by the different categorial procedures, but it should be noted that the categorial procedures do not have a single fixed ordering scheme. This is especially apparent for S, which handles questions and declaratives and main and subordinate clauses in different ways. Given the existence of such closely related but different ordering operations in the algorithm, one might expect a vulnerability to specific ordering errors in speakers, namely the imposition of a possible though inappropriate order. Speakers do make ordering errors that are interpretable from this perspective. Fay (1980b) collected and analyzed several cases of this sort. Examples 10 and 11 are from his collection.

(10) I wonder how can she tell.   [I wonder how she can tell.]

(11) Linda, do you talk on the telephone with which ear?   [Linda, with which ear do you talk (!) on the telephone?]

In example 10 there is main-clause question ordering (*How can she tell?*) in a subordinate clause—precisely the sort of ordering confusion one would expect the S procedure to be subject to. In example 11 S also seems to apply main-clause question ordering, as would have been correct in the yes/no question *Linda, do you talk on the telephone with your right ear?*. But this ordering cannot apply, because the *Wh* prepositional phrase has to appear in first position.

However, the possibility that the latter error has a conceptual cause should not be excluded. Cutler (1980a) showed that the intonation contour of this error is indeed that of a yes/no question. (Its prosody had been phonetically transcribed right after the error occurred.) It is likely that the speaker changed his mind after most of the question had been produced. A different sentence-initial PP (*with which ear*) was then erroneously accepted as a sentence-final complement of the running sentence. In that case, example 11 is a sentence blend, not an ordering error, according to Cutler.

The error in example 10 may also have an alternative interpretation. It is not different from what Garrett calls *shifts*—errors where closely adjacent words interchange. The words are typically not of the same syntactic category. Here is an example (from Garrett 1982):

(12) Did you stay up late VERY last night?   [Did you stay up VERY late last night?]

Here the stressed word *very* is shifted over *late*. This cannot be a case where the categorial procedure (AP) applied a wrong but existing ordering scheme; there is no AP ordering that puts the adverb after the adjective. The error must have a different cause. Garrett proposed that shifts arise at a later level of processing, namely where the word forms are retrieved and assigned to the corresponding syntactical positions. In other words, they arise at the level of phonological encoding. It is hard, but perhaps not impossible, to find speech errors that can be exclusively adduced to a confusion of two legal syntactic ordering schemes.

There are other failures that should probably be interpreted as errors of grammatical encoding. Fay (1980a,b, 1982) discusses various such cases. One example, from Fay (1980b), is the following:

(13) Do you think it not works [*instead of* Do you think it doesn't work?]

In this case the VP of the embedded sentence failed to insert *do* in the presence of a negation. As a consequence, the present-tense parameter was realized as an inflection on the main verb (*works*).

Fay (1982), Stemberger (1985a), and others also discuss cases of sentence blends. Such cases seem to show that a speaker can, on occasion, encode two incompatible surface structures in parallel.

Speech errors clearly tell us something about grammatical encoding, but the evidence is in no way sufficient to give full-scale support to any one computational theory. And the situation is not different for the experimental evidence to be discussed in the following sections.

7.2 Units of Grammatical Encoding

In the previous section a distinction was made between call hierarchy and destination hierarchy. The former reflects the functional aspect of grammatical encoding: inspecting the message for functions and arguments to be encoded, retrieving the appropriate lemmas, and realizing the grammatical functions they require. The latter concerns the ordering aspect of grammatical encoding; it reflects which categorial procedures do the word and phrase ordering of the retrieved functional information.

From a computational point of view, one would expect a speaker's encoding process to be functionally driven in the first place. It is the function/argument structure of the message that the speaker is encoding in lemmas and grammatical functions. Ordering procedures, which are obligatory in the language, have no such expressive function. Ford and Holmes (1978) and Ford (1982) have obtained empirical support for the notion that the call hierarchy reflects a speaker's "planning units" more clearly than the destination hierarchy.

How can these two hierarchies be distinguished in a speaker's fluent speech? Ford and Holmes concentrated on the clause structure of the two hierarchies. Take, once more, the sentence of figure 7.1: *Attila believed the world to be flat*. In the call hierarchy (or "deep structure") there is a main and a subordinate sentence or clause. The subordinate clause starts after *believed*, so that the "deep" or "basic" clause partitioning of the sentence is like this (the beginning of a clause is indicated by a slash:

/Attila believed / the world to be flat (basic clause partitioning)

But there is only one S in the destination hierarchy, so the whole sentence consists of one "surface" clause (which is also called a "finite" clause, because it contains just one tensed or finite verb):

/Attila believed the world to be flat (finite surface clause partitioning)

It is generally possible to partition a speaker's fluent speech in either basic or finite clauses. The rule of thumb is that every finite clause contains one and only one tensed or finite verb (i.e., *believed* in the example sentence), whereas every basic clause contains one and only one main verb, whether tensed or not (i.e., both *believed* and *be*); there must always be a clause break between two main verbs. An example (from Ford and Holmes 1978) shows these finite and basic clause partitionings.

Finite clause partitioning:
/I began working a lot harder / when I finally decided to come to Uni

Basic clause partitioning:
/I began / working a lot harder / when I finally decided / to come to Uni
From the definition and from these examples it appears that the beginning of a tensed clause is always also the beginning of a deep clause, but not conversely.

If indeed the call hierarchy reflects a speaker's planning units, there should be evidence for basic clause partitioning in a speaker's delivery of a sentence. What sort of evidence? Ford and Holmes improved on a technique that Valian (1971) had developed for the same purpose. A speaking subject would occasionally hear a short tone, and his task was, apart from speaking, to press a button every time a tone appeared. The reaction time from tone onset to button pushing was the dependent measure. Speakers talked freely on various general topics, such as "family life," and tones appeared at unexpected moments but on the average once every 3.5 seconds. The expectation was that at moments when a speaker was engaged in planning the reaction times would be longer, because there would be less attention available for the impinging tone stimulus.

Ford and Holmes found increased reaction times for tones that occurred toward the end of basic clauses, even when the end of the basic clause was not also the end of a surface clause. A condition, however, was that more speech would have to follow the basic clause. Their interpretation of the data was that speakers start planning the next basic clause when they reach the final syllables of the current one. The data do suggest a basic clause rhythm in a speaker's fluent production. This testifies to the psychological reality of the call hierarchy.

Ford (1982) confirmed these findings by analyzing spontaneous hesitation pauses in speakers' fluent speech. She gave speakers essentially the same task as in the previous experiment, but without tones to react to. She then registered all hesitation pauses of 200 milliseconds and longer. She found that basic clauses were preceded by hesitation pauses as often as were finite clauses; pausing preceded about one-fifth of the clauses. Also, when there was pausing, the average pause length before the two kinds of clause was not statistically different. It amounted to about one second in both cases. Since the beginning of a finite clause is, by necessity, also the beginning of a basic clause, the simple rule seems to be that basic clauses "attract" hesitation pauses. It is irrelevant whether the beginning of the basic clause is also the beginning of a finite clause. In view of the earlier findings of Ford and Holmes, one might say that a basic clause starts being planned either in a preceding pause or concurrent with the uttering of the last syllables of the preceding clause (or both).

Ford also checked whether the *number* of basic clauses in a finite clause affected the duration of silence before that finite clause. A finite clause containing just one basic clause can be called a *simple* finite clause. A clause is *complex* when it contains more than one basic clause. If a speaker had been planning the full finite clause before initiating speech, simple finite clauses should have been preceded by shorter hesitation pauses than complex finite clauses. But there was no such difference. This finding supported the conjecture that speakers do not plan more than one basic clause ahead, even if the finite clause contains more than one basic clause.

Planning ahead does *not* mean that the whole clause is grammatically encoded before it is uttered. Experiments by Lindsley (1975, 1976), Levelt and Maassen (1981), and Kempen and Huijbers (1983) have shown that even the uttering of a simple subject-verb sentence can begin before the verb has been fully encoded. The only claim made by Ford and Holmes is that a speaker is occupied with the encoding of just one clause at a time. Only at the end of the uttering of a clause is the encoding of the next one taken up.

Ford concludes this way: "... the detailed planning for a sentence proceeds in recurring phases, each of which consists of the planning of a basic clause unit. During each phase a predicate is chosen and its lexical form retrieved, the logical arguments of the predicate decided upon, and the logical arguments sequenced in the way specified by the predicate's lexical form." We can agree, except for the last part. The sequencing or ordering of phrases is determined not only by the structure of lemmas and the call hierarchy but also by the destination hierarchy. The major categorical procedures impose order on the returned constituents. The same lemma can find its arguments arranged in different orders, depending on such factors as whether it occurs in a main clause or a subordinate clause.

Taken together, these findings are supportive of the notion that the rhythm of grammatical encoding follows the semantic joints of a message —its function/argument structure—rather than syntactic joints. It is the partitioning of the message to be expressed that a speaker is attending to, and this (co-)determines the rhythm of grammatical encoding. The syntactic-ordering decisions are largely or fully automatic; they can run in parallel. Characteristic speech errors may occur when operations of syntactic ordering fail, but the complexity of these syntactic operations will not be reflected in measures of mental load, such as reaction times and hesitation pauses. This is in line with earlier studies by Goldman-Eisler (1968), Taylor (1969), and Rochester and Gill (1973), who found no effects of syntactic complexity on hesitation pauses, speech latencies, or disruptions, respectively.

Gee and Grosjean (1983) performed extensive analyses of hestitation pauses, relating them not only to clause boundaries but also to any other phrase boundaries. They also included *phonological* units in their analysis, in particular so-called intonational and phonological phrases. Prosodic units and their generation will be discussed in section 8.2 and chapter 10, but it is important here to notice that these phonological units added substantially to the account of the observed pausing patterns. Van Wijk (1987), in a reanalysis of the Gee-Grosjean results, argued that the observed pausing patterns are *exclusively* determined by the phonological encoding and the articulatory preparation of the speaker. In other words, grammatical encoding plays no role worth talking about.

Does this contradict the above conclusions on deep clauses as planning units? Not necessarily. First and foremost, the data of Gee and Grosjean were obtained on a *reading* task, whereas the data of Ford and Holmes involved spontaneous speech. The course of grammatical encoding is probably quite different in these two kinds of task. In reading, the speaker can rely heavily on the printed materials. Lexical retrieval and the building of syntactic constituents can be based largely on parsing of the visual input. Reading aloud is primarily a perceptual, phonological, and articulatory task. It is not at all surprising, then, to find no effects of message planning and its interfacing with grammatical encoding (i.e., with the call hierarchy). Second, the original Ford-Holmes data were reaction times, not pause patterns. There is no compelling reason for a phonological or an articulatory interpretation of such reaction-time data. Third, the issue is not one of either/or. It would, in fact, be quite surprising if processes of phonological encoding and articulatory preparation were *not* responsible for generating pause patterns; they are the proximal causes of pausing. What is at issue is whether, in addition, there are traces of more distal encoding operations. Mapping function/argument structures in the message onto clause-like syntactic units probably leaves such a trace in the pause pattern. Subsequent findings by Holmes (1984 and forthcoming) are consonant with this conclusion.

7.3 The Encoding of Topic and Other Nuclear Entities

7.3.1 Accessibility and The Encoding of Topic

As was discussed in section 3.4, a speaker takes a certain perspective on a conceptual structure to be expressed. There is, first, the choice of topic. When the speaker's purpose is to expand the addressee's knowledge about something, the message will highlight this topic concept, to distinguish it from the comment that is made about it. In its turn, the Formulator will encode the topic in a syntactically prominent position.

What does "syntactically prominent" mean? It can mean that the topic is encoded as grammatical subject. Remember that there is a preference hierarchy for grammatical functions, with the subject function at the top of the list (see subsection 6.2.2). It can, alternatively, mean that the topic will be encoded early in the sentence, whether or not in the role of subject. This makes good functional sense: When the speaker's intention is to expand the interlocutor's information about something, the interlocutor may want to first find or create the address to which the comment information can be attached. This is easier when the topic information appears early in the sentence, before the verb, than when it appears after the verb.

It is very generally the case that these two carriers of syntactic prominence coincide. Word-order statistics of the world's languages show that 84 percent of them place the subject in front of verb and objects (Hawkins 1983). Hence, when a subject function is chosen to encode topical information, it will usually precede the predicate containing comment information. But, as we will see shortly, it may be possible to distinguish empirically between topic "fronting" and assigning subjecthood to topics.

How does the Formulator manage to place the topic in a syntactically prominent position? I will argue that this is an automatic consequence of the Formulator's control structure. It will, in many cases, be enough for the topical concept to be first in triggering its lemma(s) for it to be encoded early in the sentence and/or in subject position. This is exactly what happened to the concept CHILD in the procedural example of section 7.1, where the sentence *the child gave the mother the cat* was generated. The concept CHILD was an early-available message fragment. Maybe the speaker had introduced it in the previous sentence, so that the concept was highly available. At any rate, it caused *child* to become the first-retrieved lemma. The further operations, which generated *the child* as a subject noun phrase in sentence-initial position, were automatic consequences of this early availability of the lemma. The early triggering of topical lemmas could, in many cases, be due to an early delivery of the topical message fragment. Wundt's principle will then automatically give it primacy in grammatical encoding as well.

Bock and Warren (1985) called this factor "conceptual accessibility." They showed that a highly available concept tends to be encoded in a prominent grammatical function. If this is the factor at work, it should not really matter whether it is topichood that makes a concept highly available. Alternatively, or in addition, there may be a preliminary encoding operation by the categorial procedure S, which checks for the fragment in the message that is explicitly marked as topic. Theories are lacking here, and we now turn to some empirical evidence showing the preference of topical or otherwise highly accessible information for sentence-initial position and for subjecthood.

The experimental work in this context has been mostly concerned with the elicitation of the passive voice. Subjects asked to describe simple events where there is an agent doing something to a patient or recipient (for instance, a dog attacking a cat) prefer the active voice (i.e., a sentence like *the dog is attacking the cat*). Agents are preferably expressed in subject position. The simplest explanation for this fact is that the subject who perceives such an event normally encodes it from the perspective of the agent (i.e., it is the dog who is doing something). In order to transmit this information to the listener, one should make the dog the topic so that the addressee can know that the predication is about the dog. The topic (i.e., the agent) is then grammatically encoded as subject, in any of the ways discussed above. If this is what happens, experimental manipulations that make the patient (the cat) topical should increase the probability that the speaker generates passive voice. Why? If the cat is topic, it will tend to be expressed sentence-initially in subject position, and this will favor the use of the passive verb lemma (subsection 6.2.2), since it is the one that maps the thematic patient onto the subject function: *the cat is attacked by the dog*.

Various types of experimental manipulation have been used to topicalize the patient, or at least to make it more accessible. A first method is to give a perceptual cue. One shows a picture of the patient either before or after presentation of the scene, but before the subject gives his description. And the control condition, of course, is to show a picture of the agent. Prentice (1967) and Turner and Rommetveit (1968) used this method and obtained the predicted results. If the agent was cued (e.g., by a picture of the dog), almost no passive responses were given; however, if the cue depicted the patient, recipient, or theme, there were a significant number of passives in the descriptions (such as *the cat is attacked by the dog*).

Other researchers gave verbal cues. Tannenbaum and Williams (1968) first presented a paragraph in which either the patient, or the agent, or neither figured centrally, and this was then followed by the scene to be described. The subject's task was either to describe the scene with an active sentence or to describe it with a passive sentence, and the time needed to complete the sentence was measured. This is a rather unnatural task, but there was a clear congruency effect in the data. Both actives and passives were produced relatively quickly when the subject of the sentence agreed with the topic induced by the preceding paragraph. Flores d'Arcais (1975) simply mentioned either the agent (e.g., the dog) or the patient (e.g., the cat) before presenting the picture of the event (e.g., a dog attacking a cat). The subjects (native speakers of Italian) were free to describe the scene with either active or passive sentences, but the verb *attack* (in Italian) had to be used. When the cue word mentioned the agent, 77 percent of the responses were active sentences; when the cue referred to the patient, 67 percent of the responses were passives.

A very natural way to induce a topic is by asking a question. The subject is asked a question about the scene—for instance, "What did the dog do?" or "What happened to the cat?". Here the interlocutor indicates which protagonist information is needed, i.e., which protagonist should be topic. This manipulation was used by Carroll (1958), who performed the first experimental study of the elicitation of passives; it was also used in a study reported in Bates and Devescovi (forthcoming). In the Bates-Devescovi study, subjects were shown short filmstrips, for instance about a hippo hitting a ladder. They were then asked about entities in the film (e.g., "Tell me about the hippo" or "Tell me about the ladder"). When the request focused on the agent, 100 percent of the responses were active sentences; when the patient was focused, 70 percent of the answers were passive sentences (e.g., *the ladder was hit over by the hippo*). Bates and Devescovi also measured response latencies, and found a clear congruency effect. Active sentences have relatively short latencies; however, when the patient is probed and the subject still uses an active sentence, the latency is relatively long, and longer than the latency for a passive response.

Question asking was also used in a study by Bock (1977). She used a recall task. Subjects were first presented with a list of sentences of various syntactic structures. They were then given a question as a recall cue for one of the sentences on the list. The questions were constructed in such a way that they would topicalize a particular entity in the sentence to be recalled. If the sentence *a psychologist cured a neurotic poodle* had been on a subject's list, the following question could be asked: *The interior decorator was afraid she would have to get rid of her neurotic pet poodle because it was ruining the furniture, but she was able to keep it after all. What happened?* Subjects tended to reproduce the sentence in the passive voice: *a* (or *the*) *neurotic poodle was cured by a psychologist.* Clearly, the context sentence here is about the poodle, not about the psychologist, and in the answer the poodle is encoded sentence-initially in subject position.

Another way to elicit passives in recall tasks is to give a recall cue relating to the patient of the memorized sentence. Variations on this procedure can be found in Prentice 1966, Turner and Rommetveit 1968, Perfetti and Goldman 1975, and Bock and Irwin 1980. Bock and Irwin, for instance, would read a list of sentences to a subject, and next prompt the sentences by way of key words. If the sentence had been *The falling tree crushed the lumberjack*, the prompt word could be either *tree* or *lumberjack*. The results of the experiment were quite clear: The reproduced sentence tended to have the constituent containing the key word in a relatively early position. When *tree* was key word, subjects would reproduce the sentence in its original form. But when the key word was *lumberjack*, many reproductions took the form *The lumberjack was crushed by the falling tree.* Similar findings were obtained for other sentence pairs that differed in word order.

The linkage of sentence-initial position and subjecthood, we saw, is not absolute. A topic or a highly accessible entity can be encoded early in the sentence without becoming a subject. This is harder in English than in languages that have freer word order. To describe a scene where some man throws some ball, a German speaker can topicalize the ball by encoding the scene as *Den Ball wirft der Mann*, where the ball is fronted (and accented) without being subject; it has accusative case. In English it is not so easy to disentangle fronting effects from the assignment of subjecthood. But Bock and Warren (1985) developed an experimental paradigm that did just that: a sentence-recall task in which the main verb of the sentence was used as the recall cue. A subject would listen to a list of sentences. In this list there were sentences taken from three binary sets. Examples are given in table 7.1.

Table 7.1
Kinds of sentences used in Bock and Warren's (1985) recall task.

Type 1 Actives versus passives	
Active:	The doctor administered the shock
Passive:	The shock was administered by the doctor
Type 2 Prepositional versus double object	
Prepositional:	The old hermit left the property to the university
Double object:	The old hermit left the university the property
Type 3 Natural versus unnatural phrasal conjuncts	
Natural:	The lost hiker fought time and winter
Unnatural:	The lost hiker fought winter and time

The two alternatives within each type always involved a different ordering of two nouns: *doctor* and *shock* in the type 1 examples, *property* and *university* in the type 2 examples, and *time* and *winter* in the type 3 examples. For types 1 and 2 these ordering alternatives expressed a different assignment of grammatical functions. In the type 1 examples, either *the doctor* or *the shock* would be subject of the sentence. In the type 2 examples, *the university* would be either prepositional object or indirect object. But no such difference in grammatical function is apparent in the type 3 alternatives—the two nouns have the same function in either order; one can only say that an order in which the shorter word comes first sounds somewhat more natural (Cooper and Ross 1975). The first question Bock and Warren asked themselves was this: When the subject recalls the sentence, will there be a tendency for the conceptually more accessible entity to be projected on a more prominent grammatical function (i.e., subject for the type 1 sentences and indirect object for the type 2 sentences)? The second question was: Will the more accessible entity tend to be expressed in a more fronted position? Only in this latter case will there be an effect for type 3 sentences. If, however, the ordering of elements is mediated only by grammatical function, there will be an effect for sentences of types 1 and 2 only, not for those of type 3.

How was the accessibility of the entities manipulated? Through imageability (Paivio, Yuille, and Madigan 1968). One of the two critical nouns in the sentence was high on imageability (according to the tables of Paivio et al.), and the other one was low on imageability. In half the sentences presented to a subject, the highly imageable noun preceded the less imageable one; in the other sentences, the order was reversed.

In the recall task, the subject was given a sentence's main verb (e.g., *administered*) as a cue for reproducing the sentence. Regrettably, the subjects were asked to write down the sentence instead of to speak it; one should be careful in generalizing the results to normal speaking conditions, where prosody could play a significant role. But the results were clear cut. There were substantial effects of imageability for the type 1 and type 2 sentences, but none for the type 3 sentences. Bock and Warren concluded that conceptual accessibility does not affect ordering directly. Rather, a more accessible entity will "claim" a more prominent syntactic function. This, in turn, may result in a more frontal syntactic position.

Clearly, Bock and Warren's method did not involve explicit topicalization of entities. Neither were any questions asked about the critical referents (such as *What did the doctor do?*), nor did they figure as cue words (as in the Bock-Irwin study). Hence, it is still possible that topicalization can be done by "mere"fronting, without assignment of subjecthood to the topical entity. In English this would require a clefting construction, as in *It is the ball that the man throws* or *As for the ball, the man throws it*. But the latter construction, especially, has the additional effect of suggesting that there is a *change* of topic (see Reinhart 1982 and the references given there). Sridhar (1988), in a cross-linguistic study, found that in many languages, such as Hungarian, subjects topicalized objects by fronting them as in the German example above.

But if this is possible, why would speakers front a topic constituent without at the same time encoding it as the grammatical subject of the sentence? One reason may be that there is a strong competitor for the subject function. Actors and agents are preferably encoded as subjects of sentences, and more often than not they will be topics as well. But if the situation (e.g., a question) requires another argument to be the topic, the conflict can be resolved by adapting the word order and keeping the canonical assignment of grammatical function. This is what happened in the German example above. The agent (*der Mann*) is still in subject role, but the ball is placed in frontal position. Reinhart (1982) put it this way: "subjects are the unmarked topics, which means that it is easier to use a sentence when we intend its subject to be a topic. But they are not obligatory topics." The notion of competition is central to the so-called competition model of MacWhinney and Bates, which will be taken up in the next subsection.

7.3.2 Encoding Nuclear and Non-Nuclear Entities: Saliency and Competition

The notion of congruency was used in the previous paragraph to express a preferred relation between message and syntactic form. A message with a topicalized recipient has a preferred (though not a necessary) relation to a passive syntactic form. Whether that grammatical encoding will obtain depends on a variety of other pressures in the encoding process—for instance, pressure to assign the subject function to a salient agent or to an otherwise prominent or highly accessible conceptual entity. Subsection 6.2.2 discussed the notion of a universal hierarchy of grammatical functions, going from subject via direct and indirect objects to obliques. Arguments "want" to be encoded through the highest-ranking function possible. And there is at the same time a pecking order of thematic roles: from agent, via theme, to source, goal, and other roles. The agent is usually encoded in the most prominent grammatical function (i.e., as the subject); source and goal generally end up in oblique prepositional phrases. A congruent grammatical encoding is one in which the arguments and modifiers in the message are distributed over grammatical functions and syntactic positions in a way that reflects their relative importance.

But what determines the saliency or importance of an entity in the message? Several factors have already been reviewed. There were discourse factors, such as whether the entity had been topicalized by an interlocutor's question, or whether it had been recently mentioned. We also saw that imageability played a role. However, a host of other factors may be involved as well. They all relate to what can be called the "human interest" of an entity—its relevance in the eye of the speaker. This is, admittedly, rather vague, but the literature contains several suggestions as to what might contribute to human interest or to the foregrounding of certain concepts. Fillmore (1977) talked about a *saliency hierarchy*. Among the factors contributing to saliency is *humanness*. Human concepts have a stronger tendency to be encoded in the major grammatical functions subject and object than nonhuman concepts. Another factor Fillmore mentioned is *change of state*. It is usually of more interest that a state changes than that it does not change. A speaker will foreground a changing object in the message, and hence increase the odds that it will be encoded as subject or object. Compare examples 14 and 15. In the former, the table is not moving and is encoded in an oblique grammatical function; in the latter it is moving and is encoded as direct object:

(14) I pushed against the table

(15) I pushed the table

Still another factor contributing to saliency, according to Fillmore, is *definiteness* (or *accessibility*, in the terms of subsection 4.5.1). A definite referent will attain a prominent grammatical function more easily than an indefinite one. In describing a scene where there are two boys and one girl, it is probably more natural to say *The girl is kissed by a boy* than *A boy is kissing the girl*, in spite of the fact that the boy is depicted as the agent.

Chafe (1977) and Clark and Clark (1977) speak of *unexpectedness* as contributing to saliency or information value. Osgood and Bock (1977) show that *vividness* is a contributing factor. MacWhinney (1977) mentions *agency*, as well as other factors. And *perceptual factors* have often been mentioned in the literature. Figures are usually more salient than grounds, closer objects more salient than faraway ones, bigger objects more salient than smaller ones, and so on.

It should not be the aim here to review the varieties of human interest. All that is at issue is the claim that foregrounded, nuclear, emphasized entities in the message typically find their grammatical encoding in higher grammatical functions or earlier in the sentence than backgrounded or non-nuclear entities. What is the empirical evidence?

Surprisingly, there is only fairly limited evidence from analyses of (elicited) spontaneous speech. Most studies have resorted to asking subjects which sentence is a more or a less appropriate one given a particular state of affairs, asking them to put printed words or constituents in some natural order, and so on. Osgood's seminal study (1971; see also Osgood and Bock 1977), and a substantial expansion of it by Sridhar (1988), are closer to spontaneous speech. In these experiments subjects were asked to describe, one by one, a sequence of short scenes or events. In Osgood's study these were acted out (by Osgood); in Sridhar's experiment they were filmed scenes. A disadvantage of both studies is that the subjects wrote rather than spoke their descriptions of the scenes. In this way the subject could not use prosodic ways of expression, and may have compensated by making another choice of syntactic forms. Still, these studies have provided interesting information about the grammatical encoding of saliency.

Osgood played a sequence of 32 events on a table in front of an audience consisting of 26 students. The events involved a set of simple familiar objects, such as various balls of different size and color, a plate, a tube, and some chips. The subjects were instructed for each demonstration to open their eyes on the signal "open" and to close them on the signal "close". This was followed by the request to describe the event they had observed in a single sentence that "a six-year-old boy 'just outside the door' would understand." They were also instructed to describe the actor (Osgood), when necessary, as "the man."

A typical event observed by the subjects was one in which an orange rolling ball is hitting an upright tube. What would be a congruent description? The ball is agent and is changing location; the tube is recipient and static. This would favor encoding the ball in subject position. On the other hand, the tube had also figured in the previous demonstration, whereas the ball had not been around for some time. This might favor making the "given" tube the topic of the sentence. Twenty-one subjects produced sentences where the ball was subject, and five gave passive sentences with the tube in subject position.

The effect of humanness or animacy was apparent all over. When Osgood held a not-previously-observed big blue ball, 20 subjects made sentences where *the man* was subject (like *The man is holding a big blue ball*). Only five found the saliency of the new big ball impressive enough to make a passive sentence (such as *A big blue ball is held by the man*). When "the man" was seen to be involved in the scene, either in a static or in an agentive role, he usually turned up in subject position.

Figure/ground organization was also very effective. One would expect figures to be encoded in more prominent grammatical functions than grounds. When the scene was just a ball on the table, nobody put the table in subject position (something like *The table is supporting the ball*). It was encoded obliquely (*on the table*) or not at all. In describing a more complicated static scene, where a ball was on an upright tube and the tube stood on a plate, subjects normally arranged the noun phrases such that the ball would be first, the tube second, and the plate third. The ball was usually encoded as subject, and the plate obliquely in a prepositional phrase.

Osgood also played saliency factors off against one another—for instance, change of state and vividness. When he presented a scene where a very big orange ball (vivid) was hit by a small black ball (change of state and agency), only three subjects created a passive sentence with the big ball in subject position. It has been a general finding (see also Sridhar 1988 and Bates and Devescovi, forthcoming) that passives are quite hard to elicit by purely perceptual means. They are primarily triggered by discourse constraints.

Sridhar (1988) filmed Osgood-type scenes and events and presented them to subjects from ten different language communities: Cantonese, Hebrew, Finnish, Hungarian, Serbo-Croatian, English, Spanish, Japanese, Kannada, and Turkish. This cross-linguistic approach made it possible to test the universality of the congruency effects we are discussing—in particular, the claim that more important, salient, or informative entities will be encoded in major grammatical functions, and relatively early in the sentence.

Sridhar obtained overwhelming support for this claim. When, for instance, the scene was a man rolling a ball on the table, the man and the ball were almost invariably encoded as subject and object, respectively, while the table, if mentioned at all, would never appear in a major grammatical function. When there was a figure and a ground, the figure was encoded earlier in the sentence than the ground in 70 percent of the responses, and this tendency was apparent in all languages. Actions were encoded more often and earlier in the sentence than changes of state, and changes of state more often and earlier than constant states. Descriptions of static scenes proceeded preferably from top to bottom, as in Osgood's ball-on-tube-on-plate example (which was included in Sridhar's film). Closer-to-ego objects were related to further-away objects, and appeared earlier in the sentence (similar evidence was presented in subsection 4.5.3 above).

Sridhar also included scenes where (quasi-)humanness could be tested without confounding it with agency. In one scene, a black ball hit a doll which was sitting on the table. The doll appeared before the ball in 67 percent of the descriptions. When, however, a scene was presented in which the black ball hit a yellow ball, only 43 percent of the descriptions had the yellow ball before the black ball. This pattern of promoting a human entity, even if it is only a thematic patient, held for 9 of the 10 languages (Kannada was the exception).

These and many more results of Sridhar's study demonstrate that speakers of vastly different languages show very similar congruency mechanics. Materials that are presumably foregrounded or "in perspective" in the message are grammatically encoded in major grammatical functions; and the more important they are (by a variety of importance criteria), the higher they climb in the grammatical-function hierarchy and the earlier they appear in the sentence.

In one study in this tradition, spoken language was elicited. Flores d'Arcais (1987b) presented moving geometrical figures of various shapes to subjects and asked them to describe each such event. When a big figure and a small one were involved in an event, the big figure was mentioned first. When one figure was leading the other in the movement, the leading figure was mentioned first. Such factors determine which entity becomes the topic of the event.

As was observed above, the different forces from the message can often be in conflict. The topic entity may not be the agent; a vivid and brand-new object may not be more than the background for an action; and so on. Such competitions must be resolved in fluent speech. In addition, different languages provide different means for resolving these conflicting tendencies. In free-word-order languages the assignment of grammatical function is relatively independent of constituent order, with nonconfigurational languages such as Malayalam (see subsection 5.1.1) as extreme cases. Speakers of such languages may resolve conflicts by mapping one message function (e.g. topicality) onto word order (sentence-initial) and another (for instance, agency) onto grammatical function (subject). But this is far less easy for speakers of languages with rather fixed word order, such as English.

Bates, MacWhinney, and co-workers (see especially Bates and Mac-Whinney 1982, 1987; MacWhinney, Bates, and Kiegl 1984; Bates and Devescovi, forthcoming) have proposed a "competition model" in which a variety of message-level aspects, including thematic structure, topicality, and foregrounding, are probabilistically mapped onto a variety of forms at the syntactic level. The probabilistic parameters of this mapping are assumed to be different for different languages. An effort is made to find out how the parameters—i.e., the preferred use of particular syntactic devices for particular aspects of the message—can be understood from the structure of the language. Though most of this work is still based on sentence-interpretation data, data on spoken production have been acquired and analyzed (Bates and Devescovi, forthcoming) by a method roughly like Sridhar's film-presentation procedure.

The competition model is claimed to describe a *direct*, though probabilistic, mapping between the functional message level and the formal grammatical level. In other words, the congruency mechanics consist of direct grammatical responses to message "stimuli." This is acceptable if "direct" doesn't mean more than that grammatical encoding is an automatic modular process, not involving intentional goal-directed choices on the part of the speaker. There must, however, be mechanisms that realize the mapping. The "direct" probabilistic mapping of the competition model thus means that the mechanism is inherently probabilistic. In other words, an individual language user's Grammatical Encoder is supposed to be a probabilistic processor.

This is surely a respectable option, in line with an equally respectable tradition of stochastic modeling in psychology. However, the probabilistic data on which the model is currently based do not require such a solution. These data are averages over subjects, not within subjects. It could very well be the case that each individual language user has a consistent *deterministic* way of encoding messages into surface structures. The probabilistic findings are then entirely due to processing differences *between* subjects. In short, the data underlying the competition model do not relieve us from the task of developing a mechanical (computational) model of grammatical encoding or from the task of checking whether a deterministic model (with parameters differing between subjects) might suffice.

7.4 Cohesive Encoding

Another important aspect of a speaker's grammatical encoding is the realization of what is commonly called *cohesion* (Halliday and Hassan 1976). In cohesive discourse the speaker makes, where necessary, the form of the current utterance dependent on what was previously said by himself or the interlocutor. This makes it possible for the addressee to interpret elements in the current utterance in relation to previous discourse (or, occasionally, to the discourse that will immediately follow). But the cohesive forces are not limited to the ways in which entities are referred to; they also permeate the speaker's syntax. In the following, some attention will be given to empirical studies of both kinds of cohesion.

7.4.1 Cohesive Reference
What grammatical means can a speaker use to establish and maintain reference? In chapter 4 we began paying attention to the ways in which a speaker can signal to the addressee what the accessibility of a referent is, given the state of the discourse model. It was suggested that the speaker marks each referent in the message in a triple way, depending on the referent's relation to the discourse model. The marking will be plus or minus "accessible", plus or minus "in discourse model", and plus or minus "in focus" (see subsection 4.5.1). Each of these markers, when correctly encoded in the surface structure, contributes in its own way to directing the attention of the listener, making it possible for her to find or create the appropriate address for the referent in the discourse model.

How are these accessibility markers grammatically encoded? Many languages encode the "accessible" marker in the noun phrase's morphology or determiner, mapping " + accessible" referents onto definite noun phrases and " − accessible" ones onto indefinite noun phrases. The index "in discourse model" is often mapped onto prosodic focus. A referent which the speaker supposes to be in the interlocutor's discourse model is then deaccented. The "in focus" feature is often realized by some sort of lexical reduction. In-focus elements tend, in particular, to be pronominalized; there can even be complete elision. But languages also have other means to encode the referent's accessibility status, such as by word order or special morphology.

Experimental and observational support for the appropriate encoding of these anaphoric features in English were reviewed in chapter 4. Here we will limit our attention to some cross-linguistic results which support the notion that these features are universally encoded by speakers. Also, there are certain commonalities between speakers of different languages in the way this grammatical encoding is realized, but there are interesting differences as well.

Osgood's (1971) study contained rich data with respect to the circumstances of definite and pronominal reference. Sridhar's (1988) work showed that Osgood's main findings also hold for languages other than English. Osgood had observed that an object introduced for the first time was described with an indefinite article in 85 percent of the cases, but when it appeared a second time the percentage dropped to 45. Sridhar also found his subjects referring to new entities by way of indefinite noun phrases, but in some languages such an indefinite NP was not very acceptable as the subject of the sentence. This was especially the case for Hungarian and for SOV languages (i.e., languages that normally have the verb after the subject and the object). In particular, the Japanese subjects evaded ordering the indefinite term before the definite one. Notice that also in English an indefinite NP is not an exciting start of a sentence (*A ball is on the table*), in agreement with Fillmore's (1977) observations. In so-called presentative contexts, such as this one, many languages favor pre-posing the verb (*There is a small ball on the table*).

With respect to reduction as a means to express that a referent is in fcous, Osgood had found that pronominalization was especially frequent when the same object participated in two events during the same demonstration. For instance, when a black ball hit a blue one, and the blue one in turn hit an orange one, the second mention of the blue ball (now in the interlocutor's focus) was mostly by means of a pronoun (as in *the black ball hits the blue ball. It hits the orange ball*). Osgood had also found a sharp decrease in the number of adjectives when the same object was described a second or a third time (*a big blue ball → the blue ball → the ball*). Sridhar confirmed this tendency for all of his ten languages, though the tendency was slight in the responses of Japanese subjects.

MacWhinney and Bates (1978) reported a systematic cross-linguistic study of spontaneously produced speech. Children of different ages as well as adults were given pictorial presentations of scenes to be described. There were three language groups: native speakers of Italian, English, and Hungarian. With respect to the feature "accessible", the finding was that English and Italian speakers made use of the indefinite article to express inaccessibility. But this was much less the case for the Hungarian speakers —presumably because in Hungarian a new referent is introduced without any article (this also explains Sridhar's finding for Hungarian, mentioned ' above). The English speakers were less fond of using the definite article than the Italians and the Hungarians, probably because the indefinite article has an additional function in the latter two languages (namely as a numeral). Subjects apparently used the definite article wherever they could, in order to evade the potential confusion of functions.

In the MacWhinney-Bates study, the borderline between full ellipsis and pronominalization turned out to be different for English and the other two languages. Where English speakers used a pronominal form in subject position, Italians and Hungarians simply elided the subject. This is mostly impossible in English. The person and number of the elided subject are clearly marked in the verb morphology of Italian and Hungarian, and hence there is no loss of information in those languages.

What about pitch accent in the MacWhinney-Bates study? Newly introduced elements were given pitch accent, as in the studies of Nooteboom and Terken (1982) and Pechmann (1984) discussed in chapter 4. But there was a substantial difference between languages. English-speaking subjects used much more prosodic stress to introduce new or contrasting entities than did Italian speakers. And the Italians stressed more than the Hungarians, who hardly used any pitch accent for the introduction of new referents. It seems that the latter two languages offer more possibilities to use word order for marking the introduction of a new element. And indeed, there was much more fronting of "new" constituents in Hungarian and Italian than in English. This gives support to the idea that the feature of being new in the discourse model is not necessarily expressed by prosodic means. Different languages can provide different grammatical encodings for this feature.

7.4.2 Cohesive Syntax

Speakers are also cohesive in their wording and syntax. Some of the evidence was reviewed in subsection 4.2.5, in particular the observational work by Schenkein (1980) and the experimental study by Levelt and Kelter (1982). The latter study showed the speaker's tendency to answer a question like *(At) what time do you close?* with an answer that was congruent in the use or nonuse of the preposition (at). These repetition effects are probably not due to the content of the answer.

Strong experimental evidence for the persistence of syntactic form was collected by Bock (1986b). We will call her experimental method the *priming/recognition procedure*. It was also profitably used for other purposes, to which we will return in the next subsection. The experimental manipulation is one of priming, but the subject is made to believe that it is a recognition test. Bock's study involved syntactic priming. The speaker was to describe a set of pictures, but each picture was preceded by a (prime) sentence, spoken by the experimenter and repeated by the subject. The question, then, was whether the syntax of the prime sentence would affect the syntax of the picture description. The camouflage of the experiment consisted in first giving the subject a "study list" also consisting of pictures and spoken sentences. Only after this was the experimental list presented, and the subject was made to believe that this was a recognition task. The instruction was to say "Yes" or "No" for each sentence or picture, depending on whether that item had appeared in the study list. But before giving that answer, the subject had to repeat the sentence or describe the picture.

The prime sentences used in Bock's study were of the same kind as types 1 and 2 in table 7.1. That is, they were actives or passives, and prepositional or double-object sentences. The pictures (examples of which are given in figure 7.2) invited either type 1 descriptions (*Lightning is striking the church*, or *The church is being struck by lightning*) or type 2 descriptions (*The man is reading a story to the boy*, or *The man is reading the boy a story*).

Bock's results were unequivocal. The picture descriptions tended to be syntactically congruent with the prime sentences. If the prime was passive,

Figure 7.2
Examples of pictures used by Bock (1986b) to elicit scene descriptions.

the description tended to be passive; if the prime was a double-object sentence, the picture description tended to be a double-object sentence, and so on.

How does such syntactic coherence arise? There is nothing in the algorithmic theory of section 7.1 that would predict this result. On that theory, syntactic variation can only result from varying the order in which message fragments are made available. But that was not at issue in Bock's experiment. As in the Levelt-Kelter experiments, it turned out that variations in grammatical encoding could be induced by other than message-level means. In Bock's experiments this was probably not a (sole) consequence of lexical priming. For instance, when the prime was a full passive, the description could be a truncated one (like *the church was struck*)—the word *by* was not repeated, but passive syntax was.

An interpretation that stays close to the Kempen-Hoenkamp algorithm is that the syntactic specialists—in particular, the categorial procedures S, VP, NP, AP, and PP—can be biased by listening to and repeating a sentence of a particular syntactic form. This pleads for the independent existence of these syntactic specialists. They can be biased in such a way that grammatical encoding operations *overrule* message-level factors.

7.5 Feedback in Grammatical Encoding

Conceptual accessibility, we saw, has an effect on grammatical encoding. A message entity that is early available or otherwise particularly salient will normally succeed in claiming a relatively prominent grammatical function. The most likely explanation for this finding is that the corresponding lemma is retrieved at an early stage. The NP procedure called by that lemma (if it is a noun or a pronoun) delivers its output according to some preference order. The default claim is subject-of-S. If that slot is already occupied, direct-object-of-S is the next preference, and so on down the grammatical hierarchy. In this way, the order of conceptual activation can affect the order of grammatical encoding. The order of grammatical encoding, in turn, affects the order of phonological encoding. The appropriate word form can be retrieved as soon as its diacritic parameters (for number, case, etc.) have become available, and this depends, in part, on the grammatical function assigned. So we see Wundt's principle at work at two levels: from message planning to grammatical encoding, and from grammatical to phonological encoding.

The present section discusses whether there is any *converse* effect. Is there evidence for feedback in the system such that (a) the accessibility of lemmas can affect conceptual ordering decisions or (b) the accessibility of word forms can affect the order of grammatical encoding? It should be remembered that the research strategy proposed in chapter 2 was to take nonfeedback as our starting hypothesis. The assumption of "informational encapsulation" was that processors would be sensitive only to their own characteristic kind of input, not to feedback from other components. In this case, conceptual decisions should be ignorant of the results of grammatical encoding, and grammatical encoding should be insensitive to what happens at the level of phonological encoding. But this is an empirical issue. Let us now review some of the supporting and contradicting evidence.

The first issue is whether conceptual ordering decisions can be affected by lower-level formulation processes. This question was put to test by Levelt and Maassen (1981), who tested, in particular, whether the relative accessibility of lexical items affected the order of mention in conjunctive constructions. The starting assumption was that the order of mention is a conceptual message-level decision. Subjects in these experiments were presented with pictures containing three geometrical forms and a fixation point. An example is given in figure 7.3. Immediately upon presentation of the picture, two of the three forms (for instance, the circle and the square) were slightly displaced upward or downward. The subject's task was to say as soon as possible what had happened. Depending on the directions of motion, typical responses were *the circle and the square went up* or *the circle went up and the square went down*. The former sentence type, labeled *noun-phrase conjunction*, was given only when the two forms moved in the

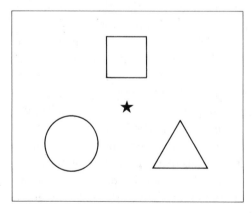

Figure 7.3
Example of the stimuli used by Levelt and Maassen (1981) to elicit two-object event descriptions.

same direction: both up or both down. The latter type, called *sentence conjunction*, was always used when the directions of movement were different. Sometimes subjects used sentence conjunction when the movements were in the same direction (*the circle went up and the square went up*), but this was less frequent and surely less congruent since it doesn't do justice to the "common fate" of the two motions. (In an additional experiment, the sentence forms were prescribed rather than left to the subjects' convenience.)

The geometrical figures had been carefully selected. Half of them had to be easy to name and the other half hard to name, and this difference had to be due to lexical accessibility rather than to better or worse recognizability or detectability. The figures were selected in preliminary experiments where subjects simply had to name individual geometrical patterns, and where naming latencies were measured. The figures indeed differed markedly in naming latency. In addition, the detectability latencies were measured for all figures. Eventually, sets of easy- and hard-to-name figures were selected that did not differ in detectability. A circle, for instance, was an easy-to-name figure, with an average naming latency of 691 milliseconds. The naming latency for *square*, however, was relatively long: 772 milliseconds on average. Hence, the square was in the hard-to-name set of figures. The experiments involved three easy-to-name and three hard-to-name figures. Their average difference in naming latency was 83 milliseconds.

Did lexical accessibility affect word order? When the event involved a circle and a square, for instance, did the speakers say *the circle and the square went up* (where the easily accessible word *circle* is in initial position), or *the square and the circle went up* (with the harder word first)? Notice that the order "easy → hard" was quite cooperative, given the task. The subjects had been asked to give their descriptions as quickly as possible. By uttering the easy word first, the speaker would gain in descriptive speed.

But nothing happened. The easy word was first in 52.5 percent of the descriptions—not significantly different from randomness. (In the additional experiment with prescribed syntactic response frames, the percentage was 50.5.) What *was* found was that when the hard word was put in initial position, the latency to initiate the sentence was reliably longer than when the easy word came first (by 40 msec, and by 51 msec in the additional experiment). In other words, the hard names were also harder to access in sentence context. Still, the speakers could not capitalize on this noticeable difference in response speed by planning their utterances accordingly.

This result supports the notion of informational encapsulation. The conceptual system is ignorant about the accessibility of lexical items. Conceptual ordering decisions will not be reversed by such factors. The situation may, however, be slightly more complicated, as we will see shortly.

Is there feedback from the level of phonological encoding to that of grammatical encoding? Here three experimental results should be reported. The first finding, also from the Levelt-Maassen experiment, has to do with the choice of syntactic frame. Remember that conjoined or "common fate" movements (both figures rising together, or both falling) were preferably expressed by noun-phrase conjunction (e.g., *triangle and square went up*). There were, however, cases where such events were described by sentence conjunction (*triangle went up and square went up*). This occurred especially when both figures were difficult to name. Why did this happen? Levelt and Maassen conjectured that when the speaker had to retrieve two difficult word forms in close succession, he may not have succeeded in finding the second one in time to utter it when it was needed. The speaker may have started saying *triangle* ..., but then failed to come up in time with the phonetic plan for *square*. The speech need then "forced" him to give up constructing a noun-phrase conjunct, and to take a different route of grammatical encoding—one where the already-retrieved verb form (i.e., *went up*) could be uttered first. In other words, the speaker *revised* the grammatical encoding of the event. This, surely *is* a feedback explanation, and it should be supported by independent evidence. Such evidence exists. An on-the-fly revision of grammatical frame should take extra time. Therefore, the durations of these utterances were measured. And indeed, these critical utterances turned out to span more time (85 milliseconds more) than their controls. In other words, trouble in phonological encoding may affect grammatical encoding.

The issue was further tested in two experiments by Bock. In a first study, Bock (1986a) used her prime/recognition technique with pictures such as that in figure 7.2a above. However, this time the prime was not a spoken sentence but a spoken word. The word was either a semantic or a phonological prime. In the case of figure 7.2a, a semantic prime could be the word *worship*. It is a close associate of *church*. Bock conjectured that that prime might induce a picture description which would have *church* in a prominent grammatical role—i.e., something like the passive *The church is being struck by lightning*. Inversely, when the prime was *thunder*, its close associate *lightning* might end up in subject position, as in the active *The lightning is striking the church*. Such a finding would be very interesting in itself, because it is not so obvious that presenting the associate would affect the *conceptual* accessibility of the referent. It would, rather, directly affect the activation of the corresponding lemma. But the consequences should be the same if the analysis in the previous paragraph is correct: A lemma that is more highly activated, whether through saliency of the corresponding concept or through association with another activated lemma, will tend to end up in a more prominent grammatical function.

A phonological prime *sounds* like the target—e.g., *search* for *church* or *frightening* for *lightning*. And these kinds of primes form the critical test for the present issue. If phonological priming affects grammatical encoding, that is strong evidence for feedback from the level of phonological encoding to that of grammatical encoding. If, for instance, the prime *search* were to induce *church* to turn up in a particular grammatical function, this could only have been mediated by the phonological form of *church*.

Bock found that semantic primes did affect grammatical encoding. The primed element tended to turn up in subject position. However, there was no effect of phonological priming. In other words, no evidence was found for feedback from phonological to grammatical encoding.

But Bock (1987b) dedicated a second study to this issue. She applied the same priming/recognition method as in the previous research, but the experiments were different in three respects: First, in addition to scenes such as those presented in figure 7.2a, Bock presented pictures like those in figure 7.4. These were designed to release *conjunctive* descriptions, such as *The woman is carrying a lamp and a plant* and *The dog and the cat are under*

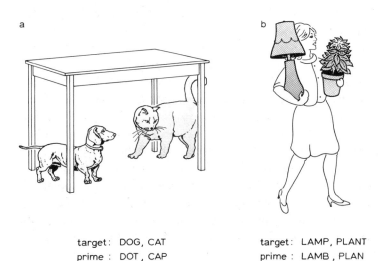

a

target: DOG, CAT
prime : DOT, CAP

b

target: LAMP, PLANT
prime : LAMB, PLAN

Figure 7.4
Examples of pictures types used by Bock (1987b) to elicit conjunctive descriptions.

the table. This is the kind of description Levelt and Maassen studies in their experiments. Second, the phonological primes were of a very strong kind. In all cases the word-initial part of the prime was identical to that of the target object. (In general, the phonological match was made as close as possible.) Examples of targets and primes are given in figure 7.4. Third, only phonological primes were used; there were no semantic primes.

This time Bock did obtain a significant phonological-priming effect. The effect, moreover, was one of *inhibition*: The primed target word tended to appear later in the sentence than the unprimed target word. For instance, when figure 7.4a was presented after the prime word *cap*, subjects tended to describe it as *The dog and the cat are under the table*, with the primed *cat* in secondary position. The effects were strongest for pictures like 7.2a. In 56.1 percent of these cases, sentences were constructed in which the primed word appeared in secondary position (i.e., not in subject position). The weakest effects were those for the conjunctive cases, as in figures 7.4a and 7.4b. In 52.9 percent of these cases the primed target word appeared in secondary position. But this was still significantly different from a random 50 percent result.

Bock also ran two control experiments. In the first one, subjects were not asked to describe the scene, but to just mention its two most prominent objects. The subjects' order-of-mention results showed the same kind and size of priming effects as had been obtained in the sentential descriptions. In the second control experiment, the subject did not have to repeat the prime word aloud, as in all previous experiments. Instead they were asked either to mouth it for themselves or to just listen to it. For both groups the results were essentially the same as in the main experiment.

What can we conclude from these excellent experiments? A first conclusion concerns the results with respect to scenes like that in figure 7.2a. These showed the strongest amount of (inhibitory) priming. The following explanation could be proposed: The phonological prime apparently inhibits the activation of the target word form. This, in turn, inhibits activation of the target lemma. This reduces the chance for that lemma to "claim" a prominent syntactic function (i.e., subject) during grammatical encoding. In other words, there is feedback from the phonological to the grammatical level of encoding. A slightly different account could bring this result in line with the feedback conjectured by Levelt and Maassen: Grammatical encoding initially proceeds without concern for potential trouble at the phonological level. But as soon as the first target name is about to be phonologically encoded, there will be a "speech need" situation if the name's phonological form is in an inhibited state due to the prime. This "trouble signal" is fed back to the level of grammatical encoding, and the syntactic frame is revised. Such revision took extra time in the Levelt-Maassen findings. Bock found a similar effect: There were dysfluencies in utterances, and these occurred mainly around the early target locations in the sentence. That is exactly the moment where syntactic revision should be taking place, if it occurs at all. On this account, the inhibition of the word form does *not* lead to inhibition of the corresponding lemma, but to a syntactic revision.

What are the theoretical implications of the results for conjunctive phrases, i.e., for the descriptions of scenes such as those in figure 7.4? It is obviously preferable to explain these in the same way as the previous ones. But the first kind of explanation above is not applicable. If indeed one lemma is inhibited by feedback from the phonological level, this will not have an effect in a situation where both lemmas end up in the same grammatical role. And that is the case in phrasal conjuncts. One cannot say anymore that the uninhibited lemma will be quicker to claim a more prominent grammatical function. For these scenes the only issue is the *order* of conjoining in the same grammatical function. That leaves us with the second account: syntactic revision in case of "speech need."

Though the revision account is the more economical one, covering both kinds of results in Bock's study as well as Levelt and Maassen's findings on feedback, one troublesome issue remains: Levelt and Maassen did *not* find an effect of lexical availability on ordering in conjunctive phrases, whereas Bock did. The difference, however, is more apparent than real. Levelt and Maassen found a nonsignificant ordering effect of 52.5 percent; Bock obtained a significant effect of 52.9 percent—a negligible difference. What remains to be dealt with is Levelt and Maassen's interpretation of their own test. Remember that they started from the assumption that the ordering decision is a conceptual one, and their hypothesis was that word-finding trouble should not lead to a revision of that decision. In retrospect, their experiments probably did not test that hypothesis. What they did test was whether phonological accessibility could affect syntactic encoding operations. These revised syntactic encoding operations would then *overrule* the conceptual input, but would not cause it to be *revised*. This interpretation is, moreover, in full agreement with the account of Bock's syntactic-biasing experiments given in section 7.3 above.

To sum up: The findings discussed in this section show the possibility of feedback from the phonological to the grammatical level of encoding. This feedback is likely to proceed as follows: Trouble at the level of access to word forms may induce a revision of syntactic frame. There are no findings that support on-line feedback at the next higher level of speech planning. The present evidence suggests that message preparation proceeds in full ignorance of the developing state of affairs at the levels of grammatical and phonological encoding.

Summary

Grammatical encoding takes a message as input and delivers a surface structure as output. It is likely that this process is highly automatic and nonintentional. A speaker will not, for every message, consider which of various grammatical alternatives would be most effective in reaching some communicative goal.

The first section of this chapter sketched a possible architecture for such automatic encoding: Kempen and Hoenkamp's (1987) Incremental Production Grammar. The algorithm has several attractive features as a model of the speaker: It is lexically driven; it generates "incrementally," from left to right, taking whatever message fragments the speaker makes available; it generates major constituents in parallel (which, as we saw, is a requirement if the fluency of speech is to be explained); it generates linguistically well-formed structures of an interesting, nontrivial variety; and so on. The model is, primarily, an existence proof. It shows the feasibility of constructing nonintentional grammatical-encoding algorithms that behave like real speakers in important respects.

The architecture of a processing system can sometimes become transparent in the ways it errs or fails. An effort was made to relate several types of speech error to joints in the Kempen-Hoenkamp architecture. Exchanges of words and of phrases could be attributed to errors in the delivery or the destination of procedural output. The algorithm could also predict the stranding of inflectional elements and of stress. These predictions met with varying but encouraging degrees of support from the error data.

Apart from destination errors, we distinguished errors of ordering. These should be attributed to the selection of possible but inappropriate ordering frames by categorial procedures in the algorithm. Such errors may indeed occur, but they certainly don't occur in large quantities. Rather more frequent are *shifts*—mostly slight mislocations of a word or a smaller segment. With Garrett, we attributed these to failures at the next level of processing, where phonological form is encoded.

The chapter then turned to various areas of experimental research in grammatical encoding. First, the studies of Ford and Holmes were mentioned. These studies suggest the existence of an encoding rhythm going from basic clause to basic clause—i.e., following the major semantic joints in the message rather than syntactic surface constituents. Second, the encoding of topical and highly accessible entities was discussed. It was shown that topical information is usually encoded early in the sentence, and preferably as grammatical subject. Also considered was how the various arguments in the thematic structure of the message would be distributed over grammatical functions, and over word-order positions. Grammatical encoding was called "congruent" if the relative importance of the various arguments and modifiers was reflected in the assignment of grammatical functions and constituent positions. Several studies were reviewed that showed that a systematic congruency mechanics exists, and that it is universal to an interesting degree. Third, some remarks were made on the generation of definiteness, pronominalization, and (de-)accentuation. These are anaphoric grammatical devices for linking the interpretation of the current utterance to what was said earlier or what is about to be said. They contribute to the coherence of discourse. Cross-linguistic evidence has shown both similarities and differences in the grammatical devices speakers use to establish coherence of reference. There is, in addition, syntactic coherence in the sense that an utterance repeats syntactic features of a previous utterance in the discourse. This phenomenon, which can be experimentally induced, shows that grammatical encoding procedures can become biased, independent of message-level input.

Finally, the issue of feedback was discussed. Can grammatical encoding affect message construction, and can phonological encoding affect grammatical encoding? The conclusions were fairly straightforward: There is no experimental support for the first kind of feedback. We can maintain the modular assumption that message construction proceeds without on-line feedback from the level of grammatical encoding. There is, however, clear evidence for the possibility of feedback from phonological to grammatical encoding. A minimal interpretation of this feedback is that it consists of revising a syntactic frame when trouble arises at the (next) level of phonological encoding.

Chapter 8

Phonetic Plans for Words
and Connected Speech

The first stage of the formulating process, grammatical encoding, is followed by a second stage in which a representation of the utterance's form is generated. It takes successive fragments of surface structure as they become available as input; it produces, incrementally, the form specifications that the Articulator will have to realize, the speaker's phonetic plan. In going from a surface string of lemmas to a phonetic plan for connected speech, the speaker generates a variety of intermediary representations. Phonological encoding is not as simple as retrieving stored phonetic plans for successive words and concatenating them. Rather, the phonetic plan is a rhythmic (re-)syllabification of a string of segments. Each word's segments and basic rhythm are somehow stored in the form lexicon. When these word patterns are concatenated, new patterns arise. Segments may get lost or added, particularly at word boundaries. Syllables may be formed that cross word boundaries. Word accents are shifted to create a more regular rhythm for the larger string as a whole, and so on. Many of these operations serve to create more easily *pronounceable* patterns. And pronounceable is what the input to the Articulator should be. The present chapter reviews some of the form specifications involved in the generation of phonetic plans. How these target representations are built by the speaker will be the subject of chapters 9 and 10.

The review will be done in two steps. Section 8.1 is concerned with the form of words. Words, as we saw in chapter 6, have morphological and phonological structure. This structure is specified in the speaker's form lexicon, or can be composed from smaller lexical elements in the course of speaking. The process by which the speaker retrieves this form information from the lexicon and uses it to create a phonetic plan for the word suggests the existence of a multi-level organization of word-form properties. Section 8.2 deals with connected speech. The phonological encoding of surface structure often requires a phonetic plan that spans several words. Such plans for connected speech have form properties of their own—segmental, rhythmic, and melodic.

Before we proceed to these discussions of lexical and supralexical form, some remarks about the phenomenological status of the generated representations are in order. These representations are, as Linell (1979) suggested, plans for phonetic acts. As such, they have a distinctly articulatory status. And these phonetic plans are, to a substantial degree, consciously accessible. They can, in particular, be present to the speaker as images of the target sound patterns; this is colloquially known as *internal* or *subvocal* speech. It is a remarkable fact that there can be internal speech without overt articulation. The conscious accessibility of phonetic plans makes it, apparently, possible for a speaker to decide freely on whether they should be articulated or not. This differs markedly from the phenomenological status of surface structure. Grammatical relations are not consciously accessible to linguistically untrained speakers, and probably not even to trained linguists when they are in the course of speaking. Surface structure cannot be monitored directly; it is automatically molded into a phonetic plan. It is, however, an empirical issue which aspects of the phonetic plan can be monitored and which cannot. Surely, not every single aspect of the form representation is accessible to the speaker.

Speakers do not always generate sound images (internal speech) for themselves when they speak, and there are probably important individual differences in this respect (McNeill 1987). The accessibility of the phonetic plan is not dependent on the presence of internal speech. In the following, the neutral terms *form representation* and *phonetic plan* will be used to indicate the output of the present component, leaving undecided whether this output is available as internal speech.

8.1   Plans for Words

A word is internally structured at two levels, the morphological and the phonological. At the morphological level a word is composed of one or more *morphemes*, such as roots, prefixes, and suffixes. At the phonological level a word consists of *syllables* and of *segments*, such as consonants and vowels. These two levels of organization entertain complex interrelations. In the following we will first consider some elementary properties of the morphological level of organization. We will then turn to the phonological level, which is organized at different "tiers." We will finish with a few remarks about the interrelationships between morphology and phonology.

8.1.1 Morphology

Morphological structure is reminiscent of surface structure. A word is a hierarchical organization of meaningful words, roots, and affixes, just as a sentence is a hierarchical organization of meaningful phrases and clauses. The morphological constituents of words combine to make *derivations* (as in *danger-ous, loud-ness, in-sufficient*), *compounds* (as in *sun-shine, dry-clean*), and *inflections* (as in *walk-ed, car-s*). In English, affixes are either prefixes (like *in-*) or suffixes (like *-ness*). Other languages, such as Arabic, also have infixes (affixes that are put into a root). In the following we will, however, restrict ourselves to English derivation, compounding, and inflection.

Derivations

Derivations in English can arise through the addition of affixes (prefixes or suffixes) to *words* or to *roots*. Each word that does not carry a word affix is itself a root (e.g., *car, sunshine*); hence, many roots are words themselves. But there are also roots that are not words because they cannot stand alone (e.g., *ceive* in *de-ceive*). Let us begin with the affixation of roots.

A root can combine with an affix to make a new root. Take the noun root *nation*. It can take the root affix *-al*, which makes it into an adjective root: *national*. This adjective root can, in turn, take an affix *-ity*, which makes it into a noun root: *nationality*. The whole construction, of course, is a word. The tree structure is this:

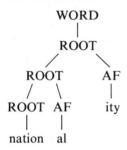

Other root affixes (called *class I affixes* by Siegel [1974] and *primary affixes* by Kiparsky [1982]) are *-ous, -ive, -ate, -ory,* and *-ify*.

It is characteristic of root affixation that it can affect the sound form of the root: The first vowel in *nation* is different from the first vowel in *national*, and in going from *national* to *nationality* the word accent shifts from the first to the third syllable.

This is different for word affixation, which is far less intrusive on the head word. Take, for instance, the word affixes *-less* and *-ness*. The word *nation* combines with *-less* to make the adjective *nationless*, and the latter word combines with *-ness* to make a noun. As a tree diagram it looks like this:

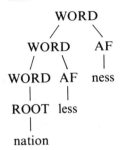

In this case the addition of affixes does not affect the vowel character or the stress pattern of the head word. Other word suffixes (alternatively called Class II or secondary suffixes) are *-er*, *-y*, *-ize*, and *-ish*.

Word and root affixes can combine in a word, but then the word affixes are always outside the root affixes. *Nation-al-ize* is possible, but *nation-less-ity* is impossible. As tree representations:

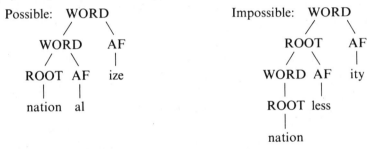

Selkirk (1982, 1984a), whose analysis we are following here, explains this very general phenomenon in English by means of the simple requirement that in a morphological tree a ROOT node may not dominate a WORD node, as is the case in the impossible tree above.

Finally, there is derivational prefixing, and the same regularity appears there. Word prefixes are *ex-* and *non-*; root prefixes are *in-* and *de-*. In mixed cases, word prefixes come to the left of root prefixes (as in *non-de-scending*). There are only a few affixes that can be both word and root affixes, e.g. *un-* and *-ment*. In *governmental*, *-ment* is a root affix, because it is followed by another root affix (*-al*); in *punishment*, it is a word affix because it follows a word affix (*-ish*). For an explanation of these and other exceptions see Selkirk 1982.

Compounds

All English compounds are made up of words from the major lexical categories (nouns, verbs, adjectives, and prepositions), and most combinations of them are possible—for example:

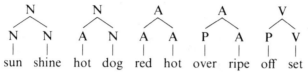

Examples of impossible combinations are NV and VA. Most compounds have a head; it is the rightmost element that has the same syntactic category as the whole compound. In all the examples above, it is the rightmost element (*shine*, *dog*, etc.). The other element usually modifies the meaning of the head, but not all compounds are transparent in this respect. The AN compound *hot dog* is less transparent than the NN compound *sheepdog*.

Also, one can form more complex compounds by combining words that are morphologically complex themselves, or by adding affixes. Examples are *black-board chalk*, *pass-ing note*, and *far-fetch-ed-ness*. The reader may take pleasure in drawing morphological trees for these and other cases.

Is compounding the conjoining of roots, or the conjoining of words? Quite probably it is the conjoining of words. If it is the conjoining of words, the resulting compound must be a word as well, because a word node cannot be dominated by a root node. If the compound is itself a word, it cannot take class I or root affixes; it can take only class II or word affixes. That seems to be generally the case. It is, for instance, all right to say *laid-backness*, but not *laid-backity*. It should further be observed that affixed words can be compounded, as in *fighter-bomber*. These, in turn, can be affixed by word affixes (*fighter-bomberless*), and so on. In other words, compounding and class II affixation seem to occur at the same "level." However, in English there may be a higher level of affixation: the level of regular inflection.

Inflections

In English the regular inflections are very simple in structure. They consist of a noun or verb stem plus an affix, and the affix is always a suffix (i.e., it follows the stem word). Take the word form that corresponds to the lemma *car* if it has the diacritic parameter "plural". It has the following morphological structure:

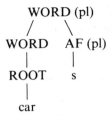

```
      WORD (pl)
     /        \
 WORD        AF (pl)
   |           |
 ROOT          s
   |
  car
```

Similarly, the verb form *swims* has this structure:

```
      WORD (sing, 3d pers, pres)
     /        \
 WORD        AF (sing, 3d pers, pres)
   |           |
 ROOT          s
   |
 swim
```

The three diacritic parameters specified in the lemma for *swim* (in this example, "singular", "3rd person", and "present tense") are together realized in the suffix -*s*. If the number would have been plural, there would have been no suffix.

Halle and Mohanan (1985) argue (contrary to Selkirk 1982) that regular inflection is not on a par with normal word affixation. A major argument is that inflections can be added to all kinds of words, whether they have affixes or not and whether they are compounds or not. But as soon an inflection is added, no further suffixes can be adjoined (as in, say, *swimsness*). Another argument is that it is hard to use an inflected word as the first word in a compound (as in *swimswater*). However, there may be semantic reasons for these facts, and there are, moreover, many exceptions (e.g., *swimming pool*). Whether there is a genuine third morphological stratum in English is a matter of dispute.

The inflectional structure of English is meager. Other languages, such as German, are far richer in inflectional morphology. But German and English have in common that they project different diacritic features of the lemma on the same suffix. The -*s* in *he thinks* expresses third person, singular, and present tense at the same time. Thus, English is called an *inflectional* language. So-called *agglutinative* languages distribute diacritic features over successive affixes, each one realizing another feature. Turkish, Finnish, Hungarian, and Japanese are languages of this kind. Speakers of agglutinative languages regularly produce new words when they speak, as was discussed in chapter 6. However, an adult speaker of an inflectional language has used almost all the derivational and inflectional forms before, and can readily retrieve them from the mental lexicon. The exceptional new words are mostly compounds. Still, the fact that almost all morphologically complex words are stored in the speaker's lexicon does not mean that the internal structure of a word has become irrelevant in its production. Speech errors and other production phenomena tell us that a word's morphology does play a role in its retrieval during speech.

The entity to which an inflection is added is traditionally called a *stem*. (In the examples above, the roots *car* and *swim* are stems.) So, we now have the notions *word*, *root*, and *stem*. Each word contains (or consists of) at least one root. Many roots can be words themselves; some cannot (such as *-ceive*). If a word is inflected, the stem is whatever the inflectional affixation applies to. Let us now turn to the phonology of words.

8.1.2   Tier-Representation in Word Phonology
A word consists of one or more syllables, and each syllable consists of one or more slots that can contain phonetic material, such as consonants or vowels. The final phonetic plan for a word represents how the phonetic material is distributed over these so-called *timing slots*. The axis of this representation is nothing but the row of timing slots. It is called the *skeletal tier* (or, alternatively, the *timing tier*). But these slots are partitioned in small chains. There is, first of all, their grouping into successive syllables. And syllables can consist of further constituents, such as onsets and rimes. This constituent organization of the slots at the skeletal tier is represented at the so-called *syllable tier*.

The phonetic content of the slots is of two kinds: *quality* (also, confusingly, called *melody* in the phonological literature) and *prosody*. The quality of phonetic content is determined by such features as whether the speech sound should be voiced or unvoiced, nasal or non-nasal, plosive or non-plosive. These qualitative features are specified at the *segment tier*. The prosodic plan, on the other hand, specifies the metrical and the intonational pattern of the intended utterance. They are specified at the *metrical* and *intonational* tiers, respectively.

It is not precisely known how the different tiers relate to one another (see Clements 1985 for various hypotheses), but figure 8.1 can be a starting point for the following discussion. The tier organization is like a set of pages glued together at the edges. Each page edge represents a tier, and each page connects two tiers. The skeletal tier connects via the right page to the segmental tier and via the left page to the syllable tier. The syllable tier, in turn, connects directly to the metrical and to the intonational tier. Later I will suggest that the segment tier at the right is the spine for a further set

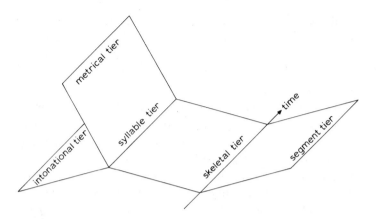

Figure 8.1
An initial representation of the coupling of tiers in an articulatory plan.

of pages, containing the *feature tiers*. Each page connects two tiers, and it displays the "association lines" between the tiers, i.e., the precise connections between the units of the two tiers involved. The following subsections will give a summary discussion of the tiers and their interconnections.

8.1.3 The Skeletal Tier

The skeletal tier is a sequence of slots, and these slots can contain phonetic content. A filled slot is a phonetic segment or a *phone*. It is not the case that a speaker pronounces one phone, then the next phone, and so on. Still, his phonetic plan consists of a sequence of phones. Each phone, however, will be realized by the articulator as constituting part of a larger articulatory gesture. The smallest such gesture is the articulation of a whole syllable.

The simplest representation of the skeletal tier is just

X X X X ...,

the sequence of timing slots to be filled. Indeed, some phonologists leave it at that (see, e.g., Halle and Mohanan 1985). Others, however, distinguish between slots that should be filled with *sonorous* content and slots that should be filled with *nonsonorous* materials. Sonorous speech sounds are relatively loud. The most sonorous ones are vowels, such as [a] and [ɔ]. Least sonorous are voiceless stops, such as [p] and [k]. Others are in between; [r], [l], [m], and [n], for instance, are in the middle range of sonority (Selkirk 1984b). A syllable always has a high-sonorous peak segment, which can be preceded or followed by other less sonorous sounds. Many phonologists indicate at the skeletal tier which slots should contain syllabic peaks; i.e., "syllabicity" is represented at the skeletal tier (Hayes 1986). Such slots are indicated by V. This, of course, derives from "vowel," but it means only "high-sonorous segment of the syllable." All other slots are indicated by C. This derives from "consonant," but it means only "low-sonorous segment of the syllable."

The syllable peak may extend over two slots, as in long vowels, but it cannot have two peaks separated by a less sonorous element. In fact, there is a general rule that, within a syllable, sonority decreases from the peak to the syllable boundaries (Selkirk's [1984b] "Sonority Sequencing Generalization"). The peak is the top of a "sonority hill," which slopes down toward the boundaries without secondary sonority peaks. One must, probably, allow for a slightly weaker version of this rule: that sonority is *nonincreasing* away from the peak. There may be juxtaposed segments of *equal* sonority.

Here we will adopt the CV notation for the skeletal tier (Clements and Keyser 1983). A sequence of slots could, for instance, look like

C V V C V.

This represents a sequence of two syllables, because there are two peaks: a long one and a short one. This particular tier could be filled by materials for the word *meter*. The first syllable has [i] as peak, a long vowel that takes two slots. It is preceded by the less sonorous [m], which fills the initial C slot. The second syllable has [r] as its peak; it is more sonorous than the [t] that precedes it. The segments, therefore, relate to the slots as follows.

```
slots:      C V V C V
            |  \/  | |
segments:   m  i   t r
```

In the following, phones or strings of phones will be put in square brackets. The phonemes of which phones in the phonetic plan are a realization are given between slashes. So, [m] is the phone in the phonetic plan that, in some syllabic environment, realizes the phoneme /m/.

8.1.4 The Syllable Tier

The slots at the skeletal tier are grouped in larger *syllable units*. These are represented at the syllable tier. The simplest representation would be one in which the slots are merely connected to successive syllable nodes. The syllabic representation for *meter* would then be the following.

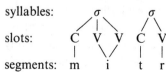

```
syllables:          σ          σ
                   /|\        / \
slots:        C   V  V    C    V
             |    \/       |    |
segments:    m    i        t    r
```

What kinds of strings can be syllables? All languages have CV or CVV syllables, most have V syllables, many have CVC syllables, and some have VC syllables. English has them all. It is, moreover, possible in English to make strings of two Vs, and of two or three Cs within a syllable (as in the monosyllabic word *scraped*).

Such strings of V and C slots within a syllable can be further partitioned into so-called *syllable constituents*. A syllable's main constituents are *onset* and *rime*. Each syllable has a rime. The rime begins with the syllable peak. If the syllable is just a V, that V is the rime. If further consonants follow the peak, they also belong to the rime. So *art* is a word, it is a syllable, and it is a rime. A rime is naturally partitioned into a *nucleus* and a *coda*. The nucleus contains the peak slot(s), the coda the remaining C slot(s). The syllable *art* has /a/ as nucleus and /rt/ as coda.

The onset of a syllable is the string of Cs preceding the peak. In *meter*; /m/ and /t/ are syllable onsets. Onsets can also be clusters of low-sonorous elements, such as /skr/ in the monosyllabic word *script*. If no C precedes the V, the onset is empty. Some of the main syllable types appear in the four-syllable word *astonishment*:

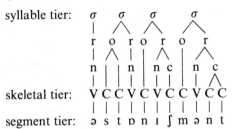

syllable tier:

skeletal tier:

segment tier:

The first syllable, /ə/, fills a single slot. Its peak is, at the same time, its nucleus, its rime, and the whole syllable. The second syllable, /stɒ/, has an onset, /st/, and it is further branching over two slots containing /s/ and /t/. The rime is nonbranching; it consists of the nucleus /ɒ/. The next syllable, /nɪʃ/, has a nonbranching onset, /n/, but a branching rime, consisting of a nucleus /ɪ/ and a coda /ʃ/. A coda can also be branching. This is the case in the fourth syllable, /mənt/. Here the onset /m/ and the nucleus /ə/ are nonbranching, but the coda fills two C slots: with /n/ and /t/, respectively, where /n/ is more sonorous than /t/. The way in which a syllable branches is, as we will shortly see, a determinant of whether it will receive stress at the metrical tier.

In English multisyllabic words, each V is part of the peak of a different syllable. Compare the words in example 1: *contract, contractor*, and *retinal*.

(1)

syllable tier:

skeletal tier:

segment tier:

Contract has two V peaks and hence two syllables; *contractor* and *nominal* have three of each. Since V here is the peak of a syllable, how are the consonants distributed over adjacent syllables? The main rule is that a V attracts as many of the consonants preceding it as it can. So, instead of *contr-act* or *cont-ract*, we have *con-tract*. The vowel of the second syllable takes on both /t/ and /r/. This rule is known as *maximization of onset*. Only the "leftovers" are for the coda of the preceding syllable. In *contract*, /n/ is the leftover C; it is subsumed under the previous syllable (*con*). Why is /n/ not also attracted into the initial consonant cluster of the second syllable? A major reason is that the phone [n] (the realization of /n/) is more sonorous than [t] (the realization of /t/). As a consequence, the resulting syllable, [ntrækt], would have two sonority peaks: [n] and [a]. This contradicts the Sonority Sequencing Generalization. There may, in addition, be language-specific restrictions on clusters. For each language, there are so-called *phonotactic rules* that specify possible and impossible clusters in syllable onset and syllable offset.

The second syllable of *contract* is *tract*. But the second syllable of *contractor* is *trac*. This is, again, due to maximization of onset. The third syllable of *contractor* doesn't like to begin with V; it tries to assemble syllable-onset consonants. It takes /t/; however, it cannot take /k/, since /kt/ is phonotactically impossible as a syllable onset in English (though not in other languages). The result is thus *con-trac-tor*. This example shows how the addition of a suffix can lead to *resyllabification*, the reassignment of elements at syllable boundaries.

Though the maximization of onset applies quite generally, there are also exceptions. In *nationlessness* there is a syllable break between *less* and *ness*; still, /sn/ is a possible syllable-initial cluster in English. In subsection 8.1.1 it was discussed that word affixes are not "sound-intrusive." Here we see that they also tend to preserve their own syllable identity. This is different for root affixes that easily attract consonants from the root (as in *plaint* → *plain-tive*).

The word *retinal* in example 1 demonstrates still another important feature of syllabification. Maximization of onset would predict the syllabification *re-ti-nal*. Still, the consonant /n/, which is syllable-initial, also participates in the foregoing syllable, so that the word contains as syllables *re*, *tin*, and *nal*. This phenomenon is called *ambisyllabicity*. Certain consonants in intervocalic position (i.e., in VCV configurations, where both Vs are unstressed) can make a *liaison* between adjacent syllables. For American English, the flapping /t/ of *retinal* is probably also ambisyllabic.

8.1.5 The Segment Tier

A speaker's phonetic plan represents which phones go in successive timing slots. The sequence of phones in a syllable specifies the articulatory gesture to be made by the speaker in order to realize that syllable. The number of different phones in the world's languages is fairly limited. Whatever its exact size, it is small enough that an International Phonetic Alphabet (IPA) could be designed by which the phonetic segments in different languages can be roughly transcribed. The IPA, given in appendix A, is used in this book to represent phonetic segments. The phone sequence *cat* will be transcribed as [kæt], *nation* as [neɪʃən], and so on.

Phones are not indivisible wholes. They represent various features of the articulatory gesture to be made. To utter a speech sound is a fairly complicated motor activity involving maneuvers of different parts of the respiratory system, the larynx, and the vocal tract. The sound may require inhalation or exhalation, it may or may not require voicing (the periodic vibration of the vocal folds), and it will require a range of vocal-tract specifications, such as positions or movements of the velum, the tongue, and the lips. A phone is an abstract representation of such gestural components. Their precise execution is not specified in the phonetic plan; that is the task of the articulatory component.

Which features, then, are specified at the segmental level? I will not give an exhaustive listing, but I will mention some major classes (see also section 11.1.3). At the respiratory level, a speaker might make a distinction between inhaling and exhaling sounds. But English and most (but not all) other languages have exhaling speech sounds only. At the laryngeal level the most important feature is *voicing*. All spoken languages make a contrast between voiced and unvoiced speech sounds. In English, [d] and [t] differ in just this feature, and so do the segments [b] and [p] and the segments [g] and [k]. At the supralaryngeal level (i.e., the level of the vocal tract), two main classes of features can be distinguished: *place* features and *manner* features.

The place features indicate where in the vocal tract the speech sound is to be made. Some examples of place features are *labial* (versus *nonlabial*), which specifies whether the lips should form a constriction, as in [m], [p], or [b]; *coronal*, which requires the constriction to be made by the tongue blade, as in [t] or [O]; and *posterior* (versus *anterior*), where the primary constriction is behind the alveolar ridge, as in [g] or [h].

The manner features specify a variety of further aspects of the articulation beyond its place. Among them are *nasal* (versus *non-nasal* or *oral*), which specifies whether the velum should be lowered so that the nasal cavity will resonate with the speech sound, as in [m] and [ŋ]; *rounded* (versus *unrounded*), meaning that the sound is to be made with protruding lips, as in [u]; and *strident* or *fricative*, which involves the generation of a spirantal noise at the place of constriction, as in [s] and [f]. The above-mentioned feature of voicing is also often considered to be a manner feature. Several of these manners and places of articulation will be further discussed in chapter 11.

A feature may or may not be *distinctive* within a language. It is distinctive if the distinction between two words in a language hinges on that feature. Voicing is distinctive in English, because it opposes words such as *bill* and *pill*, *tell* and *dell*. The manner feature *nasal* is distinctive because it discriminates the words *man* and *ban*, and *name* and *dame*, and so on. Other features are not distinctive. For English this is so for the *aspiration* feature. Compare the words *pot* and *spot*. The [p] of *pot* is pronounced such that a little puff of air follows the release; this is called aspiration. The word *spot* is pronounced without p-aspiration. But the aspiration feature is nondistinctive in English, because there are no two words whose difference hinges on that feature. There are, for instance, no two different words *p'ot* and *pot* in English, where the former is aspirated and the latter is not and where different things are meant. Whether or not /p/ should be aspirated depends only on its syllabic enviroment. They are two context-dependent variants of /p/. Variants of a speech sound differing only in nondistinctive features are called *allophones*; [p'] and [p] are allophones in English. They are allophonic realizations of the same *phoneme*, /p/. A phoneme is a segment as far as specified for its distinctive features only. So, *pot* and *spot* contain the same phoneme /p/, but realized as different (allo)phones.

It is an important question whether the more abstract notion of "phoneme" is psychologically relevant for a theory of the speaker, or whether the phone is the only relevant level of form representation. The next chapter will discuss evidence from speech errors that strongly supports the notion of the phoneme as a processing unit of phonetic planning. When the speaker intends to say *spot-and-kill* but instead happens to say *skot-and-pill*, the *phonemes* /p/ and /k/ exchange, not the allophones; the /p/ will be aspirated in *pill*, whereas it was not in *spot*. By and large it seems to be the case that the form specifications for words in the mental lexicon are *phonemic*, like /spɒt/ and /pɪl/. The speaker uses these representations to retrieve the corresponding syllabic gestures. The phonetic plans for these syllabic gestures are phonetic, i.e., in terms of allophones (e.g., [spɒt] and [pʼɪl]. The next chapter will discuss how the phonemic codes in the lexicon are used to retrieve the phonetic specifications for the syllables.

The number of distinctive features for a language is quite small, probably around 20. Each of them is a more or less independently controllable aspect of articulation. It was remarked above that a speaker does not pronounce one phone, and then the next one, and so on. Rather, he plans whole articulatory gestures of at least syllabic size. Such a gesture normally involves not only feature change but also feature maintenance. Successive syllabic slots may maintain the values of certain specific features while changing the values of others. In the word *manner*, for instance, the distinctive feature of voicing persists over the whole word. Or take nasality. The French pronunciation of the town name *Nancy* involves a sequence of [n] and [ã], where both [n] and [ã] are nasal; nasality persists over two phones, the whole first syllable of the word. It has therefore been suggested that the segment tier be used as a spine to which a whole set of *feature tiers* are linked, like the pages of a book. At least, one could make a laryngeal tier and a supralaryngeal tier, and subdivide the latter into a place tier and a manner tier. This was suggested by Clements (1985). Alternatively, one could write a separate tier or line for each distinctive feature, as is done for the voices in a musical score. We will not pursue this here. The important point is that we avoid the trap of a strictly segmental picture of articulatory planning. Articulatory gestures can span several timing units, and should be represented as such.

8.1.6 The Metrical Tier

Speaking is a rhythmic process. A speaker organizes his utterance in patterns of stressed and unstressed syllables, and can assign various degrees of stress or accent to different syllables. The production of speech is, in this respect, not unlike the production of music. Rhythmical organization is probably the most universal property of music. There is always some regular organization of beats in groups of two, three, or more, and the metrical organization is almost always hierarchical to some degree (Longuet-Higgins 1987). There is, of course, no fixed time unit in speech like a measure in music, but there is surely some hierarchical organization of beats.

At the word level of speech, multisyllabic words can also be said to have a metrical pattern, and this pattern is represented on the metrical tier. The metrical tier is associated to the syllable tier. Stress is a sound property of syllables. It is, among other things, reflected in the duration of the spoken syllable. When a syllable is stressed, it is longer than when it is not stressed. The syllable *for* is longer in *formal* than in *forlorn*. From this point of view, the metrical tier might be represented as a string of syllable-linked musical notes of different lengths, like this:

This, however, would be too suggestive. Syllable duration is not the only way in which stress variations are realized. Stress is also, in part, realized by variation in amplitude or intensity and by pitch movement. It needs a more abstract representation than a purely temporal one. There is, moreover, a relation to vowel quality. The initial phoneme /ɔ/ is realized differently in *forlorn* and in *formal*. When a vowel is unstressed in English, its quality may differ from the stressed allophone. In short, stress is an abstract category, like "phoneme". It may be realized in different ways, depending on the language and on the speaker.

An attractive way to represent a word's stress pattern on the metrical tier is by means of a so-called *metrical grid* (Prince 1983; Selkirk 1984a). It provides each syllable with one or more beats. Take the word *California*. It has a beat pattern like this:

```
     x
x    x
x  x  x   x
Ca li for nia
```

The main word stress or *word accent* is on the third syllable (*for*); there is a secondary stress on the first syllable (*ca*), and the remaining two syllables have the minimum amount of stress. We assume that, in most cases, a word's basic stress pattern is simply available to a speaker. But it is surely interesting that, when confronted with an unknown printed word, a native speaker will immediately assign a stress pattern that conforms to the rules of the language. For instance, *pefinarca* will most likely receive the same stress pattern as *California*. Speakers apply stress-assignment rules unawares; the rules are part of their knowledge of the language.

This is not the place to review the metrical rules of English (see especially Selkirk 1984a), but some major tendencies in stress assignment can be mentioned.

A first, quite general observation is that the rime of a syllable is important in stress attraction, whereas the onset plays no role in it. When a syllable has a branching rime—i.e., when the rime is anything more than a single V, like *for* in *California*—it is called a *heavy* syllable, and it will get an extra beat in its column. Syllables with just a V rime are called *light*; they do not get an extra beat for heaviness.

There is, second, a strong tendency toward stress *alternation*. Speakers dislike a sequence of two stressed syllables. If this is imminent, for instance because there is a sequence of two heavy syllables, one of them will lose a beat. On the other hand, speakers also dislike sequences of unstressed syllables, especially more than two of them. A speaker will add beats in order to break such patterns. The resulting alternating stress pattern is present in *California*, but also in most other polysyllabic words.

Third, affixes play a special role in stress assignment. Word-initial and word-final affixes are never stressed in English. Affixes can receive stress only in nonextreme positions, and only when they are root affixes. This is, for instance, the case for *al* in *nationality*.

Fourth, function words (auxiliaries, pronouns, determiners, and so on) tend to be destressed as if they were affixes. Phonologically, they are not really words at all.

Fifth, when a lemma has been assigned pitch accent in the generation of surface structure, at least one extra beat is given to the syllable that has word accent. For example, if a speaker answers the question *Were you born in Oregon?* with *No, in California*, the metrical grid for *California* will be

```
       x
       x
x      x
x  x  x    x
Ca li for nia
```

So, even if the stress pattern of *California* is stored in the speaker's word form lexicon, it can be adapted to accommodate the diacritical feature of pitch accent. Other accomodations of a word's basic metrical pattern can result from stress clashes with neighboring words (see subsections 8.2.2 and 10.2.1).

8.1.7   The Intonation Tier

So far we have seen that the phonetic plan an English speaker constructs for a word derives largely from information stored in the mental lexicon. The phonemic constitution of morphemes and words is stored in the lexicon; so, quite probably, is the (allo)phonic composition of the language's syllables. To generate the phonetic plan for a word, the speaker uses the phonemic code as a key to retrieve the phonetic syllabic code. (This process is the subject of chapter 9.) But some aspects of the word's phonetic form are not stored in the lexicon and have to be constructed time and again. For English and many other languages, this is true of a word's intonation pattern. (This pattern should be carefully distinguished from the word's stress pattern; the same stress pattern can go with very different intonation patterns.) Here are some possible intonation contours for *California* (for the notation system, see subsection 8.2.3):

(2)

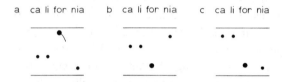

It is not hard to think up contexts in which these different contours would occur naturally. Version a can occur in the simple assertive utterance *I live in California*; version b can be used in a question, such as in *Do you live in California?*; and version c can occur in the emphatic *California again!*. The three intonational contours perform three different functions. But they are not lexically stored as three different versions of *California*; rather, they derive from the intonational phrase in which the word participates.

In all three phrases, *California* has pitch accent, and this is in all contours realized by an obstruction of pitch, either up or down, to the syllable that carries the word accent (i.e., *for*). The intonational shape of a word is largely determined by whether it has pitch accent or not and by where it occurs in the intonational phrase. More will be said on this in subsection 8.2.3.

8.1.8 Morphophonemic Relations
So far we have dealt with the morphological structure of words, and with their phonological structure. Clearly, the two are intimately related. The phonetic material that appears in the syllabic slots of the phonetic plan originates from the phonemic properties of a word's morphemes. But syllable boundaries do not always respect morpheme boundaries, and a

lot of rearrangement takes place in going from the morpheme level to the syllable level. En route, phonemes may be added or deleted, and feature values may change. All this is governed by *morphophonemic rules.* These rules will not be discussed here in any detail; we will just consider the different regular phonetic shapes the plural morpheme can take in English:

pit → pits   (addition of /-s/)
toad → toads   (addition of /-z/)
edge → edges   (addition of /-ɪz/)

Here we see the addition of different segments, and resyllabification (in the case of /-ɪz/). Such variants of the same morpheme are called *allomorphs.* The morphophonemic relations between singular and plural are known to native speakers of English, who easily apply them to nonsense words: *rit → rits, tood → toods, losh → loshes.* This means that the morphophonemic relation between singular and plural is not only stored for each noun in the speaker's lexicon, but is also abstractly stored as a set of rules that can be productively applied to new words. These rules are rather simple; they refer only to the final segment of the noun (is it voiced, coronal, strident?), and they apply in just the same way to possessives (*the pit's taste, the toad's legs, the edge's sharpness*).

   This concludes our review of the speaker's phonetic plan for single words. But the final phonetic shape of a word also depends on the context in which it appears. Words assimilate to their environment in connected speech. This may affect their segmental composition, but also their metrical properties. Moreover, words participate in the melody of the utterance.

8.2   Plans for Connected Speech

The phonetic plan for connected speech can also be represented as a layered structure. In fact, the tiers are no different than the word-level tiers. On the skeletal tier there is a sequence of high and low sonorant slots; the phones in these slots are represented at the segment tier. Their partitioning into syllables and syllable constituents is represented at the syllable tier. The stress pattern over syllables is represented at the metrical tier, and the utterance melody appears at the intonation tier. Here we will be concerned only with those aspects of the plan that make it different from a mere concatenation of word plans. There are, in fact, differences at the level of segments and syllables, at the metrical level, and at the intonation level.

8.2.1 Segments and Syllables

The phonetic plan for connected speech may involve a special choice of allomorphs, cliticization, and resyllabification. Let us consider some examples of these phenomena.

A special choice of allomorphs occurs in English *auxiliary reduction*. Auxiliaries like *have* and *is* have reduced forms, which are chosen in certain connected speech situations. Rather than saying *I have bought it*, speakers will opt for *I've bought it*. Similarly, they will say *Dick's running* instead of *Dick is running*. In these cases the reduced allomorph, /-v/ or /-z/, cannot stand alone as a word, because it is not syllabic. Rather, a new word-like unit is formed by gluing the allomorph to the preceding word to form *I've* and *Dick's*. This is called *cliticization*; /-v/ and /-z/ are *enclitics* to the preceding word. The new string is called a *phonological word*. Little is known about the lexical status of such cliticizations. Is *I've* a stored lexical element in the speaker's mental lexicon? It probably is, because of its frequent usage. But it is less likely that *Dick's* is a readily stored item with the meaning of *Dick is* (except if the speaker happens to be married to Dick and is always talking about him). At any rate, a succession of two different lexical items in surface structure may be realized as a single word-like unit in the phonetic plan for connected speech (see Kaisse 1985 and Nespor and Vogel 1986 for detailed analyses of these matters).

When words are juxtaposed in connected speech, they may be subject to resyllabification at their junctures. In fact, segments may appear which are absent when the word is spoken in isolation. Let us take an example from British English: /r/ deletion. The /r/ is not pronounced in syllable-final position, so *car* is pronounced as [ka], and *care* as [kɛ:]. But it reappears in the word when in syllable-initial position, as in *carry* or in *caring*: [kæ-ri], [kɛy-rɪŋ]. This is a word-internal phenomenon, and one wonders whether it also occurs across words in connected speech. It does. When the British English speaker says *the car is running* without cliticizing the *is*, the sequence *car is* becomes resyllabified as [kɑ-rɪz]; the /r/ of *car* is now syllable-initial and thus becomes pronounced. Similar phenomena occur in French *liaison*, as in *nous-avons*, where the /s/ reappears in syllable-initial position.

The segmental and syllabic structure of a phonetic plan for connected speech is not a mere concatenation of plans for isolated words. There can be considerable restructuring, in particular by the use of allomorphs, by cliticization, and by resyllabification. These and other restructurings are especially apparent in fast speech, to which we will return in chapter 10.

8.2.2 Metrical Structure

Words and word-like units are grouped into smaller or larger prosodic units. The main such unit in English and many other languages is the *intonational phrase*. As the term indicates, it is a unit of intonation, and as such it will be discussed in the next subsection. Take example 3.

(3) //The detective /1 remembered //2 that the station /3 could be entered /4 from the other side as well //5

The speaker of this sentence could deliver it as a sequence of two intonational phrases, *The detective remembered* and *that the station could be entered from the other side as well*—i.e., the two finite (and basic) clauses of the sentence. This partitioning is indicated by double slashes (//). But intonational phrases also have an internal metrical structure. Many authors assume the existence of so-called *phonological phrases* as metrical building blocks of intonational phrases (see especially Nespor and Vogel 1986). According to this view, each intonational phrase consists of one or more phonological phrases. These are metrical units which relate to surface structure in the following way (for English, and leaving some qualifying details aside): The first phonological phrase of a sentence begins where the sentence begins and ends right after the first lexical head of an NP, a VP, or an AP. The next phonological phrase begins just there and ends after the next such lexical head, and so recursively; any remaining "tail" after the last lexical head is added to the last phonological phrase. According to this definition, sentence 3 consists of five phonological phrases, with right boundaries at /1, //2, /3, /4, and //5. In this sentence the respective lexical heads-of-phrase are *detective*, *remembered*, *station*, *entered*, and *side*.

The phonological phrase is characterized by a metrical togetherness of adjacent words. Bock (1982), Garrett (1982), and van Wijk (1987) suggest that it is indeed a unit of phonological encoding, an output package for the articulatory component. However, others (in particular, Selkirk [1984a]) do not partition intonational phrases into such all-or-none metrical building blocks. Rather, they assume various *degrees* of metrical togetherness between adjacent words in intonational phrases. There are, on this view, no strict rules for partitioning an intonational phrase into smaller phonological packages, except that the speaker will respect a certain degree of togetherness. In other words, the speaker has certain options that he may or may not use to complete a "package" for the Articulator. Whether he will use an available option depends on various performance factors (to which we will return in chapter 10). The speaker of sentence 3, for instance, could, after planning the word group *the detective*, ignore the option for a break and add *remembered* in the same phonological phrase, thus creating *the detective remembered* as one output package.

There are, then two issues to be considered: Where are the options for a speaker to complete a phonological phrase? What makes the speaker use an available option? The latter issue will be taken up in chapter 10; here we will only consider the former.

There are better and worse options. A very good place to complete a phonological phrase is the end of a sentence (position //5 in the example above), or the end of a clause (positions //2 and //5). Ends of clauses are quite often also ends of intonational phrases. Not a good option is right after a preposition in a prepositional phrase, e.g., after *from* in *from the other side*. Several factors conspire to make a good option. Let us review some of the potential places for a break.

(i) The end of an intonational phrase. This break is obligatory.

(ii) The end of a sentence constituent. A sentence constituent is one that, in the destination hierarchy (see subsection 7.1.3), is delivered to S. This is, normally, the case for the subject and the predicate phrase of a sentence.

(iii) The end of a multi-word phrase. Ends of NPs, VPs, APs, or PPs are good options for a prosodic break.

(iv) After the lexical head of a NP, a VP, or an AP (i.e., the criterion used above to define phonological phrases). A good break point is after the main verb of the verb phrase, or after the main noun in a noun phrase, even if these are not in constituent-final position.

(v) After a content word. It is almost never the case, except in self-repairs, that a speaker breaks *within* a word. And if a speaker breaks after a word, that word is usually a content word. Function words that are not phrase-final are seldom followed by a break. The head of a prepositional phrase, for instance, is usually not followed by a break—except when the speaker has trouble accessing the following head noun.

Selkirk (1984a) represents these options by adding "silent demibeats" to the metrical grid for each of the above factors (I will use the term "silent beats" instead.) Here is one of her examples:

```
x         x              x         x
x         x          x   x         x
x x xxx x x      xx  x    x   x   x   x   x xxxxx
Mary    finished   her Russian  novel
```

The first word, *Mary*, is followed by three silent beats: one because *Mary* is a content word (v), one because it is head of phrase (iv), and one because it completes a sentence constituent (ii). The next word, *finished*, is followed by two silent beats, because it is a content word (v) and because it is head of phrase (iv). The possessive pronoun *her* is not a content word (see v), nor does it meet any other condition for the addition of a silent beat. And so forth. Such a metrical-grid representation should, of course, not be read as a direct representation of pause durations between words. Rather, it represents degrees of rhythmical togetherness of words; *her* and *Russian* are metrically more together than *finished* and *her*, for instance. The best break options are at points of least metrical togetherness. In the present example, that is between *Mary* and *finished*, and between *finished* and *her*. On a phonological phrase analysis, these are precisely the boundaries between the three phonological phrases of this sentence: *Mary*, *finished*, and *her Russian novel*.

Even if the speaker does not take every major break option, he may highlight the phrasal structure of his utterance by other metrical means. He may, for instance, slightly stretch a syllable or insert a small pause where there is a metrical caesura. He can, moreover, add prominence to the last already-prominent word in the phrase. This is called the *nuclear stress rule* (Chomsky and Halle 1968; Selkirk 1984a; subsection 5.2.2 above). Take again the example *Mary finished her Russian novel*. The noun phrase *her Russian novel* has *novel* as its lexical head, its last prominent word. Nuclear stress requires it to be more prominent than all other words in its phrase. Hence, it is given an additional beat. Similarly, the verb phrase *finished her Russian novel* also has *novel* as its last prominent word. With its additional beat, *novel* is also the most prominent word in the latter phrase, in accordance with the nuclear stress rule. Finally, *novel* is also the last word of the whole sentence. Hence, it should also be the most prominent word of the sentence. With its additional beat, it is. The resulting metrical grid looks like this:

```
                                   x
    x         x            x       x
    x         x       x    x       x
    x x xxx x x     xx x    x  x   x x  x xxxx
    Mary    finished  her Russian novel
```

Ideally speaking, then, the surface structure of sentences can be highlighted by various metrical means. Whether and to what degree that is actually done in fluent speech is a different matter. What should be kept in mind is that pitch accent will overrule everything else. If the speaker has reason to give pitch accent to *her* (for instance, to make a contrast with *his Russian novel*), then *her* will be given greatest prominence and *novel* will be almost stressless.

A final readjustment to be mentioned is one that promotes an optimal alternation of high and low stresses. The speaker will try to avoid stress clashes within a metrical group or a phonological phrase. Take for instance the adjective *abstrAct*, which has its word accent on the second syllable. In the phrase *Abstract Art*, the word accent will appear on the first syllable. Selkirk (1984a), who gives a systematic treatment of these shift phenomena, calls this "beat movement." The beat moves to the penultimate syllable of *abstract* in order to avoid a stress clash with the accent in *art*. The tendency toward alternating stress, which we already observed at the word level, apparently also holds within coherent metrical groups of words. Speakers of English dislike sequences of stressed syllables within a phonological phrase.

This section on the speaker's metrical plan would not be complete without addressing the issue of speaking *rate*. Deese (1984) found a speaking rate of 5–6 syllables per second in normal conversational speech, but speakers can accelerate substantially. There are, now and then, short stretches of high-rate speech with about 8 syllables per second. Deese was able to recognize at least a few functions served by such increases of rate. One had to do with turn-taking. Speakers speed up toward the end of a sentence and into the next one in order to keep the floor. This bridging is done to prevent an interlocutor from taking the next turn at the end of the sentence. Another function is expressive: to say something in a modest, nonassertive way. This probably happened in the following utterance: *There's a very recent paper. I'm trying to think of the author of it.* The second sentence was spoken very rapidly and with flattened intonation. Clearly, such rate parameters must be set in the speaker's phonetic plan.

Though the rhythm of connected speech builds on the metrical properties of the individual words, it has additional features of its own. There is, first, speaking rate, which may serve interactional and expressive functions. There is, second, a grouping of words in short stretches leading up to the lexical heads-of-phrase. Within these small metrical groups there will be a tendency toward alternating stress. These metrical units or phonological phrases may, third, combine to form larger patterns, whose metrical properties can (to some degree) highlight surface-structure relations, especially through nuclear stress assignment. Pitch-accent peaks are quite marked in the metrical pattern of connected speech. The larger coherent metrical patterns are usually called intonational phrases, because they constitute the domain for assigning melody to an utterance.

8.2.3 Intonation

The most characteristic form property of connected speech in intonational languages is its melody. The English speaker's lexicon, we saw, contains no intonation patterns for words, only stress patterns. The intonation of a word depends on which syllable is lexically marked for word accent, on whether the word is focused in surface structure (i.e., whether it should receive pitch accent), and on the sentence melody in which it partakes.

Intonation is, in the very first place, an expressive device. Pitch accent expresses the prominence of a concept, the interest adduced to it by the speaker, or its contrastive role. The melody of an utterance expresses a speaker's emotions and attitudes. It is a main device for transmitting the rhetorical force of an utterance, its weight, its obnoxiousness, its intended friendliness or hostility. It also signals the speaker's intention to continue or to halt, or to give the floor to an interlocutor. The expressive functions of language, though intimately tuned to its referential and predicative functions, are probably rather independently controlled.

When we discuss the speaker's intonational plan we must keep in mind that its roots are special, and that it is less representational and more directly expressive than any other aspect of speech. The present section presents only some of the bare outlines of what a speaker puts into his intonational plan. A full treatment would necessarily involve analyses of emotions and attitudes, as well as a review of the extensive intonation literature on British and American English, Dutch, Danish, Swedish, French, and other languages. This would go beyond the framework of the present book. The reader is referred to the following sources: Bolinger 1986; Brown, Currie, and Kenworthy 1980; Cruttenden 1986; Cutler and Ladd 1983; Gårding 1983; Gussenhoven 1984; Halliday 1970; 't Hart and Collier 1975; Ladd 1980, 1986; Ladd, Scherer, and Silverman 1986; Liberman and Pierrehumbert 1984; O'Connor and Arnold 1973; Pierrehumbert 1981; Scherer 1986; Thorson 1983; Vaissière 1983; Van Bezooijen 1984.

The structure of intonational phrases

The intonation contour of connected speech is organized over smaller or larger phrases, called *intonational phrases*. An intonational phrase consists of one or more phonological phrases or metrical groups, but there is no general rule dictating the size of an intonational phrase. The speaker may decide to make smaller or larger intonational phrases, depending on such factors as rate of speech, formality of the communicative situation, and so on. Still, it may help to give some examples of quite natural intonational phrases. Often the sentence as a whole is an intonational phrase, especially if it is not too long; *How are you?*, *Go and get the newspaper*, and *Henry's falling asleep* are normally pronounced as single intonational phrases. When the sentence is longer, or more complicated in structure, it may be broken into two or more intonational phrases. This is quite naturally done if the sentence contains a parenthetical, a nonrestrictive relative clause, or a tag question, as in the following examples:

(4)   1   2
//Connected speech // as will now become apparent //
                3
consists of intonational phrases //

(5)   1   2   3
-//The golden temple // which is still in use // was built by the Sikhs //

(6)   1   2
//He's your uncle // isn't he? //

The parenthetical in example 4, the nonrestrictive relative clause in example 5, and the tag question in example 6 are intonational phrases of their own. In examples 4 and 5 the inserted phrase breaks the main clause into two parts, each of which becomes an intonational phrase of its own. In example 6 the tag phrase is added to the main clause, which is an independent intonational phrase.

One intuitive test for the presence of an intonational phrase is that it can be surrounded by grammatical pauses. It is quite natural to insert such pauses at the double slash markers when reading sentences 4–6. Intonational phrases often display other metrical properties as well. The initial words are often spoken in the way of an *anacrusis*—a string of high-rate nonaccented syllables, which form sort of an "upbeat" to the phrase as a whole. This contrasts with what often happens at the end of an intonational phrase: a certain lengthening of the final syllable or of the final stressed syllable. The defining characteristic of an intonational phrase is, of course, that it displays one of a set of *tones* (meaningful pitch contours). An intonational phrase is always a sense unit of some sort: a sentence, a clause, a modifier/head combination, or a predication. Also, there is always at least one pitch accent in an intonational phrase. If no element is focused in surface structure, the pitch accent goes to the last lexical head (by the nuclear stress rule).

Examples 4–6 gave rather clear cases of intonational phrases. The clause, in particular the finite clause, is a privileged candidate for becoming an intonational phrase. A sentence modifier may then be set apart as an independent intonational phrase, as in example 7.

(7)   1   2
// Unfortunately // John had lost his purse //

A special case of intonational-phrase partitioning occurs in so-called *listing*, as in example 8.

(8)   1   2   3
//Could you bring the tent // the barbecue // the charcoal //
        4
and the icebox?//

Before we turn to the melodic properties of intonational phrases, a further crucial notion has to be introduced: the *nucleus*. Each intonational phrase has one and only one nucleus. The nucleus is the most prominent pitch accent in the intonational phrase. If there is only one pitch accent, it will be the nucleus. If there are more, the last one will usually be the most prominent. This is, for most intonational phrases, a natural consequence of the nuclear stress rule. The nuclei in example 7 are the syllables *for* and *pur*; the nuclei in example 8 are *tent*, *bar*, *char*, and *ice*. Still, the nucleus may also occur in an early position. Take the second intonational phrase in example 7, but now with John carrying contrastive accent: *jOhn had lost his purse* (as opposed to Peter). In that case, *John* has the nuclear accent in the phrase.

The nuclear syllable of an intonational phrase receives *primary accent*. All other syllables receiving an intonational accent are said to have *secondary accent*. All intonational accents (for short: accents) are made by some sort of pitch movement—a rise, a fall, or some combination of a rise and a fall. But not all stressed syllables receive an intonational accent. They can become rhythmically more prominent by vowel lengthening or extra loudness. In *Mary finished her Russian novel*, for instance, there were metrical peaks on the syllables *Ma*, *fi*, *Ru*, and *no*. Not all these will undergo pitch movement. The nucleus *no* will, of course, but the other three could be pronounced at a constant pitch level. In that case they would be stressed but not accented. We will call this *tertiary stress* (as opposed to primary and secondary accent).

Though the notion of intonational phrase is widely used and accepted, it is not uncontroversial. Ladd (1986) has reviewed its theoretical and empirical foundations.

"Interlinear-tonetic" notation
There is no standard notation system for pitch contours. Such a system should be neither too concrete nor too abstract. It would be too concrete if it were to represent the actual course of an utterance's fundamental frequency (its F_0), the vibration frequency of the speaker's glottis. The

phonetic plan does not provide that frequency course in all detail. The same pitch contour will be uttered at a higher frequency level by a female voice than by a male voice, and it is this "same" that we want to capture. Pitch contours are, moreover, equivalence classes. The same contour can be uttered with all sorts of accidental variations. What we want to capture are the *relevant* movements—those that carry the intonational meaning. These relevant movements are probably a rather limited set, as has been experimentally demonstrated by 't Hart and Collier (1975) and other phoneticians.

The system should also not be too abstract. It is probably insufficient to recognize just two classes of pitch, high and low, every pitch movement being just a switch of level. The most important meaning-bearing pitch phenomena are precisely in the shape and size of pitch movement. Those properties should be captured in the representation of the speaker's intonational plan.

In the following we will opt for so-called *interlinear-tonetic* notation (see O'Connor and Arnold 1973; see also Cruttenden 1986, whose analysis is largely followed in this section), which steers a convenient middle course between too concrete and too abstract a representation. This notation is exemplified in the following diagram:

(9)

he gave a loud appalling cry

The two horizontal lines represent the upper and lower boundaries of the speaker's pitch range. The dots represent syllables. The fat dots are stressed or accented syllables. The first stressed syllable in the example is *loud*. It has pitch accent, a jump up from *a*. This is a secondary accent, since loud is not the nucleus of the intonational phrase. The syllable *pa* is also stressed, but not through pitch movement; it is in the middle of a level pitch contour. This is a case of tertiary stress. The final syllable, *cry*, is the nucleus of the intonational phrase. It has primary pitch accent, through the step up from the previous syllable. There is, moreover, a downward movement within that syllable, all the way back to the baseline. It is called the phrase's *boundary tone*, the closing movement on the last syllable. This is, as we will shortly see, an essential part of the *tone* of an intonational phrase.

Prenuclear tune and nuclear tone

The melody of an intonational phrase can now be divided into two parts: the stretch preceding the nucleus and the part from the nucleus to the end of the phrase. These parts will be called the *prenuclear tune* and the *nuclear tone* (or just *tone*) of the intonational phrase. The intonational meaning of the phrase is essentially carried by the nuclear tone. The prenuclear tune can modify that meaning—can soften it or sharpen it—but cannot essentially change it. This means that a speaker expresses intonational meaning quite locally, mostly at the very end of the intonational phrase. This shouldn't be too surprising. The nucleus is the most prominent element in the utterance. It is an element of high interest in the interaction, one that should capture the listener's attention. It is the natural apex for the expression of intonational meaning (emotional, attitudinal, or rhetorical). The prenuclear part of the intonational phrase, on the other hand, is less prominent, often containing mostly given information to which the focused nuclear information is to be added. This distinction between the functions of tune and tone may be clarified by the following four examples.

(10)

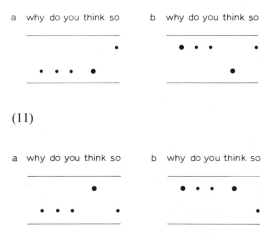

(11)

In all four examples, *think* is the nucleus; the nuclear tone stretches over *think so*, the prenuclear tune over *why do you*. Examples 10a and 10b carry the same nuclear tone, a full rise (from *think* to *so*). When the question is put in this way, it conveys the speaker's genuine interest in the answer. The nuclear tones of examples 11a and 11b are also the same; they are both full falls. Here the speaker conveys a touch of disagreement, a certain distancing from the interlocutor's position. These open versus distanced attitudes expressed by the tones in examples 10 and 11 are then further modified by the prenuclear tunes. The a tunes are low-level tunes; the b tunes are high-level. The high-level tunes tend to strengthen the character of the following tones. There is more empathy in the speaker's openness in example 10b than in 10a, and there is slightly more emphasis in the speaker's distancing in 11b than in 11a.

These are, of course, rather subtle interactions. It is not surprising to find quite diverse accounts of prenuclear tunes (alternatively called "pretonic accents"). Not only do intuitions differ substantially between authors, but it is likely that real differences in the character of these tunes exist between various dialects of English. The following discussion will be limited to a short review of the nuclear tones.

Some common tones

How is the nuclear accent made? Let us review seven of the more common tones. They have three distinguishing features, namely (i) whether they fall or rise from the nucleus, (ii) whether the nucleus itself is high or low with respect to the previous tune, and (iii) whether another pitch change occurs after the nuclear move.

Tone I: High-fall   The nucleus peaks up from the preceding level, then falls all the way down to the base level. Example:

Johnny is here

This tone expresses seriousness, in a matter-of-fact way. It is probably the most common tone for declaratives.

Tone II: Low-fall   There is a fall, but without a step up toward the nucleus. Keeping the prenuclear tune at the same mid-level pitch, the tone looks like this:

Johnny is here

This tone also expresses seriousness, but it is somewhat less involved and more businesslike.

Tone III: Low-rise   The nucleus starts at a lower level than that at which the previous tune ended. The nuclear move is a small rise, like this:

Whereas tones I and II do the "natural" thing in reaching the to-be-accented nucleus—namely, jump up—here the nuclear accent is made by stepping down. There is something contradictory in this tone: The speaker accents and plays down at the same time. Many authors interpret this as a way of reassuring. The rise at the end invites a reaction, but the addressee is given to understand that the matter is not a crucial one.

Tone IV: High-rise   The nucleus starts slightly up from the previous tune, and then rises:

This tone is used when seeking confirmation. It is mild, and it expresses genuine interest, maybe with a touch of incredulity. It also has an echoic function, seeking confirmation for what was just said, as in:

A: I saw Johnny coming in.   B: Johnny is here?

A variant of tone IV is the *full-rise*, which is indicated in parentheses. As in tone III, the nucleus starts low; but there is the high-pitched ending of tone IV. Semantically, the full-rise is more similar to the high-rise than to the low-rise.

Tone V: Fall-rise   This is a cup-like movement beginning at the nuclear syllable, and extending over any remaining syllables. The movement usually begins slightly up from the preceding tune. An example is this: Somebody asks *Isn't that a very small zoo?*, and the answer is

They've a polar bear

This tone characteristically expresses some reservation. What the speaker says is meant to be in contrast or even contradiction to what was apparently assumed or expected. The presence of the polar bear shows that the zoo is not to be belittled. The rise at the end suggests some (implicit) follow-up, the right conclusion to be drawn (*so the zoo cannot be that insignificant*). The same tone on *holidays* in *she didn't take holidays* could go well with a continuation like *she quit her job!* The tone can even affect the scope of negation, as Cruttenden (1986) showed. If somebody says *I am not going to perform anywhere*, the scope depends on the tone. With tone I on *anywhere* it means that the speaker is not going to perform at all; however, with tone V it means that the speaker *is* going to perform but not in just any place (say, only in Carnegie Hall).

Sometimes, there is another kind of meaning expressed by this tone: a self-justificatory "I told you so" or "I am telling you so". This would hold for the following sentences (nuclear vowel capitalized): *I knEw he was mean* and *You will nOtice he drinks*.

Tone VI: Rise-fall   Here the nucleus has a rising pitch obtrusion, but the phrase ends in a full fall. The tone stands out best when the nucleus is a step up from the preceding tune, like this:

Betty has her birthday

This, like the other tones with final fall (I and II), expresses completion; no continuation is invited or suggested. But in addition it expresses a great deal of enthusiasm or being impressed. The "cap" of this tone contrasts with the "cup" of tone V, and there is a related contrast in meaning. There is no reservation; rather, there is full endorsement, unrestricted commitment, overriding potential doubt or opposition.

Tone VII: Level   Here an even pitch is maintained, or at most slightly raised from the nucleus to the end of the intonational phrase. The only accent is in the step up or the step down to the nucleus. The following example is one with a step up:

I called the doctor

The most characteristic trait of this tone is its nonfinality. By not turning to baseline, as in tone I or tone II, it conveys that there is more to come. But the speaker is not inviting a reaction, either. This is, therefore, typically a neutral tone for a nonfinal phrase. It is, for instance, a good tone for listing, as in example 8 above: *Could you bring the tent, the barbecue, the charcoal,....*

The meanings of these major nuclear tones are, in part, conventional, and specific to English (or even to certain dialects of English). Still, there are aspects to these meanings that are probably more universal. Tones with a final fall express completeness, finality. Tones with a final rise express nonfinality, openness. One might say that falling tones assert the position of the speaker, whereas rising tones reach out to the addressee (to invite a reaction, to challenge, or whatever else).

Key and register
There are at least two other potentially universal aspects to intonation. The first one concerns *key*. Key is the range of movement in an intonational phrase. A speaker can make more extended falls or rises by raising his high pitch level, the peaks of his intonation (not by lowering the baseline). Brazil, Coulthard, and Johns (1980) distinguish three levels for the peak intonation: high, mid, and low. The speaker must select one of these for each and every intonational phrase. Changing key may, among other things, have a function in backgrounding and foregrounding. The three nuclei in example 5 above (repeated here as example 12) are *tem*, *use*, and *Sikhs*.

(12) The golden temple, which is still in use, was built by the Sikhs.

A natural intonation for the three intonational phrases of this sentence would involve mid, low, and high key, respectively, i.e., moderate pitch accent on *temple* (which is given information), minor pitch accent on *use* (which constitutes background information), and a major step up on *Sikhs* (which constitutes the newly focused information in the utterance). This relation between pitch range and intended attentional effect might well be universal in the world's languages. Key is probably also related to rate. Deese (1980) found that high-rate stretches of speech tended to have subdued intonation.

A second aspect is *register*. Register is the pitch level of the baseline. The scream is universally high register, and high-register speech may have a similar root: It expresses emotion and tension. It also expresses "smallness"—the register of the child, and metaphorically the register of helplessness and deference.

The key notions for the speaker's intonational plan are the intonational phrase, its nucleus, its tune, its tone, its key, and its register. They are the co-determinants of the intonational contour. The speaker surely has no intonational lexicon with whole ready-made contour templates. The closest thing to that may be something like a tone lexicon, a relatively small set (but larger than seven) of canonical tonal contours. These contours are expressive and meaningful. In the process of phonological encoding, they have to be projected onto the stretch of speech that extends from the nucleus to the end of the intonational phrase.

Summary

Phonological encoding is the speaker's construction of a phonetic plan. This chapter has outlined the structure of phonetic plans, both at the word level and at the level of connected speech. The plans for words are built on their morphology, and they involve a phonological organization at various levels or tiers. The derivational and inflectional morphology of words were reviewed, and it was suggested that, for almost all words used by a native speaker of English, this internal structure is stored in his mental lexicon.

The phonetic form of words involves qualitative and prosodic aspects. The qualitative aspects concern the phonetic material that is to fill successive slots of the skeletal tier. This material can be categorized as more or less sonorous (V or C). It is further characterized by various other phonetic features—particularly, laryngeal and supralaryngeal ones, such as manner and place features. One could, in fact, represent the quality information of segments on a set of independent "feature tiers." Successive phones are given some syllabic organization: Each syllable contains a sonorous peak, which may be flanked by less sonorous phones. A syllable's rime characterizes it as either strong or weak, and this, in turn, affects the rhythmic structure of the word in which it figures.

The prosodic aspect of a word's phonetic plan involves its metrical and intonational organization. Each word has an internal organization of more or less stressed syllables, and this is part of the stored code for the word. This metrical pattern can be conveniently represented by way of metrical grids. The syllable that carries main stress is the one that will be given pitch accent if that is specified in surface structure. A word's intonation is not lexically stored in languages like English, although it is (to some degree) in so-called tone languages. In English, the intonation of a word depends on whether it receives pitch accent and on the melody of the intonational phrase in which it partakes.

A speaker's plan for connected speech is not a simple concatenation of word plans. First, a speaker may select clitic allomorphs instead of free-standing words when producing connected speech, such as *I've* instead of *I have*. These and other forms of cliticization create new word-like units—phonological words—and usually involve some degree of resyllabification. There are also various other segmental and syllabic changes that can occur at word boundaries in connected speech.

Connected speech also involves specific metrical planning. We considered an organization into what some call "phonological phrases"—stretches of speech leading up to lexical heads of NPs, VPs, or APs. Some such metrical packaging undoubtedly exists in speech; it highlights a sentence's surface-structure organization. There are, in addition, intonational phrases, consisting of one or more of these coherent metrical units. They are domains for the assignment of intonation.

Intonation of connected speech was the final subject of this chapter. It was stressed that the function of intonation is expressive rather than representational, and that this makes it very special in a speaker's phonetic plan. We distinguished between two parts of an intonational phrase: the prenuclear part, whose tune has a qualifying or modifying function, and the remaining part from nucleus to end of phrase, whose tone carries the intonational meaning. We concentrated on different nuclear tones and their approximate expressive functions. Two further properties of a phrase's intonation were discussed: its key and its register.

Chapter 9
Generating Phonetic Plans
for Words

How does a speaker generate the phonetic form of a word, given the developing surface structure? This chapter will characterize the process of phonetic planning as the spelling out of stored form representations and their projection on pronounceable syllables. The stored representations involve, in particular, the morphological, metrical, and segmental composition of words. A major task of phonological encoding is to generate a string of syllables that the Articulator can accept and pronounce. Syllables are basic units of articulatory execution. As was outlined in the preceding chapter, they consist of phones which, when executed, are complex and temporally overlapping articulatory gestures. The adult speaker, we conjecture, has an inventory of syllables. They need not be generated from scratch over and again. Rather, these stored articulatory patterns are addressed during phonological encoding on the basis of the spelled-out word representations. Also, certain free parameters are set, such as a syllable's duration, stress, and pitch. The eventual phonetic plan is a string of such specified syllables.

This chapter deals with the phonological encoding of single words. There is a certain drawback to this: It may seem as if phonological encoding is a wasteful process. Spelling out a word's segmental makeup also makes available the stored syllabification of the word, i.e., the segments' abstract grouping in syllables and syllable constituents. Why then should there be a second phase where strings of segments are used to address stored syllable representations? The main reason for this seemingly roundabout way of phonetic planning is to be found in the generation of connected speech. A word's stored syllabification is not sacrosanct. In connected speech, words often form coalitions with their neighbors that lead to so-called resyllabification. A phrase like *I gave it*, for instance, is easily resyllabified as *I ga-vit*. This enhances the fluency of articulation. To make an optimally pronounceable phonetic plan, the Phonological Encoder needs the segmental spellout of adjacent words. And it will often come up with a different syllabification than what is stored in each word's form code. In the present chapter, however, we will by necessity look only at cases in which the word's stored syllabification corresponds precisely to the syllable pattern in the eventual phonetic plan. Resyllabification in connected speech will be addressed in the next chapter.

The mission of the present chapter is to show that the phonetic plans for words are not stored and retrieved as ready-made wholes. Rather, they result from accessing and spelling out stored multi-level representations and using these to address syllable programs. This spelling out and addressing can occasionally become confused, leading to slips of the tongue, which are as revealing for the scientist as they can be painful for the speaker.

The chapter begins with a treatment of the tip-of-the-tongue phenomenon, the tantalizing situation of almost retrieving a much-wanted word. Bits and pieces of the word form become available, but not the whole thing. It is a highly slowed down version of word-form access, and it is often revealing of the underlying processes.

In section 9.2, phonological encoding is described as involving three major levels of processing: using lemmas to retrieve a word's morphemes and metrical structure, using morphemes to access a word's syllables and segments, and using segments and clusters to address stored phonetic syllable plans. These three levels will be called *morphological/metrical spellout*, *segmental spellout*, and *phonetic spellout*. And each of these levels can be a source of characteristic speech errors.

This is further elaborated in section 9.3, which considers in a systematic way what units can and what units cannot be involved in sublexical errors. This will lead to a further refinement of our three-level analysis of phonological encoding. We will then turn to a more systematic processing account of what can happen to such units. They can be added, omitted, exchanged, and so on, and each of these phenomena should eventually be understood as a derailment of processes that underlie normal, undisturbed phonological encoding.

There are two major accounts of the causation of sublexical form errors in speech. They will be reviewed in the final sections of this chapter. In most respects the two theories are complementary rather than competitive. The error account of Shattuck-Hufnagel's (1979) slots-and-fillers theory, on which the present chapter is based to a large extent, will be given in section 9.4. The activation-spreading account—in particular, Dell's (1986, 1988)—follows in section 9.5. A short final section addresses the issue of serial ordering in these two theories.

9.1   The Tip-of-the-Tongue Phenomenon

The form of a word is usually easily activated when its lemma is accessed, but there are comical or embarrassing cases of speech need where the transition from lemma to sound form is hampered. This is known as the *tip-of-the-tongue* (TOT) phenomenon. James (1893) considered it, but Brown and McNeill (1966) were the first to study TOT states experimentally. They gave their subjects dictionary definitions of moderately unusual objects—for example,

a navigational instrument used in measuring angular distances, especially the altitude of sun, moon, and stars at sea.

The subjects had to retrieve the name of the object. Some subjects knew the instrument's name immediately; others could not remember it at all. But some felt that they knew it and that they were on the verge of producing the word. These subjects, who were in the TOT state, were asked to guess the initial letter and the number of syllables, to mention the words that had come to mind, and so on. For the above example, subjects tended to guess /s/ as the initial phoneme and two as the number of syllables, and sound-related words like *secant* and *sextet* had come to mind (meaning-related words, e.g., *compass*, also occurred). Apparently there is much lexical-form information available in the TOT state. (The target word was *sextant*.)

    In the Brown-McNeill experiment, and in later, more extensive replications (Gardiner, Craik, Bleasdale 1973; Yarmey 1973; Koriat and Lieblich 1974, 1977; Rubin 1975; Browman 1978; Reason and Lucas 1984; Kohn, Wingfield, Menn, Goodglass, Berko-Gleason and Hyde 1987; Priller and Mittenecker 1988), it was found that in about 60–70 percent of the cases the first phoneme or cluster was correctly guessed, the middle part of the word was more error-prone, and subjects did better again on the final segment. The number of syllables was correctly guessed in 60–80 percent of the TOT states, and the subject usually knew which syllable was stressed. There is, in short, a partial activation of the word-form representation, involving the word's metrical structure as well as its initial and sometimes its final segment. But a full spelling out of the word's segments is blocked.

    Jones and Langford (1987) were able to induce such blocking by giving subjects a "blocking word" after the definition. (If *sextant* were the target word, *secant* would be a good blocker.) When the blocker was given right after the definition, there was an increased chance of the subject's entering a TOT state. It was irrelevant whether the blocker was a high- or a low-frequency word; only its phonological similarity to the target word mattered. Also irrelevant were semantic blockers (e.g., *compass* if the target word were *sextant*). This supports the notion that in the TOT state there is no search for the lemma; it has already been retrieved on semantic grounds. What fails is full access to the form information. A phonological blocker further "misguides" this search.

These experiments show that the lexical-form representation is not all-or-none. A word's representation in memory consists of components that are relatively accessible, and there can be metrical information about the number and accents of syllables without these syllables' being available. Jones and Langford call this a "word sketch." Let us see what this initial sketch might look like.

9.2   Frames, Slots, Fillers, and Levels of Processing

Speech errors provide ample evidence for the independent availability of word sketches or frames and of the elements that are to fill them. Take segment exchanges, such as *I s*ould be sh*eeing him soon* (from Shattuck-Hufnagel 1979). When the speaker tried to access the first phoneme of *should*, /ʃ/, the first phoneme of *seeing*, /s/, intruded. The /s/ of *seeing* must already have been available as a word-initial segment candidate when *should* was being generated. After the mis-selection, however, the speaker did not say *I sould be eeing*. The fact that the initial phoneme of *seeing* had already been used has in no way removed the word-initial slot of *seeing*. It persists and is filled by the still-available word-initial candidate /ʃ/. There are frames with positions for morphemes, phonemes, or other elements; during speech these frames are filled with candidate elements. In the following it will be argued that the frame is an address template for a procedure or subroutine. Once a frame is filled, the address is complete and the procedure can be identified and executed. This is just another case of *productions* in Newell's sense, discussed in chapter 1: IF the filled address frame is such-and-such, THEN spell out the corresponding form information.

Let us consider three examples to clarify this notion. They are taken from three major levels of processing in word-form generation; together they give a first sketch of the system that subserves phonetic planning. The three levels of processing are *morphological/metrical spellout, segmental spellout,* and *phonetic spellout.*

9.2.1   Morphological/Metrical Spellout
Morphological/metrical spellout is a procedure that takes lemmas and their diacritical parameters or features as input and makes available both

the morphological and the metrical composition of a word. The example
involves addressing the correct inflectional form of a verb. Remember that,
in English surface structure, verb lemmas have diacritical parameters for
number, person, and tense, among other things. There is, for instance, one
lexical entry for the verb *eat*, but it contains various lexical items, such as
eat, *eats*, *ate*, and so on (see subsection 6.1.2). The diacritical parameters
serve to select the correct item within the verb's lexical entry. How does this
come about?

The form address, we suppose, is a frame consisting of slots: one slot for
the lemma as it appears in surface structure, and further slots for the
diacritical parameters. More precise, the slot for the lemma is the form
address to which the lemma points (see subsection 5.1.2). In subsection
6.2.1 the lemma's form address was represented by an arbitrary number.
Here, however, for ease of identification, we will put the lemma's name in
the address slot instead of a number. That name is, of course, not the word
form to be retrieved. Thus (with the diacritical parameters limited to the
three ones mentioned), the morphological and metrical forms for *segmented*
and *knew* are stored under addresses such as these:

lemma	number	person	tense
segment	any	any	past

lemma	number	person	tense
know	any	any	past

In both cases the address *frame* is the following template:

lemma	number	person	tense

when a lemma of category V appears in surface structure, this address
frame is automatically made available. The frame now has to be filled in
order to become an address for a morphological/metrical spelling-out
routine. When each slot is filled by an appropriate element, the lock is
opened and the morphological and metrical spelling-out routines become
available. The routines make available the morphological structure of the
item and the number of syllabic peaks (if any) for each morpheme. Also, the
peak that carries word accent is marked. For *segmented*, the procedures
generate a stem (*segment*) and a suffix morpheme (*ed*) in that order, and

they locate two syllable peaks in *segment* and one in *ed*. The second peak of *segment* is marked for word accent. For *knew*, the subroutines produce a single morpheme, with a single syllable peak which carries word accent. These results can be represented as follows:

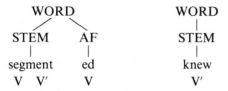

In other words, the procedures unlock two sets of form information: the morphological representation and the basic metrical pattern of a word. It is, as yet, not strictly necessary to assume that these two kinds of information are always simultaneously retrieved. But that assumption is not critical for the sketch of phonological encoding to be developed in this chapter. The crucial point is that a word's metrical information becomes available at a very early stage, as is apparent from the tip-of-the-tongue studies. This metrical information is particularly important for the generation of connected speech, as will be seen in the next chapter.

The metrical information consists of the syllabicity status of each morpheme, i.e., the number of peaks it corresponds to at the skeletal tier, plus the stress distribution over peaks. Recall from subsection 8.1.6 that a word's basic metrical pattern can involve more than two levels of stress, as represented in the word's metrical grid. It is probably correct to assume that the full metrical pattern as it is stored in the lexicon becomes available at this stage. For ease of presentation, however, the present discussion will be limited to two levels of stress: one for the peak carrying word accent and one for all other peaks. Accented peaks will be indicated by V', nonaccented ones by V.

At this level of spellout, only *stored* metrical information is made available. Pitch accent and contextually determined metrical properties of the word (subsection 8.2.2) are generated by what we will call the *Prosody Generator* in chapter 10.

No segmental information (subsection 8.1.5) is available at the present level of representation. It is only for ease of reference that the retrieved stems are written as *segment* and *knew*; we could as well have used numbers to refer to these entities. Similarly, the suffix is depicted as *ed*, but we could as well have written *pta* (for "past-tense affix").

When there are misselections in filling the address frame, the wrong address is composed and an inappropriate spellout routine is retrieved. In the speech error *that I'd hear one if I knew it* [intended was: *that I'd know one if I heard it*] (Garrett 1980b), the lemmas *hear* and *know* got exchanged by mechanisms discussed in chapter 7. The point here is that, in addressing the morphological/metrical spell-out of the first verb, the wrong lemma (*hear*) and the appropriate diacritical tense feature (present) were used as fillers. Together they precisely formed the address under which the morphology of the item *hear* was stored. Similarly, the pair of fillers (*know*, past) formed the key that opened the lock for the morphological/metrical spellout of *knew*, as in the above example.

The metrical spellout—i.e., the number of peaks for each word and their stress values—is crucial for the construction of address frames at the last, phonetic spellout level. It determines the number of syllables to be retrieved at that level (see subsection 9.2.3).

9.2.2 Segmental Spellout

The procedures for segmental spellout take the morphemic and metrical information as input and generate the segmental composition of the word. In the course of this, the segments' grouping in syllable constituents also becomes available.

The address frame of a syllabic spellout procedure contains morphological slots, such as for stem and affix. The fillers are morphemes together with their metrical information, as spelled out at the previous level of processing. Two examples are given below. They are the addresses and spellouts for the verb form *segmented* and for the plural noun *segments*.

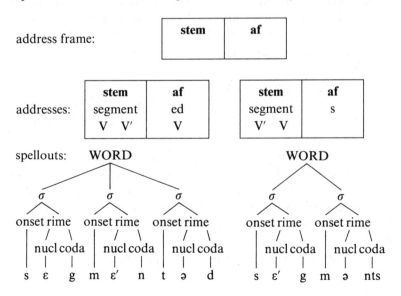

The address frames at this level are made available on the basis of the spellouts of the previous level of processing. When the slots get filled with (respectively) the stem *segment* and the affix *ed*, the address is created for the spellout of *segmented*. The retrieved procedure yields three syllables, each parsed into onset, rime, nucleus, and coda—i.e., just the syllable tier representation of the word (subsection 8.1.4). In this example, most but not all of the onsets, nuclei, and codas are single phonemes. Only the last coda is a consonant cluster: /nts/. This needs further spelling out. There is, we will assume, a *cluster spellout procedure* that takes a cluster as input and yields the individual segments or phonemes as output. So, for the cluster /nts/ this can be depicted as follows:

$$
\text{/nts/} \rightarrow \boxed{\begin{array}{c} \text{cluster} \\ \text{spellout} \end{array}} \rightarrow \text{/n/, /t/, /s/}
$$

This issue will be taken up in more detail in subsection 9.3.4.

It is probably the case that each spelled-out segment is categorized as onset, nucleus, or coda, or as part of a cluster (but see section 9.5). The reason, as we will see in subsection 9.2.4, is that in speech errors onsets can exchange with onsets, nuclei with nuclei, and codas with codas. But it is seldom that segments of different category exchange. Still, these categories can be revised in connected speech. In *I ga-vit*, the coda segment /v/ has become an onset segment.

Two further points should be noted. The first one is that the input morpheme boundaries are not preserved in the syllabic grouping of segments. The affixes *ed* and *s* are generated as parts of the syllables /təd/ and /mənts/. The second point is that the metrical information is now translated into nuclear phonemes. Compare the nuclei of the syllables /mɛn/ and /mənts/. They are different vowels at this level, /ɛ/ and /ə/, and this is a consequence of the difference in stress assignment.

What sort of addressing errors can be made at this level of processing? The critical fillers are different kinds of morphemes, such as stems and affixes. Errors occur when an inappropriate filler is used. In *take the freezes out of the steaker* [*take the steaks out of the freezer*] (from Fromkin 1973), the stem of *steaks* combined with the affix of *freezer* in addressing a segmental spellout routine. As a result, *steaker* was produced. Subsequently, the leftover stem of *freezer* and affix of *steaks* were used to address a further segmental spellout routine. The output was the two-syllable *freezes*; i.e., the affix was given its context-dependent form /-ɪz/ instead of /-s/. Such a context-dependent form is called an *allomorph*. This shows that the spellout routine does make use of the fact that the misplaced -*s* affix of *steaks* is really nothing but an unspecified plural affix at the filler level (it is written as *s* only for convenience).

Another remarkable type of speech error that arises at the present level of processing is the stress error. Cutler (1980a) reports an extensive analysis of such errors. One of her examples is *I put things in that abstr*A*ct that I cannot justify*, where the noun *abstract* erroneously carries word accent on the second syllable. How could this error arise? Cutler showed that in such errors the lexical-stress placement is always that of a related word, another derivation of the same morpheme. For the erroneous noun *abstr*A*ct*, the related word is probably the verb *abstract*, which has stress on the second syllable; for the error *articul*A*tory*, the related word is *articulation*; and so on. This systematic relation can be explained by an erroneous choice of filler in addressing the segmental spellout routine. Take the above examples *segm*E*nted* and *s*E*gment*. Assume that a speaker is trying to say *Peter segmented two segments*. At some stage the morphological/metrical spell-outs of *segmented* and of *segments* become available. To address the spellout routines for *segmented*, the speaker may erroneously choose the available morpheme

segment

V'   V

as the filler, together with the right past-tense affix. The spellout procedure then generates *s*E*g-men-ted*. It is not necessary for lexical-stress errors that the related word appear somewhere in the sentence. What is important is that the related word be somehow activated in the production process. How that can happen is the topic of subsection 9.5.2.

Before we turn to the next level of processing, notice that an English speaker may occasionally compose a well-formed address by completing a frame with the right kind of fillers and still fail to retrieve a word form. As was extensively discussed in subsection 6.1.3, English speakers do now and then produce new words. An example may have been the word *steaker* in the above speech error. This is surely a possible word in English, but it is unlikely that the speaker had it in store. Still, the speaker created a spellout on the spot. This is presumably done by analogy (Stemberger 1985b), an old, important, but still ill-understood notion in psychology and linguistics.

9.2.3   Phonetic Spellout

After retrieving a word's sequence of segments, the Phonological Encoder will use them to address phonetic plans for syllables. The phonetic plan for a syllable specifies the articulatory gesture to be executed by the Articulator. It can be characterized as a sequence of phones, but phones are not discrete nonoverlapping events. Rather, each phone is a temporal gesture itself, which typically overlaps in its execution with other phone gestures in the syllable (Browman and Goldstein 1986). Moreover, the dynamic properties of a phone depend substantially on where it appears in the syllable, and on the other phones the syllable is composed of. In other words, phones in a syllable's phonetic plan are always *allophones* (subsection 8.1.5), context-dependent realizations of phonological segments or phonemes.

It is very likely that the skilled language user has an inventory of syllable plans, a stock of frequently used motor programs. Phonetic spellout will, then, consist largely of retrieving these syllable programs. This subsection discusses how these programs can be addressed, following a notion developed by Crompton (1982). Before we turn to that, two things must be noted. The first is that stored syllable programs are not completely fixed. A syllable can be pronounced with more or less force, shorter or longer duration, different kinds of pitch movement, and so on. These are free parameters, which have to be set from case to case. This issue will be taken up in the next chapter. Second, it is probably not so that *all* of a language's possible syllables are stored in the speaker's mind. New formations are certainly possible, and we will return to that issue below.

Syllable plans have addresses, and the first step of phonetic spellout is to compose the appropriate address. An address, we assume, consists of three slots: one for an onset, one for a nucleus, and one for a coda. These slots will, one after another, have to be filled by appropriate subsequent segments as these become available from segmental spellout. Slots can also accept clusters. How clusters are formed to become fillers for slots will be taken up in subsection 9.3.4. Let us now work out these notions by way of an example.

The example concerns addressing the phonetic plans for the first syllables of the words *segmented* and *hemisphere*: *seg* and *hem*. Their addresses result from filling the following address frames:

onset	nucl	coda		onset	nucl′	coda

Where do these address frames come from? It was mentioned earlier that the metrical output of the first spellout level would be crucial input for the construction of addresses at the phonetic spellout level. The procedure can be quite simple: For each peak of metrical spellout, an address frame is triggered that contains precisely three slots—one for onset, one for nucleus, and one for coda. They come in two kinds, one for unstressed syllables and one for stressed syllables. This corresponds to the two kinds of peak in metrical spellout. The left address frame above is for an unstressed syllable, the right one for a stressed syllable.

In the segmental spellout of *seg* (see above), the first phoneme segment, /s/, was categorized as syllable onset; the second segment, /ε/, as unstressed nucleus; and the third segment, /g/, as coda. This is precisely the triple of fillers matching the slots in the left address frame:

onset	nucl	coda
/s/	/ε/	/g/

The address is now complete, and the syllable's phonetic plan can be retrieved. It consists of the syllable-specific allophones [s], [ε], and [g], and the whole phonetic plan for the syllable can be written as the spellout

[sεg]

For *hem* of *hemisphere* the story is analogus. The segmental spellout gave three phonemes: /h/, /ε'/, and /m/, for onset, nucleus, and coda. In combination they are the adequate fillers for the right address frame above. The completed address for the syllable retrieved is

onset	nucl'	coda
/h/	/ε/'	/m/

and the phonetic spellout is

[hε'm].

Note that the nuclear phone is marked for accent. In articulatory terms this may mean longer duration, more amplitude, or pitch movement.

When, by chance, an inappropriate filler is made available, an addressing error may occur. This happened when the speech error h*eft* l*emisphere* [*left hemisphere*] was made (Fromkin 1973). Here the syllabic spell-outs for both lemmas had become available. When a syllable onset had to be specified for addressing the articulatory subroutine for the first syllable, the segment /h/ was apparently more strongly activated than the segment /l/. Both were of the correct category (onset). Together with the available fillers for nucleus and coda, the syllable *heft* was erroneously addressed' and the phonetic syllable plan [hε'ft] was activated. Similarly, when the next syllable was programmed, an onset filler was needed. The /h/ had been used, but the /l/ was still available and of the right category. Together with /ε'/ and /m/, it filled the address frame to cue the syllable *lem*, releasing the articulatory plan [lɛ'm].

Also for this level of spelling-out one should wonder whether the native speaker of English will occasionally be productive. That is, will an adult speaker occasionally produce a well-formed but nonstored syllable, i.e., one he never uttered before? A rough count of the number of different syllables in English (with thanks to Hans Kerkman) yielded a number of about 6,600 over 38,000 word types. Hence, the number of English syllable types is relatively small, and could be easily stored in the speaker's lexicon. And other languages, such as Japanese, probably have much smaller numbers of different syllables. Still, some of these syllables may be quite infrequent, arising only in unusual morphemic combinations (such as in *infarct-s*, which involves the syllable [fɑrkts]). Speakers are probably able to produce new but well-formed kinds of syllables by analogy. This shouldn't surprise us, because this is presumably the way they acquired their syllable repertoire to start with. The mechanism of such new formations, however, is unknown.

A phonetic spellout mechanism, such as that proposed here (following Crompton 1982), will handle much but not all allophonic variation in language production. The different phonetic realizations of a segment or phoneme are, in large part, dependent on the different syllable environments in which it appears. But there is context beyond the syllable which may also affect a segment's phonetic realization. Moreover, a syllable's stress and pitch properties are largely contextually determined. We will defer discussion of these sources of variation to chapter 10, which deals with phonetic planning in connected speech.

9.2.4 The Unit-Similarity Constraint

All three of the examples above have shown how speech errors may arise when inappropriate fillers are made available in the addressing of spelling-out procedures. In the following we will speak of the *target* (i.e., the appropriate filler) and the *intrusion* (the inappropriate filler). What is a possible intrusion for an address slot?

The three levels of spellout—morphological/metrical, segmental, and phonetic—have provided us with different kinds of slot fillers: lemmas and diacritic features at the first level, morphemes (roots, stems, and affixes) at the second level, and syllable constituents (onsets, nuclei, and codas) at the level of phonetic spellout. Each slot required a filler of its own category. An affix cannot fill a stem slot, an onset cannot fill a coda slot, and so on. A filler must have the right password for a slot: the filler's category at the relevant level or tier of representation. As a consequence, targets and intrusions obey the following principle (Shattuck-Hufnagel 1979):

Unit-Similarity Constraint   The intruding element is of the same level of representation and category as the target element.

Lemmas exchange with lemmas, stems with stems, affixes with affixes, syllable onsets with syllable onsets, and so forth. But stems or roots never exchange with affixes, affixes do not exchange with onsets, and onsets hardly ever exchange with codas.

The three levels of processing considered so far cover a major part of a word's form-generating mechanism. But much detail is still to be provided. Before turning to an analysis of the system's control structure, we will consider whether there are more or other target-intrusion pairs. The determination of what kinds of units are displaceable can help us find out what kinds of fillers are needed in addressing the form-generating routines. So far, some anecdotal evidence has been provided for lemmas, diacritical features, stems, affixes, and syllable constituents as fillers. But what about syllables, distinctive features, or other potential fillers? The next section reviews what can and what cannot be mislocated in speech errors.

9.3   Substitutable Sublexical Units

Fromkin (1971) conjectured that almost any linguistically defined sublexical unit or feature could be subject to substitution in speech errors. Later research, however, showed that, though this may be true as a general characterization, certain kinds of speech error are exceedingly rare (Shattuck-Hufnagel and Klatt 1979; Stemberger 1983a; Dell 1986). Other experimental work has added to a further specification of what is replaceable and not (Treiman 1983, 1984; Levitt and Healy 1985). Let us review some of the main sublexical units.

9.3.1   Morphemes
All the morpheme types discussed in subsection 8.1.1 can be displaced in speech errors. Stems and whole words are exchangeable, as in nam*ing a* wear *tag* [wearing a name tag]; or a stem and a root can exchange, as in *I hate* rain*ing on a* hitch*y day* [*I hate hitching on a rainy day*] (both from Shattuck-Hufnagel 1979). So, in view of the Unit-Similarity Constraint, whole words, stems, and roots are of similar filler category. But units of this category almost never exchange with affixes. Affixes are a displaceable category of their own. They can be anticipated, as in *people read the backs*es

of boxes [*people read the backs of boxes*] (Shattuck-Hufnagel 1979). They can be persevered, as in *Ministers in the church*es [*Ministers in the church*] (Fromkin 1971). Notice in the latter example that perseveration of the affix does not create *church*s, but *church*es; i.e., the correct allomorph is produced. This shows that the shifted unit is an affix, not just the phoneme /s/.

Morpheme errors can be caused either at the level of morphological spellout or at the level of segmental spellout. The earlier example *I'd hear one if I knew it* [*I'd know one if I heard it*] is caused at the higher level, owing to an erroneous combination of lemma and diacritical feature in addressing the spellout routine. But it is unlikely that *raining on a hitchy day* arose at this level, since the two lemmas involved (*rain* and *hitch*) are of different grammatical categories. This violates the Unit-Similarity Constraint at that level of processing. Exchanging lemmas, we saw in chapter 7, are usually of the same syntactic category. It is more likely that the latter error is due to addressing failure at the level of segmental spellout, where stem and root are exchangeable. For *church* → *church*es the level is undecidable, but other affix errors are unambiguous. The perseveration *they needed to be mad*ed [*they needed to be made*] (Shattuck-Hufnagel 1979) can only be due to an addressing failure in segmental spellout. At the earlier level, *make* plus "past" had successfully triggered the routine that produces the stem *made*. In syllabic spellout, this stem combined with the persevered -*ed* affix of *needed* to produce the two-syllable form *maded*. It is therefore important in the analysis of speech errors (and of word-form production in general) to distinguish diacritical features such as "past", "plural", and "third person" from the affixes they induce.

9.3.2 Syllables

There are occasional reports of syllable replacements in the speech-error literature. Of course, all substitutions by monosyllabic morphemes are at the same time syllable replacements. The test case, however, is whether a single syllable of a multi-syllabic morpheme can be moved or replaced. Shattuck-Hufnagel (1979) presented as an example ca*ssy* pu*t* [*pussy cat*], where the syllable *pu* was moved. But she noted that such errors are highly exceptional. Dell (1986) made the same observation, and explained the exceptions in terms of a coincidence of replacements of smaller, subsyllabic units. (In the above example, this would have been syllable onset /p/ and syllable nucleus /u/.)

The sheer absence of pure syllable substitutions is especially remarkable since syllables clearly play an important role in speech errors and in fluent speech generally. MacKay (1972), for instance, observed that word blends often respect syllable boundaries, as in Wells's (1951) example *be-hortment* [*behavior/deportment*]. Fujimura and Lovins (1978) argued that syllables are the smallest relatively invariant articulatory units in speech production, and I concur with that view. But syllables are, apparently, never themselves fillers for address slots. This is in full agreement with the three-level model sketched above. At none of the three levels are fillers of the category "syllable" required to compose an address.

9.3.3   Syllable Constituents

In chapter 8 we distinguished between syllable onset and rime, and within rime between nucleus and coda. Onsets and rimes can be independently involved in speech errors. MacKay (1972) observed that in word blends breaks were more likely to occur before a syllable's vowel than after it; thus, *gr-astly* [*grizzly/ghastly*] should be more common than *mai-stly* [*mainly/ mostly*] (both examples from Fromkin 1971). Syllable onsets do move as a whole in speech errors, whether they are single phonemes or consonant clusters; note *f*ace sp*ood* [*space food*] (from Fromkin 1971).

Rimes can move as well: *f*art *very h*ide [*fight very hard*] (from Fromkin 1971). The latter, however, is a rather infrequent type of speech error. The two rime parts, nucleus and coda, can also be replaced as units, although they have a stronger tendency to stick together (Shattuck-Hufnagel 1983; Stemberger 1983a). An example of nucleus movement is *clea*p pik [*clip peak*]; coda substitution can be seen in *do a one ste*tch – *step switch* (both from Fromkin 1971).

An extensive analysis of more than 300 spontaneous speech errors involving the nucleus was reported in Shattuck-Hufnagel 1986. A major finding was that 79 percent of the errors occurred between vowels in stressed syllables, as in *the debote f*eik – *debate focuses on*, where both the target (here /eɪ/ and the intrusion (here /oʊ/) belonged to a stressed syllable. "Mixed" cases were rare, and the intruding vowel was always accommodated to the stress of the target syllable. Remember that the phonetic spellout mechanism created different addresses for stressed and unstressed syllables. A slot for a stressed nucleus will normally accept only a stressed vowel, and vice versa for a non-stress slot. This explains the low number of mixed cases in the data. It is just another demonstration of the Unit-Similarity Constraint. It does not, of course, explain the fact that errors involving two unstressed vowels are quite rare (as in *Buffo the* – *Byffy the Buffalo*, where unstressed /i/ and /oʊ/ are involved as target and intrusion). Stressed vowels are far more error-prone than unstressed ones.

A systematic experimental study of the movability of syllable constituents was done by Treiman (1983, 1984). She gave subjects different word games to play involving different types of syllables. In one game, subjects had to make two new syllables out of one. They would listen to four training examples and repeat each of them, e.g.

kig → kaz ig
buf → baz uf
tep → taz ep
nol → naz ol.

They were then asked to do the same to a set of test stimuli. A critical item could now be the syllable *skef*. What would a subject do? Either of two responses would be consistent with the training examples: *skef → skaz ef*, which separates onset and rime, and *skef → saz kef*, which separates the initial consonant from the rest. Only the first response type respects syllable constituents (onset, rime), and almost all responses were of that type, i.e., preserving the syllable's onset cluster.

Other syllable games tested the integrity of nucleus and coda. In one of these, subjects had to learn the syllable splitting again, but this time they were left no choice. The splitting had to go either as in

(1) isk → it ask

or as in

(2) isk → ist ak.

In type 1, nucleus and coda are left intact; however, in type 2 the break is made not between nucleus and coda but within the coda before the final consonant. Subjects made many more errors on type 2 than on type 1. Also, type 2 took many more trials to learn. It is apparently easier to leave the coda intact. Given this finding, Treiman could test cases where linguists disagree on where the boundary is between nucleus and coda. Remember, for instance, how *meter* was analyzed in subsection 8.1.4. There the so-called *liquid* segment /r/ behaved as a high-sonorous peak segment, i.e., as a V at the segmental tier. Now take a word like *bird* or *earth*. Is /r/ still a V, belonging to the nucleus, or is it rather a C-part of the coda? What would it do in Treiman's game? She tested such cases by examples of types 3 and 4.

(3) orth → ot irth

(4) orth → ort ith

Subjects found type 4 much easier than type 3. This pleads for the notion that the liquid is part of the nucleus rather than part of the coda; i.e., analysis i is preferred over ii:

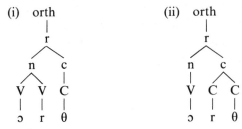

Games with nasals (e.g., *imf* → *iz amf*) gave results that were intermediary between these games with liquids and the original games 1 and 2 with obstruents (like /t/). These experimental results are in fine agreement with Stemberger's (1983b) and Shattuck-Hufnagel's (1986) finding that also in speech errors the liquids /r/ and /l/ tend to stick to the immediately preceding vowel, as in *cheeps 'n twirts* [for *chirps 'n tweets*]. In other words, they behave as parts of a displacing nucleus.

There is, finally, one syllable constituent that needs special attention: the *null-element*, be it a null-onset or a null-coda. On the surface, a syllable like *orth* or *art* doesn't seem to have an onset; it seems to have only a rime. Still, it has been suggested that there is an onset, though an empty one. Similarly, the syllable *spa* lacks a coda, but can be analyzed as having a null-coda. The main argument for these analyses is that the null-element can be anticipated or exchanged in speech errors. Shattuck-Hufnagel, discussing this matter (1979, 1983), gave examples such as *Doctor -inclair has emphasized* [*Sinclair*], where the empty onset of *emphasized* is already anticipated when the onset of *Sinclair* is prepared. Or is this simply an onset or phoneme deletion, without any relation to *emphasized*? Only careful statistical analysis can provide a decisive answer. Dell (1986) has presented statistical evidence that the null-element is not always involved in onset or coda omissions, but it is probably still needed for a complete account of the speech-error data.

In summary: There is good evidence that syllable constituents can function as fillers, and that their constituent category is crucial: Onsets exchange with onsets, rimes with rimes, nuclei with nuclei, and codas with codas, all in agreement with the Unit-Similarity Constraint.

9.3.4 Segments

Some two-thirds of sublexical speech errors involve single segments, either consonants or vowels (Shattuck-Hufnagel 1982). Many of these are, of course, just syllable onsets, nuclei, or codas. But there are still many errors where individual phonemes in onset or coda clusters are in trouble. This is, for instance, the case for the exchange error p*eel like* f*laying* [*feel like playing*] (Shattuck-Hufnagel 1982), where the phoneme /p/, but not the whole onset cluster /pl/, is mislocated. Fromkin (1973) presents an impressive list of such divisions of consonant clusters. One of her cases is *blake fruid*, where the liquids /r/ and /l/ are exchanged, leaving the rest of the syllable onsets in place.

These observations are, so far, not covered by the three-level model of section 9.2. It can handle phoneme exchanges as long as these phonemes are single syllable constituents themselves, as in h*eft* l*emisphere*. To explain errors of the above kind, however, a mechanism of *cluster composition* is required. Such a mechanism, moreover, is needed if phonetic spellout is to work. Remember that the address frames at that level contain three slots: one for syllable onset, one for the nucleus, and one for the coda. In order to retrieve a syllable like *brake*, one needs for the onset slot a cluster, /br/, not a single phoneme segment. Hence, there must be a way to build such clusters from consecutive segments spelled out at the previous level.

How can cluster composition be modeled? The present proposal is to treat it just like phonetic spellout. That is, we will assume that the speaker has an inventory of onset clusters. They are the small set of onset clusters that are phonotactically allowed in the language, such as /st/, /br/, /fl/, and /skr/ in English. Similarly, there will be a set of phonotactically possible coda clusters. A cluster can be addressed by filling the slots of a corresponding address frame. Let us work this out in some more detail for syllable-onset clusters, which are most prone to speech error.

Take the word *groom*. At the level of segmental spellout the sequence of segments /g/, /r/, /u/, /m/ is produced. At the next level they will be used to complete the onset, nucleus, and coda slots of a syllable address. What should go into the onset slot? Not just /g/, but the cluster /gr/. In subsection 8.1.4 we discussed a rule called "maximization of onset." The onset cluster will be made as large as phonotactic rules allow. Onset-cluster composition consists of collecting as many consecutive C-type ("consonantal") segments as possible and filling an address frame with the same number of slots. (When there is just one consonant, the resulting "cluster" will be a singleton.) In the example there are two consecutive consonants, /g/ and /r/. A two-slot address frame is made available and is filled with these elements. If the result is a phonotactically possible address, the corresponding cluster becomes available for insertion in the onset slot. This can be depicted as follows:

address frame:

onset C$_1$	onset C$_2$

address:

onset C$_1$	onset C$_2$
/g/	/r/

retrieved onset cluster: /gr/

For other pairs of segments no cluster will be found. For instance, if the slots were to be filled with /n/ and /t/, respectively, no cluster would be retrieved; /nt/ is not a possible onset cluster in English.

What happens if such a sequence arises by chance? Will it be pronounced? The answer is clearly No. Take Fromkin's (1971) example *flay the pictor* [*play the victor*]. The mislocated /v/ is devoiced when it appears in front of *-lay*, thus turning into /f/. There is a still-unresolved discussion in the literature on how this is caused (Fromkin 1971; Davidson-Nielson 1975; Garrett 1980a; Crompton 1982; Stemberger 1983a; Stemberger and Treiman 1986), but somewhere the segment pair (/v/, /l/) has to be turned into the phonotactically possible onset cluster /fl/, which can then be used as filler for an onset slot in phonetic spellout. A similar problem arises in explaining speech errors such as *we have a big stellar down there* [*cellar*] (Stemberger 1983a). It is likely that here the /d/ of *down* in anticipated in pronouncing the target word *cellar*, and that this results in the onset cluster /st/ rather than /sd/. The generation of these cases may develop as follows.

address frame:

onset C$_1$	onset C$_2$

addresses:

onset C$_1$	onset C$_2$
/F/	/l/

onset C$_1$	onset C$_2$
/s/	/T/

retrieved onset cluster: /fl/   /st/

The /F/ in the leftmost address slot stands for either /v/ or /f/. When either of these is followed by /l/, a legal address is formed, namely that of the cluster /fl/. In other words, the feature of voicing is irrelevant for the potential filler of this slot if the next element is /l/. Similarly, the /T/ in the rightmost address slot means either /t/ or /d/. If either of these is preceded by /s/, a legal address is created for the cluster /st/. Similarly, the legal onset cluster /sp/ may be retrieved when the pair (/s/, /P/) is inserted in the address frame. Here /P/ stands for either /b/ or /p/. This may be at the base of speech errors such as *benefit spall – small businesses* (Stemberger 1983a). In this error the /b/ of *businesses* is anticipated and fills the C_2 slot of the cluster. However, the addresses (/s/, /b/) and (/s/, /p/) are not distinctive; they both refer to the cluster /sp/, /sb/ being phonotactically impossible as an onset cluster in English. Segment specifications such as /P/, /F/, /T/, and /K/ (for /k/ and /g/) are sometimes called *archiphonemes*. They are phonemes unspecified for at least one feature.

If cluster composition can involve archiphonemic segment specifications, the obvious next question is whether archiphonemes may arise in the *spellout* of clusters at the previous level. For instance, when the word *still* is segmentally spelled out, will the onset cluster be spelled out as /s/, /t/, or rather as /s/, /T/, where /T/ is the archiphoneme unspecified for voicing? The latter would normally suffice, because at the next level of cluster composition, where the cluster /st/ is to be retrieved, nothing more is required than the pair of fillers /s/, /T/ (at least, if the above proposal is correct).

Stemberger (1982, 1983a), who raised this question, gave an affirmative answer. There is evidence from speech errors to support the idea that archiphonemes arise in cluster spellout. One case involves the word *scruffy*. According to the above analysis, its onset cluster will be spelled out as /s/, /K/, /r/. Here /K/ is an archiphoneme with the voicing feature unspecified, i.e., it stands for both /k/ and /g/. At the next stage of cluster composition, this triple /s/, /K/, /r/ will suffice for the retrieval of /skr/; there is no possible onset cluster /sgr/ in English. But what happens if, by accident, the initial segment /s/ disappears? Both /kr/ and /gr/ are possible onset clusters in English, as in *crazy* and *grasp*. If indeed /K/ appears in the cluster spellout, not only can /k/ arise when the /s/ is lost, but /g/ is possible as well because the archisegment was not specified for the voicing feature. Stemberger (1983a) gave examples such as *in your really gruffy – scruffy clothes*, where indeed the /k/ of *scruffy* is realized as /g/ when the preceding /s/ happens to disappear. One wonders, of course, how perceivable such distinctions are.

Though the notion of archiphoneme is attractive for the analysis of such cases, it should be observed that an archiphoneme is just a phoneme on our definition in subsection 8.1.5. It is a segment specified for its *distinctive* features only. The segments /g/ and /k/ cannot be distinctively used in English when they follow /s/ in an onset cluster; hence, in that context they are the same phoneme.

The conclusion so far is that individual phonemes in onset clusters, whether or not they are syllable constituents themselves, can become misplaced in speech errors. The character of these misplacements has led us to assume a process of cluster composition that creates maximal onset clusters for syllables. These can then be inserted in the onset slots at the phonetic-spellout level. In the following, cluster composition will be considered as a preliminary or first stage of phonetic spellout.

The process of onset-cluster composition can err in several ways. An extensive analysis of word-initial cluster errors, both naturally occurring and experimentally elicited, was reported by Stemberger and Treiman (1986). A major finding of this study was that the second position in onset clusters is much more vulnerable to error than the first position. It is more likely to be lost or to be subject to substitution. Errors such as (5) and (6), which involve the second position, are more frequent than cases like (7) and (8), which involve the first position.

(5) They pace – place too little emphasis on their own results [loss of second consonant in onset cluster]

(6) prace – place Bresnan's arguments . . . [substitution of second consonant]

(7) Their attention pan – span is . . . [loss of first consonant]

(8) A crate – great quest . . . [substitution of first consonant]

Also, it is more likely that a second-position consonant becomes erroneously added than a first-position consonant. Example 9 is a more frequent type of error than example 10:

(9) Oh, so you have to bruy it with the T.V. [addition of second consonant]

(10) the same as the hit frate – hit rate for low-frequency items. [addition of first consonant]

We will not pursue Stemberger and Treiman's explanation of this asymmetry in detail here. But clearly, accurate filling of the C1 position in a cluster is given precedence in phonological encoding.

A similar mechanism of cluster composition can probably be suggested for codas. Here again, only phonotactically possible clusters are to be addressed. But the mechanism must differ in that there is no maximization rule for codas.

What about complex nuclei? Earlier we noted Stemberger's and Shattuck-Hufnagel's findings that a nucleus consisting of vowel plus liquid moves as a whole (an example was *cheeps and twirts*, where the whole complex nucleus /ɜr/ was displaced). Diphthongs, according to Fromkin (1971), are also rarely split into their component segments. Stemberger

(1983a) gives as an example

(11) They mooy – they may be moving back east again

but recognizes that these cases are exceptional. For the time being, there is no reason to assume the existence of a special spellout-and-composition mechanism for complex nuclei.

A final issue to be taken up here is whether all phonemic segments are equally "mislocation-prone." The answer is: to a substantial degree yes, but with certain qualifications. Shattuck-Hufnagel and Klatt (1979) counted the frequency of occurrence of the various phonemes in fluent speech (they restricted the count to occurrences in content words because function words are only infrequently involved in speech errors). If all phonemes are equally vulnerable, their frequency of occurrence in normal speech should predict their relative frequency of misplacement in speech errors. Correlations were computed for the consonants in the MIT speech-error corpus. The chance that a phoneme target would not be produced in the intended slot correlated 0.83 with frequency of occurrence of that phoneme, accounting for almost 70 percent of the variance. This means that, by and large, there are no "strong" intruding phonemes as opposed to "weak" error-prone ones. And indeed, each phoneme appeared about as often as target as it appeared as intrusion in the error data.

However, no such result was obtained in an experiment with elicited speech errors by Levitt and Healy (1985). They found that less frequent phonemes were indeed somewhat more error-prone, and that there was a tendency for more frequent phonemes to be more intruding or "stronger." In the study by Shattuck-Hufnagel and Klatt, too, certain phonemes were "weaker" or "stronger" than expected. In particular, /s/ and /t/ belonged to the "weaker" class. They tended to become "palatalized"—i.e., /s/ tended to turn into /ʃ/ or /tʃ/, and /t/ into /tʃ/. The reverse "depalatization" error, such as from /ʃ/ to /s/, was much less likely to occur. This asymmetry was, however, not reproduced in the Levitt-Healy study, and thus cannot explain their differential phoneme-strength effect.

The slight discrepancies between the two studies are probably largely due to the fact that the experimental study involved only single phonemes occurring in onsets of monosyllabic target items (such as *ra* and *li*), whereas the phonemes' syllable positions were not restricted in the observational study of Shattuck-Hufnagel and Klatt. In other words, a phoneme may, to some degree, be a "strong" contender for one syllable position but a "weak" contender for another position. Averaged over all positions in the syllable, however, these differences wash out, and all phonemes show an about equal average strength.

There is, moreover, a complex interaction between, on the one hand, the distributional properties of phonemes over segmental slots in the syllable and, on the other hand, differential vulnerability of syllabic slots to error. This catches the eye when one considers the following observation in the original study by Shattuck-Hufnagel and Klatt: Among the "stronger," seemingly less vulnerable phonemes was /ŋ/. The authors gave the obvious reason: This segment cannot appear in word-initial or syllable-initial position, which is the most error-prone position. Summarizing, therefore, one can say that all segments are about equally strong as contenders for segmental slots, but that there may be some dependency on position.

In conclusion: Phonemic segments are displaceable units. But when they are displaced, they are *accommodated* to their new environment. This means that they are phonetically realized in accordance with their position in the cluster or syllable. This allophonic accommodation is a natural consequence of the addressing mechanism proposed (following Crompton 1982). The same mechanism precludes the displacement of *allophones*, which is, in fact, never observed.

9.3.5 Distinctive Features

Can distinctive features, such as voicing and nasality, be moved individually? There are repeated claims in the literature that this is indeed possible. The classical examples are Fromkin's (1971). A shift of the voicing feature seems to occur in g*lear* p*lue sky* [*clear blue sky*], where the voicing feature of /b/ was anticipated in the initial segment of *clear*. Two new phonemes resulted: /g/ and /p/. A nasality shift is apparent in m*ity the* d*ue teacher* [*pity the new teacher*]. The /p/ is nasalized and thus turns into /m/; the /n/ is denasalized and turns into /d/. When two new phonemes are formed, one can be sure that a feature has been replaced.

One might conjecture that most phoneme replacements are, in actuality, replacements of single features or sets of features. For instance, the exchange *is* p*ade* m*ossible* [*is made possible*] might be due to a shift of the nasality feature only, rather than to an exchange of the phoneme segments /m/ and /p/ as a whole. In *you* g*etter stop for* b*as* [*you better stop for gas*], the apparent exchange of /g/ and /b/ may in fact be an exchange of a *pair* of distinctive features: anteriority and labiality. This, however, is very unlikely. Shattuck-Hufnagel and Klatt (1979) showed that multiple-feature shifts as in the latter example are far too frequent to be predicted by independent but coinciding single-feature shifts. The only really clear cases of feature replacements, i.e., where new phonemes are formed, occur with negligible frequency; only a few cases have been reported in the literature.

Apparently, distinctive features do not function as fillers in addressing subroutines. Their role in speech production is a different one, as will be discussed in subsections 9.4.2 and 9.5.2.

So far, we have considered the replaceability of word parts that are linguistically well defined: morphemes, syllables, syllable constituents, phonemes, allophones, and distinctive features. It turned out that syllables are hardly ever involved in substitutions, and allophones never. The displacement of features is possible but exceptional. This tells us something about the kinds of fillers that should figure in a slot/filler theory of phonetic planning: They are morphemes, syllable constituents, and phoneme segments. Allophones and distinctive features are probably computed only after the slots have been filled with the appropriate units. The spellout framework developed so far accounts for just these filler types. But is our present list of fillers complete? Shattuck-Hufnagel (1983, 1987) argues that there are still other displacement-prone word parts.

9.3.6   Word Onsets and Word Ends

Syllable onsets, we saw, are among the most frequent units involved in speech errors. But are they really always syllable onsets, or should they be characterized as word onsets? In monosyllabic words one cannot distinguish between syllable onset and word onset, but in polysyllabic words one can. In a word like *ferment*, is only the word-initial /f/ error-prone, or are both syllable onsets, /f/ and /m/, vulnerable? Shattuck-Hufnagel's (1987) statistics show that word onsets are more vulnerable than other syllable onsets in a word, by a factor of 4.5. Moreover, word onsets are far more prone to particular types of errors, especially exchanges, than other parts of the word. No less than 82 percent of the consonant-interaction errors in the MIT corpus occur in word onsets.

Still, one could argue that all this may be due to the tendency of word-onset syllables to be *stressed* syllables. It could be the case that onsets of stressed syllables are especially error-prone. So, in the verb *fermEnt* the /m/ would be error-prone, whereas in the noun *fErment* it would be the /f/. Shattuck-Hufnagel (1985, 1987) tested this in a so-called tongue-twister experiment in which a subject received a card with four words printed on it. (Examples are given in table 9.1.) The task was to read the card three times, then to turn it over and to recite it three times from memory. With examples like these, subjects made occasional errors, involving (for instance) misplacements of /p/ and /f/, as in *parade fad poot farole*. In the example for tongue-twister type i the /p/ is a word onset but it is not the onset of a stressed syllable; in the example for type ii /p/ is the onset of a stressed

Table 9.1
Effects of word position and syllable stress on segmental speech errors (after Shattuck-Hufnagel 1985).

Type	Example	Number of errors	/p/ is word-initial	stressed-syllable-initial
(i)	parade fad foot parole	121	+	−
(ii)	repeat fad foot repaid	58	−	+
(iii)	peril fad foot parrot	178	+	+
(iv)	ripple fad foot rapid	8	−	−

syllable but not a word onset; in type iii it is both in a stressed syllable and a word onset; in type iv it is none of these.

The table presents the numbers of errors released in the experiment. The critical segment (/p/ in the examples) was almost never affected when it was neither word-initial nor stressed-syllable-initial (case iv). When it was stressed-syllable-initial only (case ii), there were substantially more errors. When it was word-initial only (case i), the error rate was even higher. The strongest effect resulted when the segment was both word-initial and stressed-syllable-initial (case iii). The statistics from the experiment show that the strong word-onset effect and the weaker stressed-syllable-onset effect were additive; they contributed independently to the chance of error.

Hence, word onsets do seem to have a special status as fillers, and this is in agreement with the tip-of-the-tongue results discussed in section 9.1. Still, syllable onsets are replaceable units themselves, independent of their word position. Both the experimental results and the spontaneous-error data show, however, that constituents of *stressed* syllables are especially error-prone.

It is interesting to compare this result with what Shattuck-Hufnagel (1986) found for vowel errors. There the most vulnerable position turned out to be in the syllable carrying main stress. It was far less relevant whether that syllable was word-initial or not. It would therefore be wrong to conclude that there is a special role for the word-initial syllable as a whole. Rather, it is solely the word onset (consonant or cluster) that has a special status. Shattuck-Hufnagel (1987) went a long way toward unraveling this special status. She compared consonantal errors where the intrusion came from the same planned utterance (such as exchanges) against errors where the intrusion has no obvious source in the planned utterance. These were called "interactional" and "non-interactional" errors (Dell 1986 called them "contextual" and "non-contextual" errors). An example of an interactional error is *a lung – a young lady*; a noninteractional error is *the inflation* w*ate* [rate]. An analysis of errors in polysyllabic words, in which there are also non-word-initial syllable onsets, produced an interesting result: 77 percent of the interaction errors were word-initial, whereas only 28 percent of the non-interaction errors were word-initial. Is the special vulnerability of word onsets in some way related to phrasal planning (i.e., planning that involves two words from the same phonological or intonational phrase)?

To support this idea, Shattuck-Hufnagel (1987) performed another tongue-twister experiment. There were two kinds of twisters in this experiment: phrases and lists. For each phrasal twister (e.g. *From the leap of the note to the nap of the lute*), there was a list twister (e.g. *leap note nap lute*). It turned out that in the phrasal twisters 77 percent of the interactional errors were word-initial. In list twisters, however, only 44 percent of the interactional errors were word-initial. Word-onset vulnerability is apparently a consequence of generating connected phrasal speech. These findings have been replicated and extended by Wilshire (1985), but the connected speech mechanism responsible for the robust effect is as yet unknown.

The special status of word onsets is complemented by the replaceability of word ends in speech errors—in particular, word ends that are larger than a syllable. Shattuck-Hufnagel (1983) gave as an example a case where *Howard and Claire* was delivered as *Haire and Cl*oward. There is a shift here of the word-final *oward* (or was it a word-onset exchange where the intended order was *Claire and Howard*?). However, it is extremely rare that larger-than-syllable word endings move as units in speech errors.

This review of substitutable sublexical units has led to three main conclusions: (i) Only those sublexical-unit types for which there are address slots in the spellout mechanism are susceptible to error. (ii) Consonantal clusters are spelled out into their constituent segments, but this is not so for complex nuclei. (iii) Word-onset consonants are especially error-prone when connected phrasal speech is produced. The next section will summarize the now-expanded spellout model, and will then discuss how Shattuck-Hufnagel's slots-and-fillers theory accounts for a variety of errors.

9.4   The Slots-and-Fillers Theory and the Causation of Errors

9.4.1   Processing Levels

At the level of grammatical encoding, lemmas are released one by one with their diacritical parameters as the surface structure develops. Each of these constitutes the next bit of input for phonological encoding. According to the version of the slots-and-fillers theory presented here, this planning involves three levels of processing: morphological/metrical spellout, segmental spellout, and phonetic spellout (including cluster composition). These levels of processing are illustrated in figure 9.1, which shows the course of phonetic planning for the plural noun *crampons*.

A lemma (or rather its lexical pointer) and its diacritical features constitute the address where the item's morphological and metrical information is stored. The address is the IF-statement for a production that retrieves that information. The lexical entry *crampon* contains a singular item and a plural item. The diacritic feature "plural" directs the search to the appropriate lexical item. It is assumed that all inflectional word forms that are frequently used by the speaker are stored items in the form lexicon. Also, each frequently used derivational form constitutes an independent lexical entry (Cutler 1983a; Stemberger and MacWhinney 1986). It does not take more time or effort for a speaker to access complex inflectional forms than to access simple ones. Complex forms, inflectional or derivational, don't have to be *composed*; they are as available as simple forms.

The spellout at this level consists of a string of morphemes (stems, roots, affixes), as well as metrical information such as the number of peaks for each morpheme and the stored stress distribution relating to these peaks. For *crampons* there is a stem and an affix, and there are two peaks, of which the first one has primary stress. Each peak will trigger the generation of a syllable address frame at the phonetic spellout level. Syllable address frames probably come in two kinds: stressed and unstressed.

The segmental spellout routines take the metricized root-and-affix strings as input, and produce a string of syllables, each spelled out in terms of syllable constituents: onsets, rimes, nuclei, and codas. Onset and coda clusters are further spelled out as individual segments. The eventual result is a full segmental spellout of the item. Each segment is probably labeled as onset, peak, or coda item (but see section 9.6). If a segment pertains to a cluster, it may be further labeled as, e.g., "onset C_1" (for instance, /k/ in the example) or "coda C_1" (/n/ in the example).

The phonetic spellout routines, finally, are there to find phonetic syllable plans for strings of segments. These articulatory programs for syllables are largely stored; they only have to be addressed by way of the right key. An address consists of a triple of onset, nucleus, and coda. These are filled, in turn, by appropriate segments or segment clusters. The first syllable of *crampons* is found by inserting /kr/, /æ'/, and /m/ in the slots, respectively. Cluster composition must precede this process of insertion. The mechanism of cluster composition prevents phonotactically illegal clusters from arising.

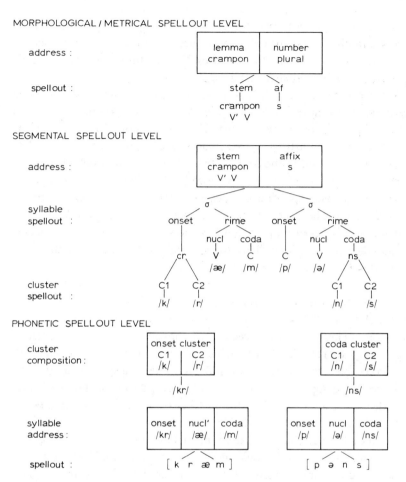

Figure 9.1
Levels of processing in generation of phonetic plan for *crampons*.

The retrieved phonetic plan for a syllable is a sequence of phones. When executed, a phone is an articulatory gesture over time. A syllable's phones are overlapping and interacting gestures. Each gesture consists of dynamic phonetic features, such as voicing and nasalizing.

There may be independently stored routines for stressed and unstressed syllables, as Crompton (1982) suggests. In *crampons*, [kræm] is a stressed syllable; [pəns] is an unstressed one. The nuclear slot of a stressed frame cannot accept an unstressed vowel such as /ə/. The appropriately filled address frames point to the correct stressed or unstressed syllable plans.

However, not everything can be stored. The syllable's stored phonetic plan is modifiable, depending on the prosodic context in which it appears. Also, there must be a mechanism for creating new, rare syllables; we will take up these issues in chapter 10. Let us now turn to the control structure proposed in the slots-and-fillers theory, and to its account of the main kinds of sublexical-form errors.

9.4.2   The Causation of Errors

On the slots-and-fillers account, errors of word form are due to failures in addressing. This is most easily seen at the phonetic-spellout level. Addressing at this level requires making triples of onset, nucleus, and coda available to complete the characteristic address frame for a syllable. Sometimes more than one appropriate filler is available for a slot, or the target filler is made available too late. The slots are then filled by a nonintended triple, and a similar but erroneous syllable is accessed.

Shattuck-Hufnagel's (1979) account of how different types of speech errors, exchanges, substitutions, additions, omissions, and shifts can arise under these circumstances involves a two-step control structure, with a *selection* step followed by a *checkoff* step. Let us consider how this is involved in the causation of the various kinds of errors.

Exchanges

Example: *a but-gusting meal* [*a gut-busting meal*]

There are two fillers available when a filler is requested for the first onset slot: /g/ and /b/. This is due to speedy segmental spellout at the previous level of processing. The most highly activated item is now selected to be copied in the onset slot. This happens to be /b/, which becomes the intrusion. After insertion, a filler is normally "checked off"; in other words, its activation is reduced to zero, and it is no longer available. This happens to /b/, but not to /g/ (which was not used). The nucleus and coda slots are correctly filled, and the syllable retrieved is [bʌt] instead of [gʌt]. At a later stage, when the next syllable-onset element is requested, /b/ is no longer available as a filler—it was checked off. But /g/ is still available and of the right kind. It fills the slot, and together with /ʌ/ and /s/ it forms the triple that accesses the syllable [gʌs]. In short: Exchanges can result when misselection is followed by normal checkoff. The original target will stay available and will fill the slot that was meant for the checked-off element.

Substitutions

Examples: *if you can change the* p*irst part* [*if you can change the first part*] (anticipation)
a phonological f*ool* [*a phonological rule*] (perseveration)

A substitution combines a misselection with a checkoff error. In the anticipation error above, when an onset element was requested, the filler /p/, to be used later, was already available, and was more strongly activated than the target filler /f/. It was copied in the onset slot. So far, the situation is the same as in exchanges. But now, /p/ was not checked off, and stayed available as onset filler. (On the activation-spreading account to be discussed in the next section, /p/ is quickly reactivated after insertion.) It could therefore be used again as onset filler when the next syllable, [pɑrt], was addressed.

In perseverations the same processing errors are made, but in reverse order. In the second example above, /f/ is correctly inserted when the onset is requested for the first syllable of *phonological*; however, it is not checked off, and it stays available to fill a later syllable-onset slot. This leads to a misselection when, for a new word, a new syllable onset is requested; the still-available /f/ is more activated than the target /r/ at that moment. As a result, the syllable [fʊl] is addressed instead of the target [rʊl].

Omissions

Example: *Doctor -inclair has emphasized* [*Doctor Sinclair has emphasized*]

As was discussed above, this type of error suggests the existence of a null filler. The first syllable of *emphasized* has the null element as syllable onset. When that null element is early available as a filler, it may be misselected to fill the onset slot of *Sinclair*'s first syllable. It is, however, not checked off, and it stays available for repeated insertion at the appropriate occasion. On this account, omissions are nothing but substitutions involving a null filler.

However, other kinds of omissions require a different account. They are the so-called *haplologies*. Fromkin (1971) calls them *telescopic errors* because the utterance becomes contracted, as in *rigous* [*rigorous*] and *tremenly* [*tremendously*]. There are also much wilder cases, such as *I have a spart for him* [*I have a spot in my heart for him*]. Crompton (1982) observed that the jumps (over the omitted part) go from one syllable-constituent boundary to another identical constituent boundary. In *rig-ous* the same transition is at issue as in *rig-orous*, namely from syllable onset to syllable nucleus. In *tremen-ly* the transition is from coda to onset, as it is in *tremen-dously*. This shows that the regular pattern of address frames is followed: onset-nucleus-coda/onset-nucleus-coda, etc. Onset *clusters* or coda *clusters* are never broken open in haplologies. The situation is highly comparable to the way in which transitions are handled in blends (see subsection 9.3.2). According to Cutler (1980b), it is often the case that the two ends meet at a common segment. An example from Fromkin (1973) is *nitness* for *Nixon witness*, where the common element is /ɪ/.

It is, as yet, unclear how whole strings of fillers get lost in the phase of phonetic spellout. One cause could be that not enough syllable frames are set up, i.e., that a peak at the level of metrical spellout fails to trigger an onset/nucleus/coda frame. The available fillers then have to compete for too few slots. Let us call this a *frame-generation error*. Another cause could be that the lost elements are so similar to nearby elements that they are not recognized as different and they are put into the same slot. Stemberger and MacWhinney (1986) induced "no-marking errors"—errors where an inflection is not pronounced when the stem displays a sound form that could be a realization of that inflection. For instance, when presented with the word *lifting* or *yielding* and asked to pronounce the past-tense form, subjects occasionally answered *lift* instead of *lifted*, or *yield* instead of *yielded*. (Such errors are also observed in spontaneous speech.) This almost never happened for verbs like *bake* or *grab*, where there is no similarity between the past-tense inflection and the sound form of the stem.

Additions

Examples: *has slides sloping in* [*has sides sloping in*]
             Glod bless you [*God bless you*]

The first kind of example is the most frequent one. The addition of /l/ to *sides*, however, is only apparently an addition. The most straightforward account is an anticipation of the onset cluster /sl/ of *sloping*. Thus, it is a substitution error. (This may also be so for example 10 above.)

The second kind of example (which is similar to example 9) is harder to account for. It is most probably due to misselection in cluster composition. When a syllable-onset filler was requested, a cluster /gl/ was inserted. How could this have come into existence? It probably started with a frame-generation error. An onset-cluster address was set up with two slots. C_1 was then correctly filled with /g/. C_2 accepted /l/, the C_2 element of the next onset cluster. This /l/ was not checked off after insertion, so it could be used a second time as C_2 filler, for the composition of /bl/. So, there was—on this account—a concatenation of an error in frame generation, a misselection, and a checkoff error. The origin of a frame-generation error is always difficult to locate. In the present case, an onset-cluster frame was correctly generated for *bless*; but it may have been generated too early.

Shifts

Examples: *Walter Conkrite* [*Walter Cronkite*]
           Frish Gotto [*Fish Grotto*]

The apparently shifted /r/ in the first example is probably not a shift at all. The error can be accounted for as an exchange of two syllable onsets:/kr/ and /k/. The second example (from Fromkin 1971) is due to a frame-generation error followed by a misselection during cluster composition. The C_1/C_2 frame set up for *Grotto* appeared too early. It then accepted (erroneously) /f/ in its C_1 slot and (correctly) /r/ in C_2. This created the onset cluster /fr/, and both /f/ and /r/ were checked off. The cluster then filled the first syllable-onset slot. For the second syllable-onset slot, only /g/ remained as a filler.

All these types of errors can also occur at higher levels of processing. There can, for instance, be exchanges, substitutions, omissions, additions, and shifts of morphemes. (Several examples were presented above.) And the mechanisms are probably quite similar, involving failures of selection, of checking off, and/or of frame generation. Frame-generation failures are least understood, however.

The development of a complete slots-and-fillers theory requires an account of how the address frames are set up to start with. This is fairly simple at the phonetic-spellout level, where the sequence of onset-nucleus-coda frames was triggered by the sequence of peaks in metrical spellout. It is also relatively simple at the cluster-composition level. There should be a frame for each cluster spelled out at the previous level. But segmental spellout has a more highly structured sequence of address frames. They can be pairs of stem and affix, or pairs of roots, or roots with several affixes, and so on. The sequence of address frames for segmental spellout must be formed on the basis of the earlier morphological spellout results. When a lemma is spelled out as stem + affix, a stem/affix frame is set up, and similarly for other spellouts. It is not impossible that certain errors result from the setting up of deviant address frames at the level of segmental spellout, as well. That will, however, not be pursued here; instead we will consider a final factor in the causation of errors: phonemic similarity.

Phonemic similarity

Segmental errors are subject to a quite general constraint: Target and intrusion tend to be similar in distinctive feature composition. An exchange such as p*aid* m*ossible* is more likely than one such as *a two-sen* p*et* [*two-pen set*]. The more features on which the target and a potential intruder differ, the smaller the chance of error. This was shown initially by Nooteboom (1967) in an analysis of Dutch speech errors, and later by MacKay (1970) for German and by Fromkin (1971) for English errors. Shattuck-Hufnagel and Klatt (1979) demonstrated it for the consonantal errors of the MIT corpus, and Shattuck-Hufnagel (1986) showed the constraint to hold as well for the vowel errors of that corpus. Levitt and Healy (1985) confirmed the feature-similarity constraint in experimentally elicited errors.

Though the constraint is evidently correct, it is less clear which common distinctive features are the main determinants of segment confusion. Van den Broecke and Goldstein (1980) performed, for consonant errors, extensive multidimensional analyses on two American-English corpora, a Dutch corpus, and a German corpus. They found a clear confirmation of the feature-similarity constraint, though some phonological feature systems were better predictors of segment confusability than others. Certain features contribute more to exchangeability of segments than others, and again, the ordering differs somewhat for different feature systems. A fair summary, however, is this: Among the most affected features in consonantal errors are the place features. Target and intrusion frequently differ in the place where the main constriction is made in the vocal tract; a /p/ easily exchanges for a /k/, for instance. In other words, place is not a great contributor to similarity. Somewhat less affected is the voicing feature; that is, it is a more important determinant of (dis)similarity. At the other end of the scale is the manner feature nasality. That feature tends to be maintained in speech errors (but not in the above example *paid mossible*); to put it differently, nasal consonants are mutually quite confusable.

Shattuck-Hufnagel (1986) performed a similar analysis for vowel errors and found an interesting parallel to the just-mentioned observations. The feature that was most easily changed in vowel errors was the place feature: back versus front. On the other hand, manner features were far less vulnerable. In particular, tense vowels (such as /i/ in *beat*) tended to replace tense vowels, and lax vowels (such as /ɪ/ in *bit*) tended to replace lax vowels. The general pattern, therefore, seems to be that place features are vulnerable in speech errors, whereas manner features are more stable. There is no ready explanation for the similarity constraint within the slots-and-filler model; however, we will return to it in the next section, where an activation-spreading account is discussed.

This subsection has reviewed the causation of errors in the slots-and-fillers model. The main characteristic of the model is the thorough separation between the setting up of structural frames and the filling of these frames with appropriate, independently spelled-out units. The model accounts for the important and empirically well-supported Unit-Similarity Constraint. It also gives a principled account of which errors are possible and which are impossible. And it explains the causation of errors by failures of two control processes: selection and checkoff. In addition, there may be failure in the mechanism that governs the setting up of the address frames.

The model was not designed to make precise quantitative predictions of various error types. In particular, it has little to say about the spellout mechanisms, i.e., the ways in which sublexical units are activated and retrieved in order to become available as fillers. Also, the checkoff mechanism—the deactivation of units after insertion—may need further scrutiny. What precisely is a checkoff error? Is it a failure to deactivate, or is it, rather, a speedy reactivation process? These and similar issues are central to the activation-spreading model. The most detailed version of that model (Dell 1986, 1988) is quite compatible with the slots-and-fillers model, and it is in many respects complementary to it.

9.5 Activation-Spreading Theory

The enormous speed with which a speaker can access the form representations in long-term memory requires an efficient control structure. In this section we will consider further how, at the three main processing levels, the stored forms are accessed in order to make them available as slot fillers for the next level. The most elaborate accounts of these processes are to be found in the so-called *spreading activation* (better: *activation-spreading*) theories, which were introduced in section 1.3 and which were considered in subsection 6.3.5 in connection with the accessing of lemmas. Word-form access has been more of a hunting ground for activation-spreading theorists than lemma access, as is apparent from publications such as Kozhevnikov and Chistovich 1965, Dell and Reich 1977, 1980, and 1981, Dell 1984, 1986, and 1988, MacKay 1982 and 1987, Meyer and Gordon 1985, and Stemberger 1985a. The most elaborate treatment is that of Dell 1986; the present section reflects his notions to a large degree.

9.5.1   The Stratified Structure of the Word-Form Lexicon

Dell's (1986) activation-spreading model is organized in four strata or levels of nodes: the semantic, the syntactic, the morphological, and the phonological. These strata consist of nodes that are permanently available in long-term memory. Nodes can be activated, and when active they spread their activation to connected nodes at other levels. At the syntactic level the nodes stand for lemmas and their diacritical features. At the morphological level they stand for stems and affixes. At the phonological level they stand for syllable constituents and phonemes. In other words, the node levels correspond rather precisely to the inputs and the outputs of the processing levels discussed in the previous section. Missing, however, is a level at which phones are represented. There is, as yet, no activation-spreading account of the generation of (allo)phones.

Spellingout, i.e., going from level to level, is done by activation spreading or priming. Take, for example, the words *reset* and *resell*. The representations at the syntactic, the morphological, and the phonological strata are presented in figure 9.2. The web of connections leading down from the two lemmas at the syntactic level are precisely their long-term form representa-

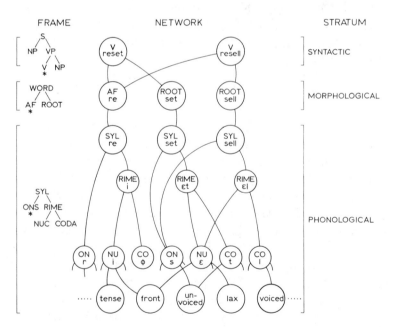

Figure 9.2
Example of strata, frames, and connected network in activation-spreading theory.

tions in the mental lexicon. The two representations share an affix at the morphological level as well as a syllable and several phonemes at the phonological level.

At each level of representation and each discrete moment in time there is one and only one *current node*. Assume that at the syntactic level the verb lemma *reset* is the current node in the developing surface structure. It is marked by an asterisk in the syntactic frame. This means that its state of activation is increased by some constant but substantial amount. At the next moment in time the increased activation is spread to the morpheme nodes *re* and *set* at the morphological stratum. This is equivalent to morphological spellout. The activation is also spread further to the connected nodes at the phonological level.

There must now be an independent structural reason for promoting a prefix node to the current node at the morphological level. In the slots-and-fillers theory this reason is the current availability of a particular slot in the developing address frame. Neither of the theories is well developed with respect to how these structural frames are set up, though Dell (1985) and MacKay (1982, 1987; see also subsection 12.1.4 below) have presented suggestions as to how an activation-spreading theory can promote a node to the current node. At any rate, a particular *kind* of node should be requested—for instance, an affix node. The requested kind of node, or the slot to be filled, is again marked by an asterisk, but now in the morphological frame. Of all the available prefix nodes in memory (i.e., in the network), the most highly activated one will be selected. Since the node for the prefix *re* was just primed, it will most probably become the current node. This increases its state of activation even more, by the fixed extra amount of activation allotted to current nodes. At the next moment, the morpheme's additional activation is spread to the phonological stratum— i.e., to the syllable and syllable-constituent nodes that are connected to the affix node. The syllable frame at this level successively requests an onset, a nucleus, and a coda.

A digression is in order here: That a syllable's onset, nucleus, and coda are requested in serial order deviates from Dell's (1986) original proposal, which says that "to simplify matters, it is assumed that onset, nucleus, and coda for a given syllable are selected simultaneously." But Dell (1988) revised this position largely on the basis of an experimental study by Meyer (1988), which makes it likely that a syllable's slots are filled in serial order. Since she found that, in accordance with Dell (1986), a word's syllables are also addressed in serial order, she could conclude that a word's phonetic plan as a whole is normally built up serially—"from left to right," so to speak.

The evidence is that one can reduce a subject's response latency in pronouncing a word by giving an appropriate prime. But Meyer found that the only effective primes were those that started at word onset. So, for the word *pitfall*, *p* is a good prime but *it* or *fall* has no effect. The priming effect, moreover, increases monotonically as longer word-initial stretches are given as primes. So, for *pitfall* the following primes are increasingly effective: *p*, *pit*, and *pitf*. Meyer developed an elegant technique to present such phonological primes.

Let us now return to the phonological encoding of *reset*. At the moment the onset of its first syllable is requested (a state of affairs indicated by an asterisk in figure 9.2), the most highly activated onset node is the phoneme /r/. It becomes the current node, and it spreads its additional current-node activation to its distinctive feature nodes. The syllable frame then requests a nucleus (and receives /i/), and a coda (the null element /∅/), which completes the first syllable. Dell (1988) allows for other syllable frames than onset-nucleus-coda, for instance a CV-frame that could accommodate the syllable /ri/ without recourse to a null element.

After a current node has been selected and its activation has been boosted and spread, the activation falls back to zero. This is equivalent to the check off mechanism in the slots-and-filler theory. It makes it unlikely that the same node is immediately available as current node again. It can be quickly reactivated, however.

A very similar story can be told about the promotion of the root morpheme *set* to current node. When after the prefix a stem node is sought at the morphological level, *set* is the most strongly activated one (*sell*, for instance, is not very active). It becomes the current node, and its activation level is boosted. The node spreads its activation to the phonological-level nodes. At that level, the current nodes required by the syllable frame are, successively, onset, nucleus, coda, onset, nucleus, coda, and so on. Each time, the most activated node of the type is selected.

An important property of the activation-spreading model is that a node's activation spreads not only to lower levels but also to higher ones. The arcs or connections in the network are perfectly bidirectional channels for the spreading of activation. Take the prefix *re*. When it becomes activated (first by priming from *reset*, then by being promoted to current node), it sends a quantum of activation back up to *reset*, but also to the lemma node *resell* and to all lemmas whose morphological spellouts begin with the prefix *re*. The slightly activated node *resell*, in turn, spreads some fraction of its newly acquired activation to the stem morpheme *sell*, and from there the activation perpetuates to the phonological level. The system would, of course, become steadily more excited in this way, and to prevent this the assumption is made that all nodes show an exponential decay of activation over time.

The control structure of spreading activation is one of parallel processing. There is simultaneous activation of whole sets of nodes at a given level of representation, and there is simultaneous activity at all levels; at each level there is always a "current" node. There are no long waiting lines in accessing the form lexicon, and that is just what is needed to account for the high-speed performance of speech generation.

9.5.2   Activation-Spreading and Speech Errors
The upward spreading of activation can now be used to explain several speech-error phenomena that are otherwise hard to understand. Here are some of them.

Malapropisms
A malapropism is the replacement of a word by another existing word that is related in form but not in meaning. This type of speech error was first analyzed (and named after Sheridan's character Mrs. Malaprop, who excelled in using wrong words) by Fay and Cutler (1977). The intruding word tends to have the same number of syllables, the same beginning, and the same stress pattern—much like a tip-of-the-tongue guess. Fay and Cutler list as examples *week* for *work*, *open* for *over*, *constructed* for *corrected*, and so on. Not all malapropisms are speech errors, of course; it happens occasionally that a speaker really doesn't know which word means what.

The activation-spreading account of real malapropisms is straightforward. We saw that *resell* is primed by the affix *re* (see figure 9.2). If there is enough time for *resell* to spread a fraction of its activation to the morpheme node *sell*, there is some minimal chance that it becomes selected as the current node instead of *set*. This chance is even higher if the activation that flowed from *reset* to *set*, and further down to the /s/ and /ɛ/ nodes, has enough time to flow back up to the root node *sell* before a new current node is selected at the morphological level. If indeed *sell* is selected as the current node, a malapropism is born: The speaker will say *resell* instead of *reset*. For these errors to occur, the rate of speaking should be low; otherwise there is not sufficient time for the backward spreading to take effect.

Lexical bias
There is a tendency in sublexical errors to create words rather than non-word strings. Speech errors such as h*old card cash* [*cold hard cash*], where

the newly formed units are words, are more likely to occur than errors such as *I s*ould be sh*eeing him soon* [*I should be seeing him soon*], where nonsense strings result.

Dell and Reich (1981) proved this statistically for a large corpus of collected speech errors, and this found reconfirmation in the work of Stemberger (1984). Baars, Motley, and MacKay (1975) gave an experimental demonstration of lexical bias. These authors were the first to generate speech errors experimentally, and their technique has been much used since. It consists of asking subjects to read a list of word pairs. In this list there are target pairs, such as *darn bore* or *dart board*. A target pair is preceded by three bias pairs in the list. A bias pair contains at least the initial phonemes of the desired error outcome. So, in order to induce the error *barn door* for *darn bore*, bias pairs such as *ball dome* are given. Under these conditions, readers produce 10–15 percent spoonerisms on the target items, saying *barn door* [for *darn bore*] or *bart doard* [for *dart board*]. What Baars et al. found in their 1975 study is that there is much more slipping for target pairs that create real words when spoonerized than for those that create nonsense words. The error *darn bore → barn door* is a much more frequent type of slip than *dart board → bart doard*. There is a lexical bias in slips of the tongue.

The activation-spreading account of lexical bias is, again, based on the flowing back of activation from lower to higher levels—in particular, from the phonological to the morphological stratum. This feedback can only prime the nodes of really existing morphemes in the language; there are no other nodes at the morphological level. There are nodes for *darn* and *bore* but not for *bart* and *doart*. In figure 9.2, there are nodes for *set* and *sell* but not for *sef*. This makes the error *resell* more likely than the error *resef*: a lexical bias. At the same time, the activation-spreading theory predicts that the lexical-bias effect should decrease at higher speaking rates. Backward spreading needs time to develop. This prediction was substantiated in an experiment by Dell (1985), who used a modified version of the technique of Baars et al. in which he varied the time available for a subject to respond. When the subject had to speak quickly, the lexical-bias effect disappeared.

The lexical-bias effect is also at the basis of the stress errors discussed in subsection 9.2.2. When the verb *segmEnt* is activated it will prime the noun *sEgment*, because they share most of the nodes at the phonological level. This explains how a related but differently stressed word can come to interfere in the generation of word accent.

The discussion about the origins of lexical bias in speech errors is still unsettled. An alternative to the activation-spreading accound is an editing account: the speaker intercepts nonwords just before uttering them. These issues will be further discussed in section 12.1.

The repeated-phoneme effect

It has often been observed that exchanges of word or syllable onsets are more likely to occur when the following phoneme is the same in each of the two syllables (Wickelgren 1969, 1976; Nooteboom 1973; MacKay 1970; Shattuck-Hufnagel 1985). Two examples are k*it to f*ill [*fit to kill*], where both exchanged consonants are followed by /ɪ/, and h*eft* l*emisphere* [*left hemisphere*], where the following vowel is /ɛ/ in both words. Dell (1984) used the technique of Baars et al. to study whether word-onset exchanges are more likely to occur when the following vowel is the same in each word than when they are different. This is indeed what he found. In addition, Dell found that the repeated phoneme need not be the vowel adjacent to the word onset; it can also be the word-final consonant. In the pair *boot coat*, for instance, the codas /t/are the same but the nuclei are not. Still, there is an increased chance that the initial /b/ and /k/ phonemes will exchange, and this must be due to their syllables' ending on the same coda.

Dell's explanation of these effects in the spreading activation model (see also Stemberger 1985a) makes use of syllable nodes at the phonological level, which mediate between morpheme nodes and nodes for syllable constituents (see figure 9.2). For *boot* and *coat*, for instance, the situation looks like this:

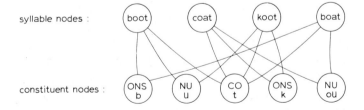

Here *boot* primes /b/, /u/, and /t/. The /t/ is, however, doubly primed; it also receives activation from *coat*, which moreover primes /k/ and /oʊ/. Together, /k/, /ʊ/, and the doubly primed /t/ feed back to the syllable node *koot*. Similarly, the syllable *boat* receives double activation from /t/, which increases the likelihood that it will become the current node in a slip. The repeated-phoneme effect should be dependent on the rate of speaking. At high rates, there is not enough time for lower-level nodes to feed back to higher-level ones. Dell (1986) found evidence of a diminished effect in exchanges when the speaking rate was increased.

Checkoff failure

Remember that Shattuck-Hufnagel (1979) explained the occurrence of substitution errors, in particular anticipations and perseverations, as resulting from a combination of a misselection and checkoff failure. A misplaced filler, once used, remains available as a filler. Its activation is, apparently, not turned back to zero. The activation-spreading model explains this, again, by means of feedback from lower to higher levels. When in the above diagram the syllable node *boot* is the current node, it spreads its activation to /b/, /u/, and /t/. The *boot*'s activation resets to zero. In their turn, however, the activated phonemes /b/, /ʊ/, and /t/ return part of their gained activation to *boot*. As a result, *boot* is reactivated shortly after it fired. This makes it a candidate for a subsequent choice as current node. The speaker may say *boot boot* instead of *boot coat*. Also, the syllable node *boat* will be activated by /b/ and /t/. This makes *boot boat*, where there is perseveration of /b/, a possible slip of the tongue. In view of this explanation, anticipations and perseverations should occur especially at low speaking rates, because then there is time to (re)activate a higher-level node from a lower-level node. At higher rates, exchanges (which require normal checkoff of used fillers) are more likely. This is exactly what Dell (1986) found when he applied the technique of Baars et al. at varying speaking rates.

Phonemic similarity

The intruding phoneme tends to be similar to the target in terms of its distinctive feature composition. This was called the phonemic similarity constraint in subsection 9.4.2. The activation-spreading theory can account for this phenomenon if a level of distinctive feature nodes is introduced. This level is depicted as the bottom level of nodes in figure 9.2. The explanation goes like this: Each activated phoneme node will spread its activation to the corresponding set of feature nodes, i.e., to nodes representing features such as voicing, place of articulation, and nasality. In their turn, the activated feature nodes will return activation to all phoneme nodes that share these features. Hence /s/ will, through its distinctive feature node "unvoiced", activate /t/; /i/ will, via the feature node "front", activate /ɛ/; and so on. In this way, similar phonemes increase their mutual availability as candidate fillers. This enhances the chance that an intrusion will be similar to a target.

However, the functional significance of a feature stratum is not altogether clear. The sets of feature nodes connected to a phoneme node cannot represent the allophonic feature composition of the segment in its specific environment. If that were the case, the segmental dislocations that the model describes would be replacements of (allo)phones by (allo)phones. But we know that phones do not exchange in speech errors; only phonemes do, and they become accommodated to their new environment. Hence, the feature sets represent phonemes; they are not phonetic output parameters. But this means that the activation-spreading theory in its present state does not generate a phonetic plan; at least the lowest level of planning, the phonetic specification of syllables, is still missing.

The present review of the activation-spreading theory (especially Dell's) doesn't do justice to one of its main strengths: its quantitative formal nature. Dell (1986) reported two computer simulations of the theory. There are parameters for the rate of activation spreading and for decay of activation. At each (discrete) moment in time, each node summates the incoming activation from all nodes it is connected to. There is a constant extra quantum of activation (called *signaling activation*) for the node that becomes the "current node." This is a fairly limited and fixed set of parameters. Independent of these is a speaking-rate parameter: the time (or the number of discrete time units) allotted for the generation of a syllable. Dell made the fruitful assumption that the rate of activation spreading is constant and independent of speaking rate. This independence made it possible to predict the nontrivial result that lexical bias would increase with slower speaking rate, and that high speaking rates would favor exchanges over perseverations and anticipations. As we saw above, these model predictions were experimentally verified.

Dell has been very careful not to overstate the power of his model. For instance, some of the properties of errors reviewed above do not fall out naturally from the model's assumptions. In particular, the model does not account for the special status of word onsets in speech errors, nor does it predict the extra vulnerability of stressed syllables and of syllable onsets. It is, of course, relatively easy to state these facts in terms of the model. One can manipulate the parameters in such a way that more activation is spread from a lemma to its word onset, to its accented syllable, and to syllable-initial consonants than to its other phonological constituents; but then the model is used only as a formal language to *describe* the data, not as their *explanation*. On these issues, see especially Dell 1988.

9.6   Serial Order in Phonological Encoding

According to the slots-and-fillers model, a word's segmental spellout by and large preserves its linear order; i.e., there is an ordered string of segments (Shattuck-Hufnagel 1979). When, at the next level, segments (or clusters) are required to fill successive syllable slots (i.e., onset, nucleus, and coda slots), the string of segments can be used in the given order. If the word is *pitfall*, the segmental spellout is the string /p/, /ɪ/, /t/, /f/, /ɔ/, /l/. These segments will then be used in the same order to fill the slots of two successive syllable frames, and the correct syllable plans [pit] and [fɔl] will be addressed. For this procedure to work, the segments need not be categorized in terms of onset, nucleus, or coda. The segment /t/ will never end up in the onset slot, because of its serial position. It is not necessary to label it as "coda segment".

If this procedure were followed strictly, speech errors wouldn't arise. The error *fitpall*, for instance, couldn't occur. Clearly, the ordering is not always fully specified (as Shattuck-Hufnagel of course recognized), since such errors do occur. This, however, requires a measure to prevent errors (such as *piftall*) where an onset and a coda segment are exchanged. Such errors, which violate the Unit-Similarity Constraint, are exceedingly rare. Are spelled-out segments categorized in terms of their function in the syllable (onset, nucleus, or coda)?

So far we have followed Dell's suggestion that segments are indeed labeled in terms of their syllabic function. And this is an obvious requirement in the activation-spreading theory. There is no guarantee in that theory that the order of maximally activated phonemic nodes corresponds precisely to the word's order of phonemes. When, for instance, the current node must be an onset segment, it could well be the case that the strongest activated phoneme is one that should end up as coda. To prevent this, Dell labeled phonemes according to syllabic function (see figure 9.2). When an onset is required, the most highly activated onset node is selected as the current node. This guarantees that the Unit-Similarity Constraint applies at this level. It is impossible to misselect an onset for a coda, or inversely; an onset intrusion must itself be an onset segment, and similarly for nucleus and coda intrusions.

Meyer (1988), however, suggests that this may be overkill. First, her experiments show that there is rather strict linear ordering in the making available of a word's segments. Dell's 1986 model may have to be modified to account for this finding. Second, syllabic slots may accept only certain *kinds* of segments. This is clearest for the nucleus slot. It will accept only phonemes of high sonority value (in particular, vowels). A spelled-out vowel need not be labeled as being of category "nucleus" to be recognized as a possible nucleus filler. Also, certain phonemes can never become onsets (e.g., /ŋ/ in English), and others will never be codas, depending on the language. Finally, cluster composition can play a distinct role. Subsection 8.1.3 mentioned Selkirk's Sonority Sequencing Generalization: A syllable's sonority slopes down from the peak in both directions. This means that an onset cluster, such as /sm/ or /skr/, has its phonemes in increasing order of sonority. Similarly, a coda cluster, such as /ld/ or /nt/, consists of phonemes that are decreasing in sonority value. To the extent that this property holds, it distinguishes onset clusters from coda clusters. If the onset slot of a syllable address accepts only sonority-increasing clusters whereas a coda slot takes only clusters that are sonority-decreasing, that will suffice to prevent violations of the Unit-Similarity Constraint as far as onset and coda clusters are concerned. It is not necessary, then, to categorize phonemes as "onset cluster element" or "coda cluster element".

This chapter began with an expression of concern that the phonological encoding of words may appear to be a wasteful process. At the level of segmental spellout, a word's syllabic composition becomes available. At the next level of processing, the spelled-out segments are used to address syllable plans of the same composition. Why can't there be a short-cut? The main answer to this is that in connected speech a word's spelled-out syllabic composition is often not preserved in the resulting string of syllable plans. Strings like *gave it him* are resyllabified in fluent speech (*ga-vi-tim*). They become new, so called phonological words. And this enhances the ease and the fluency of articulation. But we can now add a second point: If it is not strictly necessary to label each spelled-out segment with respect to its function in the syllable (i.e., as onset, nucleus, or coda element), phonological encoding may not require a full spellout of a word's syllabic composition at the segmental-spellout level to start with. On that view, syllables will appear only at the final stage of phonological encoding: the phonetic-spellout level. Further research is needed to settle this point.

Summary

Phonological encoding is a process by which the phonological specifications of lexical items are retrieved and mapped onto a fluently pronounceable string of syllables. Unpacking a word's phonological specifications and using them to retrieve the appropriate syllable programs involves various levels of processing. Studies of the tip-of-the-tongue phenomenon, in which this process of phonological unpacking is blocked or slowed, support this view. An initial sketch of the word can be available while further segmental details are still lacking.

There are two rather complementary accounts of phonological encoding: the slots-and-fillers theory, with Shattuck-Hufnagel as its mother, and the activation-spreading theory, with Dell as one of its fathers. Our review started from the slots-and-fillers perspective. It was proposed that there are three levels of processing in phonological encoding. At the first level, lemmas and their diacritical features are the fillers for addressing and spelling out the stored morphological and metrical composition of words. At the next level, this information is used to address and spell out the word's segmental composition. At the third level, a word's string of segments is used to address one or more phonetic syllable programs. These syllable programs are specifications of articulatory gestures, built up out of consecutive but mutually overlapping phone gestures.

At each level, independently defined address frames are set up that "request" slot fillers of particular types. For morphological/metrical spell-out, the address frames consist of slots for lemmas (or, rather, their lexical pointers) and their diacritical features. A frame is set up for each successive lexical category in surface structure. At the level of segmental spellout, frames are set up that contain slots for morphemes, such as stems, prefixes, and affixes. At the level of phonetic spellout, the frames for addressing syllable programs consist of onset-nucleus-coda triples. One such frame is set up for each peak in metrical spell-out. A preliminary process at this level is cluster composition, in which segments are combined to make phonotactically acceptable onset or coda clusters.

Each level, therefore, requests its own types of fillers: lemmas and diacritical features for morphological/metrical spellout, morphemes for segmental spellout, phonemic segments and syllable constituents for phonetic spellout. Neither syllables nor distinctive features or allophones are used as fillers for the addressing of stored form representations.

The slots-and-fillers theory accounts for the occurrence of speech errors by assuming occasional failures of two control processes: filler selection and filler checkoff. There may, in addition, be errors in the generation of address frames. The theory gives a natural account of the Unit-Similarity Constraint, the observation that target and intrusion in errors are almost always of the same structural level and category. And, closely related to this, it correctly distinguishes between possible and impossible speech errors.

How are fillers made available? By spellout in the slots-and-filler approach. More elaborate accounts of filler activation at the different levels of processing are proposed in the connectionist or activation-spreading theories. Dell's account, in particular, is formal and quantitative enough to predict the kinds and (to some extent) the relative frequencies of word-form errors, both in observational data and in experimentally induced slips of the tongue. It also provides explanations for various other speech-error phenomena, such as lexical bias effects and effects of speaking rate. In this theory, the different kinds of fillers are represented as nodes at different strata or levels of representation—among them a level for word or lemma nodes, a stratum for morpheme nodes, and a phonological stratum where there are nodes for syllables, syllable constituents, and phonemes. Between levels, nodes are connected by arcs along which the activation of a node is spread to nodes at a lower level, but also to nodes at a higher level. This layered network is a theory of the structure of the word-form lexicon and of the way in which it is accessed. Essential for its operation is the parallel activation of structural frames that control the order in which activated nodes are boosted, a central concept from the slots-and-fillers theory. As it stands, the activation-spreading theory does not yet account for the generation of (allo)phones as they appear in the final phonetic plans for syllables.

The final section of this chapter reconsidered the mechanism of serial ordering in phonological encoding. The more ordering there is of segments at the segmental-spellout level, the less need there is for segments to be labeled in terms of their syllabic functions. Such labeling can also be made superfluous by taking the sonority of segments and clusters into account. Maybe a word's syllabic composition appears only at the final, phonetic spellout level.

Chapter 10
Generating Phonetic Plans
for Connected Speech

The generation of connected speech involves more than the mere concatenation of word forms retrieved from memory. Words participate in the larger gesture of the utterance as a whole, and the speaker's phonetic plan expresses this participation in myriad ways.

There are, first, morphological and segmental accommodations of various sorts. A speaker will choose allomorphs that are tuned to the context. In chapter 8 auxiliary reduction was given as an example. Speakers normally prefer *I've bought it* over *I have bought it*, and *he'll go* over *he will go*. They may also cliticize other elements to neighboring words. Small words such as *to* and *of* are reduced and cliticized under certain conditions, as in *I wanna go* or *a bottle'o milk*. Segments may get lost, changed, or added at word boundaries, as in *jus fine* for *just fine* and *got [tʃ]ou* for *got you*. This often goes with resyllabification at word boundaries. In short, the syllable plans retrieved in connected speech often do not conform to the syllabification of the individual words' citation forms. This is because it is a main function of phonological encoding to prepare for fluent connected articulation. Long strings of spelled-out "citation" forms must be translated into fluently pronounceable strings of syllables.

Second, there is the speaker's prosodic planning. Words participate in the overall metrical structure of the utterance; they are grouped in smaller or larger rhythmic phrases. This phrasal togetherness is realized by the manipulation of the loudness, the duration, and the pitch of successive syllables in the utterance, and by the insertion of pauses. The speaker will, in particular, chunk his running speech in intonational phrases, which are the domain for the assignment of pitch contours. In the speaker's phonetic plan, words participate in this melodic line, creating peaks or troughs when they carry pitch accent. The melodic line is, in addition, expressive of attitude and emotion over and above the propositional meaning expressed in the utterance.

The present chapter will review how prosodic plans for connected speech are generated by the speaker, and how these affect the generation of word form. These two aspects of phonetic planning are closely interwoven. It is, for instance, impossible to generate a metrical structure for an utterance as a whole without having access to the syllabicity of the constituent words. In turn, however, the computed metrical parameters for the overall utterance must eventually be realized in the phonetic spellout of the individual words. There is a back-and-forth between stages of word-form spellout and stages of prosodic planning. But very little is known about the processes involved in the phonological encoding of connected speech.

The chapter will begin with a rough sketch of a possible architecture underlying the generation of connected speech (section 10.1). A *Prosody Generator* figures rather centrally in this architecture. It produces incrementally, and in close interaction with word-form spellout, the metrical and intonational parameters of an utterance. These are, we will suppose, eventually fed to the phonetic spellout procedures. After this global sketch of the architecture we will turn to a more detailed treatment of the Prosody Generator and of its metrical and its intonational planning (sections 10.2 and 10.3, respectively). Section 10.4 will discuss how the Prosody Generator affects the processes of segmental and phonetic spellout—in particular, how it mediates in the syllabification and the segmental accommodation of words in connected speech.

10.1   A Sketch of the Planning Architecture

10.1.1   Processing Components
In the "blueprint for the speaker" (figure 1.1), the box labeled "phonological encoding" represents a processor that is supposed to generate phonetic plans for connected speech. Let us begin by filling that box with some further details, as in figure 10.1.

The main input to phonological encoding is the unfolding surface structure. First, its terminal nodes with their diacritical parameters are pointers to word-form addresses. The previous chapter outlined how these word forms are retrieved from memory and transformed into phonetic plans. The main steps in this process—morphological/metrical spellout, segmental spellout, and phonetic spellout, are depicted on the left side of figure 10.1. Second, the surface phrase structure plays an important role in the generation of phonetic plans for connected speech. It is the main input to the *Prosody Generator*—a processing component that computes, among other things, the metrical and intonational properties of the utterance.

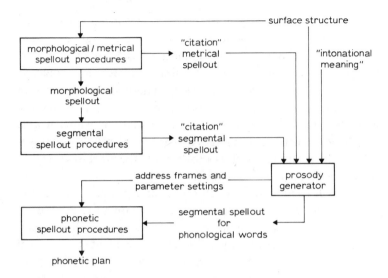

Figure 10.1
An outline of the architecture for the phonological encoding of connected speech.

Additional input to the Prosody Generator is what we called "intonational meaning" in chapter 8: rhetorical intentions, emotions, and attitudes. They cause the Prosody Generator to select certain tunes and tones, and to set key and register. Further essential input is the metrical spellout—i.e., each word's number of syllabic peaks, the location of the one that carries word accent, and the word's diacritical pitch-accent feature (if any). This, in combination with the relevant phrase-structural information, suffices to compute a metrical grid (see subsection 8.2.2) for the utterance, as well as a pitch contour.

   Some aspects of phonological encoding are under executive control. Intonational meaning may perhaps be considered a form of executive control. The speaker can also, within bounds, freely insert pauses and vary the rate of speech. Speech rate is an important factor in phonological encoding. Not only does it affect the size of phonological and intonational phrases; it also has consequences at the segmental and phonetic levels, as we will see. When speech is fast, phonetic spellout is affected across the board. In the previous chapter we saw that Dell (1986) made the fruitful assumption that speaking rate does not affect the speed of spreading activation; it only affects the number of syllable frames to be filled per second. More generally, we will assume that the rate parameter sets the speed of frame production at all levels of processing in phonological encoding. In the terms activation-spreading: It determines how long a "current" node stays current.

Let us now turn to the output of the Prosody Generator. It was argued in the previous chapter that the address frames of phonetic spellout are triggered by metrical spellout, each peak initiating the construction of a syllable frame. This can now be further specified. Figure 10.1 expresses the assumption that the string of peaks is channeled through the Prosody Generator. The phonetic spellout procedure subsequently receives a highly enriched signal. It specifies for each successive syllable frame its duration, its loudness, and its contribution to the pitch contour. It also inserts pauses. Phonetic spellout, then, is not the mere retrieval of a stored phonetic syllable plan; it is also a parametrization of that plan in terms of duration, loudness, and pitch movement.

There is reason to assume that prosody generation also affects segmental spellout. Phrasal boundaries can become determinants of how a word's syllables will be spelled out. A good example is the French phenomenon of *liaison*.* There are many French words in which the final consonant is, as a rule, not pronounced (e.g.,*trè(s), cour(t), peti(t)*). But this final consonant may fail to delete when the next word in connected speech begins with a vowel (as in *très intelligent, court ajournement, petit enfant*). This bears some resemblance to what happens with the word *an* in English. As a rule, its final /n/ is not pronounced, except if the next word begins with a vowel (*a ball, an animal, an intelligent animal*). So far this just shows that the segmental spellout of a word's final syllable may be dependent on the onset of the next word. This in itself is an important property of connected speech; it shows that segmental spellout is not merely a word-internal process but can be dependent on context. The case of liaison demonstrates, in addition, that there are phrasal conditions on this context-dependency. The following examples from Kaisse 1985 will illustrate this:

très intelligent
(very intelligent)

trè(s) intelligent et modeste
(very intelligent and modest)

In the first of these examples there is normal liaison; the /s/ is pronounced. In the second, however, there is no liaison if *très* modifies the whole conjunction *intelligent et modeste*, i.e., if the phrasal composition is (*très*

---

* For an experimental study of liaison see Zwanenburg, Ouweneel, and Levelt 1977.

(*intelligent et modeste*)). The phrase boundary between *très* and *intelligent* apparently blocks liaison in this case.* The precise formulation of the phrasal relations that allow or block liaison is not at issue here (see Kaisse 1985 for a detailed analysis), but only the fact that phrasal relations between subsequent words can, on occasion, affect their segmental spellout. It should, furthermore, be noticed that liaison (or, for that matter, /n/-deletion in *an*) is, within broad limits, independent of speaking rate. They are general phenomena of connected speech.

In summary: The Prosody Generator computes phrasal conditions relevant to segmental spellout, as well as a range of prosodic parameters for phonetic spellout. Before turning to these activities of the Prosody Generator in sections 10.2 through 10.4, we will consider where some further phenomena of connected speech are generated in the framework of figure 10.1.

10.1.2   Casual Speech

It is essential to distinguish between phenomena of connected speech, of casual speech, and of fast speech (Kaisse 1985). Connected speech need neither be casual nor fast. There are general properties of connected speech that arise independent of its speed or its formality. French liaison is such a case, and so are many of the metrical and intonational phenomena to be discussed in this chapter.

Casual speech differs from formal speech, but it need by no means be fast. There is slow casual speech, just as there is fast formal speech. Casual speech is a *register*,[†] a variety of the language, which may have characteristic syntactic, lexical, and phonological properties. A speaker may or may not have several such registers at his or her disposal ("motherese" and "telegraphic speech" are two examples). In casual talk the speaker is biased not only toward using a particular subset of his lexicon (e.g., *cop* rather than *policeman*) but also toward using particular allomorphs (e.g., *I've* rather than *I have*). We will assume that not only the former lexical choices but also the latter allomorphic ones are made during grammatical encoding. In other words, they are indicated at the level of surface structure, and hence are contained in the input to phonological encoding. The surface structure's terminal nodes point to the intended "casual" forms.

---

*But one wonders what Kaisse's data base for this claim was. Native speakers of French seem to have difficulties with the particular example.

[†] This use of the term *register* should not be confused with the notion of pitch level discussed in chapter 8.

Still, some aspects of casual speech have their origins in phonological encoding itself. When a speaker says *lea'me alone*, he is not using a casual allomorph of *leave*, but rather deleting a syllable-final consonant. This is, no doubt, a casual-speech phenomenon that arises at the level of word-form planning. We will, however, assume that phonological phenomena of casual speech are only *indirectly* caused by the casual register. The casual register allows for much faster speech than the formal register, and it is only at high rates that forms like *lea'me alone* arise. The proximal cause of such phonological phenomena is therefore rate, not casuality of register. Hence, the present chapter should concentrate on general phenomena of connected speech and of fast speech only.

10.1.3 Fast Speech

Among the most prominent properties of fast speech are *reduction* and *assimilation*. Reductions can arise at different levels of processing. A speaker can increase his rate of communication by generating short messages, by using a telegraphic register, and/or by accessing reduced (casual) allomorphs. All this is planned above the level of phonological encoding.

A speaker can also gain speed by reducing small unaccented words, such as pronouns and prepositions: *Give'm attention, Think o'money.* Such reductions may originate at the level of segmental spellout, following some very general rules of reduced spellout. These rules are sensitive to the character of immediately adjacent elements (e.g., *a bottle o'milk* but not *a bottle o'applejuice*) and to prosodic phrase structure (e.g., *Think o'money* but not *What are you thinking o'? Money?*).

Speed can also be gained by reducing segments across the board. A speaker can, for instance, reduce all word-initial unstressed vowels, as in *p'tato* or *t'mato* (Zwicky 1972). This depends neither on adjacent words nor on phrase structure. There are, however, restrictions on the kinds of new clusters that arise. For instance, *m'ternal* and *r'member* are unlikely reductions (Zwicky 1972; Kaisse 1985). These restrictions are, however, not phonotactic in the sense that only well-formed onset clusters are allowed; /pt/ and /tm/ are ill formed as syllable onsets in English. It is likely, therefore, that this kind of reduction takes place *after* the syllable plans are addressed. The correct syllables ([pə], [tə]) are addressed, but these unstressed syllables are given such minimal settings for their duration and loudness parameters that their vowels just about disappear in articulation. Why such extreme minimal settings are not possible for [mə] or [ri] is unclear, but it probably has to do with the high-sonorous onsets of these syllables.

To sum up: There can be reduction at all three spellout levels. The surface-structure input can induce morphological spellout to address reduced allomorphs, segmental spellout can generate reduced forms following general structure-dependent rules, and phonetic spellout can be subject to extreme parameter settings for the duration and loudness of a syllable.

Assimilation is a quite general phenomenon in connected speech, but it spreads wider in fast speech than in slow speech. It involves the change of some segment under the influence of another one, and the change makes the two speech sounds more similar. The phrase *ten books*, for example, is pronounced as [tɛm bʊks], where /n/ assimilates to the adjacent /b/ by adopting its bilabiality feature. Most forms of assimilation are to be located at the segmental spellout level. There can be substantial structure dependency in assimilation, as is testified by the much studied case of *wanna* (the assimilation of *want* and *to*). Assimilation is possible in *Who do you want to (wanna) succeed*, but not in *Who do you want to succeed you?* (Dogil 1984). (See also example 9 below.) The dependency on phrasal relations, however, is quite different for different kinds of assimilation. This will be taken up again in section 10.4.

Assimilation should be distinguished from *coarticulation*. Adjacent speech sounds interact because of the physiology and the mechanics of articulation. These interactions become more intense at higher speech rates; they depend on the time allotted to the articulation of syllables. These parameters are set at the phonetic spellout level. Coarticulation, therefore, occurs at the same level as the vowel reduction in *p'tato*, discussed above.

Reduction and assimilation often combine with *cliticization*, which is also widespread in connected speech but which is especially prominent when talk is fast. Cliticization consists of adjoining reduced materials to immediately adjacent words. The assimilation *wanna* above is such a case. Cliticization is necessary where a reduced morpheme has no syllabicity of its own. The allomorph *-ve* in *I've* and *you've* is nonsyllabic; it generates no peak in metrical spellout. It cannot be a free-standing word. It must, therefore, attach to the preceding word during segmental spellout. The result is a *phonological word*. The domain of segmental spellout is the phonological word (Nespor and Vogel 1986). The Phrase *I've* is not spelled out for *I* and *have* and subsequently reduced. It is, rather, the phonological word *I've* that is spelled out (as /aɪv/). By and large, each word form pointed to by the surface structure is a phonological word, with nonsyllabic allomorphs as a main exception. In addition, new phonological words can arise during phonological encoding, with cliticization as a main case. The Prosody Generator computes these new phonological words on the basis of phrasal configurations in surface structure and syllabicity information from metrical spellout. It can also decide to further reduce and adjoin elements, even if they are both syllabic. The above assimilation *wanna* is such a case; it has become a single phonological word, and it is spelled out as such during segmental spellout.

These few remarks on fast speech have served to provisionally localize some major phenomena of fast speech, such as reduction, assimilation, and cliticization, in the framework of figure 10.1. More definite conclusions about the origins of these phenomena during fluent speech await thorough process analyses. Only when we understand the structure that controls the generation of connected speech will we be able to propose a more definite partitioning of the system.

10.1.4   Shifts

Another phenomenon to be localized in the scheme of figure 10.1 was already touched upon in chapter 7 in the discussion of Garrett's (1982) example:

(1) Did you stay up late vEry last night?

Garrett called this kind of speech error, where a word jumps over one or two adjacent ones, a *shift*. Garrett's view of shifts, with which I concur, is that they are caused not at the level of grammatical encoding but during phonological encoding. Shifts ignore the syntactic-category constraints that are so characteristic of word exchanges. The interchanged words in example 1, *very* and *late*, are of different syntactic categories, and so are *it* and *making* in the following example (from Stemberger 1985a):

(2) We tried it mAking ... mAking it with gravy.

Here it is a closed-class word (*it*) that is anticipated; an open-class one is jumped over. Garrett observed that closed-class elements (such as pronouns, prepositions, and articles) predominate in shifts, and this also holds for Stemberger's data.

Where can shifts be located in the framework of figure 10.1? My suggestion is in the transition from surface structure to morphological/metrical spellout. As surface structure is incrementally produced, its terminal pointers become available "from left to right." They will be fillers for successive address frames, and each completed address will occasion the retrieval of an item's morphological/metrical form information. Even if the surface structure's terminal elements are generated in impeccable order, a "later" element may happen to be spelled out more rapidly than an earlier element.

One would expect such anticipations especially in the case of highly fre-quent words, whose forms are more easily accessed than the forms of rare words. Stemberger (1985a) confirmed this prediction. It should, in addi-tion, be noted that closed-class words are very high in frequency, which accounts for their preponderance in shifts.

One consequence of order reversals in morphological/metrical spellout is that there is a concomitant reversal of order in the metrical patterns received by the Prosody Generator. This predicts that a shifted word's pitch accent will stick to it, and that is what one observes in examples 1 and 2. Garrett (1982), Cutler (1980a), and Stemberger (1985a) observed and confirmed this property of shifts. It contrasts with errors in grammatical encoding, which, as we saw in subsection 7.1.2, usually show stranding of pitch accent.

Misordering at the level of morphological/metrical spellout can prob-ably also account for affix shifts, as in the following (from Garrett 1982):

(3) I had forgot about*en* that

Here the affix of *forgot-ten* jumped over *about*, to which it attached. Presumably, the two morphological spellout procedures for *forgotten* and *about* ran more or less in parallel. The morpheme *about* became available just after the stem *forgot*, and just before its suffix *ten*. If this account is anywhere near correct, however, it is still surprising that such sublexical shift errors are not much more frequent in fluent speech.

This completes the initial sketch of the phonological encoding architec-ture underlying the generation of connected speech. The following three sections will deal more specifically with the workings of the Prosody Generator.

10.2   The Generation of Rhythm

The rhythm of connected speech appears in the alternation of more or less stressed syllables and the insertion of pauses. There are several ways in which a speaker can stress a syllable. One is to make it louder than neighboring syllables, another is to stretch it in time, and still another is to give it an accenting pitch movement. Though independently variable, these three tend to go together. It makes sense, therefore, to begin by considering the generation of rhythm at a fairly abstract level, namely as the generation of a pattern of stresses and pauses. This abstract pattern was called *metrical structure* in chapter 8.

Let us recapitulate what kinds of metrical structure are built by the speaker. There are, first, the words, with their internal stress patterns. The basic stress patterns are retrieved from memory during metrical spellout. One of a word's syllables is marked for word accent; it will attract pitch accent, if there is to be any. In addition to retrieved words, the Prosody Generator will have to deal with other phonological words created by cliticization. Second, there are phonological phrases to be built. They can be seen either as "absolute" prosodic units—successive stretches of speech leading up to lexical (nonpronominal) heads-of-phrase (Nespor and Vogel 1986)—or as "relative" units leading up to stronger or weaker break options (Selkirk 1984a). Third, there are intonational phrases. One could say that they run from one *actual* prosodic break (i.e., a *taken* break option) to the next. These phrases are the domain for the assignment of meaningful pitch contours. There is, finally, the utterance as a whole, which may have utterance-initial or utterance-final metrical properties relevant to turn-taking, such as anacruses or utterance-final lengthenings.

A main principle for a processing theory of rhythm is that, at all these levels, production should take place *incrementally*. This means that the metrical pattern should be created as surface phrase structure and morphological/metrical spellout become available. The Prosody Generator should not buffer large amounts of input in order to make current decisions dependent on later materials. It should, rather, be able to work with very little lookahead. In the following we will successively consider the metrical planning of (phonological) words, of phonological phrases, and of intonational phrases from this incremental point of view. We will then turn to aspects of timing, i.e., the duration of segments and syllables in the contexts of words, phrases, sentences, and larger units, and finally to the issue of isochrony, i.e., the presumed regular temporal spacing of stressed syllables in the connected speech of "stress-timed" languages.

10.2.1 Phonological Words

In speakers of languages (such as English) that have limited lexical productivity, the basic or "citation" metrical pattern of most words is stored in the mental lexicon. This metrical pattern is one of the first features to be spelled out in word-form access. The Prosody Generator accepts it as the basis for further metrical processing. If the lexical pointer to the form address has the diacritical feature "pitch accent", this information is also transmitted to the Prosody Generator. A first task, then, is to translate this information as an extra beat on the peak that carries word accent. This procedure is exemplified in the following, which depicts the pitch accenting of *California*:

(4) **Basic metrical grid**   **Pitch-accented grid**

```
                                          x
              x                           x
      x   x                       x   x
      x  x  x    x        →       x  x  x    x
      Ca li for nia               Ca li for nia
```

In this example the word *California* is written out for convenience only; the adjustment of the metrical pattern can be made before the individual syllables have been spelled out.

In subsection 10.2.2 I will argue that this accenting operation needs no lookahead whatsoever—i.e., that it can be done incrementally, as new words are metrically spelled out. This is slightly different for operations that prevent stress clashes. In chapter 8 the example phrase *abstract art* was given, which is pronounced with alternating stress—*Abstract Art*—in spite of the fact that the "citation" accentuation of the adjective is *abstrАct*. A "beat movement" (Selkirk 1984a) prevents a stress clash between two adjoining syllables. The same type of beat movement can be observed in the phrase *sixteen dollars*. The stored accent pattern for the constituent words are *sixtEEn* and *dOllars*, but in the phrase there is alternating stress: *sIxteen dOllars*. This movement operation is depicted in the following:

(5) **Beat movement**   (i)   (ii)

```
              x    x                    x        x
      x   x     x   x            x   x     x   x
      x   x     x   x    →       x   x     x   x
      six teen dol lars          six teen dol lars
```

Beat movement does require some minimal amount of lookahead. It is of two sorts. First, since the condition for the shift is a threatening succession of two stressed syllables in subsequent words, the metrical pattern of the second word must be at hand in order to effectuate a beat movement in the first one. This requires that the Prosody Generator minimally buffer the metrical patterns of two subsequent words (but see subsection 10.2.2). Of course, it does not always do so. But if it doesn't (because of a high speech rate, or for some other reason), there will be no beat movement. Second, there are phrasal restrictions on beat movement. If the utterance to be developed is

(6) Dimes I have sixteen, dollars just one

there will be no beat movement. It is prevented by the phrase boundary following *sixteen*. This shows that the input for the beat-movement operation is not only the metrical structure of two consecutive words but also phrasal information. The latter information is quite local in nature, however. The only relevant feature is whether or not there is a phrasal boundary following the first word of the pair (and if so, of what kind it is).

The Prosody Generator can also create new phonological words by cliticization. Unstressed closed-class words are easily cliticized to adjoining open-class words, and the tendency to cliticize increases with the rate of speech. The sentence *They have it* will normally be uttered with *it* cliticized to the lexical head of phrase *have*—i.e., with *have-it* as a single phonological word. The phonological word is the domain of syllabification. The phonetic spellout for *have-it* will not consist of the syllables [hæv] and [ɪt], but of [hæ] and [vɪt].

Can cliticizations be incrementally generated? That is, can the Prosody Generator produce these phonological words without lookahead? Let us begin with the dominant case of *enclitics* (cases where the "little" word follows the "big" word to which it adjoins). The above *have-it* is an example. In English, most enclitics derive from unstressed monosyllabic closed-class words, particularly pronouns, auxiliaries, and particles. But there are two cases to be distinguished:

(i) Cliticization is, of course, obligatory or necessary when the "little" element is nonsyllabic. This is generally the case for cliticized auxiliaries. It was suggested above that auxiliary forms such as *'ve* and *'ll* are allomorphs of the full forms. These allomorphs are already referred to by appropriate lexical pointers in surface structure, and are directly addressed at the level of morphological/metrical spellout. The metrical pattern of such an element is empty, since these morphemes have no syllabic peak. The only thing to be done by the Prosody Generator is to add the empty element to the previous nonempty one. Having access to the developing surface-structural information, the Prosody Generator recognizes the empty element as the metrical realization of a particular lexical pointer. It is in this way that phonological words such as *I've* and *you'll* arise initially. At the next stage, the Prosody Generator must occasion the correct segmental spellouts of these prosodic words. The recognition of such nonsyllabic elements, and the subsequent decision to adjoin them to their predecessors, is obviously a completely local affair; there is no relevant "later" information. This conclusion leaves unimpeded the possibility that, during grammatical encoding, the choice of such an allomorph might depend on the following syntactic context. Compare, for instance, the sentences 7 and 8, which are derived from an example in Pullum and Zwicky 1988:

(7) I know where it's located

(8) I know where it is

In sentence 7, the nonsyllabic allomorph is generated. However, sentence 8 requires the full form; *I know where it's* is ill formed. This difference suggests that later context can be relevant for the choice of allomorph.*

(ii) When the "little" word is syllabic and can stand alone as a phonological word, the Prosody Generator can still cliticize it to the foregoing "big" word. A much-studied case is the infinitival particle *to*. It is easily cliticized in a sentence like the following:

(9) Who do you want to see?

　　　/wɒntə/

　　　/wɒnə/

Here the new phonological word *want-to* is formed, which becomes spelled-out as /wɒn-tə/ and, by further reduction, as /wɒnə/. This kind of *to*-cliticization is quite general (consider *ought-to*, *used-to*, and *supposed-to*, all of which show resyllabification, testifying to their status as phonological words). Still, the Prosody Generator cannot leave it at completely local decisions, i.e., decisions involving only the pair $X + to$. This is apparent from example 10, where the same pair, *want to*, cannot be adjoined:

(10) Who do you want to see this memo?

Examples 9 and 10 are from the work of Pullum and Zwicky (1988), who present a concise review of the extensive literature on *to*-contraction. The upshot of this literature is that there are phrase-structural conditions on the cliticization of infinitival *to*. The Prosody Generator must refer to surface structure in order to decide whether these conditions are fulfilled. However, the main question for our present purposes is whether these are local conditions or whether they can involve much later parts of surface structure. Pullum and Zwicky conclude their review of the evidence with the statement that "a very small portion of the surface syntactic context, local in terms of both adjacency and bracketing ... is relevant for the determination of whether a given word sequence can have the contracted pronunciation." In other words, little lookahead is required for the Prosody Generator to cliticize these structure-dependent cases. It should be added that for other varieties of encliticization, as well, there is no convincing counterevidence against this locality assumption.

The situation is only slightly different for *procliticization*, where the "little" word is adjoined to the following "big" word. This is far less widespread in English. The pronoun *it* in subject position can, in certain

---

*Because *is* is an auxiliary in sentence 7 only, there is also a *local* syntactic difference.

dialects of English, adjoin to the following auxiliary or main verb, as in *'t is winter* or *'t went away*. And there are dialects of English in which one can adjoin an indefinite article to the head noun (as in *anapple*, which then becomes syllabified as [ə-næpl]). Utterance-initial conjunctions, as in *And go now*, can also procliticize: *Ngonow*. These kinds of cliticization, of course, require a lookahead of one word, but probably no more. The phrase-structural condition on procliticization is probably just the absence of a major phrase boundary right after the potential clitic. Cliticization blocks in a sentence such as *John, who hated it, went away*, where [twɛnt] cannot be formed.* The one-word metrical and structural lookahead required here is the same as the minimal lookahead required for beat movement. And if this lookahead fails (for instance, because the "big" word is not retrieved in time), there will be no procliticization. The speaker will say *it – went away*, not *'t – went away*.

In conclusion: The speaker can generate phonological words incrementally. The phrase-structural and metrical conditions for cliticization are, it seems, locally available; a lookahead of no more than one word is required.

Two further closing remarks should be made on the generation of phonological words. The first one concerns the distinction made above between reduced auxiliaries and clitics of other kinds. Auxiliary clitics, such as *'ve* and *'ll*, it was argued, are indicated at the surface-structure level. Their lexical pointers have a diacritic feature that selects for the reduced allomorph. The reduction of most other small elements, such as *to* and it, was not treated as allomorphic; it was considered purely a matter for the Prosody Generator. Why not include the auxiliaries in this more general "late" account of reduction and cliticization? Kaisse (1985) gave various reasons for giving a lexical account of auxiliary reduction. A first one is that the reduced forms of auxiliaries are irregular, and therefore are probably stored as such. Take, for instance, the reduced forms of *will* and *would*: *'ll* and *'d*. No other English *w*-words reduce in this manner. (It would yield something like *'ch* for *which*.) A second reason is that there are slight distributional differences between the full and reduced forms of auxiliaries, testify-

---

* In addition to the phrase boundary after *it*, there are two other factors that might preclude cliticization here. First, *it* is not the subject of *went away*. Second, there is no c-command relation between *it* and *went*. A surface-structure constituent *A* c-commands a constituent *B* if, of every constituent of which *A* is a proper part, *B* is also a proper part, but without *B*'s being a proper part of *A*. Kaisse (1985) argues for the role of c-command conditions on cliticization. Both factors, however, are strictly local in surface structure.

ing to their lexical status. One can say *Where's the lions?*, but there is no correct slow-speech equivalent *Where is the lions?*

The other remark concerns the difference between inflections and clitics. If a reduced auxiliary is treated as a spelled-out morpheme that becomes cliticized, why not treat inflections in just the same way? To produce the form *walked*, there should be two lexical pointers in surface structure: one for the stem *walk* and one for the past inflection *-d*. The Prosody Generator would then encliticize the latter to the former, and induce the regular segmental spellout /wɔkt/. This would indeed be very similar to the production of *I've*. When inflections are treated as just a kind of closed-class elements, one also has an easier account of inflectional-shift errors, such as Garrett's example *I had forgot about*en *that*. The inflection *en* shifts, just as any closed class element can shift. Still, there are strong reasons for distinguishing inflections from clitics. These reasons are reviewed by Zwicky and Pullum (1983). Among them are the following: (i) Clitics are not very "choosy" about their hosts, whereas inflections are. The clitic auxiliary *'s* can attach to any kind of host, not only to a subject noun or pronoun. Here it adjoins, for instance, to a preposition: *The person I was talking to's going to be angry with me.* Inflectional suffixes, in contrast, attach only to a specific host category. Plural *s*, for instance, attaches only to noun stems. (ii) There is much irregular inflection (*give – gave*) but no irregular cliticization. (iii) Clitics can attach to other clitics, as in *I'd've done it*, but inflections cannot attach to inflections (except in speech errors such as *people read the backses of boxes*). These and other reasons make it necessary to distinguish carefully between the etiologies of inflections and those of clitics.

10.2.2 Phonological Phrases, the Grid, and Incremental Production
As the surface structure unfolds "from left to right," the speaker incrementally constructs phonological words. Can he also incrementally group these words into larger prosodic phrases—in particular, into phonological and intonational phrases? In this subsection I will argue that this is almost always possible, in spite of a theoretical counterargument. The speaker can normally construct these phrases without much "preview" of later surface structure. Let us begin with phonological phrases.

Chapter 8 presented a strict view and a more lenient view of phonological phrases. On the strict view (Nespor and Vogel 1986), an utterance is a concatenation of phonological phrases. They are, roughly, defined as stretches of speech leading up to and including a lexical head of phrase. The more relativistic conception (Selkirk 1984a) is that the phonological phrase is a stretch of speech leading up to a weaker or stronger "break option." Let us consider the incrementality issue from both points of view. We will begin with the strict view, and consider example 3 of chapter 8, repeated here as example 11:

(11) //The detective /1 remembered //2 that the station /3 could be entered /4 from the other side as well //5.

All single and double slashes indicate phonological phrase boundaries.

As a first approximation, the incremental construction of a phonological phrase by the Prosody Generator can be straightforward:

Main Procedure Concatenate phonological words until one appears that is or contains a lexical head of phrase (i.e., head of NP, VP, or AP). Terminate the phrase right after that phonological word, except if the conditions for the Coda Procedure apply.

Ignoring for the moment the Coda Procedure, we can observe that this Main Procedure gives the correct result for positions /1 through /4: *detective*, *remembered*, *station*, and *entered* are lexical phrase heads. The head-of-phrase function is locally indicated in the developing surface structure (see subsection 5.1.3). The procedure requires no preview.

There is a problem, however, for the last phonological phrase. Its lexical head is *side*, but the phrase continues till after *as well*. How does the Prosody Generator know that the phrase should not be ended after *side*? Should it, for instance, know that there is no further lexical head of phrase in the offing? That would be a "preview" requirement.

That, however, is not necessary. The local surface-structural information (i.e., just between *side* and *as*) tells the Prosody Generator that (i) the current PP is finished and (ii) the new phrase is not a VP, a PP, an AP, or an NP. This suffices to add any newly created phonological words to the current phonological phrase. And it involves, again, strictly local information. The more general formulation can be the following:

Coda Procedure If a phonological word containing a lexical head of phrase completes that major constituent but is followed by a minor constituent boundary (i.e., not a VP, a PP, an AP, or an NP boundary), then add the following phonological words to the current phonological phrase until no more words follow or until a major constituent begins.

In sentence 11, this procedure will add the minor constituent *as well* to the current phrase *from the other side*. It will, in fact, complete it, since no more words follow. But the speaker might have continued with, say, *through a gate*. In that case he would have had to round off the current phrase after *well* and begin a new one, because *through* opens a major (PP) constituent.

The Main and Coda Procedures guarantee incrementality of phonological phrase construction for most cases. One remaining problem concerns "nonlexical" heads of major constituents—in particular, pronoun heads of NPs. What, for instance, if example 11 had ended as follows?

/ 4 from the other side of it //5

The coda procedure does not apply here, because a new major constituent begins after *side*: the PP *of it*. Still, *of it* cannot be an independent phonological phrase, because its NP has (and is) a "nonlexical" head: the closed-class word *it*. So, it is to be added to the current phrase. But to decide this, the Prosody Generator should be able to "preview" the upcoming nonlexical head *it*. There are at least two possible reactions to this problem. The first one is to consider *side-of-it* as an encliticization, i.e., as a single phonological word. In that case the Main Procedure will build the correct phonological phrase. The phonological word *side-of-it* contains a lexical head of phrase (*side*); hence, the boundary follows that phonological word. Whether this solution suffices remains to be seen. It may, in particular, not be the case that encliticization of such phrases materializes in slow speech. A second reaction could be this: Major constituents with nonlexical heads tend to have this head in first or second position (*I saw it*, or *I heard of it*), because pronouns do not take complements to the left. The preview required, therefore, spans no more than two closed-class words, i.e., two syllable peaks.

Our provisional conclusion, therefore, is that phonological phrases can be incrementally produced. No substantial buffering of surface structure is required. The phrases can be produced as the surface structure unfolds "from left to right."

Let us now turn to the "lenient" view of phonological phrases. It should be remembered (see chapter 8) that in Selkirk's (1984a) theoretical framework the phonological phrase is only a derived notion. What really matters is the distribution of "silent beats" over the between-word positions of the metrical grid. When two words are separated by many beats, one can speak of a phonological phrase boundary. The number of silent beats between words is determined by a variety of factors, which we called "break options." According to the theory, the main break options are the end of an intonational phrase; the end of a sentence constituent; the end of a multiword NP, VP, PP, or AP; after a lexical head of NP, VP, or AP; and after a content or open-class word (see subsection 8.2.2). If each of these factors contributes one silent beat when it applies, the sentence *Mary finished her Russian novel* displays the following distribution of silent beats:

(12) Mary xxxx finished xx her Russian x novel xxxxx

The size of the beat strings determines whether particular metrical phenomena can take place. For instance, stress clashes between adjoining words will be prevented (by beat movement) only if they are separated by no or few beats. The size of the strings also determines the use of various boundary markers, such as pitch movements, pauses, glottal stops, and syllable lengthening. (For a systematic study of these boundary markers in reading that strongly confirms the relevance of the just-mentioned factors, see de Rooy 1979.)

The issue of incrementality now involves two questions: (i) How much lookahead is needed for the Prosody Generator to insert the correct number of silent beats between one word and the next? (ii) How much lookahead is needed to compute each new word's stress level? Let us take up these questions in this order.

The number of silent beats inserted after a word depends on the number of prevailing break options. For each of the options we should, therefore, ask: Can it be locally recognized, or does it need structural lookahead? The least obvious factor in this respect is the first one, end of intonational phrase. We will return to it in subsection 10.2.3, where we will conclude that its status as a factor is circular. The end of a sentence constituent—i.e., a constituent immediately dominated by S (subject phrase, predicate phrase) —is locally given in surface structure. This also holds for the end of a multiword NP, VP, AP, or PP; the Prosody Generator must remember only that the phrase was multiword. Lexical heads of NP, VP, and AP are also immediately recognizable as such as the surface structure unfolds, and so are content-word lemmas. This means that, at the end of each word, the Prosody Generator can, without preview of later surface structure, determine which of these conditions are fulfilled. The answer to the first question is, therefore, that the distribution of silent beats can be incrementally computed.

The second question requires discussion of the metrical processes involved in the generation of a metrical grid. Take beat movement, demonstrated in example 5 with the generation of *sIxteen dOllars*. According to Nespor and Vogel (1986), the domain of beat movement is the phonological phrase; i.e., there will be no beat movement if the two words are separated by a phonological phrase boundary, as in sentence 6. In terms of grids, a separation by two or more silent beats will probably suffice to block beat movement. The Prosody Generator can compute the beat movement for the first word if it knows this word's stress distribution, the number of silent beats following the word, and the second word's stress distribution. Since the silent beats are computed without lookahead, the only preview required is the second word's metrical form. Can it be known with just a one-word lookahead? It can in most cases, though it is theoretically not obvious. The case would be trivial if beat movement were to depend only on the "citation" metrical patterns of the two words involved. In that case, a preview of the next word's metrical spellout would suffice for the Prosody Generator to take a decision on beat movement. But according to Selkirk's theory, beat movement applies to materials that are already metrically processed to some extent, not to the spelled-out base forms. If this preprocessing is a condition for beat movement, one should first find out how much lookahead the preprocessing requires.

This preprocessing, called *text-to-grid-alignment* by Selkirk, involves various kinds of stress-assignment rules. For our present purposes we can refrain from reviewing most of them. With only two exceptions, they concern the composition of the citation forms of words, including word compounds. We are, however, assuming that the native English speaker has these basic patterns stored for all words he uses, except the extremely infrequent ones. A speaker can probably apply the rules when he forms a brand-new word, but normally he won't have to refer to them in his incremental phonological encoding. The two exceptions are the "Pitch-Accent Prominence Rule" and the "Nuclear-Stress rule." Can these rules be applied incrementally?

The *Pitch-Accent Prominence Rule* says that a pitch-accented syllable should be more prominent than any syllable that is not associated with pitch accent. Moreover, this rule overrides any other metrical rule.

This latter addition makes the rule very simple to apply in incremental fashion. When the Prosody Generator receives the basic metrical pattern of a pitch-accented word, it will process the diacritical pitch-accent feature by adding one or more extra beats to the syllable carrying word accent. This was already discussed (see example 4). In order to apply the rule correctly, the Prosody Generator must take care of two things. First, so many extra beats have to be given to the pitch-accented syllable that it is more prominent than any earlier non-pitch-accented word in the current intonational phrase. This requires a record of previous stress assignments, but no lookahead. Second, any following word in the phrase that has no pitch accent should be given less prominence. That is what "overriding" means. But at the moment of assigning pitch accent, the Prosody Generator need not know these following words. It will implement this requirement as further words are received for processing. In short, pitch accent can be assigned on a purely incremental basis.

The *Nuclear-Stress Rule* says: Assign primary stress to the last nonanaphoric word in a major category or sentence (at least, this is one of its many formulations).

Selkirk's (1984a) treatment of this rule in terms of metrical grids was discussed in chapter 8 above. In each major phrase, so many beats are added to the accented syllable of the last word that it becomes the most stressed word in the phrase. Take the sentence *The sixteen dollars were lost.* After beat movement on *sixteen*, the grid looks like this:

```
(13)       x        x           x
           x   x     x   x   x   x
       x   x   x     x   x   x   x
       the six teen dol lars suf ficed
```

The subject NP, *the sixteen dollars*, has *dollars* as its last word. To have primary stress in the phrase (i.e., more stress than *sixteen*), it needs one additional best:

```
(14)                 x
           x         x           x
           x   x     x x     x   x
       x   x   x     x x     x   x
       the six teen dollars suf ficed
```

But the Nuclear-Stress Rule will apply again on the level of the sentence as a whole. Here *sufficed* is the last word of the constituent. It needs two extra beats to surpass the stress of *dollars*. The end result is this:

```
(15)                             x
                     x           x
           x         x           x
           x   x     x   x   x   x
       x   x   x     x   x   x   x
       the six teen dol lars suf ficed
```

What does the Prosody Generator have to know in order to apply the Nuclear-Stress Rule? Can it generate the correct metrical pattern just going from left to right without knowledge of later surface structure? It can in the following way: In going from left to right, the Generator checks whether each word completes a major constituent. If a word does so, its stress is increased just enough to surpass the stress of all other words in the phrase. This, of course, requires a record of previous stress assignments in the phrase. But it requires no preview. The nuclear stress on *dollars* is independent of what follows. It is, in particular, independent of the later nuclear stress on *sufficed*. But the Prosody Generator must keep a record of previous surface structure. When it gets to *sufficed* and notices that it completes a sentence, it must know where the sentence began, since *sufficed* is to be given more stress than any other element in the sentence. In short: The incremental assignment of nuclear stress requires memory of phrase structure and of previous stress assignments, but no lookahead.

One complication (which doesn't affect this conclusion) is the assignment of pitch accent. If the phrase doesn't contain a pitch accent, the procedure goes as outlined. If there is a pitch accent, the rule doesn't apply; it is "overridden." If there are two or more pitch accents and the phrase-final word has a pitch accent, then the Nuclear-Stress Rule applies again, and it gives the phrase-final pitch-accented element the highest prominence.

It is, therefore, safe to say that the metrical "preprocessing" does not require lookahead, but only memory. Thus, beat movement can always apply with one-word lookahead, i.e., after the next word's "preprocessed" metrical pattern has been computed. And this preprocessing requires no lookahead. Beat Movement is one of three "grid euphony rules," which create the alternating rhythm in speech. We will leave the other two rules, Beat Addition and Beat Deletion, untouched here. They do not change the picture, as they require no more preview than the stress level of the next word's first syllable.

However, potential "domino" effects must be discussed. Consider Beat Movement again. The current word's stress pattern shifts because of the next word's. But then, couldn't the current word's adapted stress pattern affect the previous word's? Theoretically, it could. For example:

(16) sixtEEn abstrAct pAIntings →

      sixtEEn Abstract pAIntings →

      sIxteen Abstract pAIntings

Here, the clash with *pAIntings* requires *abstrAct* to become *Abstract*. This, however, causes a stress clash with *sixtEEn*, which requires it to change to *sIxteen*. And indeed, this would be the "ideal delivery" of this phrase. This ideal delivery requires a two-word lookahead. But there is, of course, no theoretical upper limit on the domino effect; *any* amount of lookahead may be required. What is the psycholinguistic consequence?

What we called "preprocessing" (i.e., the assignment of pitch accent and nuclear stress to basic word patterns) is not subject to the domino effect. A speaker can always do this incrementally, without any previewing. Making speech really rhythmic, however, means applying the euphony rules, and this does theoretically require infinite lookahead. In practice, however, cases like example 16 are rare—it is, actually, pretty hard to construct four- or five-word cases. With a one-word preview, the speaker can almost always come up with the correct rhythmic result. Whether he actually does is another issue, to which we will return in subsection 10.2.5.

When there is good reason for the speaker to approach "ideal delivery" of the utterance, he will presumably buffer more than a single word, so that cases such as example 16 will be recognized in due time. The conjecture can be made that one consequence of using a formal register is to increase the "window" or buffer of phonological encoding. We should, in addition, predict that, in fast speech, rhythm rules are the first to be disturbed, leaving the assignment of pitch accent and nuclear stress intact.

10.2.3 Intonational Phrases

"Break options" were mentioned in the discussion of the assignment of silent beats in the previous subsection. The speaker may or may not express silent beats, depending on register and rate of speech. The expression can take the form of lengthening a phrase-final syllable, inserting a small pause, making a pitch movement, and so on. But in all these cases the speaker basically continues; he does not really take a break. When the speaker does take a break, however, he factually completes an intonational phrase. This means that he selects an appropriate nuclear tone, and that after the break (which is usually followed by a pause of more than 200 milliseconds) he resets the baseline pitch to begin a new intonational phrase (if any). The former point will be taken up in section 10.3, the latter in the next chapter. The question here is: What determines whether a speaker will take a break option?

The break decision is, to some extent, under the speaker's executive control. The speaker may want to be highly intelligible to his listener(s), so he may speak slowly in short, high-keyed intonational phrases. He will then take every major break option to complete an intonational phrase. (The *reductio ad absurdum* of this speaking style can be observed in stewardesses' announcements during airline trips.) This freedom in taking break options immediately defeats all efforts to give a principled linguistic definition of intonational phrases (see also Ladd 1986). Intonational phrases are, to some extent, pragmatic devices under the speaker's intentional control.

There is, second, a general relation with speaking rate. Fewer options are taken at high rates than at low rates. A speaker concatenates much more in fast speech than in slow speech. In fact, the speeding up of speech is due largely to the leaving out of pauses. In addition, there is apparently a tendency to avoid making very short or very long intonational phrases, i.e., to distribute breaks evenly (Grosjean, Grosjean, and Lane 1979; Gee and Grosjean 1983). The reason for this tendency is unclear, but together with the just-mentioned relation to speaking rate it implies that speakers prefer to make intonational phrases within a particular range of duration. An intonational phrase should ideally span some 2 seconds and range between 1 and 3 seconds. Deese's (1984) data on spontaneous speech are in agreement with these estimates. The following example, taken from his table 6–5, gives the pause durations between intonational phrases and the duration of each phrase in milliseconds:

(17)

	1,249		1,831

.../ 1,580 /before they discover that/ 499 /the bankers and the landowners/

                       1,593
680 /are going to take all the profits/

                       3,060
230 /and then insist that the Holbrook family owes them/

          1,910   1,535
510 /so the idyll of farm life/ 420 /proves an illusion as well/

Such a tendency to equal durations (if it can be substantiated for spontaneous speech at all) may have its *raison d'être* in articulatory motor programming, either in the size of the Articulatory Buffer, or in the convenient amount of air to be inhaled, or in both.

A third set of factors are syntactic. Speakers usually break when they reach a sentence boundary. Taking pauses and change of pitch as evidence, Deese (1984) found that 76 percent of the sentence boundaries in his large sample of spontaneous speech were prosodically marked. Still, it should be noticed that an intonational phrase *can* cross a sentence boundary. Chapter 8 above mentioned the boundaries of parentheticals, tag questions, nonrestrictive relative clauses as attractors of intonational breaks. They are all sentential constituents. Another syntactic factor discussed in chapter 8 is the succession of three or more constituents of the same type (*the barbecue, the charcoal, and the icebox*), which invites "listing intonation"—i.e., one intonational phrase per constituent.

A fourth factor is semantic in origin. A speaker may be inclined to break shortly after a very prominent pitch accent. The latter will then become the nucleus of the intonational phrase.

A final factor is, one could say, an "operational" one: the availability of new surface-structure fragments. If, at a potential break point, no further surface materials have become available for phonological encoding, the speaker must take the option in order to gain processing time. The lack of new ammunition may have different causes, as we have seen; there may be planning trouble at the message level, or at the level of grammatical encoding.

It should now be clear why I have called the intonational-phrase boundary a "circular" factor as a phonological break option: The decision to break *creates* the intonational-phrase boundary; it is in no way determined by it.

10.2.4 Metrical Structure and Phonic Durations

Metrical structure reflects itself, in part, in varying durations of segments, syllables, words, phrases, and pauses. The relation is not a simple one. A stressed syllable tends to be longer than an unstressed one, but a phrase-final unstressed syllable may also be stretched. Strings of silent beats in metrical structure will probably correspond to pauses, but Selkirk (1984a) suggests a more complicated relation: that the number of silent positions following a word will reflect itself in the sum of the last syllable's lengthening and the following pause. Thus, both metrical stress and silence may be mapped onto syllable length. The Prosody Generator should compute durational parameters for successive syllables and for the pauses between them. These parameters should be fed to the phonetic spellout mechanism, which generates the phonetic plans for successive syllables. Little is known about the computation of these temporal phonetic parameters, but a host of empirical studies, especially on syllable duration, are relevant to this issue. We will successively consider studies of syllable length in words, in phrases, and in larger utterances, and will complete this section with a few remarks on pauses.

It is a well-established fact that syllables in longer words tend to be shorter than the same syllables in shorter words. Nooteboom (1972) retrieved a publication by Roudet (1910), who gave measurements for the syllable [pâ] in French words of increasing length:

	centiseconds
pâte	27
pâté	20
pâtisserie	14
pâtisserie St. Germain	12

And this finding has been repeatedly reconfirmed by phoneticians (see, e.g., Lindblom 1968; Lehiste 1970). Lehiste (1970) suggested that this phenomenon might be due to a tendency of speakers to make words equally long. Syllables in longer words would then necessarily be shorter

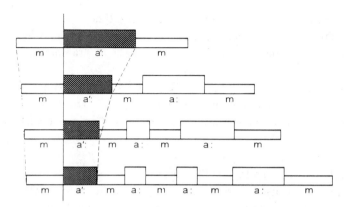

Figure 10.2
Duration of a stressed vowel in a word's initial syllable as a function of the
number of syllables following the word. (After Nooteboom 1972.)

than syllables in shorter ones. But Nooteboom (1972) showed that this is
not so. It is not the *total* number of syllables in a word that determines a
particular syllable's duration, but the number of syllables *following*. To
show this, Nooteboom had subjects pronounce nonsense words containing one stressed syllable *mAm* plus zero or more preceding and following
syllables, all of the type *mam*. Figure 10.2 shows the average findings for
zero, one, and two syllables following the stressed one. Only the number
of syllables *following* had a substantial effect. The stressed vowel's duration
is about halved going from zero to two following syllables. The consonant
duration is also reduced, but only by about 20 percent. (See Gay 1981
for a similar result.) Fujimura (1981) calls the less reducible parts of an
articulatory gesture "icebergs." A syllable is not stored with fixed relations
between the durations of its parts. Lengthening and shortening a syllable
affects its icebergs (in particular, its C parts) far less than it affects the waves
in between (in particular, its peak or V part). But different consonants are
"icebergy" to different degrees, and they tend to be softer in syllable-final
position (Cooper and Danly 1981).

Nooteboom's results were confirmed by Nakatani, O'Connor, and Aston
(1981) for stressed syllables only. Otherwise there was no tendency to compress syllables in longer words or to stretch short words. Word duration
was strictly a linear function of the word's number of syllables.

Taken together, these results make it likely that there is no preferred
duration parameter stored with the word as a whole. Rather, for each syllable the duration parameter is set as a function of the number of syl-

lables to follow in the word. The number of syllables (or peaks) in a word becomes available during metrical spellout. This can therefore be a basis for the Prosody Generator's computation of these parameters. Clearly, the Generator needs a full word's lookahead to decide on its first syllable's temporal parameter. Syllable length is, moreover, a function of metrical stress. Nakatani et al. (1981) found that the syllable carrying word accent is longer than a word's other syllables, and that this difference is more marked if the word is pitch accented.

  But syllable length also depends on conditions outside the word—in particular, on the number of syllables following in the phrase. Fujimura (1981) gives the following examples:

It was yEllow ice cream

It was yEllow, I screamed

In the second utterance, where *yEllow* is phrase-final, that word is uttered at a far slower rate than in the context of the first utterance. Phrase-final lengthening of syllables has been shown repeatedly (Klatt 1975; Kloker 1975; Umeda 1975; Cooper 1976; Cooper and Cooper 1980; Cooper and Danly 1981; Nakatani et al. 1981; see also the short review by Vaissière 1983). Nakatani et al. (1981) found that stressed syllables become progressively longer toward the end of a (phonological) phrase. But this was not so for unstressed syllables, which are not sensitive to phrase position. On the other hand, both stressed and unstressed syllables did show the word-final lengthening effect.

  Cooper and Danly (1981) reported that the phrase-position effect is stronger in the final phrase of an utterance (as in example 18 below) than in a nonfinal phrase (example 19):

(18) Bob made a counter-offer to the largest *bid*

(19) The couple made the largest *bid* on the cottage

This may be due to Nuclear Stress, which can only occur sentence-finally. If so, it confirms the finding of Nakatani et al. (1981) that a syllable's length varies with its degree of stress.

  Also closely related to the phrase-position effect is what one could call the "word-in-isolation effect." Words in isolation are substantially longer than words in phrases. This may be a special case of the phrase-position effect; an isolated word is, of course, the last one in its phrase. Whether isolated words are *as long as* (other) phrase-final words remains to be tested.

  Phrase-final syllable lengthening can be computed by the Prosody Generator without much foresight. It concerns the last phonological word in the phrase; from there, the phrase boundary is "visible" to the Prosody Generator. A progressive lengthening of stressed syllables over the course of the entire intonational phrase, as reported by Nakatani et al., asks for a different kind of explanation. If it can be substantiated at all in more natural speech situations (Nakatani et al. used a modified form of Nooteboom's task), one might conjecture that the speaker "blindly" increases the duration of successive stressed syllables till he reaches the end of the intonational phrase, and that he then resets the durational parameter to the initial value for the next phrase. Another possible explanation involves nuclear stress. Phrase-final stresses naturally "grow" toward the end of the sentence, owing to the mechanics of the Nuclear-Stress Rule. And more heavily stressed syllables tend to be longer. The mechanics of nuclear-stress assignment do not require much preview, as we have seen.

Let us now turn to effects above the phrase level. Lehiste (1975) reported that readers stretch the last sentence of a (read) paragraph. It is not known whether this generalizes to turn-final sentences in spontaneous speech. Turn-taking intentions play an important role in spontaneous speech. A sentence-*shortening* effect, reported by Deese (1980, 1984), was mentioned in chapter 8 above. In contrast with the other studies mentioned in this section, Deese analyzed natural conversations. He found that they contained stretches of accelerated speech with a speaking rate of about ten syllables per second (the normal rate was five to six syllables per second). These could be expressive of modesty, or they could serve a floor-keeping function: "I am approaching the end of my sentence, but not of my utterance; there is more to come." Indeed, speakers finished them with the appropriate "continuation rise" as a boundary tone.

These utterance-level findings are, essentially, findings on speaking rate. And speaking rate is, to some extent, under direct intentional control. The speaker increases his rate mainly by cutting back on pausing. Compression of syllable duration hardly ever surpasses 25 percent.

This brings us to pausing. Let us first recall the study by Gee and Grosjean (1983), discussed in section 7.2. They analyzed the distribution of pauses in materials that were obtained in a reading task. In this task subjects read simple sentences, one by one, at different rates of speaking. Pause lengths could be perfectly predicted from a complex index, involving syntactic and prosodic features. The more such features coincided at a break, the longer the pause. The main prosodic features were whether the break involved a boundary between phonological phrases or between intonational phrases, but allowance was also made for a break before the (phonological) word carrying sentence-final nuclear stress. Van Wijk (1987) published a reanalysis of these findings, which we already touched upon in section 7.2. He argued that prosodic factors alone sufficed to make the same predictions: The least pausing should occur between a content word and a function word adjoined to it. One could say that this protects the integrity of phonological words. The next larger pause option is between content words within a phonological phrase. Still larger pauses may be expected at boundaries between phonological phrases. Here van Wijk distinguished between "neutral" and "marked" phrases boundaries, which are both predictors of pausing. The latter type can only be interpreted as intonational phrase boundaries, because they may involve a nuclear pitch movement, such as a continuation rise. Still, van Wijk denies that Gee and Grosjean's intonational-phrase boundary feature is relevant. At any rate, however, it seems that the prosodic phrasing structure alone suffices to predict the pausing pattern in a reading task.

So far, we may conclude that speakers who can prepare for "ideal delivery"—and this is the case when the task is to read a single sentence—make their pausing durations dependent on the phonological phrase structure. One might want to test whether the number of silent beats of Selkirk's algorithm would be an equally good predictor of pause durations. One would also want to see further evidence for her conjecture that the number of silent beats following a word predicts the *sum* of syllable-final lengthening and following pause—i.e., evidence for a negative correlation between syllable lengthening and pausing. Some indirect evidence for the latter conjecture can be found in Scott 1982.

But one should never forget that pausing is multiply determined (see O'Connell and Kowal 1983 for a review). Pauses and nonpauses may, in particular, serve subtle communicative functions, as Kowal, Bassett, and O'Connell (1985) showed in an analysis of the reading and interviewing styles of two media professionals. In reading, sentence-final pauses were almost always made; in fact, the whole pausing pattern followed the norms of "ideal delivery". However, omission of pauses between sentences, and probably extension of the intonational phrase over the sentence boundary, occurred in almost 40 percent of the cases in the interviews. This happened especially in high-speed, ego-involved utterances. On the other hand, pauses can be inserted at odd places to create rhetorical effects, to suggest spontaneity, and so forth. There is much executive control in the management of pausing; one should not expect strict phonological rules to govern the distribution of silence in speech.

Also, one should exercise much restraint in generalizing findings on prosody in reading aloud to spontaneous speech.

10.2.5 Isochrony

It has been argued that English is a *stress-timed* language (Pike 1945) in which speakers tend to produce stressed syllables at regular and roughly isochronous intervals. Other languages, such as French and Spanish, are supposed to be *syllable-timed*, i.e., to give about equal duration to each syllable. Traditionally, the interval that begins at a stressed or salient syllable and ends just before the next stressed syllable is called a *foot* (Abercrombie 1967). The following example (from Halliday 1970) shows a partitioning in feet:

each / fOOt in / tUrn con / sIsts of a / nUmber of / sYllables /

Stress-timing would mean that feet tend to be equally long. This notion of the foot as a prosodically relevant entity has been largely abandoned in linguistics, and I see no role for it in a theory of language production either. The modern notion of foot is entirely internal to the phonological word (Nespor and Vogel 1986). Still, it is an empirical issue whether the spacing of stressed syllables in English tends toward isochrony.

How could isochrony be attained in the production of speech? In two ways. Speakers could, first, stretch or compress syllable durations, depending on the number of syllables in a foot. When there are many syllables in a foot, they should be pronounced at a higher rate than when there are only a few. Second, speakers could add, delete, or shift accents so as to make feet that are about equally long. As things stand, there is only conflicting evidence for the hypothesis that speakers vary syllable durations in order to establish isochrony. But there is good reason to suppose that speakers shift accents to create a more even distribution of stressed syllables. Let us discuss these two ways of establishing isochrony in turn.

Lehiste (1977) reviewed the isochrony research and concluded that some findings spoke for and other findings spoke against isochrony. She mentioned in particular that speakers often violate isochrony in order to mark syntactic boundaries (see Cutler and Isard 1980 for some experimental evidence).

Since the publication of Lehiste's review, some further studies have appeared, again with ambivalent results. Nakatani et al. (1981) found absolutely no evidence for isochrony in their experimental data. Their measurements concerned so-called reiterated speech, in which a subject would read an adjective-noun pair like *remote stream* and pronounce it as *mamAmAm*. The pair was embedded in a sentence, like *the remote stream was perfect for fishing*, and the rest of the sentence was spoken normally; the full stretch of speech would therefore be *the mamAmAm was perfect for fishing*. The adjective-noun pairs were constructed in such a way that they contained shorter or longer feet. (The above sentence, for instance, contains the one-syllable foot/mout/.) Nakatani et al. analyzed the durations of one-, two-, three-, and four-syllable feet as spoken by their most fluent subjects. If there is a tendency toward isochrony, the foot duration should not increase linearly with the number of syllables. But it did. Each syllable added a fixed amount of time (about 150 msec) to a foot's duration, irrespective of the foot size. Each syllable consisted of precisely two segments, [m] and [æ], so that the average segment duration was about 75 msec. The relevance of this will soon be apparent.

Jassem, Hill, and Witten (1984), on the other hand, found some evidence for isochrony in a detailed segment-by-segment analysis of the recorded materials that go with Halliday's (1970) course in spoken English. They found that segments (and thus syllables) were significantly shorter in long feet than in short feet, and that the average segment rate was 13.3 per second (which corresponds to an average segment duration of 75 msec). The speech rate in the two studies considered here was therefore precisely the same. Still, the findings on isochrony differ. Nakatani et al. caution against overgeneralizing their findings. In particular, their experimental materials were reiterated adjective-noun phrases; they did not contain function words. It could be that some degree of isochrony is obtained by manipulating the duration of function words only.

There are other interesting findings in the study by Jassem et al. One of them is that there is no isochrony in so-called *anacruses* (short stretches of high-rate speech). As was mentioned above, Deese (1984) showed that such stretches are quite normal in spontaneous speech. It is relevant here that whatever there is in isochrony breaks down at these high speaking rates. There may be isochrony in trot, but there is none in gallop.

Dauer (1983) compared the isochronous tendencies of five different languages, including "stress-timed" English and "syllable-timed" Spanish. The materials were literary texts read by native speakers. That choice is regrettable, because literary texts may very well have been *designed* to be rhythmic. Still, the results were somewhat surprising. The variability of inter-stress intervals (i.e., feet) was the same for stress-timed as for syllable-timed languages. English feet were as variable in duration as Spanish feet. And for all languages the average foot length was statistically the same, namely between 400 and 500 msec. But is this isochrony? On the present interpretation, isochrony can only mean that foot length is not a linear function of the number of syllables it contains; the more syllables there are in a foot, the shorter they should be. Dauer showed, however, that for her data the function is a linear one. Each additional syllable added 110 msec to the interstress interval, and in all languages. In other words, there was no isochrony, even for readings of literary texts.

The contradicting results of Dauer and Jassem et al. leave the issue as undecided as it was to start with. There is, at any rate, no reason so far to conjecture an internal clock or pacemaker that induces the speaker to deliver speech in isochronous feet. In spite of her own data, Dauer aligns herself with such a notion.

The second possible way for a speaker to establish isochrony is by manipulating the placement of stress. Beat Movement does just that, as do Selkirk's other euphony rules. They promote a rhythm of alternating stresses, and thus they promote isochrony. This view of isochrony is linguistically far better motivated than the previous one. It should, in particular, be noticed that it has no consequences for syllable length. Isochrony is established by evading strings of adjoining stressed syllables or of adjoining unstressed syllables, not by squeezing more or fewer syllables into a fixed temporal frame.

The data one would need in order to prove this version of isochrony would be that euphony adjustments are indeed made in spontaneous speech. For instance, is it statistically more often the case that speakers shift clashing stresses apart (as in *sIxteen dOllars*) than that they shift them together (as in the unlikely *he becOmes sIxteen*)? Two recent studies were devoted to this issue, one by Cooper and Eady (1986) and one by Kelly and Bock (1988).

Cooper and Eady report five experiments in which they created conditions for beat movement, such as clashing stresses. The following two sentences, for instance, appeared on a list to be read by subjects:

(20) Thirteen corporations submitted bids to build the new shopping mall

(21) Thirteen companies submitted bids to build the new shopping mall

In example 20, *thirteen* can be normally pronounced with main stress on the second syllable, since it is followed by two unstressed syllables. In example 21, however, there is the risk of clashing stresses, since *company* begins with a stressed syllable. An isochrony or beat-movement tendency on the part of the speaker would induce the pronunciation *thIrteen*. And

Cooper and Eady constructed several other cases where metrical analysis would predict a shift toward a more isochronous rhythm. All the sentences were read aloud, and the critical syllables were analyzed with respect to their duration and pitch (F_0); a stressed syllable should be of longer duration and/or of higher pitch than an unstressed one. The results of this extensive and careful study were completely negative. There was no measurable difference between examples 20 and 21 insofar as the syllables of *thirteen* were concerned. And, similarly, there was no evidence for stress shifts in any of the other conditions tested. Are we being deceived by metrical phonology?

Kelly and Bock (1988) restored confidence. Their experimental approach was very different. They provided their subjects with sentences containing a two-syllable nonsense word, such as *colvane*. In the context of a given sentence, the nonsense word would function either as a noun or as verb. In examples 22 and 23, for instance, *colvane* plays the role of a noun, whereas it figures as verb in examples 24 and 25.

(22) Use the colvane proudly.   [noun, trochaic biasing context]
(23) The proud colvane proposed.   [noun, iambic biasing context]
(24) Planes will colvane pilots.   [verb, trochaic biasing context]
(25) The pins colvane balloons.   [verb, iambic biasing context]

Kelly and Bock predicted that noun function would induce a trochaic word accent, i.e., *cOlvane*, following the majority rule for English nouns (*tIger*, *sOldier*, etc.). Conversely, they expected the nonsense verb to receive iambic accent, i.e., *colvAne*, in accordance with the majority rule for English verbs (*convEne*, *expEct*). The critical variable in the experiment, however, was the metrical context in which the nonsense word appeared. The noun in example 22 is preceded by a normally unstressed syllable (*the*) and followed by a stressed one (*proud*). This environment would support the expected trochaic rhythm of the "noun" *colvane*. But in example 23 the trochaic rhythm *cOlvane* would clash with the metrical context. It would create a stress clash between *proud* and *col*. The context biases for a iambic pattern: *the prOud colvAne propOsed*. Similarly for the nonsense verbs in examples 24 and 25: In the former, the context biases toward a trochaic word accent, contrary to the normal iambic pattern for verbs; in the latter, however, the context supports the iambic verb pattern.

In the Kelly-Bock experiment, subjects read such sentences and their speech was tape-recorded. The critical nonsense words were then excised from the tapes, and two judges categorized the word accents as either iambic or trochaic. The results, which were consistent between the two judges, amounted to this: Although trochaic patterns dominated, nouns (as in examples 22 and 23) received significantly more trochaic pronunciations than verbs (as in examples 24 and 25). Trochaic biasing contexts (as in examples 22 and 24) released more trochaic pronunciations than iambic biasing contexts (as in examples 23 and 25). The latter result shows that speakers do tend to impose an alternating stress rhythm, in spite of the fact that they have preferential accentuations of verbs and of nouns. There is a tendency toward isochrony, in that stress clashes are, to some extent, evaded by adjusting a word's metrical pattern.

The question remains why these results are so different from those obtained by Cooper and Eady. A first point to be noticed is that Kelly and Bock's contextual biasing effect, though highly significant, is not exceedingly strong. The trochaic biasing context released 84 percent trochaic patterns, the iambic context 77 percent. When effects are this small, one needs many observations to detect them. Kelly and Bock had more than 50 times as many observations per condition than Cooper and Eady. A second potentially important difference was that Kelly and Bock used perceptual judgments of stress, whereas Cooper and Eady had physical measurements. Perceived stress is a complex function of a syllable's composition, loudness, duration, pitch movement, and (maybe) precision of articulation. All these features were available to the judges, and they were able to weigh them. Cooper and Eady had only duration and pitch measurements, and may thus have missed other subtle features contributing to stress. Third, Cooper and Eady used real words. It may be the case that the effect observed by Kelly and Bock is even smaller when real words are used.

Together, these two studies strongly invite further experimental exploration of metrical euphony rules, including experiments that involve spontaneous speech rather than reading aloud. Almost all experimental research in prosody involves reading tasks, but in reading the normal conditions for incremental speech planning are not met. Results on a speaker's prosodic planning and lookahead in reading cannot be generalized to normal spontaneous speech.

A study by Cutler (1980b), finally, provides interesting evidence that a speaker's tendency to impose an even distribution of stresses can induce characteristic speech errors. In particular, Cutler studied spontaneous errors involving either syllable omission (as in example 26) or stress shifts (as in example 27).

(26) Next we have this bicEntial rug [bicentEnnial]

(27) We do think in spEcific terms [specIfic]

Cutler checked whether errors like these established more isochrony than there would have been in the target utterance. For instance, the target utterance for example 26 would have had the following foot structure; the error foot structure is given as a comparison:

Target: / Next we / have this bicen/tennial / rug /

Error: / Next we / have this bi/cential / rug /

The foot containing the error (the second foot) is closer in number of syllables to the surrounding feet than is the second foot in the target sentence. Hence, the error establishes more isochrony than the target would have displayed. Cutler found that this tendency toward more isochrony was highly significant for her corpus of syllable omission errors.

In a similar test for stress errors (such as in example 27), Cutler established that the resulting patterns of feet were more isochronous than the target patterns.

Where could these errors arise in the model framework of figure 10.1? Example 26 involves the deletion of a syllable. One might guess that the Prosody Generator skips the delivery of an unstressed syllable frame to the phonetic spellout level. The error in example 27 is harder to account for. As Cutler (1980a) showed, such stress-placement errors originate in the simultaneous activation of a morphologically related word. For *specific*, the related word would be *specify*, which has word accent on the first syllable. One might conjecture that the metrical patterns of both words were spelled out in metrical spellout, and that both stress patterns were simultaneously fed to the Prosody Generator, which then made its choice in such a way that euphony or rhythm could be established with least effort. This explanation, however, falls short of accounting for word-stress errors that involve a mixture of the metrical patterns of the two concurring words (as in *articulAtory*, which has the number of syllables of *artIculatory* but the accent placement of *articulAtion*). The ways of the Prosody Generator are still quite enigmatic.

This completes our review of isochrony, the main conclusion of which is that the Prosody Generator's metrical planning promotes an alternating distribution of more-stressed and less-stressed syllables. This establishes some degree of isochrony. The original notion of isochrony, however, finds rather little support. Syllable lengths are seldom or never adapted for the purpose of spacing stressed syllables evenly over time.

This also completes our review of metrical planning, the first main job of the Prosody Generator in the generation of connected speech. We sketched how a metrical pattern could be computed for phonological words, and for phrases up to the level of intonational phrases. We analyzed whether this generation could be done incrementally, without more preview of surface structure than a single word. The answer was encouraging, in spite of the fact that the euphony operations, which establish rhythm, theoretically require infinite lookahead. We also considered one of the Prosody Generator's main types of output: a pattern of stress and durational parameters for successive syllables and silences. These parameters are to be implemented during the phonetic spellout operations. They are sensitive to a syllable's position in a word, phrase, paragraph, or turn. Finally, empirical research on isochrony was reviewed. There is only very limited support for the original idea that a speaker adjusts the lengths of unstressed syllables so as to make intervals between stressed syllables more isochronous. There is a better empirical basis for supposing that, at least to some extent, speakers like to impose an even distribution of stressed syllables.

10.3   The Generation of Intonation

The second main job for the Prosody Generator is to compute pitch contours for successive intonational phrases. The melody of an intonational phrase, as we saw in subsection 8.2.3, is the result of a variety of forces. It expresses the speaker's affective involvement, especially in key and register. Its tune is raised when a new topic is introduced, or in response to the interlocutor's introduction of a new topic. It also expresses, by way of continuation rise or final fall, whether the speaker intends to continue or not. It signals, through pitch accents, where there is prominent, new, or contrastive information. And it is, through its nuclear tone, an important instrument for expressing the utterance's illocutionary force.

There is no process model that provides an on-line computation of the sentence melody resulting from all these forces. In the following we will, therefore, set ourselves a fairly limited task. We will consider some of the factors affecting each of the global and local properties of sentence melody, and the effects they have. The global properties are declination, key, and register. The local ones are prenuclear tune and nuclear tone. The main message of this section will be that intonational planning can probably be done incrementally, without much lookahead. But "euphony" or melody can be improved when there is a small amount of preview. This is in full harmony with what we found for metrical planning in the previous section.

10.3.1   Declination

There is evidence that, at least in many languages, pitch gradually drifts down in the course of an intonational phrase. Cohen and 't Hart (1965) called this phenomenon *declination*. An example is given in figure 10.3. It is as if the pitch movements that go with pitch accent and nuclear tone are superimposed on a generally downward-drifting "declination line." Willems (1983) measured an average declination of 0.3 semitones per second for spontaneous British English speech (there are twelve semitones in an octave). The variability in such measurements is, however, so large that doubts about the universality of the declination phenomenon are warranted (Lieberman, Katz, and Jongman 1985; see also Ladd 1984 on the statistical claims with respect to declination).

Where declination is systematic, it may be due not to the speaker's phonetic plan but rather to physiological factors such as diminishing subglottal air pressure (see chapter 11). At the end of an intonational phrase, the speaker inhales and the pitch level is reset to the higher starting position. As a result, a kind of sawtooth pattern of declination arises over successive intonational phrases.

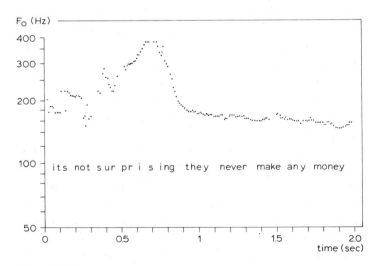

Figure 10.3
The gradual declination of pitch over an intonational phrase. The pitch-accent peak is superimposed on the "declination line." (From Cohen et al. 1982.)

But it has been suggested that some planning of declination is possible. There is, in particular, some evidence that declination is steeper for short utterances than for long ones (Ohala 1978; Cooper and Sorensen 1981; De Pijper 1983; Collier and Gelfer 1983). The latter finding is, on first view, not easy to reconcile with an incremental theory of intonation. How can the speaker know in advance how long his intonational phrase is going to be, if he has not even generated the full surface structure for that phrase? It is too early, however, to draw dramatic conclusions. First, the effect is most apparent in reading. But in reading a speaker does have a preview in the most literal sense. Second, the causal relation (if any) between phrase length and slope of declination may be inverse. If a speaker, for whatever reason, makes his pitch decline rapidly, he will sooner feel the urge to reset. This may induce him to take an early break option. Consequently, the running intonational phrase will be a short one.

10.3.2   Setting Key and Register

The range of pitch movement in an intonational phrase—the key—depends in particular on the "news value" of that phrase. When a phrase expresses "main-track" or foregrounded information (subsection 4.3.5), the key will, as a rule, be higher than when it expresses "side-track" or background information. Brown, Currie, and Kenworthy (1980) found that the key is also higher when a speaker introduces a new topic, and that the pitch excursions diminish when a topic becomes exhausted. They also showed that the baseline of the pitch range (i.e., the register) is lifted as a whole when a speaker introduces a new topic. Key and register are, moreover, lifted together when the speaker has a strong ego involvement in what he is saying. That ego involvement can be due to general communicative tension (Heeschen, Ryalls, Hagoort, and Bloem, forthcoming), to surprise, or to enthusiasm. A higher register is also chosen to express friendliness, helplessness, and so on.

These settings of key and register do not require any lookahead. As far as register is concerned, the Prosody Generator will set a global pitch parameter for phonetic spellout. This is the default pitch level for successive syllables. Pitch excursions for pitch accenting or nuclear tones are then programmed as deviations from the baseline. The key (i.e., the size of the pitch excursions) may be set as a global parameter to be instantiated every time a pitch accent is to be made. In this way, foregrounded and backgrounded information may be globally opposed by a speaker. Alternatively, the size of the excursion may be set anew for each syllable requiring a pitch excursion, depending on the accessibility or the contrastiveness of the particular lexical item.

10.3.3 Planning the Nuclear Tone

A tone, as we saw in chapter 8, is not an indivisible whole. There is, first, the *nuclear pitch movement*: a step up or down to the nucleus, plus a fall or rise (or steady level) from the nucleus. There is, second, a *boundary tone*: the pitch movement that takes place at the final syllable of the intonational phrase. These two pitch movements can be separated by several syllables, or they can follow one another within a single syllable. This is exemplified in figure 10.4, which gives three cases of tone V (the fall-rise). In figure 10.4a the nuclear movement is on *po*, the boundary tone on *leave*. In figure 10.4b the nucleus is still *po*, but now *bear* is the end-of-phrase syllable, and it carries the boundary tone. In figure 10.4c *bear* is both the nucleus and the boundary syllable, and both pitch movements are then projected on that same single syllable.

These two components of a tone can probably be set independently, and they play different expressive roles. The nuclear pitch movement is mostly a focusing device. It indicates the most prominent lexical item in the intonational phrase. But in addition it has an illocutionary function:

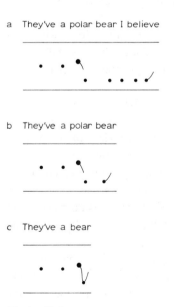

a They've a polar bear I believe

b They've a polar bear

c They've a bear

Figure 10.4
Decreasing separation of nuclear pitch movement and boundary tone.

expressing matter-of-factness, being reassuring, or the like. The boundary tone can perform several different functions. It can indicate a mood of finality or nonfinality. It can express the utterance's illocutionary force, the kind of commitment the speaker is making. It can express the speaker's intention to finish a turn or to continue. And it can be expressive of attitude, as in the rising tone of friendliness.

In order to generate the nuclear pitch movement, the Prosody Generator must select the nuclear syllable. How much lookahead is needed to do this? In subsection 10.2.2 we saw that the assignment of pitch accent or nuclear stress requires no lookahead. But in order to assign a nuclear pitch movement, the Prosody Generator must know which pitch-accented or nuclear-stressed syllable is the last one of the intonational phrase. Here we should return to the conclusion of subsection 10.2.3: "the decision to break *creates* the intonational phrase boundary; it is in no way *determined* by it." In other words, every time the speaker reaches a pitch-accented or nuclear-stressed syllable, a decision can be made to give it the nuclear tone and to break at the next convenient break option. This requires no lookahead whatsoever. In particular, the convenient break option need not be in view. There is only the decision that it should be taken as soon as it appears. It was suggested in subsection 10.2.3 that very prominent pitch accents, in particular, may induce a speaker to decide on a break.

The fact that lookahead is not a necessary condition for positioning the nuclear pitch movement by no means excludes the possibility that speakers do look ahead in deciding where to begin the nuclear tone. As we have seen for metrical planning, lookahead can increase the "euphony" of speech. Especially in slow speech, where the generation of surface structure can be far ahead of phonological encoding, a more ideal delivery can be planned when the speaker has preview of a sentence boundary. He can then decide to complete the intonational phrase at that sentence boundary, and hence to make the nuclear pitch movement at the last pitch-accented or nuclear-stressed syllable of the sentence.

The generation of the boundary tone obviously requires no more lookahead than a single syllable. It is made on the last syllable before the break; only that break must be in view.

The Prosody Generator must, in some way or another, know what nuclear tone to impose. It depends, we saw, on a multitude of factors. Some of these factors are probably indicated at the message level. Illocutionary force, mood, and modality are planned by the speaker when he generates a message to be expressed (see subsection 3.5.1). At the level of surface structure these are translated in part into syntactic sentence mood (declarative, interrogative, imperative), in part into the use of modal verbs or adverbials, and in part into indicators for nuclear pitch movements and boundary tones (see section 5.2). These indicators or parameters in surface structure are recognized by the Prosody Generator, or so we assume.

Still, it is unlikely that these parameters are the sole determinants of nuclear tone. Take, for instance, the choice of boundary tone. Many questions are asked with a falling boundary tone (Brown et al. 1980; de Pijper 1983). Consider example 28a, with its low-fall nuclear tone.

(28)

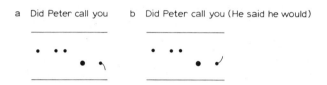

Let us assume that the falling boundary tone was indicated at the level of surface structure. This indication will easily be overruled if the speaker decides, shortly before finishing the sentence, not to finish his turn but to add another clause (*He said he would*). He will now make a continuation rise as boundary tone on *you*, as in example 28b. This looks like direct executive control rather than replanning of a surface structure. Also, the emotional and attitudinal aspects of tone, such as friendly rising boundary tones, are probably directly induced by the emotional system without mediation through message and surface structure. The Prosody Generator will, in some as yet unknown manner, integrate these various sources of activation in making the final choice of tone.

10.3.4 Planning the Prenuclear Tune
The nucleus can be the only accented syllable in the intonational phrase. The default tune is then an about constant mid-level pitch. There are, of course, always small pitch variations. There is, in particular, systematic covariation with metrical stress. Stressed syllables tend to be somewhat higher in pitch level than unstressed ones. Or, more precisely: Metrical stress is, in part, realized through variation in pitch. The default tune requires no more lookahead than is required for assigning metrical stress. But a tune's course can be "improved" when there is lookahead. De Pijper (1983) found that when a tune without accents spans several syl-

lables, a reader will show *inclination*. That is, he will make a gradual rise of pitch up to the nucleus. Default tune and inclining tune are depicted in example 29, where the nucleus has tone 1.

(29)

The amount of lookahead needed for an inclining tune is, of course, rather limited. A speaker can incline almost "blindly"; the only risk is that he may come up against his pitch ceiling, as sportscasters sometimes do. In other words, the speaker should not incline too much as long as the nucleus is not yet in sight.

If an intonational phrase introduces a new topic in the conversation, its first stressed syllable and the subsequent tune can be quite high-pitched, at least in British English (Brown et al. 1980). More generally, a high-pitched tune signals a speaker's special involvement with what is said. Also, *wh*-questions and certain kinds of emphatic utterances (*Who will be at the party?; Do come to the party*) have high pitch-initial tunes. That high starting level can, of course, be set without specific lookahead.

A tune may also contain one or more additional pitch accents. Depending on the amount of lookahead, these pitch accents are realized individually or in conjunction. If there is one further pitch accent in the tune, these two cases can be illustrated as in example 30a and 30b, where the nuclear tone is a high-fall and a low-fall, respectively.

(30) (a) individual realization   (b) "hat pattern"

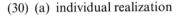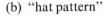

These two patterns are alternative realizations for sentences such as *We mIght be able to gO*, with *might* and *go* accented. In example 30a, the tune falls back to mid-level immediately after pitch-accented *might*, and the level is maintained until the nuclear tone is made on *go*. Example 30b depicts a so-called hat pattern ('t Hart and Collier 1975); the speaker accents *might* by way of a rise and *go* by way of a step down to mid-level, and in between these the tune maintains a high pitch level. Lookahead is a condition for producing the hat pattern. The speaker must know at the first pitch accent that another one is going to follow. There are no clear differences in intonational meaning between the two patterns in example 30, but the hat pattern is more euphonious. It constitutes a more aesthetically pleasing delivery of two subsequent accents. The hat pattern is a more likely pitch contour when two accents are to be made in close succession. But even then a speaker often makes individual realizations. Brown et al. (1980) found that in such cases the fall back to mid-level between the pitch peaks was often not fully realized; they called this phenomenon, in which the syllables between the peaks stayed somewhat raised in pitch, *tonal sandhi.*

The pitch-movement parameters that the Prosody Generator incrementally computes for prenuclear tune and nuclear tone affect the phonetic spellout procedures directly. Successive syllables are set to rise or to fall in pitch, or by default to stay level with the previous syllable. The sizes and slopes of the rises and falls are programmed, as well as their precise timing; it is quite critical where in the syllable a rise or fall is made ('t Hart and Collier 1975).

This completes the rather brief treatment of intonational planning. Metrical and intonational planning go hand in hand. The metrical peaks are the main loci of pitch movement, and the planning of intonational phrases is as much a metrical as an intonational affair. We have, moreover, seen that both forms of prosodic planning can be done incrementally. It is not necessary for a speaker to buffer long stretches of surface structure in order to program the prosody of connected speech. But if such buffering is possible, as it is in slow speech or in reading, the Prosody Generator can generate a more euphonious output, more rhythmic phrasing, and larger melodic lines.

10.4 The Generation of Word Forms in Connected Speech

The consideration of the generation of word forms in the previous chapter was limited to the spellout of stored ("citation") forms. The present section will reconsider word-form spellout as it occurs in connected speech. The present chapter began with the argument that in connected speech the syllabic and segmental composition of word forms are context dependent. Segmental and phonetic spellout depend on prosodic decisions. The domain of syllabification, in particular, is not the citation form but the phonological word (see subsection 10.2.1). The Prosody Generator must, therefore, construct phonological words before complete phonetic spellout is possible. But the construction of phonological words is impossible without access to segmental information. This issue will be taken up first in the present section; we will then move to some aspects of phonetic spellout in context.

10.4.1 Segmental Spellout in Context

To account for context-dependent segmental spellout, such as occurs in assimilation (e.g., /tɛm bʊks/), in cliticization, and in reduction (e.g., *a bottle o'milk*), we must assume that segmental spellout is a two-step process.

The first step is basically as described in subsection 9.2.2. When the morphological slots of an item's address frame are filled with the appropriate morphemes, the item's stored syllabic and segmental composition is spelled out.

The second step involves the Prosody Generator. It receives, for each successive lexical item, the spellout from the first step. The metrical information is independently fed into the Prosody Generator from metrical-spellout and phrase-structural information, and a partitioning is made into phonological words. The most frequent case (in English) is that a single input item becomes a single phonological word. But with the limited lookahead discussed in subsection 10.2.1, phonological words consisting of two or even more lexical items can be built up. The segmental strings of these items are concatenated and modified, following quite general phonological rules. In addition, assimilations at phonological word boundaries are generated (as in/tɛm bʊks/).

This modified segmental output forms, for each phonological word, the input to the phonetic spellout procedures. Syllable frames are addressed in just the way proposed in subsection 9.2.3., with metrical and intonational parameters set for each of them.

Two examples may help to clarify the two-step procedure at the level of segmental spellout. The first is a case of what was called *obligatory* cliticization in subsection 10.2.1; the second is an instance of *optional* cliticization.

Cliticization is obligatory if the "little" element is nonsyllabic. Auxiliary forms such as *'ve* and *'ll* are allomorphs of the full forms, and we have considered reasons to suppose that they are indicated as such in the surface-structure representation. So, if the speaker uses a casual speech register to generate the sentence *They have called*, the first two morphemes accessed will be *they* and *'ve*. The first step of segmental spellout will, for these elements, yield the following:

(31)

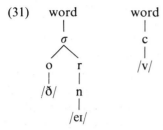

When the Prosody Generator receives this pair, it will initiate a second step that consists of attaching the nonsyllabic coda-branch /v/ of the second word to the rime of the first word. This gives the following:

(32)

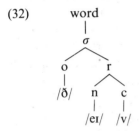

The triple of syllable constituents—onset, nucleus, and coda—then becomes input to phonetic spellout. Because this phonological word consists of one syllable, the Prosody Generator generates one syllable frame for the phonetic spellout procedure. That syllable frame is "enriched" with metrical and intonational information, as was discussed in subsections 10.2 and 10.3.

The Prosody Generator can impose an optional encliticization when the register is casual and the speech rate relatively high. When the speaker is generating the sentence *John got to swim in the morning*, the first step of spelling out the lexical items *got* and *to* produces their "citation" syllabic structures. In a second step, the Prosody Generator combines them into one phonological word, which involves resyllabification. These steps are shown in the following diagrams.

(33)

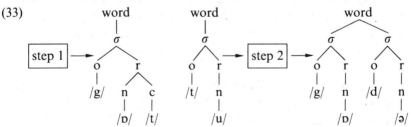

Here we see both deletion (of /t/) and change (/t/ → /d/, /u/ → /ə/) of segments. This, together with the loss of one word boundary (i.e., a silent beat), will probably simplify the eventual phonetic pattern.

It was stated above that these phonological adaptations are quite regular. This is more a hypothesis than an established fact. But there is reason to make that hypothesis. If some form of accommodation or encliticization is irregular (i.e., specific to a particular word or a pair of words), it is probably lexicalized. That is, the encliticization is stored as such in the lexicon. Examples of this are the contraction of *do not* to *don't* and that of *will not* to *won't*. These are rather irregular encliticizations in English. In other words, if the Prosody Generator is to deal with one of these constructions, it must have stored its irregular shape. But such storage is precisely what the lexicon is for. The lexicon is the repository of forms: the Prosody Generator can adapt them to context. One should also not exclude the possibility that frequently occurring regular encliticizations are stored as such; /gɒdə/ may be such a case, and the even more frequent /wɒnə/ (for *want to*) is a good candidate.

We will not consider in any detail the rules governing step 2. They are different for different languages, and even for English they are not well known (but see Dogil 1984, Kaisse 1985, Nespor and Vogel 1986, and Pullum and Zwicky 1988). It should be repeated, however, that these rules are sensitive to local phrase structure. There will be no encliticization of the kind illustrated in diagram 33 when *got to* occurs in the sentence *John got, to be sure, to swim every morning*. The parenthetical phrase boundary following *got* blocks the formation of the phonological word /gɒdə/. Local phrase-structural conditions govern the applicability of encliticization and assimilation rules. Generally speaking, the phonological operations in step 2 prepare a segmental output string that can be pronounced with less articulatory effort than the input string.

The step 2 procedures compute the segmental consequences of metrical structure. The Prosody Generator receives an item's stored metrical information. In addition, it receives an item's pitch-accent feature, if any. The resulting metrical planning (see section 10.2) can also have consequences at the segmental level. For instance, a syllable's vowel may be a different segment when it is stressed than when it is unstressed. These consequences of metrical planning are presumably also implemented at step 2.

10.4.2   Phonetic Spellout in Context

The first input to phonetic spellout is a string of address frames, each containing three slots: one for onset, one for nucleus, and one for coda (but see subsection 9.5.1). Each frame is "enriched" by prosodic information; it contains parameters for the syllable's duration, loudness, and pitch movement. Also, silent pauses between frames are indicated. The second input to phonetic spellout consists of triples of onset, nucleus, and coda, which are to fill the frames. These triples are produced by the above step 2 procedures and, when necessary, cluster composition (subsection 9.3.4). One may wonder again, as we did in section 9.6, whether it is strictly necessary that all segments and clusters be explicitly labeled in terms of syllabic function before they can be used as fillers. But we will not pursue this issue again.

Each address frame that is filled by the appropriate syllable constituents forms an address where the "standard" phonetic plan for that syllable can be found. The actual phonetic plan results from the imposition of the prosodic parameters that were attached to the address frame.

These parameter settings are responsible for some characteristic phenomena of fast speech. When a syllable's duration is set to be very short, as may happen in fast speech, vowel length will be reduced rather more than consonant length in the phonetic plan (see subsection 10.2.4). This vowel reduction can, in extreme cases, annihilate the syllable's syllabicity, as we observed in reductions such as *p'tato* and *t'mato*. When durations are short, the phonetic plan will also show more temporal overlap of adjacent phones. Take the word *cue*, where the vowel requires the articulatory feature of lip rounding. In slow speech, that lip rounding can be realized in the course of the diphthong. In fast speech, however, the lip rounding will have to start with the initial consonant in order to be realized at all. In other words, there is, to some extent, coarticulation of the onset consonant and the following vowel. A syllable's phonetic plan specifies at what moments various articulatory gestures are to be initiated. These temporal relations are crucially dependent on the syllable's duration.

It is quite probably the case that phonetic spellout is organized per phonological word. Though syllable frames are successively filled by their triples, as they become available, it is likely that the whole phonetic plan for a phonological word is collected before it is delivered to the Articulator. In other words, the Articulator cannot start pronouncing a phonological word's first syllable if it has not received the whole phonetic word plan. Meyer's (1988) evidence in support of this assumption was mentioned in chapter 9: If the Articulator were to begin as soon as a (phonological) word's first syllable is made available, a word's first syllable would be a good prime, but its first syllable plus part of its second syllable

would not. Meyer, however, found that a word like *pitfall* was primed
more strongly by *pitf* than by *pit*. Similarly a word like *pedagogue* was
more strongly primed by *peda* than by *pe*. If the phonetic spellout is not
delivered until all of a phonological word's syllables have been planned,
one would further expect that phonological encoding takes more time
when there are more syllables in a word. This in fact seems to be the case.
(The evidence, collected by Klapp and his co-workers, will be reviewed in
section 11.1, where we will consider the interfacing of phonological encoding and articulation.)

   This section has discussed some aspects of word-form planning in the
context of connected speech. The obvious dependency of spoken words
on context and rate made it necessary to consider mechanisms that adapt
spelled-out stored forms to their contexts of occurrence. Such mechanisms help to create fluently pronounceable phonetic plans in connected
speech. The Prosody Generator plays a central role in this adaptation by
creating phonological words and by setting appropriate parameters for
phonetic spellout. Phonetic spellout is probably made available to the
Articulator per phonological word.

Summary

This chapter reviewed the speaker's phonological encoding of connected
speech. It began with a sketch of the processing architecture underlying
the phonetic planning of connected speech (figure 10.1). A Prosody Generator that interacts with the spellout procedures introduced in the previous chapter was introduced. It accepts various kinds of input. There is,
first, surface phrase-structural and pitch-accent information, which is
relevant for prosodic planning. There is, second, the metrical spellout, on
which metrical planning is based. There is, third, executive, attitudinal,
and emotional input, which affects such aspects of phonetic planning as
speaking rate, intentional pausing, general loudness level, tune, and tone.
Finally, there is input from segmental spellout, which can be modified by
the Prosody Generator to create new phonological words.

   The Prosody Generator produces two kinds of output. The first kind is
a string of address frames for phonetic spellout. Each address frame is enriched by parameters for the syllable's set duration, its loudness, its pitch
movement, and (may be) its precision of articulation. The second kind of
output consists of the fillers for these address frames: segments that can
fill onset, nucleus, or coda slots. Phonetic spellout then consists in the re-

trieval of stored phonetic syllable plans and their subsequent parametrization for duration, loudness, etc. As soon as all syllables for a phonological word have been planned, the Articulator can take over.

A major task for the Prosody Generator is the generation of rhythm. It generates phonological words, phonological phrases, and intonational phrases. I went a long way to show that the Prosody Generator needs little lookahead to create these structures. It can, mostly, be done incrementally. This means that it is not necessary to buffer more than one or two successive lexical elements in order to assign them their appropriate metrical weight. But if more buffering is possible—such as at lower speaking rates—the resulting metrical pattern can become more euphonious than if buffering is limited. I discussed, in particular, how new phonological words are generated by cliticization. I also outlined basic procedures for the generation of phonological and intonational phrases. And I considered these procedures in the alternative framework of metrical grids. The section on the planning of rhythm was then completed by reviewing what happens to segment and syllable durations in different word and phrase contexts, and by reviewing the shaky evidence for isochrony as it was originally defined. What there is in terms of isochrony, I argued, is due to metrical euphony rules rather than to stretching and shrinking of unstressed syllables.

Another main task of the Prosody Generator is to compute a pitch contour for the utterance. This can also be done without much preview, both for the more global and for the more local aspects of pitch. Among the more global aspects are declination, key, and register. I discussed, in particular, the counterintuitive suggestion in the literature that the speaker adapts his slope of declination to the length of the intonational phrase. There is no convincing ground for accepting this as a fact. For the more local phenomena of tune and tone, the state of affairs is very similar to metrical planning. Very little preview or buffering is required to assign an appropriate pitch curve to an intonational phrase. But with more lookahead more melodic lines can result, such as hat patterns and inclinations.

The final section returned to the connected speech phenomena of encliticization and assimilation. The generation of word forms in context causes striking deviations from the words' citation forms. New phonological words are formed out of pairs or triples of lexical items, and all sorts of accommodations can arise at boundaries between phonological words. The mechanism responsible for these contextual adaptations—a system of rules operating on the output of segmental spellout—was outlined. The rules can enforce the merging and resyllabification of items, depending on the phrase-structural relations between them. It is this restructured material that forms the input to phonetic spellout. The eventual result is a phonetic plan for connected speech.

Fluent articulation is probably man's most complex motor skill. It involves the coordinated use of approximately 100 muscles, such that speech
sounds are produced at a rate of about 15 per second. These muscles are
distributed over three anatomically distinct structures: the *respiratory*,
the *laryngeal*, and the *supralaryngeal*. The respiratory system, with the
lungs as its central organ, regulates the flow of air, the source of energy
for speech production. The laryngeal structure, including the vocal cords,
is responsible for the alternation between voicing and nonvoicing and for
the modulation of pitch. The supralaryngeal structure or *vocal tract*, with
the velum, the tongue, the jaw, and the lips as its major moveable parts,
exercises two functions in articulation. The first is to constrict or interrupt the air flow in particular ways so as to produce fricative, plosive, and
other consonants. The second is to serve as a resonator, modulating the
timbre of the successive speech sounds. The timbre depends, in particular, on the shape of the oral, nasal, and pharyngeal cavities. The second
section of this chapter presents a short review of these three vocal organs
and of their roles in the articulatory realization of the phonetic plan.

Almost all vocal organs, from the lungs to the lips, subserve other
functions than speech alone. The respiratory system's main function is
breathing—the uptake of oxygen from air and the emission of waste
products such as carbon dioxide and vapor. The larynx, by glottal control, protects the respiratory system from intrusions of food. The supralaryngeal structures are used in the mastication and swallowing of food.
Though largely the same musculature is involved in the production of
speech, the pattern of coordination is totally different. Theories of speech
articulation have to account for this "speech mode" of coordination.
They specify the nature of speech motor control, the way in which
phonetic plans are executed by the vocal organs. The third section of this
chapter reviews some of the major theories of speech motor control.

Though these theories are quite divergent, there is rather general agreement about the relatively invariant or context-free nature of phonetic or articulatory plans. It is the executive motor system that realizes the intended articulatory target depending on the prevailing context.

The Articulator is special as a processing component in that it does not map an input representation onto an output representation. Rather, it *executes* its input representation—an utterance's phonetic plan. The result is a motor pattern, not a mental representation of anything. The phonetic plan, we saw, specifies the articulatory gestures for successive syllables, with all their segmental and prosodic parameters. This plan, the Formulator's output, may become available at a rate that is not exactly tuned to the actual rate of articulation, which is the rate *specified* in the phonetic plan. As a rule, some buffering will be required to keep the phonetic plan (i.e., the motor program) available for execution. We will begin the present chapter by reviewing some work on the management of this so-called Articulatory Buffer, which forms the interface between phonological encoding and articulation.

11.1 Managing the Articulatory Buffer

The interface of phonological encoding and articulation involves a system that can temporarily store a certain amount of phonetic plan. Chapter 10 suggested that the Phonological Encoder delivers plans for phonological words as smallest units to the Articulator. As the phonetic plan becomes available to the Articulator, it can be incrementally unfolded in terms of motoneural instructions. But there are very strict temporary restrictions on the course of articulation. Sustaining a fluent, constant rate of speaking requires a storage mechanism that can buffer the phonetic plan (the speech motor program) as it develops. It can, presumably, contain a few phonological phrases. Moreover, it *must* contain a minimal amount of program in order for speech to be initiated—probably as much as a phonological word. The present section will discuss some studies that have dealt with the management of this store, in particular the work done by Klapp, Sternberg, and their colleagues.

It has long been known that when single words or digits are read aloud, the voice-onset latency, measured from the onset of the stimulus, increases with the number of syllables in the utterance (Eriksen, Pollack, and Montague 1970). Klapp, Anderson, and Berrian (1973) discovered that this *syllable latency effect* was due not to the input (visual) process but to the preparation of the articulatory response. They first replicated

Table 11.1
Pronunciation latencies for one- and two-syllable words, in msec. (Data from Klapp et al. 1973, 1976.)

Number of syllables	Word naming	Categori-zation	Picture naming	Simple reaction	Utterance duration
One syllable	518.4	695.6	619.3	310.8	495
Two syllables	532.8	697.4	633.3	312.5	494
Difference	14.4	1.8	14.0	1.7	−1

the syllable latency effect by having subjects pronounce visually presented one- and two-syllable words which contained the same number of letters (e.g., *clock* and *camel*). The word-naming latencies were significantly different by an average of 14 milliseconds (see table 11.1, first column). This could not have been due to a difference in word-perception times, since the difference disappeared in a semantic-categorization experiment where no articulation of the words was required. In the latter experiment, half of the subjects had to say Yes when the word was an animal name (such as *camel*) and No otherwise; the other half were instructed to say Yes when the word was an object name (such as *clock*) and No otherwise. The Yes response latencies, given in the second column of table 11.1, are virtually identical for the one-syllable and the two-syllable words. Here only the *input* words differ in the number of syllables; the subjects' utterances don't. Klapp et al. did get a syllable latency effect when the stimulus was a picture (of a clock, a camel, etc.) to be named. The latencies for this condition are given in the third column of the table. Two-syllable names took, on the average, 14 msec longer to be initiated than one-syllable names. This is the same latency difference as was found for the reading of printed words. Similar syllable latency effects have been found in the reading of digits. Reading four-syllable numbers (e.g. 27) goes with longer voice onset latencies than reading three-syllable numbers (e.g. 26); see Klapp 1974 for experimental data and further references.

Where do these latency differences arise in the preparation of the articulatory response? Do they come into being *before* the phonetic plan is delivered to the Articulatory Buffer? Or are they rather articulatory in nature? That is, do they come about when the phonetic plan for the word is retrieved from the Articulatory Buffer and "unpacked" to be executed? I will argue that much of the syllable latency effect arises before the delivery of a word's plan to the buffer. But I will subsequently discuss evidence that the size of a phonetic plan (though not necessarily its number of syllables) also affects the latency of its retrieval from the buffer. In addition, there is a small but consistent number-of-syllables effect in the unpacking of a retrieved phonetic plan. That evidence comes from the work of Sternberg and colleagues.

It should be remembered that a speaker can prepare a phonetic plan without factually initiating the utterance. Waiting for a traffic light, the speaker can prepare to say "green" as soon as the light changes, and can keep the response in abeyance. When the light turns green, the reaction time can be as short as 300 msec. This is, then, the time needed to initiate the response. Such a response is called a *simple reaction*. Is the syllable latency effect one of phonological encoding, or one of response initiation? In order to test this, Klapp et al. used a simple reaction task. The word was presented on the screen for reading, but the speaker was told not to utter the word until a Go signal appeared, 3 seconds after stimulus onset. This gave the speaker the time to program the response, which he then kept ready in the Articulatory Buffer. When pronunciation latencies were measured from the Go signal, the numbers in the fourth column of table 11.1 were obtained. Under these circumstances there was no difference in pronunciation latency between one-syllable and two-syllable words. The syllable effect, therefore, is a real programming or phonological encoding effect, not an initiation effect.

But what is it that takes more time in the programming of a two-syllable word than in that of a one-syllable word? Were the two-syllable words in the experiments of Klapp and his colleagues simply longer than the one-syllable words, and could this be the reason that their encoding took more time? It is known from experiments with nonverbal motor reactions that longer responses require more preparation time. However, utterance duration cannot explain the syllable latency effect. In a subsequent study, Klapp and Erwin (1976) measured the utterance durations of the one- and two-syllable words of the 1973 study. The values are presented in the final column of table 11.1. There is virtually no difference. This may seem surprising in view of the syllable-dependent duration of utterances discussed in the previous chapter, but subjects may have had the tendency to make individual words about equally long when they pronounced them in a list-like fashion. That they did the same in the 1973 experiment is likely but cannot be taken for granted.

Assuming that response duration cannot have been the cause of the planning difference, Keele (1981) suggested that the difference stems from the hierarchical nature of the motor program (i.e., the phonetic plan). In particular, the Prosody Generator has to establish the relative timing of syllables in a multisyllabic word. This might involve a higher pro-

gramming load for *camel* than for *clock*. It appears from studies with
nonverbal responses (e.g. tapping) that the more complex the required
timing relations in a response (e.g. the tapping rhythm) the longer the
response latencies (Klapp and Wyatt 1976). On this view, the syllable
latency effect can be attributed to the extra time needed by the Prosody
Generator to compute the durational relations between the syllables of
bisyllabic words.

An alternative and simpler explanation is the one proposed in the previous chapter: In the phonetic spellout of a phonological word, syllable
programs are addressed one by one, in serial order. Hence, the number of
syllables in a phonological word will determine the duration of phonetic
spellout. If only plans for whole words are delivered to the Articulator,
monosyllabic words will become available for articulation earlier than
multisyllabic ones. There is an interesting deviance from Wundt's principle here. The Articulator cannot start working as soon as a word's first
syllable has been programmed; it must await the whole word before it can
start executing its first syllable's phonetic program.

Let us now turn to latency studies of articulatory unpacking and execution. Sternberg, Monsell, Knoll, and Wright (1978) asked their subjects
to pronounce lists of words, usually ranging in number from one to
five. The words were visually presented one after another. Then, after a
4-second delay, a Go signal (an illuminated square) appeared on the
screen, and the subject had to repeat the list as quickly as possible. This
was therefore a simple reaction task. The subject had only to retrieve a
prepared phonetic plan from the Articulatory Buffer and to initiate its
execution, just as in the simple-reaction-task condition of Klapp et al.
(1973). A major experimental question was whether the number of items
in the buffer would affect the voice-onset latencies, measured from the Go
signal.

Sternberg et al. used all sorts of lists—for instance, weekdays in
normal or random order, digits in ascending or in random order, and lists
of nouns. In all cases the result was essentially the same: As the number
of items in the list increased, the voice-onset latency increased by about
10 msec per additional item. Initiation of pronouncing a one-word "list"
took about 260 msec; for a two-word list the latency was 270 msec; for a
three-word list it was 280 msec, and so on.

Sternberg and colleagues interpreted this result as a *retrieval* effect. The
Articulatory Buffer, they supposed, is like a pot containing the items,
each with an order number. To retrieve item 1, the speaker draws an item
at random and inspects it to see whether it is item 1. If it is not, he draws

another item for inspection, and so on until item 1 turns up. At this moment the item's phonetic plan is unpacked, and the commands are issued to the neuromotor apparatus. All tested items, including the correct one, are dropped back into the pot, and the search for the next item begins. On this model, the average time to find word 1 on the list obviously depends on the number of items in the buffer. When there is only one, it is retrieved on the first draw; when there are two, retrieval requires one or two draws (1.5, on average); when there are three it takes an average of 2 draws; and so on. If a draw takes 20 msec, each additional item on the list will increase the mean voice-onset latency by 10 msec.

This model makes a further interesting prediction: that retrieving the second item will take just as much time as retrieving the first, because all the items were dropped back into the pot. Retrieving item 2 is just as complicated as retrieving item 1. In particular, it will depend in the same way on the number of items on the list. Each additional item will add 10 msec to the average retrieval time of item 2. In fact, this will hold for every item on the list. Therefore, speaking will be slower for a long list than for a short list. The speaking duration per item will increase by 10 msec for every additional word on the list. And this is almost exactly what was found. Sternberg and colleagues showed, moreover, that these increases of 10 msec, 20 msec, and so on were affecting the final parts of the words. We will return to this observation shortly.

In one experiment, Sternberg et al. compared the subjects' performances on lists of one-syllable words and lists of two-syllable words. They matched the words carefully (e.g., *bay* with *baby*, *rum* with *rumble*, and *cow* with *coward*). A first finding in this experiment was that, for all list lengths (1, 2, 3, and 4), the voice onset for lists of one-syllable words was about 4.5 msec shorter than that for lists of two-syllable words. Notice that this differs from the results of Klapp et al. given in column 4 of table 11.1. Their one-word "lists" showed the same simple reaction times for one- and two-syllable words. This difference has never been satisfactorily explained, and I will not add to the conjectures. Sternberg et al. speculated that, having *retrieved* item 1 from the buffer, the speaker has to *unpack* it further to make its constituent motor commands available for execution. This unpacking depends on type and size. A two-syllable word, for instance, involves more unpacking than a one-syllable word. And if the list begins with a two-syllable word rather than with a one-syllable word, unpacking the first syllable's plan will require a few additional milliseconds. This is because *some* unpacking of the second syllable is to be done before articulation of the first syllable can be initiated.

Taken together, the syllable latency effect seems to have a double origin. Klapp's 14-msec syllable effect is one of phonological encoding, whereas Sternberg's 4.5-msec effect is one of unpacking. Sternberg's theory of the Articulatory Buffer says that it becomes loaded with a hierarchically organized phonetic plan or motor program (see also Gordon and Meyer 1987). The units of this program are the words in the list (or, rather, the phonological phrases, as will be discussed). Each unit in the buffer consists of fully specified subprograms for its syllables and their constituent phones. The *retrieval* from the Articulatory Buffer involves complete buffer units—i.e., full phonetic plans for the words (or phrases) in the list. After retrieval of a unit, its phonetic plan or motor program has to be *unpacked* so that all its motor commands become available for execution. This takes more time for a more complex unit than for a simple unit, more time for a two-syllable word than for a one-syllable word, and perhaps—at the next level—more time for a word beginning with a consonant cluster than for one beginning with a single consonant.

An untenable alternative view would be that the Articulatory Buffer contains word-level *addresses* (equivalent to our lemma addresses) but no further phonetic plan. Upon retrieving a unit, the word's address would be opened (roughly equivalent to our spellout procedures), making its articulatory plan available. On this view the buffer would not be an articulatory one. In order to reject this theory, Sternberg, Monsell, Knoll, and Wright (1980) compared utterance latencies and durations for lists of words and lists of nonwords. If the units in the buffer are nonwords whose articulatory programs are still to be constructed after retrieval (instead of being spelled out from store), one would expect a relatively long voice-onset latency for the uttering of the first item and a relatively long duration for the uttering of the list as a whole. The lists of nonwords were phonotactically carefully matched to the lists of words. The experimental procedure was in critical respects the same as in the earlier study. The results for onset latencies and utterance durations turned out to be almost indistinguishable for word lists and nonword lists. Sternberg et al. concluded that in both cases the buffer contained fully assembled programs for all units in the list, whether words or nonwords. Hence, it is a genuine *articulatory* buffer.

According to Sternberg et al., the stages of programming (i.e., phonological encoding), retrieval from the buffer, and unpacking are, finally, followed by a *command and execution* stage. Here the motor commands are issued to the neuromotor machinery, and the response is executed. A word's duration is its execution time. Sternberg, Wright, Knoll, and Monsell (1980) asked themselves: Is the execution time affected by the retrieval time, or is a word's execution time simply a fixed quantity? When the processes of retrieval and execution are completely disjunct in time, one would expect a short silence before each subsequent word of the list is uttered. The length of this pre-word pause would depend on the number of items in the list; there would be an additional 10 msec for each additional item.

Are these multiples of 10 milliseconds in extra retrieval time indeed projected on pauses between words? They are not. What speakers do is expand the final part of the previous word; they "cover up" the retrieval time by lengthening the execution of the utterance. Sternberg et al. carefully analyzed what happened to lists of two-syllable words. It turned out that the retrieval times were almost completely absorbed by the words' second syllables. The second syllable of the word *copper* was longer when the word appeared in the middle of a five-word list than when it occurred in the middle of a three-word list, but the first syllable was just about equally long in the two cases. The obvious interpretation is that the retrieval process takes place just before the next word is uttered, and that fluency of speech is achieved by stretching the final part of the previous word. This supports Selkirk's (1984a) notion that silent beats can be realized as much by syllable drawl as by pausing.

It was mentioned above that phonological phrases rather than words are the motor units in the Articulatory Buffer. Sternberg called them *stress groups*. This idea, which arose in the 1978 study by Sternberg et al., was based on some further experimental results. In one experiment Sternberg et al. interpolated function words between the nouns of a list. The list *bay-rum-cow*, for instance, would be presented as *bay and rum or cow*. Would this "count" as a five-item list, or as a three-item list? Analysis of the data showed that it behaved like a three-item list. Since there were three stressed words in each of the lists, the conjecture was made that the motor planning units in the Articulatory Buffer are, in fact, "stress groups." A stress group here is nothing but a small phonological phrase containing just one stressed element, for instance *and rUm*. The conjecture is, therefore, fully consonant with the notion, developed in chapter 10 above, that phonological phrases are important units of phonological encoding. It is likely that the buffer is successively filled with phonological words, but that larger phonological phrase units are formed when the buffer is heavily loaded.

Table 11.2
Phases in speech motor control.

Stage 1: Assembling the program
This is the stage of phonological encoding, with a phonetic plan as output (see chapters 8–10). The phonetic plan is a detailed motor program, delivered phonological word by phonological word. When the task requires, phonetic plans can be stored in the Articulatory Buffer. The preferred units of storage are phonological phrases.

Stage 2: Retrieving the motor programs
When the speaker decides to start a prepared utterance, its motor units (i.e., the phonetic plans for the phonological phrases) are retrieved from the Articulatory Buffer. The time needed to retrieve each unit depends on the total number of units in the buffer.

Stage 3: Unpacking the subprograms
Once retrieved, the phonetic plan for a phonological phrase has to be unpacked, making available the whole hierarchy of motor commands. The more complex a motor unit, the more time unpacking takes.

Stage 4: Executing the motor commands
At this stage the motor commands are issued to the neuromotor circuits and executed by the musculature. Syllables can be drawled to absorb retrieval latencies.

The picture emerging from these studies is summarized in table 11.2.

To what extent is this picture valid for spontaneous speech? Of course, people do reproduce lists now and then in everyday life (for instance, telephone numbers). It should, in addition, be noted that in the experiments the lists were uttered as prosodic wholes—as intonational phrases with normal declination and boundary tones (Sternberg, Wright, Knoll, and Monsell 1980). There can, moreover, be no doubt that stages 1 and 4—phonological planning and execution—are always part of normal speech. The question is, rather, how much buffering and unpacking has to be done in normal fluent speech.

Clearly, a speaker can start uttering a phonological phrase before all its details have been programmed. This is apparent from cases of prelexical hesitation. A speaker may have to stop in the midst of a phonological phrase that has begun with quite normal prosody, as in *I saw him in ... eh, in ... eh, in Vallauris.* Here the full program for the place name was, clearly, not yet assembled, let alone buffered, when it was needed for execution. Still, the preposition of the phonological phrase (*in*) was uttered normally. Execution can follow phonological encoding at a very short distance, a distance smaller than a full phonological phrase. This distance is probably the size of a phonological word (the smallest "chunk" delivered by the Phonological Encoder), and buffering will be minimal or absent. On the other hand, grammatical and phonological encoding may occasionally go through a speedy phase, so that a greater amount of ready-made program becomes available than can be executed at a normal speaking rate. Articulatory buffering is an important facility under such circumstances.

11.2   The Vocal Organs and the Origins of Speech Sounds

The execution of a phonetic plan involves the coordinated use of a highly complex musculature. Figure 11.1 depicts the structures involved in speech production. The discussion below will follow the figure's partitioning into respiratory, laryngeal, and supralaryngeal structures.

11.2.1   The Respiratory System

In normal breathing, the lungs contain some 3 liters of air. We inhale and exhale about half a liter at a time. In speech, far more air can be exhaled at a time; 3.5 liters is not abnormal. This, of course, requires deeper inhalation. The inhalation during speech is quick; taking up no more than 15 percent of the breathing cycle (versus 40 percent in normal breathing). In speech, most of the respiratory cycle is spent on exhalation, which can easily take 10 or 15 seconds (versus 3 seconds in normal breathing).

Inhalation and exhalation are controlled by various muscles in the thorax and the abdomen. When the inspiratory muscles contract, the cavity enclosed by the ribs increases in volume, and the resulting pressure gradient causes air to flow into the lungs. During normal breathing, exhalation is mainly brought about by relaxing the inspiratory muscles. The elastic shrinking back of the thorax is enough to create the slight overpressure necessary for expiration. In speech, however, the inspiratory muscles keep being innervated during the initial phase of exhalation, holding back the air, so to say. Then they suddenly relax, and the expiratory muscles of the thorax take over to compress the volume even more. Still later during the exhalation or speaking phase the abdominal muscles may start contracting. As a result, the diaphragm is pushed upward into the thoracial cavity, decreasing its volume even more. This complex interplay of muscular activity during exhalation causes a rather constant air pressure during speech production. Still, there is a slightly decreasing slope in this pressure. It is the main cause of pitch declination in the course of an utterance (see subsection 10.3.1).

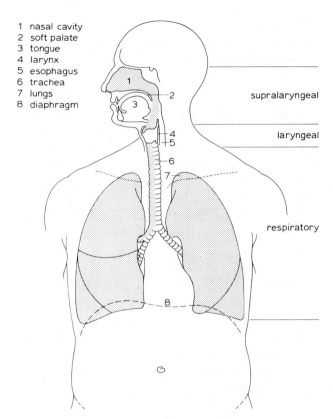

1 nasal cavity
2 soft palate
3 tongue
4 larynx
5 esophagus
6 trachea
7 lungs
8 diaphragm

supralaryngeal

laryngeal

respiratory

Figure 11.1
The respiratory, laryngeal, and supralaryngeal structures involved in speech
production.

11.2.2 The Laryngeal System

The larynx is responsible for phonation in speech, not only for normal voicing but also for whispering and for other less common registers (such as a man's falsetto). Figure 11.2a presents a posterior view of the larynx. It sits on top of the trachea, a tube connecting it to the lungs. The larynx as a whole can be moved up and down and forward and backward by various extrinsic muscles attached to the mandible, the skull, and the thorax. These movements can easily be traced by touching the Adam's apple, the protruding part of the thyroid cartilage; they are especially pronounced during swallowing. At the top of the larynx is the epiglottis, which can cover the larynx's exit. This is done at moments of swallowing, when food is transported from the mouth to the esophagus and the stomach. At these moments two other laryngeal closures are made as well: The glottis is shut by the vocal folds, and the false vocal cords (slightly above the glottis) are moved together so as to make a firm closure. During speech and normal breathing, the false vocal cords are wide apart.

The centerpiece of the larynx is the structure around the *vocal folds* (also called *vocal cords*). Figure 11.2b gives a sagittal view of this part. The *glottis* is the area between the vocal folds. It can be opened or closed. The vocal folds, each about 2 centimeters long, can be pulled apart at the posterior side to make an angular opening. They cannot move at the anterior side, where they are both attached to the *thyroid cartilage* (directly behind the Adam's apple). But they can be drawn apart at the posterior side, because each is attached to an *arytenoid cartilage* and these two cartilages can be abducted or adducted by sets of muscles attached to them (the posterior and lateral *cricoarytenoid muscles*, respectively). The vocal folds themselves are also largely muscle tissue, except for where they touch (and maximally vibrate); these parts of the folds are ligaments. There are two kinds of muscles in the folds: (i) The *longitudinal thyromuscularis* shortens the fold when it contracts; the arytenoid cartilage, to which it is attached, is accordingly displaced in the forward direction. The antagonist muscles, which pull the cartilages back into place, are the *crycothyroid muscles.* Their contraction causes the folds to become longer and more tensed. (ii) The *vocalis* is attached to the ligament tissue, and can influence the curvature of the ligament.

Voicing occurs when the folds are pulled together while air pressure is built up by the respiratory system. When the pressure is sufficiently high, the folds burst apart and release a puff of air. This, in turn, causes a temporal reduction in subglottal air pressure, which makes the glottis close

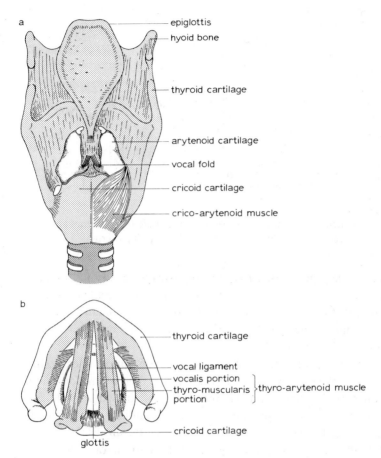

a

— epiglottis
— hyoid bone

— thyroid cartilage

— arytenoid cartilage

— vocal fold

— cricoid cartilage

— crico-arytenoid muscle

b

— thyroid cartilage

— vocal ligament
— vocalis portion
— thyro-muscularis portion } thyro-arytenoid muscle

— cricoid cartilage

glottis

Figure 11.2
(a) A posterior view of the larynx. (b) A superior view of the vocal folds and the cartilages they are attached to. (After Calvert 1980.)

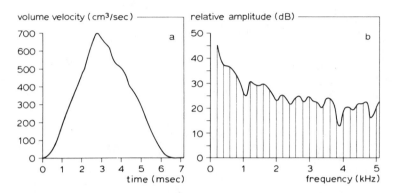

Figure 11.3
(a) Increase and decrease of air flow in a single glottal puff. (After Denes and
Pinson 1963.) (b) Spectral analysis for a 200-Hz glottal puff pattern.

again. The cycle repeats itself rhythmically (this is called the "Bernoulli
effect"), and the glottis releases a periodic sequence of puffs of air. The
average frequency of these puffs is about 200 Hz in a woman's voice and
110 Hz in a man's. The actual frequency at any one moment is called the
speech sound's *fundamental frequency*, or F_0.

During one puff, the outflow of air first increases almost linearly, then
decreases again the same way. Figure 11.3a shows this pattern for a single
puff. If one could listen to regular repetitions of this pattern alone, it
would resemble the sharp sound of an oboe reed, not the smooth sound
of a tuning fork. The latter sound is created when the air displacement is
sinusoidal. Physically speaking, the sawtooth pattern of figure 11.3a
when continuously repeated, can be constructed as the sum of a set of
sinusoidal components: The same sound would be produced by a battery
of tuning forks of the following sort: a big tuning fork vibrating at frequency F_0 (say, 200 Hz); a somewhat smaller tuning fork, precisely an
octave higher (i.e., vibrating at 400 Hz); a still smaller fork, vibrating a
fifth higher (i.e., at 600 Hz); and even smaller forks at 800 Hz, 1,000 Hz,
1,200 Hz, and so on. (One can ignore the very small forks vibrating at
frequencies of more than 5,000 or 6,000 Hz.)

Figure 11.3b presents the sound intensity in decibels produced by each
tuning fork, one bar for each fork. The intensity is high for the 200-Hz
fork, and it decreases for the higher-frequency forks. Since the regular
string of glottal puffs is precisely imitated by this battery of tuning forks,
figure 11.3b can be seen as the *spectral analysis* of the sawtooth vibration
pattern consisting of puffs such as in figure 11.3a. In other words, it is the

spectral analysis of a 200-Hz vibration produced by the glottis. The sound consists of a pure (sinusoidal) 200-Hz tone plus decreasing amounts of each of its overtones (400, 600, and 800 Hz, etc.). These higher components give the sound its sharp timbre. The fundamental frequency component (200 Hz in the present example) is also called the first *harmonic*; the first overtone (400 Hz) is the second harmonic, and so on. In figure 11.3b the intensity for each harmonic is presented by a vertical bar. The undulating line connecting the bars is called the *spectral envelope*. When the glottis vibrates at a different frequency than 200 Hz, the spectral envelope is by and large the same; only the spacing of bars varies. The spectral envelope is a useful characterization of the *timbre* of a periodic speech sound, irrespective of its pitch.

The pitch contours of speech are realized by varying F_0. The vibration frequency of the vocal folds can vary over a range of about two octaves (professional singers can do much better), but it usually doesn't surpass one octave in normal speech. This frequency is a complex function of various factors. F_0 covaries with subglottal pressure. This is, as we have seen, a main cause of pitch declination in speech. F_0 is also—and more substantially—affected by the length and the tension of the vocal cords. These two factors have opposite effects: lengthening decreases F_0, tensing increases F_0. When the crycothyroid muscles stretch the folds, there is both lengthening and tensing, but the tensing effect overrides the lengthening effect, just as when one stretches an elastic band. As a consequence, there is an increase in the fundamental frequency. The small muscles controlling the tension of the folds can adjust far more rapidly than the big inspiratory and expiratory muscles. Thus, the fine, speedy pitch movements in speech depend mainly on laryngeal muscles.

The loudness of speech is determined largely by the intensity of vocal-fold vibration. This intensity depends, in part, on subglottal pressure. The higher the pressure, the faster the flow of air and the louder the speech sound. The intensity of vibration also depends, to a substantial degree, on the size of the glottal opening. It is not strictly necessary for the glottis to be totally closed at the moments between the air puffs. The Bernouilli effect will also arise when there is a slight V-shaped opening between the folds. As a consequence, some air will escape without transmitting its energy to the folds, and the vibration is weakened. The difference in energy expenditure between loud and soft speech, measured in volumes of air displaced per unit time, is probably quite small.

In whispering, the glottis is opened so much that no periodic vibration of the folds occurs any more, but it is still so narrow that a hissing noise

1 nasal cavity
2 palate
3 velum
4 oral cavity
5 alveolar ridge
6 lips
7 teeth
8 tongue
9 nasopharyngeal port
10 uvula
11 tonsils
12 pharynx
13 epiglottis
14 larynx
15 cricoid cartilage
16 vocal fold
17 thyroid cartilage
18 trachea
19 esophagus

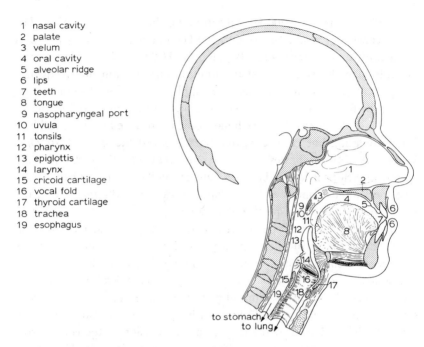

Figure 11.4
The vocal tract. (After Calvert 1980.)

results when the air passes through it. When speech is articulated this way, the voiced parts of speech are replaced by "hissed" parts.

11.2.3 The Vocal Tract

The supralaryngeal system, or vocal tract, consists of the structures between the epiglottis and the lips and nose. Figure 11.4 depicts these structures.

The vocal tract consists of three main cavities: the *pharynx* or *throat*, the *oral cavity*, and the *nasal cavity*. The pharynx and the oral cavity are flexible in shape; the nasal cavity is a rather fixed structure. The size and shape of these three cavities determine the *resonance* properties of the vocal tract. The place and manner of constricting the outflowing air stream determine the proper *articulation* of speech segments.

Resonation

Each of the three cavities can resonate with the buzzing sound produced by the vocal folds. Consider the nasal cavity. It participates in shaping the timbre of a speech sound when there is an open connection with the

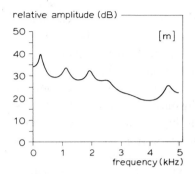

Figure 11.5
Spectral envelope for the nasal sound [m].

pharynx. This occurs when the *velum* or *soft palate*, a very flexible organ, is moved forward to open the *nasopharyngeal port*. This is its normal position in breathing. A speech sound produced with this port open has a characteristic nasal timbre. It is an articulatory feature of the consonants [m], [n], and [ŋ], and of nasalized vowels such as that in *chance* or that in French *en*.

This special timbre arises because the nasal cavity affects the energy spectrum of the sound produced by the vocal folds. The spectrum of the buzzing sound produced in the glottis was given in figure 11.3b. There is a string of decreasing intensity peaks, extending from F_0 to about 5,000 Hz. The nasal cavity will dampen or attenuate the energy in the high-frequency ranges and will amplify the energy in the very low range (around 200 Hz). The resulting spectral envelope is like the one given in figure 11.5, which is an analysis of the sound [m].

The nasal cavity is never the only resonator involved in shaping a speech sound's timbre. The *pharynx*, which is the mediating structure between the larynx and the nasal cavity, is necessarily involved in the production of all nasal and all non-nasal sounds. The shape of the pharynx or throat is not fixed. It can, first of all, constrict itself. This happens especially during the peristaltic movement that transports food from the mouth to the esophagus. It can, second, be raised and widened by a special set of levator muscles. And, third, its shape changes depending on the position of the soft palate. Each shape of the pharynx will have its own effect on the timbre of a speech sound.

The resonating properties of the *mouth* depend on the positions of the mandible, the tongue, the lips, and the velum. All of these are independently movable. The *mandible* can be moved up and down, forward and backward, and sideways. It is mainly the up-and-down movement that is relevant to speech; it can drastically decrease or increase the volume of the oral cavity. When the volume is small, the higher frequencies are amplified; when it is large, the lower frequencies are more prominent.

The *tongue*, probably the most essential organ in the articulation of speech, is a highly flexible instrument. Phylogenetically, its role is to displace food within the mouth, especially during mastication, and to transport liquid and chunks of food to the pharynx. It is also the seat of an important sensory function: taste. The tongue is moved by, and largely consists of, *extrinsic* and *intrinsic* muscles. The extrinsic muscles attach to bones of the skull and the larynx. A large part of the tongue's body is formed by the *genioglossus*, an extrinsic muscle extending from the frontal cavity in the mandible to the back, the middle, and the front of the tongue. It can strongly affect the shape of the oral cavity by retracting or protruding the tongue, and by depressing or lifting it. The intrinsic muscles, which run both longitudinally and laterally through the tongue's body, can affect its finer shape in numerous ways: They can make the tongue longer and narrower, they can widen and flatten the tongue, they can move the tip up or down, and they can make the upper surface concave or convex. All these movements are relevant for resonation and for the articulation of consonants.

The *lips* can affect the timbre of speech most markedly by spreading (as in *pit*) and by rounding (as in *put*). The rounding of the lips, and their protruding, is effected by a circular intrinsic muscle around the mouth opening, the *orbicularis oris*. Other muscles can move the lips in and out, and draw the corners of the mouth up or down. The muscles of the lips and other facial muscles play an important role in the facial expression during speech communication. These expressions can provide visual backchannel signals to the interlocutor (see subsection 2.1.2).

The *velum* is the only movable part of the mouth's *palate*. The palate consists of the teeth ridge or *alveolus*, the *hard palate*, which forms the roof of the oral cavity, and the *soft palate* or velum. The velum's main function in speech, we saw, is to open and close the nasal cavity. In doing so, it also affects the shape of the mouth.

The shapes of the three vocal-tract cavities—in particular, the mouth —determine the characteristic timbres of a language's vowels. The main oral contributors to a vowel's timbre are the positions of the tongue and the lips. As far as the lips are concerned, it is especially their rounding (and their slight protruding) that matters. The tongue's contribution to the sound quality of vowels depends largely on the activity of the extrin-

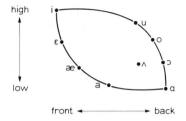

Figure 11.6
Tongue positions for eight vowels. (After Denes and Pinson 1963.)

sic muscles that regulate the position of the body of the tongue, which can vary between high (close to the palate) and low and between the front and the back of the mouth. These positions, and the English vowels that go with them, are diagrammed in figure 11.6.

The vowels in figure 11.6 differ systematically in their spectral properties. The spectral envelopes of the four vowels [ɛ], [ʌ], [i], and [æ] are given in figure 11.7. Figure 11.7a gives the spectrum for [ɛ]. It can be seen from this figure that the vocal tract resonates especially with frequencies in the ranges of 500, 1,700, and 2,400 Hz. These peaks in the spectrum are called the first, second, and third *formants*, or F_1, F_2, and F_3. (Remember that the vibration frequency of the vocal folds was called F_0.) As Stevens (1983) has pointed out, F_1 and F_2 are typically quite far apart for a front vowel such as [ɛ]. In order to appreciate this, compare the spectrum for [ɛ] with that for the back vowel [ʌ], given in figure 11.7b. Here F_1 and F_2 are quite close together. In other words, front vowels typically show a concentration of resonance in the high frequency range, whereas back vowels have their energy concentrated in the low frequency range.

High and low vowels also differ systematically in their spectral envelopes. Figures 11.7c and 11.7d give the spectra for the high vowel [i] and the low vowel [æ], respectively. Both are front vowels, with the characteristic spreading of F_1 and F_2. Their crucial difference, according to Stevens (1983), is in the position of F_1. High vowels such as [i] have their first formant in the very low frequency range, whereas the frequencies of the first formants of low vowels such as [æ] are substantially higher.

These static pictures of vowel spectra should not give the illusion that vowels do not change their spectral properties during articulation. In fluent speech the characteristic spectrum of a vowel arises only for a short moment, if at all. The degree to which the vocal tract approaches the ideal configuration for a particular vowel depends on the context in

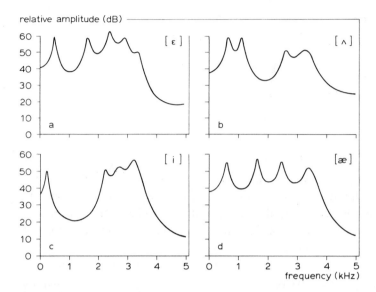

Figure 11.7
(a–d, respectively) Spectral envelopes for the vowel sounds [ε], [ʌ], [i], and [æ].
(After Stevens 1983.)

which the vowel appears, and on the rate of speech. There are, moreover, vowels that are characterized by a *changing* spectrum. They are called *diphthongs*. The English diphthongs are [aɪ] as in *night*, [ɔɪ] as in *toy*, [eɪ] as in *sake*, [aʊ] as in [owl], and [oʊ] as in *phone*. The pronunciation of a diphthong involves gliding the body of the tongue from one position to another.

Not only vowels, but also consonants reflect in their sound quality the configuration of shapes in the vocal tract. This is especially apparent in voiced consonants that involve periodic vibration of the vocal chords. Examples are [b], [d], [g], [v], and [z], as well as the nasal consonants [m], [n], and [ŋ]. But unvoiced consonants, such as [p], [t], [k], [f], and [s], also have their own characteristic frequency spectra, which can change rather drastically in the course of their articulation (Schouten and Pols 1979). Every speech sound has a slowly or rapidly changing timbre, which depends on the changing shape (and hence the changing resonance properties) of the vocal tract.

Articulation
The vocal tract can be constricted at different *places* and in different *manners* (see subsection 8.1.5). The most visible place of constriction is the lips; [p], [b], [m], and English [w] are produced with a *bilabial* constriction.

Constriction is also possible between the lower lip and the upper teeth. When a constriction is made in this place, the speech sound is called *labio-dental*. The phones [f] and [v] are the two labio-dentals in English; [w] is a labio-dental in various other languages.

When the place of articulation is between the tongue blade and the upper teeth, the speech sound is called a *dental*; the English consonants [ð] and [θ] are dentals. Still further back, and thus less visible, is the place of articulation for a rather heterogeneous set of speech sounds: [t], [d], [s], [z], [n], [l], [r], and [j]. They are all made with a constriction somewhere along the gums or alveolar ridge; thus, they are called *alveolars*.

When the main constriction of the vocal tract is made somewhere along the hard palate, the speech sound is *palatal*; [ʃ] and [ʒ] are cases in point. For some palatal consonants, the main constriction borders on the alveolar ridge; these speech sounds are called *palato-alveolar*, and among them are [tʃ] and [dʒ]. All speech sounds in which the tongue blade is used in the major constriction, ranging from dental to palatal, are called *coronal*.

Velars have the velum as the place where the main constriction is made. The three velar speech sounds in English are [k], [g], and [ŋ] (but [w] also often involves a secondary or even a main constriction at this place of articulation).

There are languages that involve the uvula, the fleshy clapper-like appendix of the soft palate, in certain consonants. This is, for instance, the case for French [r] and for Spanish, Dutch, and Hebrew [x]. This place of articulation is, correspondingly, called *uvular*. The deepest place of articulation is the glottis. The main constriction for [h] is just there; it is a *glottal* speech sound. All speech sounds with a main constriction behind the alveolar ridge are called *posterior* (as opposed to *anterior*).

Each place of articulation can go with different *manners of articulation*. One manner is to create a momentary but complete closure of the vocal tract at the place of articulation. The built-up air pressure is subsequently released, which creates a plosive effect. Speech sounds of this kind are called *plosives* or *stops*. Examples are English [b] and [p], [d] and [t], [dʒ] and [tʃ], and [g] and [k], which come in pairs, each consisting of a voiced and an unvoiced consonant. The distinction between *voiced and unvoiced* is, therefore, also considered to be a manner aspect of articulation. In their turn, voiced stops can have the additional manner of being *nasalized*. The English nasal stops are, we saw, [m], [n], and [ŋ].

Another manner feature involves rounding of the lips, as in the above-mentioned *put*, where the vowel [ʊ] is *rounded* as opposed to the [ɪ] in *pit*. English [w] is also rounded.

When there is no complete closure but rather a constriction so narrow that audible air turbulence is created, the manner of articulation is called *fricative*, *strident*, or *spirant*. The English fricatives also come in pairs of voiced and unvoiced consonants. They are [v] and [f], [ð] and [θ], [z] and [s], [ʒ] and [ʃ], and [ɦ] and [h]. The latter two are allophones; the voiced [ɦ] appears in intervocalic position, as in the word *Ohio*. The stop consonants [dʒ] and [tʃ] behave like fricatives after the moment when the air is released. In that sense they are hybrids of stops and fricatives; some phoneticians call them *affricatives*. Stops, fricatives, and affricatives are three varieties of *obstruents*.

When the constriction is still less narrow, so that no audible spiration results, very rapid changes of resonance (which resemble diphthongs) can be created. This is the *semi-vowel* manner of articulation. English [j], as in *yet*, and [w], as in *wet*, are semi-vowels, and so is [r] in many English dialects. A very special case is [l], whose manner of articulation is called *lateral*. It involves a temporary central alveolar constriction, with the air passing by laterally.

This section has reviewed the major vocal organs involved in the production of speech. More details can be found in Calvert 1980. The central issue for a theory of articulation is, of course, how a speaker's phonetic plan becomes realized as a coordinated motor activity. If the plan is roughly as suggested in the previous chapter, how are the respiratory, laryngeal, and supralaryngeal muscle systems set to bring about the intended articulatory pattern? The phonetic plan is a motor program at a still abstract level. The string of syllable gestures is parametrized for rhythmic and prosodic variables, for variables of rate and force, and for the precision of articulation to be attained. But in order for this motor program to run, its articulatory features must be realized by the musculature of the three main structures reviewed in this section. The same feature can often be realized in different but equivalent ways. There is a flexibility in motoneural execution that makes it possible to realize a particular articulatory feature in spite of varying boundary conditions. This context dependency of the motor execution of speech has puzzled phoneticians greatly. The next section will review some of the theories that have been proposed to account for this flexibility in the motor control of speech.

11.3   Motor Control of Speech

The speaker's phonetic or articulatory plan, as it eventually emerges from phonological encoding, is strongly based on syllables. A syllable's phones are articulatory gestures whose execution depends heavily on their position in the syllable and on the other phones with which they are more or less coarticulated. If indeed, as I will argue, the syllable is a unit of motor execution in speech, how much articulatory detail is specified in the phonetic plan? A complete theory of motor control will, in final analysis, have to account for the fine detail of neuromuscular activity in speech. There has been a strong tendency in the literature to include all or most of this detail in the articulatory or phonetic plan (also referred to as "motor program"), which then would prescribe the full detail of individual muscle contractions.

More recent developments in motor-control theory, however, have made this view less attractive. Studies of handwriting (van Galen and Teulings 1983; Thomassen and Teulings 1985; Kao, van Galen, and Hoosain 1986) have shown that there are astonishing invariants in the execution of a program under different modes of execution. One well-known example is the constancy in letter shape and writing speed between writing on paper and writing on a blackboard. At the level of individual muscle activity, the neuromotor patterns for these two modes of writing are totally different. But even ignoring such dramatic differences, it is a general property of motor execution that it is highly adaptive to context. Handwriting immediately adapts to the resistance of the paper, just as gait adapts to the resistance of the walking surface. In the same way, the execution of speech motor commands adapts to peripheral context—for instance, a pipe in the mouth.

It is, therefore, attractive to assume that the commands in the articulatory plan involve only the *context-free* or invariant aspects of motor execution, and that the context-dependent neuromuscular implementation of the program is left to a highly self-regulating neuromotor execution system. This system *translates* the program codes into appropriate neuromuscular activity (Gallistel 1980). Without such context-dependent translation, one must assume that a different motor program is prepared for each context of execution. Since contexts of motor execution can vary infinitely, this would involve an immense drain on information-processing resources in the planning of motor activity. In the following, this division of labor between programming and execution will be accepted. But there is a danger in this approach: The neuromuscular execution system is easily made a *deus ex machina* that will take care of everything the theorist cannot explain. Shifting the account for a motor system's adaptability to a self-regulating executive system creates the obligation to causally explain these self-regulations. However, this distinction does exclude several theories of the nature of speech motor commands—in particular, the following two.

11.3.1 Location Programming

The theory of *location programming* assumes that the program consists of a sequence of target locations for the articulatory musculature. Each phone involves such a set of target positions. The theory is attractively simple. It is known that a muscle's target length can be encoded in the muscle spindle. The alpha/gamma loop, which is a peripheral reflex arc, will then automatically realize this target length, irrespective of the starting length of the muscle (see figure 11.8 for more detail).

To realize a phonetic segment, several muscles will be set for a particular target length. As soon as all the target positions for that phone have been reached, the next set of locations will be commanded, and so on till the end of an utterance's program. The program specifies a sequence of targets, but they are not explicitly timed; there is no *intrinsic timing* in the plan. The duration of moving from one phonetic target to the next depends only on the mechanical properties of the musculature involved, i.e., on executive factors beyond the phonetic plan. This is called *extrinsic timing*.

I argued for intrinsic timing in chapters 8 and 10. At various stages of phonological encoding, durational parameters are set that reflect the utterance's composition in prosodic units (such as phonological words and phrases, intonational phrases, and turns). These parameters are eventually transmitted to the phonetic spellout procedures and implemented in syllable programs. As a result, the phonetic plans for successive syllables are *intrinsically* timed. How this timing is realized will depend on the internal composition of the syllable. A syllable containing many consonants (such as *scratch*) will always be longer than one with few (such as *at*). Such syllable-specific durational properties are part of the stored syllable program. But they will be modified by the higher-level rhythmic parameters. Kohler (1986) provides an explicit model for this two-level intrinsic syllable timing. Though the location-programming theory gives a natural account of syllable-specific differences in duration (e.g., *scratch* takes more time than *at* because there is a longer sequence of target posi-

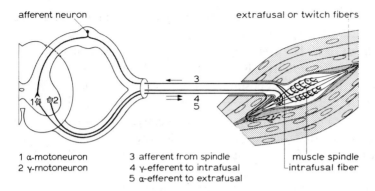

1 α-motoneuron
2 γ-motoneuron
3 afferent from spindle
4 γ-efferent to intrafusal
5 α-efferent to extrafusal
muscle spindle
intrafusal fiber

Figure 11.8
The alpha/gamma loop in muscle-tone control. A skeletal muscle's main fibers, the *extrafusal* or *twitch fibers*, are innervated by alpha motoneurons originating in the spine. Interspersed between the twitch fibers are so-called *intrafusal* fibers, whose contraction is controlled by gamma-motoneurons, which also originate in the spine. Wrapped around intrafusal fibers are *muscle spindles*. These afferent neurons fire when the intrafusal fibers are more contracted than their neighboring extrafusal fibers. This "difference information" is returned to the alpha motoneurons in the spine. It causes them to send impulses to the extrafusal fibers, which contract as a result. This causes a decrease of spindle activity, because a better match is obtained between the stretching of extrafusal and intrafusal fibers. The equilibrium point is reached when this match is complete. The alpha/gamma loop allows for fine control of the muscle's target length. The gamma system can, by contracting its low-mass intrafusal fibers, quickly "dictate" a target length to the muscle as a whole. The muscle's twitch fibers— the real mass of the muscle—will, through the alpha/gamma loop, adapt their length to the preset intrafusal fiber lengths. Measurements show that the innervation of a muscle's alpha and gamma neurons is about simultaneous. But the lightweight intrafusal muscle system, which is never loaded, reaches its target length relatively quickly. The extrafusal main body of the muscle adapts more slowly.

tions to be realized), it provides no possibility of implementing the higher-level rhythmic parameters.

The theory can, however, explain an aspect of coarticulation. The spatio-temporal route through which the articulators move in order to reach, say, a vowel's target position in a CVC syllable will depend on the previously reached target position: that of the syllable-initial consonant. Similarly, the route out of the vowel's target configuration will depend on the character of the syllable's coda. So, the vowel gesture [a] will be different in *car* and *father* because it starts and ends differently in these environments.

The theory fails to account for other aspects of context-dependent motor execution. It can, in particular, not deal with *compensatory* movements in speech articulation. If a speaker says *aba*, he moves both his jaw and his lips to realize the closure of [b]. The location-programming theory explains this by specifying the phone [b] as a set of target lengths for the musculature controlling the positions of the mandible and the lips. But it cannot explain the following: If the jaw is fixed in the open position (phoneticians do such cruel things), the lips will still get closed when the speaker is pronouncing *aba*. The speaker compensates for the jaw movement by making a more extensive closing movement with the lips. In other words, a different target position is set for the lips. Nothing in the theory predicts this. We will shortly return to this compensatory behavior, which has been a major argument for developing the notion of context-dependent motor execution.

Nobody entertained the location-programming theory in this idealized form. MacNeilage (1970) came closest, but in later papers (MacNeilage and Ladefoged 1976; MacNeilage 1980) he rejected it.

11.3.2 Mass-Spring Theory

A close relative of the location-programming theory is the *mass-spring theory*, which was developed to explain the control of limb movements (Fel'dman 1966a,b). An experimental test of this theory for pointing gestures, the results of which were essentially negative, is reported in Levelt, Richardson, and La Heij 1985. Lindblom used the theory to explain motor control in speech as early as 1963, and it was later used by Fowler and Turvey (1980) and by Fowler, Rubin, Remez, and Turvey (1980).

In its simplest form, the theory treats the agonist and the antagonist of a limb as stretchable springs that "want" to reach their normal resting position (the *zero position*). The limb will rotate around the joint, and will eventually reach a steady-state position which is determined by the equi-

librium of torques resulting from the pull of the agonist and the antagonist, as well as by gravity. In order for a limb's target location to be
programmed, the zero positions of the agonist and the antagonist have
to be tuned. This is done by setting a muscle's target length by means of
the above-mentioned spindle system. Each muscle will then strive for its
target length, until an equilibrium is reached between the pulls of the
different muscles controlling the limb's movement. Normally, none of the
muscle target lengths will have been reached in the limb's steady state.
Here the mass-spring theory differs from the location-programming
theory, according to which the muscles do reach their "tuned" target
positions.

An advantage of the mass-spring theory is that there is not a *single* tuning to reach a particular steady state; rather, there is an *equivalence class*.
The same steady-state position can be reached by tuning the agonist and
the antagonist to become very short as can be reached by setting them
both for some medium length. The muscles are more tensed in the former
case than in the latter, and the limb's target position is, correspondingly,
reached more quickly in the former case than in the latter. This is the way
in which movement *timing* can be controlled in the mass-spring model.

Like the location-programming theory, the mass-spring theory in its
simple form fails in that it cannot handle compensatory adjustment to
context. When one speaks with a pipe in one's mouth, the tongue's target
positions for various vowels are different than when the pipe is not there.
When an adult speaker is given a biteblock between his teeth, he immediately produces quite acceptable vowels. This can only be done when
the vowels are articulated with substantial deviations from their normal
target positions (Lindblom, Lubker, and Gay 1979; Gay and Turvey
1979; Fowler and Turvey 1980). The articulation of consonants also
adapts to such hampering circumstances (Folkins and Abbs 1975; Kelso,
Tuller, and Harris 1983; Kelso, Saltzman, and Tuller 1986).

Similarly, the laryngeal system adapts immediately when the speaker
looks up or down, or tilts his head, or turns it sideways. And the respiratory system is equally adaptive; it has to function quite differently in contexts of standing, sitting, and lying down. The mass-spring model does
not predict compensation when a limb's (or an articulator's) movement is
mechanically interfered with; the interfering force is simply added to the
set of forces between which an equilibrium is established. The eventual
rest or steady-state position will, as a result, be different from the case
where there is unhampered movement (Levelt et al. 1985), but there will
be no adequate compensation for this difference. In particular, no other

articulator will "take over," as the lips do when compensating for an immobilized jaw in the articulation of [b].

There are still other problems with theories that involve the programming of target lengths for muscles or target rest positions for articulators. One is that most phones cannot be characterized by just a target *position*; they are *gestures* in time. Diphthongs are diphthongs by virtue of a gliding change of the vocal tract's configuration. The place of articulation of consonants may seem to be a definable target position, but the manner of articulation requires particular temporal characteristics of the way that target position is approached or left. This is not controllable by location programming. The mass-spring theory at least allows for control of the speed at which the rest position is reached. But full control of the *trajectory* of movement also requires more than the simple mass-spring account (Saltzman and Kelso 1987).

An additional problem for a mass-spring account of articulation (which may be solvable) is to work out the equations for soft tissue such as the tongue. The theory was initially developed to account for the rotation of limbs around joints, but many of the speech articulators have peculiar damping and stiffness properties that are hard to model. Both Lindblom (1963) and Fowler et al. (1980) have considered these problems. Their solutions are quite different, however, as we will see.

In spite of the various problems of the mass-spring model (in particular, its failure to account for compensation), elements of this model will turn up again as part of another conception of motor control: the theory of coordinative structures. Before we turn to that theory, however, three other theories of articulatory motor control will be reviewed.

11.3.3 Auditory Distinctive-Feature Targets
If the motor command codes are more abstract than target positions of articulators, what is their nature? It has been suggested that their nature is *auditory* or *acoustic* (Nolan 1982; Stevens 1983; Kent 1986). According to this view, the speaker's codes are images of the intended sound structure. With the syllable as a motor unit, the speaker would code the auditory properties of the syllable's sequence of phones. Stevens (1983) suggested that these properties can best be characterized by a set of phonetic *distinctive features*. These are highly perceivable and contrastive dimensions of variation in speech sounds. Linguistically relevant contrasts are made along precisely these dimensions; /b/ contrasts with /n/ in the perceivable dimension of nasality, and with /p/ in the even more per-

ceivable dimension of voicing. The target for the realization of a phone is the set of its linguistically distinctive perceptual features.

In order to be perceptually distinctive, the features should be *acoustically* realized by the production apparatus. Consider, for instance, the acoustic condition for perceiving a stop consonant. Stevens (1983) argued that a major condition for perceiving a stop is the rapidity of spectral change. Take the perceptual distinction between [ba] and [wa]. Only the consonant in [ba] is perceived as a stop or plosive, and, as Stevens showed, this is concomitant with the rapid spectral change in going from the syllable-initial consonant to the vowel. Another of Stevens' examples is the feature of nasality, already discussed in subsection 11.2.3 (see figure 11.5). The clear perceptual distinction between nasal and non-nasal sounds is, according to Stevens, based on the presence of resonance in the very low frequency spectrum. These and other perceptually distinctive features are *acoustic goals* that the speaker tries to achieve. For each phone in a syllable, a small set of such acoustic goals must be realized.

An attraction of this theory is that it puts the goals of articulation in the ear of the listener. The relation between motor programs of speech and perceptual analysis of speech sounds is, on this view, not arbitrary but systematic. This systematicity has been stressed time and again, but it is usually interpreted in the reverse way. Lindblom (1983), for instance, argues that "languages tend to evolve sound patterns that can be seen as adaptations to the motor mechanisms of speech production." The set of possible speech sounds is not exclusively determined by perceptual distinctiveness (though Lindblom stresses, like Stevens, that this is an important criterion); the biomechanical properties of the production apparatus severely limit the class of possible sound-form distinctions languages can employ. Somewhat further back in history, Liberman, Cooper, Shankweiler, and Studdert-Kennedy (1967) also made this reverse move in their motor theory of speech perception. According to this theory, the listener, in analyzing a speech sound, constructs a model of the articulatory movements by which the speaker could have produced it. The perceptual targets of analysis are speech motor patterns. A very similar view was expressed by Halle and Stevens (1964) in their analysis-by-synthesis theory of speech perception. This is exactly the reverse of the acoustic theory of speech motor production, where the goals of production are distinctive perceptual patterns.

Though one should be sympathetic to the view that there are quite systematic relations between perception and production of speech sounds (there is even important neurological support for this view; see Ojemann

1982), one should be worried when students of perception conjecture motor targets while students of production surmise perceptual targets. It is like Joseph and Mary each assuming, erroneously, that the other is taking care of the Holy Child. A major problem for an acoustic or an auditory theory of motor commands is, as MacNeilage (1980) points out, that it fails "to generate consequences for the control of actual movements." When the target is, for instance, a very low-frequency resonance component in the acoustic signal, which is perceived as nasality, why would the speaker open the nasopharyngeal port?

11.3.4   Orosensory Goals, Distinctive Features, and Intrinsic Timing

One step toward dealing with this problem was suggested by Perkell (1980; see also Stevens and Perkell 1977). Though the "distal" goals of speech motor programming are indeed sensory distinctive features, such as voicing, obstruency, and nasality, the speaker has learned how these goals can be attained by realizing more proximal goals. These are called *orosensory goals*. Each distinctive feature corresponds to a particular aspect of articulation that can be *sensed* by the speaker.

Take, for example, the feature of obstruency, which is a property of all stop consonants. The speaker has learned that the distal auditory goal of plosion can be realized by increasing the intraoral air pressure, and there are oral sensors that register this pressure. Hence, the proximal articulatory goal is to reach that air-pressure level. How that goal is attained will, in turn, depend on other features that have to be realized simultaneously. If there is, for instance, the manner feature "coronal", as in [t], the air pressure will be increased by making a constriction between the tongue and the alveolar ridge. If, however, a labial feature has to be realized, as in [p], the pressure will be increased by constricting the vocal tract at the lips. In both cases, however, the orosensory goal for making a stop consonant is the same: an increase in sensed air pressure. The goal is, therefore, still quite abstract; it does not involve the specification of concrete muscle contractions.

In order to take care of these executive aspects, Perkell assumed subsequent stages of motor control at which the abstract motor commands are reorganized and are translated into contraction patterns for the muscles. The point of departure is the abstract orosensory feature matrix, which specifies for each subsequent segment (consonant, vowel) of the utterance the orosensory features that must be realized (see figure 11.9). This is the level of abstract motor commands. There is intrinsic timing at this level; segment durations are in some way globally specified.

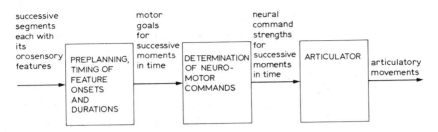

Figure 11.9
Three main components of Perkell's (1980) model of speech production.

At the subsequent stage, the motor goals for each small segment in time are specified. These goals depend in two ways on context. First, the realization of the motor goal for a feature can be dependent on other features. A vowel's duration, for instance, will depend on the place feature of the following consonant. If that consonant has an anterior place of articulation, the vowel can be shorter than if the consonant has a posterior place of articulation (as in *lob* versus *log*). Second, the realization of certain features has to be initiated quite some time before the goal is in fact reached. This requires coarticulation of features from different segments. An example is the rounding feature in vowels such as [u]. When the word *crew* is not pronounced too slowly, the lips are already rounded when the first consonant [k] appears. (Compare the pronunciation of *crew* with that of *crow*, where the vowel is unrounded.) Bell-Berti and Harris (1979) measured a fixed time anticipation of lip rounding in vowels. The reorganization at this "preplanning stage" takes care of the correct timing of the various feature onsets and durations.

These timed motor goals are, at the next stage, translated into neuro-motor commands for the articulatory muscles. These neuromotor commands control the contraction patterns of the muscles. The command strengths, Perkell argues, depend not only on the motor goals but also on feedback from the articulators. This feedback should be the basis for the compensatory behaviors discussed above. Perkell discussed various kinds of feedback that may be involved here. Among them are the muscle spindle feedback loop (see figure 11.8), various kinds of orosensory feedback, and maybe some auditory feedback (as will be discussed in the next chapter). However, no account is given of how these feedback loops reshape the neuromotor command patterns so as to produce the critical compensation phenomena. The last stage depicted in figure 11.9 involves the factual speech articulation.

Perkell's answer to the question of how the distal auditory target is reached is, in short, that the speaker has learned to replace it with orosensory goals. This replacement does not occur during the moment-to-moment control of speech; the "proximal" motor commands are directly in terms of orosensory goals. The child, however, has to acquire the correct orosensory goals by auditory feedback. Also, auditory feedback is necessary to maintain the fine tuning of the orosensory goals; there is noticeable deterioration in cases of long-lasting acquired deafness.

There have been rather heated discussions in the literature about motor-control models of this type (Fowler 1980; Hammarberg 1982; Fowler 1983; Parker and Walsh 1985). Whether or not the primary or abstract level of motor commands already specifies the *timing* of motor execution was central to these discussions. According to Perkell's model, it does (to some extent); however, the related models of Moll and Daniloff (1971), Daniloff and Hammarberg (1973), and Hammarberg (1976) do not make such a claim. In the latter models, the abstract motor commands are timeless segments consisting of bundles of features; temporal features are added only at the later stages of motor execution. Fowler (1980) called such theories *extrinsic-timing* theories. She argued for *intrinsic timing*, such that the "abstract" motor command units should already be fully specified in terms of their temporal shape. This makes it unnecessary to reorganize the motor commands, as is done in Perkell's "preplanning" stage. The abstract phonetic plan for a segment already specifies its entire gestural shape over time.

But how can one account for coarticulation if Perkell's second stage is eliminated? According to Fowler, coarticulation is nothing but the simultaneous realization of phones whose temporal specifications overlap in time. The motor command for the vowel [u], for instance, specifies an early onset of rounding, which may then temporally overlap with preceding phones, as is the case in *crew*. The temporally specified motor commands for successive segments of an utterance are superimposed or added. Fowler (1983) speaks of *vector summation*. The resulting muscular innervation is some linear or nonlinear function or "sum" of the innervations proceeding from the individual commands. It will, further, depend on the biomechanics of the moving parts how the resulting muscular excursions will be related to the two (or more) input commands. Typically the "summation" is nonlinear (Fujisaki 1983). This means that the degree to which one command is realized depends on the strength of the other commands. In short: Where segmental gestures overlap in time, they are simply *co-produced*. Fowler (1986b), in response to Diehl's (1986) critique of this co-production hypothesis, cites empirical evidence in support of vector summation. A further development of Fowler's approach can be found in Browman and Goldstein 1986.

11.3.5 Auditory Targets with Model-Referenced Control

Returning now to theories where the *proximal* targets are auditory goals, we should consider the theory proposed by Lindblom, Lubker, and Gay (1979). It contains a serious effort to deal with the problem—signaled by MacNeilage (see subsection 11.3.3)—of explaining how an auditory goal is translated in actual control of movements.

Lindblom et al. report in detail on their biteblock experiments, which show unequivocally that the formant structure of vowels is essentially unchanged when the speaker has a biteblock between his teeth. This must involve compensatory positioning of the tongue, since (as Lindblom et al. showed) without such compensation substantially different formant structures would appear in the biteblock condition. The compensation is there on the very first trial, and on the very first puff of air released by the glottis. These latter findings exclude two explanations for the biteblock results. The first one is that the speaker learns in the course of successive trials by listening to himself and by making successive approximations. No such learning over trials occurred. The second explanation, also excluded, is that the speaker uses immediate auditory feedback from what happens during the first few glottal pulses to immediately correct the vowel he is making. The almost perfect compensation is not based on auditory feedback; it is there from the very beginning of the articulation.

Lindblom et al. then go on to argue that the targets of the motor commands are *sensory*—i.e., that the target for a vowel is the way in which the vowel should be perceived. This representation is quite abstract, and it is far removed from the many equivalent ways in which this sensory impression can be produced. But these equivalent ways (for instance, with and without a biteblock) do share certain features. For vowels the shared feature is the so-called *area function*, which is a measure of how the shapes existent in the vocal tract determine the tract's resonance spectrum. The neurophysiological code for a particular sensory vowel quality is, then, in terms of the vowel's area function.

How does a speaker create the correct vocal-tract shape whether he has a pipe, or food, or a biteblock, or new dentures, or nothing in his mouth? Lindblom et al. assume that the brain is informed about the state of the vocal tract by proprioception, in particular by tactile feedback from the mucous skin in the oral cavity (although there are other forms of orosensory feedback; see Stevens and Perkell 1977). This tells the brain what the shape of the tract is like. Given the area function, the brain can then compute the sensory effect when a tract of that shape is used as a resonator. If this internally generated sensory representation is critically different from the sensory *target* of the motor command, the speaker can adapt the shape of the tract—for instance by moving the tongue—and compute the sensory representation that goes with this new constellation. When the approximation to the target is satisfactory, the vowel can be articulated and it will be correct right away.

In other words, the speaker has an internal *model* of the relevant properties of his vocal tract. By proprioceptive feedback from the actual vocal tract, he can set the parameters in this model and compute the expected sensory outcome of using the actual vocal tract of that shape. If the computed sensory outcome is not satisfactory, the actual shape can be adapted by appropriate efferent activity.

This theory is, of course, not limited to the control of vowel production. It should also be possible to internally simulate or predict the sensory effects of consonants that evolve from some articulatory gesture. And indeed, immediate adaptation phenomena have also been observed in the articulation of consonants. Folkins and Abbs (1975), for instance, interfered with jaw movement by means of some mechanical contraption. If this interference was unexpectedly applied when a word containing an intervocalic [p] had to be said, the speakers still produced complete lip closure by stretching both the upper and the lower lip more than usual. More recently, Kelso, Saltzman, and Tuller (1986) obtained similar results for the pronunciation of [b]. We will presently return to these results.

It should be obvious that the internal model that simulates the sensory results is based on extensive experience with listening to one's own speech. It is, therefore, not surprising that Oller and MacNeilage (1983) did not find full compensation in biteblock experiments with a four-year-old and a nine-year-old. Deaf people, of course, lack such a model.

Motor control of this type is called *model-referenced control* (Arbib 1981). It is a form of closed-loop control because it involves a feedback loop. The proprioceptive information is fed back to set the parameters of the internal vocal-tract model.

Fowler and Turvey (1980) pointed out that the theory of Lindblom et al. is underspecified in one major respect: When there is a relevant difference between the intended sound and the one simulated by the internal model, some adaptation of the vocal tract has to be initiated; but nothing in the theory tells us how an *appropriate* adaptation is generated. It is most improbable that this proceeds by trial and error. It should, rather, be derived from the *character* (not the mere size) of the difference between the intended and the simulated speech sound.

At the same time, Fowler and Turvey (1980) argued that the theory is also *over*specified, i.e., unnecessarily complex. Model-referenced control could as well be conceived of as follows: The model computes, by proprioceptive feedback, the present state of the vocal tract. Given the intended sound (i.e., the code or command in the motor program), it should be able to compute a vocal-tract shape that will create the intended sound. It will then send efferent control signals to the vocal-tract musculature, which will move it from the actual to the computed configuration. This alternative, of course, requires a solution to the problem of how to effectuate a change from the actual situation to one that will produce a particular intended sound.

In spite of claims to the contrary (Kelso, Holt, Kugler, and Turvey 1980), there is nothing in the theory of Lindblom et al. that makes it inconsistent with existing data. Fowler and Turvey (1980) recognized this and stated (rather more carefully than Kelso et al.) that there may be *a priori* grounds for preferring a different theory. We will now turn to that theory.

11.3.6 Coordinative Structures

It has long been known that rather complex motor coordination is possible without much central control. The classical farmhouse demonstration is the decapitated running chicken. There are trains of motor activity, involving the coordinated use of whole sets of muscles, that can apparently run off automatically. These are traditionally call *synergisms*. Lenneberg (1967) applied this notion to speech production. One synergism that he analyzed in detail is respiration during speech. According to Lenneberg there is a special "speech mode" of respiration, which is quite different from nonspeech respiration (see subsection 11.2.1): There are long stretches of exhalation, and only short moments of inhalation (only 15 percent of the respiratory cycle time, versus 40 percent in normal breathing). There is about four times as much air displacement during the cycle in speech as in nonspeech breathing. The outflow of air has a relatively constant rate in speech, but not in normal breathing. The coordination patterns of the respiratory muscles are distinctly different in speech and nonspeech breathing.

Not only the respiratory system, but all vocal organs have other uses than speech. Mastication and swallowing involve largely the same muscles as speech, but the muscles' coordination differs substantially between the speech and nonspeech modes. A muscular organization that is set to act as an autonomous functional system is called a *coordinative structure* (Easton 1972; Turvey 1977).

A coordinative structure can be seen as a system with a severely reduced number of degrees of freedom. Each individual muscle can act in several different ways at any moment, but most of these cannot occur if the muscle functions as part of a coordinative structure. In swallowing, for instance, the oral and pharyngeal muscles contract in a strict temporal order. This organization is both automatic (it can even be released as a reflex action) and functional (it is set to perform a particular *kind* of task: transporting stuff from mouth to the esophagus). There are only a few degrees of freedom left in this system. It will, for instance, behave slightly differently in swallowing a big object than in transporting a small object or some fluid.

A coordinative structure, therefore, is not totally rigid in its action. It is set to perform an *equivalence class* of actions that will all produce the same functional *kind* of result. Which particular motor activity within the equivalence class is performed depends on the context of action. For swallowing the context has to do with the kind of food transported; for walking it has to do with the resistance between feet and floor; for eye tracking it has to do with direction and speed of the visual target, and so forth. Coordinative structures can be considered as hinges between abstract, context-free motor commands and concrete, context-adapted motor execution. The abstract command specifies the kind of act required; the coordinative structure's execution takes care of the peripheral context in which the result has to be produced.

Considered in terms of its coordinative structure, walking appears to involve a *hierarchy* of subsystems, involving the muscle systems of the arms, the legs, the feet, and the toes. A similar hierarchical organization is still largely intact in the unfortunate running chicken mentioned above. Also, coordinative structures tend to produce *cyclic* behavior. This is obvious in walking and breathing. It is at this point that mass-spring accounts become integrated with coordinative-structure theories of motor control. Cyclicity can be a quite natural result of mass-spring activity; when there is little damping of the movement, the system will overshoot its (eventual) steady state and swing back and forth for some time. As in walking, this swinging can be functionally integrated in the coordinative structure's behavior.

Coordinative-structure accounts of speech motor control often stress its cyclic and hierarchical nature. There are two major cyclic phenomena in speech. One is the breathing rhythm, the special cyclic synergism of inspiration and expiration studied by Lenneberg (1967). The other is the syllable rhythm, which is largely a property of vocal-tract functioning.

Considered as a coordinative structure, the vocal tract in its speech mode is set to produce a string of syllables. That is the structure's characteristic kind of output. Which particular syllables are to be uttered has, of course, to be in the motor command; however, the functional organization of the vocal tract in speech motor control is such that the motor commands need not contain anything that is *common* to all syllables. Brodda (1979) and Sorokin, Gay, and Ewan (1980) have argued that the normal syllable rate in the world's languages (5–6 per second) is a consequence of the biomechanics of the vocal tract. It is the *eigenfrequency* of the system, especially of the mandible's movements. At this rate the movements absorb a minimum of muscular energy. This need not be in the motor program; it can be *extrinsically* timed.

But the *deviations* of this syllable rate must be programmed. This is *intrinsic* timing, because these temporal parameters are part of the phonetic plan. The way the extrinsic parameters are coded in the phonetic plan may be rather abstract. Shorter durations, such as in unstressed (versus stressed) syllables, can be obtained by making less extensive movements of the relevant articulators. This, in turn, may be realized by setting less extreme local targets for these articulators. This means that in the articulatory plan, duration can be, in part, *spatially* coded.

Speech motor control is also hierarchical. Take again the syllable as a programming unit. Its execution involves, on the coordinative-structure account, at least two subsystems: one for the realization of the peak and one for the execution of the less-sonorous flanking consonants. It has been argued that these involve rather separate muscular systems which can largely operate in parallel. This will be taken up in subsection 11.3.7.

The notion of coordinative structures is currently popular in theories of speech motor programming. (See especially Kelso et al. 1983, 1986; Fowler 1980, 1983, 1986a; Fowler et al. 1980.) On this view, motor commands are serially ordered instructions for phonetic acts or articulatory "tasks." Each act is specified in a context-free way. For instance, [b] involves the task of closing the lips with a certain force. But it is not fixed beforehand how much the share of jaw and lip movement should be in accomplishing this task. In fact, there is an infinitude of different ways to accomplish it. The task itself, however, is *minimally* specified; there is no need to detail features of the phonetic act, which will be automatically taken care of at lower levels of motor execution, namely by the so-called *articulator network* (Saltzman and Kelso 1987). It will, in a highly self-organized way, adapt to the accidentals of context and find the least energy-consuming way to reach the goal. At least, such is the claim. If the jaw cannot move, the lips will compensate by moving more.

Recently, substantial progress has been made in developing the mathematics of such self-organizing motor systems (Saltzman and Kelso 1987). There are usually more articulator variables than there are task variables (two lips and one jaw can move in order to realize a single degree of lip opening). The mathematics must therefore specify how the articulator variables are *redundant* in executing the task, i.e., how the articulators' motor patterns are mutually restraining in the "articulator network." There must be a reduction of degrees of freedom in a coordinative system, as was exemplified above by the swallowing reflex. General mathematical procedures for effecting such reductions are now available.

Furthermore, the theory must specify how the articulator network can "know" the state of its articulators, i.e., their position and their direction and velocity of motion. It has been suggested that there is no feedback to be monitored in a coordinative structure's mass-spring system (Fowler, Rubin, Remez, and Turvey 1980), but this cannot be correct. Compensation behavior requires some sort of feedback. Saltzman and Kelso (1987) provide such a feedback system. Figure 11.10 presents it in the form of a

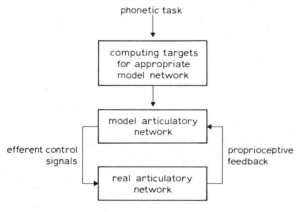

Figure 11.10
Model-referenced control in the coordinative-structures theory.

diagram. Notionally, it is not essentially different from Lindblom's model-referenced control (see above), and it is similar to Neilson and Neilson's (1987) "adaptive model theory." The articulator network consists of the real articulators and of a model of these articulators. The parameters for the model articulators' muscle tonus, position, and velocity, which constitute the model's initial state, are derived from proprioceptive feedback (see below). The task induces the *model's* behavior; the model articulators move in their mutually restrained way in such a way that the task is accomplished in the model. The spatio-temporal and force properties of the model's motions are fed on-line to the *real* articulators, which faithfully execute them. By proprioception the resulting spatio-temporal properties of these real movements are fed back to the model, which can detect any significant deviations from the model movements. If there is some significant deviation, the model will compensate in order to reach the set goal. The corrected model articulations are fed to the real articulators, which execute the compensatory move, and so on.

Let us see how this works out for the jaw-lip compensation. The task is to close the lips for [b]. The mathematics of the coordinate system distributes the closing movement in some optimal (energy-preserving) way over jaw and lip movements. These movements are performed in the model, and the real articulators follow faithfully until the jaw is (experimentally) braked in its course of motion. Proprioception reports this deviant motion pattern back to the model, which then computes a different distribution of movement for the three articulators such that the same effect—lip closure—is obtained. These corrected movement patterns are transmitted to the real articulators, which execute them.

This, at least, is the story when the model has no advance proprioceptive information about the imminent obstruction. What the model should do in such a case, according to Lindblom and MacNeilage (1986), is give the initial reaction of *exerting more force* on the jaw so that the apparent resistance is overcome. If the feedback is still deviant, the other articulators take over full compensation. Lindblom and MacNeilage noted the finding by Abbs and Cole (1982) that initially more force is indeed exerted on the perturbed articulator. This also precedes the compensation in the other articulators.

But with a biteblock in the mouth, there is at least some proprioceptive feedback *before* the movement is initiated. There is high tonus in the masseter muscles, but no corresponding movement of the mandible. The initial parameters of the model will be set accordingly, and compensation can be immediate. And this is indeed what is found in the biteblock experiments.

The elementary articulatory elements of a coordinative structure are mass-spring systems, but they are joined together to operate as a whole that can perform a particular phonetic task. The coalition of articulators can be a different one for each task. Any single articulator can participate in several different coordinative structures. As we saw, the jaw is part of the coordinative structure that takes care of pronouncing [b]. It is also part of the structure that takes care of producing [z]. But these are two distinct coordinative structures. Kelso, Tuller, Vatikiotis-Bateson, and Fowler (1984) performed compensation experiments for both [b] and [z]. When the task was to pronounce [b] and the jaw's movement was restrained, there was increased, compensatory lip movement. However, when the task was to pronounce [z] and the jaw's movement was similarly braked, no compensatory movement occurred in the lips. This shows that the jaw-lip coupling is specific to the phonetic task at hand. A coordinative structure is a functional, not a "hard-wired," coalition of articulators.

A dooming conclusion, however, is that each recurring phonetic segment requires its own coordinative structure. One would, of course, like to see some higher-order *organization* of elementary coordinative structures (the hierarchical control structure promised by theorists in this camp). A good candidate for a second-order level of organization is one that takes care of producing a language's possible syllables. The motor control of syllables may be hierarchically organized, as is walking or typing. Syllabic organization will be the subject of the next subsection.

This short review of the theories of speech motor control makes one thing abundantly clear: There is no lack of theories, but there is a great need of convergence. Theories differ both in the nature of the commands they conjecture and in their modeling of motor execution. One point of convergence among the theories, however, is the view that, whereas speech motor commands are relatively invariant, the executive motor system can take care of adaptations to the immediate context of execution without being instructed to do so. A related inevitable development is toward accounts involving model-referenced control. Finally, most theorists sympathize with the notion of the syllable as a unit of speech motor execution.

11.3.7 The Articulation of Syllables

The syllable is in many ways an *optimal* articulatory motor unit. It allows the consonants to be co-produced with the peak without too much articulatory interference. The reason is, as Öhman (1966), Perkell (1969), Fowler, Rubin, Remez, and Turvey (1980), and Lindblom (1983) have argued, that consonants and vowels often involve disjunct articulators.

The production of most vowels depends on the positioning of the tongue body by means of the extrinsic muscles—in particular, the genioglossus. Most consonants that involve the tongue at all (in particular, the coronals) are articulated by means of the intrinsic muscles, which affect the shape rather then the body position of the tongue. Whereas moving the tongue body around is a relatively slow process, most consonantal articulators can be adjusted fairly rapidly. To the extent that the muscles involved in the production of consonants and vowels are indeed disjoint, the movements can be co-produced without interference. On this view, articulation can be seen as the production of a stream of syllable peaks, with consonantal articulation superimposed.

If Brodda (1979) and Lindblom (1983) are correct in supposing that syllable rate is largely determined by the *eigenfrequency* of the moving parts involved in vowel production (the mandible and the tongue body), this steady stream of syllable peaks is the outcome of an energy-saving production mechanism. Indeed, Fowler et al. (1980) conjecture that there is a *continuous* stream of vowel articulation, which is handled by a relatively independent muscular organization. This is the "carrier wave" for the articulation of consonants. One should, of course, be careful not to overstate the disjunction of consonant and vowel articulators. There are various articulators, such as the jaw, which are actively involved in both consonant and vowel production, as Fowler (1986b) admits.

But the economy of the syllable organization is not only based on the co-producibility of consonants and vowels. There is also a tendency to distribute consonants over the syllable in such a way that consonant articulation will involve a minimum of spatial excursion of articulators, and that means a minimum of energy expenditure. The languages of the world, according to Lindblom's claim, tend to arrange the segments of a syllable in such a way that adjacent segments involve *compatible* articulators. This not only holds between the peak and its flanking consonants; it may also hold between adjacent consonants. Compatibility is present in consonant clusters such as [sp], [sk], [pl], [skr], and [spl]; it is not in clusters like [pb], [kg], and [tfd]. Clusters of the latter kind hardly ever appear in syllables.

Also, as was discussed in sections 8.1 and 9.6, syllables are "hills of sonority." The more *sonorant* consonants in a syllable tend to be positioned closer to the peak than the less sonorant ones. The sonorants [r] and [l], for instance, tend to directly precede or follow the peak, whereas [t] or [s] can be separated from the peak by one or two intermediate consonants. The syllable *tram* is a rather more likely one than *rtam*, and *slam* is more likely than *lsam*.

A syllable, in other words, is a production unit designed for optimal co-articulation of its segments. As a consequence, a maximum of perceptual distinctiveness is produced by means of a minimal amount of articulatory effort.

Summary

This chapter has dealt with one of man's most complex motor skills: the fluent articulation of speech. Articulation is the motor execution of a phonetic plan. Before it becomes articulated, a phonetic plan can be temporarily buffered. The first section of the chapter discussed the management of this so-called Articulatory Buffer, which presumably compensates for fluctuating differences between the rate of formulating and the rate of articulating.

In order for speech to be initiated, some minimal amount of phonetic plan (probably a phonological word) must have been assembled and delivered to the Articulator. The work of Klapp et al. showed that, correspondingly, onset latency is longer for two-syllable words than for one-syllable words. A condition for this so-called syllable effect is that the speaker cannot have prepared and buffered the articulatory response. The phonetic spelling out of a word's syllables is a serial process. Hence, preparing a two-syllable word for articulation takes longer than preparing a one-syllable word.

Sternberg and colleagues extensively studied the mechanism of retrieving the program from the Articulatory Buffer and unpacking it. The time needed to retrieve an articulatory program is a linear function of the number of items (probably phonological phrases) in the buffer. A further finding was that unpacking a two-syllable word takes slightly more time than unpacking a monosyllabic word. A likely interpretation of the latter phenomenon is that a word's articulation cannot start right after its first syllable has been unpacked. Rather, part of the second syllable must have been made available as well. It may be a necessary condition for making a fluent articulatory liaison between a word's syllables. It was, finally, found that the whole duration of the execution of an utterance's phonetic plan depends not only on the number of its syllables but also on the total number of items (words or short phrases) in the buffer. The more items there are in the buffer, the harder it is to retrieve each of them. The extra time needed to retrieve the next item is often gained by drawling the current item's last syllable. In fluent speech, the role of the Articulatory Buffer may be rather limited. Still, articulatory buffering is not just a laboratory effect.

Next we turned to the vocal organs involved in speech production. They are organized in three major structures. The respiratory system controls the steady outflow of air during speech; it provides the source of acoustic energy. It has its own mode of functioning during speech – a mode that differs markedly from normal nonspeech breathing. The laryngeal system, with the vocal folds as its central part, controls voicing and loudness in speech. During voicing it generates a periodic train of air puffs, which provide the wide frequency spectrum on which resonation builds. The supralaryngeal system or vocal tract contains the chambers in which resonation develops, in particular the nasal, oral, and pharyngeal cavities. Their shapes determine the timbre of vowels and consonants. The vocal tract, moreover, is the main contributor to the proper articulation of speech segments. There are different places where the vocal tract can be constricted, and there are different manners in which these constrictions are made or released. The combinations of places and manners of articulation provide a rich variety of possible speech sounds; each language uses only a subset of these.

The third section of the chapter concerned the organization of speech motor control. The major questions concerned the nature of a motor command and the way in which such a command is executed. These questions are not independent; most theories of speech motor control couple the answers in some way or another.

A first theory considers motor commands to be target positions for articulators. This location-programming theory was criticized because it is not sufficiently abstract. Target positions are highly context dependent. A segment's articulation depends not only on the immediately abutting segments but also on incidental contextual factors, such as food in the mouth, clenched teeth, and tilt of the head. Since contextual variation is unlimited, preparing a phonetic or articulatory program would become an unduly complex affair. A similar critique applies to a simple mass-spring account of motor execution. On that account, an "intended" position will not be reached when external forces interfere with the movement of articulators. Each such context would require a different motor command.

All other theories agree on the abstract, relatively invariant nature of motor commands in speech (the articulatory plan). It is only the executive apparatus that adapts the motor commands to the prevailing physical context.

We then reviewed theories according to which the abstract commands are to reach certain auditory goals. On these theories, speakers build sensory images of the sounds they intend to produce. Lindblom's theory, in particular, goes into much detail about how such an image can guide motor activity. There is model-referenced control. This means that the speaker has an internal model of his own vocal apparatus. For each configuration of the model, the resulting sensory image can be derived and compared against the goal image. The notion of model-referenced control is especially useful for dealing with so-called compensation phenomena. When an articulator is hampered in its movements, another can "take over" so that the intended sound is nevertheless produced.

Other theories, though sympathetic to the notion of auditory targets as distal goals, take motor commands to involve more proximal goals. Perkell suggests the existence of orosensory goals, i.e., goals definable in terms of the sensory experience of one's own vocal tract. It is claimed that auditorily important distinctive features, such as obstruency and nasality, have close orosensory correlates.

In the coordinative-structures theory, finally, it is supposed that the executive system consists of a hierarchy of task-oriented structures. Each such coordinative structure is a group of muscles temporarily set to function as a unit. The phonetic plan is a string or hierarchy of articulatory tasks, and each articulatory task requires a different coalition of cooperating muscles. Within such a coalition, the muscular innervations are coupled by some function that severely limits their degrees of freedom but which guarantees a particular kind of result. That result is obtained whatever the initial states of the individual muscles, or whatever the limiting external conditions, such as a pipe in the mouth obstructing jaw movement. Model-referenced control is an essential aspect of coordinative structures, and so is a mass-spring account of movement control. The executive system has a great deal of intelligence, on the coordinative-structures account of articulation. Though much work is still to be done to decipher this "wisdom of the body," recent developments in the mathematics of coordinative control show that there is life in the enterprise.

The final section of the chapter was devoted to the articulation of syllables. It was argued there that syllables are important articulatory units.

Not only is it likely that major aspects of a syllable's phonetic plan are stored (and retrieved during phonetic spellout); it is also likely that syllables are optimally organized to facilitate high-speed co-articulation of their segments. This minimization of articulatory effort goes with a maximization of perceptual distinctiveness, even at high rates of speaking.

Chapter 12
Self-Monitoring and Self-Repair

Speakers monitor what they are saying and how they are saying it. When they make a mistake, or express something in a less felicitous way, they may interrupt themselves and make a repair. This is apparent not only in spontaneous conversations, but in all kinds of discourse. Here are three examples. The first was reported by Schegloff, Jefferson, and Sacks (1977):

(1)
A: And he's going to make his own paintings.
B: Mm hm,
A: And – or I mean his own frames
B: Yeah

In spite of B's *mm hm*, a sign of acceptance, A became aware that she had said *paintings* instead of *frames*, and corrected this on her next turn.

The second and third examples are pattern descriptions obtained in an experiment reported in Levelt 1982a,b. The subjects were asked to describe patterns such as the one shown in figure 12.1. They were told that their descriptions would be tape recorded and given to other subjects, who were to draw the patterns on the basis of these recordings (see also subsection 4.4.2 and figure 4.5). One subject was in the process of indicating the connection between the yellow node and the pink node and said

(2) And above that a horizon –, no a vertical line to a pink ball

This is much like the repair of an error in example 1, but here the speaker was very quick in effectuating the repair; the trouble item (*horizontal*) was not even completed. Another subject, going from the yellow node to the blue one, said

(3) To the right is blue – is a blue point

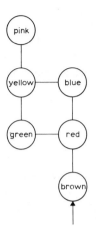

Figure 12.1
One of a set of patterns to be described. The nodes had real colors in the experiment. (After Levelt 1982a.)

This is, clearly, not the correction of an error. Rather, the speaker has made the description of the blue node more precise—more appropriate to the task. The distinction between error repairs (such as in examples 1 and 2) and appropriateness repairs (example 3) is an important one, as will become apparent in this chapter. The three examples show that speakers can monitor and repair their own speech. And this self-monitoring doesn't need the interlocutor's feedback. Speaker A in example 1 discovered her error even though B ignored it. The other two repairs were also made spontaneously; there was no interlocutor to initiate the repair by asking *What?* or *What do you mean?*.

The first section of this chapter will deal with this process of self-monitoring. How dependent is fluent speech on self-monitoring? What does a speaker monitor for? How does a speaker become aware of trouble in his own speech? We will, in particular, consider two theoretical accounts of monitoring: the editor theories and the connectionist models. In section 12.2 we will turn to what the speaker does upon detecting trouble. He may, sooner or later, interrupt his speech to initiate a repair. This usually creates a problem for the interlocutor or the listener. The normal flow of speech is interrupted, and the interpretation of the ongoing speech has to be changed or qualified. Speakers often signal this to their listeners by sudden pausing and by the use of editing expressions, such as *er, rather, no,* and *I mean.* We will analyze this process of self-interruption and the systematicity in the employment of editing expressions. Finally, the speaker will initiate the repair proper. Section 12.3 will discuss the way in which speakers construct their repairs. Contrary to certain claims in the linguistic literature, repairs are constructed in a highly regular fashion. They are subject to strict linguistic rules and strict conversational rules.

12.1 Self-Monitoring

12.1.1 What Do Speakers Monitor for?

That speakers can attend to various aspects of the action they are performing is apparent from the kinds of spontaneous self-repairs speakers make. Some major targets of monitoring seem to be the following.

Is this the message/concept I want to express now?

An example from the above-mentioned set of pattern descriptions (Levelt 1983) is this:

(4) We go straight on, or – we enter via red, then go straight on to green.

Here the speaker realized that his linearization was not adequate; he should have mentioned the brown entry node before moving to the green one. He stopped and restarted the right way.

Also, a particular message may, on closer inspection, not be correct or adequate with respect to the intention. This seems to have been the case in the following utterance (from Schegloff 1979):

(5) Tell me, uh what – d'you need a hot sauce?

Here the speaker probably started to say *what do you need?*, but it was apparently more adequate to issue a different directive, a Yes/No question. The original utterance was interrupted on the fly, and a somewhat different speech act was performed.

In these and similar cases the speaker's trouble is at the conceptual level. The speaker can directly monitor the messages he prepares for expression, and he may reject a message before or after its formulation has started. In the former case no overt repair will result, though there may be some hesitation. In the latter case the original utterance will sooner or later be replaced by a formulation of the alternative message.

Is this the way I want to say it?

Even if the speaker is sure about the information to be conveyed, he may get second thoughts about the way it should be expressed, given the discourse record—i.e., given the topic and content of previous discourse, given what was literally said earlier, and so on (see section 4.2). Consider the following example from the pattern descriptions:

(6) To the right is yellow, and to the right – further to the right is blue

Here the speaker started expressing the intended concept, but then realized that the move described previously had also been to the right. By adding *further* the speaker made his utterance more cohesive with previous discourse.

The speaker may also realize that what he is saying involves a potential ambiguity for the listener. Again, the intended concept was expressed, but it was, in retrospect, not sufficiently contextualized. The following example from Schegloff et al. 1977 is a case in point:

(7) Hey, why didn't you show up last week. Either of you two.

Here the speaker addressed the interlocutors with a question about not showing up last week. But then he realized that the communicative situation could be ambiguous. He had intended to address the interlocutors not as a group but as individuals. That ambiguity was taken away by the repair.

At this level, in short, the speaker's monitoring concerns the contextual appropriateness and sufficiency of the information expressed. Closely related to this focus of monitoring is the next one.

Is what I am saying up to social standards?
One's choice of words will, normally, depend on the level of formality required by the context of discourse. In court one will say *policeman* rather than *cop*; this is a choice of *register*. There is some evidence that speakers monitor their speech for unacceptable deviations from standards of formality and decency. In particular, Motley, Camden, and Baars (1982) have shown experimentally that speakers are very good at catching taboo words before they are uttered.

Am I making a lexical error?
The speaker's message may be as intended and contextually appropriate; still, flaws of formulation may appear, and speakers do monitor their speech for these errors. The most frequently caught error of this kind is the *lexical error*. Consider an example from the pattern descriptions; it appeared in one subject's description of the pattern shown in figure 12.1:

(8) Left to pink – er straight to pink

Here the speaker almost certainly intended to express the concept "straight". The previous utterance had introduced the yellow node, and it is even impossible to go left from there. Still, the wrong lemma, *left*, became activated (owing to causes discussed in chapter 6). The speaker caught the error and corrected it. Here is another case, from Levelt and Cutler 1983:

(9) Well, let me write it back–er, down, so that . . .

Speakers monitor for lexical errors of any grammatical category, but not all lexical errors are caught.

Are my syntax and my morphology all right?

Certain formulating errors are due not so much to lexical access as to other trouble in grammatical encoding; and sometimes speakers do become aware of deviant syntax or morphology, as is evident from their repairs. Note the following instances:

(10) What things are this kid – is this kid going to say incorrectly? (from Levelt and Cutler 1983)

Here the speaker noticed an error of agreement and corrected it.

(11) Why it is – why is it that nobody makes a decent toilet seat? (from Fay 1980b)

Here an ordering error, either an error of syntax or a shift, was caught and immediately corrected.

Am I making a sound-form error?

Trouble in phonological encoding is often recognized by speakers, as is apparent from spontaneous repairs. Cases 12 and 13 are examples of segmental and suprasegmental phonological trouble that was apparently quickly noticed by the speaker.

(12) A unut – unit from the yellow dot   (from Levelt 1983)

(13) . . . from my prOsodic – prosOdic colleagues   (from Culter 1983b)

Below we will discuss experimental evidence presented by Baars, Motley, and MacKay (1975) which demonstrates that speakers can notice and intercept an imminent nonword before uttering it.

Has my articulation the right speed, loudness, precision, fluency?

There is some minimal evidence that speakers monitor their speech delivery for parameters of this sort, but it does not stem from spontaneous self-corrections. It is exceptional indeed for a speaker to spontaneously repeat a word with more precision, or more slowly, or more loudly. Such corrections are typically induced by the interlocutor, who says *what?*, knits his brows, or otherwise signals that the speaker's delivery was not optimal. There is some experimental evidence for self-monitoring of loudness. Speakers immediately increase the loudness of their speech when it becomes masked by loud noise—this happens naturally at cocktail parties, but it can also be provoked experimentally (Siegel and Pick 1976).

It is surely possible to make more fine-grained distinctions between foci of self-monitoring. Schegloff et al. (1977) mention, for instance, the monitoring of word selection, of person reference, and of next-speaker selection (example 7 is a case of the latter). Cutler (1983b) reports interesting findings about speaker's monitoring of pitch-accent placement. The main conclusion here can, even without these finer distinctions, be straightforward: Speakers can monitor for almost any aspect of their own speech.

12.1.2 Selective Attention in Self-Monitoring

Do speakers actually attend simultaneously to all these aspects of their speech? This is most unlikely, and there are data to support the view that (i) much production trouble is not noticed by the speaker, that (ii) monitoring is context-sensitive, i.e., contextual factors determine which aspects of speech will be given most scrutiny by the speaker, and (iii) a speaker's degree of attention for self-generated trouble fluctuates in the course of an utterance.

There is both indirect and direct evidence that the meshes of a speaker's trouble net are too wide to catch all queer fish in his own speech. Nooteboom (1980) analyzed Meringer's (1908) corpus of speech errors and found that 75 percent of the registered phonological errors and 53 percent of the lexical errors were repaired by speakers. This is indirect evidence, because a speaker may detect all errors but still not bother to correct each and every one of them.

More direct evidence can be found in Levelt 1983, which reports on color-naming errors in a pattern-descriptions task. Remember that the subject's task was to give a description that would allow another subject to draw the pattern. It was, therefore, essential for a speaker to give correct color names in all cases. All 2,809 pattern descriptions, produced by a total of 53 subjects, were checked for errors in color naming. There were 472 such errors. A speaker would occasionally say *yellow* instead of *green*, *orange* instead of *pink*, *green* instead of *blue*, and so forth. Of these errors, only 218 were repaired by the speaker. That is 46 percent, which corresponds well to Nooteboom's 53 percent for lexical errors. So, even where it is a speaker's given task to produce the correct color name, only about half of the errors are caught. This is most probably due to failures in detection.

Not all sources of trouble are given equal attention. The context of discourse is an important determinant of the kind of flaws a speaker will try to prevent, intercept, or correct. One would expect a speaker to attend most carefully to trouble that is potentially disruptive for the ongoing discourse. Evidence pointing in this direction was provided by Cutler (1983b), who analyzed a corpus of lexical-stress errors (such as the one in example 13 above). About 50 percent of these errors were spontaneously repaired. The likelihood of repair depended on how disruptive the error might be for the listener. A potentially disruptive stress error is one in which there is also a segmental change, in particular a change in vowel quality. That holds for *prOsodic* in example 13, where the second vowel is reduced to [ə] and is no longer perceivable as [ɒ]. It does not hold for the stress error *sarcAsm*, where both vowels keep their intended vowel quality. That the former kind of stress error is in fact far more disruptive for the listener than the latter was experimentally confirmed by Cutler and Clifton (1984). They found that potentially disruptive stress errors were spontaneously repaired in 63 percent of the cases, whereas no more than 23 percent of nondisruptive stress errors were repaired.

It should, of course, be noted that this evidence is indirect. The speaker may have noticed a nondisruptive stress error without bothering to repair it. A disquieting finding in this connection is Nooteboom's, mentioned above. One would expect lexical errors to be more disruptive for discourse understanding than phonological errors; but only 53 percent of the lexical errors were spontaneously repaired, as against 75 percent of the phonological ones. Did Meringer's speakers not bother to correct their lexical errors? This is most unlikely. They probably didn't notice them to start with. But then there is a problem with the notion that speakers will attend most to flaws that are most disruptive for their listeners. Did Meringer carefully register all the repairs? His research target was speech errors, not repairs. The case is, clearly, undecided, but we will shortly return to it when we consider theories of self-monitoring.

Much more direct evidence for the context sensitivity of monitoring proceeds from various experimental studies by Baars, Motley, and others. All these studies used, in one way or another, the speech-error-inducing technique discussed in subsection 9.5.2. A subject is presented with a series of biasing word pairs, such as *ball dome*, and is asked to read these pairs silently. They are then followed by the target pair, for instance *darn bore*, which is to be read aloud. When the word-initial phonemes of the target pair are the same as those of the bias pairs but the order is reversed, speakers make occasional errors on the target pair, saying (e.g.) *barn door* instead of *darn bore*. The technique has been used not only to study the generation of speech errors but also to study the selective attention of speakers in monitoring for such errors.

A good instance of such a study is the original one, in which Baars, Motley, and MacKay (1975) studied the lexical-bias effect (the finding that errors that are real words are more likely to occur than errors that are nonwords). In subsection 9.5.2 above, we considered the activation-spreading account for this finding: Backward spreading of activation can only affect lexical nodes; there are no such nodes for nonwords. But the original interpretation of the lexical-bias effect (Baars et al. 1975) was a different one. They concluded that speakers edit their speech for lexical status before it is uttered. A nonlexical slip is intercepted just before it is uttered, but a lexical slip may pass through the sieve. We will return to this editing theory shortly; the important point here is that Baars et al. were able to show that this monitoring of nonlexical slips is subject to selective attention. Lexical bias is not a necessary effect; it depends on the contextual setting. When *all* pairs of items in the list were nonwords, there was no bias against nonword slips. Word and nonword slips appeared at equal rates. But as soon as some pairs of real words were added to the list (the target pairs were left unchanged; i.e., they consisted of nonwords), the lexical bias appeared again—the slips tended to be words. If a speaker's task deals exclusively with nonsense words, he apparently doesn't bother to attend to the lexical status of his output; however, this changes drastically when normal words appear in the testing materials. This finding is hard to reconcile with the activation-spreading account of the lexical-bias effect, which applies equally to both conditions.

The same technique was also helpful in establishing other context sensitivities in a speaker's selective attention. Some of these findings can be accounted for by activation spreading, but for others this is less easy. Here we will take them on their face value as contextual effects on a speaker's self-monitoring. The alternative theories of monitoring will be taken up in subsequent paragraphs.

Motley (1980) used interference items of a sort that might introduce a certain *semantic* bias in a speaker's editing. For instance, the target pair *bad-mug* might be preceded by semantically biasing pairs such as *irate-wasp* and *angry-insect*. These may weaken the resistance against a slip such as *mad-bug*. And that is what Motley found. Such slips were edited out less often when the context was semantically biasing than when it was semantically neutral. Similarly, *syntactic* biases could be induced—i.e., biases for particular syntactic constructions, such as adjective-noun (Motley, Baars, and Camden 1981).

It is also interesting that Motley (1980) was able to create a biasing *conversational setting*. In this experiment he used target pairs preceded by "standard" phonological interference (biasing) items. The target items were of two kinds. One kind is exemplified by *shad-bock*, which when preceded by appropriate interference items may lead to the slip *bad-shock*; this was the "electrical" kind of target. The other targets were "sexy" ones, such as *lood-gegs* and *goxi-firl* (the intended slips are obvious). The two target types were mixed in the list. Half the subjects were attached to fake electrodes and told that mild shocks could be given. The luckier half of subjects underwent no such threat, but had an attractive and provocatively attired female experimenter. The resulting slips corresponded to the condition of treatment. In the electrical condition, "electrical" speech errors prevailed; in the sexy condition, "sexy" speech errors were dominant. Because all these speech errors were induced by *phonological* interference items, Motley concluded that the difference was an editing effect. When one expects things electrical, a phonological slip that produces such an item will not be filtered out by the editor, and similarly for sexy items. There is an attentional bias in the subject.

In conclusion: A speaker can attend to different aspects of his speech output. In this way, potential flaws can be intercepted before they are overtly uttered. This is called *prearticulatory editing*.

There is, further, evidence that a speaker's attention to his own output fluctuates in the course of an utterance. The evidence proceeds from an analysis of the 472 color-name errors mentioned above (Levelt 1983). For each of these errors it was determined where it occurred in the ongoing phrase. More precisely, it was determined how many syllables separated the erroneous color word from the end of the syntactic constituent (usually a noun phrase) to which it belonged. For example, the erroneous color words in examples 14, 15, 16, and 17 are zero, one, two, and three syllables away from the end of the phrase (which is marked by a slash).

(14) And then you come to *blue* / – I mean green

(15) There is a *yellow* node / to the right of the red one

(16) To the right is a *black* crossing / from which you can go up or down

(17) You enter at a *green* nodal point /

It was then determined how many color-name errors in these different positions were noticed by the speaker and repaired (as in example 14). The results are given in figure 12.2, which shows clearly that the error-detection rate increases sharply toward the end of the phrase. Of the phrase-final color-name errors, 57 percent were detected and repaired;

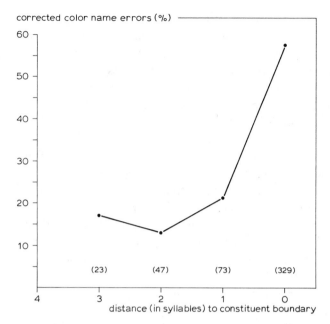

Figure 12.2
Proportion of color name errors detected and repaired by speakers for different positions in the current phrase. Numbers in brackets depict the total number of color name errors for that position. (After Levelt 1983.)

for non-phrase-final errors, the percentage was no greater than about 15. In other words, a speaker's selective attention to his own output increases toward the ends of phrases. During speech a speaker's attentional resources are mainly used for message planning, but by the ends of phrases attention can momentarily shift in order to evaluate the current speech output.

I have dealt with selective attention in monitoring, but I have delayed the discussion of theories of monitoring. There is no one generally accepted theory of self-monitoring in speech, but the main classes of theories have been foreshadowed here. There are *editor theories* of monitoring, and there are *connectionist theories* such as activation-spreading accounts. Let us take these up in turn.

12.1.3 Editor Theories of Monitoring

The major feature of editor theories is that production results are fed back through a device that is *external* to the production system. Such a device is called an *editor* or a *monitor*. This device can be distributed in the sense that it can check in-between results at different levels of processing. The editor may, for instance, monitor the construction of the preverbal message, the appropriateness of lexical access, the well-formedness of syntax, or the flawlessness of phonological-form access. There is, so to speak, a watchful little homunculus connected to each processor. Distributed editing has been proposed by Laver (1973, 1980), De Smedt and Kempen (1987), and van Wijk and Kempen (1987).

A major problem with distributed editing is reduplication. The editor that evaluates the output of a particular processing component must incorporate the same kind of knowledge as the component it monitors; how else could it evaluate the component's output? Hence, for each level of processing there is a reduplication of knowledge: the processor's and the monitor's. Distributed editors are, moreover, not on speaking terms with the notion of components as autonomous specialists. Section 1.3 proposed a partitioning of the system such that a component's mode of operation is minimally affected by the output of other components. This principle is undermined when each processing component is controlled by some monitoring agent.

A more restricted editing device was proposed by Motley, Camden, and Baars (1982). It cannot inspect all intermediary output in the generation of speech, but only the prearticulatory output. Editing follows phonological encoding, according to these authors. The editor can intercept or veto troublesome output before it becomes articulated—hence the notion of "prearticulatory editing."

Some evidence for the existence of such an editor was reviewed in the previous subsection, but particularly important in this respect is the study by Motley et al. (1982). In an experiment very much like the above-mentioned one by Motley (1980), they induced socially less appropriate speech errors (e.g., *tool kits* → *cool tits*). In these cases a speaker could either (i) not make the error, or (ii) make the error, or (iii) make a partial error. A partial error is one in which there is no full exchange, but rather an anticipation or perseveration, such as *cool kits* or *tool tits*. Of these two, the former is socially more appropriate than the latter. Motley et al. found that the appropriate partial speech error was made more frequently than the inappropriate one, and they explained this by a mechanism of prearticulatory editing. The speaker, they conjectured, would internally generate the full taboo error (*cool tits*) and start articulating it. If there were enough time to recognize the taboo word, they might be able to intercept it and correct it before uttering it. The result would be the innocent partial error (*cool kits*).

This conjecture predicts two nontrivial results. The first one is that speakers will be more prone to manufacturing innocent partial errors when the potential taboo word comes second than when it comes first. It comes second in the just-mentioned example; it would come first in a case like *fits tall* → *tits fall*. In the latter case there will hardly be enough time for the editor to recognize and intercept the taboo word. And indeed, this is what was found in the reported experiment. The second result predicted is that, because a *potential* taboo word is recognized by the speaker, the speaker should give the corresponding emotional reaction. The authors measured their speakers' galvanic skin response, which is known to reflect emotional arousal. This prediction is quite nontrivial for the following reason: An innocent partial speech error, such as *cool kits*, could have been produced as a simple error of anticipation without any intervention of an editor. In that case no taboo word would have been generated in phonological encoding, and the speaker would have had no reason to show an emotional response. The prearticulatory-editing explanation, however, presupposes that the full error (*cool tits*) was internally generated, and that it would have produced the corresponding galvanic skin response despite the fact that no overt taboo word ever appeared. Again, this is what Motley et al. found. There is also good clinical evidence for the existence of prearticulatory editing in agrammatic patients (Garnsey and Dell 1984).

Unlike distributed editors, the prearticulatory editor is not omnipresent in the language-production system. It cannot evaluate intermediary results, and it leaves the operation of most processing components unaffected. Whether this editor involves reduplication is not resolved. It must, of course, be able to evaluate semantic, syntactic, phonological, and other aspects of prearticulatory or internal speech. How can this be conceived without implicating reduplication?

An obvious solution is to identify the editor with the language-understanding system. A speaker can attend to his own speech in just the same way as he can attend to the speech of others; the same devices for understanding language are involved. In Levelt 1983 I elaborated this proposal by supposing that there is a double "perceptual loop" in the system—that a speaker can attend to his own *internal* speech before it is uttered and can also attend to his self-produced *overt* speech. In both cases the speech is perceived and parsed by the normal language-understanding system. This view of self-monitoring is depicted in figure 12.3, which is nothing but a condensed version of figure 1.1. It should be

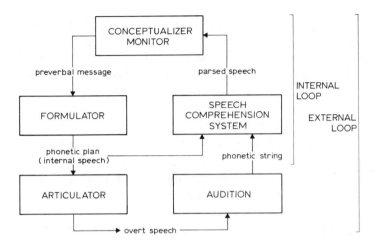

Figure 12.3
The perceptual loop theory of self-monitoring.

noted that the language-understanding system is not only able to derive a message from its speech input, it is also able to detect deviations from linguistic standards. When we listen to the speech of others we can discern deviant sound form, deviant morphology, and deviant syntax. According to the perceptual-loop theory, the same mechanism is involved in monitoring one's own internal or overt speech.

The major advantage of this approach is that no *additional* editing devices have to be conjectured. There are no special-purpose editors to check the outputs of lemma access, of grammatical encoding, of segmental spellout, and so forth. Only the final (prearticulatory) phonetic plan or internal speech and the overt speech produced can be attended to by the language-understanding system. The aspects of the self-produced speech to which a speaker will be especially sensitive will then depend on the context, in agreement with the findings of Motley and colleagues.

This is important, because MacKay (1987) has argued against editor theories on the ground that the errors one detects in one's own speech are different *in kind* from those one detects in the speech of others. MacKay compared Nooteboom's (1980) counts in the Meringer data on self-correction and in Tent and Clark's (1980) data on error detection in other-produced speech. As mentioned, Nooteboom found a 75-percent correction rate for phonological errors and a 53-percent rate for lexical errors. Tent and Clark, who asked their subjects to exactly transcribe the sentences they heard (and these sentences could contain various kinds of errors), found that a phonemic mispronunciation was noticed far less often than a morphemic or a syllabic error.

But this argument is invalid. Apart from the fact that the two data sets are highly incomparable (for instance, white noise was added to Tent and Clark's experimental sentences), it is obvious that the attentional criteria are quite different in listening and speaking. A listener's first concern is to extract meaning from the speech signal, even in spite of ill-formedness. A speaker, however, must guard not only the meaningfulness of his speech but also its satisfaction of grammatical standards. His attention will be tuned accordingly.

Moreover, the monitoring of other-produced speech is itself highly dependent on context. The detection rate for errors of different types is highly dependent on the kind of task assigned to the listener (Bond and Small 1984). When a listener is instructed to monitor for errors of a particular kind, the chances of detection rise sharply (Cooper, Tye-Murray, and Nelson 1987). In short: A difference between the detection distribution for self-monitoring and that for the monitoring of others can hardly be used as an argument against the perceptual-loop model. Both distributions depend on context and on task, and in normal conversational situations these contexts are systematically different for self-monitoring and other-monitoring.

The perceptual loop consists, according to figure 12.3, of two pathways, one involving perception of self-produced overt speech and one involving internal speech. Can these two routes be distinguished experimentally? Are there, in particular, qualitative differences in the features picked up by these two systems, and are there differences in speed of feedback?

An inventive study by Lackner and Tuller (1979) produced affirmative answers to both of these questions. Subjects were given a string of four syllables (for instance, pi-di-ti-gi) and asked to repeat this sequence again and again over a period of 30 seconds. The speaking of these syllables was paced by means of a light flashing once per second. This is a tongue-twister-like situation, and speakers occasionally made errors in pronouncing the syllables. They were asked to push a button every time they noticed an error. In this way two aspects of monitoring could be registered: the detection or nondetection of a self-produced error, and the latency of detection (measured as the time interval from speech onset to button press). The experiment was designed to compare a condition where there was overt feedback with one where there wasn't. The latter condition was realized by using earphones to present the speakers with strong white noise, which largely or fully masked the self-produced overt speech.

Are there qualitative differences in self-monitoring between these two conditions? Lackner and Tuller used three kinds of tongue-twisting strings. Apart from the type given above (involving CV syllables differing in onset consonants), they gave strings where CV and V syllables alternated (e.g., *pi-æ-ti-o*) and strings consisting of V syllables only (e.g., *æ-i-o-u*). For the first two kinds of strings, errors could be categorized as *place-of-articulation* errors (e.g., *di* for *gi*), as *voicing errors* (e.g., *di* for *ti*), or both (e.g., *di* for *pi*). Did the detection rates for these three kinds of error differ between the two testing conditions? They did. The detection rate of voicing errors was markedly lower in the auditory masking condition than in the unmasked condition. There was, however, hardly any difference in detection rate for place-of-articulation errors or for combined errors. Trouble in voicing is, apparently, far better perceived via overt speech than via internal speech. This result is not surprising from the perceptual-loop point of view. In the articulatory plan, the distinction between voiced and unvoiced plosive consonants hinges on a tiny difference in the moment of voice onset after the release of the obstruction in the vocal tract. This, however, creates a substantial acoustic effect, which can be picked up by the external loop. Similarly, Lackner and Tuller found that errors in vowel quality were detected much better when there was no masking. In the masking condition, vowel errors that involved small deviations from the target vowel (e.g., [ɛ] for [ɪ]) often went unnoticed.

There were also differences in detection latencies between the two conditions. Although one would expect the masking condition to be more difficult and therefore to create longer latencies, the reverse turned out to be the case. Detection latencies were shorter in the masked condition. And this is as it should be. The overt-speech loop is longer; extracting features from overt speech requires both articulation and acoustic analysis. These processes are not involved in the internal loop. Masking noise suspends the longer external loop.

Lackner and Tuller argued that, in normal speaking situations, both loops are involved. This should predict that the detection latencies for self-produced errors will be shorter than those for other produced errors, since some self-produced errors will be detected via the internal loop. An experiment comparing the detection latencies of self-produced and other-produced errors showed that this was indeed the case. For the kinds of materials used in the above experiment, detection latencies were more than 100 milliseconds shorter in self-monitoring than in other-monitoring.

Is the perceptual loop short enough to intercept an error? The external loop isn't, of course; a word is evaluated only when it is articulated. The effectiveness of the internal loop, however, depends on how far phonetic planning is ahead of articulation. We have seen that it can be one or even a few phonological phrases ahead. The more articulatory buffering, the more opportunity for self-monitoring. But what about fast-running speech, where buffering is presumably minimal?

Let us assume that the internal loop and the Articulator can simultaneously start working on a phonological word delivered by the Phonological Encoder. How much time does the Articulator use to unpack the phonetic program and to initiate articulation? The only measures we have are the latencies in the fourth column of table 11.1. These were the simple reaction latencies in the experiments of Klapp et al. They were about 310 msec. But these latencies included perceiving the Go signal (say, 80 msec). The Articulator's own latency can therefore be estimated at about 200–250 msec. This means that there is at least this much time between the delivery of the phonetic plan and the initiation of articulation. Is this long enough for the internal loop to recognize the word and, in case of trouble, to send an interruption signal to the Articulator?

How long does it take to recognize a word in running speech? The results of Marslen-Wilson and Tyler (1981, 1986) indicate that, on the average, recognition is possible about 200 msec after word onset. This corresponds roughly to the length of a syllable or a monosyllabic word. This short time holds for listening to *overt* running speech; i.e., it includes the time taken by the auditory process. Recognition of one's own *internal* speech can, therefore, be even speedier, say with a latency of 150–200 msec. This would leave the internal loop with 0–100 msec to send an interrupt signal to the Articulator in case of trouble. In other words, the internal loop may in many cases be short enough for effective word-level monitoring in fluent speech—i.e., short enough to interrupt articulation before the troublesome word is spoken. And this is the extreme case where there is no buffering. If there is more phonetic plan available in the buffer, there should be no timing problem whatsoever.

This, however, requires optimal attentional conditions. These are not always given, as we saw in the previous subsection. The speaker may then still be too late in intercepting the trouble item. This can lead to repairs such as the following:

(18) To the left side of the purple disk is a *v* – a horizontal line

Here execution (of the word *vertical*) had just set in before speech could be halted. Such a repair shows that self-monitoring indeed need not be based on overt speech. The erroneous word had been planned, as is evident from the initial [v] (and the context of pattern descriptions), but too little of the word was pronounced to make recognition via the external loop possible.

Summing up: We have seen good evidence for both prearticulatory and postarticulatory editing. That there is prearticulatory editing is apparent from partially intercepted errors such as example 18, but especially from the experiments of Motley et al., whose nontrivial predictions about partial repairs and psychophysiological responses were fully confirmed. That there is, in addition, monitoring of *overt* speech is apparent from the results of Lackner and Tuller, which show a differential sensitivity to self-produced errors under conditions of auditory feedback versus impeded feedback. There is, in short, evidence for the existence of both the external and the internal feedback loop.

Before we turn to the connectionist accounts of self-monitoring, one additional remark should be made: Not all self-monitoring during speech is mediated by the perceptual loops. Speakers can also monitor their messages before they are formulated. They can attend to the appropriateness, the instrumentality, and the politeness of the speech act they are planning. This is an entirely conceptual activity; it need not involve any formulation or parsing.

12.1.4 Connectionist Theories of Monitoring

It is characteristic of connectionist accounts that there are no mechanisms external to the speech-production apparatus involved in the control of one's own speech. In positive terms: The system's self-control is due to the same inherent feedback that is presumably operative anyhow in the generation of speech. That is, the bottom-up priming from lower-level nodes to higher-level nodes in the network (see subsection 9.5.1). There is no editor watching the production system's output.

Even strong proponents of an activation-spreading account, such as Dell (1986) and Stemberger (1984), do not dogmatically exclude other kinds of feedback—e.g., through the language-understanding system. Still, one naturally tries to push the notion as far as possible. The most far-reaching network account of monitoring is that of MacKay (1987). His *node structure theory* explains error detection along the following lines.

MENTAL NODES

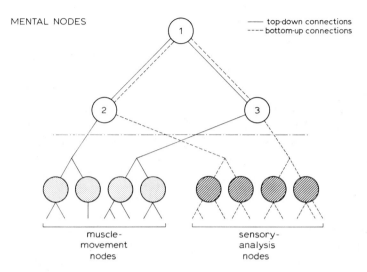

Figure 12.4
Common and specific nodes in MacKay's (1987) node structure theory.

Language production and language understanding are largely sub-served by one and the same *node structure*, a layered network of mental nodes. This is schematically represented in figure 12.4, which pictures a very small part of the network. The three mental nodes represented in the upper portion of the figure are common to production and perception. The two node types in the bottom part of the figure are specific. They are, respectively, "muscle-movement nodes" and "sensory-analysis nodes". These nodes are involved in articulation and audition, respectively.

The network for language has several layers of mental nodes. There are layers of "propositional nodes," of "conceptual nodes," of "lexical nodes," of "syllable nodes," of "phonological nodes," and of (distinctive) "feature nodes." All these layers of mental nodes are shared by the production system and the comprehension system. An activated mental node primes all nodes connected to it. These, in turn, prime—to some lesser extent—the nodes connected to them, and so on. The theory is quite similar to Dell's (1986) in that it assumes bidirectional priming between layers of mental nodes. It is also similar in another respect. In Dell's theory, a node could become "current node," which would boost its activation level. When, for instance, a syllable-onset phoneme was structurally required at some moment in time, the most strongly primed onset phoneme would become the current node. The same principle is used in the node-structure theory. The most primed node in a particular domain (e.g., the domain of onset phonemes) will become the "activated" node at the moment it is structurally required. An "activated" node in the node-structure theory is equivalent to a "current" node in Dell's spreading activation theory.

Also, errors arise in the same way in the two theories: The "wrong" node becomes "current" or "activated." This happens when the "wrong" node is the most strongly primed one of its kind at the moment such a node's activation is needed. This can have several causes. The speaker may want to say *the green light* but may happen to say *the red light*. When the speaker prepares his proposition, mental nodes for the modifier and entity concepts GREEN and TRAFFIC LIGHT are, at some moment, activated. They prime nodes connected to them—for instance, COLOR (from GREEN) and RED (from TRAFFIC LIGHT). They also prime nodes at the next, lexical level. The node for *green* is primed by GREEN and by COLOR. The node for *red* is primed by RED and by COLOR. It may happen that *red*'s priming just exceeds *green*'s at the moment an adjective is needed. In that case *red* will become the current or activated adjective node, though GREEN had been the only "current" concept node of type "modifier." Bottom-up priming may be another cause of erroneous activation.

How is an error detected in the node-structure theory? Through backward priming. When *red* is erroneously activated, it spreads its activation back to the concept node RED, which undergoes a sudden increase of priming. And this precisely is *perception* in the node-structure theory: the bottom-up priming of mental nodes. In this way, MacKay claims, an error is perceived almost immediately, and a corrective action can start before articulation of the error has been initiated. The mechanism of such a corrective action is, as yet, not very well defined in the node-structure theory.

When we compare the editing account and the connectionist account, the most worrisome diagnosis is that, as they stand, both are very hard to disconfirm. We saw that the initial editor theories suffered from reduplication of knowledge. This was repaired in the perceptual-loop account, where the monitoring device is just the speaker's language-understanding system. In MacKay's node-structure theory, even more economy is attained by equating the mental networks for the production and the understanding of language. This is a bold step not followed in the present book. There is, on my view, too much empirical evidence, both experimental and clinical, for a substantial separation of processors involved in the producing and the understanding of language.

Still, there are no doubt intimate connections between the speaking system and the listening system (Cutler 1987). One showpiece is the phenomenon of *delayed auditory feedback*, extensively studied and discussed by MacKay (for a review of this work, see MacKay 1987). The basic phenomenon is this (Lee 1950): A speaker listens to his own speech over earphones. The speech is amplified and delayed. When the delay is of the order of 200 milliseconds, serious dysfluencies arise in the speaker's speech delivery. It becomes a kind of stuttering, with repetitions and delays of speech sounds and drawls in the articulation of vowels. Here speech perception immediately interferes with speech production, and this wouldn't be possible without short-circuited connections between the two systems.

MacKay's account of this effect is, in essence, this: It is an essential property of the node-structure theory that an activated node is completely inhibited shortly after its activation. As a consequence, it will not be the most active node at the next moment in time. This opens the way for another node in the same domain to become the next activated or current node. The phase of inhibition is, however, short. Nodes representing phonemes or distinctive features can be reactivated some 150 or 200 msec after inhibition. And that is what happens systematically in a situation of delayed auditory feedback. The sensory nodes (figure 12.4) that react to the speech that is fed back prime precisely the same mental nodes that had been active some 200 msec earlier. This priming is substantial because of the amplification of the speech. In many cases, the same node will then again be selected as the current node, because it has again become the most primed of its kind. This then leads to repetition of the same motor activity–i.e., to stuttering.

Other things are more problematic for the node-structure theory's account of self-monitoring. The theory implies that every error is detected almost immediately; bottom-up priming is always direct and automatic. This, however, is not in agreement with the findings in Levelt 1983 that error detection can be substantially delayed. This will be the first issue taken up in the next section.

Also difficult to handle are some of the set effects Motley and his colleagues established. One of the hardest is the finding by Baars, Motley, and MacKay (1975) that the lexical-bias effect disappeared when only nonwords were used in the error-eliciting procedure (see subsection 12.1.2). There is as much bottom-up priming of lexical nodes in the latter case as when real words are used, but no lexical bias arises. Self-monitoring may not be as automatic as the node-structure theory suggests. A subject may have reasons to bother about lexical status, or not to bother. And the same holds for his attitude with respect to other features of his speech.

12.2   Interrupting and the Use of Editing Expressions

When a speaker detects trouble that is sufficiently alarming according to the speaker's current standards, the decision will be taken to interrupt speech and to initiate a repair. There are two issues to be considered here. The first one is the temporal relation between detection and interruption: Does a speaker complete certain parts of speech before halting, or is interruption immediate? The second is whether and how the speaker signals to the addressee that trouble is at hand and that some repair is about to be made.

12.2.1   Interrupting the Utterance

The present evidence on spontaneous self-interruptions allows us to maintain the following *Main Interruption Rule*. (One minor but interesting exception to the rule will be discussed below.)

Main Interruption Rule:
Stop the flow of speech immediately upon detecting trouble.

This rule was first suggested and discussed by Nooteboom (1980) in his analysis of the repairs in the Meringer (1908) corpus. A detailed empirical analysis of the rule on the basis of almost 1,000 tape-recorded spontaneous self-repairs in the visual-pattern descriptions discussed above was presented in Levelt 1983. Some of the main findings of that analysis will be summarized here.

There is a variable distance between the troublesome item and the point of self-interruption. The speaker may discover trouble and interrupt himself before the trouble item is uttered. That is probably the case in a *covert* repair, such as the following:

(19) Here is a – er a vertical line

We do not know in this case what the troublesome item was. Maybe the speaker was about to say *horizontal*. At any rate, there was some reason to interrupt and restart. The repair is called "covert" because we don't know what was being repaired; 25 percent of the repairs in the corpus were of this kind. Not knowing the source of trouble, we cannot be sure about the delay between the source of the trouble and the moment of

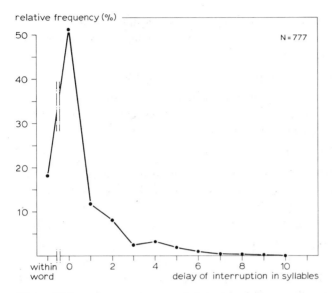

Figure 12.5
Distribution of interruption moments in number of syllables after trouble item.
(After Levelt 1983.)

interruption. In the following we will, therefore, ignore these covert repairs and limit ourselves to *overt* repairs. The troublesome items will be italicized.

In overt repairs, interruption can take place during the utterance of the troublesome item, or right after it, or one or more syllables later. Figure 12.5 shows the distribution of interruption moments in the overt repairs of the pattern-description data. If indeed interruption follows on the heels of detection, the curve in figure 12.5 also reflects the distribution of error detection.

Let us begin with the immediate within-word interruptions. The following repair is an example:

(20) We can go straight on to the *ye-*, to the orange node

About 18 percent of the overt repairs in the corpus were of this type. Interruption can also occur just after the troublesome item, as in the following:

(21) Straight on to *green* – to red

This is, in fact, very common. It is the most frequent place of interruption, occurring in 51 percent of all self-repairs.

But interruption can also be delayed by one or more words. This happens in the remaining 31 percent of the overt repairs. In example 22, the troublesome element was *green*.

(22) And from *green* left to pink – er from blue left to pink

Interruption occurred only three words later. An infrequent case of such delayed interruptions (4 percent out of the 31 percent) was one in which the interruption occurred within a word, as in the following:

(23) And *over* the gray ball a pur- or er right of the gray ball a purple ball

The Main Interruption Rule says that, in all these cases, the speaker halted immediately upon becoming aware of trouble. Delays in interruption, therefore, are ascribed to delays in *detection*. An alternative to the rule would be that speakers do not interrupt immediately, but prefer to complete the current word, phrase, clause, or whatever constituent. The evidence does not favor such an alternative. Any smaller or larger constituent can be interrupted for repair. This is the case in example 20, where there is not only interruption of a word but also interruption of a noun phrase; there is no delay. And when there is delay, there need be no constituent completion. Example 23 demonstrates this. There is delay, but neither the integrity of the word nor that of the noun phrase (*a purple ball*) is respected. Delayed interruptions with incomplete constituents are quite common in spontaneous self-repairs.

Still, one could make a statistical argument. Speakers may have *some* tendency to delay interruption till after completion of the current phrase. If there is such a tendency, delayed interruptions in repairs will respect phrase boundaries more often than immediate interruptions. However, the reverse turned out to be the case. Interruptions immediately after the troublesome item respected phrase boundaries in 74 percent of the cases, whereas delayed interruptions coincided with phrase boundaries in 66 percent of the self-interruptions. Hence, there is no reason to suppose that a speaker delays interruption in order to complete the current phrase.

But do speakers respect the integrity of *words* when they interrupt? Nooteboom (1980), in his analysis of the Meringer data, found that words are almost never broken up; speakers tend to delay interruption until at least the current word has been completed. It should be remembered, however, that Meringer was interested in speech errors rather than in the way speakers self-interrupt. It is, in particular, very hard for even an attentive listener to register exactly where a speaker interrupts his own speech. The repairs in my pattern-description data were all tape-recorded; this made it possible to determine precisely where the self-interruption took place. It turned out that 22 percent of interruptions occurred within words. Words are not sacred cows in self-repair.

Still there is something special about within-word interruptions. Words that are real errors are much more prone to interruption than words that are merely not fully appropriate or words that are correct. Compare the following three examples:

(24) First a *bro- –* er a yellow and a green disk

(25) To the left of it a *blanc*, or a white crossing point

(26) *Left* to the pink disk, or right to the pink disk

In example 24, the word *brown* is wrong and the speaker interrupts it for repair. In example 25, the word *blanc* is not an error. It is, rather, somewhat inappropriate because the speaker always used *white* to describe white nodes. Note that the speaker does not interrupt *blanc*. Erroneous words were interrupted more than three times as often in the pattern-description data as merely inappropriate words. Example 26 is still different. There is an error word (*left*), but the speaker was late in detecting the trouble. If detection occurred when the word *disk* was being uttered, the speaker should have interrupted that word, according to the Main Interruption Rule. The data show, however, that words are seldom broken up in such cases of delayed interruption. The bulk of within-word interruptions are cases where the broken-up word is an error itself.

Can this be adduced to the *detection* of trouble? Hardly. There is no reason to assume that the detection of error (as in example 24) occurs more frequently within the troublesome word than the detection of inappropriateness (as in example 25). And it is even less likely that when detection of trouble is late, as in example 26, it won't occur within a word. That is, we have a real exception to the Main Interruption Rule: Words that are not errors themselves tend to be completed before interruption. One would be inclined to a pragmatic interpretation of this finding. By interrupting a word, a speaker signals to the addressee that that word is an error. If a word is completed, the speaker intends the listener to interpret it as correctly delivered.

Are syllable boundaries respected when a speaker halts within a word? Compare the following repairs:

(27) Then follows a *horizon-*, no, a vertical line

(28) Over the *gree-*, no I am wrong, left of the green disk . . .

(29) I go *f-*, all the way straight

In example 27, the word is broken up but the syllable boundary is respected. In examples 28 and 29, syllable boundaries are not respected; this is quite common in self-interruptions. But there is a difference between the latter two examples. In example 28 the pronounced part of the word is itself a *possible* syllable. In that sense the interruption respects the phonotactic constraints of the language. This is not so for example 29, where the speaker produced just a fricative (probably the first consonant of *further*) that was not a possible syllable. A careful analysis by ear of all 172 within-word interruptions in the data revealed that 39 percent were of this latter kind, i.e., the production of a sound that was not a well-formed syllable in the language. When speakers interrupt an erroneous word, they are quite inconsiderate with respect to its phonological integrity. Here the Main Interruption Rule—stop as soon as trouble is detected—appears to be respected.

The Main Interruption Rule, in short, can be maintained with one exception: Speakers tend to complete the current *correct* word upon detection of trouble. An important consequence of the rule is that delayed interruption signals delayed detection of trouble. But delayed detection of trouble cannot be accounted for by the node-structure theory as it stands.

12.2.2   The Use of Editing Expressions

The speaker's self-interruption is usually followed by a short pause or by what is called an *editing expression* (Hockett 1967). Editing expressions—simple ones such as *er, that is, sorry, I mean* and elaborate ones such as *oh, that's impossible; I will start again, OK?*—play a significant role in signaling to the addressee that there is trouble, and what kind of trouble it is. James (1972, 1973), for instance, analyzed the uses of *uh, oh,* and *ah,* and how they differ semantically. The interjection *uh* or *er* signals, according to James, that something has been temporarily forgotten. DuBois (1974) argued that the phrase *that is* is used to specify a referent in a repair, as in the following:

(30) He hit Mary – that is, Bill did.

The use of *rather,* according to DuBois, is for "nuance editing," as in

(31) I am trying to lease, or rather, sublease my apartment.

And *I mean* is used when there is an out-and-out mistake:

(32) I really like to – I mean – hate to get up in the morning.

These are constructed cases, not observed ones, but they strongly suggest that there are special editing expressions for signaling straight mistakes or errors (as in example 32) and others for signaling appropriateness problems (as in examples 30 and 31). What do the repair data tell us?

It is indeed the case that a speaker's use of editing expressions is quite different after an error than after a mere inappropriateness. The most remarkable difference in my data (Levelt 1983) is that errors were followed by editing expressions in 62 percent of the cases, whereas for appropriateness repairs the percentage was only 28. And this makes communicative sense. In the case of an error (as in example 32), the speaker may want to warn the addressee that the current message is to be replaced. But in the case of an inappropriateness (for instance, an underspecification, as in examples 30 and 31), no such drastic steps are imminent. The addressee will only be given an additional specification. This distinction was already apparent in the speaker's tendency to interrupt erroneous words but not inappropriate words.

The repair data also showed a systematic difference in the kinds of editing expressions used. Errors were mostly followed by *er*, *or*, and *no*. The latter two tell the addressee that an alternative is about to come, and that something is being rejected. Such oppositions are not often created in appropriateness repairs. The most frequent appropriateness-editing term in the Dutch data was *dus* (literally *thus*)—a connective that normally presupposes the correctness of the previous propositions and introduces some consequence or state of affairs that is compatible with it. In other words, the speaker self-interrupts but tells the listener to continue the same line of interpretation. This editing term was never used when the occasion for repair was an error. Also, speakers excused themselves (by *sorry* or the like) after errors, but almost never after cases of inappropriateness.

A very special editing term is *er*. It is the most frequently used editing expression, used in 30 percent of all repairs. It is also the only editing expression that is practically universal; it exists, with only minor phonetic variations, in many if not all languages. The latter should make one suspicious; *er* would be the only universal word. But is *er* a word, or is it rather a neutral sound that is likely to occur under certain speaking conditions?

Analysis of the pattern-description repair data reveals that there is one dominant factor determining the use of *er*: the actuality or recency of trouble. The most frequent use of *er* was in covert repairs, such as

(33) We start with a green – er – green point.

Here trouble is clearly present, though we cannot tell precisely what kind of trouble. Of the covert repairs in the corpus, two-thirds contained an editing expression. Of these, *er* was by far the most frequent one, occurring in 84 percent of the cases. The next most frequent use of *er* was right upon the interruption of a word, as in

(34) Right to *lef* – er to yellow.

If an editing term was used in these cases, it was *er* in 80 percent of the cases. The use of *er* declined when the delay between the trouble spot and the interruption increased. When the troublesome word has just been completed, as in example 35, *er* was no longer the most frequent editing term; still, 35 percent of the editing expressions were *er*.

(35) Left – er – right in front of me

When the interruption was delayed by one or more words, as in example 36, the use of *er* dropped to 21 percent.

(36) From white I go *straight* to – er – right to blue.

Another way of expressing the same result is that the difference between the use of *er* and the use of other editing expressions is that *er* is used when the delay between the troublesome word and the interruption is short (in fact, the average delay for *er* is 1.7 syllables); the other expressions are used at larger delays (average: 4.3 syllables). The interjection *er* apparently signals that at the moment when trouble is detected, the source of the trouble is still actual or quite recent. But otherwise, *er* doesn't seem to mean anything. It is a symptom, not a sign.

12.3 Making the Repair

After self-interruption there is a moment of suspense. The speaker's *er* may help him to keep the floor, and various editing expressions may be used for the same purpose or to indicate the kind of trouble at hand. This moment of suspense will be used to prepare the correction. It is, at the same time, a moment of trouble for the listener. The running interpretation of the flow of speech is suddenly interrupted, and the listener has a *continuation problem*. How much of the interrupted utterance is to be reinterpreted or qualified? Or is it just a moment of hesitation after which speech will continue normally?

It will be argued in this section that speakers make repairs in such a way that their listeners' continuation problems are maximally accommodated. Speakers repair, first, in a linguistically principled way. The repair entertains a simple and systematic syntactic relation to the interrupted utterance. This makes it possible for the listener to derive an interpretation for the *pair* of original utterance and correction. Second, speakers include more or less of the original utterance in their correction, which is an important way of letting the listener know whether the occasion for repair is an error or an inappropriateness. Third, the very first word of the repair is usually enough to allow the listener to determine where the repair is to be inserted in the original utterance. Fourth, the speaker can focus the replacement by assigning it pitch accent. The next four subsections will deal with these four systematic properties of repairs. In a final section some attention will be given to less conventional ways of self-repairing.

12.3.1   The Syntactic Structure of Repairs

It has often been observed that speakers restart their speech at a phrase boundary or a constituent boundary (DuBois 1974; Nooteboom 1980). This is the *constituent rule*. The rule is not only correct, it is also trivial. A check of the 957 repairs in my corpus (Levelt 1983) shows that there are only minor exceptions, but a further analysis makes it clear that this adherence to the rule is due to the language rather than to the way speakers repair. In a right-branching language, such as English or Dutch, almost any word in a sentence marks the beginning of a syntactic constituent. This is exemplified in the following.

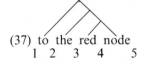

(37) to the red node
      1   2   3   4   5

If a repair were to start at position 1 in example 37, it would initiate a prepositional phrase. Beginning at position 2 or 3, it would introduce a noun phrase. Whether position 4 is also to be taken as the beginning of a noun phrase depends on one's theory. The important thing to observe is that when syntactic branching predominantly proceeds to the right, as in example 37, new phrases are started in subsequent positions. Only phrase *endings* coincide. In example 37, all phrases end in position 5. In the pattern descriptions, 89 percent of all the occurring words were phrase initial. It is, in other words, quite hard for a speaker to violate the constituent rule while making a repair.

What is worse, the rule does not guarantee that the repair is well formed. Just as we have intuitions about the well-formedness of sentences, we can have rather strong feelings about whether a repair "fits" or doesn't "fit." The following (constructed) example may help to demonstrate this point:

(38) Is the doctor seeing – er – the doctor interviewing patients?

This repair sounds rather funny; it is intuitively ill formed. Still, it respects the constituent rule; the repair starts with a noun phrase (*the doctor*). Is there something in the repair itself (*the doctor interviewing patients*) that makes it a problematic case? No; the same repair can be fine in the following context:

(39) Is the nurse – er – the doctor interviewing patients?

This repair is intuitively well formed. Well-formedness of a repair is, apparently, not a property of its intrinsic syntactic structure. It is, rather, dependent on its relation to the (interrupted) original utterance. The constituent rule ignores that relation.

What sort of relation is a repair to maintain with the original utterance? The relation is, in essence, quite simple. Syntactically speaking, an utterance and its repair constitute a kind of *coordination* (Levelt 1983; De Smedt and Kempen 1987), and the syntactic rules of coordination have to be followed. This state of affairs can be captured in a *Well-Formedness Rule* for repairs. The rule is somewhat abstract on first appearance, but is easily explained. In the rule, O means the original utterance, R means the repair proper, and C is a string of zero or more words that is to complete the original utterance. The rule ignores the use of editing expressions.

Well-Formedness Rule for repairs
An original utterance plus repair ⟨OR⟩ is well formed if and only if there is a string C such that the string ⟨OC*or*R⟩ is well formed, where C is a completion of the constituent directly dominating the last element of O (*or* is to be deleted if that last element is itself a connective such as *or* or *and*).

To demonstrate this rule, we will apply it to the just-discussed ill-formed and well-formed cases.

In the ill-formed repair given as example 38, O, the original utterance, is *Is the doctor seeing*. The interrupted constituent in the original utterance is the verb phrase (*seeing* . . .). It can, for instance, be completed by an NP such as *the surgeon*; let us take this as C, the completion. Then follow *or* and the repair R, *the doctor interviewing patients*. The result is this:

(40) Is the doctor seeing the surgeon or the doctor interviewing patients?

This coordination is as ill formed as the repair in example 38.

What about the well-formed case (example 39)? There O is *Is the nurse*. Its last word is *nurse*, which itself completes the NP constituent, so the completion C can be empty. R is the repair *the doctor interviewing patients*, and the coordination specified by the rule will be the following:

(41) Is the nurse or the doctor interviewing patients?

This is all right as a coordination. For these examples, therefore, the biconditional rule appears to work.

How does it work for naturalistic data? An analysis of the pattern-description repairs showed that the rule was adhered to with only minor exceptions—i.e., speakers usually made repairs that were syntactically well formed. Let us apply it to the following observed repair:

(42) From purple up to, straight up to red

This repair is, according to the rule, syntactically well formed because the corresponding coordination is. O is *from purple up to*. Its last word (*to*) introduces a prepositional phrase; let us complete it with *green* (= C). R is *straight up to red*. The coordination thus becomes

(43) From purple up to green or straight up to red

which is well formed.

So far, the conclusion is warranted that, in contrast with what has been suggested in the linguistic literature about repairs, self-repair is a syntactically regular process. In order to repair, the speaker tends to follow the normal rules of syntactic coordination.

This does not mean, of course, that the Well-Formedness Rule cannot be violated in a speaker's repair behavior. The study of speech errors has made it abundantly clear that just about any linguistic rule is occasionally violated by speakers. Such irregularities are especially likely to arise when there are attentional lapses, or when there are high processing demands (such as in fast speech). Repair situations are almost always "loading" moments for a speaker. It is, therefore, quite surprising how *regular* speakers' repairs usually are.

But just as one can experimentally elicit speech errors, one can also experimentally elicit ill-formed repairs. Van Wijk and Kempen (1987) designed an inventive experimental procedure to induce repairs in syntactically well-controlled sentences. The speaker's task was to describe an event depicted in a picture. An example of such a picture is given in figure 12.6a. It can be described as follows:

(44) The bald man with the spectacles pushes the sad clown.

The subject was first made familiar with the possible agents and re-

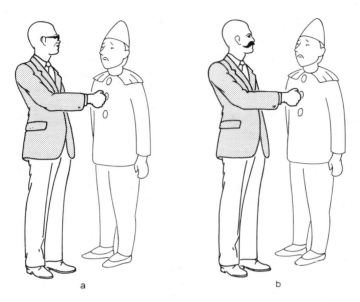

Figure 12.6
Pictures used in van Wijk and Kempen's (1987) repair elicitation experiment.

cipients, and with the kinds of actions depicted in the pictures. They were introduced as *the man, the clown,* etc., so that no naming problems would arise during the experiment. In the main experiment, the protagonists in a picture did not appear simultaneously, but one after the other. The picture was built up over time. If the man appeared first in the picture of figure 12.6a, the subjects usually started making an active sentence. When the clown appeared first, followed by the pushing man, the sentence being uttered usually became a passive one (*The sad clown is pushed by the bald man with the spectacles*). In this way different syntactic constructions could be induced. The important variable, however, was this: At some moment during the speaker's utterance the picture was changed. Some attribute of the one protagonist or the other, or the action depicted, was altered. The man with spectacles, for instance, suddenly became a man with a moustache, as in figure 12.6b. When the change came some time after the speaker had uttered *with the spectacles*, he normally halted and repaired to replace *spectacles* by *moustache*. A typical repair was the following:

(45) The bald man with the spectacles – er with the moustache pushes the sad clown.

Clearly, example 45 adheres to the Well-Formedness Rule; the corresponding coordination would be *The bald man with the spectacles or with the moustache pushes the sad clown*, which is fine. But van Wijk and Kempen developed this technique especially to induce very delayed repairs. When the pictorial change occurred late in the speaker's utterance, ill-formed repairs might occur, such as the following:

(46) The bald man with the spectacles pushes – er – with the moustache pushes the sad clown.

This is ill formed because the corresponding coordination would be something like *The bald man with the spectacles pushes a child or with the moustache pushes the sad clown*, which is horrible. And indeed cases like example 46 do arise regularly under such experimental conditions.

On the basis of these and related experimental results, van Wijk and Kempen conjectured that speakers have, essentially, two ways of making a repair. The first one they call a *reformulation*; the speaker creates a new syntactic construction. An instance of this is example 42 above, where *up* is reformulated as *straight up*, which involves a syntactic addition. These repairs systematically adhere to the Well-Formedness Rule. Reformulations occur at the level of grammatical encoding, in the realm of syntax.

The second repair strategy is *lemma substitution*. A lemma substitution fully preserves the syntax of the original utterance; only a word is replaced. There is no further grammatical re-encoding. Examples 45 and 46 are of this kind. According to van Wijk and Kempen, they may but need not adhere to the Well-Formedness Rule. And indeed, two such cases also appeared in my naturalistic data: example 47 (presented here) and example 56 (below).

(47) right of *purple* is – er – of white is purple

The Well-Formedness Rule creates a coordination like *right of purple is green or of white is purple*, which is ill formed. Further scrutiny of naturalistic data is needed to substantiate the systematic occurrence of such repairs. And if they occur more than occasionally, one should check whether they are experienced as well formed by speakers of the language; only if they are need a subsidiary well-formedness rule be added to the grammar of repair.

12.3.2 Ways of Restarting

One can adhere to the Well-Formedness Rule and still restart in very different ways after self-interruption. The repair may or may not include parts of the original utterance, and these parts can be smaller or larger. A very major determinant of how speakers restart is the *repair occasion*, i.e., the type of trouble the speaker is dealing with. Earlier we distinguished between two major classes of trouble: out-and-out *error* and *inappropriateness*. In the former case the repair must undo the mistake; in the latter case some further specification is needed in order to say the same thing in a more felicitous way. The way in which speakers begin their repairs is systematically different for these two kinds of repair occasion. To demonstrate this, three ways of restarting should be distinguished.

The first one will be called *instant repairing*. In these cases there is a single troublesome word, and the speaker retraces to just that word and replaces it with a new item. In other words, the repair begins with the replacement, as in example 48.

(48) Again left to the same *blanc* crossing point – white crossing point

Here the very first word of the repair, *white*, replaces the troublesome item, *blanc*. Notice that, in this example, there is delayed interruption (till after *crossing point*). Instant repairs do not require immediate interruption. Of all the error and appropriateness repairs in my corpus, 42 percent are instant repairs.

The second way of restarting is to retrace to and repeat some word prior to the trouble element. This is called *anticipatory retracing*. An example is the following:

(49) And left to the *purple* crossing point – to the red crossing point

The troublesome item is *purple*, but after interruption the speaker retraces to the beginning of the prepositional phrase, thus "leading in" the replacement of *purple* by *red*. This happens in 35 percent of the error and appropriateness repairs.

The third way of restarting is by making a *fresh start*. The speaker neither instantly replaces the trouble element nor retraces to an earlier word. Rather, he starts with fresh material that was not part of the original interrupted utterance, as in example 50.

(50) From yellow down to *brown* – no – that's red

The speaker says neither just *red* or *to red*; he starts with a new construction: *that's* .... Fresh starts appear in 23 percent of the error and appropriateness repairs in the repair corpus. A special kind of fresh start is one in which the speaker starts with fresh material but then still copies part of the original utterance; the following is an example:

(51) The road begins with a – or it goes on and it begins with a green crossing.

Table 12.1
Ways of restarting for appropriateness repairs and error repairs. (Data from Levelt 1983.)

	Instant repairs	Anticipatory retracings	Fresh starts
Appropriateness repairs ($N = 290$)	30%	25%	44%
Error repairs ($N = 399$)	51%	41%	8%

After the editing expression *or*, the speaker introduces fresh material (*it goes on and it*), then repeats part of the original utterance (*begins with a*). This special kind of fresh start is called a *prespecification*.

How does a speaker restart when he has made an error, and how when the trouble has been an inappropriateness? Table 12.1 gives the results for these two classes of repair occasions in the pattern-description data.

The table shows a considerable difference in the ways of restarting for the two categories of repair occasion. Repairs of errors are usually made either instantly or by anticipation. It is exceptional to make a fresh start after a mistake; example 50 is such a case. It should be added that three-fourths of the fresh starts in the category of appropriateness repairs are prespecifications, such as in example 51. Such prespecifications hardly ever occur among error repairs.

The upshot of these findings is that most error repairs leave the original utterance unaffected but for the erroneous element. Nothing is changed or added that is not strictly necessary. Repairs of all-out mistakes are *conservative*. When, however, the trouble is an inappropriateness, such as an ambiguity or an underspecification, the speaker tends to introduce fresh materials. Either he will say the same thing differently by creating a new sentence or phrase, or he will make a prespecification (which involves the insertion of fresh syntactic materials into the original utterance). The latter is, in fact, the dominant procedure for appropriateness repairs. Insertions of fresh materials almost always follow the Well-Formedness Rule. This also holds for van Wijk and Kempen's (1987) experimental data. A different way to put this is that in cases of inappropriateness speakers tend to *reformulate* what they had said. In cases of error they *preserve* their original formulation and only exchange the troublesome element.

One might expect that the way of restarting is also influenced by the amount of delay before interruption. It would, for instance, make sense to give an instant repair after an immediate interruption; the troublesome word would then immediately be followed by its correction. Detailed analyses of the repair data showed, however, that there is no such systematic dependency. The way of restarting is by and large independent of where the original utterance was interrupted.

12.3.3 Restarting and the Listener's Continuation Problem

There is another aspect of restarting that deserves particular attention. Not only the speaker but also the listener is in trouble when an utterance is interrupted. It is well known that listeners interpret speech "on-line" as much as possible (see, for instance, Marslen-Wilson and Tyler 1981). That is, listeners tend to syntactically, semantically, and pragmatically integrate each new word of an utterance into whatever they have understood so far. This integration is done very quickly, even *during* the delivery of the word. When an utterance is interrupted by the speaker, the listener's problem is how to insert the new repair information into the developing interpretation of the original utterance.

It would be ideal if the listener could know how to do this as soon as the first word of the repair appears. In particular, a repair's first word (after whatever editing terms) can, first, be the instant replacement for a trouble item, as in example 48. In that case the listener would want to know that this is the case, as well as which word in the original utterance is to be replaced. The first word can also be the beginning of an anticipatory retracing. How can the listener know that this is so, and which element in the original utterance is the target of retracing? A third alternative is for the first word to be the beginning of a fresh start. That is important to know, because the listener will then interpret it as an addition rather than as a change. Finally, the interruption may be due to a covert repair. In that case the first word after the restart is either just the next word of the current sentence, as in example 52, or an item overlapping with the original utterance, as in examples 19, 33, and 53. For the listener, the latter case is like an anticipatory retracing.

(52) Left of the black dot – er – which was already mentioned

(53) A vertical line to a – to a black disk

Does the way in which speakers restart reveal to their listeners right away which of these four cases is at hand? The answer is, by and large, Yes. In particular, speakers adhere to two conventions of restarting, which will now be discussed. Both conventions relate the first word of the repair to some earlier word in the original utterance.

The Word-Identity Convention
If the first word of the repair is identical to some word *w* of the original utterance, the repair is to be interpreted as a continuation of the original utterance from *w* on. (If there is more than one such word in the original utterance, take the last one.)

The idea of this convention is easily exemplified. Case 54 adheres to the convention; case 55 doesn't.

(54) Right to *yellow* – er – to white
       |_____|

Here the first repair word, *to*, also appears in the interrupted utterance. The intended interpretation, therefore, is *right to white*. The continuation of interpretation means, in particular, that the local syntax at the point of insertion is acknowledged. In the case of

(55) And at the bottom of the *line* a red dot – a vertical line
       |_____|

the convention prescribes the interpretation *and at the bottom of the line a vertical line*, and that is not what the speaker intended. Before discussing whether violating cases such as 55 are just exceptional or rather quite frequent, I will introduce the second convention, which applies to cases where the first word of the repair differs from all the words in the original utterance.

The Category-Identity Convention
If the syntactic category of the first word of the repair is identical to the syntactic category of some word *w* of the original utterance, the repair is to be interpreted as a continuation from *w* on, with the first repair word replacing *w*. (If there is more than one such word in the original utterance, take the last one.)

The latter convention is followed in example 56 but violated in example 57.

(56) Down from white is a *red* node and from – pink node
       |_____|

By the convention, the interpretation should be *down from white is a pink node*, since the adjective *pink* is to replace the adjective *red* in the original utterance. This is indeed the intended interpretation.

(57) And then again a *stretch* to a red patch – stripe
       |_____|

Here the convention prescribes the interpretation *and then again a stretch to a red stripe*, the noun *stripe* replacing the last noun (*patch*) in the original utterance. This was not intended by the speaker; *stretch* was to be replaced.

Do speakers follow these conventions? Examples 55 and 57 are real exceptions in the data. The Word-Identity Convention was violated in 13 percent of the cases in which it should have applied. In most of these cases not the last but an earlier identical word had to be taken. The Category-Identity Convention was violated in 9 percent of the cases, and again in most of these cases an earlier category-identical word had to be taken (as in example 57). In quite a number of cases, the Word-Identity Convention was violated but the Category-Identity Convention was respected. In fact, in no more than 7 percent of the cases did speakers violate both constraints at the same time. In other words, in a large majority of cases speakers begin their repair in such a way that the listener can immediately insert the repair in the right slot of the original utterance. This guarantees unhampered on-line interpretation of utterance-plus-correction. And the repair's prosody reveals this fact. When the "bridged" parts in repairs 54–57 are spliced out of the tape, normal fluent speech arises (Levelt 1984b).

The reader may have noticed the similarity of the two conventions. The Word-Identity Convention is probably a special case of the Category-Identity Convention. However, it makes psychological sense to keep them apart. In the case of word identity, the listener knows that the repair is going to be an anticipatory retracing—there will be a lead-in to the correction, and a "leisurely" interpretation is possible. In case of mere category identity, there is instant replacement—which probably requires more alertness on the part of the listener.

The above conventions do not solve all of the listener's continuation problems. If the conditions for neither convention are met, the repair can be either a fresh start or a covert repair of the type shown in example 52. In the former case a new syntactic construction is at hand; in the latter case the syntax of the utterance is simply continued. This is an important difference in on-line interpretation. The problem, however, is smaller than it appears to be. In the large majority of repairs the listener can determine which is the case on the basis of the editing term used. In 92 percent of all covert repairs (i.e. hesitations) of this sort, speakers used *er* as an editing term, whereas only 6 percent of the fresh starts were introduced by *er*. Two-thirds of the fresh starts had no editing term at all, which shouldn't surprise us: Fresh starts are the mark of appropriateness repairs, and in most cases appropriateness repairs go without editing expressions.

In conclusion, therefore, it can be said that, with a low rate of exceptions, speakers solve their addressees' continuation problem when a repair is at hand. No later than upon the first word of the repair the listener can know how to relate the repair to the interrupted utterance. Whether the listener in fact uses that information when dealing with the speaker's trouble is another issue; it is not a concern of this book.

12.3.4 Prosodic Marking in Self-Repair

Following a suggestion by Goffman (1981), Cutler (1983b) drew a distinction between repairs that are prosodically marked and those that are unmarked. A repair is prosodically unmarked when "the speaker utters the correction on, as far as possible, the same pitch as the originally uttered error [or trouble item]." Also, in unmarked repairs, the amplitude and the relative duration of the repair mimic those of the trouble item. A repair is prosodically marked when the prosody of the trouble item and its correction differ substantially. Marking can be done by creating a contrast in pitch contour, in loudness, or duration. Cutler found that repairs of phonetic errors are, as a rule, unmarked. For instance, for the repair

(58) Well it'll all have to be *unsiled* – unsigned

the speaker does not make a prosodic contrast between *unsigned* and the erroneous *unsiled*. Marking typically occurs in lexical repairs, such as

(59) You're *happy* to – wElcome to include it

(where pitch accent is, as usual, indicated by capitalizing the vowel).

Still, in Cutler's corpus only 38 percent of the lexical repairs were prosodically marked. What, then, governs a speaker's decision to mark a repair? To deal with this question, we (Levelt and Cutler 1983) analyzed all of the tape-recorded lexical repairs in the pattern-description corpus. There were 299 such repairs for which the independent markedness judgments of the two authors agreed. Of these, 134 (45 percent) were marked.

A first analysis concerned the interrupt/restart pattern of the repair. Did a speaker mark the replacing word more often when interruption was immediate, i.e., within or right after the trouble word? Or did a speaker do more marking in instant repairs than in anticipatory retracings and fresh starts? It turned out that none of these factors had anything to do with prosodic marking in repairs. In other words, prosodic marking in no way reflects the *syntax* of the repair operation.

Rather, repair prosody is *semantically* motivated. This appears, first, from a comparison of error and appropriateness repairs. Of the error repairs, 53 percent were prosodically marked, whereas only 19 percent of the appropriateness repairs were. It should be remembered that repairs of errors are made to *reject* what was said earlier. This, we saw, is also apparent from the use of editing terms such as *no*, *or*, and *sorry*, and from the tendency to break off the error word. Prosodic marking *accentuates* this contrast. Repairing for inappropriateness, however, does not involve rejection as much as it involves further specification; no contrast is established to what was said before.

Still, the question should be raised why only 53 percent of these error repairs are marked. Don't they all involve a semantic contrast? Yes, they do, but there are degrees of contrast. The speaker and the listener will often be mutually aware of the set of alternatives for a trouble item. The sense of contrast will be highest when this set is small, as in the case of antonyms (*left* – no, *rIght*). It will be less when the number of alternatives to the trouble word is large.

The repair data we studied made it possible to test this notion of degrees of contrast. Among the lexical corrections there were many color-name repairs. The experimental patterns involved eleven different colors; hence, the number of alternatives to a particular color was ten. There were also a substantial number of errors in directional terms. These almost always exchanged *left* and *right*, *horizontal* and *vertical*, or *up* and *down*— i.e., antonyms. In most of these cases, therefore, there was just one alternative. If the degree of contrast matters, one would predict more prosodic marking in the repairs of directional terms than in the color-name repairs. And indeed, this turned out to be the case. Seventy-two percent of the direction-term repairs were marked, versus 50 percent of the color-name repairs. The degree of semantic contrast, therefore, is an important contributing factor to prosodic marking in self-repairs.

These findings place the origins of prosodic marking in repairs at the message level. The speaker intends to give contrastive prominence. This, in turn, induces prosodic focus in grammatical encoding (see subsection 5.2.2), which becomes phonologically realized as pitch accent.

In addition to this genealogy of prosodic marking in repairs, there may well be a personal stylistic factor. Certain speakers became quite upset with themselves when they made a mistake; they would, so to say, cry out the corrections. One speaker even marked every single repair. Others preferred to make their repairs more or less in passing, as if the listener rather than the speaker was to blame for the misunderstanding. What would you do, dear reader?

12.3.5   Repairing on the Fly

There are many more ways of repairing than those reviewed above. Actually, the boundaries between repairing and nonrepairing are quite fuzzy. There are parentheticals and expansions that come, sort of, as afterthoughts. One wouldn't call the following a repair:

(60) He conquered Babylon, the great Alexander.

It is, clearly, a well-formed utterance. If it were a repair, the Well-Formedness Rule would classify it as ill formed. (*He conquered Babylon and the great Alexander* is ill formed if *he* and *the great Alexander* are co-referential.) But other cases are less clear. What about the following?

(61) That's the only thing he does is fight.   (from Kroch and Hindle 1982)

(62) It seems to be a good marriage, of her parents.   (C. van Wijk, personal communication)

(63) Who did you think else would come?   (from Garrett 1980a)

In all these cases the speaker repairs (or seems to repair) something on the fly, without an explicit stop and restart operation (see van Wijk and Kempen 1987 for a review of such cases). Speakers are apparently willing to stretch or even distort their syntax to cope with local trouble, just to maintain fluent delivery of their speech.

How universal are the mechanisms of self-repair that we have reviewed in this chapter? Though the present base of data and analyses is still fairly limited, there is reason to suppose that the organization of repair is quite invariant across languages and cultures. This is, in particular, argued by Schegloff (1987) on the basis of a comparison of repair behavior in Tuvaluan (South Pacific), Quiche (Guatemala), and Thai. According to Schegloff these universal patterns of conduct proceed from "plausibly generic organizational contingencies of interaction."

Summary

Speakers attend to what they are saying and how they say it. They can monitor almost any aspect of their speech, ranging from content to syntax to the choice of words to properties of phonological form and articulation. But they do not continuously attend to all these things simultaneously. Attention is on the one hand selective, and on the other hand fluctuating. Which aspects of speech are attended to is highly dependent on the context and on the task. A speaker can be set to attend to certain kinds of errors or dysfluencies, and to ignore others. Also, the detection rate fluctuates with the developing phrase structure of the current utterance; monitoring is more intense at ends of phrases.

There are, essentially, two classes of monitoring theories: the editing theories and the connectionist theories. The editing theories put the monitor outside the language-production system; the connectionist accounts make it internal to the system. The most parsimonious version of the former type is the perceptual-loop theory, which identifies the monitor with the language user's speech-understanding system. According to this theory, the speaker can monitor both his internal speech and his overt speech (via the internal and the external perceptual loop, respectively). But there is no monitoring access to intermediary results of formulating. The connectionist type of account is most specifically worked out in MacKay's node-structure theory. It assumes that the systems for language production and language understanding are largely coincident networks of connected nodes. Error detection is due to bottom-up priming within this network. Both kinds of theories have their strengths and weaknesses, and both are hard to disconfirm.

After noticing some flaw in content or in well-formedness, a speaker may interrupt himself and begin a repair operation. There is evidence that self-interruption follows immediately upon the detection of trouble. Speakers do not wait till after the completion of a syntactic, a lexical, or a phonetic unit. There is, however, one exception to this Main Interruption Rule: Speakers respect the integrity of words—at least, of words that are themselves correct. Erroneous words, on the other hand, are frequently broken off in self-repairs.

The moment of suspense after self-interruption is often filled with some editing expression, most frequently *er*. This *er* is a symptom of the actuality of trouble. It appears especially when the troublesome item is immediately recognized by the speaker. Other editing terms tend to reveal the *kind* of trouble at hand. When there is an all-out mistake, editing expressions are used that involve rejection or excuse (*no, sorry*). When what was said was merely not fully appropriate, editing expressions are not much used, and when used they tend to stress the continuity of interpretation (*that is*).

When the speaker resumes speech after this interlude, he carefully relates the repair to the interrupted original utterance. There is, first, a syntactic relation between these two. The original utterance and the repair are, essentially, delivered as two conjuncts of a coordination. The syntax of repairing is governed by a rule of well-formedness, which acknowledges this coordinative character of repairs. The rule is usually followed in naturally occurring repairs. But it can, as can any linguistic rule, be violated.

A second observation is that the way of repairing depends on the occasion. In correcting all-out errors, speakers tend to preserve the original syntax in the repair. They can cite parts of the original utterance without change, except of course for the item(s) to be replaced. When the occasion of repair is an inappropriateness, speakers often reformulate, either by inserting fresh materials into the original utterance or by starting with a new utterance. Error repairs are conservative; appropriateness repairs are rather innovative reformulations.

A third property of the way speakers restart their speech is that they give cues about how to relate the repair to the original utterance. When the repair is to be understood as the continuation of the original utterance from some word on, the first repair word reveals which word that is. In most other cases the editing term tells the listener how to solve this continuation problem.

Not all repairs are neatly made as stop-and-restart operations. Speakers can preserve fluency by repairing "on the fly," but usually at the expense of syntactic well-formedness.

It is often the interlocutor who makes the speaker aware of some trouble in his speech, by asking *what?* or *what do you mean?* or by giving nonverbal signals. A speaker not only monitors his own speech directly; he also monitors it indirectly by attending to the interlocutor's reactions.

Appendix
Symbols from the
International Phonetic
Alphabet, with examples

a	stop, cop	m	man, him
ɑ	balm, rather	n	nose, annoy
æ	fat, placid	ŋ	wing, sink
ʌ	but, flood	oʊ	go, soul
aɪ	eye, kite	ɔ	walk, law
aʊ	owl, how	ɒ	want, astronaut
b	boss, hobo	ɔɪ	boil, voice
tʃ	cembalo, pitch	p	pie, nap
d	do, had	r	rim, parrot
dʒ	wedge, rage	s	simon, boss
eɪ	bait, day	ʃ	ship, facial
ə	among, readily	t	town, walked
ɛ	weather, any	θ	thin, myth
f	felt, left	ð	then, weather
g	go, leg	u	roof, flew
h	hat, how	ʊ	look, full
ħ	Ohio, ahead	ɜr	bird, worst
i	evil, bee	v	voice, give
ɪ	if, remit	w	why, quail
j	yet, canyon	x	(Spanish) proteger, (Dutch) kachel
k	case, back	z	zeal, haze
l	lip, bill	ʒ	leasure, garage

Bibliography

Abbs, J. H., & Cole, K. J. (1982). Considerations of bulbar and suprabul-bar afferent influences upon speech motor coordination and programming. In S. Grillner, B. Lindblom, J. Lubker, & A. Person (Eds.), *Speech motor control.* Oxford: Pergamon Press.

Abercrombie, D. (1967). *Elements of general phonetics.* Edinburgh University Press.

Anderson, J. R. (1976). *Language, memory, and thought.* Hillsdale, NJ: Lawrence Erlbaum.

Anderson, J. R. (1983). *The architecture of cognition.* Cambridge, MA: Harvard University Press.

Appelt, E. A. (1985). *Planning English sentences.* Cambridge University Press.

Arbib, M. A. (1981). Perceptual structures and distributed motor control. In V. Brooks (Ed.), *Handbook of physiology. The nervous system: Vol. 2. Motor control.* Bethesda, MD: American Physiological Society.

Atkinson, J. M., & Drew, P. (1979). *Order in court.* London: MacMillan.

Austin, J. L. (1962). *How to do things with words.* Oxford: Clarendon Press.

Baars, B. J., Motley, M. T., & MacKay, D. (1975). Output editing for lexical status from artificially elicited slips of the tongue. *Journal of Verbal Learning and Verbal Behavior, 14,* 382–391.

Baddeley, A. (1986). *Working memory.* Oxford: Clarendon Press.

Barth, E. M., & Wiche, R. T. P. (1986). *Problems, functions and semantic roles.* Berlin: De Gruyter.

Barwise, J., & Perry, J. (1983). *Situations and attitudes.* Cambridge, MA: MIT Press.

Bates, E., & Devescovi, A. (forthcoming). Competition and sentence production. In B. MacWhinney & E. R. Bates (Eds.), *Cross-linguistic studies of sentence processing.* Cambridge University Press.

Bates, E., & MacWhinney, B. (1982). Functionalist approaches to grammar. In E. Wanner & L. Gleitman (Eds.), *Language acquisition: The State of the art.* Cambridge University Press.

Bates, E., & MacWhinney, B. (1987). Competition, variation, and language learning. In B. MacWhinney (Ed.), *Mechanisms of language acquisition.* Hillsdale, NJ: Lawrence Erlbaum.

Bates, E., Masling, M., & Kintsch, W. (1978). Recognition memory for aspects of dialogue. *Journal of Experimental Psychology: Human Learning and Memory, 4,* 187–197.

Bauer, L. (1983). *English word-formation.* Cambridge University Press.

Beattie, G. (1978), Floor apportionment and gaze in conversational dyads. *British Journal of Social and Clinical Psychology, 17,* 7–16.

Beattie, G. (1980). Encoding units in spontaneous speech: Some implications for the dynamics of conversation. In H. W. Dechert & M. Raupach (Eds.), *Temporal variables in speech.* The Hague: Mouton.

Beattie, G. (1983). *Talk: An analysis of speech and non-verbal behavior in conversation.* Milton Keyes: Open University Press.

Beattie, G. (1984). "Are there cognitive rhythms in speech?"—A reply to Power, 1983. *Language and Speech, 27,* 193–195.

Beattie, G., & Butterworth, B. (1979). Contextual probability and word frequency as determinants of pauses in spontaneous speech. *Language and Speech, 22,* 201–211.

Beaugrande, R. de. (1980). *Text, discourse, and processes.* Norwood, NJ: Ablex.

Bell-Berti, F., & Harris, K. (1979). Anticipatory coarticulation: Some implications from a study of lip rounding. *Journal of the Acoustical Society of America, 65,* 1268–1270.

Berg, T. (1987). The case against accommodation: Evidence from German speech error data. *Journal of Memory and Language, 26,* 277–299.

Bierwisch, M. (1965). Regeln für die Intonation deutscher Sätze. In M. Bierwisch (Ed.), *Studia Grammatica VII. Untersuchungen über Akzent und Intonation im Deutschen.* Berlin: Akademie-Verlag.

Bierwisch, M. (1982). Linguistics and language error. In A. Cutler (Ed.), *Slips of the tongue and language production.* Berlin: Mouton.

Bierwisch, M. (1986). On the nature of semantic form in natural language. In F. Klix & H. Hagendorf (Eds.), *Human memory and cognitive capabilities: Mechanisms and performances.* Amsterdam: North-Holland.

Bock, J. K. (1977). The effect of pragmatic presupposition on syntactic structure in question answering. *Journal of Verbal Learning and Verbal Behavior, 16,* 723–734.

Bock, J. K. (1982). Towards a cognitive psychology of syntax: Information processing contributions to sentence formulation. *Psychological Review, 89,* 1–47.

Bock, J. K. (1986a). Meaning, sound, and syntax: Lexical priming in sentence production. *Journal of Experimental Psychology: Learning, Memory, and Cognition, 12,* 575–586.

Bock, J. K. (1986b). Syntactic persistence in language production. *Cognitive Psychology, 18,* 355–387.

Bock, J. K. (1987a). Coordinating words and syntax in speech plans. In A. Ellis (Ed.), *Progress in the psychology of language* (Vol. 3). London: Lawrence Erlbaum.

Bock, J. K. (1987b). An effect of the accessibility of word forms on sentence structures. *Journal of Memory and Language, 26*(2), 119–137.

Bock, J. K., & Irwin, D. E. (1980). Syntactic effects of information availability in sentence production. *Journal of Verbal Learning and Verbal Behavior, 19,* 467–484.

Bock, J. K., & Warren, R. K. (1985). Conceptual accessibility and syntactic structure in sentence formulation. *Cognition, 21,* 47–67.

Boehme, K. (1983). *Children's understanding of German possessive pronouns.* Unpublished doctoral dissertation, Nijmegen University.

Bolinger, D. (Ed.). (1972). *Intonation: Selected readings.* London: Penguin.

Bolinger, D. (1983). Where does intonation belong? *Journal of Semantics, 2,* 101–120.

Bolinger, D. (1986). *Intonation and its parts.* London: Edward Arnold.

Bond, Z. S., & Small, L. H. (1984). Detecting and correcting mispronounciations: A note on methodology. *Journal of Phonetics, 12,* 279–283.

Boomer, D. S. (1965). Hesitation and grammatical encoding. *Language and Speech, 8,* 148–158.

Boomer, D. S., & Laver, J. D. M. (1968). Slips of the tongue. *Journal of Disorders of Communication, 3,* 2–12. (Reprinted in Fromkin, V. A. (Ed.). (1973). *Speech errors as linguistic evidence.* The Hague: Mouton.)

Brazil, D., Coulthard, M., & Johns, C. (1980). *Discourse intonation and language teaching.* Burnt Mill, Harlow: Longman.

Bransford, J. D., & Johnson, M. K. (1973). Considerations of some problems of comprehension. In W. G. Chase (Ed.), *Visual information processing.* New York: Academic Press.

Bresnan, J. (1978). A realistic transformational grammar. In M. Halle, J. Bresnan & G. A. Miller (Eds.), *Linguistic theory and psychological reality.* Cambridge, MA: MIT Press.

Bresnan, J. (Ed.). (1982). *The mental representation of grammatical relations.* Cambridge, MA: MIT Press.

Broadbent, D. E. (1975). The magic number seven after fifteen years. In A. Kennedy & A. Wilkes (Eds.), *Studies in long term memory.* London: John Wiley.

Brodda, B. (1979). *Något om de Svenska ordens fonotax och morfotax.* (Paper No. 38). University of Stockholm, Institute of Linguistics.

Browman, C. P. (1978). Tip of the tongue and slip of the ear. Implications for language processing. *UCLA Working Papers in Phonetics, 42,* 1–149.

Browman, C. P., & Goldstein, L. M. (1986). Towards an articulatory phonology. *Phonology Yearbook, 3,* 219–252.

Brown, G., Currie, K. L., & Kenworthy, J. (1980). *Questions of intonation.* London: Croom Helm.

Brown, G., & Yule, G. (1983). *Discourse analysis.* Cambridge University Press.

Brown, P., & Dell, G. S. (1987). Adapting production to comprehension: The explicit mention of instruments. *Cognitive Psychology, 19,* 441–472.

Brown, R. (1973). Schizophrenia, language and reality. *American Psychologist, 28,* 395–403.

Brown, R., & McNeill, D. (1966). The "tip of the tongue" phenomenon. *Journal of Verbal Learning and Verbal Behavior, 5,* 325–337.

Bruner, J. S. (1983). *Child's talk: Learning to use language.* New York: Norton.

Bühler, K. (1934). *Sprachtheorie.* Stuttgart: Fisher.

Bürkle, B., Nirmaier, H., & Herrmann, Th. (1986). *Von dir aus ... Zur hörerbezogenen lokalen Referenz.* (Bericht 10). Mannheim: University of Mannheim, Forschergruppe Sprechen und Sprachverstehen im Sozialen Kontext.

Butterworth, B. (1972). *Semantic analyses of the phasing of fluency in spontaneous speech.* Unpublished doctoral dissertation, University of London.

Butterworth, B. (1975). Hesitation and semantic planning in speech. *Journal of Psycholinguistic Research, 4,* 75–87.

Butterworth, B. (1980a). Some constraints on models of language production. In B. Butterworth (Ed.), *Language production: Vol. 1. Speech and talk.* London: Academic Press.

Butterworth, B. (1980b). Evidence from pauses in speech. In B. Butterworth (Ed.), *Language production: Vol. 1. Speech and talk.* London: Academic Press.

Butterworth, B. (Ed.). (1980c). *Language production: Vol. 1. Speech and talk.* London: Academic Press.

Butterworth, B. (1982). Speech errors: Old data in search of new theories. In A. Cutler (Ed.), *Slips of the tongue and language production.* Berlin: Mouton.

Butterworth, B. (1983a). Lexical representation. In B. Butterworth (Ed.). *Language production: Vol. 2. Development, writing and other language processes.* London: Academic Press.

Butterworth, B. (Ed.). (1983b). *Language production: Vol. 2. Development, writing and other language processes.* London: Academic Press.

Butterworth, B. (forthcoming). Lexical access in speech production. In W. Marslen-Wilson (Ed.), *Lexical representation and process.* Cambridge, MA: MIT Press.

Calvert, D. R. (1980). *Descriptive phonetics.* New York: Decker.

Carr, T. H. (1979). Consciousness in models of human information processing: Primary memory, executive control, and input regulation. In G. Underwood & R. Stevens (Eds.), *Aspects of consciousness: Vol. 1. Psychological issues.* London: Academic Press.

Carroll, J. M. (1958). Process and content in psycholinguistics. In R. Patton (Ed.), *Current trends in the description and analysis of behavior.* University of Pittsburgh Press.

Carroll, J. M. (1983a). Nameheads. *Cognitive Science, 7,* 121–153.

Carroll, J. M. (1983b). Toward a functional theory of names and naming. *Linguistics, 21,* 341–371.

Chafe, W. L. (1970). *Meaning and the structure of language.* University of Chicago Press.

Chafe, W. L. (1976). Giveness, contrastiveness, definiteness, subjects, topics, and point of view. In C. N. Li (Ed.), *Subject and topic.* New York: Academic Press.

Chafe, W. L. (1977). The recall and verbalization of past experience. In R. W. Cole (Ed.), *Current issues in linguistic theory.* Bloomington: Indiana University Press.

Chafe, W. L. (1979).The flow of thought and the flow of language. In T. Givon (Ed.), *Syntax and semantics: 12. Discourse and syntax.* New York: Academic Press.

Chafe, W. L. (1980). The deployment of consciousness in the production of a narrative. In W. L. Chafe (Ed.), *The pear stories. Cognitive, cultural, and linguistic aspects of narrative production.* Norwood, NJ: Ablex.

Chomsky, N., & Halle, M. (1968). *The sound pattern of English.* New York: Harper and Row.

Clark, E. V. (1970). How young children describe events in time. In G.B. Flores d'Arcais & W. J. M. Levelt (Eds.), *Advances in psycholinguistics.* Amsterdam: North-Holland.

Clark, E. V. (1974). Normal states and evaluative viewpoints. *Language, 50,* 316–332.

Clark, E. V. (1977). From gesture to word: On the natural history of deixis in language acquisition. In J. S. Bruner & A. Garton (Eds.), *Human growth and development*. Oxford: Wolfson College.

Clark, E. V. (1987). The principle of contrast: A constraint on language acquisition. In B. MacWhinney (Ed.), *Mechanisms of language acquisition*. Hillsdale, NJ: Lawrence Erlbaum.

Clark, E. V. (1988). On the logic of contrast. *Journal of Child Language, 15,* 317–335.

Clark, E. V., & Clark, H. H. (1979). When nouns surface as verbs. *Language, 55,* 767–811.

Clark, H. H. (1970). Word associations and linguistic theory. In J. Lyons (Ed.), *New horizons in linguistics*. Baltimore: Penguin.

Clark, H. H. (1973). Space, time, semantics, and the child. In T. E. Moore (Ed.), *Cognitive development and the acquisition of language*. New York: Academic Press.

Clark, H. H. (1979). Responding to indirect speech acts. *Cognitive Psychology, 4,* 430–477.

Clark, H. H. (1985). Language use and language users. In G. Lindsey & E. Aronson (Eds.), *The handbook of social psychology*. New York: Harper and Row.

Clark, H. H., (1987). Four dimensions of language use. In M. Bertuccelli-Papi & J. Verschueren (Eds.), *The pragmatic perspective*. Amsterdam: John Benjamins.

Clark, H. H., & Clark, E. (1977). *Psychology and language. An introduction to psycholinguistics*. New York: Harcourt Brace.

Clark. H. H., & Gerrig, R. J. (1984). On the pretense theory of irony. *Journal of Experimental Psychology: General, 113,* 121–126.

Clark, H. H., & Haviland, S. E. (1977). Comprehension and the given-new contract. In R. O. Freedle (Ed.), *Discourse production and comprehension*. New York: Academic Press.

Clark, H. H., Schreuder, R., & Buttrick, S. (1983). Common ground and the understanding of demonstratives. *Journal of Verbal Learning and Verbal Behavior, 22,* 245–258.

Clark, H. H., & Schunk, D.H. (1980). Polite responses to polite requests. *Cognition, 8,* 111–143.

Clark, H. H., & Wilkes-Gibbs, D. L. (1986). Referring as a collaborative process. *Cognition, 22,* 1–39.

Clements, G. N. (1985). The geometry of phonological features. *Phonology Yearbook, 2,* 225–252.

Clements, G. N., & Keyser, S. J. (1983). *CV Phonology. A generative theory of the syllable*. Cambridge, MA: MIT Press.

Cohen, A. (1965). Versprekingen als verklappers bij het proces van spreken en verstaan. *Forum der Letteren, 6,* 175–186.

Cohen, A. (1968). Errors of speech and their implication for understanding the strategy of the language users. *Zeitschrift für Phonetik, 21,* 177–181.

Cohen, A., Collier, R., & Hart, J. 't (1982). Declination: Construct of intrinsic feature of speech pitch? *Phonetica, 39,* 254–273.

Cohen, A., & Hart, J. 't (1965). Perceptual analysis of intonation patterns. *Proceedings of the Vth ICA, A16.* Liege, Belgium.

Collier, R., & Gelfer, C. E. (1983). Physiological explanations of F0 Declination. In M. P. R. Van den Broecke & A. Cohen (Eds.), *Proceedings of the Tenth International Congress of Phonetic Sciences.* Dordrecht: Foris.

Cooper, W. E. (1976). *Syntactic control of timing in speech production.* Unpublished doctoral dissertation, Massachusetts Institute of Technology.

Cooper, W. E., & Danly M. (1981). Segmental and temporal aspects of utterance-final lengthening. *Phonetica, 38,* 106–115.

Cooper, W. E., & Eady, S. J. (1986). Metrical phonology in speech production. *Journal of Memory and Language, 25,* 369–384.

Cooper, W. E., & Paccia-Cooper, J. M., (1980). *Syntax and speech.* Cambridge, MA: Harvard University Press.

Cooper, W. E., & Ross, J. R. (1975). World order. In R. E. Grossmann, L. J. San, & T. J. Vance (Eds.), *Papers from the parasession on functionalism.* Chicago Linguistic Society.

Cooper, W. E., & Sorensen, J. M. (1981). *Fundamental frequency in sentence production.* New York: Springer.

Cooper, W. E., Tye-Murray, N., & Nelson, L. J. (1987). Detection of missing words in spoken text. *Journal of Psycholinguistic Research, 16,* 233–240.

Crompton, A. (1982). Syllables and segments in speech production. In A. Cutler (Ed.), *Slips of the tongue and language production.* Berlin: Mouton.

Cruse, D. A. (1986). *Lexical semantics.* Cambridge University Press.

Cruttenden, A. (1986). *Intonation.* Cambridge University Press.

Cutler, A. (1980a). Errors of stress and intonation. In V. A. Fromkin (Ed.), *Errors in linguistic performance.* New York: Academic Press.

Cutler, A. (1980b). Syllable omission errors and isochrony. In H. W. Dechert & M. Raupach (Eds.), *Temporal variables in speech. Studies in honour of Frieda Goldman-Eisler.* The Hague: Mouton.

Cutler, A. (Ed.). (1982a). *Slips of the tongue and language production.* Berlin: Mouton.

Cutler, A. (1982b). *Speech errors: A classified bibliography.* Bloomington: Indiana Linguistics Club.

Cutler, A. (1983a). Lexical complexity and sentence processing. In G. B. Flores d'Arcais & R. J. Jarvella (Eds.), *The process of language understanding*. Chichester: John Wiley.

Cutler, A. (1983b). Speakers' conceptions of the function of prosody. In A. Cutler & D. R. Ladd (Eds.), *Prosody: Models and measurements*. Heidelberg: Springer.

Cutler, A. (1987). Speaking for listening. In A. Allport, D. G. MacKay, W. Prinz, & E. Scheerer (Eds.), *Language perception and production: Relationships between listening, speaking, reading and writing*. London: Academic Press.

Cutler, A., & Clifton, C., Jr. (1984). The use of prosodic information in word recognition. In H. Bouma & D. G. Bouwhuis (Eds.), *Attention and performance: X. Control of language processes*. Hillsdale, NJ: Lawrence Erlbaum.

Cutler, A., & Isard, S. (1980). The production of prosody. In B. Butterworth (Ed.), *Language Production: Vol. 1. Speech and talk*. London: Academic Press.

Cutler, A., & Ladd, D. R. (Eds.). (1983). *Prosody: Models and measurements*. Heidelberg: Springer.

Cutler, A., & Pearon, M. (1986). On the analysis of prosodic turn-taking cues. In C. Johns-Lewis (Ed.), *Intonation in discourse*. London: Croom Helm.

Daniloff, R. G., & Hammarberg, R. E. (1973). On defining coarticulation. *Journal of Phonetics, 1*, 239–248.

Danks, J. H. (1977). Producing ideas and sentences. In S. Rosenberg (Ed.), *Sentence production: Developments in research and theory*. New York: John Wiley.

Dauer, R. M. (1983). Stress-timing and syllable-timing reanalyzed. *Journal of Phonetics, 11*, 51–62.

Davidson-Nielson, N. (1975). A phonological analysis of English *sp, st, sk*, with special reference to speech error evidence. *Journal of the IPA, 5*, 3–25.

Deese, J. (1980). Pauses, prosody, and the demands of production in language. In H. W. Dechert & M. Raupach (Eds.), *Temporal variables in speech. Studies in honour of Frieda Goldman-Eisler*. The Hague: Mouton.

Deese, J. (1984). *Thought into speech: The psychology of a language*. Englewood Cliffs, NJ: Prentice-Hall.

Dell, G. S. (1980). *Phonological and lexical encoding in speech production: An analysis of naturally occurring and experimentally elicited speech errors*. Unpublished doctoral dissertation, University of Toronto.

Dell, G. S. (1984). Representation of serial order in speech: Evidence from the repeated phoneme effect in speech errors. *Journal of Experimental Psychology: Learning, Memory, and Cognition, 10*, 222–233.

Dell, G. S. (1985). Positive feedback in hierarchical connectionist models: Applications to language production. *Cognitive Science, 9*, 3–23.

Dell, G. S. (1986). A spreading activation theory of retrieval in sentence production. *Psychological Review, 93*, 283–321.

Dell, G. S. (1988). The retrieval of phonological forms in production: Tests of predictions from a connectionist model. *Journal of Memory and Language, 27*, 124–142.

Dell, G. S., & Reich, P. A. (1977). A model of slips of the tongue. *The Third LACUS Forum, 3*, 448–455.

Dell, G. S., & Reich, P. A. (1980). Toward a unified theory of slips of the tongue. In V. A. Fromkin (Ed.), *Errors in linguistic performance: Slips of the tongue, ear, pen, and hand.* New York: Academic Press.

Dell, G. S., & Reich, P. A. (1981). Stages in sentence production: An analysis of speech error data. *Journal of Verbal Learning and Verbal Behavior, 20*, 611–629.

Denes, P. B., & Pinson, E. N. (1963). *The speech chain.* Baltimore: Bell Telephone Laboratories.

De Pijper, J. R. (1983). *Modelling British English intonation: An analysis by resynthesis of British English intonation.* Dordrecht: Foris.

De Rooy, J. J. (1979). *Speech punctuation: An acoustic and perceptual study of some aspects of speech prosody in Dutch.* Unpublished doctoral dissertation, Utrecht University.

De Smedt, K., & Kempen, G. (1987). Incremental sentence production, self-correction, and coordination. In G. Kempen (Ed.), *Natural language generation: Recent advances in artificial intelligence, psychology and linguistics.* Dordrecht: Kluwer.

Deutsch, W. (1976). *Sprachliche Redundanz und Objektidentifikation.* Unpublished doctoral dissertation, University of Marburg.

Deutsch, W., & Jarvella, R. J. (1983). Asymmetrien zwischen Sprachproduktion und Sprachverstehen. In C. F. Graumann & T. Herrmann (Eds.), *Karl Bühlers Axiomatik.* Frankfurt: Klostermann.

Deutsch, W., & Pechmann, T. (1978). Ihr, dir, or mir? On the acquisition of pronouns in German children. *Cognition, 6, 155–168.*

Deutsch, W., & Pechmann, T. (1982). Social interaction and the development of definite descriptions. *Cognition, 11*, 159–184.

Diehl, R. L. (1986). Coproduction and direct perception of phonetic segments: A critique. *Journal of Phonetics, 14*, 61–66.

Dik, S. C. (1978). *Functional grammar.* Amsterdam: North-Holland.

Dik, S. C. (1987). Linguistically motivated knowledge representation. In M. Nagao (Ed.), *Language and artificial intelligence.* Amsterdam: Elsevier Science Press.

Dixon, R. M. W. (1972). *The Dyirbal language of North Queensland.* Cambridge University Press.

Dogil, G. (1984). Grammatical prerequisites to the analysis of speech style: fast/ casual speech. In D. Gibbon & H. Richter (Eds.), *Intonation, accent and rhythm*. Berlin: De Gruyter.

Doherty, M. (1987). *Epistemic meaning*. Heidelberg: Springer.

Donders, F. C. (1868). Die Schnelligkeit psychischer Prozesse. *Archiv Anatomie und Physiologie*, 657–681.

DuBois, J. W. (1974). Syntax in mid-sentence. *Berkeley Studies in Syntax and Semantics* (Vol. I: III.1-III.25). Berkeley: University of California, Institute of Human Learning and Department of Linguistics.

Duncan, S., & Fiske, D. W. (1977). *Face-to-face interaction: Research, methods and theory*. Hillsdale, NJ: Lawrence Erlbaum.

Easton, T. A. (1972). On the normal uses of reflexes. *American Scientist, 60*, 591–599.

Ehrich, V. (1982). The structure of living space descriptions. In R. J. Jarvella & W. Klein (Eds.), *Speech, place and action. Studies in deixis and related topics*. Chichester: John Wiley.

Ehrich, V. (1985). Zur Linguistik und Psycholinguistik der sekundären Raumdeixis. In H. Schweizer (Ed.), *Sprache und Raum*. Stuttgart: Metzlersche Verlagsbuchhandlung.

Ehrich V. (1987). The generation of tense. In G. Kempen (Ed.), *Natural language generation*. Dordrecht: Martinus Nijhoff.

Ehrich, V., & Koster, C. (1983). Discourse organization and sentence form: The structure of room descriptions in Dutch. *Discourse Processes, 6*, 169–195.

Eibl-Eibesfeldt, I. (1974). Similarities and differences between cultures in expressive movements. In S. Weitz (Ed.), *Non-verbal communication*. Oxford University Press.

Eibl-Eibesfeldt, I. (1984). *Die Biologie des menschlichen Verhaltens: Grundriss der Humanethologie: Vol. 1*. Munich: Piper.

Eriksen, C. W., Pollock, M. D., & Montague, W. E. (1970). Implicit speech: Mechanisms in perceptual encoding? *Journal of Experimental Psychology, 84*, 502–507.

Fauconnier, G. (1985). *Mental Spaces: Aspects of meaning construction in natural language*. Cambridge, MA: MIT Press.

Fay, D. (1980a). Performing transformations. In R. Cole (Ed.), *Perception and production of fluent speech*. Hillsdale, NJ: Lawrence Erlbaum.

Fay D. (1980b). Transformational errors. In V. A. Fromkin (Ed.), *Errors in linguistic performance: Slips of the tongue, ear, pen, and hand*. New York: Academic Press.

Fay, D. (1982). Substitutions and splices: a study of sentence blends. In A. Cutler (Ed.), *Slips of the tongue and language production*. Amsterdam: de Gruyter.

Fay, D., & Cutler, A. (1977). Malapropisms and the structure of the mental lexicon. *Linguistic Inquiry*, *8*, 505–520.

Feigenbaum, E. (1963). The simulation of verbal learning behavior. In E. Feigenbaum & J. Feldman (Eds.), *Computers and thought*. New York: McGraw-Hill.

Fel'dman, A. G. (1966a). Functional tuning of the nervous system with control of movement or maintenance of a steady posture. II. Controllable parameters of the muscles. *Biophysics*, *11*, 565–578.

Fel'dman, A. G. (1966b). Functional tuning of the nervous system with control of movement or maintenance of a steady posture. III. Mechanicographic analysis of the execution by man of the simplest motor tasks. *Biophysics*, *11*, 766–775.

Fillmore, C. J. (1968). The case for case. In E. Bach & R. T. Harms (Eds.), *Universals of linguistic theory*. New York: Holt, Rinehart and Winston.

Fillmore, C. J. (1973). May we come in? *Semiotica*, *9*, 98–115.

Fillmore, C. J. (1977). The case for case reopened. In P. Cole & J. M. Sadock (Eds.), *Syntax and semantics: Vol. 8. Grammatical relations*. New York: Academic Press.

Fillmore, C. (1982). Towards a descriptive framework for spatial deixis. In R. J. Jarvella & W. Klein (Eds.), *Speech, place, and action: Studies in deixis and related topics*. Chichester: John Wiley.

Flores d'Arcais, G. B. (1975). Some perceptual determinants of sentence construction. In G. B. Flores d'Arcais (Ed.), *Studies in perception*. Milan: Martello.

Flores d'Arcais, G. B. (1987a). Automatic processes in language comprehension. In G. Denes, C. Semenza, P. Bisiacchi, & E. Andreewsky (Eds.), *Perspectives in Cognitive Neuropsychology*. Hillsdale, NJ: Lawrence Erlbaum.

Flores d'Arcais, G. B. (1987b). Perceptual factors and word order in event descriptions. In G. Kempen (Ed.), *Natural language generation: New results in artificial intelligence, psychology and linguistics*. Dordrecht: Martinus Nijhoff.

Flores d'Arcais, G. B., & Schreuder, R. (1987). Semantic activation during object naming. *Psychological Research*, *49*, 153–159.

Fodor, J. A. (1975). *The language of thought*. Hassocks: Harvester Press.

Fodor, J. A. (1983). *The modularity of mind*. Cambridge, MA: MIT Press.

Fodor, J. A. (1985). Précis of the modularity of mind. *The Brain and Behavioral Sciences*, *8*, 1–42.

Fodor, J. A. (1987). Modules, frames, fridgeons, sleeping dogs, and the music of the spheres. In J. L. Garfield (Ed.), *Modularity in knowledge representation and natural-language understanding*. Cambridge, MA: MIT Press.

Fodor, J. A., Bever, T. G., & Garrett, M. F. (1974). *The psychology of language: An introduction to psycholinguistics and generative grammer*. New York: McGraw-Hill.

Fodor, J. A., Garrett, M. F., Walker, E. C. T., & Parkes, C. H. (1980). Against definitions. *Cognition, 8*, 263–367.

Folkins, J. W., & Abbs, J. H. (1975). Lip and motor control during speech: Responses to resistive loading of the jaw. *Journal of Speech and Hearing Research, 18*, 207–220.

Ford, M. (1982). Sentence planning units: Implications for the speaker's representation of meaningful relations underlying sentences. In J. Bresnan (Ed.), *The mental representation of grammatical relations*. Cambridge, MA: MIT Press.

Ford, M., & Holmes, V. M. (1978). Planning units in sentence production. *Cognition, 6*, 35–53.

Foss, D. J., & Hakes, D. T. (1978). *Psycholinguistics. An introduction to the psychology of language*. Englewood Cliffs, NJ: Prentice-Hall.

Fowler, C. A. (1980). Coarticulation and theories of extrinsic timing. *Journal of Phonetics, 8*, 113–133.

Fowler, C. A. (1983). Realism and unrealism: a reply. *Journal of Phonetics, 11*, 303–322.

Fowler, C. A. (1986a). An event approach to the study of speech perception from a direct-realist perspective. *Journal of Phonetics, 14*, 3–28.

Fowler, C. A. (1986b). Reply to commentators. *Journal of Phonetics 14*, 149–170.

Fowler, C. A., & Housum, J. (1987). Talkers' signalling of "new" and "old" words in speech and listeners' perception and use of the distinction. *Journal of Memory and Language, 26*, 489–504.

Fowler, C. A., Rubin, P., Remez, R. E., & Turvey, M. T. (1980). Implications for speech production of a general theory of action. In B. Butterworth (Ed.), *Language production: Vol. 1. Speech and talk*. London: Academic Press.

Fowler, C. A., & Turvey, M. T. (1980). Immediate compensation in bite-block speech. *Phonetica, 73*, 306–326.

Francik, E. P., & Clark, H. H. (1985). How to make requests that overcome obstacles to compliance. *Journal of Memory and Language, 24*, 560–568.

Franck, D. (1980). Seven sins of pragmatics: Theses about speech act theory, conversational analysis, linguistics and rhetorics. In A. Foolen, J. Hardeveld, & D. Springorum (Eds.), *Conversatieanalyse*. Nijmegen: Xeno.

Freud, S. (1904). *Zur Psychopathologie des Alltagslebens. Über Vergessen, Versprechen, Vergreifen, Aberglaube und Irrtum*. Frankfurt am Main: Fischer, 1954. (An English translation of Chapter V: Slips of the tongue, appeared in V. A. Fromkin (Ed.). (1973). *Speech errors as linguistic evidence*. The Hague: Mouton).

Friederici, A., & Levelt, W. J. M. (1986). Cognitive processes of spatial coordinate assignment. *Naturwissenschaften, 73*, 455–458.

Frijda, N. (1972). Simulation of human long-term memory. *Psychological Bulletin, 77*, 1–31.

Fromkin, V. A. (1971). The non-anomalous nature of anomalous utterances. *Language, 47*, 27–52. (Reprinted in: V. A. Fromkin (Ed.). (1973). *Speech errors as linguistic evidence.* The Hague: Mouton).

Fromkin, V. A. (Ed.). (1973). *Speech errors as linguistic evidence.* The Hague: Mouton.

Fromkin, V. A. (Ed.). (1980). *Errors in linguistic performance. Slips of the tongue, ear, pen, and hand.* New York: Academic Press.

Fry, D. (1969). The linguistic evidence of speech errors. *BRNO Studies of English, 8*, 69–74.

Fujimura, O. (1981). Temporal organization of articulatory movements as a multi-dimensional phrasal structure. *Phonetica, 38*, 66–83.

Fujimura, O., & Lovins, J. B. (1978). Syllables as concatenative phonetic units. In A. Bell & J. B. Hooper (Eds.), *Syllables and segments.* Amsterdam: North-Holland.

Fujisaki, H. (1983). Dynamic characteristics of voice fundamental frequency in speech and singing. In P. F. MacNeilage (Ed.), *The production of speech.* New York: Springer.

Gallistel, C. R. (1980). *The organization of action: A new synthesis.* Hillsdale, NJ: Lawrence Erlbaum.

Gardiner, J. M., Craik, F. I., & Bleasdale, F. A. (1973). Retrieval difficulty and subsequent recall. *Memory and Cognition, 1*, 213–216.

Gårding, E. (1983). A generative model of intonation. In A. Cutler & D. R. Ladd (Eds.), *Prosody: Models and measurements.* Heidelberg: Springer.

Garfield, J. L. (Ed.). (1987). *Modularity in knowledge representation and natural-language understanding.* Cambridge, MA: MIT Press.

Garnham, A., Shillcock, R. S., Brown, G. D. A., Mill, A. I. D., & Cutler, A. (1982). Slips of the tongue in the London-Lund corpus of spontaneous conversations. In A. Cutler (Ed.), *Slips of the tongue and language production.* Berlin: Mouton.

Garnsey, S. M., & Dell, G. S. (1984). Some neurolinguistic implications of pre-articulatory editing in production. *Brain and Language, 23*, 64–73.

Garrett, M. F. (1975). The analysis of sentence production. In G. Bower (Ed.), *Psychology of learning and motivation: Vol. 9.* New York: Academic Press.

Garrett, M. F. (1976). Syntactic processes in sentence production. In R. J. Wales & E. Walker (Eds.), *New approaches to language mechanisms.* Amsterdam: North-Holland.

Garrett, M. F. (1980a). Levels of processing in sentence production. In B. Butterworth (Ed.), *Language production: Vol. 1. Speech and Talk.* London: Academic Press.

Garrett, M. (1980b). The limits of accommodation: Arguments for independent processing levels in sentence production. In V. A. Fromkin (Ed.), *Errors in linguistic performance: Slips of the tongue, ear, pen, and hand.* New York: Academic Press.

Garrett, M. F. (1982). Production of speech: Observations from normal and pathological language use. In A. W. Ellis (Ed.), *Normality and pathology in cognitive functions.* London: Academic Press.

Garrod, S., & Anderson, A. (1987). Saying what you mean in dialogue: A study in conceptual and semantic coordination. *Cognition, 27,* 181–218.

Garrod, S., & Sanford, A. (1983). Topic dependent effects in language processing. In G. B. Flores d'Arcais & R. J. Jarvella (Eds.), *The process of language understanding.* Chichester: John Wiley.

Gay, T. (1981). Mechanisms in the control of speech rate. *Phonetica, 38,* 148–158.

Gay, T., & Turvey, M. T. (1979). Effects of efferent and afferent interference on speech production: Implications for a generative theory of speech-motor control. *9th International Congress of Phonetic Sciences.* Copenhagen: Institute of Phonetics.

Gazdar, G. (1979). *Pragmatics: Implicature, presupposition, and logical form.* New York: Academic Press.

Gazdar, G., Klein, E., Pullum, G., & Sag, I. (1985). *Generalized phrase structure grammar.* Oxford: Blackwell.

Gee, J. P., & Grosjean, F. (1983). Performance structures: A psycholinguistic and linguistic appraisal. *Cognitive Psychology, 15,* 411–458.

Glaser, W. R., & Düngelhoff, F. J. (1984). The time course of picture-word interference. *Journal of Experimental Psychology: Human Perception and Performance, 10,* 640–654.

Goffman, E. (1981). *Forms of talk.* Oxford: Blackwell.

Goguen, J. A., & Linde, C. (1983). *Linguistic methodology for the analysis of aviation accidents.* (NASA Contractor Report 3741).

Goldman, N. (1975). Conceptual generation. In R. Schank (Ed.), *Conceptual information processing.* Amsterdam: North-Holland.

Goldman-Eisler, F. (1958). Speech production and the predictability of words in context. *Quarterly Journal of Experimental Psychology, 10,* 96–106.

Goldman-Eisler, F. (1967). Sequential temporal patterns and cognitive processes in speech. *Language and Speech, 10,* 122–132.

Goldman-Eisler, F. (1968). *Psycholinguistics: Experiments in spontaneous speech.* New York: Academic Press.

Good, D. A., & Butterworth, B. (1980). Hesitancy as a conversational resource: Some methodological implications. In H.W. Dechert & M. Raupach (Eds.), *Temporal variables in speech.* The Hague: Mouton.

Goodglass, H., Theurkauf, J. C., & Wingfield, A. (1984). Naming latencies as evidence for two modes of lexical retrieval. *Applied Psycholinguistics, 5,* 135–146.

Goodwin, C. (1981). *Conversational organization: Interaction between speakers and hearers.* New York: Academic Press.

Gordon, H., & Meyer, D. E. (1987). Hierarchical representation of spoken syllable order. In A. Allport, D. G. MacKay, W. Prinz, & E. Scheerer (Eds.), *Language perception: Relations between listening, speaking, reading and writing.* London: Academic Press.

Grice, H. P. (1957). Meaning. *Philosophical Review, 66,* 377–388.

Grice, H. P. (1968). Utterer's meaning, sentence meaning and word meaning. *Foundations of Language, Vol. 4,* 225–242.

Grice, H. P. (1975). Logic and conversation. In P. Cole & J. L. Morgan (Eds.), *Syntax and semantics: 3. Speech acts.* New York: Academic Press.

Grice, H. P. (1978). Some further notes on logic and conversation. In P. Cole (Ed.), *Syntax and Semantics: Vol. 9. Pragmatics.* New York: Academic Press.

Grimes, J. E. (1975). *The thread of discourse.* The Hague: Mouton.

Grosjean, F. (1983) How long is a sentence? Prediction and prosody in the on-line processing of language. *Linguistics, 21,* 501–529.

Grosjean, F., Grosjean, L., & Lane, H. (1979). The patterns of silence: Performance structures in sentence production. *Cognitive Psychology, 11,* 58–81.

Grosz, B. J. (1981). Focussing and description in natural language dialogues. In A. K. Joshi, B. L. Webber, & I. A. Sag (Eds.), *Elements of discourse understanding.* Cambridge University Press.

Grosz, B. J., Joshi, A., & Weinstein, S. (1983). Providing a unified account of definite noun phrases in discourse. *Proceedings of the 21st Annual Meeting of the Association for Computational Linguistics.* Association for Computational Linguistics.

Grosz, B. J., & Sidner, C. L. (1985). Discourse structure and the proper treatment of interruptions. *Proceedings of the International Joint Conference on Artificial Intelligence.* Los Altos, CA: Morgan Kaufman.

Gruber, J. S. (1965). *Studies in lexical relations.* Bloomington: Indiana Linguistics Club.

Gumperz, J. J., & Hymes, D. (Eds.). (1972). *Directions in sociolinguistics.* New York: Holt, Rinehart and Winston.

Gussenhoven, C. (1984). *On the grammar and semantics of sentence accents.* Dordrecht: Foris.

Hale, K. (1981). *On the position of Warlpiri in a typology of the base.* Bloomington: Indiana Linguistics Club.

Halle, M., & Mohanan, K. P. (1985). Segmental phonology of modern English. *Linguistic Inquiry, 16,* 57–116.

Halle, M., & Stevens, K. N. (1964). Speech recognition: A model and a program for research. In J. A. Fodor & J. J. Katz (Eds.), *The structure of language: Readings in the philosophy of language.* Englewood Cliffs, NJ: Prentice-Hall.

Halliday, M. A. K. (1967a). Notes on transitivity and theme in English: II. *Journal of Linguistics, 3,* 199–244.

Halliday, M. A. K. (1967b). *Intonation and grammar in British English.* The Hague: Mouton.

Halliday, M. A. K. (1970). *A course in spoken English: Intonation.* Oxford University Press.

Halliday, M. A. K., & Hassan, R. (1976). *Cohesion in English.* London: Longman.

Hammarberg, R. (1976). The metaphysics of coarticulation. *Journal of Phonetics, 4,* 353–363.

Hammarberg, R. (1982). On redefining coarticulation. *Journal of Phonetics, 10,* 123–137.

Hankamer, J. (forthcoming). Morphological parsing and the lexicon. In W. D. Marslen-Wilson (Ed.), *Lexical representation and process.* Cambridge, MA: MIT Press.

Harley, T. A. (1984). A critique of top-down independent levels of speech production: Evidence from non-plan-internal speech errors. *Cognitive Science, 8,* 191–219.

Hart, J. 't, & Collier, R. (1975). Integrating different levels of intonation analysis. *Journal of Phonetics, 3,* 235–255.

Hawkins, J. (1983). *Word order universals.* New York: Academic Press.

Hawkins, J. (1984). Modifier-head or function-argument relations in phrase structure? *Lingua, 63,* 107–138.

Hawkins, P. R. (1971). The syntactic location of hesitation pauses. *Language and Speech, 14,* 277–288.

Hayes, B. (1986). Inalterability in CV Phonology. *Language, 62,* 321–351.

Heeschen, C., Ryalls, J., & Hagoort, P. (forthcoming). Psychological stress in Broca's versus Wernicke's aphasia. *Journal of Clinical Linguistics and Phonetics.*

Henderson, A., Goldman-Eisler, F., & Skarbek, A. (1966). Sequential temporal patterns in spontaneous speech. *Language and Speech, 9,* 207–216.

Herrmann, T. (1983). *Speech and situation: A psychological conception of situated speaking.* Heidelberg: Springer.

Herrmann, T., Bürkle, B., & Nirmaier, H. (1987). *Zur hörerbezogenen Raumreferenz: Hörerposition und Lokalisationsaufwand.* (Bericht 12). University of Mannheim, Forschergruppe Sprechen und Sprachverstehen im sozialen Kontext.

Herrmann, T., & W. Deutsch (1976). *Psychologie der Objektbenennung.* Bern: Huber.

Hill, C. (1982). Up/down, front/back, left/right: A contrastive study of Hausa and English. In J. Weissenborn & W. Klein (Eds.), *Here and there: Crosslinguistic studies on deixis and demonstratum.* Amsterdam: John Benjamns.

Hockett, C. F. (1967). Where the tongue slips there slip I. *To honor Roman Jakobson: Vol. 2.* The Hague: Mouton.

Hoenkamp, E. (1983). *Een computermodel van de spreker: Psychologische en linguistische aspecten.* Unpublished doctoral dissertation, Nijmegen University.

Holmes, V. M. (1984). Sentence planning in a story continuation task. *Language and Speech, 27*(2), 115–134.

Holmes, V. M. (forthcoming). Hesitations and sentence planning. *Language and Cognitive Processes.*

Hopper, P. I. (1979). Aspect and foregrounding in discourse. In T. Givon (Ed.), *Syntax and Semantics: Vol. 12. Discourse and syntax.* New York: Academic Press.

Hotopf, W. H. N. (1980). Semantic similarity as a factor in whole-word slips of the tongue. In V. A. Fromkin (Ed.), *Errors in linguistic performance: Slips of the tongue, ear, pen, and hand.* New York: Academic Press.

Humphreys, G. W., Riddoch, M. J., & Quinlan, P. T. (1988). Cascade processes in picture identification. *Cognitive Neuropsychology, 5,* 67–104.

Huttenlocher, J., & Kubicek, L. F. (1983). The source of relatedness effects on naming latency. *Journal of Experimental Psychology: Learning, Memory and Cognition, 9,* 486–496.

Isaacs, E. A. & Clark, H. H. (1987). References in conversation between experts and novices. *Journal of Experimental Psychology: General, 116,* 26–37.

Jackendoff, R. (1972). *Semantic interpretation in generative grammar.* Cambridge, Mass: MIT Press.

Jackendoff, R. (1977). $\bar{X}$ *Syntax: A study of phrase structure.* Cambridge, MA: MIT Press.

Jackendoff, R. (1983). *Semantics and cognition.* Cambridge, MA: MIT Press.

Jackendoff, R. (1987a). On Beyond Zebra: The relation of linguistic and visual information. *Cognition, 26,* 89–114.

Jackendoff, R. (1987b). *Consciousness and the computational mind.* Cambridge, MA.: MIT Press.

Jaffe, J., Breskin, S., & Gerstman, L. J. (1972). Random generation of apparent speech rhythms. *Language and Speech, 15,* 68–71.

James, D. (1972). Some aspects of the syntax and semantics of interjections. *Papers from the Eighth Regional Meeting.* Chicago Linguistic Society.

James, D. (1973). Another look at, say, some grammatical constraints on, ok, interjections and hesitations. *Papers from the Ninth Regional Meeting.* Chicago Linguistic Society.

James, W. (1892). *Textbook of psychology.* London: Macmillan.

James, W. (1893). *The principles of psychology: Vol. 1.* New York: Holt.

Jarvella, R. J, & Herman, S. J. (1972). Clause structure of sentences and speech processing. *Perception and Psychophysics, 11,* 381–384.

Jarvella, R. J., & Klein, W. (Eds.). (1982). *Speech, place and action. Studies in deixis and related topics.* Chichester: John Wiley,

Jassem, W., Hill, D. R., & Witten, I. H. (1984). Isochrony in English speech: Its statistical validity and linguistic relevance. In D. Gibbon & H. Richter (Eds.), *Intonation, Accent, and Rhythm.* Berlin: De Gruyter.

Jefferson, G. (1978). Sequential aspects of story-telling in conversation. In J. Schenkein (Ed.), *Studies in the organization of conversational interaction.* New York: Academic Press.

Jefferson, G. (1985). An exercise in the transcription and analysis of laughter. In T. A. van Dijk (Ed.), *Handbook of discourse analysis: Vol. 3.* London: Academic Press.

Johnson-Laird, P. N. (1983). *Mental models.* Cambridge University Press.

Johnson-Laird, P. N., & Garnham, A. (1980). Descriptions and discourse models. *Linguistics and Philosophy, 3,* 371–393.

Jones, H. G. V., & Langford, S. (1987). Phonological blocking in the tip of the tongue state. *Cognition, 26,* 115–122.

Jorgensen, J., Miller, G. A., & Sperber, D. (1984). Test of the mention theory of irony. *Journal of Experimental Psychology: General, 113,* 112–120.

Kaisse, E. M. (1985). *Connected speech: The interaction of syntax and phonology.* New York: Academic Press.

Kamp, H. (1984). A theory of truth and semantic representation. In J. Groenendijk, Th. Jansen, & M. Stokhof (Eds.), *Truth, interpretation and information.* Dordrecht: Foris.

Kao, H. S. R., Galen, G. P. van, & Hoosain, R. (Eds.). (1986). *Graphonomics: Contemporary research in handwriting.* Amsterdam: North-Holland.

Keele, S. W. (1981). Behavioral analysis of movement. In V. Brooks (Ed.), *Handbook of physiology. The nervous system: Vol. 2. Motor control.* Bethesda, MD: American Physiological Society.

Keenan, E. L. (1976). Toward a universal definition of "subject". In C. N. Li (Ed.), *Subject and topic*. New York: Academic Press.

Keenan, J., MacWhinney, B., & Mayhew, D. (1977). Pragmatics in memory: A study of natural conversation. *Journal of Verbal Learning and Verbal Behavior, 16*, 549–560.

Kelly, M. H., & Bock, J. K. (1988). Stress in time. *Journal of Experimental Psychology: Human Perception and Performance, 14*, 389–403.

Kelso, J. A. S., Holt, K. G., Kugler, P. N., & Turvey, M. T. (1980). On the concept of corrdinative structures as dissipative structures: II. Empirical lines of convergence. In G. E. Stelmach & J. Requin (Eds.), *Tutorials in motor behavior*. Amsterdam: North-Holland.

Kelso, J. A. S, Saltzman, E. L., & Tuller, B. (1986). The dynamical perspective on speech production data and theory. *Journal of Phonetics, 14*, 29–59.

Kelso, J. A. S., Tuller, B., & Harris, K. S. (1983). A "dynamic pattern" perspective on the control and coordination of movement. In P. F. MacNeilage (Ed.), *The production of speech*. New York: Springer.

Kelso, J. A. S., Tuller, B., & Harris, K. S. (1986). A theoretical note on speech timing. In J. S. Perkell & D. Klatt (Eds.), *Invariance and variability in speech processes*. Hillsdale, NJ: Lawrence Erlbaum.

Kelso, J. A. S., Tuller, B., Vatikiotis, E., & Fowler, C. A. (1984). Functionally specific articulatory cooperation following jaw perturbations during speech: Evidence for coordinative structures. *Journal of Experimental Psychology: Human Perception and Performance, 10*, 812–832.

Kempen, G. (1987). A framework for incremental syntactic tree formation. *Proceedings of the Tenth International Joint Conference on Artificial Intelligence*. Los Altos, CA: Morgan Kaufmann.

Kempen, G. (1988). Language generation systems. In I. Batori, W. Lenders, & W. Putschke (Eds.), *Computational linguistics: An international handbook on computer oriented language research and applications*. Berlin: de Gruyter.

Kempen, G., & Hoenkamp, E. (1982). Incremental sentence generation: Implications for the structure of a syntactic processor. In J. Horecky (Ed.), *Proceedings of the Ninth International Conference on Computational Linguistics*. Amsterdam: North-Holland.

Kempen, G., & Hoenkamp, E. (1987). An incremental procedural grammar for sentence formulation. *Cognitive Science, 11*, 201–258.

Kempen, G., & Huijbers, P. (1983). The lexicalization process in sentence production and naming: Indirect election of words. *Cognition, 14*, 185–209.

Kenstowicz, M., & Kisseberth, C. (1979). *Generative phonology*. New York: Academic Press.

Kent, R. D. (1986). Is a paradigm change needed? *Journal of Phonetics, 14*, 111–115.

Kintsch, W. (1974). *The representation of meaning in memory*. Hillsdale, NJ: Lawrence Erlbaum.

Kintsch, W., & Bates, E. (1977). Recognition memory for statements from a classroom lecture. *Journal of Experimental Psychology: Human Learning and Memory, 3*, 150–168.

Kiparsky, P. (1982). From cyclic phonology to lexical phonology. In H. van der Hulst (Ed.), *The structure of phonological representations: Part I*. Dordrecht: Foris.

Klapp, S. T. (1974). Syllable-dependent pronounciation latencies in number naming, a replication. *Journal of Experimental Psychology, 102*, 1138–1140.

Klapp, S. T., Anderson, W. G., & Berrian, R. W. (1973). Implicit speech in reading, reconsidered. *Journal of Experimental Psychology, 100*, 368–374.

Klapp, S. T., & Erwin, C. I. (1976). Relation between programming time and duration of the response being programmed. *Journal of Experimental Psychology: Human Perception and Performance, 2*, 591–598.

Klapp, S. T., & Wyatt, E. P. (1976). Motor programming within sequences of responses. *Journal of Motor Behavior, 8*, 19–26.

Klatt, H. (1975). Vowel lengthening is syntactically determined in a connected discourse. *Journal of Phonetics, 3*, 129–140.

Klein, W. (1978). Wo ist hier: Präliminarien zu einer Untersuchung der lokalen Deixis. *Linguistische Berichte, 58*, 18–40.

Klein, W. (1979). Wegauskünfte. *Zeitschrift für Literaturwissenschaft und Linguistik, 9*, 9–57.

Klein, W. (1982). Local deixis in route directions. In R. Jarvella & W. Klein (Eds.), *Speech, place, and action: Studies in deixis and related topics*. Chichester: John Wiley.

Klein, W. (1984). Bühler's Ellipse. In C. F. Grauman & Th. Herrmann (Eds.), *Karl Bühlers Axiomatik*. Fünfzig Jahre Axiomatik der Sprachwissenschaften. Frankfurt: Klosterman.

Klein, W., & Stutterheim, C. von (1987). Quaestio und referentielle Bewegung in Erzählungen. *Linguistische Berichte, 109*, 163–183.

Kloker, D. (1975). Vowel and sonorant lengthening as cues to phonological phrase boundaries. *Journal of the Acoustical Society of America, 57* (Suppl. 1), 33–34.

Kohler, K. J. (1986). Invariance and variability in speech timing: From utterance to segment in German. In J. S. Perkell & D. Klatt (Eds.), *Invariance and variability in speech processes*. Hillsdale, NJ: Lawrence Erlbaum.

Kohn, S. E., Wingfield, A., Menn, L., Goodglass, H., Berko Gleason, J., & Hyde, M. (1987). Lexical retrieval: The tip of the tongue phenomenon. *Applied Psycholinguistics, 8*, 245–266.

Koriat, A., & Lieblich, I. (1974). What does a person in a "TOT" state know that a person in a "don't know" state doesn't know. *Memory and Cognition, 2,* 647–655.

Koriat, A., & Lieblich, I. (1977). A study of memory pointers. *Acta Psychologica, 41,* 151–164.

Kosslyn, S. M. (1980). *Image and mind,* Cambridge, MA: Harvard University Press.

Kowal, S., Bassett, M. R., & O'Connell, D. C. (1985). The spontaneity of media interviews. *Journal of Psycholinguistic Research, 14,* 1–18.

Kozhevnikov, V. A., & Chistovich, L. A. (1965). *Speech: Articulation and Perception.* Clearinghouse for Federal Scientific and Technical Information. Joint Publications Research Service. Washington, DC: U.S. Department of Commerce.

Krauss, R. M., & Weinheimer, S. (1964). Changes in reference phrases as a function of frequency of usage in social interaction: A preliminary study. *Psychonomic Science, 1,* 113–114.

Kroch, A., & Hindle, D. (1982). On the linguistic character of non-standard input. *Proceedings of the 20th Annual Meeting of the Association for Computational Linguistics.* Association for Computational Linguistics.

Kucera, H., & Francis, W. N. (1967). *Computational analysis of present-day American English.* Providence: Brown University Press.

LaBerge, D., & Samuels, S. J. (1974). Toward a theory of automatic information processing in reading. *Cognitive Psychology, 6,* 293–323.

Labov, W. (1972). *Language in the inner city.* Philadelphia: University of Pennsylvania Press.

Labov, W., & Fanshel, D. (1977). *Therapeutic discourse,* New York: Academic Press.

Lackner, J. R., & Tuller, B. H. (1979). Role of efference monitoring in the detection of self-produced speech errors. In W. E. Cooper & E. C. T. Walker (Eds.), *Sentence processing: Psycholinguistic studies presented to Merrill Garrett.* Hillsdale, NJ: Lawrence Erlbaum.

Ladd, D. R. (1980). *The structure of intonational meaning.* Bloomington: Indiana University Press.

Ladd, D. R. (1984). Declination: A review and some hypotheses. *Phonology Yearbook, 1,* 53–74.

Ladd, D. R. (1986). Intonational phrasing: The case for recursive prosodic structure. *Phonology Yearbook, 3,* 311–340.

Ladd, D. R., Scherer, K., & Silverman, K. (1986). An integrated approach to studying intonation and attitude. In C. Johns-Lewis (Ed.), *Intonation in discourse.* London: Croom Helm.

Lakoff, R. (1970). Tense and its relations to participants. *Language, 46*, 838–849.

Laver, J. D. M. (1973). The detection and correction of slips of the tongue. In V. A. Fromkin (Ed.), *Speech errors as linguistic evidence*. The Hague: Mouton.

Laver, J. D. M. (1980). Monitoring systems in the neurolinguistic control of speech production. In V. A. Fromkin (Ed.), *Errors in linguistic performance: Slips of the tongue, ear, pen, and hand*. New York: Academic Press.

Lee, B. S. (1950). Effects of delayed speech feedback. *Journal of the Acoustical Society of America, 22*, 824–826.

Lehiste, I. (1970). *Suprasegmentals*. Cambridge, MA: MIT Press.

Lehiste, I. (1975). The phonetic structure of paragraphs. In A. Cohen & S. G. Nooteboom (Eds.), *Structure and process in speech perception*. Heidelberg: Springer.

Lehiste, I. (1977). Isochrony reconsidered. *Journal of Phonetics, 5*, 253–263.

Lenneberg, E. H. (1967). *Biological foundations of language*. New York: John Wiley.

Levelt, W. J. M. (1974). *Formal grammars in linguistics and psycholinguistics*. (3 Vols.). The Hague: Mouton.

Levelt, W. J. M. (1978). A survey of studies in sentence perception: 1970–1976. In W. J. M. Levelt & G. B. Flores d'Arcais (Eds.), *Studies in the perception of language*. Chichester: John Wiley.

Levelt, W. J. M. (1981). The speaker's linearization problem. *Philosophical Transactions Royal Society London B295*, 305–315.

Levelt, W. J. M. (1982a). Linearization in describing spatial networks. In S. Peters & E. Saarinen (Eds.), *Processes, beliefs, and questions*. Dordrecht: Reidel.

Levelt, W. J. M. (1982b). Cognitive styles in the use of spatial direction terms. In R. J. Jarvella & W. Klein (Eds.), *Speech, place, and action: Studies in deixis and related topics*. Chichester: John Wiley.

Levelt, W. J. M. (1983). Monitoring and self-repair in speech. *Cognition, 14*, 41–104.

Levelt, W. J. M. (1984a). Some perceptual limitations on talking about space. In A. van Doorn, W. van de Grind, & J. Koenderink (Eds.), *Limits of perception: Essays in honour of Maarten A. Bouman*. Utrecht: VNU Science Press.

Levelt, W. J. M. (1984b). Spontaneous self-repairs in speech: Processes and representations. In M. P. R. van den Broecke & A. Cohen (Eds.), *Proceedings of the Tenth International Congress of Phonetic Sciences*. Dordrecht: Foris.

Levelt, W. J. M., & Cutler, A. (1983). Prosodic marking in speech repair. *Journal of Semantics, 2*, 205–217.

Levelt, W. J. M., & Kelter, S. (1982). Surface form and memory in question answering. *Cognitive Psychology, 14*, 78–106.

Levelt, W. J. M., & Kempen, G. (1975). Semantic and syntactic aspects of remembering sentences: A review of some recent continental research. In A. Kennedy & A. Wilkes (Eds.), *Studies in long-term memory*. London: John Wiley.

Levelt, W. J. M., & Maassen, B. (1981). Lexical search and order of mention in sentence production. In W. Klein & W. J. M. Levelt (Eds.), *Crossing the boundaries in linguistics. Studies presented to Manfred Bierwisch*. Dordrecht: Reidel.

Levelt, W. J. M., Richardson, G., & La Hey, W. (1985). Pointing and voicing in deictic expressions. *Journal of Memory and Language, 24*, 133–164.

Levelt, W. J. M., Schreuder, R., & Hoenkamp, E. (1978). Structure and use of verbs of motion. In R. N. Campbell & P. T. Smith (Eds.), *Recent advances in the psychology of language*. New York: Plenum Press.

Levelt, W. J. M., & Schriefers, H. (1987). Stages of lexical access. In G. Kempen (Ed.), *Natural language generation. New results in artificial intelligence, psychology and linguistics*. Dordrecht: Martinus Nijhoff.

Levelt, W. J. M., Zwanenburg, W., & Ouweneel, G. R. E. (1970). Ambiguous surface structure and phonetic form in French. *Foundations of Language, 6*, 260–273.

Levinson, S. C. (1983). *Pragmatics*. Cambridge University Press.

Levitt, A. G., & Healy, A. F. (1985). The roles of phoneme frequency, similarity, and availability in the experimental elicitation of speech errors. *Journal of Memory and Language, 24*, 717–733.

Lewis, D. K. (1969). *Convention: A philosophical study*. Cambridge, MA: Harvard University Press.

Liberman, A. M., Cooper, F. S., Shankweiler, D. S., & Studdert-Kennedy, M. (1967). Perception of the speech code. *Psychological Review, 74*, 431–461.

Liberman, M., & Pierrehumbert, J. (1984). Intonational invariance under changes in pitch range and length. In M. Aronoff & R. T. Oehrle (Eds.), *Language and sound structure: Studies in phonology presented to Morris Halle by his teacher and students*. Cambridge, MA: MIT Press.

Lieberman, P., Katz W., & Jongman, A (1985). Measures of intonation of read and spontaneous speech in American English. *Journal of the Acoustic Society of America, 77*, 649–657.

Lindblom, B. (1963). *On vowel reduction*. (Speech Transmission Laboratory Report 29). Stockholm: Royal Institute of Technology.

Lindblom, B. (1968). *Temporal organization of syllable production*. (Quarterly Progress and Status Report 2–3). Stockholm: Royal Institute of Technology.

Lindblom, B. (1983). Economy of speech gestures. In P. F. MacNeilage (Ed.), *The production of speech*. New York: Springer.

Lindblom, B., Lubker, J., & Gay, T. (1979). Formant frequencies of some fixed-mandible vowels and a model of speech motor programming by predictive simulation. *Journal of Phonetics, 7*, 147–161.

Lindblom B., & MacNeilage, P. (1986). Action theory: Problems and alternative approaches. *Journal of Phonetics, 14,* 117–132.

Linde, C., & Goguen, J. (1978). The structure of planning discourse. *Journal of Social and Biological Structures, 1,* 219–251.

Linde, C., & Labov, W. (1975). Spatial networks as a site for the study of language and thought. *Language, 51,* 924–939.

Lindsley, J. R. (1975). Producing simple utterances: How far do we plan? *Cognitive Psychology, 7,* 1–19.

Lindsley, J. R. (1976). Producing simple utterances: Details of the planning process. *Journal of Psycholinguistic Research, 5,* 331–351.

Linell, P. (1979). *Psychological reality in phonology.* Cambridge University Press.

Longuet-Higgins, H. C. (1987). *Mental Processes.* Cambridge, MA: MIT Press.

Lounsbury, F. G. (1954). Transitional probability, linguistic structure, and systems of habit-family hierarchies. In C. E. Osgood & T. Sebeok (Eds.), *Psycholinguistics: A survey of theory and research problems.* Bloomington: Indiana University Press.

Lyons, J. (1977). *Semantics* (2 Vols.). Cambridge University Press.

Lyons, J. (1981). *Language, meaning and context.* Bungay: Fontana Press.

MacKay, D. (1970). Spoonerisms: The structure of errors in the serial order of speech. *Neuropsychologia, 8,* 323–350 (Reprinted in V. A. Fromkin (Ed.). (1973). *Speech errors as linguistic evidence.* The Hague: Mouton.)

MacKay, D. (1972). The structure of words and syllables: Evidence from errors in speech. *Cognitive Psychology, 3,* 210–227.

MacKay, D. (1982). The problem of flexibility, fluency, and speed-accuracy trade-off in skilled behavior. *Psychological Review, 89,* 483–506.

MacKay, D. (1987). *The organization of perception and action: A theory for language and other cognitive skills.* New York: Springer.

Maclay, H., & Osgood, C. E. (1959). Hesitation phenomena in spontaneous English speech. *Word, 15,* 19–44.

MacNeilage, P. F. Motor control and serial ordering of speech. *Psychological Review,* 1970, *77,* 182–196.

MacNeilage, P. F. (1980). Emerging concepts in speech control. In G. S. Stelmach & J. Requin (Eds.), *Tutorials in motor behavior.* Amsterdam: North-Holland.

MacNeilage, P., & Ladefoged, P. (1976). The production of speech and language. In: E. C. Carterette & M. P. Friedman (Eds.), *Handbook of perception: Vol. 7.* New York: Academic Press.

MacWhinney, B. (1977). Starting points. *Language, 53*, 152–168.

MacWhinney, B., & Bates, E. (1978). Sentential devices for conveying givenness and newness: A cross-cultural developmental study. *Journal of Verbal Learning and Verbal Behavior, 17*, 539–558.

MacWhinney, B., Bates, E., & Kiegl, R. (1984). The impact of cue validity on sentence interpretation in English, German, and Italian. *Journal of Verbal Learning and Verbal Behavior, 23*, 127–150.

Makkai, A. (1972). *Idiom structure in English.* The Hague: Mouton.

Malinowski, B. (1920). Classificatory particles in the language of Kiriwina. *Bulletin of the School of Oriental Studies, 1*, 33–78. (London Institution).

Mangold, R. (1986). *Sensorische Faktoren beim Verstehen überspezifizierter Objektbennennungen.* Frankfurt: Peter Lang.

Marshall, J. C. (1984). Multiple perspectives on modularity. *Cognition, 17*, 209–242.

Marslen-Wilson, W., & Komisarjevsky Tyler, L. (1980). The temporal structure of spoken language understanding. *Cognition, 8*, 1–71.

Marslen-Wilson, W., Levy, E., & Komisarjevsky Tyler, L. (1982). Producing interpretable discourse: The establishment and maintenance of reference. In R. J. Jarvella & W. Klein (Eds.), *Speech, place, and action: Studies in deixis and related topics.* Chichester: John Wiley.

Marslen-Wilson, W., & Tyler, L. (1981). Central processes is speech understanding. *Philosophical Transactions of the Royal Society London, B259*, 317–332.

Martin, J. G., & Strange, W. (1968). The perception of hesitation in spontaneous speech. *Perception and Psychophysics, 3*, 427–432.

McNeill, D. (1979). *The conceptual basis of language.* Hillsdale, NJ: Lawrence Erlbaum.

McNeill, D. (1987). *Psycholinguistics: A new approach.* Cambridge, MA: Harper and Row.

Meringer, R. (1908). *Aus dem Leben der Sprache.* Berlin: Behr.

Meringer, R., & Mayer, K. (1895). *Versprechen und Verlesen.* Stuttgart: Goschensche Verlag. (Re-issued, with introductory essay by A. Cutler and D. A. Fay (1978). Amsterdam: John Benjamins.)

Meyer, A. (1988). *Phonological encoding in language production: A priming study.* Unpublished doctoral dissertation, Nijmegen University.

Meyer, D. E., & Gordon, P. C. (1985). Speech production: Motor programming of phonetic features. *Journal of Memory and Language, 24*, 3–26.

Miller, G. A. (1956). The magical number seven, plus or minus two: Some limits on our capacity for processing information. *Psychological Review, 63*, 81–97.

Miller, G. A. (1969). A psychological method to investigate verbal concepts. *Journal of Mathematical Psychology, 6*, 169–191.

Miller, G. A. (1978). Semantic relations among words. In M. Halle, J. Bresnan, & G. A. Miller (Eds.), *Linguistic theory and psychological reality*. Cambridge, MA: MIT Press.

Miller, G. A. (1982). Some problems in the theory of demonstrative reference. In R. J. Jarvella & W. Klein (Eds.), *Speech, place, and action: Studies in deixis and related topics*. Chichester: John Wiley.

Miller, G. A., & Johnson-Laird, P. N. (1976). *Language and perception*. Cambridge, MA: Harvard University Press.

Mittelstaedt, H. (1983). A new solution to the problem of subjective vertical. *Naturwissenschaften, 70*, 272–281.

Mohanan, K. P. (1982). Grammatical relations and clause structure in Malayalam. In J. Bresnan (Ed.), *The mental representation of grammatical relations*. Cambridge, MA: MIT Press.

Moll, K. L., & Daniloff, R. G. (1971). Investigation of the timing of velar movements during speech. *Journal of the Acoustical Society of America, 750*, 678–684.

Montague, R. (1974). *Formal philosophy: Selected papers*. New Haven: Yale University Press.

Morton, J. (1969). The interaction of information in word recognition. *Psychological Review, 76*, 165–178.

Morton, J. (1979). Word recognition. In J. Morton & J. Marshall (Eds.), *Psycholinguistics: Series 2. Structures and processes*. London: Elek.

Motley, M. T. (1980). Verification of "Freudian slips" and semantic prearticulatory editing via laboratory-induced spoonerisms. In V. A. Fromkin (Ed.), *Errors in linguistic performance: Slips of the tongue, ear, pen, and hand*. New York: Academic Press.

Motley, M. T., Baars, B. J., & Camden, C. T. (1981). Syntactic criteria in prearticulatory editing: Evidence from laboratory-induced slips of the tongue. *Journal of Psycholinguistic Research, 10*, 503–522.

Motley, M. T., Camden, C. T., & Baars, B. J. (1982). Covert formulation and editing of anomalies in speech production: Evidence from experimentally elicited slips of the tongue. *Journal of Verbal Learning and Verbal Behavior, 21*, 578–594.

Munro, A. (1977). *Speech act understanding*. Unpublished doctoral dissertation, University of California, San Diego.

Nakatani, L. H., O'Connor, J. D., & Aston, C.H. (1981). Prosodic aspects of American English speech rhythm. *Phonetica, 38*, 84–106.

Neilson, M. D., & Neilson, P. D. (1987). Speech motor control and stuttering: A computational model of adaptive sensory-motor processing. *Speech Communication, 6*, 325–333.

Nespor, M., & Vogel, I. (1986). *Prosodic phonology.* Dordrecht: Foris.

Newell, A., & Simon, H. A. (1972). *Human problem solving.* Englewood Cliffs, NJ: Prentice-Hall.

Nolan, F. J. (1982). The role of action theory in the description of speech production. *Linguistics, 20,* 287–308.

Noordman, L. G. M. (1979). *Inferring from language.* Heidelberg: Springer.

Noordman-Vonk, W. (1979). *Retrieval from semantic memory.* Heidelberg: Springer.

Nooteboom, S. (1967). Some regularities in phonemic speech errors. *Annual Progress Report. Institute for Perception Research IPO, 2,* 65–70.

Nooteboom, S. (1972). *Production and perception of vowel duration.* Unpublished doctoral dissertation, Utrecht University.

Nooteboom, S. (1973). The tongue slips into patterns. In V. Fromkin (Ed.), *Speech errors as linguistic evidence.* The Hague: Mouton.

Nooteboom, S. (1980). Speaking and unspeaking: detection and correction of phonological and lexical errors in spontaneous speech. In V. A. Fromkin (Ed.), *Errors in linguistic performance.* New York: Academic Press.

Nooteboom, S., & Terken, J. M. B. (1982). What makes speakers omit pitch accents? An experiment. *Phonetica, 39,* 317–336.

Norman, D. A., & Rumelhart, D. E. (1975). *Explorations in cognition.* San Francisco: Freeman.

Nunberg, G. (1979). The non-uniqueness of semantic solutions: Polysemy. *Linguistics and Philosophy, 3,* 143–184.

Ochs-Keenan, E. (1976). The universality of conversational implicature. *Language in Society, 5,* 67–80.

O'Connell, D., & Kowal, S. (1983). Pausology. In W. A. Sedelow & S. Y. Sedelow (Eds.), *Computers in Language Research: Part I. Formalization in literary and discourse analysis.* Berlin: Mouton.

O'Connor, J. D., & Arnold, G. F. (1973). *Intonation of colloquial English.* (2nd ed.). London: Longman.

Ohala, J. J. (1978). Production of tone. In V. Fromkin (Ed.), *Tone: A linguistic survey.* New York: Academic Press.

Öhman, S. E. G. (1966). Coarticulation in VCV utterances: Spectrographic measurements. *Journal of the Acoustical Society of America, 39,* 151–168.

Ojemann, G. A. (1982). Interrelationships in the localization of language, memory, and motor mechanisms in human cortex and thalamus. In R. A. Thompson & J. R. Green (Eds.), *New perspectives in cerebral localization.* New York: Raven Press.

Oldfield, R. C. (1963). Individual vocabulary and semantic currency: A preliminary study. *British Journal of Social and Clinical Psychology, 2*, 122–130.

Oldfield, R. C., & Wingfield, A. (1965). Response latencies in naming objects. *Quarterly Journal of Experimental Psychology, 17*, 273–281.

Oller, D. K., & MacNeilage, P. F. (1983). Development of speech production. In P. F. MacNeilage (Ed.), *The production of speech*. New York: Springer.

Olson, D. R. (1970). Language and thought: Aspects of a cognitive theory of semantics. *Psychological Review, 77*, 257–273.

Osgood, C. E. (1971). Where do sentences come from? In D. Steinberg & L. Jakobovits (Eds.), *Semantics: An interdisciplinary reader in philosophy, linguistics and psychology*. Cambridge University Press.

Osgood, C. E. (1980). *Lectures on language performance*. New York: Springer.

Osgood, C. E., & Bock, J. K. (1977). Salience and sentencing: Some production principles. In S. Rosenberg (Ed.), *Sentence production: Developments in research and theory*. Hillsdale, NJ: Lawrence Erlbaum.

Paivio, A., Yuille, J. C., & Madigan, S. (1968). Concreteness, imagery, and meaningfulness values for 925 nouns. *Journal of Experimental Psychology, 76*, (1, Pt. 2).

Palermo, D. S., & Jenkins, J. J. (1964). *Word association norms*. Minneapolis: University of Minnesota Press.

Parker, F., & Walsh, T. (1985). Mentalism vs physicalism: A comment on Hammarberg and Fowler. *Journal of Phonetics, 13*, 147–153.

Partee, B., & Rooth, M. (1983). Generalized conjunction and type ambiguity. In R. Bäuerle, C. Schwarze, & A. von Stechow (Eds.), *Meaning, use and interpretation of language*. Berlin: De Gruyter.

Pechmann, T. (1984). *Überspezifizierung und Betonung in referentieller Kommunikation*. Unpublished doctoral dissertation, Mannheim University.

Perdue, C. (Ed.). (1984). *Second language acquisition by adult immigrants: A field manual*. Rowley, MA: Newbury House.

Perfetti, C. A., & Goldman, S. R. (1975). Discourse functions of thematization and topicalization. *Journal of Psycholinguistic Research, 4*, 257–271.

Perkell, J. S. (1969). *Physiology of speech production: Results and implications of a quantitative cineradiographic study*. Cambridge, MA: MIT Press.

Perkell, J. S. (1980). Phonetic features and the physiology of speech production. In B. Butterworth (Ed.), *Language Production: Vol. 1. Speech and talk*. London: Academic Press.

Petrie, H. (1988). *Semantic and syntactic processes in speech production*. Unpublished doctoral dissertation, University of London.

Pierrehumbert, J. (1981). Synthesizing intonation. *Journal of the Acoustical Society of America, 70*, 985–995.

Pike, K. (1945). *The intonation of American English*. Ann Arbor: University of Michigan Press.

Pinker, S. (1985). *Language learnability and language development*. Cambridge, MA: Harvard University Press.

Posner, M. I., & Snyder, C. R. R. (1975). Attention and cognitive control. In R. Solso (Ed.), *Information processing and cognition: The Loyola symposium*. Hillsdale, NJ: Lawrence Erlbaum.

Power, M. J. (1983). Are there cognitive rhythms in speech? *Language and Speech, 26*, 253–261.

Power, M. J. (1984). Are there cognitive rhythms in speech?—A reply to Beattie (1984). *Language and Speech, 27*, 197–201.

Premack, D. (1976). *Intelligence in ape and man*. Hillsdale, NJ: Lawrence Erlbaum.

Prentice, J. L. (1966). Response strength of single words as an influence in sentence behavior. *Journal of Verbal Learning and Verbal Behavior, 5*, 429–433.

Prentice, J. L. (1967). Effects of cuing actor vs. cuing object on word order in sentence production. *Psychonomic Science, 8*, 163–164.

Priller, J., & Mittenecker, E. (1988). Experimente zum Unterschied von "Wort auf der Zunge" und "Gefühl des Wissens". *Zeitschrift für experimentelle und angewandte Psychologie, 35*, 129–146.

Prince, A. (1983). Relating to the grid. *Linguistic Inquiry, 14*, 19–100.

Prince, E. (1981). Toward a taxonomy of given-new information. In P. Cole (Ed.), *Radical pragmatics*. New York: Academic Press.

Pullum, G. K., & Zwicky, A. M. (1988). The syntax-phonology interface. In F. J. Newmeyer (Ed.), *Linguistics: The Cambridge Survey*. Cambridge University Press.

Pylyshyn, Z. W. (1984). *Computation and cognition: Toward a foundation for cognitive science*. Cambridge, MA: MIT Press.

Reason, J., & Lucas, D. (1984). Using cognitive diaries to investigate naturally occurring memory blocks. In J. E. Harris & P. E. Morris (Eds.), *Everyday memory, actions and absent-mindedness*. London: Academic Press.

Recanati, F. (1986). On defining communicative intentions. *Mind and Language, 1*, 213–242.

Redeker, G. (1986). *Language use in informal narratives: Effects of social distance and listener involvement*. Unpublished doctoral dissertation, University of California, Berkeley.

Reichenbach, H. (1947). *Elements of symbolic logic*. New York: Free Press.

Reinhart, T. (1982). Pragmatics and linguistics: An analysis of sentence topics. *Philosophica, 27*, 53–94.

Reinhart, T. (1984). Principles of Gestalt perception in the temporal organization of narrative texts. *Linguistics, 22*, 779–809.

Rochester, S. R., & Gill, J. (1973). Production of complex sentences in monologues and dialogues. *Journal of Verbal Learning and Verbal Behavior, 12,* 203–210.

Rochester, S., & Martin, J. R. (1979). *Crazy talk. A study of the discourse of schizophrenic speakers.* New York: Plenum Press.

Rosch, E. (1975). Cognitive reference points. *Cognitive Psychology, 7*, 532–547.

Rosch, E., Mervis, C. B., Gray, W., Johnson, D., & Boyes-Braem, P. (1976). Basic objects in natural categories. *Cognitive Psychology, 8*, 382–439.

Ross, J. R. (1970). On declarative sentences. In R. A. Jacobs & P. S. Rosenbaum (Eds.), *Readings in transformational grammar.* Waltham, MA: Ginn.

Roudet, L. (1910). *Eléments de phonétique générale.* Paris: Librairie Universitaire H. Welter.

Rubin, D. C. (1975). Within word structure in the tip-of-the-tongue phenomenon. *Journal of Verbal Learning and Verbal Behavior, 14*, 392–397.

Rumelhart, D. E., McClelland, J. L., & the PDP Research Group. (1986). *Parallel distributed processing.* (2 Vols.). Cambridge, MA: MIT Press.

Ryave, A. L. (1978). On the achievement of a series of stories. In J. Schenkein (Ed.), *Studies in the organization of conversational interaction.* New York: Academic Press.

Sacks, H. (1978). Some technical considerations of a dirty joke. In J. Schenkein (Ed.), *Studies in the organization of conversational interaction.* New York: Academic Press.

Sacks, H., Schegloff, E. A., & Jefferson, G. (1974). A simplest systematics for the organization of turn-taking in conversation. *Language, 50*, 696–735.

Sadock, J., & Zwicky, A. (1985). Speech act distinctions in syntax. In T. Shopen (Ed.), *Language typology and syntactic description: Vol. 1. Clause structure.* Cambridge University Press.

Saltzman, E., & Kelso, J. A. S. (1987). Skilled actions: A task-dynamic approach. *Psychological Review, 94*, 84–106.

Sanford, A. (1985). *Cognition and cognitive psychology.* London: Weidenfeld and Nicholson. (Also: Hillsdale, NJ: Lawrence Erlbaum).

Sanford, A. and Garrod, S. (1981) *Understanding written language: Explorations of comprehension beyond the sentence.* Chichester: John Wiley.

Schaffer, D. (1983). The role of intonation as a cue to turn taking in conversation. *Journal of Phonetics, 11*, 243–259.

Schank, R. C. (1972). Conceptual dependency: A theory of natural language understanding. *Cognitive Psychology, 3*(4), 552–631.

Schank, R. C. (1975). *Conceptual information processing.* Amsterdam: North-Holland.

Schegloff, E. A. (1972). Sequencing in conversational openings. In J. J. Gumperz & D. H. Hymes (Eds.), *Directions in psycholinguistics.* New York: Holt, Rinehart and Winston.

Schegloff, E. A. (1979). The relevance of repair to syntax-for-conversation. In T. Givón (Ed.), *Syntax and semantics.* (Vol. 12). New York: Academic Press.

Schegloff, E. A. (1987). Between macro and micro: Contexts and other connections. In J. Alexander, B. Giesen, R. Munch, & N. Smelser (Eds.), *The micromacro link.* Berkeley: University of California Press.

Schegloff, E. A., Jefferson, G., & Sacks, H. (1977). The preference for self-correction in the organization of repair in conversation. *Language, 2,* 361–382.

Schegloff, E. A., & Sacks, H. (1973). Opening up closings. *Semiotica, 7,* 289–327.

Schenkein, J. (1980). A taxonomy for repeating action sequences in natural conversation. In B. Butterworth (Ed.), *Language production: Vol. 1. Speech and talk.* London: Academic Press.

Scherer, K. (1986). Vocal affect expression: A review and a model for future research. *Psychological Bulletin, 99,* 143–165.

Schiffrin, D. (1985). Everyday argument: The organization of diversity in talk. In T. A. van Dijk (Ed.), *Handbook of discourse analysis.* (Vol. 3). London: Academic Press.

Schlesinger, I. M. (1977). *Production and comprehension of utterances.* Hillsdale, NJ: Lawrence Erlbaum.

Schmerling, S. (1976). *Aspects of English sentence stress.* Austin: University of Texas Press.

Schneider, W., & Shiffrin, R. M. (1977). Controlled and automatic human information processing: I. Detection, search and attention. *Psychological Review, 84,* 1–66.

Schouten, M. E. H., & Pols, L. C. W. (1979). Vowel segments in consonantal contexts: A spectral study of coarticulation. *Journal of Phonetics, 7,* (Part I) 1–23, (Part II) 205–224.

Schreuder, R. (1978). *Studies in psycholexicology: With special reference to verbs of motion.* Unpublished doctoral dissertation, Nijmegen University.

Schriefers, H. (1985). *On semantic markedness in language production and verification.* Unpublished doctoral dissertation, Nijmegen University.

Scollon, R., & Scollon, S. B. K. (1981). *Narrative, literacy and face in interethnic communication.* Norwood, NJ: Ablex.

Scott, D. (1982). Duration as a cue to the perception of a phrase boundary. *Journal of the Acoustic Society of America, 71,* 996–1007.

Searle, J. R. (1979). *Expression and meaning: Studies in the theory of speech acts.* Cambridge University Press.

Selkirk, E. (1972). *The phrase phonology of English and French.* Unpublished doctoral dissertation, Massachusetts Institute of Technology.

Selkirk, E. (1982). *The syntax of words* (Linguistic Inquiry Monograph 7). Cambridge, MA: MIT Press.

Selkirk, E. (1984a). *Phonology and syntax: The relation between sound and structure.* Cambridge, MA: MIT Press.

Selkirk, E. (1984b). On the major class features and syllable theory. In M. Aronoff & R. T. Oehrle (Eds.), *Language and sound structure: Studies in phonology presented to Morris Halle by his teacher and students.* Cambridge, MA: MIT Press.

Senft, G. (1985). Klassifikationspartikel im Kilivila—Glossen zu ihrer morphologischen Rolle, ihrem Inventar und ihrer Funktion in Satz und Diskurs. *Linguistische Berichte, 99,* 373–393.

Seuren, P. A. M. (1978). Grammar as an underground process. In A. Sinclair, R. J. Jarvella, & W. J. M. Levelt (Eds.), *The child's conception of language.* Heidelberg: Springer.

Seuren, P. A. M. (1985). *Discourse semantics.* Oxford: Blackwell.

Seuren, P. A. M. (1988). Presupposition. In A. von Stechow & D. Wunderlich (Eds.), *Handuch der Semantik/Handbook of semantics.* Frankfurt: Athenäum.

Seymour, P. H. K. (1979). *Human visual cognition.* New York: St. Martin's Press.

Shattuck-Hufnagel, S. (1979). Speech errors as evidence for a serial order mechanism in sentence production. In W. E. Cooper & E. C. T. Walker (Eds.), *Sentence processing: Psycholinguistic studies presented to Merrill Garrett.* Hillsdale, NJ: Lawrence Erlbaum.

Shattuck-Hufnagel, S. (1982). Three kinds of speech error evidence for the role of grammatical elements in processing. In L. K. Obler & L. Menn (Eds.), *Exceptional language and linguistics.* New York: Academic Press.

Shattuck-Hufnagel, S. (1983). Sublexical units and suprasegmental structure in speech production planning. In P. F. MacNeilage (Ed.), *The production of speech.* New York: Springer.

Shattuck-Hufnagel, S. (1985). Context similarity constraints on segmental speech errors: An experimental investigation of the role of word position and lexical stress. In J. Lauter (Ed.), *On the planning and production of speech in normal and hearing-impaired individuals: A seminar in honour of S. Richard Silverman* (ASHA Reports, 15).

Shattuck-Hufnagel, S. (1986). The representation of phonological information during speech production planning: Evidence from vowel errors in spontaneous speech. *Phonology Yearbook, 3,* 117–149.

Shattuck-Hufnagel, S. (1987). The role of word onset consonants in speech production planning: New evidence from speech error patterns. In E. Keller & M. Gopnik (Eds.), *Sensory processes in language*. Hillsdale, NJ: Lawrence Erlbaum.

Shattuck-Hufnagel, S., & Klatt, D. (1979). The limited use of distinctive features and markedness in speech production: Evidence from speech error data. *Journal of Verbal Learning and Verbal Behavior, 18*, 41–55.

Shepard, R. N., & Metzler, J. (1971). Mental rotation of three-dimensional objects. *Science, 171*, 701–703.

Shepard, R. N., & Hurwitz, S. (1984). Upward direction, mental rotation, and discrimination of left and right turns in maps. *Cognition, 18*, 161–193.

Siegel, D. (1974). *Topics in English morphology*. New York: Garland.

Siegel, G. M., & Pick, H. L. (1976). Auditory feedback in the regulation of voice. *Journal of the Acoustical Society of America, 56*, 1618–1624.

Slobin, D. (1982). Universal and particular in the acquisition of language. In E. Wanner & L. R. Gleitman (Eds.), *Language acquisition: The state of the art*. Cambridge University Press.

Smith, E., & Medin, D. L. (1981). *Categories and concepts*. Cambridge, MA: Harvard University Press.

Sonnenschein, S (1982). The effects of redundant communications on listeners: When more is less. *Child Development, 53*, 717–729.

Sonnenschein, S. (1984). The effect of redundant communication on listeners: Why different types may have different effects. *Journal of Psycholinguistic Research, 13*, 147–166.

Sorokin, V. N. Gay, T., & Ewan, W. G. (1980). Some biomechanical correlates of jaw movement. *Journal of the Acoustical Society of America, 68*(S1), S32(A).

Sowa, J. F. (1984). *Conceptual structures*. Reading, MA: Addison-Wesley.

Sperber, D., & Wilson, D. (1986). *Relevance: Communication and cognition*. Oxford: Blackwell.

Sridhar, S. N. (1988). *Cognition and sentence production: A cross-linguistic study*. New York: Springer.

Steedman, M. J. (1982). Reference to past time. In R. J. Jarvella & W. Klein (Eds.), *Speech, place and action: Studies in deixis and related topics*. Chichester: John Wiley.

Steedman, M. J., & Johnson-Laird, P. N. (1980). The production of sentences, utterances and speech acts: Have computers anything to say? In B. Butterworth (Ed.), *Language production: Vol. 1. Speech and talk*. London: Academic Press.

Stemberger, J. P. (1982). The nature of segments in the lexicon: Evidence from speech errors. *Lingua, 56*, 43–65.

Stemberger, J. P. (1983a). *Speech errors and theoretical phonology: A review.* Bloomington: Indiana Linguistics Club.

Stemberger, J. P. (1983b). The nature of /r/ and /l/ in English: Evidence from speech errors. *Journal of Phonetics, 11*, 139–147.

Stemberger, J. P. (1984). *Lexical bias in errors in language production: Interactive components, editors, and perceptual biases.* Unpublished manuscript, Carnegie-Mellon University, Pittsburgh.

Stemberger, J. P. (1985a). An interactive activation model of language production. In A. W. Ellis (Ed.), *Progress in the psychology of language: Vol. 1.* Hillsdale, NJ: Lawrence Erlbaum.

Stemberger, J. P. (1985b). *The lexicon in a model of language production.* New York: Garland Publishing.

Stemberger, J. P., & MacWhinney, B. (1986). Form-oriented inflectional errors in language processing. *Cognitive Psychology, 18*, 329–354.

Stemberger, J. P., & Treiman, R. (1986). The internal structure of word-initial consonant clusters. *Journal of Memory and Language, 25*, 163–180.

Sternberg, S., Monsell, S., Knoll, R. L., & Wright, C. E. (1978). The latency and duration of rapid movement sequences: Comparisons of speech and typewriting. In G. E. Stelmach (Ed.), *Information processing in motor control and learning.* New York: Academic Press.

Sternberg, S., Wright, C. E., Knoll, R. L., & Monsell, S. (1980). Motor programs in rapid speech: Additional evidence. In R. A. Cole (Ed.), *Perception and production of fluent speech.* Hillsdale, NJ: Lawrence Erlbaum.

Stevens, K. N. (1983). Design features of speech sound systems. In P. F. Mac-Neilage (Ed.), *The production of speech.* New York: Springer.

Stevens, K., & Perkell, J. S. (1977). Speech physiology and phonetic features. In M. Sawashima & F. S. Cooper (Eds.), *Dynamic aspects of speech production.* University of Tokyo Press.

Svartvik, J., & Quirk, R. (Eds.). (1980). *A corpus of English conversation.* Lund: CWK Gleerup.

Tannenbaum, P. H., Williams, F., & Hillier, C. S. (1965). Word predictability in the environments of hesitations. *Journal of Verbal Learning and Verbal Behavior, 4*, 134–140.

Tannenbaum, P. H., & Williams, F. (1968). Generation of active and passive sentences as a function of subject and object focus. *Journal of Verbal Learning and Verbal Behavior, 7*, 246–250.

Tanz, C. (1980). *Studies in the acquisition of deictic terms.* Cambridge University Press.

Taylor, I. (1969). Content and structure in sentence production. *Journal of Verbal Learning and Verbal Behavior, 8*, 170–175.

Tent, J., & Clark, J. E. (1980). An experimental investigation into the perception of slips of the tongue. *Journal of Phonetics*, *8*, 317–325.

Terken, J. M. B. (1984). The distribution of pitch accents in instructions as a function of discourse structure. *Language and Speech*, *27*, 269–289.

Thomassen, A. J. W. M., & Teulings, H. L. (1985). Time, size and shape in handwriting: Exploring spatio-temporal relationships at different levels. In J. A. Michon & J. Jackson (Eds.), *Time, mind and behavior*. Heidelberg: Springer.

Thorson, N. (1983). Two issues in the prosody of standard Danish. In A. Cutler & R. D. Ladd (Eds.), *Prosody: Models and measurements*. Heidelberg: Springer.

Treiman, R. (1983). The structure of spoken syllables: Evidence from novel word games. *Cognition*, *15*, 49–74.

Treiman, R. (1984). On the status of final consonant clusters in English syllables. *Journal of Verbal Learning and Verbal Behavior*, *23*, 343–356.

Turner, E., & Rommetveit, R. (1968). Focus of attention in recall of active and passive sentences. *Journal of Verbal Learning and Verbal Behavior*, *7*, 543–548.

Turvey, M. T. (1977). Preliminaries to a theory of action with reference to vision. In R. Shaw & J. Brandsford (Eds.), *Perceiving, acting, and knowing: Toward an ecological psychology*. Hillsdale, NJ: Lawrence Erlbaum.

Tyler, L., & Wessels, J. (1983). Quantifying contextual contributions to word-recognition processes. *Perception and Psychophysics*, *34*, 409–420.

Umeda, N. (1975). Vowel duration in American English. *Journal of the Acoustical Society of America*, *58*, 434–445.

Vaissière, J. (1983). Language-independent prosodic features. In A. Cutler & D. R. Ladd (Eds.), *Prosody: Models and measurements*. Heidelberg: Springer.

Valian, V. V. (1971). *Talking, listening and linguistic structure*. Unpublished doctoral dissertation, Northeastern University, Boston.

Van Bezooijen, R. (1984). *Characteristics and recognizability of vocal expression of emotion*. Dordrecht: Foris.

Van den Broecke, M. P. R., & Goldstein, L. (1980). Consonant features in speech errors. In V. A. Fromkin (Ed.), *Errors in linguistic performance: Slips of the tongue, ear, pen, and hand*. New York: Academic Press.

Van der Sandt, R. A. (1982). *Kontekst en presuppositie*. Nijmegen Institute of Semantics.

Van Dijk, T. A. (1985). *Handbook of discourse analysis*. (4 Vols.). London: Academic Press.

Van Galen, G. P., & Teulings, H. L. (1983). The independent monitoring of form and scale factors in handwriting. *Acta Psychologica*, *54*, 9–22.

Van Wijk, C. (1987). The PSY behind PHI: A psycholinguistic model for performance structures. *Journal of Psycholinguistic Research*, *16*, 185–199.

Van Wijk, C., & Kempen, G. (1987). A dual system for producing self-repairs in spontaneous speech: Evidence from experimentally elicited corrections. *Cognitive Psychology*, *19*, 403–440.

Vorberg, D. (1985). Unerwartete Folgen von zufälliger Variabilität: Wettlauf-Modelle für den Stroop-Versuch. *Zeitschrift für experimentelle und angewandte Psychologie*, *32*, 494–521.

Wales, R., & Toner, H. (1980). Intonation and ambiguity. In W. Cooper & E. Walker (Eds.), *Sentence processing: Psycholinguistic studies presented to Merrill Garrett*. Hillsdale, NJ: Lawrence Erlbaum.

Walton, D. N. (1982). *Topical relevance in argumentation*. Amsterdam: John Benjamins.

Webber, B. L. (1981). Discourse model synthesis: Preliminaries to reference. In A. K. Joshi, B. L. Webber, & I. A. Sag (Eds.), *Elements of discourse understanding*. Cambridge University Press.

Webelhuth, G. (1985). German is configurational. *The Linguistic Review*, *4*, 203–246.

Weissenborn, J., & Klein, W. (Eds.). (1982). *Here and there: Cross-linguistic studies on deixis and demonstration*. Amsterdam: John Benjamins.

Wells, G., MacLure, M., & Montgomery, M. (1981). Some strategies for sustaining conversation. In P. Werth (Ed.), *Conversation and discourse: Structure and interpretation*. London: Croom Helm.

Wells, R. (1951). Predicting slips of the tongue. *The Yale Scientific Magazine*, *26*, 9–30. (Also in V. A. Fromkin (Ed.), (1973). *Speech errors as linguistic evidence*. The Hague: Mouton.)

Whorf, B. L. (1956). *Language, thought, and reality*. Cambridge, MA: MIT Press.

Wickelgren, W. A. (1969). Context-sensitive coding, associative memory, and serial order in (speech) behavior. *Psychological Review*, *76*, 1–15.

Wickelgren, W. A. (1976). Phonetic code and serial order. In E. C. Carterette & M. P. Friedman (Eds.), *Handbook of Perception: Vol. 7*. New York: Academic Press.

Willems, N. (1983). *English intonation from a Dutch point of view: An experimental investigation of English intonation produced by Dutch native speakers*. Dordrecht: Foris.

Williams, E. (1983). Semantic and syntactic categories. *Linguistics and Philosophy*, *6*, 423–446.

Wilshire, C. (1985). Speech error distributions in two kinds of tongue twisters. Unpublished bachelor thesis, Monash University, Clayton, Victoria.

Wilson, D., & Sperber, D. (1981). On Grice's theory of conversation. In P. Werth (Ed.), *Conversation and discourse: Structure and interpretation*. London: Croom Helm.

Wilson, D., & Sperber, D. (1988). Mood and the analysis of non-declarative sentences. In J. Dancy, J. Moravsik, & C. Taylor (Eds.), *Human agency: Language, duty and value*. Stanford University Press.

Wingfield, A. (1968). Effects of frequency on identification and naming of objects. *American Journal of Psychology, 81*, 226–234.

Winterhoff-Spurk, P., Herrmann, T., & Weindrich, D. (1986). Requesting rewards: A study of distributive justice. *Journal of Language and Social Psychology, 5*, 13–31.

Wunderlich, D. (1976). Towards an integrated theory of grammatical and pragmatical meaning. In A. Kasher (Ed.), *Language in focus: Foundations, methods and systems. Essays in memory of Yehoshua Bar-Hillel*. Dordrecht: Reidel.

Wunderlich, D. (1979). *Foundations of linguistics*. Cambridge University Press.

Wunderlich, D. (1981). Linguistic strategies. In F. Coulmas (Ed.), *A Festschrift for native speaker*. The Hague: Mouton.

Wunderlich, D., & Reinelt, R. (1982). How to get there from here. In R. Jarvella & W. Klein (Eds.), *Speech, place, and action: Studies in deixis and related topics*. Chichester: John Wiley.

Wundt, W. (1896). *Grundriss der Psychologie*. Leipzig: Kröner.

Wundt, W. (1900). *Die Sprache* (2 Vols.). Leipzig: Kröner.

Yarmey, A. D. (1973). I recognize your face but I can't remember your name: Further evidence on the tip-of-the-tongue phenomenon. *Memory and Cognition, 1*, 287–290.

Yngve, V. H. (1970). On getting a word in edgewise. In M. A. Campbell (Ed.), *Papers from the Sixth Regional Meeting, Chicago Linguistic Society*. University of Chicago Press.

Zubin, D. A., & Choi, S. (1984). Orientation and gestalt: Conceptual organizing principles in the lexicalization of space. In D. Testen, V. Mishra & J. Drogo (Eds.), *Papers from the Parasession on Lexical Semantics*. Chicago Linguistic Society.

Zwanenburg, W., Ouweneel, G. R. E., & Levelt, W. J. M. (1977). La frontière du mot en Français. *Studies in Language, 1*, 209–221.

Zwicky, A. M. (1972). On casual speech. In P. M. Peranteau, J. N. Levi, & G. C. Phares (Eds.), *Papers from the Eighth Regional Meeting of the Chicago Linguistic Society*, 607–615.

Zwicky, A. M., & Pullum, G. K. (1983). Cliticization versus inflection: English n't. *Language, 59*, 502–513.

Author Index

Subject Index

Phonological
  encoding, 7, 11–12, 18, 20, 24, 26, 102,
    161–162, 165, 166, 171, 179, 181, 187,
    231, 233, 236, 239–242, 246, 255, 259,
    275–276, 278–279, 282–284, 303, 316,
    318–412 *passim*, 414, 416, 419–422,
    435–436, 462, 468–469
  feature, 23, 350
  phrase, 259, 303–307, 317, 373, 378–381,
    390–391, 411, 419–421, 454, 473
  priming, 279–280, 354
  word, 302, 317, 361, 370–380, 389–392,
    398, 406–421 *passim*, 454, 473
Phonotactic
  possibility, 294, 335–338, 344, 362, 369,
    482
  rule, 294
Phrasal Focus Rule, 174–176, 178–179
Phrase. *See* Intonational, Phonological,
  Phrase structure
Phrase structure, 163, 166–167, 169, 179–
  180, 365, 369, 373, 384, 391, 408, 498
Pitch accent, 7, 12, 100, 149–151, 166,
  174–178, 237, 244, 299–300, 306–307,
  310, 315, 317, 323, 364, 374, 382–386,
  389, 398–400, 404–405, 410. *See also*
  Accent, Accentuation
  and accessibility of referent, 270, 273
  contrastive, 172, 177, 247, 273, 307, 309,
    401, 495–496
  default, 177
  as diacritic feature, 165, 180, 191, 233,
    366, 373, 382, 408
  and focus, 100, 174, 243, 246, 496
  monitoring, 463
  and prominence, 307, 386
  and nuclear stress, 308–309, 384–385,
    402
Pitch-Accent Prominence Rule, 382
Pitch-Accent Rule, 175
Pitch
  contour, 7, 171, 255, 300, 307–310, 316,
    364, 366, 373, 398, 405, 411, 427, 498
  modulation, 413
  movement, 298, 309–310, 327–328, 367,
    372, 381, 385, 391, 396, 399–405, 409–
    410, 427
  obstruction, 300
  raising, 113, 315
  stranding, 247, 282, 372
  withholding, 147
Place features, 295, 316, 350, 443

Planning
  articulatory, 297, 420–421
  conceptual, 5, 11, 20, 24, 204. *See also*
    Macroplanning, Microplanning
  of connected speech, 364–412
  of discourse, 115, 119
  message, 11, 119, 126, 259, 275, 467
  metrical, 304, 317, 373, 397–399, 402, 408,
    410–411
  motor, 420, 435, 443–444
  phonetic, 296, 318, 321, 329, 341, 343–
    346, 359, 365, 473
  prosodic, 18, 364–365, 396, 405, 410
  speech act, 108–109, 474
  and syntax, 258–259
  unit, 23, 256–257, 259, 420
  utterance, 3–4, 18, 277, 282
Planning discourse, 112
Pleas, 61
Pledging, 61, 64
Plosive speech sounds, 290, 413, 433, 441,
  472
Plural. *See* Number
Polite requests, 66–69, 135
Politeness, 3–6, 21, 30, 37, 65–69, 124, 474
Posterior speech sounds, 296, 433
Pragmatics, 39
Prearticulatory editing. *See* Editing
Precision of articulation, 22, 396, 410, 434,
  462
Predication, 70–71, 89, 90, 98–99, 113–115,
  150–154, 159, 171, 261, 308
Prefix. *See* Morpheme
Prenuclear tune, 311–312, 403–405
Preposition, 48, 122, 166–167, 178, 192,
  194–195, 198, 236, 251, 273, 288, 369,
  371, 378, 421
Prepositional object, 238, 248, 264, 274
Prepositional phrase, 11, 167, 169, 178, 180,
  192, 195, 238, 266, 268, 304, 485, 487,
  490
Presentatives, 272
Prespecification in self-repairs, 491
Presupposition, 102, 113, 117–119, 171,
  175, 212, 216, 219. *See also* Backward
  suppletion
  existential, 118
  factive, 118
Pretonic accent. *See* Prenuclear tune
Preverbal message, 9, 11, 14–15, 72–74,
  76, 78, 93, 101, 105, 107–110, 157, 160,
  170, 179–181, 186